I0006171

No. 96.

HYDROGRAPHIC OFFICE.

THE COAST

OF

BRITISH COLUMBIA

FROM JUAN DE FUCA STRAIT TO PORTLAND CANAL,

TOGETHER WITH

VANCOUVER AND QUEEN CHARLOTTE ISLANDS.

SECOND EDITION.

WASHINGTON:
GOVERNMENT PRINTING OFFICE.
1907.

DEC 11 1907

CONTENTS.

PREFACE.

This publication, a revision of the first edition, incorporating the latest information from all reliable sources, has been prepared by Lieutenant Commander Glennie Tarbox, U. S. Navy.

It cancels the previous edition, all supplements, and all Hydrographic Office Notices to Mariners up to and including No. 49 of 1906.

As much of the area herein described has not been carefully surveyed (some portions hardly explored), mariners are earnestly requested to notify the United States Hydrographic Office, directly or through one of its branch offices, of any new information obtained, or of any errors and omissions discovered in the present edition.

CHAS. C. ROGERS,
Commander, U. S. Navy, Hydrographer.

U. S. HYDROGRAPHIC OFFICE,
Washington, D. C., December 8, 1906.

NOTE.

In this work, the bearings, courses, and trend of the land as given, are true; but for convenience, the corresponding magnetic directions, to the nearest degree, generally follow in parentheses (variation in 1906).

The directions of winds refer to the points from which they blow; of currents, the points toward which they set.

Distances are expressed in nautical miles, or in yards, the mile being approximately 2,000 yards.

The soundings are referred to mean low water, unless it is otherwise stated.

The latest information as to lights should always be sought in the light lists.

126°

INFORMATION RELATING TO NAVIGATIONAL AIDS AND GENERAL NAVIGATION.

THE CORRECTION OF CHARTS, LIGHT LISTS, AND SAILING DIRECTIONS.

The following-named publications are issued by the United States Hydrographic Office as guides to navigation: Charts, Chart Catalogues, Sailing Directions, Light Lists, Tide Tables, Notices to Mariners, Pilot Charts, and Hydrographic Bulletins. Of these, the Notices to Mariners and the Hydrographic Bulletins are free to mariners and others interested in shipping. The Pilot Charts are free to contributors of professional information, but sold to the general public at 10 cents a copy. The other publications of the office are sold under the law at cost price.

The Charts, the Sailing Directions, and the Light Lists are all affected by continual changes and alterations, concerning which information is published weekly to all parts of the world in the Notices to Mariners.

The Charts should always be, so far as our knowledge permits, absolutely correct to date; and the Light Lists should be noted for the recent alterations and additions. The Sailing Directions, however, can not, from their nature, be so fully corrected, and in all cases where they differ from the charts, the charts must be taken as the guide.

Charts.—When issued from the Hydrographic Office, the charts have received all necessary corrections to date.

All small but important corrections that can be made by hand are given in the Notices to Mariners, and should at once be placed on the charts to which they refer.

Extensive corrections that can not be conveniently thus made are put upon the plates, and new copies are issued to the ships to replace the old, which are directed to be destroyed to prevent the possibility of their being used in the navigation of the ship.

The dates on which extensive corrections are made are noted on the chart on the right of the middle of the lower edge; those of the smaller corrections at the left lower corner.

In all cases of quotations of charts these dates of corrections should be given, as well as the number of the chart (found in the right lower corner), in order that the edition of the chart referred to may be known.

The Light Lists are corrected before issue, and all changes are published in the weekly Notices to Mariners.

The navigating officer should make notations in the Light Lists and paste in at the appropriate places slips from the Notices to Mariners.

The Light Lists should always be consulted as to the details of a light, as the description in the Sailing Directions may be obsolete, in consequence of changes since publication.

The Sailing Directions are corrected before issue, and subsequently should be kept corrected by means of the Notices to Mariners.

Supplements are published from time to time and contain all the information received up to date since the publication of the volume to which they refer, canceling all previous Notices to Mariners.

The existence of Supplements or Notices to Mariners is to be noted in the tabular form inside the cover of each volume.

To enable the books to be more conveniently corrected, Supplements and Notices to Mariners are printed on one side only, and two copies are issued to each ship—one to be cut and the slips pasted in at the appropriate places, the other to be retained intact for reference.

To make the notations and paste in the slips, as the Notices to Mariners are received, is one of the duties of the navigating officer demanding faithful attention.

It must, however, be understood that Sailing Directions will rarely be correct in all details, and that, as already stated, when differences exist, the chart, which should be corrected from the most recent information, should be taken as the guide, for which purpose, for ordinary navigation, it is sufficient.

The Tide Tables, which are published annually by the United States Coast and Geodetic Survey, give the predicted times and heights of the high and the low waters for every day in the year at 70 of the principal ports of the world, and, through the medium of these by means of tidal differences and ratios, at a very large number of subordinate ports. The Tables for the Atlantic and the Pacific coast ports of the United States are also published separately.

It should be remembered that these tables aim to give the times of high and low water, and not the times of turning of the current or of slack water, which may be quite different.

Notices to Mariners, containing fresh information pertaining to all parts of the world, are published weekly and mailed to all United States ships in commission, Hydrographic branch offices and agencies, United States consulates, and foreign hydrographic offices. Copies are furnished free by the main office or by any of the branch offices on application.

With each Notice is sent also a separate sheet, giving the items relating to lights contained in the latest Notice, intended especially for use in correcting the Light Lists.

Pilot Charts of the North Atlantic and North Pacific oceans are published near the beginning of each month. These charts give the average conditions of wind and weather, barometer, percentage of fog and gales, and routes for steam and sailing vessels for the month of issue; ice and derelicts of the preceding month; ocean currents and magnetic variation for the year; storm tracks of preceding years; and much other useful information. They are furnished free only in exchange for marine data or observations.

Hydrographic Bulletins, published weekly, are supplemental to the North Atlantic Pilot Chart and contain the latest news of wrecks and derelicts along the American coast and ocean routes, Arctic ice, reports of the use of oil to calm the sea, and other information for mariners. They are to be had free upon application.

THE USE OF CHARTS.

Accuracy of chart.—The value of a chart must manifestly depend upon the character and accuracy of the survey on which it is based, and the larger the scale of the chart the more important do these become.

To judge of a survey, its source and date, which are generally given in the title, are a good guide. Besides the changes that may have taken place since the date of the survey in waters where sand or mud prevails, the earlier surveys were mostly made under circumstances that precluded great accuracy of detail; until a plan founded on such a survey is tested it should be regarded with caution. It may indeed be said that, except in well-frequented harbors and their approaches, no surveys yet made have been so minute in their examination of the bottom as to make it certain that all dangers have been found. The fullness or scantiness of the soundings is another method of estimating the completeness of the survey, remembering, however, that the chart is not expected to show all soundings that were obtained. When the soundings are sparse or unevenly distributed it may be taken for granted that the survey was not in great detail.

Large or irregular blank spaces among soundings mean that no soundings were obtained in these spots. When the surrounding soundings are deep it may fairly be assumed that in the blanks the water is also deep; but when they are shallow, or it can be seen from the rest of the chart that reefs or banks are present, such blanks should be regarded with suspicion. This is especially the case in coral regions and off rocky coasts, and it should be remembered that in waters where rocks abound it is always possible that a survey, however complete and detailed, may have failed to find every small patch or pinnacle rock.

A wide berth should therefore be given to every rocky shore or patch, and instead of considering a coast to be clear, the contrary should be assumed.

Fathom curves a caution.—Except in plans of harbors that have been surveyed in detail, the 5-fathom curve on most charts may be considered as a danger line, or caution against unnecessarily approaching the shore or bank within that line on account of the possible existence of undiscovered inequalities of the bottom, which only an elaborate detailed survey could reveal. In general surveys of coasts, or of little-frequented anchorages, the necessities of navigation do not demand the great expenditure of time required for so detailed a survey. It is not contemplated that ships will approach the shores in such localities without taking special precautions.

The 10-fathom curves on rocky shores is another warning, especially for ships of heavy draft.

A useful danger line will be obtained by tracing out with a colored pencil or ink the line of depth next greater than the draft of the ship using the chart. For vessels drawing less than 18 feet the edge of the sanding serves as a well-marked danger line.

Charts on which no fathom curves are marked must especially be regarded with caution, as indicating that soundings were too scanty and the bottom too uneven to enable the lines to be drawn with accuracy.

Isolated soundings, shoaler than surrounding depths, should always be avoided, especially if ringed around, as it is doubtful how closely the spot may have been examined and whether the least depth has been found.

The chart on largest scale should always be used on account of its greater detail and the greater accuracy with which positions may be plotted on it.

Caution in using small-scale charts.—In approaching the land or dangerous banks regard must always be had to the scale of the chart used. A small error in laying down a position means only yards on a large-scale chart, whereas on one of small scale the same amount of displacement means a large fraction of a mile.

Distortion of printed charts.—The paper on which charts are printed has to be damped. On drying distortion takes place from the inequalities of the paper, which greatly varies with different paper and the amount of the original damping, but it does not affect navigation. It must not, however, be expected that accurate series of angles taken to different points will always exactly agree when carefully plotted on the chart, especially if the lines to objects be long. The larger the chart the greater the amount of this distortion.

Mercator's chart.—Observed bearings are not identical with those measured on the mercator chart (excepting only the bearings North and South, and East and West on the equator) because the line of sight, except as affected by refraction, is a straight line, and lies in the plane of the great circle, while the straight line on the chart (except the meridian line) represents, not the arc of a great circle, but the loxodromic curve, which on the globe is a spiral terminating at the pole, or, if the direction be East and West, a circle of latitude.

The difference is not appreciable with near objects, and in ordinary navigation may be neglected. But in high latitudes, when the objects are very distant, and especially when lying near east or west, the bearings must be corrected for the convergence of the meridians in order to be accurately placed on the mercator chart, which represents the meridians as parallel.

On the polyconic chart, since a straight line represents (within the limits of 15 or 20 degrees of longitude) the arc of a great circle or the shortest distance between two points, bearings on the chart are identical with observed bearings.

The Mercator projection is evidently unsuited to surveying, for which purpose the polyconic projection is used by the Hydrographic Office and the Coast and Geodetic Survey, and the gnomonic projection by the British service.

Notes on charts should always be read with care, as they may give important information that can not be graphically represented.

Buoys.—It is manifestly impossible to rely on buoys always maintaining their exact positions. Buoys should therefore be regarded as warnings, and not as infallible navigating marks, especially when in exposed places; and a ship's position should always, when possible, be checked by bearings or angles of fixed objects on shore.

Gas buoys.—The lights shown by gas buoys can not be implicitly relied on; the light may be altogether extinguished, or, if intermittent, the apparatus may get out of order.

Lights.—All the distances given in the light lists and on the charts for the visibility of lights are calculated for a height of 15 feet for the observer's eye. The effect of a greater or less height of eye can be ascertained by means of the table of distances of visibility due to the height, published in the light lists.

The glare of a powerful light is often seen far beyond the limit of visibility of the actual rays of the light, but this must not be confounded with the true range. Refraction, too, may often cause a light to be seen farther than under ordinary circumstances.

When looking out for a light, the fact may be forgotten that aloft the range of vision is much increased. By noting a star immediately over the light a very correct bearing may be afterwards obtained from the standard compass.

On first making a light from the bridge, by at once lowering the eye several feet and noting whether the light is made to dip, it may be determined whether the ship is on the circle of visibility corresponding with the usual height of the eye or unexpectedly nearer the light.

The intrinsic power of a light should always be considered when expecting to make it in thick weather. A weak light is easily obscured by haze and no dependence can be placed on its being seen.

The power of a light can be estimated by its order, as stated in the light lists, and in some cases by noting how much its visibility in clear weather falls short of the range corresponding to its height. Thus, a light standing 200 feet above the sea and recorded as visible only 10 miles in clear weather is manifestly of little brilliancy, as its height would permit it to be seen over 20 miles if of sufficient power.

Fog signals.—Sound is conveyed in a very capricious way through the atmosphere. Apart from the influence of the wind large areas of silence have been found in different directions and at different distances from the origin of sound, even in clear weather; therefore, too much confidence should not be felt as to hearing a fog signal. The apparatus, moreover, for sounding the signal often requires some time before it is in readiness to act. A fog often creeps imperceptibly toward the land and is not observed by the lighthouse people until upon them; a ship may have been for many hours in it and approaching the land in confidence, depending on the signal, which is not sounded. When sound travels against the wind it may be thrown upward. A man aloft might then hear it, though inaudible on deck.

Taken together, these facts should induce the utmost caution in closing the land in fogs. The lead is generally the only safe guide and should be faithfully used.

Tides.—A knowledge of the times of high and low water and of the amount of vertical rise and fall of the tide is of great importance in the case of vessels entering or leaving port, especially when the channel depths are less than or near their draft. Such knowledge is also useful at times to vessels running close along a coast in enabling them to anticipate the effect of the tidal currents in setting them on or off shore. This is especially important in fog or thick weather.

The predicted times and heights of the high and low waters, or differences by which they may be readily obtained, are given in the tide tables for all the important ports of the world. The height at any intermediate time may be obtained by means of Table 2 for most of the principal tidal stations of the United States given in Table 1, and for the subordinate stations of Table 3 by multiplying its values by the ratio of mean ranges, provided the duration of rise and fall is sensibly the same at the subordinate as at the principal station. The intermediate height may also be obtained by plotting the predicted times and heights of high and low water and connecting the points by a curve. Such knowledge is often useful in crossing a bar or shallow flats.

Planes of reference.*—The plane of reference for soundings on Hydrographic Office charts made from United States Government surveys and on Coast and Geodetic Survey charts of the Atlantic coast of the United States is mean low water; on the Pacific coast of the United States as far as the strait of Fuca, it is the mean of the lower low waters; and from Puget sound to Alaska the Survey has adopted the harmonic or Indian tide plane, which is roughly that of the lowest low waters observed.

On most of the British Admiralty charts the plane of reference is the low water of ordinary springs; on French charts, the low water of equinoctial springs.

In the case of many charts compiled from old or various sources the plane of reference may be in doubt. In such cases, or whenever not stated on the chart, the assumption that the reference plane is mean low water gives the largest margin of safety.

Whichever plane of reference may be used for a chart, it must be remembered that there are times when the tide falls below it. Low water is lower than mean low water about half the time, and when a new or full moon occurs at perigee the low water is lower than the average low water of springs. At the equinoxes the spring range is also increased on the coasts of Europe, but in some other parts of the world, and especially in the Tropics, such periodic low tides may coincide more frequently with the solstices.

Wind or a high barometer may at times cause the water to fall below even a very low plane of reference.

On coasts where there is much diurnal inequality in the tides the amount of rise and fall can not be depended upon, and additional caution is necessary.

Mean sea level.—The important fact should be remembered that the depths at half tide are practically the same for all tides, whether neaps or springs. Half tide, therefore, corresponds with mean sea level. This makes a very exact plane of reference, easily found, to which it would be well to refer all high and low waters.

The tide tables give, in Table 3, for all the ports, the plane of reference to which tidal heights are referred and its distance below mean sea level.

If called on to take special soundings for the chart at a place where there is no tidal bench mark, mean sea level should be found and the plane for reductions established at the proper distance below it, as ascertained by the tide tables, or by observations, or in some cases, if the time be short, by estimation, the data used being made a part of the record.

* The distinction between "rise" and "range" of the tide should be understood. The former expression refers to the height attained above the datum plane for soundings, differing with the different planes of reference; the latter, to the difference of level between successive high and low waters.

Tidal streams.—In navigating coasts where the tidal range is considerable especial caution is necessary. It should be remembered that there are indrafts to all bays and bights, although the general run of the stream may be parallel with the shore.

The turn of the tidal stream offshore is seldom coincident with the time of high and low water on the shore. In some channels the tidal stream may overrun the turn of the vertical movement of the tide by 3 hours, forming what is usually known as tide and half tide, the effect of which is that at high and low water by the shore the stream is running at its greatest velocity.

The effect of the tidal wave in causing currents may be illustrated by two simple cases:

(1) Where there is a small tidal basin connected with the sea by a large opening.

(2) Where there is a large tidal basin connected with the sea by a small opening.

In the first case the velocity of the current in the opening will have its maximum value when the height of the tide within is changing most rapidly, i. e., at a time about midway between high and low water. The water in the basin keeps at approximately the same level as the water outside. The flood stream corresponds with the rising, and the ebb with the falling of the tide.

In the second case the velocity of the current in the opening will have its maximum value when it is high water or low water without, for then there is the greatest head of water for producing motion. The flood stream begins about three hours after low water, and the ebb stream about three hours after high water, slack water thus occurring about midway between the tides.

Along most shores not much affected by bays, tidal rivers, etc., the current usually turns soon after high water and low water.

The swiftest current in straight portions of tidal rivers is usually in the middle of the stream, but in curved portions the most rapid current is toward the outer edge of the curve, and here the water will be deepest. The pilot rule for best water is to follow the ebb tide reaches.

Countercurrents and eddies may occur near the shores of straits, especially in bights and near points. A knowledge of them is useful in order that they may be taken advantage of or avoided.

A swift current often occurs in a narrow passage connecting two large bodies of water, owing to their considerable difference of level at the same instant. The several passages between Vineyard sound and Buzzards bay are cases in point. In the Woods Hole passage the maximum strength of the tidal streams occurs near high and low water.

Tide rips are made by a rapid current setting over an irregular bottom, as at the edges of banks where the change of depth is considerable.

Current arrows on charts show only the most usual or the mean direction of a tidal stream or current; it must not be assumed that the direction of a stream will not vary from that indicated by the arrow. The rate, also, of a stream constantly varies with circumstances, and the rate given on the chart is merely the mean of those found during the survey, possibly from very few observations.

FIXING POSITION.

Sextant method.—The most accurate method available to the navigator of fixing a position relative to the shore is by plotting with a protractor sextant angles between well-defined objects on the chart; this method, based on the " three-point problem " of geometry, should be in general use.

For its successful employment it is necessary: First, that the objects be well chosen; and, second, that the observer be skillful and rapid in his use of the sextant. The latter is only a matter of practice.

Near objects should be used either for bearings or angles for position in preference to distant ones, although the latter may be more prominent, as a small error in the bearing or angle or in laying it on the chart has a greater effect in misplacing the position the longer the line to be drawn.

On the other hand, distant objects should be used for direction because less affected by a small error or change of position.

The three-arm protractor (station pointer of the British service) consists of a graduated brass circle with one fixed and two movable radial arms, the three beveled edges of the arms, if produced, intersecting at the exact center of the instrument. The edge of the fixed arm marks the zero of the graduation which enables the movable arms to be set at any angles with the fixed arm.

To plot a position, the two angles observed between the three selected objects are set on the instrument, which is then moved over the chart until the three beveled edges pass respectively and simultaneously through the three objects. The center of the instrument will then mark the ship's position, which may be pricked on the chart or marked with a pencil point through the center hole.

The tracing-paper protractor, consisting of a graduated circle printed on tracing paper, is an excellent substitute for the brass instrument and in some cases preferable to it, as when, for instance, the objects angled on are so near the observer that they are more or less hidden by the circle of the instrument. The paper protractor also permits the laying down for simultaneous trial of a number of angles in cases of fixing important positions. Plain tracing paper may also be used if there are any suitable means of laying off the angles.

The value of a determination depends greatly on the relative positions of the objects observed. If the position sought lies on the circle passing through the three objects (in which case the sum of the observed angles equals the supplement of the angle at the middle object made by lines from the other two) it will be indeterminate, as it will plot all around the circle. An approach to this condition must be avoided. Near objects are better than distant ones, and, in general, up to 90° the larger the angles the better, remembering always that large as well as small angles may plot on or near the circle and hence be worthless. If the objects are well situated, even very small angles will give for navigating purposes a fair position, when that obtained by bearings of the same objects would be of little value.

Accuracy requires that the two angles be simultaneous. If under way and there is but one observer, the angle that changes less rapidly may be observed both before and after the other angle and the proper value obtained by interpolation.

A single angle and a range give in general an excellent fix, easily obtained and plotted.

Advantages of sextant method.—In war time, when the compass may be knocked away or rifle fire make it undesirable to expose the person more than necessary, a sextant offers great advantages, as angles can be obtained at any point where the objects are visible. This contingency makes it especially desirable that all navigating officers of men-of-war should become expert in this method of fixing a ship's position.

In many narrow waters, also, where the objects may yet be at some distance, as in coral harbors or narrow passages among mud banks, navigation by sextant and protractor is invaluable, as a true position can in general be obtained only by its means. Positions by bearings are too rough to depend upon, and a small error in either taking or plotting a bearing might under such circumstances put the ship ashore.

In all cases where great accuracy of position is desired, such as the fixing of a rock or shoal or of fresh soundings or new buildings as additions to the chart, the sextant should invariably be used. In all such cases angles should be taken to several objects, the more the better; but five objects is a good number, as the four angles thus obtained not only prevent any errors, but they at once furnish a means of checking the accuracy of the chart itself. If a round of angles can be taken, the observer's accuracy is also checked. In the case of ordinary soundings a third angle need be taken only occasionally; first, to check the general accuracy of the chart, as above stated; second, to make certain that the more important soundings, as at the end of a line, are correctly placed.

If communication can be had with the shore, positions may be fixed with great accuracy by occupying with theodolite or sextant two known points of the chart. The third angle of the triangle, that between the two points at the position sought, should be measured as a check.

The compass.—It is not intended that the use of the compass to fix the ship should be given up; in ordinary piloting the compass, with its companion, the alidade, may be more usefully employed for this purpose, although less accurate than the sextant.

If the accuracy of the chart be doubtful, the compass should be used in preference to the sextant.

In fixing by the compass it should always be remembered that the position by two bearings only, like that by two angles only, is liable to error. An error may be made in taking a bearing, or in applying to it the deviation, or in laying it on the chart. A third or check bearing should, therefore, be taken of some other object, especially when near the shore or dangers. A common intersection for the three lines assures accuracy.

Compass bearing and sextant angle.—When only two objects are visible, a compass bearing and a sextant angle may be used, and a better fix obtained than by two bearings.

Doubling the angle on the bow.—The method of fixing by doubling the angle on the bow is invaluable. The ordinary form of it, the so-called "bow and beam bearing," the distance from the object at the latter position being the distance run between the times of taking the two bearings, gives the maximum of accuracy, and is an excellent fix for a departure, but does not insure safety, as the object observed and any dangers off it are abeam before the position is obtained.

By taking the bearings at two points and four points on the bow, a fair position is obtained before the object is passed, the distance of the latter at the second position being, as before, equal to the distance run in the interval, allowing for current. Taking afterwards the beam bearing gives, with slight additional trouble, the distance of the object when abeam; such beam bearings and distances, with the times, should be continuously recorded as fresh departures, the importance of which will be appreciated in cases of being suddenly shut in by fog.

A table of multipliers of the distance run in the interval between any two bearings of an object, the product being its distance at the time of the second bearing, is given in the light list and in Bowditch.

Danger angle.—The utility of the danger angle in passing outlying rocks or dangers should not be forgotten. In employing the horizontal danger angle, however, caution is necessary, as, should the chart be inaccurate, i. e., should the objects selected be not quite correctly placed, the angle taken off from it may not serve the purpose. It should not, therefore, be employed when the survey is old or manifestly imperfect.

The vertical danger angle may be conveniently used when passing elevated points of known heights, such as lighthouses, cliffs, etc. The computation of the distance corresponding to the height of the object and its angular elevation requires for small distances merely the solution of a plane right triangle; the natural cotangent of the angle multiplied by the height in feet gives the distance in feet. The convenient use of this method, however, requires tables such as those published by Captain Lecky in his little book entitled "The Danger Angle and Offshore Distance Tables."

This book very usefully extends the vertical angle method to finding a ship's position at sea by observing the angular altitude of a peak of known height and its bearing. The tables give heights up to 18,000 feet and distances up to 110 miles. When the angles are not too large they should be observed "on and off the limb" and the index error of the sextant thus eliminated, in preference to correcting for it the single altitude. It must be remembered that in high latitudes the bearing of a distant object needs correction for the convergence of the meridians before being laid down on a mercator chart. The correction may be found by the following formula, using the approximate position: The sine of the correction equals the product of the sine of half the difference of longitude by the sine of the middle latitude. It is applied on the equatorial side of the observed bearing, and its effect is always to increase the latitude of the observer.

Soundings taken at random are of little value in fixing or checking position and may at times be misleading. In thick weather, when near or closing the land, soundings should be taken continuously and at regular intervals, and, with the character of the bottom, systematically recorded. By laying the soundings on tracing paper, according to the scale of the chart, along a line representing the track of the ship, and then moving the paper over the chart parallel with the course until the observed soundings agree with those of the chart, the ship's position will in general be quite well determined. This plan was suggested by Lord Kelvin, whose admirable sounding machine renders the operation of sounding possible in quite deep water without slowing down the ship and consequent loss of time.

Dumb compass.—All ships should be supplied with the means of taking accurate bearings both by day and by night. The standard compass is not always conveniently placed for the purpose; in such case some species of alidade or dumb compass is of great importance. The utility of such an instrument in ascertaining the change of bearing of an approaching ship's light should not be forgotten.

Sumner's method.—Among astronomical methods of fixing a ship's position the great utility of Sumner's method should be well understood, and this method should be in constant use. The Sumner line—that is, the line drawn through the two positions obtained by working the chronometer observation for longitude with two assumed latitudes, or by drawing through the position obtained with one latitude a line at right angles to the bearing of the body as obtained from the azimuth tables—gives at times invaluable information, as the ship must be somewhere on that line provided the chronometer is correct. If directed toward the coast, it marks the bearing of a definite point; if parallel with the coast the distance of the latter is shown. Thus the direction of the line may often be usefully taken as a course. A sounding at the same time with the observation may often give an approximate position on the line. A very accurate position can be obtained by observing two or more stars at morning or evening twilight, at which time the horizon is well defined. The Sumner lines thus obtained will, if the bearings of the stars differ three points or more, give an excellent result. A star or planet at twilight and the sun afterwards or before may be combined; also two observations of the sun with sufficient interval to admit of a considerable change of bearing. In these cases one of the lines must be moved for the run of the ship. The moon is often visible during the day and in combination with the sun gives an excellent fix.

The morning and evening twilight observations, besides their great accuracy, possess the additional advantage of greatly extending the ship's reliable reckoning beyond the limits of the ordinary day navigation and correspondingly restricting the dead-reckoning uncertainties of the night. An early morning fix in particular is often of great value.

Observations of the stars at night require the use of the star telescope in order to define the horizon. Though the same degree of accuracy as at twilight can not be expected, night observations are a very valuable dependence and should be assiduously practiced.

Piloting.—The navigator, in making his plan for entering a strange port, should give very careful previous study to the chart and should carefully select what appear to be the most suitable marks for use, also providing himself with substitutes, to use in case those selected as most suitable should prove unreliable in not being recognized with absolute certainty. It must be remembered that buoys seen at a distance in approaching a channel are often difficult to place or identify, because all may appear equally distant, though in reality far apart. Ranges should be noted, if possible, and the lines drawn, both for leading through the best water in channels and also for guarding against particular dangers; for the latter purpose safety bearings should in all cases be laid down where no suitable ranges appear to offer. The courses to be steered in entering should also be laid down and distances marked thereon. If intending to use the sextant and danger angle in passing dangers, and especially in passing between dangers, the danger circles should be plotted and regular courses planned, rather than to run haphazard by the indications of the angle alone, with the possible trouble to be apprehended from wild steering at critical points.

The alidade or dumb compass should invariably be mounted in entering or leaving port and kept faithfully set to the magnetic direction of the ship's head, changing promptly with every change of course, so that the observed bearings may be magnetic, and therefore ready for the chart without the necessity of waiting to apply corrections. The chart should be on the bridge in readiness for reference or use in plotting positions.

The ship's position should not be allowed to be in doubt at any time, even in entering ports considered safe and easy of access, and should be constantly checked, continuing to use for this purpose those marks concerning which there can be no doubt until others gradually and unmistakably declare themselves.

The ship should ordinarily steer exact courses and follow an exact line, as planned from the chart, changing course at precise points, and, where the distances are considerable, her position on the line should be checked at frequent intervals, with recordings of time and patent log. This is desirable even where it may seem unnecessary for safety, because if running by the eye alone and the ship's exact position be suddenly required, as in a sudden fog or squall, fixing at that particular moment may be attended with difficulty.

The habit of running exact courses with precise changes of course will be found most useful when is is desired to enter port or pass through inclosed waters during fog by means of the buoys; here safety demands that the buoys be made successively, to do which requires, if the fog be dense, very accurate courses and careful attention to the times , the patent log, and the set of the current; failure to make a buoy as expected leaves as a rule no safe alternative but to anchor at once, with perhaps a consequent serious loss of time.

It is a useful point to remember that in passing between dangers where there are no suitable leading marks, as, for instance, between two islands or an island and the main shore, with dangers extending from both, a mid-channel course may be steered by the eye alone with great accuracy, as the eye is able to estimate very closely the direction midway between visible objects.

In piloting among coral reefs or banks, a time should be chosen when the sun will be astern, conning the vessel from aloft or from an elevated position forward. The line of demarcation between the deep water and the edges of the shoals, which generally show as green patches, is indicated with surprising clearness. This method is of frequent application in the numerous passages of the Florida keys.

Changes of course should in general be made by exact amounts, naming the new course or the amount of the change desired, rather than by ordering the helm to be put over and then steadying when on the desired heading, with the possibility of the attention being diverted and so of forgetting in the meantime, as may happen, that the ship is still swinging. The helmsman, knowing just what is desired and the amount of the change to be made, is thus enabled to act more intelligently and to avoid wild steering, which in narrow channels is a very positive source of danger.

Coast piloting involves the same principles and requires that the ship's position be continuously determined or checked as the landmarks are passed. On well-surveyed coasts there is a great advantage in keeping near the land, thus holding on to the marks and the soundings, and thereby knowing at all times the position, rather than keeping offshore and losing the marks, with the necessity of again making the land from vague positions. and perhaps the added inconvenience of fog or bad weather, involving a serious loss of time and fuel.

The route should be planned for normal conditions of weather, with suitable variations where necessary in case of fog or bad weather or making points at night, the courses and distances, in case of regular runs over the same route, being entered in a notebook for ready reference, as well as laid down on the chart. The danger circles for either the horizontal or the vertical danger angles should be plotted, wherever the method can be usefully employed, and the angles marked thereon; many a mile may thus be saved in rounding dangerous points, with no sacrifice in safety. Ranges should also be marked in, where useful for position or for safety, and also to use in checking the deviation of the compass by comparing, in crossing, the compass bearing of the range with its magnetic bearing, as given by the chart.

Changes of course will in general be made with mark or object abeam, the position (a new "departure") being then, as a rule, best and most easily obtained. The alidade, kept set to the ship's magnetic heading, should be at all times in readiness for use, and the chart where it may be readily consulted by the officer of the watch. The sextant should also be kept conveniently at hand.

A continuous record of the progress of the ship should be kept by the officer of the watch, the time and patent log reading of all changes of course and of all bearings, especially the two and four point bearings, with distance of object when abeam, being noted in a book kept in the pilot house for this especial purpose. The ship's reckoning is thus continuously cared for as a matter of routine and without the presence or particular order of the captain or navigating officer. The value of thus keeping the reckoning always fresh and exact will be especially appreciated in cases of sudden fog or when making points at night.

Where the coastwise trip must be made against a strong head wind, it is desirable, with trustworthy charts, to skirt the shore as closely as possible in order to avoid the heavier seas and adverse current that prevail farther out. In some cases, with small ships, a passage can be made only in this way. The important saving of coal and of time, which is even more precious, thus effected by skillful coast piloting makes this subject one of prime importance to the navigator.

Change in the variation of the compass.—The gradual change in the variation must not be forgotten in laying down on the chart courses and positions by bearings. The magnetic compasses placed on the charts for the purpose of facilitating the plotting become in time slightly in error, and in some cases, such as with small scales or when the lines are long, the displacement of position from neglect of this change may be of importance. The date of the variation and the annual change, as given on the compass rose, facilitate corrections when the change has been considerable. The compasses are reengraved when the error amounts to a degree. More frequent alterations on one spot in a copper plate would not be practicable.

The geographical change in the variation is in some parts of the world so rapid as to need careful consideration, requiring a frequent change of the course. For instance, in approaching Halifax from Newfoundland the variation changes 10° in less than 500 miles.

Local magnetic disturbance of the compass on board ship.—The term "local magnetic disturbance" has reference only to the effects on the compass of magnetic masses external to the ship. Observation shows that disturbance of the compass in a ship afloat is experienced in only a few places on the globe.

Magnetic laws do not permit of the supposition that the visible land causes such disturbance, because the effect of a magnetic force diminishes so rapidly with distance that it would require a local center of magnetic force of an amount absolutely unknown to affect a compass half a mile distant.

Such deflections of the compass are due to magnetic minerals in the bed of the sea under the ship, and when the water is shallow and the force strong, the compass may be temporarily deflected when passing over such a spot; but the area of disturbance will be small unless there are many centers near together.

The law which has hitherto been found to hold good as regards local magnetic disturbance is that north of the magnetic equator the north end of the compass needle is attracted and south of the magnetic equator repelled by any center of disturbance.

It is very desirable that whenever a ship passes over an area of local magnetic disturbance the position should be fixed, and the facts, as far as they can be ascertained, reported.

Use of oil for modifying the effect of breaking waves.—Many experiences of late years have shown that the utility of oil for this purpose is undoubted and the application simple.

The following may serve for the guidance of seamen, whose attention is called to the fact that a very small quantity of oil skillfully applied may prevent much damage both to ships (especially of the smaller classes) and to boats by modifying the action of breaking seas.

The principal facts as to the use of oil are as follows:

1. On free waves, i. e., waves in deep water, the effect is greatest.

2. In a surf, or waves breaking on a bar, where a mass of liquid is in actual motion in shallow water, the effect of the oil is uncertain, as nothing can prevent the larger waves from breaking under such circumstances, but even here it is of some service.

3. The heaviest and thickest oils are most effectual. Refined kerosene is of little use; crude petroleum is serviceable when nothing else is obtainable; but all animal and vegetable oils, such as waste oil from the engines, have great effect.

4. A small quantity of oil suffices, if applied in such a manner as to spread to windward.

5. It is useful in a ship or boat, either when running, or lying-to, or in wearing.

6. No experiences are related of its use when hoisting a boat at sea or in a seaway, but it is highly probable that much time would be saved and injury to the boat avoided by its use on such occasions.

7. In cold water the oil, being thickened by the lower temperature and not being able to spread freely, will have its effect much reduced. This will vary with the description of oil used.

8. For a ship at sea the best method of application appears to be to hang over the side, in such a manner as to be in the water, small canvas bags, capable of holding from 1 to 2 gallons of oil, the bags being pricked with a sail needle to facilitate leakage of the oil.

The positions of these bags should vary with the circumstances. Running before the wind, they should be hung on either bow—e. g., from the cathead—and allowed to tow in the water.

With the wind on the quarter the effect seems to be less than in any other position, as the oil goes astern while the waves come up on the quarter.

Lying-to, the weather bow, and another position farther aft, seem the best places from which to hang the bags, using sufficient line to permit them to draw to windward while the ship drifts.

9. Crossing a bar with a flood tide, to pour oil overboard and allow it to float in ahead of the boat, which would follow with a bag towing astern, would appear to be the best plan. As before remarked, under these circumstances the effect can not be so much trusted.

On a bar, with the ebb tide running, it would seem to be useless to try oil for the purpose of entering.

10. For boarding a wreck, it is recommended to pour oil overboard to windward of her before going alongside. The effect in this case must greatly depend upon the set of the current and the circumstances of the depth of water.

11. For a boat riding in bad weather from a sea anchor, it is recommended to fasten the bag to an endless line rove through a block on the sea anchor, by which means the oil can be diffused well ahead of the boat and the bag readily hauled on board for refilling, if necessary.

ILLUSTRATIONS AND BRIEF RULES.*

[*In the illustrative figures, the flowing lines represent the spreading oil and the arrows denote the direction of the wind and sea.*]

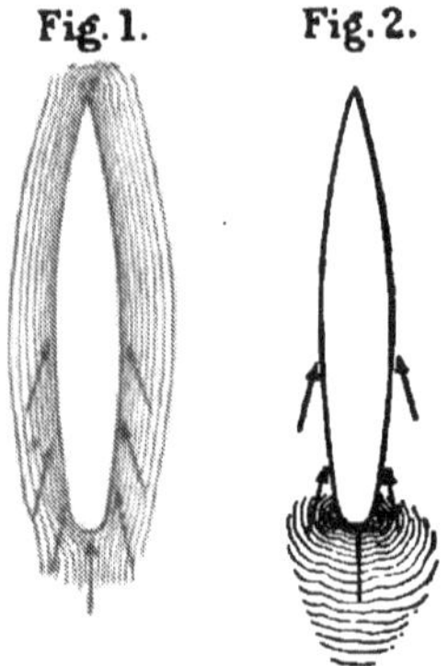

Scudding before a gale, Figure 1, distribute oil from the bow by means of oil bags or through waste pipes; it will thus spread aft and give protection both from quartering and following seas.

If distributed only astern, Figure 2, there will be no protection from the quartering sea.

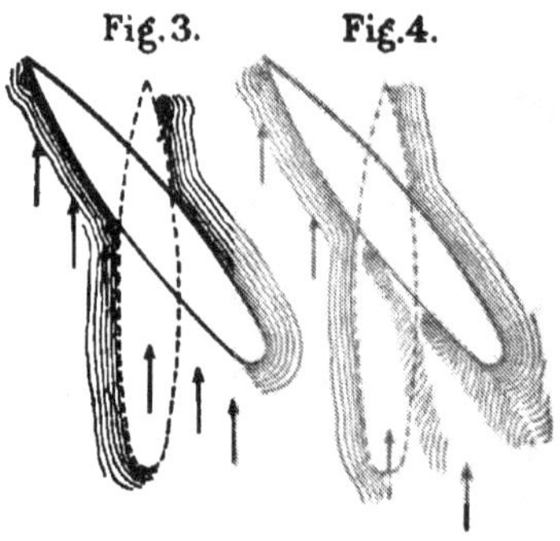

Running before a gale, yawing badly and threatening to broach-to, Figures 3 and 4, oil should be distributed from the bow and abaft the beam, on both sides.

In Figure 3, for instance, where it is only distributed at the bow, the weather quarter is left unprotected when the ship yaws.

In Figure 4, however, with oil bags abaft the beam as well as forward, the quarter is protected.

*From prize essay of Capt. R. Karlowa, of Hamburg-American Steamship Co.

Fig. 5. Fig. 6.

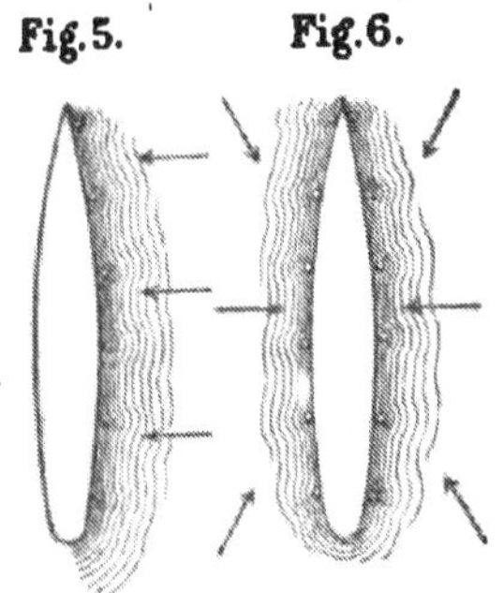

Lying-to, Figure 5, a vessel can be brought closer to the wind by using one or two oil bags forward, to windward. With a high beam sea, use oil bags along the weather side at intervals of 40 or 50 feet.

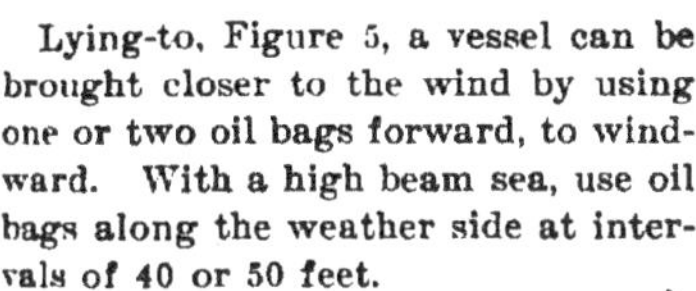

In a heavy cross sea, Figure 6, as in the center of a hurricane, or after the center has passed, oil bags should be hung out at regular intervals along both sides.

Fig. 9. Fig. 11.

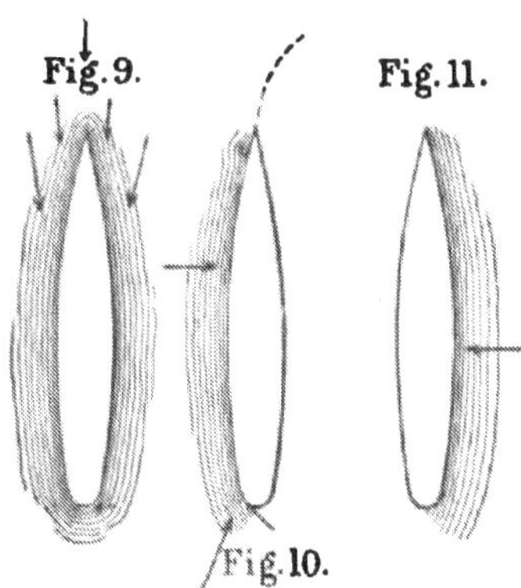

Fig. 10.

Steaming into a heavy head sea, Figure 9, use oil through forward closet pipes. Oil bags would be tossed back on deck.

Lying-to, to tack or wear, Figure 10, use oil from weather bow.

Cracking on, with high wind abeam and heavy sea, Figure 11, use oil from waste pipes, weather bow.

Fig. 7. Fig. 8.

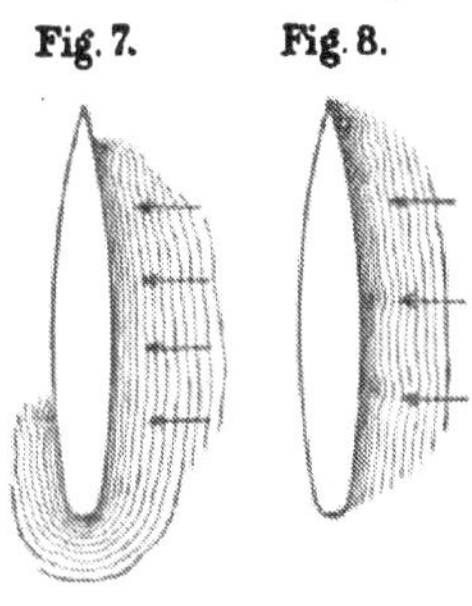

Drifting in the trough of a heavy sea, Figures 7 and 8, use oil from waste pipes forward and bags on weather side, as in Figure 8.

These answer the purpose very much better than one bag at weather bow and one at lee quarter, although this has been tried with some success, see Figure 7.

Fig. 12.

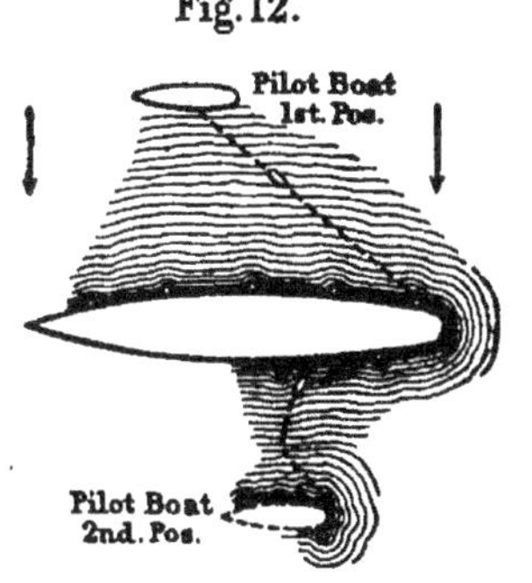

A vessel hove-to for a pilot, Figure 12, should distribute oil from the weather side and lee quarter. The pilot boat runs up to windward and lowers a boat, which pulls down to leeward and around the vessel's stern. The pilot boat runs down to leeward, gets out oil bags to windward and on her lee quarter, and the boat pulls back around her stern, protected by the oil. The vessels drift to leeward and leave an oil slick to windward, between the two.

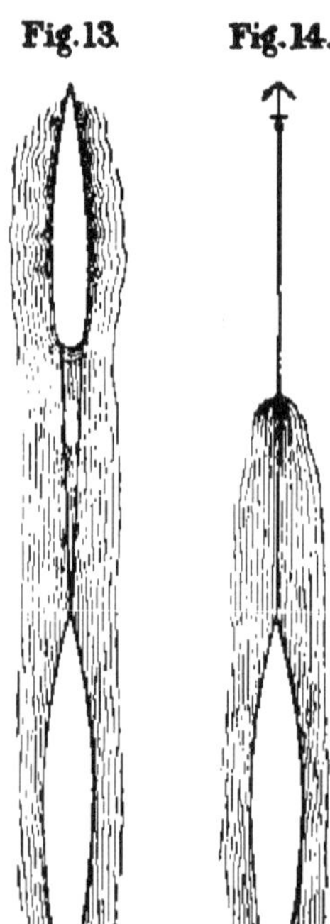
Fig. 13. Fig. 14.

Towing a vessel in a heavy sea, oil is of the greatest service and may prevent parting the hawser. Distribute from the towing vessel, forward on both sides, Figure 13. If used only aft, the tow alone gets the benefit.

At anchor in an open roadstead, use oil in bags from jib boom, or haul them out ahead of the vessel by means of an endless rope rove through a tail block secured to the anchor chain, Figure 14.

CHAPTER I.

GENERAL REMARKS—WINDS, CURRENTS—CLIMATE, METEOROLOGY—PRODUCTS—PASSAGES.

British Columbia, a province of the Dominion of Canada, was constituted a Crown colony in 1858, and entered the Confederation in 1871. It includes Vancouver island (first constituted a British colony in 1849), also the numerous islands and adjacent mainland of North America lying between Roberts point in Georgia strait, lat. 49° N., and the center of Portland canal, lat. 54° 40′ N. to 56° N. The average breadth of British Columbia is about 250 miles, and the area, including Vancouver island and Queen Charlotte islands, is roughly estimated at 370,000 square miles.

Vancouver island became a Crown colony in 1858, and was united to British Columbia (the mainland colony) as one colony under the name of British Columbia in 1866. Previous to 1858 the island had been for the most part in the hands of the Hudson's Bay Company, who held their lands in the island under a royal charter granted in the reign of Charles II.

Population.—The population by the last official census, 1901, was 178,657, classed as follows: Whites, 139,212; Indians, 24,576; Chinese, 14,869.

Aborigines inhabiting the coast have great skill in the building and management of canoes; they are a polygamous race, and subsist chiefly by hunting and fishing; those of southern Columbia are dark, and wear their hair long, while those of the more northern districts are of a clearer tint. The coast Indians live in substantial one-story dwellings of ax-hewn timber, divided into several compartments, of which one is occupied by each family. Inland the houses or wigwams are made of skins, tent cloths, and mats; in severe weather they take shelter in underground houses (circular pits) from 20 to 40 feet in diameter, and 8 or 10 feet deep, covered over with a substantial earthed roof, with a 3-foot circular aperture in the center, forming the only outlet for the inhabitants and smoke.

The British Columbia Indians are not treaty Indians and receive no assistance of any kind from the government. They live on reservations selected from the Crown lands of the province. Their numbers begin to show a small increase instead of decrease as has hitherto been the case.

The supplying of intoxicants to the Indians is strictly forbidden by law, under heavy penalties.

Products.—British Columbia contains extensive tracts of arable land, and a large auriferous district. Gold was first discovered on Thompson river in 1858.

Wheat, barley, oats, potatoes, peas, vegetables, and fruits flourish in British Columbia. The fisheries are very rich, salmon is abundant, the export of which, chiefly in tins, constitutes one of the principal sources of wealth in the country, and gives employment to upward of 19,000 people. Three salmon hatcheries are established in these waters.

Houlican (Oolachan), a fish somewhat resembling the herring, cod, herring, halibut (of enormous size), sardines, anchovy, haddock, and oysters are also found.

The fur trade, which, until the year 1860, was entirely monopolized by the Hudson's Bay Company, is considerable. Among the numerous fur-bearing animals the principal are the sea otter, marten, silver fox, black fox, and red fox.

The forests are of great extent, producing valuable timber, of which the Douglas pine (commonly called Oregon pine), white pine, maple, Scotch fir, and cedar are the principal; the Douglas pine, yielding spars 100 to 150 feet in length, and 2 feet in diameter, is exported in large cargoes. Besides the above, the yellow cypress, poplar, arbor vitæ, yew, oak, arbutus, alder, dogwood, cherry, crab apple, willow, and cottonwood are found. Cattle, horses, sheep, and other farm animals thrive generally in all parts.

In the year 1903, the total value of the mineral products of British Columbia amounted to $17,495,954, the principal items being gold $5,873,036, silver $1,521,472, copper $4,547,535, lead $689,744, coal $4,332,297.

Coal is found on the mainland and on Vancouver island, the mines on the latter being at Ladysmith, Nanaimo, Wellington, near Departure bay, and at Cumberland, near Comox. The quality is bituminous, but the coal from the Cumberland mines, containing a higher percentage of carbon, is a better steaming coal than that from the Nanaimo and Wellington mines. All these local coals give off a large quantity of smoke.

Anthracite coal, giving off but little smoke, is stated to have been recently discovered in the vicinity of Cumberland.

Bunker coal can be obtained (to order) at Esquimalt, Victoria, and Vancouver; also at Seattle, Tacoma, and Portland.

In 1903, the output of coal was 1,450,663 tons.

Communications.—Steamers run daily from Vancouver, Burrard inlet, to Victoria and Nanaimo; weekly to San Francisco; fortnightly to Portland; and at irregular intervals to all points up and down the coast.

Also, regularly to Japan and China, every fortnight in summer and every four weeks in winter; and to Australia every month.

From Victoria, steamers run to Port Essington and Port Simpson fortnightly; also, regularly to Port Angeles, 18 miles distant; Port Townsend, 38 miles; Seattle, 100 miles; Tacoma, 128 miles; Vancouver, 72 miles; New Westminster, 73 miles; Nanaimo, 72 miles; and San Francisco, 750 miles (every 5 days). Steam vessels also run from Victoria to Alaska every fortnight throughout the year. From Sydney (Saanich peninsula) a steamer runs daily to Port Guichon, on the mainland, 38 miles distant.

Railroads.—The Canadian Pacific railway crosses the heart of the British possessions in the North American continent, and is 3,054 statute miles in length between Quebec and Vancouver in Burrard inlet, the western terminus; the distance being accomplished in about 5 days 22 hours, and trains leave twice daily from both places.

A branch runs from Vancouver to English bay, and from Port Moody to New Westminster, whence it connects with Tacoma, Portland, San Francisco, and the whole of the American railroad system.

On Vancouver island there are railroads between Victoria and Wellington, near Departure bay; Victoria and Sydney, in the northern part of Saanich peninsula; and between Union wharf, Baynes sound, and the coal mines at Cumberland, near Comox.

Telegraphs.—Victoria is connected by land lines to all stations on the Esquimalt and Nanaimo railroad, and the line extends beyond the terminus of the railroad at Wellington as far as Comox, a distance of 80 miles.

Submarine cables cross Juan de Fuca strait from Becher bay to Port Crescent, and from Albert head to Port Angeles; another cable crosses Georgia strait from Departure bay to English bay.

The Pacific cable from Fanning island lands at Bamfield creek, thence by submarine cable to Alberni, crosses Vancouver island by a land line to Departure bay, connecting there to cable across the strait of Georgia.

A submarine telephone cable, connecting Victoria and Vancouver, crosses the various straits between Vancouver island and the mainland, in sections commencing at Telegraph cove, Vancouver island, and landing on the mainland at a point in Hale passage abreast Lummi island; the islands connecting these sections are San Juan, Shaw, Orcas, and Lummi.

Shipping trade.—The number of foreign seagoing vessels entering British Columbian ports during 1903 was 2,837, of a total tonnage of 2,060,879 tons. The number of coasting trade vessels arriving at all ports during 1903 was 16,557, with an aggregate tonnage of 4,523,450 tons.

Exports and imports.—In 1901–2 the total value of the imports was $19,391,256, and the exports $18,385,335.

Standard time of British Columbia is that of the meridian of 120° W. from Greenwich. In all tide tables for this area it is counted from 0 to 24 hours from midnight to midnight.

Correct time can be obtained from all Canadian Pacific railway telegraph stations, notice being given on the previous day. The signal is made by telegraph from Montreal at 11.56 a. m. Eastern standard time (75° W.), corresponding to 8.56 a. m. Pacific standard time (120° W.).

Pilots.—Towboats will be found cruising at the entrance of Juan de Fuca strait or in Neah bay; the masters of these boats are licensed pilots for the strait.

There is a licensed system of compulsory pilotage for merchant vessels for the ports of Victoria, Esquimalt, Vancouver, the Fraser river, Nanaimo, Departure bay, and Port Augusta.

Pilotage is not compulsory for the inland waters of Alaska, except as provided in the United States laws governing the Steamboat Inspection Service.

Speaking generally, there are no regular pilots for the inner channels, but reliable licensed pilots for the usual steamer routes may be obtained at Seattle on inquiry.

Quarantine.—Vessels arriving, bound to ports in British Columbia, are required to report at William Head quarantine station for inspection by the health officer.

The United States national quarantine station is at Port Discovery. Vessels subject to inspection are boarded at Port Townsend.

Rescue stations.—Depots, with provisions and other necessaries for shipwrecked mariners, have been established in Juan de Fuca strait, at Cape Beale lighthouse, in approximately lat. 48° 47½′ N., long. 125° 13½′ W., and Carmanah lighthouse, in approximately lat. 48° 36¾′ N., long. 124° 46½′ W.

Notice boards have been erected at intervals between cape Beale and Port San Juan (about 12 miles eastward of Carmanah lighthouse), on Nootka island, and near Estevan point, giving information, for the use of shipwrecked mariners, respecting the direction and distance of the nearest lighthouse, and also of the nearest Indian village where assistance can be obtained.

Cape Beale and Carmanah lighthouses are telegraph and signal stations.

Docks.—The graving dock at Esquimalt is 450 feet long over all, and 430 feet on the blocks; 65 feet wide at the entrance, with a depth of 26½ feet over the sill at high water, ordinary spring tides. This dock is closed by a caisson which, if necessary, can be placed on the outer side of the outer invert, giving an additional length to the dock of 30 feet.

H. B. M. S. Warspite, drawing 26 feet, was docked on July 18, 1891. The depth on the sill that night was 28½ feet.

The Admiralty have the right of priority of use of the Esquimalt dock.

There is a patent slip at Esquimalt capable of taking up a ship of 2,500 tons; there is also a patent slip at Victoria.

The United States Government dry dock at Port Orchard is 640 feet long over all, 573½ feet on the blocks, 93⅝ feet wide at the entrance; has 30 feet over the sill, and 28½ feet on the blocks.

In connection with the workshops which are at Tacoma, a floating dock is moored, in 8 fathoms, in Quartermaster harbor on the north side of the channel. The dock, capable of receiving vessels of large tonnage, is 325 feet long, 100 feet broad, and 80 feet between side walls; lifting power 8,000 tons. Repairs can be effected.

Climate.—The climate of British Columbia varies considerably, according to the locality; in the southern parts and on Vancouver island it is temperate during summer, the thermometer seldom rising on the hottest day above 80° F., or falling below 20° F. in winter; and it may, in fact, be said that this region possesses the climate of England without its humidity. In the central part of the province, however, the drought, heat, and cold are greater, the heat sometimes being very intense. It is, however, remarkably healthy both in summer and winter, there being no malaria or ague either during the hottest weather or in the dampest localities. Generally speaking, the summers are dry at Vancouver island, but with occasional showers; the winters bring a good deal of rain, and snow falls more or less each year.

In the northern part of the province along the coast the atmosphere is excessively humid, and rain falls heavily.

The climate of the mainland coast opposite Vancouver island differs somewhat from that of the SE. portion of the island. In summer the temperature averages slightly higher, and in winter somewhat lower, while the rainfall is greater immediately along the coast.

The lower Fraser valley (New Westminster district) does not receive in summer the cold breezes from the Olympian mountains which blow across Victoria, nor does it receive in winter so much of the genial warmth of the ocean air. As a general thing, ice forms on the river for a short time and snow begins to fall in January, and continues to do so intermittently till March, the ground not being continuously covered with it.

At Esquimalt the highest summer temperature is about 72° F. (in August), June, July, and August being the warmest months of the year. The lowest temperature is about 23½° F., the coldest months being December, January, and February. The greatest daily range occurs in March, and the smallest in October.

The temperature on Vancouver island during summer is lower than on the mainland, owing to the prevailing SE. winds blowing from the snow-capped mountains on the American side and across Queen Charlotte sound. The waters of the sound are peculiarly cold at this season.

The barometric variations are neither great nor frequent, the range for the year averaging about 1.5 inches.

The climate of Port Simpson is uncertain, no two seasons being the same, or appearing to follow any general law. During one summer fine weather may be experienced for six weeks at a time, and on such occasions a serene atmosphere, with magnificent sunsets, will be experienced. The following summer may prove one of almost constant rain, with a succession of gales from southeastward.

Along the shores of Chatham sound the rainfall is not so great as within the inlets. The temperature during July and August, 1892, varied from 62° to 48° F. The mean temperature of the sea was 4° lower than the mean temperature of the atmosphere at Port Simpson during these periods, but at Metlakatla and Nass bays it was 8° lower than the atmosphere, probably due to the influence of the cold water from the rivers which flow into those bays.

The navigator Vancouver in his voyages (1790–1795) describes as follows: "In Portland canal the sun's rays in August, between 9 a. m. and 3 p. m., are very powerful, and, reflected from the snow, caused occasionally intense heat. When the sun is obscured by the mountains, the atmosphere at once conveys a sensation of chilliness. During that month, just before sunrise, the thermometer often registers 32° F., water left in basins within a tent being frozen during the night. The vapor developed by the heat of the sun during the early portion of the day, becoming condensed on the mountainous shores of the inlet, usually falls as a drizzling rain from 3 p. m. to about midnight."

The climate of Queen Charlotte islands and the offlying islands of the coast of British Columbia is influenced by the warm body of water which washes their shores, the winter is less severe and the climate is milder on the islands than within the inlets. The vapor arising from this body of warm water is condensed upon the high mountains which form the shores of the mainland, and falls in drizzling, almost constant, rain so prevalent in these waters.

Ice.—Fraser river is sometimes, but rarely, frozen over at New Westminster. The lakes in the vicinity are frozen over, and ice forms at the heads of the several inlets where the water is comparatively fresh, but on the coast it does not form sufficiently thick to impede navigation.

Within the inlets on the coast, north of Vancouver island, ice is formed during the winter of from 8 to 12 inches in thickness, and occasionally extends as far as 25 miles from the heads of the inlets.

Skeena river is frozen over during the winter in the upper part, in severe winters as far as Port Essington. Nass river also freezes over, and down to its mouth in severe winters.

Rainfall.—The average annual rainfall appears to be about 55 inches; heavy rains generally occur in December and January.

Fogs—Juan de Fuca strait.—Although fogs in this region are not of such frequent occurrence as on the neighboring coast of California (where they prevail almost uninterruptedly during summer, and as late as the middle of October), yet from August to November they occur in Juan de Fuca strait, and are sometimes very dense over the entrance for several days together. They are generally accompanied by calms or very light winds from NW., which render them the more dangerous to sailing vessels closing the land.

Fog on the coast north of Vancouver island.—Fogs are prevalent especially during the summer months. The NW. winds which prevail during that season condense the vapor which arises from the comparatively warm water surrounding Queen Charlotte islands and the coast of Alaska. During the prevalence of NW. winds this vapor is dispersed, but during calms or with light winds, and especially with SW. winds succeeding NW. winds, it approaches quickly from seaward in the form of dense fog or drizzling mist and rain.

At times fog will be found at the entrances to the sounds during the forenoon, dispersed near noon by the heat of the sun, the afternoons becoming clear and fine.

In the outer part of Queen Charlotte sound it has been observed that the fog sweeping in from seaward often broke up after passing the groups of islands blocking the mouth of the sound, making a line of fog bank stretching between the Gordon and Millar groups, and leaving the area SE. of this line comparatively clear.

Smokes from forest fires cause much inconvenience during the dry season, and are a great impediment to navigation. In some seasons they have extended from Georgia strait to Portland inlet. When combined with fog they become very dense. In recent years, however, their prevalence has considerably diminished, some seasons being almost entirely free from them; they are cleared away by rains.

Fog signals—Caution.—Sound is conveyed in a very capricious way through the atmosphere. Apart from the wind, large areas of silence have been found in different directions and at different distances from the origin of the sound, even in clear weather. Therefore, too much confidence should not be felt in hearing a fog signal.

The apparatus, moreover, for sounding the signal often requires some time before it is in readiness to act. A fog often creeps imperceptibly toward the land, and is not observed by the people at a lighthouse until it is upon them; whereas, a ship may have been for many hours in it, and approaching the land. In such a case no signal may be sounded. When sound has to travel against the wind, it may be thrown upward; in such a case a man aloft might hear it when it is inaudible on deck. Under certain conditions of atmosphere when a fog signal is a combination of high and low notes, one of the notes may be inaudible. Mariners are therefore warned that fog signals can not be implicitly relied upon, and that the lead should never be neglected. Particular attention should also be given to placing " lookout men " in positions in which the noises from within the ship are least likely to interfere with the hearing of the sound of a fog signal, as experience shows that though such a signal may not be heard from the deck, or bridge, when the engines are moving, it may be heard when the engines are stopped, or from some quiet position. When near a steep shore, the echo of the vessel's steam whistle, or siren, may give warning of the nearness of land, the elapsed time giving an approximation to its distance.

Winds—Juan de Fuca strait.—Within Juan de Fuca strait, in the winter season, the winds usually assume its direction either up or down. During summer, the prevailing winds from NW. or SW. take a direction up the strait; while the SE. gales of winter blow fairly out.

Although a westerly wind may be blowing within the strait, it frequently, during the change of the seasons, blows heavily outside at the same time from SSW., or sometimes suddenly changes to that direction from a light easterly wind on opening the entrance, which makes that part of the coast of Vancouver island (between Port San Juan and Bonilla point) a dangerous lee shore to a ship without steam power.

The coast winds in summer prevail from SW. and NW., the former during the early months, and the latter blowing fresh and with great regularity during June, July, and August. In September and the early part of October the winds are very uncertain and there is generally a great deal of calm, gloomy weather.

The barometer usually stands above 30.00 inches during summer; should it fall to 29.90 a southeasterly wind with thick rainy weather may be expected, but of short duration, and clearing up with a westerly wind as soon as the barometer rises.

The winter winds are SE. or SW., more frequently the former; they set in toward the end of October and continue until the middle of April. SE. gales are generally preceded by a short interval of calm, cloudy weather; they spring up gradually from East or ESE.

veering to the southward, accompanied by rain and thick weather, the barometer falling rapidly; when the barometer becomes stationary the wind shifts suddenly to SW. and blows heavily with clear weather, but with frequent squalls of rain; the barometer begins to rise immediately the wind veers to SW., from which quarter it generally blows from 12 to 20 hours.

The violence and duration of these SE. gales is always proportioned to the fall of the mercury; with the barometer at 29.50 a strong gale may be looked for from this quarter; it seldom falls below 29.20, when very bad weather is certain to follow. On two or three occasions, in as many years, it has been known to fall to 28.90, and has been followed by SE. gales of great violence.

A SE. gale sometimes springs up, though very seldom, with the barometer above 30.00 inches. On such occasions the wind has always been preceded by calm, cloudy weather and rain, with a high but falling barometer; such gales are not violent and are of short duration.

SE. gales are always accompanied by thick, dirty weather, and rain; but they seldom continue from that quarter for more than 12 or 18 hours, unless the barometer falls very low, and they almost always shift to SW.

When the SW. gale of winter is not preceded by one from SE., the barometer seldom falls; it either remains stationary, when the gale may be expected to continue longer, or rises slowly, when it will gradually subside and fine weather follow. SW. gales are accompanied by heavy banks of clouds, with passing showers of rain, and sometimes snow.

The barometer has been known to fall during winter as low as 29.45, and has been followed by no gale or bad weather, but on such occasions there has been a heavy fall of snow on the hills, and a sudden fall of 15° in the temperature.

A fine northerly or northeasterly wind frequently occurs at intervals during the months of December, January, and February; it is always accompanied by a high barometer (above 30.00), and at such times a continuance for several days together of clear, cold, frosty weather may be looked for; the barometer on these occasions will sometimes rise as high as 30.70, and the fine weather will then probably last a fortnight or more.

Winds in the strait of Georgia.—The prevailing summer wind in the strait of Georgia is from NW., or the same as on the outside coast, and between May and September it blows strong and steady, commencing about 9 a. m. and dying away toward sunset. These winds do not generally extend much below Roberts point, among the Haro archipelago they become variable and baffling, while in the main channels of Rosario and Haro the westerly wind entering the strait of Fuca is deflected to SW., and vessels running up these channels with a fair wind almost always find it ahead on entering the strait of Georgia. During winter there is a good deal of moderate, calm, and gloomy weather, but gales from SE. and SW. are frequent.

Winds on the coast north of Vancouver island.—The prevailing winds during the summer on the coast northward of Vancouver island are from the NW., preceded during the earlier summer months by SW. winds.

During the winter months SE. and SW. winds prevail.

Gales from the SE. prevail at all seasons, and are more frequent and severe than those experienced on the coast of Vancouver island. The summer gales are of shorter duration than those of winter, and seldom last more than 48 hours. At the fall of the year, gales from the SE., lasting for 8 days have been experienced.

The strength of the summer winds depends greatly upon local circumstances. Down the channels, which lie in a NW. and SE. direction, with high land on both shores, they frequently blow with great strength. The wind usually begins at sunrise, increases in strength throughout the day until about 3 p. m., and then gradually declines toward sunset. The nights, as a rule, are calm during the summer months; but, if the wind prevail but slightly from the NW. during the night, it will probably blow hard from that quarter on the following day.

The barometer stands at about 30.10 during the prevalence of NW. winds. Gales from the SE. are usually preceded by a falling barometer, but not invariably. A sensation of dampness in the atmosphere is the usual precursor, and the reading of the wet and dry bulbs, though as a rule not differing greatly upon this coast, more closely approximate each other.

If during the summer the barometer fall one-tenth of an inch, especially if it has been standing at higher than 30.20, a gale from the SE. is probable.

These gales usually begin at ESE., veering to the southward with a falling barometer; the wind remaining at SE. and SSE. for a long or short period, according to the season of the year. With a rising barometer the wind shifts to the SW. with violent squalls, and then hauling more westerly blows itself out. A strong SE. gale, of short duration, has been experienced, during the summer, with the barometer previously registering 30.17 and falling to 30.12.

Winds in Queen Charlotte islands.—Southeast winds are prevalent, and are almost invariably accompanied with thick, rainy weather; those from the opposite quarter generally bring fine weather. The weather is uncertain, and can not be depended on for 24 hours at a time.

The heaviest rainfall is local, taking place on the western mountains of Queen Charlotte islands. It may often be noted that while heavy rain is falling on the mountains the sky is comparatively clear over the strait to the eastward. From this circumstance the NE. part of Graham island is not subject to a heavy rainfall. Snow occasionally falls in winter.

Currents.—Outside a distance variously estimated to be 25 to 50 miles from the southwestern coast of Vancouver island, a southeasterly current has been found to prevail more or less throughout the year, being most marked during the summer and autumn months, westerly and northwesterly winds blowing almost constantly during the summer. Inshore of this southeasterly current, along the western coast of Washington and Vancouver island, and across the entrance to the strait of Juan de Fuca, there is a northwesterly current. The velocity of this current varies considerably, being increased in southerly and southeasterly weather and diminished during the northwesterly winds that prevail during the summer months; during severe northwesterly gales is is probable that the direction of this current is reversed, but resumed when the weather moderates.

Near the entrance to the strait this northwesterly set is augmented by the ebb current out of the strait, which from the latest information sets in a general WNW. direction. The flood current, coming from the southward and setting across the entrance to the strait, also aids in producing and maintaining this northwesterly set.

Caution.—Off the entrance to the strait of Juan de Fuca the set of both the flood and the ebb stream, together with the indraft caused by Barkley, Clayoquot, and other sounds, accounts for the large amount of wreckage seen between Carmanah and cape Cook, and mariners are warned that with strong southeasterly to southwesterly winds there is a dangerous set onto this dangerous coast with its many outlying dangers. Sailing vessels, therefore, when making the strait of Juan de Fuca during the winter months, especially during November and December, and experiencing easterly and southeasterly winds, which then prevail, should endeavor to hold a position between SSW. and WSW. from Tatoosh Island light, and on no account open up the entrance of the strait until an opportunity occurs of getting well inside.

Tides.—On the coast and in the channels of British Columbia there are usually two high and two low waters, unequal in height, during the lunar day, the low waters differing from one another to a much greater extent than the high waters. The inequality varies principally with the declination of the moon. When the moon is near the equator the tides are generally nearly equal and have the least diurnal range. When the moon is near its greatest declination, north or south, the tides are very unequal and usually have the greatest range of the month.

The relative height of consecutive high waters or of consecutive low waters may be ascertained by noting the declination and the transit of the moon, there being two cases:

1. With north declination the higher high water occurs near the time of the moon's lower transit, and the lower low water follows the higher high water.

2. With south declination the higher high water occurs near the time of the moon's upper transit, and the lower low water follows the higher high water. (These rules do not apply to Juan de Fuca strait, Georgia strait, and their estuaries.)

At times, for two or three days together, the inequality of the low waters is so great as to destroy the smaller tide, and the water either stands for a long time after the proper time of the first high water and then continues to rise to the second, or, if the first high water should be the higher for the day, the water stands after the proper time of the succeeding or higher low water and then falls to the lowest level. Sometimes, instead of remaining stationary, the water will rise with varying rate from the lowest level to the highest, and there will be apparently but one tide in the day; but there are generally two defined tides.

The tides on the west coast of Vancouver island and in the channels north of it, between Queen Charlotte sound and Georgia strait, are more regular in time than those to the east and can not be referred to the same standard port.

The larger tide of the day occurs during the daytime when the sun is north of the equator, and during the night when it has south declination.

Tidal currents.—The tidal currents off the entrance to Juan de Fuca strait are rotary, and under conditions of equal rise and fall set about East at high water, circling round, through South, to West at low water, and continuing round through North to East again at high water.

The direction of the stream, as well as its strength, depends greatly on the range of the tide causing it. With a strong ebb current out of the strait the stream, from about 2 hours after to about 4 hours before high water, sets between SW. by S. and W. by S., when it gradually changes through West until at high water it is running NNW. From high water to 2 hours after, the stream is nearly slack, and changes quickly, though East, to South and West.

Observations, made in July, 1901, gave evidence of a steady westerly set, the rate of the east-going stream being never found to be much more than half that of the west-going stream.

The tidal wave traveling up the west coast of North America causes the flood stream to set obliquely across the entrance to Juan de

Fuca strait toward the Vancouver island shore, while a part of it turns sharply into the strait at cape Flattery. This latter stream, running with considerable velocity, sometimes 3 or 4 knots, over Duntze and Duncan rocks, sets also over to the Vancouver island shore as well as maintaining a general direction up the strait, and passes through the various channels among the islands of the Haro archipelago into the strait of Georgia, its effect being felt as far to the northward as Bute and Toba inlets. At cape Mudge and Stuart island, where Discovery passage and Cardero channel, respectively, open into Georgia strait, it is met by the stream which enters by Queen Charlotte sound. The effect is felt at some distance from cape Mudge, whirls and overfalls being frequently met with. The ebb stream has always been found to run to the southward through the Haro archipelago and out of Juan de Fuca strait for 2½ hours after low water by the shore. The ebb is stronger than the flood.

Outside the strait, along the shores of Washington and Vancouver island, the flood sets to the northward at a rate ranging from 1 to 1½ miles per hour; inside the strait, as far as Race rocks, the currents have a velocity of 2 to 4 miles per hour, depending on the range of the tides and the direction and force of the winds, the flood having a greater velocity along the northern shore than along the southern.

The ebb sets westnorthwestward after leaving the strait. It is felt most along the southern shore, and between New Dungeness and Port Crescent there is a southerly set that should be guarded against.

Along the Vancouver island shore the currents turn 1½ to 2½ hours earlier than on the Washington side of the strait. At Race rocks and Discovery island the currents have a velocity of 3 to 6 miles per hour and continue to run 1 to 2½ hours after high and low water. Eastward of Race rocks, in the wider part of the strait, the velocity is much less.

United States system of buoyage.—The following uniform system of buoyage has been adopted for the coasts and harbors of the United States:

In approaching the channel, etc., from seaward, red buoys, with even numbers, will be found on the starboard side of the channel, and must be left on the starboard hand in passing in.

In approaching the channel, etc., from seaward, black buoys with odd numbers, will be found on the port side of the channel, and must be left on the port hand in passing in.

Buoys painted with red and black horizontal stripes will be found on obstructions, with channel ways on either side of them, and may be left on either hand in passing in.

Buoys painted with white and black vertical stripes will be found in mid-channel, and must be passed close-to to avoid danger.

All other distinguishing marks to buoys will be in addition to the foregoing, and may be employed to mark particular spots, a description of which will be given in the printed list of buoys.

Perches with balls, cages, etc., will, when placed on buoys, be at turning points, the color and number indicating on which side they shall be passed.

Different channels in the same bay, sound, river, or harbor, will be marked as far as practicable by different descriptions of buoys. Principal channels will be marked by nun buoys; secondary channels, by can buoys; and minor channels, by spar buoys. When there is but one channel, nun buoys, properly colored and numbered, are usually placed on the starboard side, and can buoys on the port side, of it.

The rule for coloring buoys is applicable to beacons, and other day marks, marking the sides of channels. In other places, beacons and day marks will be constructed with special reference to the background against which they are seen.

Canadian system of buoyage.—Throughout the ports of British Columbia all buoys on the starboard side of the channel, entering from seaward, are painted red, and, if numbered, marked with even numbers, and must be left on the starboard hand when passing in.

All buoys on the port side, entering from seaward, are painted black, with odd numbers, if any, and must be left on the port hand when passing in.

Buoys painted with red and black horizontal bands will be found on obstructions or middle grounds, and may be left on either hand.

Buoys painted with white and black vertical stripes will be found in mid-channel, and must be passed close-to, to avoid danger.

All other distinguishing marks to buoys are in addition to the foregoing, and indicate particular spots; a detailed description of which is given when the mark is first established.

Perches with balls, cages, etc., will, when placed on buoys, be at turning points, the color and number indicating on which side they are to be passed.

Spar buoys will in some cases be surmounted by a ball, which will invariably be painted red, and will indicate that it is a starboard buoy, and must be left on the starboard or right hand when entering a channel or harbor.

The rule for coloring buoys is equally applicable to beacons, spindles, and other day marks, so far as it may be practicable to carry it out.

In British Columbian waters the buoys are not withdrawn in winter.

United States storm signals.—The following signals are in use by the Weather Bureau of the United States Department of Agriculture for announcing the approach of wind storms:

A storm signal.—A red flag with black center indicates that the storm is expected to be of marked violence.

A red pennant displayed with the flags indicates easterly winds—that is, from northeast to south, inclusive, and that the storm center is approaching. If the pennant is above cautionary or storm signal, winds from the northeast quadrant are expected; if below, winds from the southeast quadrant.

A white pennant displayed with the flags indicates westerly winds—that is, from north to southwest, inclusive, and that the storm center has passed. If the pennant is above the cautionary or storm signal, winds from the northwest quadrant are expected; if below, from the southwest quadrant.

Night signals.—By night a red light will indicate easterly winds; a white light above a red will indicate westerly winds.

The information signal consists of a red pennant, and indicates that the displayman has received information of a storm covering a limited area, dangerous only for vessels about to sail for certain points. The signal will serve as a notification to shipmasters that important information will be given them upon application to the displayman.

Canadian storm signals.—Storm signals are displayed from a gallows, usually erected on the post office, and consist of a black cone and a black cylindrical drum by day, and red and white lights at night.

By day.—(1) Cone with point down indicates the probability of a gale, at first from an easterly direction. (2) Cone with point uppermost indicates that a gale, at first from the westward, is expected. (3) The addition of the drum above the cone as in (1) indicates the expectation of a severe easterly gale. (4) The addition of the drum below the cone as in (2) indicates that a severe westerly gale may be expected.

By night.—(5) A red light indicates as in (1) and (3) by day. (6) A white above a red light indicates as in (2) and (4) by day.

Kelp will be seen on the surface of the water, growing on nearly every danger with a bottom of rock or stones, during the summer and autumn months, especially in those channels where the water is in constant motion; but during the winter and spring this useful marine plant is not always to be seen, and in close harbors where there is little motion in the water is often absent, in British Columbian waters.

It should be an invariable rule never to pass through kelp. In general, by keeping clear of kelp you keep clear of danger, but this must not prevent attention to the lead, as the rule sometimes fails; kelp is always a sign of danger, and unless the spot where it grows has been carefully sounded, it is not safe for a ship to pass over it. A heavy surge will occasionally tear the kelp away from rocks; and a moderate stream will ride it under water, when it will not be seen. When passing on the side of a patch of kelp, from which the stems stream away with the current, care should be taken to give it a wide berth, because the kelp showing with a strong tide is on one side of and not over the rocks. The least water will usually be found in a clear spot in the middle of a thick patch of fixed kelp.

It is perhaps well to point out that kelp not attached to rock floats on the water in heaps, whereas kelp attached to rocks streams away level with the surface, while the leaves give an occasional flap.

INNER PASSAGES.

Caution.—When navigating the inner waters of British Columbia it should be constantly borne in mind that many of the main channels and most of the minor passages have only been roughly examined; detached bowlders from the broken shores, and pinnacles of rock are still frequently found. Whenever, therefore, a broad and clear channel is known to exist, there is no justification in using, without necessity, one of more doubtful character, even if there be some saving in distance; and a ship should always be maintained in the safest possible position in a channel, as well as when going in or out of port.

Victoria to Burrard inlet.—The best route from Victoria to Burrard inlet is south of Trial and Discovery islands, through the main channel of Haro strait, and northward of Stuart and Waldron islands into the strait of Georgia. Only those with good local knowledge should attempt to navigate the inner channels.

The usual route for moderate-sized steamers between Victoria and Burrard inlet, is south of Trial island, westward of Chain and Chatham islands, by Mayor and Baynes channels, then to the northward, passing on either side of Zero rock and Darcy shoals, through Sydney channel and Moresby passage, between Prevost and Pender islands, and through Active pass into the strait of Georgia. By using this route weaker tidal streams will be experienced than are found in Haro strait and Swanson channel.

Victoria to Alaska.—From Victoria, or the strait of Juan de Fuca, it is usual for vessels to pass through Haro strait and enter Georgia strait, eastward of Saturna island, or through Active pass. The latter should be used only by steam vessels.

Strait of Georgia to Queen Charlotte sound.—Steamers usually pass southward of Ballenas islands, and also the Sisters, from whence a course is shaped for Discovery passage, the only navigable channel from the gulf of Georgia to the northwestward. Vessels may have to wait for slack water in Seymour narrows, for which Menzies and Duncan bays to the southward of the narrows, and Plumper bay to the northward, will be found convenient anchorages.

Proceed mid-channel through Johnstone strait; there is a clear channel both northward and southward of Helmcken island, the only prominent danger being Ripple rock; the latter, named Race channel, is that generally used, passing between Ripple rock and Camp point on Vancouver island.

When navigating Broughton strait do not pass more than 400 yards southward of Cormorant island to clear Nimpkish bank, and keep the southwestern shore of Haddington island aboard at a distance of ¼ mile to avoid the ledge extending eastward from Ledge point. Care should be taken when rounding Pulteney point, the SW. extreme of Malcolm island, off which foul ground extends for 1½ miles.

From Broughton sound to Queen Charlotte sound two routes are used. At night and in thick weather the better passage is through Goletas channel and Christie passage and thence through New channel, because they allow a closer and safer approach to the shores; this is the route commonly used. But in daytime with clear weather the route through New channel, in spite of the dangers on either hand, may be safely used. During July, August, and September dense fogs occur, and westerly winds bring a heavy swell.

From Queen Charlotte sound to Dixon entrance.—The route usually followed by steamers is by way of Fitzhugh sound, Lama passage, Seaforth channel, Milbank sound, Finlayson and Grenville channels, and Chatham sound. The passage from Queen Charlotte sound to Fitzhugh sound is between the dangerous Sea Otter group on the west and the rocks off the entrance to Smith sound. At its narrowest part, off Egg island, this passage is only 3 miles wide. Westerly winds bring a heavy swell, and, as dense fogs are frequent in this vicinity, too great care can not be taken in its navigation.

Caution.—Coming from the northwestward, Storm islands have a striking resemblance to Pine island and great caution should be exercised not to turn into Sealed passage between Storm islands and Pine island. This passage is blocked by Blind reef, which breaks in heavy weather.

Vessels entering from the westward use North passage between the Sea Otter group and Calvert island.

Fitzhugh sound is about 40 miles long, averages about 3 miles wide, and has deep water.

When passing from Seaforth channel to Milbank sound it is usual to pass ½ to ¾ mile northward of White rocks.

Finlayson channel is about 24 miles long, 2 miles wide, and has deep water; Hiekish narrows is 500 yards wide in the narrowest part. When passing Hewitt rock keep the NE. shore aboard, distant about 200 yards.

Grenville channel is reached from the westward through Campania sound, by Squally or Whale channels, or by the inner passages and Wright sound. Except when bound up Skeena river the passage south of Gibson island is preferable, thence by Arthur passage to Chatham sound, to Dixon entrance, and Port Simpson.

Dixon entrance to Cross sound.—The main channels at present used and touching at various points of Alaskan territory are, by the inland passages, as follows:

Passing through Revillagigedo channel, Tongass narrows, and Clarence strait, the route leads by way of Stikine strait to Wrangell harbor. From Wrangell harbor the route continues by way of Sumner strait and Wrangell strait into Frederick sound. Wrangell strait has a least depth of 10 feet at low water. It is well buoyed, but the navigation is difficult. Vessels too large to make the passage through Wrangell strait continue westward through Sumner strait, round cape Decision, and go northward through Chatham strait, or westward to sea by way of cape Ommaney. In either case, if bound for Sitka direct, the route would lead northward by Chatham strait and through Peril strait.

If bound to Juneau and Skagway stand through Frederick sound and Stephens passage to Juneau and Douglas in Gastineau channel; thence by Stephens passage to the western end of Douglas island; if bound to the head of Lynn canal pass up Favorite channel. If bound to Sitka pass through Saginaw channel, down Chatham strait, and by Peril strait. Peril strait should on no account be undertaken without a pilot. Vessels may pass out by Chatham or Sumner straits and continue outside to Sitka.

OCEAN PASSAGES.

Vancouver and Yokohama—Full-powered steam vessels.—The tracks recommended are as follows:

From Vancouver to Yokohama, during summer months, from Juan de Fuca strait steer to cross the meridian of 140° W. in lat. 51° N., keeping on that parallel to the one hundred and seventieth meridian, thence steering to cross 160° E. in lat. 48° N., 150° E. in lat. 43½° N., and to make the coast of Japan at Kinkwasan light in about lat. 38° 20′ N.

During winter months follow the same track to the one hundred and sixtieth meridian east, thence steering to cross 150° E. in lat. 44½° N., passing about 50 miles southeastward of Shikotan (Skotan), and to make the coast of Japan as before at Kinkwasan light.

These routes are usually northward of the westerly winds, and in the track of the cold westerly current throughout.

From Yokohama to Vancouver, at all seasons, cross the meridian of 150° E. in lat. 40° N., 160° E. in 44½° N., 170° E. in 47½° N., and the one hundred and eightieth meridian in lat. 49° N.; thence keeping on that parallel to 140° W., and from there steering for the entrance of Juan de Fuca strait. This route is usually in a warm easterly current throughout.

Sail or auxiliary steam.—Leaving Juan de Fuca strait, stand to the southwestward into the NE. trades, and run to the westward between the parallels of 15° and 20° N. From May to November, when in longitude about 180°, stand for Japan, but from December to April do not stand direct for Japan till in about 146° E., and allow for the Japan stream setting to the northeastward.

Vancouver to Valparaiso.—Full-powered steamers should proceed direct.

Sail or auxiliary steam.—**In winter** SE. and SW. winds prevail on the coast of California as far south as about lat. 25° N., and those bound from Vancouver island to Valparaiso at that season should stand down the coast, keeping at about 100 miles from it until near the latitude of San Francisco, and thence gradually edge to the westward so as to pass westward, and in sight, of Guadalupe island, where in all probability the NE. trade wind will be met; then steer to sight Clipperton island, passing westward of it; in about this latitude the NE. trade wind will be lost.

If steam power is available the belt of variable winds and calms, which at this season on the meridian of 120° W. is 250 to 350 miles wide, should be crossed on a southerly course so as to pick up the northern edge of the SE. trade winds in about long. 110° W. (well to windward); but if depending on sail alone a vessel will probably not be able to cross the equator much to windward of long. 118° W., and every effort should be made not to cross farther than that to the westward, as the result would be that the vessel would not weather Elizabeth to Pitcairn islands, in the vicinity of which light, baffling winds from South to SE. would be experienced.

The SE. trade wind at this time of the year will, in all probability, be met with between latitudes 5° N. and 3° N., the higher latitude during the early winter months (November and December), and the lower latitude toward March, when the ship should be kept full, making, as nearly as the wind will permit, a due South (true) course.

In about lat. 6° S. the trade wind generally becomes more easterly in direction, sometimes hauling as far around as E. by N. Cross the twentieth parallel (South) in long. 120° or 121° W. in order to pass well to windward of Ducie island, and, standing to the SE., cross the meridian of Easter island in about lat. 33° S. and the one hundredth meridian in lat. 36° S. Calms and variable winds will be experienced in the vicinity of the thirtieth parallel, setting into the NW. quarter as the vessel gets more to the southward, and on this account the one hundredth meridian should never be crossed northward of lat. 36° S. The fortieth parallel should be reached before making easting; thence steer to pass southward of Juan Fernandez and on to Valparaiso.

In summer.—In summer a course farther west may be pursued, passing the latitude of San Francisco in about 130° W. Thence a sailing vessel should be kept farther from the land to avoid the calms and light, variable winds experienced at this season along the coast of lower California and in the bay of Panama. After meeting the NE. trade wind in about lat. 30° N. stand to the southward, making a South (true) course on the meridian of 125° W., not only to avoid the calms above mentioned, but also the hurricanes which during August and September are liable to be met with eastward of that meridian. Occasionally, but rarely, these storms are met with west of long. 125° W.

The NE. trade wind will be lost at this season in lat. 11° or 12° N., and the belt of doldrums will be found to be not so wide as during the winter months. The SE. trade wind will at this season be met with in about lat. 8° N., and if, as is most likely to be the case at the commencement, the wind be well to the southward, stand to the eastward in order to recover some of the ground lost by keeping farther to the westward in the NE. trades. Endeavor to cross the equator in from long. 118° to 120° W.; soon after crossing the wind will haul more to the eastward, when stand to the southward to weather Ducie island, and reach the fortieth parallel before making easting, so as to fall in with the northwesterly winds, as calms and variable winds are met with north of that parallel. After passing the meridian of 90° W. haul up for Juan Fernandez, and thence for Valparaiso.

Valparaiso to Vancouver—Full-powered steam vessels.—Proceed direct.

Sail and auxiliary steam.—The best route to pursue when making this voyage is the same at all times of the year. Leaving Valparaiso stand to the northwestward passing to the eastward of St. Felix, and crossing the seventeenth parallel in long. 90° W. After falling in with the SE. trade wind steer to cross the equator in about 118° W. After falling in with the NE. trade wind steer to cross the twentieth parallel in long. 137° W. and the thirtieth parallel in long. 140° W. Thence edge away to the eastward, crossing the fortieth parallel in long. 138° W., and make for lat. 47° N., long. 130° W., before steering direct for Juan de Fuca strait. (Distance by this route 7,350 miles.)

In May and June the NE. trade wind is often very weak north of the twentieth parallel, and frequently a belt of calm exists between the twentieth and thirtieth parallels.

Panama to Vancouver island—Steam routes.—Direct. Along the California coast and to the northward, steamers should follow the coast from point to point, as nearly as possible, always keeping within 15 miles of the land. By this means the strong NW. wind will frequently be avoided, as calms will often be found close in with the shore when there is a wind to seaward.

Auxiliary steam.—Vessels with auxiliary steam power bound from Panama to Vancouver island should stretch off on a W. by N. (true) course (or, until the parallel of 12° N. is gained, a little more northerly), passing the meridian of Acapulco in about lat. 13° N. The eastern limit of the NE. trade wind is uncertain, but it will generally be met with in about long. 103° W., i. e., at about 300 miles from the land. When first falling in with it the W. by N. course should be maintained, as by steering more to the northward the trade wind will be found to hang to the north and northwest. The meridian of 110° W. should be crossed in lat. 14° N., after which steer to cross the one hundred and thirtieth meridian in about lat. 30° N., when steer northward as far as lat. 40° N., or until the westerly winds are reached, and thence gradually edge away for the port.

Sailing.—A vessel unaided by steam power will experience considerable difficulty and delay in getting out of the bay of Panama, owing to the light baffling winds and calms which are met with there at all seasons. Between October and April the prevailing wind in the gulf is from the northward; for the remainder of the year the wind hangs more to the westward, and land and sea breezes are felt, varied by calms and occasional squalls from southwest. Northward of lat. 5° N., between the eightieth and one hundred and tenth meridians, is a region of calms and light winds varied by squalls of wind and rain; but southward of lat. 5° N., between the coast of the mainland and the Galapagos islands, westward of the meridian of 80° W., the wind is between South and West all the year round, and, except between the months of February and June, is fairly strong.

A vessel should, therefore, at all seasons make the best of her way to the southward, keeping as nearly as possible on the meridian of 80° W. until lat. 5° N. is reached, when, if the wind will allow, make a SW. course. Should the wind be westward of SW. stand to the southward, but if southward of SW. stand to the westward, and should the wind be light and variable with rain make every endeavor to get to the southward. When lat. 2° N. is reached, a vessel may, between June and January, stand to the westward, carrying SW. winds as far as 85° W., after which the wind will haul to the southward and southeastward, settling into the SE. trade wind.

Pass northward of the Galapagos islands, keeping on the parallel of 2° N. until the meridian of 105° W. is reached, when edge away to pass westward of Clipperton island, in the neighborhood of which the NE. trade wind will be met with, when stand to the NW. to cross the parallel of 20° N. in long. 120° W., after which pursue the same course as if bound from Valparaiso.

Between January and April, however, it is better to cross the equator between the Galapagos islands and the mainland before standing to the westward. Southward of lat. 1° N. the wind will be found to haul to the eastward as the vessel leaves the coast. At this season vessels should keep to the southward of the equator until westward of long. 105° W., when proceed as before directed.

Vancouver to Panama—Full-powered steam.—Direct.

Sailing.—Sailing vessels making this passage between the months of December and May, inclusive, when the prevailing winds on the west coast of Mexico are from the the northward, and the current favorable, should stand down the coast of California, keeping about 100 miles off, and at about 150 miles off the coast of Mexico, shaping a course to make the island of Hicaron, about 50 miles westward from Mariato point, which is a good landfall for vessels bound to Panama from the westward.

Between the months of June and November, inclusive, when calms, variable winds, and oftentimes hurricanes prevail on the west coast of Mexico, sailing vessels should stand well out to sea after passing San Francisco, shaping a course to cross the equator in about long. 104° W., thence standing on to the southward, until sure of reaching Panama on the other (starboard) tack.

Southeastern Australia to Vancouver and back—Full-powered steamers.—Direct as possible, passing southeastward of New Caledonia, and calling at Fiji and Honolulu for coal, if necessary.

Sail and auxiliary steam routes.—Pass north or south of New Zealand, or through Cook strait, according to the direction of the wind on leaving, preferably through Cook strait, if from Sydney or Bass strait, but south of New Zealand if passing south of Tasmania.

Run to the eastward on about the parallel of 40° S., until in about 160° W.; then stand to the northeastward into the SE. trades. Run through both trades and when in the westerlies beyond the NE. trades, proceed direct.

When passing through the calms of Capricorn and Cancer, and through the equatorial doldrums, a northerly course should be steered to get through them as quickly as possible, and in an auxiliary steam vessel steam should be used.

A vessel on leaving New Zealand could at once stand to the northward through the trades, especially in July, August, and September, but better winds would probably be experienced by following the former route.

On the route back, stand to the southwestward into the NE. trade, and thence proceed as direct as possible, crossing the equator in about 170° W., and passing westward of the Fiji islands and southeastward of New Caledonia.

17203——4

CHAPTER II.

STRAIT OF JUAN DE FUCA, ADMIRALTY INLET, PUGET SOUND, HOOD CANAL, AND POSSESSION SOUND.

VARIATION IN 1906.

Cape Flattery	23° 40′ E.	Port Townsend	23° 15′ E.
Victoria	23 30′ E.	Seattle	23° 00′ E.

Juan de Fuca strait, between the south coast of Vancouver island and the north coast of Washington, has its entrance between the prallels of 48° 23′ N. and 48° 36′ N., on the meridian of 124° 45′ W., and is the connecting channel between the ocean and the inland passages extending southward to Puget sound and northward to the inland waters of British Columbia and southeast Alaska. The strait of Juan de Fuca is liable to all those sudden vicissitudes of weather common to high northern latitudes, and in few parts of the world is the caution and vigilance of the navigator more necessary than in entering it.

The commerce of this region is extensive, both foreign and domestic. Vast quantities of lumber and fish, together with grain and coal, are exported, while the manufacturing and shipbuilding industries are becoming important. Several transcontinental railroads have their western terminals on Puget sound and Georgia strait, and there are several trans-Pacific lines of steamers, foreign and domestic, in addition to the coasting and local steamers and sailing vessels.

The breadth of the strait at its entrance, between cape Flattery on the south and Bonilla point on Vancouver island, is 13 miles; from its entrance it has an average breadth of 12 miles for a distance of 50 miles in an ESE. direction, and thence to Whidbey island, its eastern boundary, a breadth of 15 to 18 miles. From the ocean to Whidbey island the mid-channel distance is 83 miles.

The shores are bold, abrupt, and covered with a heavy growth of timber and dense underbrush. They may be approached safely within ½ mile.

The strait in the center is of great depth, but within 1½ miles of either shore there is, generally, under 40 fathoms, and on the northern side, when 5 miles eastward of Port San Juan, 8 to 12 fathoms will be found within 1 mile of the shore.

On the northern or Vancouver island shore of the strait the hills rise gradually and are densely wooded, but near the coast attain to no great elevation; on the southern side are the almost perpetually snow-clad mountains known as the Olympian range.

At the eastern limit of the strait the western face of Whidbey island is very steep; it is about 250 feet high, and appears flat, as does the whole country eastward to the sharp-cut outline of the Cascade range, stretching northward, where the snow peak of mount Baker is distinctly seen, and to the southward, where the higher peak of mount Rainier attracts the eye.

During dry summers forest fires envelop the country in a vast smoke that lasts for 2 or 3 months. At such times it is frequently impossible to make out the shore at ½ mile distance. The strong westerly winds coming up the strait disperse it for awhile, but only to fan the fires and give them renewed force and activity.

On both sides of the strait are several anchorages or stopping places which may be taken advantage of by those meeting with adverse winds; those on the southern side, before reaching the harbors of Admiralty inlet, are Neah and Clallam bays, Port Angeles, New Dungeness bay, Washington harbor, and Port Discovery; on the northern side, westward of the Race islands, are Port San Juan, Sooke inlet, and Becher bay, eastward of which excellent anchorage may be always obtained during westerly winds.

The northern shore should be avoided, as it is the lee shore for most gales, and with the exception of Esquimalt harbor there are no anchorages for strangers that afford shelter from all winds.

In clear weather, no difficulty will be experienced in approaching the entrance of the strait from any direction, as the land on both sides is high, and cape Flattery, the southern point at the entrance, is very prominent, particularly from the southward because of the low land between Mukkaw and Neah bays.

The approaches to Juan de Fuca strait are marked by lights at cape Beale and Carmanah on the Vancouver side, and at Destruction island, Umatilla reef, and cape Flattery on the American side of the strait. These all, with the exception of Cape Beale light, have fog signals; nevertheless, in thick weather, the lead should be the chief dependence.

Soundings.—The outer limit of the 100-fathom curve is about 35 miles in a SSW. direction from cape Beale and cape Flattery. Westward of Barkley sound it is at an average distance of 25 miles offshore until westward of Clayoquot sound. Southward of Umatilla Reef lightvessel it is at an average distance of 20 miles from the lightvessel and Destruction island, except in a narrow submarine valley, with greater depths, beginning at a point about 10 miles southwestward from the lightvessel and extending northward, expanding to a width of over 5 miles between Carmanah point and cape Flattery, and thence into the straits. The outer limit of this valley is about 10 miles westward of cape Flattery.

On the Vancouver shore the 50-fathom curve is not less than 10 miles offshore at the entrance to Clayoquot sound, and to the eastward increases this distance rapidly to 25 miles off the western side of Barkley sound. Off the entrance to Barkley sound there is a bank, averaging 6 miles in width with a depth of 36 to 50 fathoms, surrounding a deep pocket that begins 7 miles from cape Beale and extends in a southwesterly direction for about 22 miles, with depths varying from 50 to 102 fathoms, and an average width of 5 miles. Southward of cape Beale the 50-fathom curve is about 4 miles offshore and extends toward cape Flattery, inclosing Flattery bank. From Duntze rock the 50-fathom curve passes ¾ mile westward of Cape Flattery lighthouse and then rapidly increases its distance from the coast to 8 miles, and is 3 miles westward of Umatilla Reef lightvessel. The depths inside 100 fathoms decrease rapidly to 30 fathoms, where the bottom becomes more uniform. To the southward of cape Flattery the 30-fathom curve is about ¾ mile inside the 50-fathom curve until abreast of Flattery rocks, where it is less than 1 mile westward of Umatilla Reef lightvessel.

Fogs.—The fogs are generally heavier near the entrance, decreasing in density and frequency up the strait. Near the entrance the fog sometimes stands like a wall, and vessels entering the strait run out of it into clear bright weather even before passing Tatoosh island. These fogs frequently extend a long distance seaward, and when combined with the smoke from the forest fires become exceptionally dense. The wind gradually works the fog into the strait, and it will follow the northern shore past Port San Juan to Sombrio river; occasionally it will reach as far as Sooke inlet and at times to Race rocks. As a rule, however, the fog follows farther into the strait along the southern shore, at times as far as Port Townsend. Frequently the northern shore is clear when the southern shore is enveloped in fog.

Wind.—In summer the prevailing northwesterly winds draw into the strait, increasing toward evening, and sometimes blowing a 10-knot breeze before midnight; this occurs, however, only when the winds are strong outside, and sailing vessels may be a week between cape Flattery and Admiralty inlet.

In winter southeasterly winds draw out of the strait, causing a heavy cross sea off the entrance, the heavy southwesterly swell meeting that coming out. Under these conditions vessels may make Neah or Clallam bays and await more favorable weather. The weather off the entrance in winter is, as a rule, exceptionally severe, and wrecks are of frequent occurrence. The heavy and broken sea is probably due to the shoaling off the entrance, the irregularity and velocity of the currents, and the conflict between the wind drawing out of the strait and that along the coast. Heavy rains occur in this region during the summer, and squalls of hail and sleet during the winter.

Currents.—The flood current enters Juan de Fuca strait from the ocean and sets eastward through the strait into Admiralty inlet, to the southward, and through the channels of Washington sound, to the northward, and meets the flood current from the northwestward around Vancouver island to the southward of cape Mudge.

Throughout the strait and at the entrance to Admiralty inlet, Haro strait, Rosario strait, and the smaller channels of Washington sound, the currents continue to run from 1½ to 2½ hours, depending on the range of the tides, after high and low water by the shore.

From the entrance of Juan de Fuca strait to Race rocks the velocity is from 2 to 4 knots, varying with the range of the tides and with the winds. Eastward of Race rocks the velocity is from 1½ to 3 knots till near the entrance to Admiralty inlet, where it varies from 2 to 4 knots. Heavy tide rips occur at the entrance of Admiralty inlet, and they may be looked for on all the banks in the strait; they are particularly heavy off cape Flattery, Race rocks, point Dungeness, and point Wilson.

Rescue stations.—Depots, with provisions and other necessaries for shipwrecked mariners, have been established at Cape Beale lighthouse and Carmanah lighthouse.

Notice boards have been erected at intervals between cape Beale and Port San Juan (about 12 miles eastward of Carmanah lighthouse), giving information, for the use of shipwrecked mariners, respecting the direction and distance of the nearest lighthouse, and also of the nearest Indian village where assistance can be obtained.

Cape Beale light.—Situated on a small islet at the extremity of cape Beale, which is a bold rocky point, 120 feet high (the tops of the trees being 300 feet above high water), is a square lighthouse, built of wood and painted white, 42 feet high, from which is exhibited, at a height of 178 feet above the sea, a white light, revolving every 30 seconds, with a red sector between the bearings S. 66° E. (East mag.) and S. 2° W. (S. 22° E. mag.), visible 19 miles. The light is in, approximately, lat. 48° 47′ 23″ N., long. 125° 13′ 14″ W. The lighthouse is a signal station, and has telegraphic and telephonic communication with Victoria.

Caution.—The light should not be brought to bear southward of S. 72° E. (N. 84° E. mag.), so as to avoid the foul ground which extends off Barkley sound.

The coast eastward of cape Beale trends SE. by E. for 21 miles to Carmanah lighthouse.

Carmanah light.—On the southern extremity of the point immediately westward of Carmanah, and about 2 miles NW. of Bonilla point, is situated a square, wooden tower, painted white, lantern red, white dwelling attached, 46 feet high, from which is exhibited, at a height of 173 feet above the sea, a flashing white light every minute, showing 3 flashes with intervals of 15 seconds between, followed by an interval of 30 seconds, during the greater part of which the light is eclipsed. The light should be visible 19 miles, and is in, approximately, lat. 48° 36′ 43″ N., long. 124° 44′ 59″ W.

Fog signal.—Carmanah fog signal is a horn, worked by steam and compressed air, giving blasts of 6 seconds' duration separated by silent intervals of 24 seconds.

The fog-signal station, of wood and painted white, with red roof, is situated in front of, and a little below, the lighthouse. It faces to the southward; the horns (which are in duplicate) are 125 feet above high water.

A signal station, also, for the purpose of enabling passing steamers to communicate during fogs, is established at Carmanah lighthouse. This consists of a steam whistle, and passing vessels may communicate by whistle sounds, using the Morse or Continental telegraphic codes.

The signal and rescue station at Carmanah lighthouse, with which vessels may communicate by means of the International code of signals, is under the following rules and regulations:

Vessels exhibiting their distinctive numbers will have their names transmitted to Victoria (for publication only) free of charge.

Dispatches to or from vessels within signaling distance, by flags of the International code, will be duly delivered as addressed, at tariff rates.

Dispatches will be charged for at the regular telephone rates, but no charges will be made for signaling between the flag station and vessels at sea.

Dispatches may be delivered in cipher by special request, otherwise they will be transmitted in ordinary language.

Destruction island lies about 45 miles to the southward of cape Flattery and about 3 miles off the Washington coast. It is 90 feet high, flat-topped, and covered with brush, with a few clumps of trees; it is about ½ mile long and at its southern part about 300 yards wide.

Light.—On the southwesterly part of Destruction island, in approximately, lat. 47° 40′ N. long. 124° 30′ W., is exhibited a flashing white light, showing a flash every 10 seconds, from a height of 147 feet above the sea, and visible 18 miles.

The lighthouse consists of a conical iron tower, 80 feet high, painted white, upper part black; with two oilhouses 25 yards, two dwellings about 180 yards, and a barn 225 yards, in a NE. direction, and a fog-signal building about 43 yards in a NW. direction, from it. These buildings are painted white, with brown roofs.

The fog signal is a steam siren that gives blasts of 5 seconds' duration, separated by silent intervals of 55 seconds.

Umatilla Reef lightvessel, moored about 2½ miles southwestward of Umatilla reef, in 25 fathoms of water, is about 33 miles NNW. of Destruction Island lighthouse, and about 14 miles SSE. of Cape Flattery lighthouse. The lightvessel shows two fixed white lights, one from each masthead, 39 feet above the sea, and visible 13 miles.

The lightvessel is schooner-rigged, with two masts and no bowsprit, a black funnel and a fog-signal apparatus between the masts, and a white circular gallery at each masthead under the lantern. The hull is painted red, with UMATILLA REEF in large black letters on each side, 67 in black figures on each bow and quarter.

Fog signal is a steam whistle which gives a blast every 30 seconds, thus: Blast 3 seconds, silent interval 27 seconds. If the whistle be disabled, a bell will be rung by hand.

The coast from cape Flattery trends south for a distance of 25 miles; the land is mountainous and heavily wooded. At a distance of 13 miles are the Flattery rocks, a group of bare, rugged islets, the outer rock lying 2½ miles off cape Alava.

Caution.—Seamen are again cautioned that when navigating the inner waters of British Columbia it should be constantly borne in mind that many of the main channels and most of the minor passages have only been roughly examined; detached bowlders from the broken shores, and pinnacles of rock, are still frequently found. Whenever, therefore, a broad and clear channel is known to exist, there is no justification for using, without necessity, one of more doubtful character, even if there be some saving in distance; and a ship should always be maintained in the safest possible position in a channel, as well as when going in or out of port.

SOUTHERN SHORE OF JUAN DE FUCA STRAIT.

Cape Flattery, or Classet, is a remarkable point of land, and in clear weather distinctly seen 35 miles, rising gradually from the sea to a thickly wooded mountain nearly 2,000 feet high, with an irregular-shaped summit, and falling again 3 or 4 miles eastward. When seen from the southward or southwestward it has the appearance of an island, being separated by low land from hills of the same or greater elevation, which rise again immediately southward of it.

Flattery was the name given to this cape by Cook in 1788; but Vancouver, in 1792, says it was known to the natives by the name of Classet.

On a nearer view, the headland itself, with offlying rocks over which the sea is almost constantly breaking, presents an uninviting appearance; it is a rugged sea-worn cliff of no great elevation, rising gradually to its more prominent feature, a densely wooded mountain. From the cape the coast trends eastward for 4 miles to Neah bay.

There is generally a heavy swell with irregular tides, and vessels should not approach the shore within a mile.

Tides.—It is high water, full and change, at cape Flattery, at 0 h. 0 m.; the ebb commences to run 2 hours after high water and continues for 6 hours.

Tatoosh island lies about half a mile NNW. from cape Flattery. The main island is about ¼ mile in diameter, with three smaller ones and several reefs awash close-to on its northwestern face. It is 108 feet high, flat-topped, and bare. A reef, the outer rock of which is usually awash, extends ¼ mile westward.

The passage between the island and the cape is dangerous; sailing vessels should give the island a berth of 3 miles.

Cape Flattery light.—On the summit of Tatoosh island stands Cape Flattery lighthouse, from which is exhibited, at a height of 155 feet above the sea, a fixed white light, with a fixed red sector between S. 16° E. (S. 40° E. mag.) and S. 9° E. (S. 33° E. mag.), covering Duncan and Duntze rocks. A dark sector, on the side toward the Washington shore, extends over an arc of 91° from N. 82° W. (S. 74° W. mag.) to N. 9° E. (N. 15° W. mag.); eastward of Chibadehl rocks it is not visible north of N. 88° W. (S. 68° W. mag.). Approximate lat. 48° 23′ 30″ N., long. 124° 44′ 06″ W.

The lighthouse is a white, conical tower rising from a gray sandstone dwelling, lantern painted black; another dwelling stands about 25 yards northeastward, and the fog-signal station about 27 yards northward, of the lighthouse.

Fog signal is a steam whistle which sounds blasts of 8 seconds' duration separated by silent intervals of 52 seconds.

Signal station.—A storm signal station has been established on Tatoosh island near the lighthouse; the building is white with black roof. Vessels can communicate by the International code. The station has telephonic communication and vessels can be reported, or may send or receive messages.

Fuca pillar, 140 feet high and 50 feet in diameter, lies $\frac{8}{10}$ mile S. 15° E. (S. 39° E. mag.) of the lighthouse on Tatoosh island. It is a leaning, rocky column, and only 120 yards from the cliffs, which are 120 feet high. It shows well when a vessel is approaching Tatoosh island from the northwestward, and is last seen from the strait when the face of the cape is just open of the eastern tangent of Tatoosh island.

Duncan rock lies N. 14° W. (N. 38° W. mag.) 1 mile from Cape Flattery lighthouse; it is a few feet above water, but the sea always breaks over it. There is deep water between it and the island, but vessels should not use the passage unless carried by the tidal streams into such a position as would cause danger in trying to avoid it. A shoal of 4 fathoms lies southeastward of Duncan rock with Cape Flattery lighthouse bearing S. 2° W. (S. 22° E. mag.), distant 1,550 yards.

Duntze rock, with 3 fathoms water over it, lies about ¼ mile N. 19° W. (N. 43° W. mag.) of Duncan rock, and the sea frequently breaks on it. The cross sea which is created in this neighborhood during bad weather strongly resembles heavy breakers, extending a considerable distance across the strait. In the immediate neighborhood of cape Flattery, and among these rocks, the tides are strong and irregular.

Swiftsure bank, on which a depth of 13 fathoms was reported to exist, is situated 13 to 15 miles NW. from Cape Flattery lighthouse. This bank was carefully sounded over by H. B. M. S. Egeria, in 1901, when the least depth found was 20 fathoms; there is a considerable area having depths of from 21 to 25 fathoms.

Buoy.—A whistling buoy, painted in black and white vertical stripes, is moored in 23 fathoms, 12¾ miles N. 51° W. (N. 75° W. mag.) from Cape Flattery lighthouse. This buoy will prove a useful aid to vessels entering or leaving the strait.

Reported shoal.—A sounding of 26 fathoms, bottom very coarse sand, has been obtained in lat. 48° 46′ N., long. 126° 36′ W. Another cast taken immediately afterwards gave no bottom at 98 fathoms.

Directions.—Vessels from the southward or westward bound for Juan de Fuca strait, except the coasting steam vessels which all carry pilots, should make cape Flattery; there is no inducement to hug the coast, on which a long rolling swell frequently sets, and this swell meeting the southeasterly gales of winter, causes a confused sea.

The cape and its offlying rocks should be given a berth of at least 3 miles, as the tidal stream sometimes sets over Duncan and Duntze rocks with great velocity; the currents furnish an additional reason why these dangers should not be too closely approached.

It is equally necessary when entering or leaving the strait to avoid the coast of Vancouver island between Port San Juan and Bonilla point, when there is any appearance of bad weather.

It is recommended to pass at the distance of at least 10 miles from the coast of the mainland southward of cape Flattery, unless working to windward against a fine northerly wind, which is frequently found during summer, when it may be safely approached, but not closer than 3 miles.

When nearing the strait at night, or in thick weather, be certain of the latitude. Within a distance of 25 to 30 miles from cape Flattery or the Vancouver island coast, the steady set to the northwestward across the entrance to the strait should be particularly guarded against, especially during the winter months, when southeasterly and southerly winds prevail. Sailing vessels making the strait during bad weather should endeavor to hold a position between SSW. and WSW. from Cape Flattery light, and on no account open up the entrance of the strait until an opportunity occurs of getting well inside. It is necessary also to remember that, though it may be blowing strongly from the SW. or SSW. outside, on rounding cape Flattery an easterly wind may be found blowing out of the strait, and a vessel would then find the Vancouver island coast a dangerous lee shore.

With southwesterly or westerly gales it will be more desirable to run in and seek shelter than to remain outside. If the land has been made either to the southward of cape Flattery or on the Vancouver island shore within a moderate distance of the entrance, or if the latitude can be relied upon within 2 or 3 miles, it will be advisable to run for the strait. The powerful light on Tatoosh island will, except in very thick weather, or fog, be seen, and as soon as a vessel is actually within the strait, where there is comparatively smooth water, with sufficient sea room, she can run boldly up the center for Race light, or if preferred, by the assistance of that on Tatoosh island, maintain position in the strait.

When Cape Flattery light is brought to bear to the northward of West it is shut in by the land about Neah bay, and Race Island light becomes obscured by Beechey head when bearing southward of E. by S.; therefore, when either of these lights are obscured the distance from either coast will be closely known, and in the latter case a ship will be getting too close to the northern shore.

When intending to go outside the Race islands, pass the land about Beechey head at a distance of at least 2 miles.

Steamers taking Race passage give Church point a berth of about ½ mile, and keep the land aboard about that distance until up with Bentinck island, when the latter should be closed and kept within ¼ mile, or just outside of the kelp. The passage between Bentinck island and the Vancouver coast is choked with rocks, and strong tidal streams set through.

Coming from the westward with a heavy westerly or northwesterly gale, thick weather, and uncertain of the latitude, it would be prudent to lie-to at not less than 30 miles from the entrance of the strait, or on the edge of the bank of soundings. These gales seldom last more than 12 hours, and if they veer toward the SW. the weather will clear, and vessels may bear up for the strait.

With a SE. gale the land may be closed, as smoother water will be obtained, and the bank of soundings off the Vancouver island shore will indicate pretty accurately the distance from the land. Gales from this quarter sometimes continue in the winter season for 30 hours.

It is of great importance in making the strait during bad weather to strike the outer edge of the bank of soundings, as the ship's distance from the land will then be accurately known.

Should sailing vessels be overtaken by one of the dense fogs which sometimes hang over the entrance of the strait, they should not close the land, but stand off sufficiently far to avoid the set of the current and tidal streams near cape Flattery.

When 8 or 10 miles eastward of Port San Juan there is anchoring ground in 12 fathoms 1 mile from the shore, and if the fog is very dense a stranger should anchor; it should be noted, however, that not infrequently the weather is clear a few miles within the strait while the entrance is totally obscured.

Neah bay, about 5 miles westward of cape Flattery, is formed between Koitlah point and Waaddah island; the latter, ½ mile long in a NW. and SE. direction, is narrow and covered with pine trees. Koitlah point is 4 miles east from cape Flattery.

The bay offers a safe and convenient anchorage to vessels meeting SW. or SE. gales at the entrance to the strait, and is sheltered from W. by N. round by South to ENE. The western shore is steep, but a reef extends more than 200 yards off Koitlah point, and a sand bank which dries extends ¼ mile at low water from abreast the cliffs. The head of the bay is a low sandy beach, on which the surf generally breaks. Off the SW. side of Waaddah island extends a reef and shoal water for a distance of ¼ mile, and the holding ground is not so good on the island side. The passage between the island and Baaddah point is only 250 yards wide with a least depth of 3¾ fathoms; this channel is used only by small vessels having local knowledge.

The proximity to the entrance to the strait and ease of access at all times make this anchorage very valuable; there is usually some swell, especially in northerly or westerly weather, when it is rather uncomfortable.

Lights.—On the northwestern extremity of Waaddah island, from an arm on a white stake, 20 feet above high water, is exhibited a fixed white light.

From a white gallows frame on Baaddah point, 16½ feet above water, is exhibited a fixed white light.

Whistling buoy.—A buoy, painted red, with NEAH BAY on it in white letters, and fitted with an automatic whistle, is moored in 21 fathoms at the entrance to Neah bay about 1¼ miles E. by N. from Koitlah point. The tidal streams set strongly past the buoy.

Anchorage.—The anchorage space is about 1 mile by ½ mile with depths varying from 4 to 10 fathoms, sandy bottom.

A good berth will be found in Neah bay, in 6 fathoms, sandy bottom, with the outer point of Waaddah island N. 56° E. (N. 32° E. mag.), and Koitlah point N. 56° W. (N. 80° W. mag.); a short distance within this position kelp grows in large patches all over the bay, and care is necessary in selecting a berth. Large sailing vessels may anchor in 7 or 8 fathoms a little outside the above bearings, in the center of the bay, with the outer point of the island N. 79° E. (N. 55° E. mag.).

Tides.—It is high water at full and change in Neah bay at 0 h. 33 m.; springs rise 7½ feet, neaps rise 6¾ feet.

Signal station.—A weather signal station has been established on Baaddah point; it displays signals for the approach of all dangerous winds, and is equipped with the International code flags. Messages signaled by the International code will be transmitted by telegraph. Vessels showing their numbers will be reported to Seattle, Portland, and San Francisco.

Neah is a small settlement at the head of the bay. There is a post-office here, and communication may be had with sound ports by telegraph and steamers. Freight and passengers are landed in small boats or canoes. Lighterage charges are about $4 per ton. Provisions can be obtained in small quantities.

Directions.—In entering pass westward of the whistling buoy and give Waaddah island a berth of 600 yards.

Vessels should leave this bay on any indication of a NE. wind, and if too late and unable to weather Waaddah island, they may run between it and the main; the passage is 250 yards in breadth, and the least water 21 feet; they must be careful to avoid the ledge off the SW. end of Waaddah, and in hauling out should give the eastern side of the island a berth of at least ¼ mile. Vessels have ridden out NW. gales close to the SE. end of Waaddah in 6 fathoms, but it is more prudent to get out into the strait at the commencement of the gale. During strong westerly or southwesterly gales, or after they have been blowing outside, a considerable swell rolls into the bay, which renders it at such times a disagreeable though not unsafe anchorage; small vessels may go close in and get smooth water, even among the kelp, which grows in 4 and 5 fathoms.

Clallam bay.—This bay is 15 miles SE. by E. ½ E. from Neah bay, the intervening coast being nearly straight and the shore bold. The only remarkable feature is Sail rock 150 feet high, lying a short distance offshore and 2 miles eastward of Waaddah island.

Temporary anchorage and shelter may be had, during easterly or southeasterly winds, in the center of the bay in from 8 to 10 fathoms.

The bay is easily recognized by Slip point, its eastern bluff, which is the western termination of a bold coast ridge, about 1,000 feet high.

Slip Point light.—A fixed white light, 30 feet above high water and 6 feet above the ground, is shown from a white framework structure, with brown roof, erected on Slip point.

Fog signal.—In the same building is a fog trumpet, operated by compressed air, which gives one blast every 20 seconds, thus: Blast 2 seconds; silent interval 18 seconds.

East and West Clallam are two small settlements on the eastern and western ends of the bight. Communication may be had with sound ports by steamer and telegraph.

Storm-warning displays are made from a staff at West Clallam.

Tides.—High water occurs 1 h. 6 m. later, and low water 0 h. 57 m. later than at cape Flattery.

The coast from Clallam bay continues in an ESE. direction for 8 miles to Pillar point, so called from its terminating in a bare columnar-shaped rock, somewhat remarkable from its contrast to the general characteristics of the country (thickly wooded from summit to water line), where few objects present themselves by which seamen may accurately fix their positions. The coast on the eastern side of this point forms a small bight, in which there is a considerable stream and an Indian village, and then trends E. by S. for 17 miles to Striped peak; a small river, the Lyre, enters the strait just westward of Low point, 6 miles westward from the peak.

Striped peak is rather remarkable from a landslip occurring down its face; at 1½ miles westward from the peak, and ⅓ mile off the western point of Crescent bay (merely an indentation), lies a rock with 3 feet over it, and on which the sea breaks at low water. This rock is marked by a red nun buoy.

Light.—On Low point, the eastern point of Lyre river, is exhibited a fixed white post-lantern light as a guide for vessels calling at the small town of Gettysburg at the mouth of the Lyre river.

Port Crescent, about 15 miles eastward from Pillar point, is a small semicircular bight about 1 mile in diameter. The anchorage is of small extent and suitable only for small vessels. Port Crescent village, at the head of the bight, has a post-office, and communication may be had with sound ports by steamer and telegraph.

Light.—The western head of the bay is marked by a fixed red post-lantern light, 40 feet above high water.

Crescent reef.—A reef with 3 feet of water over it lies about ⅝ mile northward of the western point at the entrance; it extends about

$\frac{5}{8}$ mile in an east and west direction, with a narrow channel between it and the point.

Buoy.—The reef is marked by a red nun buoy placed about 50 yards N. by E. from the shoalest part of the reef.

A. reef extends about 400 yards northwestward from Tongue point, the eastern point at the entrance.

Storm-warning signals are made from a staff at Port Crescent.

Telegraph cable.—The submarine cable from Becher bay, Vancouver island, is landed in Crescent bay.

Freshwater bay, 3 miles eastward from Striped peak, between Observatory and Angeles points, is nearly 1 mile deep, and more than 2 miles wide in an east and west direction, and the depth varies from 6 to 12 fathoms. Observatory point has several rocks extending a short distance off it; the western side of the bay is a high, bold shore. Angeles point, the eastern entrance point, is low; the river Elwha, flowing through it, forms a delta, and has caused a bank with a depth of water on it varying from 2 fathoms close inshore to 10 fathoms at a distance of 1 mile. There is anchorage within the line of the points in from 6 to 9 fathoms, but the bay is little used on account of its lack of shelter and its nearness to Port Angeles.

Port Angeles is $6\frac{1}{2}$ miles eastward of Angeles point, 56 miles eastward of cape Flattery, and about 27 miles to the westward of point Wilson. It is included between Ediz hook, a low, narrow sand spit about 3 miles long, and the southern shore, and is about $2\frac{1}{2}$ miles long with a width of $1\frac{1}{4}$ miles at its entrance.

The harbor is easy of access and is frequently used by vessels when weather-bound or awaiting orders. It is protected from all but easterly winds, which have little effect.

The best anchorage is in 7 to 12 fathoms, sticky bottom, off the wharves.

Port Angeles.—On the southern shore of the port is the town of Port Angeles, a port of entry, a deputy collector being stationed here. From 15 to 22 feet can be taken alongside the ends of the piers. Communication may be had with sound ports by steamer and telegraph.

Storm-warning signals are displayed from a staff and are plainly visible to vessels in the harbor and strait.

Tides.—It is high water, full and change, at 1 h. 51 m. Springs rise $5\frac{1}{2}$ feet.

Telegraph cable.—A submarine cable crosses Juan de Fuca strait from Albert head to Port Angeles; it lands $1\frac{1}{2}$ miles westward of Ediz Hook lighthouse. Vessels should not anchor near the cable.

Ediz Hook light.—From the extremity of Ediz hook, northerly side of Port Angeles, is exhibited, 41¾ feet above high water, a fixed white light, which should be visible 11¾ miles.

The lighthouse is a square tower rising from a dwelling, painted white, dome of lantern black.

Approximate position: Lat. 48° 08′ 24″ N., long. 123° 24′ 07″ W.

Fog signal.—The fog-signal station is a white bell tower about 108 yards N. by W. from the lighthouse. During thick or foggy weather a bell will be struck by machinery once every 15 seconds.

New Dungeness bay.—The shore from Port Angeles runs to the eastward as far as Green point, a distance of about 5 miles, and thence to the northeastward for 8 miles to New Dungeness lighthouse.

The bay is formed by a sand spit, like Ediz hook, which extends in a northeasterly direction from the mainland for a distance of 3½ miles. This spit is low and narrow, and covered with grass.

Dungeness shoal extends to the northeastward from the end of the spit for a distance of ¾ mile. It has 11 feet over it at low water; at the change of the stream a heavy tide rip runs over it.

Buoy.—The extremity of this shoal is marked by a red nun buoy which should be left to starboard by vessels entering the bay or bound up the strait.

On the inside of the bay, about a mile from the extremity of the hook, another narrow sand spit runs to the southward, toward the main shore, forming a large, inner, shoal bay with a narrow opening, through which the water forms a rapid, going in and coming out. Abreast of this point is a small stream, on the western side of which is a bluff 60 feet high, and on it a village of Clallam Indians; from the stream fresh water can be obtained at low water.

The shore eastward of this stream is low, swampy, and covered with brush and trees; off it are extensive mud flats, which uncover at low water for over half a mile, and which extend as far as Port Williams and Washington harbor.

Light.—On the outer end of New Dungeness spit, from a conical tower, rising from a grayish-yellow dwelling, is exhibited, 90¾ feet above high water, a fixed white light, which should be visible 15¼ miles.

Approximate position: Lat. 48° 10′ 55″ N., long. 123° 06′ 31″ W.

The tower, upper part black, lower part white, lantern red, is 89 feet high. The fog-signal building is 150 yards northeasterly, and a white barn 33 yards southwesterly, from the tower.

Fog signal.—The fog signal consists of a 12-inch steam whistle which, in thick or foggy weather, is sounded thus: Blast of 6 seconds' duration; silent interval of 12 seconds; blast of 3 seconds' duration; silent interval of 39 seconds.

Anchorage.—The usual and best anchorage in New Dungeness bay is to bring the lighthouse to bear N. 18° E. (N. 5° W. mag.), ½ mile distant, in 8 fathoms, sandy bottom. With the lighthouse bearing N. 11° W. (N. 34° W. mag.), ¾ mile distant, the same depth and bottom are found; from this position a vessel can readily get under way and clear the point. A SE. wind drawing out of the strait blows directly into this bay, but the bottom will hold any vessel with good ground tackle; the only difficulty will be to get the anchors out of the mud after riding a couple of days to a gale.

Tides.—It is high water, full and change, at New Dungeness at 3 h. 3 m.; springs rise 5 feet.

Washington harbor.—The coast from New Dungeness trends SE. for about 6 miles to Washington harbor. The shore is low and flat and bordered by an extensive mud flat which averages nearly 1 mile in width. The harbor is about 3¾ miles long in a NNW. and SSE. direction, with an average width of 1 mile. Its entrance is almost closed by a long sand spit extending from the eastern side, leaving a narrow, winding channel through which only 11 feet can be carried with local knowledge. The depths inside range from 6 to 19 fathoms.

The harbor is therefore of little importance when there are so many good ones in the neighborhood.

Port Discovery, where Vancouver anchored and refitted his ships, and from whence he commenced his exploration of these regions in May, 1792, lies in the eastern part of the bight between New Dungeness and point Wilson. It is not readily made out by vessels in the strait because the entrance appears blocked by Protection island, lying 2 miles NW. of it. The harbor is an extensive inlet trending in a SSE. direction for about 6 miles, with an average width of 1½ miles. The general depth of water is from 20 to 30 fathoms.

Anchorage may be had in 20 fathoms, soft bottom, on the western side 2 miles south of Clallam point, the western point of entrance, and also near the head of the inlet, into which empties the Salmon river.

A spit extends a short distance off Clallam point; when working up, the prominent points should be avoided, as the soil breaking away from the neighboring cliffs has formed a bank off most of them.

Tides.—It is high water, full and change, in Port Discovery at 2 h. 30 m.; springs rise 7 feet.

The United States National Quarantine station is situated at Clallam point.

Protection island.—This island lies immediately off the entrance to Port Discovery and shelters it from NW. winds. It is about 1½ miles long in a NE. and SW. direction, and about 1 mile wide.

The highest part is near the western end where it is about 200 feet high, though the fir trees by which it is covered make it look much higher. The coast is very steep, and the eastern portion of the island is cultivated.

From its southwestern extremity a shoal extends for over ¼ mile, with depths of less than 5 fathoms ½ mile from the point.

Buoy.—This is marked by a black can buoy moored in 5½ fathoms about ¾ mile westward of the end of the spit known as Kanem point. The northern and western sides of the island are shoal for a distance of ½ mile.

Dallas bank.—Extending 2½ miles northward from Protection island is Dallas bank, on which vessels may anchor in from 4 to 10 fathoms. Dallas shoal, with a depth of 3 fathoms over it, is reported to be about 2½ miles northward of the western end of Protection island.

Between Protection island and the mainland there is a broad safe passage.

The coast runs from cape George, the eastern point of entrance to Port Discovery, in a general ENE. direction to point Wilson. About midway is Middle point, projecting out from the coast line nearly ⅓ mile. This stretch of coast lies at the base of high yellow cliffs between 400 and 500 feet high.

Currents.—The currents in this neighborhood are confused, due to the proximity of the entrance to Admiralty inlet, Dallas bank, and the passage to Port Discovery.

Libby rock, with a depth of 10 feet over it, lies ½ mile NNW. of Middle point. Northward of the rock, and outside the foul ground off Middle point, is moored, in 8 fathoms, a red nun buoy, marked 4.

Quimper peninsula.—Between Port Discovery on the west and Port Townsend on the east lies a peninsula averaging 3 miles in width and about 10 miles long. It is undulating and has many large farms.

Point Wilson.—This point lies at the entrance to Admiralty inlet, of which it forms the western point. It is also the northwestern point of the entrance to Port Townsend.

The high, yellow, clay cliffs surmounted by heavy forest run from Port Discovery to Port Townsend, and reach a height of 400 or 500 feet near Rocky point; they are very steep and break down suddenly under a hill 250 feet high, ⅜ mile before reaching the extremity of point Wilson. This point stretches out toward Admiralty head and is formed of low sandy hillocks covered with coarse grass.

On the extremity of the point are the lighthouse buildings.

Between Rocky point and point Wilson the 5-fathom curve is less than ¼ mile distant, except within ⅜ mile of point Wilson, where it reaches out ½ mile over a very rough, rocky, and shingly bottom, with a field of kelp to mask it. The kelp field is well off the point on the northern side of the bight just westward of the low extremity. The 10-fathom curve lies about ⅔ mile from the shore. Directly off the point toward Admiralty bay, a depth of 20 fathoms is found 100 yards from the beach, and the currents make by it with great velocity. During ebb tides a very strong eddy current sets to the eastward alongshore from Middle point, and even as far as Port Discovery. Vessels working out from Port Townsend, with the strong summer winds, should stand well under the SE. shore of point Wilson, carrying 3 fathoms within 250 yards of the beach SW. of the lighthouse, and round the point close aboard.

Sunken rock.—A dangerous sunken rock has been reported as lying about ½ mile offshore and about ¾ mile west of point Wilson.

Buoy.—To mark the foul ground off Wilson point is moored a red nun buoy, marked 6, in 14 fathoms of water. Vessels should not go inside of the buoy.

Point Wilson light.—On the end of the spit making off to the eastward from point Wilson, westerly side of the entrance to Admiralty inlet, is exhibited from a white square tower rising from a dwelling, also white, the lantern and dome being painted black, a fixed white light varied by a red flash every 20 seconds. The light is 50 feet above the water and should be visible 12½ miles.

Approximate position: Lat. 48° 08′ 39″ N., long. 122° 45′ 14″ W.

Fog signal.—From a white building in front of the dwelling is sounded a 12-inch steam whistle, thus: Blast, 8 seconds; silent interval, 52 seconds.

Partridge point.—This is the western point of Whidbey island, the eastern boundary of the strait of Juan de Fuca. It may be considered the northern point of the entrance to Admiralty inlet and Puget sound, although Admiralty head and point Wilson are, strictly considered, the two points of entrance.

The seaward slope is very steep and shows large areas of sand and sandy soil. The land is level on the summit, and is covered with spruce, fir, and cedar. There are two noticeable cultivated farms on the shore about 3 miles to the northward of the point. The point is so round that it is not easily recognized on coming from the west, but from the south and north it is well marked and prominent. Its face is composed of yellow sand, which, being blown up the hill by the strong westerly winds, has formed a very peculiar ridge on the outer face of the top. This is so narrow that it can hardly be traveled, and in many places it is 35 feet above the ground inside; yet, being overgrown with bushes, the ridge is now permanent.

A bowlder reef extends ½ mile from the point and, in summer, is marked by kelp.

Off the end of this reef, in from 5 to 10 fathoms, the tidal streams are very strong, and there are overfalls at the changes.

Buoy.—About 1 mile westward of Partridge point, marking the end of the reef, is moored a red bell buoy, in 15 fathoms of water.

Partridge bank, a ridge about 1 mile wide, extending 3¼ miles in a NW. and SE. direction, is situated NW. of Partridge point, its southeastern end being about 1¾ miles from the point.

The shoalest part of the bank, a small patch with 14 feet over it, lies 3¼ miles N. 50° W. (N. 73° W. mag.) from Partridge point, and the same distance S. 5° E. (S. 28° E. mag.) from Smith Island lighthouse.

Buoy.—Near this 14-foot patch is moored a black can buoy. Vessels bound into Admiralty inlet should leave this buoy on the port hand.

ADMIRALTY INLET, PUGET SOUND, AND HOOD CANAL.

General description.—Under special names the great body of water now known to the commercial world under the general designation of "Puget sound" may be described as a series of vast interior canals giving unsurpassed facilities for navigation in the very heart of a prosperous section of the country.

"Puget sound," in the broad acceptation of the term, lies between latitudes 47° 03′ N. and 48° 11′ N., and between longitudes 122° 10′ W. and 123° 10′ W.

Admiralty inlet has its entrance 14 miles east from New Dungeness light, between Wilson point on the south and Partridge point on the north; connecting Juan de Fuca strait with Puget sound and Hood canal, it runs in a general SSE. direction for about 17 miles to point No Point and the southern end of Whidbey island, with an average width of 3 miles.

Its eastern shore, formed by Whidbey island, affords neither anchorage nor shelter. The western shore is more broken and irregular, the principal inlets being Port Townsend at its northern end and Port Ludlow at its southern end. Port Townsend, Port Hadlock, and Port Ludlow are the principal towns.

At 16 miles within the entrance Hood canal open out southward.

Puget sound extends about 35 miles in a general southerly direction from the southern end of Whidbey island, and then turns southwestward, ramifying by eight principal arms through an area 22 miles square. The extreme northwestern arm, named Case inlet, reaches within 2 miles of the head of Hood canal, and between them lies comparatively low ground and a large lake.

At its northern end it connects with Possession sound and the inland waters east of Whidbey island that lead through Deception pass into Rosario strait.

The principal towns on the sound are Seattle, Tacoma, and Olympia.

The shores of these inlets are generally bluffs, ranging from 50 to 500 feet in height, and their tops are covered with trees and thick undergrowth to the very edge. It is difficult to recognize the different points because of the sameness in the appearance of the shores.

The depth of water is everywhere great and anchorage difficult to obtain at any distance from shore.

Tidal currents.—In Admiralty inlet the tidal streams run at a rate of from 1 to 3 knots, and turn at about 2½ hours after high and low water by the shore.

Directions (general).—The navigation of these waters is perfectly simple in clear weather with the aid of the chart, the channels being broad, open, and generally free from outlying dangers. In thick weather the use of whistle echoes is common by those having local knowledge, and in certain localities the lead is of use. A mid-channel track is generally safe, but strangers are advised to employ pilots, especially in the narrow passages of the southern part of the sound.

Admiralty head lies 5½ miles SE. from Partridge point, and directly opposite the entrance to Port Townsend. It is a nearly vertical, rocky cliff, 80 feet high, the summit being marked by the cluster of white lighthouse buildings; it falls away to the northward to low, marshy ground and a large lagoon.

Light.—From Admiralty head is exhibited a fixed white light, at a height of 127 feet above the sea, which should be visible 17¾ miles.

The tower, cylindrical, painted white, and 32 feet high, is connected by a covered passageway with a white two-story dwelling. The lantern is black. There is a white oil house about 17 yards southward of the dwelling.

The light is in, approximately, lat. 48° 09′ 40″ N., long. 122° 40′ 46″ W.

Admiralty bay is formed by a sweep of the shore line, forming a semicircle with a diameter of more than 3 miles. It is used only occasionally for anchorage, just to the eastward of the lighthouse, where the bottom is hard and sandy in irregular ridges, and with depths of from 15 to 25 fathoms. It is an uncomfortable anchorage, for it is open to the full sweep of the southeasters, and at all times the current is running out. This current is so strong that even in the summer winds a vessel rides to it. With the wind from the southward a vessel would lie in the trough of the sea.

Sailing vessels should not approach Admiralty head or bay, because in calm weather they encounter the strong and irregular currents near it, and they may be embayed under the eastern shore.

Port Townsend is just within the entrance of Admiralty inlet, now almost universally known as Puget sound, and is a port of entry for the Puget Sound district. It is a safe harbor, but from its extent it is subject to a disagreeable sea in heavy winds, and with a strong southeaster landing is oftentimes impracticable and the sea dangerous for boats.

The entrance to the harbor itself lies between point Wilson and Marrowstone point, the latter distant 3⅝ miles from the former. Inside of the line between point Wilson and Marrowstone point the width of the port is contracted by point Hudson, which lies S. ¾ E. 1⅝ miles from point Wilson. From the entrance the mid-channel direction of the port is nearly SW. for 3 miles, with an average width of 2 miles to abreast the most westerly indentation, and then S. by E. for 3½ miles, with an average width of 1¼ miles.

The shores of the port are moderately high, bright cliffs, with some breakdowns. The summits are covered with forest trees, except near the town.

Between Wilson and Hudson points there is a deep bight, the bluff shore receding ½ mile westward, and carrying deep water for more than ¼ mile inside the line of the points, except near point Hudson.

Point Hudson is a broad, low, gravel spit, stretching out ¼ mile from the high cliffs of the town of Port Townsend. Part of the town is built on this low point and the customhouse is but a short distance from the wharves. A large sawmill is on the extremity of the point; extensive wharves project from the front of the town into deep water, and landing is readily and safely made. A quarter mile off these wharves there is a deep channel carrying 10 to 16 fathoms of water, through which the currents run with considerable velocity. Off the northern side of the point the 3-fathom curve extends out over ½ mile for ⅝ mile NNW.

Within recent years a shoal has made out 250 to 300 yards north of point Hudson.

Buoy.—To mark the shoal north of Hudson point, a red spar buoy has been moored in 30 feet of water, with Hudson Point light bearing SW. ¼ S., distant 350 yards.

Rock.—A vessel drawing 18 feet is reported to have struck on a rock from which the Port Townsend customhouse bears approximately N. 29° W. (N. 52° W. mag.), distant nearly ⅜ mile.

Light.—A fixed red light, 12 feet above the sea, is exhibited from a white post about 15 feet from the end of Hudson point.

Compass range.—To aid mariners in determining the errors of their compasses, the true bearing of mount Baker from the customhouse at Port Townsend is N. 43° 05′ 07″ E.

Prohibited anchorage.—Because of the submarine cables laid in Port Townsend, vessels are forbidden to anchor within the areas inclosed by the undermentioned imaginary lines:

(*a*) A line drawn from Point Wilson lighthouse in a N. 66° E. (N. 43° E. mag.) direction to the shore northward of Admiralty Head lighthouse, and another line drawn to the southward of this line and parallel to it at a distance of ⅜ mile.

(*b*) A line drawn from Marrowstone Point lighthouse in a N. 6° E. (N. 17° W. mag.) direction to the shore southward of Admiralty Head lighthouse, and another line drawn to the westward of this line and parallel to it at a distance of ⅜ mile.

(*c*) A line drawn from a point on shore ⅝ mile southwesterly from Wilson Point lighthouse in a S. 54° E. (S. 77° E. mag.) direction to the shore westward of Marrowstone Point lighthouse, and another line northeastward of this line and parallel to it at a distance of ⅜ mile.

A United States Branch Hydrographic office is established at Port Townsend. Bulletins are posted giving information of value to mariners, who are also enabled to correct their instruments and charts from standards. No charge is made for this service.

Weather signals of the United States Weather Bureau are shown from a staff on the customhouse.

Repairs.—Small repairs can be made to machinery up to 700 indicated horsepower; 4 tons of metal can be run at one time; cylinders of 50 inches and 12 feet long can be cast and bored; boilers can be made; shafting of 12 inches can be turned. Masts and boats can be built.

Quarantine.—Vessels bound for ports in Washington are boarded here.

Anchorage.—The usual anchorage is 1 to 1½ miles southward of Hudson point in 8 to 10 fathoms, muddy bottom. In southerly gales better anchorage is afforded in the bight northward of the military post, in 8 to 10 fathoms, muddy bottom; the cliffs afford some protection.

Tides.—It is high water, full and change, approximately at 3 h. 49 m.; springs rise 6½ feet, neaps range 4 feet.

Port Townsend is the standard port of reference for tides in these waters.

Tide tables are published yearly by the United States Coast and Goedetic Survey which give data for this region.

Fort Townsend.—About 3 miles southward of Port Townsend, on the western shore, is Fort Townsend, an abandoned military post, the buildings of which are visible from the anchorage off the town.

Kala point, on the west side of the bay, and within 1¾ miles of the head, is a low point, projecting ¼ mile from the steep, high hillside out into very deep water; it lies S. by W. about 3½ miles from point Hudson. Half a mile south of Kala point a small stream, called the Chimikim creek, opens between two high and steep cliffs; the shoal water extends ¼ mile outside this mouth.

Irondale, on the western shore and about a mile from the head of the bay, exports some pig iron.

Walan point is a very low and marshy projection on the eastern side of the bay, and stretches ¼ mile out into very deep water. It lies 2¾ miles southward from point Hudson. Between it and Kala point, on the western side, the bay is a mile wide, and the depth of water 14 and 15 fathoms, over soft, sticky bottom.

The head of the bay is visible from point Hudson over Walan point, and is distant 5¼ miles in a straight line. It is ¾ mile between the high cliffs on the east and west, and deep water continues to the head. In the SW. angle there is a shoal pocket, formed by a low and very narrow spit ⅓ mile long, with a rocky islet at the entrance. Port Hadlock sawmills are located here. They ship a considerable amount of lumber. The smoke from them can be generally seen from the mouth of the bay. In the SE. angle there is a narrow channel opening into a large flat, mostly bare at low water, and bounded by a beach nearly 100 yards across and ½ mile long, which separates Port Townsend from Oak bay. Across this creek there is a portage frequently used by the Indians.

Kilisut harbor is a narrow inlet, with a narrow, shoal, and winding entrance, that penetrates Marrowstone island in a southerly direction for about 3 miles. The entrance has a depth of 11 feet, but local knowledge is necessary to enter. At high water this harbor is connected by a crooked boat channel with Oak bay, to the southward.

Directions.—Vessels bound into Port Townsend from Juan de Fuca strait must keep clear of the rocky shoal off the northern side of point Wilson, but as soon as point Hudson is opened by point Wilson the latter may be passed within 120 yards with a depth of 20 fathoms, hard bottom; through this deep channel a strong current runs. When abreast of point Wilson a steamer should steer S. 12° E. (S. 35° E. mag.) to clear the shoal ground to the northward of point Hudson; but a sailing vessel may keep a little inside this course until within ½ mile of point Hudson, and then gradually keep away about ¼ mile from the shore in from 5 to 10 fathoms of water over hard bottom, and as the point opens run quite close, with the summer wind directly offshore, to save making a tack. There is a depth of 10 to 15 fathoms a little more than ⅛ mile offshore. Stand on about ½ mile to the SW., parallel with the city front, and anchor anywhere off the wharves in from 10 to 12 fathoms, and ¼ mile distant. In winter anchor farther out, to clear point Hudson in getting under way with a southeaster.

When sailing vessels are coming down the sound bound into this port with the ebb current, they should pass Marrowstone point nearly ¾ mile before heading in for the town, and so avoid a very strong eddy which comes out of the bay along and under the high shore westward of this point. If the wind be light and the ebb current strong, pass the point quite close-to; run along the outside of the current rip, and try to get upon Mid-channel bank as soon as practicable, to avoid being set up the sound by the next flood.

In summer sailing vessels not employing tugs will frequently drift about the entrance for days without a breath of wind and with very strong currents.

In winter the SE. storms blow with great violence in this high latitude, and a vessel lying off Port Townsend must move to an anchorage under the cliffs near the old military post to get a comfortable berth, in 10 fathoms of water, soft bottom.

Mid-channel bank.—This bank lies on the line between Marrowstone and Wilson points. Within the 10-fathom curve it stretches halfway from Marrowstone island toward Wilson point, and the least water found on it is 5¾ fathoms. The bottom is clear, hard sand.

Marrowstone point is a low, sandy point extending out 300 yards from the bluff and forms an indentation on its southern face, where anchorage may be had in 12 fathoms, with a current or eddy invariably running to the northward.

Fortifications have been built on the higher part of the point, and the trees cleared away to some extent, thus altering its appearance.

Light.—A fixed red light is shown from a white post, near high-water mark, on the extremity of Marrowstone point, elevated 22 feet above the sea. The post stands in front of, and close to, a white house with red roof.

The fog signal is a bell struck by machinery every 15 seconds.

Craven rock lies close to the shore, about 1⅓ miles southward of Marrowstone point.

Bush point is on the eastern shore of Admiralty inlet; it is low and projects half a mile from the general direction of the shore, and has one or two clumps of trees and bushes, with low ground behind and the ground rising therefrom and densely wooded. There is deep water close to the point, and anchorage may be had on the northern side in 15 fathoms, sandy bottom, but the streams are strong and irregular.

Light.—A fixed white light, elevated 25 feet above the sea, is exhibited on Bush point.

Nodule point, abreast Bush point, on the opposite shore, is a rounding bluff point, covered with trees, 1½ miles northward of the southern end of the island which forms the NE. shore of Oak bay. Directly off this point there is good anchorage in 12 to 15 fathoms.

Oak bay opens northwestward and extends nearly to Port Townsend. It has bluff shores nearly all around, the SW. face being limestone. When beating out of the inlet with a favorable stream do not work into the bay for the sake of a long tack.

Olele point is the southern point of entrance to Oak bay, and is heavily wooded.

Basalt point, lying about ¾ mile southward of Olele point, is a rounding jagged point, covered with trees to the shore line and rising to a moderate hillock.

Klas rock lies ¼ mile N. 36° E. (N. 13° E. mag.) of Basalt point and the same distance offshore. It is a patch of rocks 175 yards in extent and marked with kelp. There is deep water all around this danger and 16 fathoms may be carried inside of it.

Mutiny bay, on the eastern side of Admiralty inlet, in the indentation between Bush point and Double bluff, has a narrow bank of 8¼ to 13½ fathoms in its northern part, which affords good fishing.

Double bluff is a promontory 1 mile wide and 1½ miles long, between Mutiny bay on the west and Useless bay on the east. The cliffs are 300 to 400 feet in height, and the greater part of the surface back from the face is covered with trees, but near the water it is destitute of trees, except one large clump, which marks it conspicuously in going up the sound.

Shoals extend nearly 600 yards westward from the bluff, and are usually marked by kelp.

Useless bay, on the eastern side of Double bluff, is nearly 5 miles broad at the mouth and 2½ miles deep to the northeastward. It lies wide open to the SW. The shores are in part bluff and in part low, with a fringe of marsh around nearly the whole bay. At the head of the bay there are two long, narrow sand spits, behind which lies Deer lagoon, a large shallow sheet of water, full of marsh isles and having a shoal outlet between the sand spits.

Scatchet head.—The southern end of Whidbey island terminates in two headlands with cliffs of yellow clay. Scatchet head, the western one, is about 140 feet high. At the base of the cliff are some large granite bowlders.

Possession point, the eastern headland, reaches an elevation of about 300 feet.

Between Scatchet head and Possession point there is a shallow bight running back 1½ miles, named Cultus bay, which dries at low water.

Shoals extend ½ mile offshore just westward of Scatchet head and over ¼ mile offshore from the head to Possession point.

A shoal bank extends to the southward from the headlands, the 5-fathom curve being ½ to 1 mile offshore, from which the water deepens gradually to the southward, the 20-fathom curve being 3 miles offshore. A rock awash at low water lies 225 yards south of Possession point.

Port Ludlow.—Southward of Basalt point and 2 miles westward of Foulweather bluff is the opening to Port Ludlow, on the western side of the entrance to Hood canal. This bay has a broad entrance open to the northeastward, and extends in a southerly direction for 2 miles, narrowing gradually to its head.

The head of the bay is a small landlocked basin, nearly ½ mile in extent, with good anchorage in 6 to 8 fathoms, mud bottom.

The coast is for the most part low, with a gently rising country behind, covered with Oregon pine.

Tala point, which lies on the eastern side of the entrance to Port Ludlow and separates it from Hood canal, is a bluff head about 200 feet high, covered on top with Oregon pine.

From this point there is a bar of hard sand nearly ¼ mile wide, within the 5-fathom curve, stretching in a curve to Colvos rocks, which lie about halfway between Tala and Basalt points.

Buoy.—A black spar buoy is moored on the bar, in 3 fathoms, nearly ½ mile northward from Tala point.

Colvos rocks, a cluster of three rocks, lie at the extremity of the sand bar stretching from Tala point. The nearest rock to the western shore of the bay lies nearly ½ mile SE. from Basalt point; it is 25 feet high and steep-to on its NW. side. The southeastern rock is the largest, and from it a shoal of rock and hard sand stretches to the SE. for ½ mile.

Buoy.—The extremity of this shoal is marked by a red nun buoy moored in 3 fathoms ½ mile southeastward of Colvos rocks.

Snake rock.—Abreast the Colvos rocks, and nearly ¼ mile from the shore, there is a large rock, named Snake rock, 150 yards in extent and awash at high water.

Directions.—The deepest channel into Port Ludlow is between Colvos rocks and Snake rock, the channel being 600 yards wide between the 5-fathom curves, with depths of 11 to 16 fathoms in mid-channel.

The usual channel is between the red and black buoys marking Colvos rocks and Tala point, with depths ranging from 3½ to 4¾ fathoms.

Tides.—Springs rise 7½ feet, neaps range 6 feet.

Foulweather bluff.—This is one of the most noticeable of the many cliffs in Puget sound. It is the northern extremity of the peninsula which separates Admiralty inlet from the entrance to Hood canal. It is the landmark for making Port Ludlow at the entrance to that canal, and Port Gamble, 5 miles inside. The northern face is about ½ mile broad, with nearly vertical, sandy, clay cliffs about 225 feet high, and covered on the summit with heavy firs and a very dense undergrowth. It slopes toward the east to a bluff 40 feet high, but on the side next to Hood canal the cliff is steep.

On the southwestern side of the bluff two small points make out, with a little recession between them. The northern one is low.

Rock.—A rock awash at the lowest tides lies off the face of the bluff, a little to the east of the middle of the face, and 3 fathoms of water is found outside this danger.

Point No Point lies about 4 miles ESE. from Foulweather bluff; it is low and just above high water, with a gully and small stream opening just at the western part. To the southward the shore is nearly straight for 10 miles, with increasing height to the cliffs, and a low, narrow, marshy line under them to Pilot point, 2½ miles distant. The land behind it is 200 or 300 feet high and moderately wooded. Deep water runs close to the point. Under the south side of the point there is good anchorage in 10 fathoms.

Light.—On point No Point a fixed white light is exhibited at an elevation of 23 feet above the sea; it is visible in clear weather from a distance of 9¾ miles.

The lighthouse is a square white tower with a black lantern, with watch room and fog-signal building attached. White dwelling about 65 yards to the westward.

Fog signal.—A trumpet gives 2 blasts every 30 seconds, thus: Blast 3 seconds, silent interval 3 seconds, blast 3 seconds, silent interval 21 seconds.

Apple Tree cove.—This cove lies about 7 miles to the southward of point No Point and to the southwestward of Apple Cove point, a low point rising behind to higher, wooded ground. From 5 to 12 fathoms, over sticky mud bottom, are found fully ½ mile from the shore, and a depth of 6 fathoms is carried well into the cove. The head of the cove is 1½ miles from the point, and vessels may avoid adverse currents by anchoring on the bank. The head of the bay is marshy; no fresh water can be obtained here.

Edmund point.—Nearly abreast Apple Tree cove, on the eastern side of the sound, and about 6 miles to the southward of Possession point, is Edmund point. It is a low, round point with a lagoon inside it. There is a bluff to the southward.

From Edmund point the shore runs in a NNE. direction for a distance of about 9 miles to Elliot point, on the eastern side of the entrance to Possession sound. The shore is low but, as a general thing, steep-to.

Point Wells.—This point, 1¼ miles south of Edmund point, is low and makes out from the high bluff behind it. Though contracted, there is anchorage in the bight between the points.

President point and Jefferson point.—On the western side of the sound and on the northern side of the entrance to Port Madison, there is a moderately high and bluff shore, the land behind it rising from the bluffs and covered with wood. It begins at President point and continues 1 mile southward to point Jefferson, whence the shore makes a sharp turn and runs to the westward for more than 3 miles.

The southern shore of Jefferson point is a low broken cliff.

Stretching off the shore between President point and Jefferson point for more than ½ mile there is a 9-fathom bank which affords excellent anchorage when drifting with light airs and adverse currents. Under the southern side of Jefferson point the kelp extends, as a rule, to the 5-fathom curve.

Port Madison is on the western side of Puget sound between point Jefferson and the northern end of Bainbridge island, and is about 3 miles deep with a breadth of 2 miles at its entrance.

The northern shore is formed by broken, white cliffs with low beaches between. The cliffs on the western shore are low, the buildings of the Indian reservation near the entrance to Agate passage being the most prominent mark.

The southern shore is composed of broken cliffs except where indented by the narrow arm that runs about 1 mile to the southward, on the eastern shore of which is situated the Port Madison lumber mills.

The entrance leading to the mill port of Port Madison is about ¾ mile westward of Point Monroe light. The channel is narrow with only 13 feet of water. The anchorage is limited, but wharf facilities are ample. Provisions and water can be obtained and tugs are available.

Monroe point.—This, the NE. point of Bainbridge island and the SE. point of entrance to Port Madison, is a low, narrow, sandy spit, curving from the outer shore of the island to the northwestward and then to the southwestward, being separated from the cliffs by not more than 400 yards.

Very shoal water extends to the 3-fathom curve, whence the depth increases quickly to 20 fathoms.

Light.—A fixed red light, 25 feet above the sea, is shown from a white stake near high-water mark, and about 150 yards from the end of the spit making off from Monroe point.

Bainbridge island, 9 miles long in a north and south direction, lies in a deep bight of Great peninsula, and its eastern coast forms the western shore of Puget sound abreast West point and Elliott bay. It is moderately high, has some high bluffs along the eastern shore, but is broken by several indentations, forming anchorages and harbors.

Skiff point, 3 miles to the southward of Monroe point, is broad and rounding, and projects fully ½ mile into the sound. The point is low, rising uniformly to the ridge to the westward. The bluff to the northward is moderately high; the water off the point is deep.

Murden cove is just under Skiff point. The northwestern shore is low; the southern shore has steep clay cliffs. The inner part of the cove has shoal water, but inside of the line of the two points there is anchorage in 10 to 15 fathoms.

Yemoalt point is the southern point of Murden cove. It is a low point, with gently rising land behind it. The cliffs to the northward and southward are moderately high and broken. There is deep water off the point.

Eagle harbor is a narrow indentation in the eastern shore of Bainbridge island, about 5 miles south of Monroe point. It is about 1 mile long and about ½ mile wide, and affords excellent anchorage in 5 to 6 fathoms, muddy bottom. The northern side of the entrance is Wing point, very narrow and low.

The entrance is deep but only about 200 yards wide between Wing Point reef and the spit on the southern side at the entrance, and caution is necessary in entering.

Wing Point reef extends southeastward for about ½ mile from Wing point, and there is a 16-foot spot and depths of less than 4 fathoms over ¾ mile from the point.

A spit, bare at low water, extends about 300 yards northward from the southern point at the entrance and nearly 500 yards in a northwesterly direction, with depths of 2 feet and less.

Buoys.—A red nun buoy is moored near the southern end of Wing Point reef and about ½ mile from the point.

A horizontally striped can buoy is moored, in 21 feet of water, about 183 yards southwestward of the 16-foot spot, known as Tyee shoal.

A black can buoy, numbered 0, is moored S. 71° W. (S. 48° W. mag.) from Wing point, to mark the northeastern edge of the shoal making off from the south entrance point.

A black can buoy, numbered 1, is moored, in 21 feet of water, N. 89° W. (S. 68° W. mag.) from Wing point, to mark the extremity of the shoal making to the northwestward from the south entrance point.

Vessels should give Wing point a good berth, say ¾ mile, until within ½ mile of Blakely rock. Wing Point reef is sometimes marked with kelp, but this can not be depended on.

Blakely harbor is a small and narrow indentation a little over 1 mile south of Eagle harbor and just north of Restoration point.

It is nearly a mile long with an entrance width of nearly ½ mile; the depths range from 18 fathoms at the entrance to 3½ fathoms near the head.

The usual anchorage is near the entrance in 9 to 16 fathoms, sticky bottom.

Blakely, at the head of the port, is a large mill port and exports considerable lumber. Provisions, water, and tugs can be obtained. A steamer makes regular trips to Seattle.

Blakely rock.—A little more than ½ mile from the entrance to Blakely harbor and nearly ¾ mile to the northward of Restoration point lies Blakely rock, a ledge some 400 yards in extent, the highest part being 15 feet above high water. There is shoal water and foul ground for about 300 yards to the northward of the rock, the shoal being marked by kelp; the southern side is steep-to. A ridge, with 5 to 9 fathoms over it, connects Blakely rock with Wing Point reef.

Directions for Eagle harbor and Blakely harbor.—Coming from the northward, pass 1 mile eastward of Wing point, and, crossing the ridge midway between the buoy marking Tyee shoal and Blakely rock (the rock distant ½ mile), proceed on into Blakely harbor, or head up for Eagle harbor, as required.

Coming from the southward, round Restoration point at not less than 600 yards, and, proceeding between the northern side of the point and Blakely rock, steer for either harbor as requisite.

Restoration point, the southeastern extremity of Bainbridge island, is remarkable in appearance. The point is low, flat, and about 10 feet above high water for 300 yards back from its extremity, when it rises to a height of 100 feet and is covered with trees.

Decatur reef, partly bare at low water, extends about 300 yards eastward from Restoration point. At 100 yards from the end of the ledge there is 6 fathoms of water, and 16 fathoms at ¼ mile.

Buoy.—The end of the reef is marked by a red spar buoy, in 8 fathoms, about ¼ mile S. 44° E. (S. 67° E. mag.) from Restoration point.

Orchard point is the low, rocky point at the south side of the entrance to Rich passage into Port Orchard. Behind it the land rises into a moderate hillock with a low neck to the southward, and a cove inside the passage to the westward. Off this point the water is deep.

Light.—A fixed white light is exhibited on Orchard point, elevated 25 feet above the sea.

Port Orchard, lying between Bainbridge island and the mainland of Great peninsula, is a narrow sound of considerable extent; it is connected at its northern end with Port Madison by Agate passage and at its southern end with Puget sound by Rich passage. The southern portion is known as Sinclair inlet, from the northwestern side of which a narrow channel, Port Washington narrows, leads to Dye inlet, an inner landlocked basin.

Dogfish bay, a shallow and winding inlet, opens from the northwest corner of the port.

The depths in the main body of Port Orchard range from 6 to 30 fathoms with few dangers, and these as a rule near the shore. The shores are rather low and wooded.

Charleston, Bremerton, and Sydney, on the shores of Sinclair inlet, are the most important of the settlements in Port Orchard.

Naval station.—At Bremerton is located a naval station of the United States, where there are large repairing shops.

Dock.—The United States Government dry dock is 640 feet over all, 608.2 feet over the blocks, and 92.7 feet wide at the entrance; it has a depth of 30 feet over the sill and 28½ feet on the blocks.

Buoys.—A red spar buoy has been moored in 30 feet of water to mark the outer edge of the mud bank lying on the eastern side of the entrance to the dry dock. Mooring buoys have been placed off the entrance to the dock.

Shoal.—Shoal water extends to the southward of Herron point, northern side of entrance to Port Washington narrows, for a distance of ¼ mile.

Communication may be had by regular steamers and by telegraph and telephone with Seattle.

Tides.—Springs rise 9½ feet, neaps range 6 feet.

Agate passage, the northern entrance to Port Orchard, leads from the southwest part of Port Madison. This channel is very narrow, only 100 yards wide in places, and is obstructed by a shoal in the northern end with depths of only 6 to 7 feet; the currents are strong; the channel proper has from 3 to 4 fathoms.

Rich passage, the southern entrance to the port, is the one in general use. Its outer end is between Beans point, the southern extremity of Bainbridge island, and Orchard point. The passage is about 3 miles long and its width varies from ¾ mile at its eastern end to ¼ mile at its western end. The depths range from 5 to 18 fathoms.

Swirls and tide rips are formed in the passage but are not dangerous to navigation.

Orchard rocks, which cover and uncover, lie on the NE. side of the channel near the outer end of Rich passage, and about ¼ mile from Bainbridge island.

Beacon.—On the highest portion of Orchard rocks stands an iron spindle, 18 feet high, surmounted by a barrel painted black and white in horizontal stripes.

Buoys.—About 600 yards south of Orchard Rocks beacon is moored, in 6 fathoms, a red nun buoy, numbered 4.

On the northern side of the entrance to Rich passage, and about 700 yards from the southern shore of Bainbridge island, is moored, in 7½ fathoms, a red nun buoy, numbered 2. This buoy marks a submerged rock, having 4 fathoms of water over it, which lies at the southern extremity of Bainbridge reef.

Yukon harbor, with the town of South Colby on its southern shore, lies about two miles south of Orchard point. Anchorage may be had in 5 to 9 fathoms, bottom sand.

Meadow point, on the eastern side of Puget sound, and nearly opposite Monroe point, is a small, low, grassy point, with a marshy lagoon inside and higher ground rising behind.

West point is a sharp, low, grassy point, 2¼ miles SW. of Meadow point, projecting nearly 1 mile into the sound.

Light.—On the extremity of West point is exhibited a light which flashes alternately red and white, interval between flashes 10 seconds, elevated 23¾ feet above high water, and visible 10 miles.

The tower is square and painted white, lantern black. White dwellings 200 feet in rear of tower.

Fog signal.—A trumpet sounds blasts of 5 seconds' duration, separated by silent intervals of 25 seconds.

Shilshole bay and creek.—Between the two above-mentioned points is Shilshole bay, and at the head of the bay Shilshole creek empties, draining Union lake, 3 miles to the eastward. The shoal water extends farthest at the mouth of the creek.

Anchorage may be had in Shilshole bay in 15 fathoms, over sandy bottom, with West Point lighthouse bearing about SSW., distant ¾ mile.

There is a good anchorage in 7 to 10 fathoms about 250 yards from the shore between West point and Shilshole creek, with good protection from southeasters.

A dredged channel having a depth of 10 feet at low water connects Shilshole bay with the docks at Ballard, on the northern shore of Salmon bay.

It is proposed to extend this channel to lake Washington.

Elliott bay.—On the eastern side of the sound and on the southern side of West point, Elliott bay opens with a width of 5⅓ miles, contracts rapidly to 2⅓ miles, and then continues with that width for 2 miles to the edge of the extensive flats at the mouth of the Duwamish river.

On the southern side of the high wooded bluff commencing just eastward of West point there is a long, bright horizontal cut, which is halfway between the water and the top; it is a good landmark. This bluff is named Magnolia bluff and it makes a long rounding sweep for 1¼ miles to the southeastward from the lighthouse. It reaches nearly 400 feet in elevation and continues with decreasing height for 1⅜ miles nearly ESE. to a sharp recession of the shore which makes in to the northward for ¾ mile. This recession forms a moderately wide cove, bare at low water, called Smith cove. Under the foot of Magnolia bluff and nearly ¾ mile SSE. of its highest break, there is a large granite bowlder inside the low-water line, and locally known as Four Mile rock. The broken bluff abreast this rock is 220 feet high and the land behind it rises to nearly 400 feet. From the eastern side of Smith cove the shore for 3 miles is nearly straight and runs SE. It is comparatively low, but the land behind rises rapidly to the top of the ridge between this bay and Union lake, the extreme height being 440 feet. After rounding West point a vessel should keep about ½ mile off the northern shore, the general course to Seattle being S. 57° E. (S. 80° E. mag.), and the distance 5¼ miles from the light on West point.

Duwamish river.—This is a moderately large stream rising in the Cascade range, and running a general course to the northwestward to Elliott bay. A tributary from the north drains the extensive lakes, Washington and Sammamish, and in its valleys and at the lakes there have been developed extensive deposits of coal and iron. The whole country is well wooded. The great mud flats at the head of Elliott bay are formed from the sediment brought down by this river.

A railroad trestle crosses these flats near their edge.

Seattle, the largest and most important city on the sound, covers nearly the whole northeastern shore of the bay. In 1904 the population was 132,000. Its commerce, both domestic and foreign, is extensive, and it is the terminus of, or connects with, several transcontinental railroads. It is the terminus of several lines of trans-Pacific steamers, and connects with points north and south both by rail and water.

There is an extensive system of wharves along the front of Seattle, and vessels go directly there to discharge and load. These wharves extend into deep water. Mooring buoys have been placed for those waiting dock room. The public boat landing is at the foot of Madison street.

Anchorage.—Vessels are not allowed to anchor northward of a line from the coal bunkers to Duwamish head. Few vessels anchor on account of the depth. Dues for use of the mooring buoys are collected by the harbormaster. Vessels anchoring off the town find the best ground near the southern part of the town, where there is a depth of 15 to 20 fathoms over muddy bottom, about 400 yards off the wharves. It drops off suddenly from 15 fathoms.

Coal.—Vessels are rapidly coaled at a wharf, by chutes, alongside which there is a depth of 30 feet; the wharf is 700 feet long. Six thousand tons are kept in stock.

Steam tugs.—The tug service is good throughout the sound.

Pilotage is not compulsory. Reliable pilots for the sound and for the inside passage to Alaska can be obtained.

Docks.—There is a floating dock 230 feet over all, 55 feet wide, with a lifting capacity of 3,000 tons. There is also a marine railway 300 feet on the blocks, 80 feet wide, with a lifting capacity of 3,500 tons.

Repairs of any kind can be made. Shafting 12 inches in diameter and 40 feet long can be turned; iron castings of 30 tons and bronze castings of 10 tons can be made. Masts and boats can be built.

Supplies of all kinds can be obtained. Water may be had alongside the wharves or from water boats.

Weather signals are displayed here.

Tides.—It is high water, full and change, at Seattle at 4 h. 44 m.; springs rise 10 feet, neaps 8½ feet. The tidal currents in the harbor have little velocity.

Directions.—When a sailing vessel is getting under way from the anchorage off Seattle, the usual summer winds compel the first tack to be to the southward toward the edge of the great mud flat. If it be high water this flat can not be distinguished, and the lead must be kept going. When a depth of 15 fathoms is struck go about, for the water shoals to 3 fathoms very suddenly.

If the stream be ebb, those bound out of the sound should stand well into the inlet, and if bound up the sound should work close under and around Duwamish head to Alki point. Vessels should pass to the northward of the bell buoy marking the shoal extending off from Duwamish head. If the stream be flood, those bound out of the inlet should work under the north shore and close to West point; if bound up the sound, they should work under the north shore about 3½ miles to Magnolia bluff, or to the Four Mile rock, or until they can fetch well clear of Alki point. If calms prevail, a tug is employed to tow vessels in or out.

Duwamish head is steep, about 320 feet high, the summit sparsely covered with Oregon pine. The beach at low water extends 300 yards northward and shoal water to the 3-fathom curve, which is 600 yards from the bluff, whence the depth rapidly increases to 20 fathoms. Along the east side of the bluff the water is deep close inshore. Under the eastern side of the head is the town West Seattle, with a large sawmill and extensive wharfage facilities.

Buoy.—A red bell buoy is moored in 6 fathoms about ⅓ mile northward of Duwamish head, to mark the shoal extending off that point.

Alki point.—The south point of the entrance to Duwamish bay is Alki point. From the northwestward, just before reaching West point, Alki point is seen as a moderately low, bare, nearly flat-topped mound, with a steep cliff nearly 60 feet high toward the water, and a short, low point outside of it, which is the real point. Inside of the curiously shaped mound there is a low neck with large straggling pine trees, and behind this the land again rises.

On the north side of Alki point a vessel anchoring in 20 fathoms over sandy bottom can not have a greater scope of chain than 35 fathoms without being too close to the shore. The beach is smooth and very regular, being composed of sand and gravel.

Light.—A fixed white light, elevated 12 feet above high water, on a white stake, is exhibited on Alki point.

Williams point is the first small, low, sandy point, 3 miles from Alki point. The land rises rapidly behind it and it is pine-covered. It is the north point of Fauntleroy cove.

Brace point forms the south side of Fauntleroy cove. It is a small, low, sandy, gravelly point, backed by rapidly rising ground, covered with Oregon pine. When running north, before a vessel reaches Pully point, Brace point is seen as a moderately high, wooded point just eastward of Alki point, the land behind the first rise falling a little and then rising to the eastward.

Fauntleroy cove.—This slight indentation is between Williams point and Brace point; the distance apart of these points is a little over ¾ mile. Good anchorage may be had here in 10 and 12 fathoms. Fresh water is easily obtained in the vicinity.

Pully point is 4 miles from Brace point. It is a low point with a flat, rounding hillock behind it, and upon which stands one large, high tree in the middle and two or three smaller ones straggling on each side. The extremity of the point is sand and gravel and it pitches sharply off into very deep water, the 50-fathom curve lying but a short distance outside, with 120 fathoms in mid-channel. There is deep water on the north and south sides; strong currents sweep by it.

Light.—A fixed white light, 16 feet above high water, is shown from a post on the SE. corner of the wharf at the outer end of Pully point.

Blake island, at the northern entrance to Colvos passage, is about 1 mile in extent, not high, but covered with wood, except at the eastern point, which is low and pebbly. The eastern side of the island is low, with straggling trees, and the land rises to near the western side. On the northern side of the island the water is shoal for a distance of ¼ mile. There is anchorage in 17 to 18 fathoms close under the eastern point, with bottom of soft mud.

Allen bank.—Stretching from the SE. face of Blake island there is a bank with less than 20 fathoms of water reaching all the way across to point Vashon, at the northeastern part of the entrance to Colvos passage. The bottom is variable; in some places mud and in others hard sand. The depth is greater near the island and decreases to as little as 8½ fathoms 1 mile N. by E. ½ E. of point Vashon. This bank has proven of great service to vessels losing the wind and having adverse currents; more especially when Colvos passage was the channel used by all vessels.

Vashon island.—This is the largest island in the waters of Admiralty inlet and Puget sound. It is high, with steep shores, covered with wood and undergrowth. It is 11 miles in length, north and south, and ranges from 1 to 6½ miles in breadth. It may be considered as lying in a great expansion of the sound 12 or 14 miles long and 10 miles wide. Between the eastern and southeastern sides of the island and the mainland is the 2-mile-wide channel of the main inlet, reaching as far as Commencement bay. Around the shores of the island there is a belt of kelp in the latter part of the summer and autumn, but it is torn away by the storms of the winter and spring.

The easternmost projection of the coast of Vashon island is a curiously shaped peninsula, named Maury island, 4½ miles long and 1½ miles wide, lying at the SE. part of Vashon island. This peninsula is high and wooded.

The NW. part is connected with Vashon island by a low, sandy neck of land 100 yards wide. The bight on the northern side of this neck is Tramp harbor.

In the earlier years of the navigation of these waters by large sailing vessels, Colvos passage was universally used, but in recent years the development of Tacoma and the use of tugs have changed the whole traffic to the main channel between Vashon island and the main shore to the eastward. In this channel the streams are not strong, the chances for anchoring are few, and it is sometimes calm while there is a fine breeze blowing through Colvos passage.

The main channel on the east side of Vashon island is the best to work in with a head wind.

Vashon point, the northern point of the island, is a high rounding bluff, covered with Oregon pine. North of Vashon island there is good anchorage about ¾ mile offshore, with protection from southeasters.

Dolphin point is a high bluff, covered with Oregon pine to the base. Good anchorage is reported in from 7 to 14 fathoms.

Beals point, 2½ miles from Dolphin point, is a wooded point, rising gradually to several hundred feet, but it does not project far into the channel; there is deep water close off it.

Heyer point is about 2¼ miles south of Beals point. Between it and Maury island is a broad open bight named Tramp harbor, with a very low shore on the southern part and nearly connected with the head of Quartermaster harbor. In this bight there is anchorage in 15 to 18 fathoms, over fine gray sand; this is a good anchorage, and there is fresh water.

Robinson point is the easternmost projection of Maury island; it stretches well over toward the eastern shore of the channel, which it reduces in width to 2 miles. The extremity of the spit is 150 yards outside the trees, with intervening marshy ground, and then a bluff, which is about 30 feet high, covered on the top with trees. The bluff rises to about 70 feet.

The steep shore runs to the southwestward for about 4 miles, ending in point Piner.

Light.—A fixed red light, elevated 40 feet above the sea, is exhibited from a white post on Robinson point. A white dwelling stands 165 yards to the southward of the light.

Fog signal.—A steam whistle gives blasts of 6 seconds' duration, separated by silent intervals of 54 seconds.

Quartermaster harbor, lying between Maury island and Vashon island, is 3½ miles long and over ½ mile wide, with 5 to 10 fathoms, over gray sand and mud. This bay offers excellent shelter, plenty of water, and good holding ground.

On the eastern side of the entrance a shoal extends nearly 300 yards offshore. Its outer edge is marked by a red nun buoy moored in 8 fathoms of water.

About ¼ mile north of the buoy, on the eastern side of the channel, lies a 3¾-fathom spot.

On the western side of the channel, about 400 yards offshore, are several shoal spots with depths of 9 to 17 feet.

Dock.—A floating dock, used in connection with the workshops at Tacoma, is moored in 8 fathoms in the eastern part of the harbor. The dock is 325 feet over all, 80 feet between side walls, 23 feet over the sill, and has a lifting capacity of 8,000 tons.

Colvos passage.—Before the general use of steam tugs on these waters and before the development of Tacoma as the terminus of a transcontinental railroad, this passage was the almost invariably used ship channel for vessels to and from Puget sound. It is formed by the western shore of Vashon island and the eastern shore of Great peninsula. It is 11½ miles long and nearly straight on a course S. by W., and has a very regular width of 1 mile, with high bluff shores, varied by numerous small, low, sand points making out a short distance from the face of the bluff and all having very deep water off them. The mid-channel depths are from 50 to 65 fathoms over fine gray sand and gravel. A vessel may anchor anywhere under either shore if she has room to swing. The best anchorage is under the eastern shore, near the northern entrance, about 1½ miles inside of point Vashon. There is here a slight receding and breaking down of the bluff and a vessel will find excellent anchorage in 5 to 10 fathoms of water. This anchorage is known as Fern cove, and the low point forming the southern shore is point Peter.

There is usually more wind in this passage than in the broad passage to the eastward of Vashon island, and much stronger currents, while at the northern entrance, between point Vashon and Blake island, is the anchoring ground of Allen bank, already described. There are no known dangers in this passage.

Southworth point.—The northern entrance of Colvos passage is 1 mile wide between point Vashon and point Southworth, the latter being nearly west from the former. It is low near the water, but rises to a high wooded bluff. It has deep water close under its SE. side, but anchorage may be had off the northern face with strong currents.

Dalco point.—This is the southwestern point of Vashon island, where Colvos passage opens to the southward. The southernmost point of the island is Neill point, which is nearly a mile to the eastward of Dalco point. The former point is a moderately high, wooded bluff with no definite point, being a rounding shore.

Neill point, as seen when off point Defiance, is a high sloping bluff covered with trees to the beach without any bright exposed part.

Dalco passage.—The passage between Neill point and point Defiance is known as Dalco passage. The currents in it are very variable.

Brown point.—This forms the northern point of the entrance to Commencement bay. On the outermost point to the northward it is low and gravelly with gently rising wooded ground behind a marshy spot inside the low point. On the southern face of the point the shore rises gradually and irregularly in exposed, white, clay cliffs from 25 to 200 feet high within ⅝ mile from the point. There is very deep water 100 yards off the point.

Light.—A fixed white light is exhibited, at a height of 20 feet, from a white frame on Brown point.

Fog signal.—A bell is struck by machinery every 20 seconds.

Dash point.—The low point 1⅓ miles NE. ¾ N. of point Brown is Dash point, slightly breaking the general line of the shore to the northeastward. There is a slight bight with deep water between them.

Commencement bay.—South of Robinson point the width of the inlet or sound expands to 3½ miles, with high, bluff, wooded shores on both sides; on the northwestern shore the bluffs are unbroken; on the southeastern they are broken by small streams entering the sound. In this expansion of the sound the water is deep to either shore, and in the center it is about 100 fathoms.

At the southern part of this basin Commencement bay opens to the southeastward with its entrance between point Brown on the northern side and the shore east of point Defiance on the southern. It is 1¾ miles wide at the entrance and about 2 miles deep. At the head of the bay there is an extensive mud flat, and low land, formed by the deposits brought down by the Puyallup river. This is a large stream flowing from the Cascade range and nearly parallel with Duwamish river.

Throughout the bay the depth of water is very great, ranging from 88 fathoms in the middle of the entrance to 30 fathoms close under either shore, and 20 fathoms close to the edge of the mud flats, which are dry at low water.

No special directions are needed to enter or leave this bay.

Anchorage.—The depths as a rule are too great for convenient anchorage, but vessels may anchor under the northern shore about 1 mile eastward of Brown point. Vessels are not allowed to anchor between the western shore of the bay and a line extending from the St. Paul and Tacoma Mill Company's wharf to the Tacoma Warehouse and Elevator Company's elevator without written permission from the harbormaster.

Mooring buoys have been placed off the Tacoma water-front and are in charge of the harbormaster, a fee being charged for their use.

Tides.—It is high water, full and change, at 4 h. 45 m.; springs rise 10½ feet, neaps 9 feet.

The eddy currents in Commencement bay are so very irregular that to steer by courses in thick weather is almost useless. There is a peculiar film of whitish water on the surface of the bay during the ebb tide and during the first quarter of the flood tide; this rarely leaves the bay, and is said to be caused by the glacial waters brought down by the Puyallup river. When in or off the entrance to this bay the snow-covered summit of mount Rainier shows distinctly over the low ground at the head of the bay.

Tacoma, the second city in size and importance on the sound, is situated on the southern shore at the head of the bay. It has considerable commerce, both foreign and domestic, and exports large amounts of coal, grain, lumber, and flour. It is one of the terminals of the Northern Pacific railroad, which has extensive wharves and repair shops here.

Repairs of all kinds can be made. In connection with the repair shops at Tacoma, there is moored in Quartermaster harbor, on the farther side of the sound and about 5 miles from Tacoma, a large floating dock.

Supplies of all kinds can be obtained. Fresh water may be had alongside the wharves or from water boats.

Coal.—Vessels coal alongside wharves, at which the depth is 23 to 33 feet at low water. Coal is loaded for shipment through chutes at the rate of 100 to 150 tons per hour. Coal can be obtained in any reasonable quantity on short notice.

Wharves.—There is an extensive system of wharves with plenty of water alongside, and the facilities for handling cargo are ample.

Weather signals are made here and are plainly visible from the harbor.

Pilots and towboats can be obtained.

PUGET SOUND SOUTHWARD OF TACOMA.

Southward of point Defiance the sound is composed of a number of inlets, passages, and islands, at present of little commercial value outside of the lumbering interests. The depths are generally great and there are but few dangers. The shores are generally well wooded and moderately low.

These waters are navigated by small steamers with headquarters at Seattle, Tacoma, or Olympia, occasional small sailing vessels, and by tugs engaged in towing logs to the sawmills.

The navigation is very simple in good weather, but in thick and foggy weather it requires a full local knowledge of the currents and the peculiarities of the echoes from all points passed by the steamboats. With a knowledge of the tides and currents the captains and pilots run in foggy or thick smoky weather by courses and time-distances, and when approaching any point they ascertain its distance and bearing by the echo of their steam whistle from the shores. No minute sailing directions could be drawn up to take the place of the local knowledge and experience of the pilots, and general directions are only suggestive in good weather, for the chart is the best guide.

The Narrows.—This is a relatively narrow passage connecting the broader channels of the sound lying to the northward and the narrower channels and passages to the southward and westward. Through it pass all the waters of Puget sound.

The Narrows is about ¾ mile wide and 5 miles long in a general north and south direction; its shores are high, bold, and in some places rocky; the tops of the cliffs are wooded.

Midway through the Narrows is a high, long, rounding point, known as point Evans, and close under it is a sunken rock with kelp around it and in patches alongshore.

Evans rock lies about 180 yards offshore, has about 4½ feet upon it at extreme low tides, and the pilots of the steamboats have special marks for passing close to it. It is locally know as the "Bowlder."

At the extreme low tides of the year, about June, this rock shows just above the water for a few minutes at the slack.

Tidal currents.—In mid-channel the regular flood and ebb currents are always found to run from ½ to 1 hour after high or low water. There are generally considerable tide rips, especially at spring tides, with strong swirls, which make the water very rough and dangerous for small boats, more particularly when the winds are contrary to the currents.

On the east side of the Narrows and south of point Defiance a strong eddy current is found on the flood tide from about abreast of point Evans to point Defiance. This eddy is much used by small steamers, but great care must be exercised when close to point Defiance, if bound through Dalco passage to Tacoma, to haul out gradually to meet the strong flood at the point, either bows on, or quartering on the starboard bow, instead of running into it almost at right angles. The line between the flood and the eddy is well marked by the rip.

On the west side of the Narrows, between point Evans and Gig harbor, there is a strong eddy current on the ebb tide. This eddy is always taken advantage of by steamboats and small craft, but the pilots of boats using this eddy must be careful to keep clear of the "Bowlder," or Evans rock. On the west side of the Narrows, between point Evans and point Fosdick, there is slack water very close under the shore during the flood, but only the smallest craft can take advantage of it.

Point Defiance, the northeastern entrance point to the Narrows, is at the extremity of the nearly straight line of coast forming the southwestern side of Commencement bay. It is about 4 miles W. by N. from Brown point and 1¼ miles SW. from Dalco point. It rises by several steps. Between high- and low-water mark there is a narrow ledge or shelf of rock bare at low water. The face of this rock is almost perpendicular, with 5 fathoms of water alongside, and at 70 yards off 10 fathoms over rocky bottom. Above this rocky ledge there is a rise of 40 feet, a slope reaching 50 feet higher, and a third rise of 100 feet, above which the head is densely wooded, and the ground rises gradually inland. The face of the cliff is too steep for trees, and is a bright yellow color. The northern face of the point looks directly into Colvos passage. On the eastern side of the point the trees come down to the beach, which is very narrow and covered at high water. There is deep water close under the point, and strong eddies exist around the point on the flood.

Gig harbor.—On the western side of the Narrows, at the northern entrance, and opposite point Defiance, there is a small boat harbor, with a depth of 10 feet of water in the entrance and 5 fathoms inside. The entrance is very narrow.

Day Island anchorage.—At the southern entrance to the Narrows and on its eastern side, about 4 miles to the southward of point Defiance, is a small cove. Anchorage may be had in 15 fathoms, but there are strong swirling currents which make it an uncomfortable berth. Small craft may anchor in 7 to 8 fathoms ¼ mile northward of Day island, which forms the western side of the cove. There is a small patch of kelp, with bowlders, close off Day island. Vessels may anchor to the southwestward of Day island, clear of the kelp, but the currents are strong.

Hale passage, between Fox island and the mainland, enters on the western shore about 5 miles southward from point Defiance. It is about 4 miles in length and varies in width from 1 mile at its eastern end to ⅜ mile at its western end, where it connects with Carr inlet.

Whollochet bay.—This is a moderately wide bay, opening into the northern side of Hale passage, opposite the middle of the northern shore of Fox island, and 1 mile westward of Fosdick point, at the southern entrance of the Narrows. The immediate shores of this bay are low, rising to wooded high land; it affords a good and sheltered anchorage.

Carr inlet has its entrance between Fox and McNeil islands, about 8 miles southward of point Defiance, and extends northwestward about 6 miles and then northeastward for 8 miles more, terminating in flats at its head.

Good anchorage is afforded near the head in 8 to 15 fathoms, soft bottom, and in several coves on its southern and eastern shores. A mid-channel course may be followed with safety.

McNeil island is about 3 miles long, east and west, and about 2 miles wide north and south. It is high and wooded, with high bluff shores, broken at the eastern end.

Pitt passage, which separates McNeil island from the mainland to the westward, is obstructed, near its middle, by Pitt island and the shoals surrounding it, and at its northern end by Wyckoff shoal, which extends off from the northwestern part of McNeil island.

Toliva shoal lies in the middle of the fairway, ⅞ mile south of Gibson point, the southernmost part of Fox island, and 1 mile from the eastern shore of the sound. This danger, about 150 yards in extent, consisting of two rocks with 14 feet of water over them, is marked by kelp. The tide rip upon the shoal is very great, and with a little wind it raises a confused short swell, sufficient to swamp a small boat.

The shoal lies nearly in mid-channel and may be passed on either side, giving the buoy a berth of over 300 yards.

Buoy.—A nun buoy, painted in red and black horizontal stripes, is moored, in 4½ fathoms in the center of Toliva shoal.

Steilacoom is a small town on the eastern shore of the sound about 9 miles to the southward of point Defiance. It is situated on a bluff, and in approaching in thick weather the whistle echo is very good. There is communication by rail and telegraph.

When approaching from the northward keep under the eastern shore to avoid Toliva shoal, and, if bound for Steilacoom, anchor off the town in 15 fathoms, hard bottom, about 400 yards offshore. As the holding ground is poor and the currents strong, it is not advisable to anchor here. The tide rip with a little wind makes it dangerous for boats.

Steilacoom river, locally known as Chambers creek, empties into the sound about 1 mile northward of the town.

Tides.—It is high water, full and change, at Steilacoom at 4 h. 46 m.; springs rise 11 feet, neaps 9¼ fet.

Ketron island, narrow, 1¼ miles long, lies parallel with the shore, 1 mile southward of Steilacoom, with a passage on the east side named Cormorant pass, ½ mile wide, with a depth of 25 fathoms, muddy bottom. The island is from 60 to 100 feet high, with steep sides, and is covered with tall Oregon pine.

Anderson island is moderately high and wooded, with deep water around its shores. It is a little over 3 miles from Steilacoom and is 4 miles long, north and south, and about 2½ miles broad. The southern end reaches well down into the southern part of the sound opposite the mouth of the Nisqually river, only ¾ mile from the Nisqually flats. There are good passages all around the island, with the broadest toward Nisqually, forming the Nisqually reach, and the narrowest toward McNeil island, this latter forming Balch passage.

Oro bay.—In the southeast side of Anderson island there is an indentation ¾ mile deep, and nearly 1 mile wide between the points of entrance. The line of soundings across the entrance is 25 fathoms, with good water close to either point, but deeper under the southern point. The 5-fathom curve reaches nearly ⅓ mile into the bay, with muddy bottom.

Caution.—In rounding the southern point of Anderson island, give it a good berth, as foul bottom exists there.

Balch passage, between Anderson and McNeil islands, is the channel most used by vessels bound to Olympia; it connects at its western end with Drayton passage. It is about 2 miles long with an average width of ½ mile. The Washington State penitentiary, on the southeastern shore of McNeil island, is a prominent object.

Eagle island, small, low, and wooded, lies near the middle of the passage, and about ⅓ mile from the shore of Anderson island. A 5-foot shoal lies about 300 yards WNW. of the island. Vessels may pass on either side, but the northern channel offers more room.

Light.—A fixed white light, 25 feet above water, is exhibited from a white stake close to the water's edge on the southern point of Eagle island.

Drayton passage, westward of Anderson island, is about 2½ miles long in a NE. and SW. direction and 1 mile wide. To the northward it connects with Pitt and Balch passages, to the southward with Nisqually reach. With the exception of a spit making out ¼ mile from its western shore, a little more than 1 mile from Devils head, it is free from all dangers.

Titusi bay, on the western shore of Drayton passage, though small, offers good anchorage in 7 to 8 fathoms, muddy bottom.

Nisqually reach.—That portion of the sound lying between Anderson island and the mainland is known as Nisqually reach. The southern end of Anderson island is known as Lyle point; this is a long, rounding, moderately low point, with trees growing down to high-water mark. Under its western side is Thompson cove. There are strong tide rips off the point during the flood tide.

Nisqually flats.—These extensive flats lie in the broad southern bend of the sound south of Anderson island. They are 3½ miles in extent, east and west, and about ¾ mile wide. They lie off the broad, low, marshy valley through which the Nisqually river and its ramifications reach the sound. There is very deep water along the northern edge of the flats, but especially toward the eastern limit.

Nisqually.—This place is 5 miles south of Steilacoom, on the same side of the sound. It is at the mouth of a small stream and at the eastern edge of the extensive Inskip bank (Nisqually flats).

Nisqually landing is 1 mile north of the Nisqually river, where Signalilchew creek empties. There is one sawmill on the creek. This creek is the natural outlet of the chain of lakes on the prairies; one of these lakes, American lake, is several miles long.

Devils head.—This is a bluff about 80 feet above the water and covered with trees that reach a height of 100 feet. There are trees under the bluff down to the very narrow sand beach. It is the southern point of the unnamed peninsula between Carr inlet on the east and Case inlet on the west.

Johnson (Moody) point is the extremity of the promontory between the broad waters toward Drayton passage and Nisqually reach and the narrow arm of the sound on the west, named Henderson inlet. It is a low, sandy point, with some unpainted shanties under the trees and bluff, which are inside and behind the low shore.

Light.—A fixed white light, elevated 25 feet above high water, is exhibited on Johnson point.

Case inlet extends NNW. from Johnson point for 4 miles and then northward for 10 miles more, terminating in flats at the head, which is only 2 miles distant from the head of Hood canal. For about 7 miles from the entrance the western shore is formed by Hartstene island, at the northern end of which is the entrance to Pickering passage.

Herron island, steep and bluff on its western face, lies near the eastern shore of the inlet and about 4 miles from its entrance.

The waters of the inlet are deep, decreasing gradually toward the head. Good anchorage may be had anywhere north of Hartstene island in 6 to 15 fathoms, muddy bottom.

Henderson inlet, immediately westward of Johnson point, extends to the southward for 4½ miles, its southern half being filled with shoals and flats. The average width is about ½ mile, and there is good anchorage inside the entrance in 5 to 6 fathoms, muddy bottom. A spit extends about ¼ mile from the western point of entrance in the direction of Itsami shoal.

Itsami shoal lies 1 mile WSW. from the northernmost extremity of Johnson or Moody point and ¾ mile from the nearest shore of Hartstene island. It is a rocky patch, having 5 feet on it, with kelp spreading out to a depth of 3½ fathoms. There are 8 to 14 fathoms between the shoal and the western shore of Johnson point, and 6 fathoms between it and Dickerson point.

Buoy.—Itsami shoal is marked by a nun buoy, painted red and black in horizontal stripes, which is moored in 4 fathoms on the northern side of the kelp.

Dana passage.—From Itsami shoal the passage is contracted to about ½ mile wide, with mid-channel depths of 13 to 20 fathoms over coarse gray sand, shells, and gravel, and good water close to the shores. The eastern shore is indented and moderately low, but covered with Oregon fir; the western shore is formed by the southern side of Hartstene island and is higher than the eastern shore. There are very strong currents in this passage during spring tides. There is foul bottom close to Brisco point, and the edge of the channel is steep-to.

Brisco point is 60 feet high, wooded, and has good water close to it on the eastern side, but the 3-fathom curve extends 300 yards south from the point, with a fringe of kelp in 4 fathoms. The channel immediately on the western side of the point is Peale passage.

Dofflemyer point is low and cleared on the north, with cliffs 80 feet high on the south.

Light.—A fixed white light is exhibited on Dofflemyer point from a white post at a height of 20 feet.

Point Cooper, at the western side of the entrance to Budd inlet, projects to the northward; it is low and sharp, and rises to 80 feet in ½ mile toward the south. It divides Budd inlet from Eld inlet; the 3-fathom curve extends 300 yards from the point, narrowing the entrance to Eld inlet.

Budd inlet, at the head of Puget sound, and about 26 miles from Tacoma, is 6 miles long and 1 mile wide, extending to the southward from Dana passage and terminating in flats that are bare at low water. The average depth in the outer or northern part of the inlet is 6 fathoms over a muddy bottom. The inner end of the inlet becomes very shoal, the 3-fathom curve being 1½ miles from the town of Olympia, at its head. A mud flat dries out from the town for a distance of ¾ mile.

Through this flat a dredged channel leads to the wharves at Olympia. This channel has a depth of 12 feet and a least width of 150 feet, with a turning basin 500 feet wide at its inner end.

Lights.—The eastern edge of the cut is marked by two fixed red post lights, one at its northern end, the other 200 yards from the wharf at Olympia.

Olympia shoal lies about ⅜ mile off the western shore and ¼ mile northward of Butler cove, a small bight in the western shore about 4 miles south of Cooper point. This rocky patch bares at extreme low water.

Buoy.—The shoal is marked by a red nun buoy moored in 4 fathoms about 200 yards NE. of it.

Many vessels go to the wharf at Olympia at high water and lie there in the soft mud at low water.

Olympia is the capital of Washington. It has educational institutions, manufacturing establishments, sawmills, etc. The lumber output of the country is large and extensive deposits of coal have been found.

A wharf projects northward from the town through the middle of the flats, about ½ mile beyond the old wharf, into 6 feet of water at the lowest tides. Dredging is in progress.

Tumwater is a village about 1 mile south of Olympia, on the Deschutes river, where the water power of the falls is utilized by mills for various products of manufacture.

Tides.—It is high water, full and change, at Olympia at 5 h. 30 m.; springs rise 14 feet.

Eld inlet, immediately west of Budd inlet, resembles the latter in character. It is somewhat narrower than Budd inlet, and extends about 6 miles in a general SSW. direction. Good anchorage may be had anywhere inside the entrance in 4 to 7 fathoms, with soft bottom. A mid-channel course is clear to the flats at the head. Give Cooper point, the eastern point at the entrance, a berth of at least ¼ mile.

Peale passage, between Hartstene and Squaxin islands, extends in a general NNW. direction about 4 miles from Dana passage, connecting with Pickering passage. The passage is shoal, but local knowledge can carry a draft of 10 feet through it at low water. Strangers should take a pilot.

Squaxin passage, southward of Squaxin and Hope islands, is about 1 mile long in a WNW. direction. It leads to the entrance of Totten and Hammersley inlets. The northern shore is foul, and at its western end a rock, with 15 feet over it, lies nearly in mid-channel. The passage is narrow and strangers should proceed with caution.

The southern shore should be favored throughout; at the western end, the northern end of Steamboat island should be favored to avoid the rock in mid-channel. The tidal currents have considerable velocity.

The passage between Hope and Squaxin islands is foul and should not be used.

Totten inlet extends southwestward from the western end of Squaxin passage for about 8 miles, with a varying width of from ¼ to 1¾ miles. The depths range from 4 to 14 fathoms. Skookum inlet is a small, shoal, and narrow inlet on the western shore. There is good anchorage between the entrance of Totten inlet and the mouth of Skookum inlet.

Hammersley inlet, the entrance to which is about 1 mile north of the western entrance of Squaxin passage, is a narrow, tortuous, and shoal inlet, navigated only by light-draft steamers with local knowledge; the tidal streams are very strong.

Lights.—A fixed white light is shown from a white stake, 25 feet above high water, near the town of Arcadia, on the southerly side of the entrance to Hammersley inlet.

A fixed white light is shown from an arm on a white stake on Church point, northern side of Hammersley inlet, about 3 miles W. ⅛ N. from Arcadia light.

Pickering passage extends northward and eastward from the entrance to Hammersley inlet, between the mainland and the western side of Squaxin island and western and northwestern sides of Hartstene island. It is about 8 miles long and ¼ to ½ mile wide. The shores are low and wooded, and the depths vary from 6 to 15 fathoms. Except for the shoals extending eastward from the mouth of Hammersley inlet the passage is free from outlying dangers and a mid-channel course can be followed with safety.

Directions—Defiance point to Olympia.—No written directions can give an adequate description of these waters. In clear weather, with the aid of the chart, maintain a mid-channel course throughout. In foggy weather, or in the dense, smoky weather of a dry summer, it is impossible to see a ship's length ahead, and the irregular currents greatly increase the difficulty. At such times only a most thorough local knowledge will prevent disaster.

From Defiance point a mid-channel course for 7 miles will bring a vessel up to Toliva shoal, which may be passed on either side.

The usual route is to pass northward of the shoal and proceed by Balch and Drayton passages. Eagle island, in Balch passage, may be passed on either side, but the passage northward of it is the wider, and a mid-channel course through it should be held until Drayton passage is well open, so as to avoid the shoal westward of Eagle island.

If bound through Nisqually reach, keep over toward Anderson island to avoid Nisqually flats, and then steer a mid-channel course until up with Johnson point. Round Johnson point at a distance of ¼ mile, and, passing northward and westward of Itsami shoal, keep in mid-channel through Dana passage, giving the southern shore a berth of at least ¼ mile until up with Dofflemyer point, whence a mid-channel course up Budd inlet will lead to the light at the entrance of the dredged channel to Olympia.

Hood canal.—This large arm opens on the western side of the sound, about 15 miles inside of point Wilson, between Foulweather bluff and Tala point. It extends in a SSW. direction for 44 miles and then trends sharply ENE. for 11 miles more, terminating in flats that uncover at low water.

The shores of the canal are bold, high, and wooded, rising to much greater heights than anywhere else in the sound. This is particularly the case on the western shore, where the western shore of Dabop bay attains an elevation of 2,600 feet in less than 2 miles from the water. These high flanking mountains of the Olympus range are known as the Jupiter hills.

The waters of the canal are deep, except at the heads of the bays and mouths of the streams. The bottom is mud throughout.

The tidal currents reach a maximum velocity of 3 knots.

Hoods head.—This is the island-like mass on the western side of Hood canal, 3 miles inside Foulweather bluff. It is connected by a low, narrow strip of sandy beach, ½ mile long, with the western shore. There is anchorage in 15 fathoms, muddy bottom, northwestward of the head and ⅓ mile from the shore.

The northern face of the head is a very steep, bare cliff, and the southern face a rounding, high, bare cliff. The land behind the cliffs is covered with pine. At the eastern point of the head a low, sandy point makes out for 300 yards and terminates in a very sharp point, called point Hannon, off which is deep water with strong whirls during the strength of the current.

Port Gamble is a landlocked bay on the eastern side of the canal, about 5 miles from the entrance. It is about 2 miles long and ½ mile wide, with an average depth inside of 5 fathoms. The entrance, between two low, grassy, sand spits, is only 300 yards wide; the channel is 120 yards wide between the 3-fathom curves, and its greatest depth, for ½ mile, is 8½ fathoms.

On the western point of the entrance is a sawmill; the wharves on the western point are built out so that vessels have deep water between them and the eastern point.

Considerable lumber is shipped from Port Gamble. Provisions and water are obtainable. A tug can be had.

Light.—A fixed white light is shown from a post planted in 20 feet of water on the eastern side of the entrance to Port Gamble. The light is 12 feet above high water.

Squamish harbor.—About 1 mile SSW. of Hoods head is Termination point, with high wooded land behind it and a long narrow beach in front. Southwestward from Termination point is Squamish harbor, an open bight in the western shore of the canal. Case shoal, about 1 mile long and ¼ mile wide, lies parallel with, and ¼ mile from, the western shore. There is a 6-fathom channel inside this shoal and around its northern end.

The Sisters are two rocks, each about 150 yards in extent and covered at half tide, that lie about ¾ mile SSW. from Termination point. A rock with 7 feet over it is reported to exist about ⅓ mile N. 89° W. (S. 68° W. mag.) from the southernmost Sister and about the same distance offshore.

Seabeck bay.—Southward from Termination and Salsbury points the canal runs for 12 miles in a SW. by S. direction, with a general width of 1½ miles, gradually decreasing to the point of the Toandos peninsula on the western side of the canal. The shores are bold, and there is good water close under them and no known danger. The depth ranges from 30 to 70 fathoms; the currents are strong.

The eastern point of the Toandos peninsula is Hazel point, and here the canal takes a direction nearly W. by S. for 5 miles. Under the southeastern shore of this reach and directly abreast Oak head lies Seabeck bay. This bay is an indentation 1 mile long in a southerly direction, and is therefore open to the northward. At its narrow head there is the mouth of a small stream. On the east side of the bay the shore is moderately low; on the west there is a long point which forms the protection to the bay. On the old charts this projection was called Seabeck point; on the recent ones it is named point Misery. At the entrance the harbor is more than ¾ mile wide, with 15 fathoms over sandy bottom in the middle; near the head it is contracted, but a depth of 5 fathoms of water is carried well up to the mill which is on the eastern side.

There is a small settlement, a lumber port, near the head of the bay with a wharf having 7 feet of water alongside it. About 1 mile northward of the settlement is a wharf with 16 feet alongside, where wood and water can be obtained.

Oak head is the southernmost projection of Toandos peninsula. It is high and abrupt, with deep water close under the shore. It is almost 2 miles northward from point Misery, with 60 fathoms of water in mid-channel between.

Fishermans bay.—Just on the east side of Oak head there is a long, narrow cove making in NNW. for ¾ mile. There is a little spit at the west side of the entrance and the water is not deep.

Dabop bay is the largest inlet in the canal and extends about 10 miles in a northerly direction westward of Oak head. The bay has very bold shores, deep water, and very high hills on its western side. Near its head it divides into two arms; the western is named Quilcene bay, and is shallow and marshy at its head, where there is a settlement named Quilcene, on the left bank of Big river.

Quilcene is connected with Port Townsend by rail.

Dusewallips river.—Abreast of Oak head, on the western side of Dabop bay, the river empties, and has formed a flat delta and a broad shoal in front. This shoal is 2 miles long and ½ mile wide, with deep water close up to it. Between this shoal and Tskutsko point, the nearest part of the Toandos peninsula, the width of the bay is nearly 2 miles and the depth is 80 fathoms over muddy bottom.

Quatsap point, 4 miles WSW. of Oak head and on the western side of the canal, is a moderately low head, under the southern side of which is a broad, open bay 1 mile wide, with an extensive flat extending out to the line of the NE. and SW. points. This bay receives the Duckabush river, which brings down much detritus.

Hamahama river empties on the west side of the canal 12 miles SW. of Oak head. It is marked by a delta fronted by a shoal 1 mile long and ½ mile wide; there is a depth of 15 fathoms close to the shoal, while the 20-fathom curve reaches out nearly to mid-channel to the southeastward. This river drains a large lake 4 or 5 miles behind the high mountains over the shore, and into this lake flows a large stream from the Olympus range.

The Great Bend of Hood canal is 22½ miles by the mid-channel course from point Misery. Here the breadth of the canal expands to 2 miles for a like distance and thence runs nearly 15 miles to the head in a general NE. direction, decreasing in width to ½ mile at Sisters point on the north side. The shores are bolder on the port hand going up; the water continues deep to within 2½ miles of the head, where there is a depth of 3 fathoms only. The head, known as Lynch cove, is filled with mud flats and the width decreases to ½ mile.

Annas bay.—This is the southernmost part of Hood canal at the Great bend and it receives the water of the Skokomish river, which has brought down so much sediment that the eastern half of the bay is a great sand and mud flat, with deep water around the outer edge to the west and north. There is deep water between the western edge of this bank and the western main shore 1 mile distant. On the point on the southern side of the shore of the inlet and forming the eastern side of Annas bay is the village of Union, from which there is a road through to Oakland on Hammersley inlet. The Skokomish is a large mountain stream coming around the SE. flank of the Olympus mountains. It drains a large lake named Cushman, high up the flanks of mount Ellinor.

Tides.—It is high water, full and change, at Union at 5 h. 0 m.; springs rise 11 feet.

Ayres point is the head which forms the farthest projection of the peninsula from the northward into the canal at Annas bay. It is a high, rounding point and has deep water close under it.

Sisters point is a high, rounding bluff on the north shore of the canal 4 miles east of Ayres point at the Great bend. It projects from the northward and contracts the canal, leaving a channel only ¼ mile wide, with deep water over gravelly bottom.

Clifton.—This village is at the extreme head of Hood canal. There is a road thence to Oakland, another to Lightville, at the head of Case inlet, and a third to Seabeck bay.

Possession sound.—The southern entrance to this now important and extensive series of broad, deep channels lies between Possession point, the southernmost point of Whidbey island, and the main shore opposite, unmarked by any special projection or object. Scatchet head and Possession point have already been described.

Light.—On Elliot point is exhibited a flashing white light every 5 seconds, at an elevation of 33 feet above the water, which is visible 11 miles.

The light is shown from an octagonal lantern with a black roof, surmounting a white, square, two-story wooden tower attached to the western front of a white, square, one-story wooden fog-signal building with a brown pyramidal roof. A white, one and one-half story, wooden dwelling with brown roof is located to the southeastward, and a similar dwelling is located southwestward from the fog-signal building. A white windmill is situated to the southward of the western dwelling.

Fog signal.—A Daboll trumpet sounds blasts of 4 seconds' duration, separated by silent intervals of 16 seconds.

The northern entrance to this sound is the intricate and narrow Deception pass. The sound receives several important watercourses, Snóhomish river from the SE., Stillaguamish river about the middle, with Skagit river from the NE. It also connects to the northward by the Swinomish slough with Padilla bay, and thence with Guemes channel and Bellingham bay.

The depth throughout the sound is great, except at the deltas of the rivers, which bring down an immense amount of alluvial material which forms mud flats. That from the Skagit river has nearly filled the sound and reduced the channel to a width of ¼ mile with only 7 fathoms of water in some places. There are numerous villages and towns on the rivers and shores of the sound, and, beside the traffic by sailing vessels, regular communication is kept up by steamer from Seattle with all the towns and settlements.

The shores present the general features of Puget sound, but the channels are narrower. There are no known dangers in the channels. The deltas of the rivers are low and muddy, and behind them there is a dense forest and undergrowth.

From Possession point the sound runs NNE. for 3½ miles to abreast point Elliot, with an average width of about 2 miles, and then expands into an irregular basin about 5½ miles in diameter. This basin is locally known as Port Gardner. The eastern portion of this basin is filled by the extensive flats formed by the Snohomish river. The channels through these flats, forming the mouths of the river, are being improved by the United States Government; they are navigable by light-draft river steamers.

The water is generally deep and the only anchorage afforded is off the town of Everett, close inshore, in 10 to 15 fathoms.

Everett, located practically on the site of Port Gardner, is on the eastern shore of the sound, about 4 miles from point Elliot. Work is in progress for the improvement of the harbor and its wharf facilities.

Provisions, water, and coal can be obtained, and minor repairs can be made. There is a marine railway with a capacity of 1,500 tons.

It is on the line of the Northern Pacific railroad, and has communication with Seattle by steamers.

Gedney island, in the middle of the basin, is about 1¼ miles long in a NW. and SE. direction and about ½ mile wide. The island is high, wooded, and prominent. From its southeastern end a shoal makes out, the 5-fathom curve being ¾ mile from the point. The southern side of the island is shoal for nearly ¼ mile from the beach.

A ridge, with 5 to 17 fathoms over it, connects Gedney island with Camano island.

Tulalip bay is a small, shallow cove on the main shore nearly abreast of Allen point, at the entrance to Port Susan. The buildings of the Indian reservation are located here. The channel to the wharf is marked by two spar buoys, one red, the other black.

Camano island, between Port Susan and Saratoga passage, is irregular in shape and about 13½ miles long, the southeastern part consisting of a long, narrow tongue terminating in Camano head, about 300 feet high. The southernmost projection of the head is known as Allen point. At its northern end the island is separated from the mainland by sloughs which are dry at low water.

Port Susan, on the eastern side of Camano island, has a total length of about 11 miles. It is 2 miles wide at the entrance and opens out to a width of 5 miles near the head, where extensive flats, bare at low water, extend out for over 3 miles. There is deep water throughout the port until near the head, where anchorage may be had off the extreme western edge of the flats in 10 fathoms. Care should be exercised in approaching and anchoring, as the flats rise abruptly from deep water.

A channel, dry at low water, has been dredged across the flats to the southern mouth of Stillaguamish river; it is used by light-draft vessels at high water.

Light.—A fixed white lantern light, elevated 15 feet above high water, is shown from a post on the eastern side of the southern pass of the Stillaguamish river.

Buoys.—The channel across the flats is marked by red spar buoys, which should be left to the eastward.

Saratoga passage is the broad, deep strait leading from Port Gardner between Camano island on the east and Whidbey island on the west; from Camano head to the mills of Utsalady it is 18 miles long. The strait averages 2 miles in width; the shores are bluff and covered with Oregon pine. The depths decrease uniformly from 100 fathoms at the entrance to 17 and 18 fathoms at the head.

Allen point.—This is the southeastern end of Camano island, and forms the northern point of entrance to Saratoga passage. It rises inland to the tops of the trees, estimated to be 160 feet above the water. A landslide has left a low outer cliff with a few trees upon it; then a second cliff of white clay which rises 100 feet above the water and is covered with high pine trees. This point is called by steamboat men Camano head.

Sandy point, on Whidbey island, the southern point of entrance, is moderately long, low, and has no bushes. The bluff behind it rises by three steps, with straggling trees. There is a house at the inner, or western, end of the low beach of the point, with a cleared space on the rising ground, and a white house in the upper part of the clearing. It was formerly known as Joe Brown's point.

Light.—A fixed white light is exhibited from a stake on Sandy point.

East point, 6 miles northwestward from Sandy point, on the western side of the passage, is a short, grassy spit, backed by a high, wooded bluff. The tops of the trees are about 150 feet above the water.

Point Lowell, on the southwestern shore of Camano island, lies 1½ miles north of East point. To the eastward of point Lowell is a small cove named Algers bay.

Rocky point, the eastern point of entrance to Holmes harbor, is 1¼ miles west of East point. Rocky point rises gradually from the water's edge to a height of 80 feet. The trees have been cut away and scrub now covers it. About ¼ mile from the point is Hackney island, low and rocky, the shoal extending to a distance of ½ mile NW. from the point. Hackney island is about 50 yards in extent at low water; at extreme low water the whole shoal is bare.

Holmes harbor, from its entrance west of Rocky point, extends in a southerly direction for about 5 miles. The water is deep, but anchorage may be had in 17 fathoms, muddy bottom, at its head.

In entering give Rocky point a berth of at least ¾ mile.

Watsak (Snakeland) point lies on the western side of Saratoga passage, about 8½ miles NNW. of Rocky point. From it extends to the northward a narrow, shoal spit for a distance of ¼ mile.

Buoy.—A black can buoy is moored, in 4 fathoms, about 100 yards from the end of the spit.

Penn cove extends WSW. from Watsak point for 3½ miles, the head of the cove being about 1½ miles from Partridge point, the western extremity of Whidbey island. There are several small settlements on the shore of the cove. It affords good anchorage, in 8 to 14 fathoms, just inside the entrance.

Oak harbor, the entrance to which is 2½ miles NNW. from Watsak point, is a small, irregular cove about 1½ miles long and ¾ mile wide. The cove is shallow, with a narrow, winding channel leading to the wharf at Oak Harbor, a small settlement at the head. Vessels of 10 feet can reach the wharf, but strangers should not attempt the channel.

Maylor spit extends northwestward from the eastern shore of the harbor and is marked by two lights.

Lights.—At Oak harbor a fixed white light is exhibited on the southeastern end of Maylor spit, where it joins the land, and a fixed red light on its northwestern end.

Buoys.—The channel is marked by black spar buoys, which should be left to the westward.

Forbes point is the end of the peninsula separating Oak harbor and Duncan bay. It is foul, and a rock, bare at low water, lies ½ mile south of it.

Buoy.—A red nun buoy is moored, in 4 fathoms of water, about 50 yards southward of the rock.

Crescent harbor, or **Duncan bay,** just eastward of Oak harbor, is a semicircular bight about 2 miles in diameter. Shoals extend ½ mile eastward from Forbes point and ¾ mile westward from point Polnell; with these exceptions the harbor is clear, and furnishes good anchorage in 10 to 11 fathoms with muddy bottom.

Polnell point.—This is the eastern boundary of Crescent harbor; it is low, and foul on the western side. When seen from the southward it looks like a bluff-faced islet.

Utsalady, the most important place on Possession sound, is on the northern end of Camano island, 27 miles from the southern entrance to the sound.

Skagit bay, the entrance to which lies between point Polnell and point Demock, the latter being the northwestern point of Camano island, is about 8 miles long in a NW. and SE. direction. The greater portion is filled with flats, bare at low water, and intersected by the numerous channels through which the Skagit river empties.

Between the flats and Whidbey island, the latter being shoal for a distance of 100 to 200 yards, there is a narrow channel decreasing in width from 1 mile at its southern end to ¼ mile at its northern end. The channel is about 8 miles long from its southern end to abreast Hope island, beyond which it expands into a basin, connected westward with Juan de Fuca and Rosario straits by Deception passage, and eastward with Similk bay.

The tidal currents through this channel are strong. The depths vary from 7 to 23 fathoms.

Buoys.—The channel over the flats from Utsalady to Stanwood, Stillaguamish river, is marked by spar buoys moored in 12 to 15 feet at high water.

The channel over the flats to the mouth of the Skagit river is marked by spar buoys, in 12 to 16 feet at high water. They should be passed close-to.

Lights.—The southern pass of Skagit river is marked by two lights, both of which should be left on the starboard hand in entering. The first is a fixed red post-lantern light on the southern side of the dredged channel; the second is a fixed white post-lantern light on the eastern side about ⅓ mile from the mouth of the pass.

Near the northern end of the flats, and about 2 miles south of Hope island, is the entrance to the dredged channel leading into Swinomish slough. At its northern end it connects with Padilla bay.

The entrance to the dredged channel lies between two red beacons, which should not be approached closer than 200 yards.

Lights.—A fixed white light is shown from each end of the jetty on the northern side of the dredged channel leading to La Conner.

A fixed red light is shown on the eastern side of the passage, known as the Hole-in-the-Wall, about 1 mile from La Conner.

A fixed red light is shown, on the eastern side of the channel, from the point situated about ¼ mile south of La Conner.

La Conner is the only town on the slough.

Ala spit, abreast the western end of Hope island, is low, with a sand spit extending 350 yards offshore. Anchorage may be had northward of Hope island.

Deception pass, between Whidbey and Fidalgo islands and a northern entrance to Skagit bay and Possession sound, is about 2 miles in length; near its western end it is obstructed by an island, nearly in mid-channel. Vessels pass south of the island. This channel is used only by vessels with local knowledge and at, or near, slack water. The tidal currents render this passage dangerous.

Slack water occurs about 1½ hours after high and low water at Port Townsend.

Light.—A fixed white light is exhibited from the southwestern extreme of Fidalgo island. The light is ½ mile westward of the narrowest part of the pass. It is close to the edge of the bluff and 40 feet above high water.

NORTHERN SHORE OF JUAN DE FUCA STRAIT.

The coast from point Bonilla to Owen point runs 10 miles ESE. It is nearly straight, rocky, and bluff, with high mountains rising immediately behind it, all heavily wooded.

Vessels are apt to lose much of their wind close to the shore.

Port San Juan, officially known as Port Renfrew, is the first anchorage on the northern shore within the entrance of Juan de Fuca strait. The opening, which is remarkable from seaward, appears as a deep gap between two mountain ranges; the entrance is 13 miles NE. ⅜ E. from Cape Flattery lighthouse.

The entrance points lie 1½ miles ESE. and WNW. from each other; the port trends 3½ miles NE. by E. and is 1¼ miles wide, terminating in a beach of muddy sand. Gordon river and Cooper inlet enter the port through this beach; very small coasters enter them toward high water and find shelter within.

On the western side of the port, rocks and broken ground extend for 1 mile within Owen point and nearly 400 yards from the shore; one rock, awash, lies 1,000 yards ENE. from Owen island and 550 yards from the shore. The hill named Pandora peak does not show as a peak within the port.

Owen point, the western entrance point, has at about 200 yards from it a low flat rock named Owen island, awash at high water.

Observatory rocks, off the eastern entrance point (San Juan point), are high pinnacles with two or three trees growing on them, and some smaller offlying rocks, the outermost of which lies 300 yards from the shore. At 800 yards within these rocks and 300 yards from the shore is another reef partly out of water, named Hammond rocks.

Buoy.—The entrance to Port San Juan is marked by a whistling buoy, painted red, moored in 14 fathoms of water. This buoy is nearly in the middle of the entrance, and vessels may leave it on either hand.

A substantial wharf, protected by a breakwater, 900 feet in length with 15 feet alongside, has been built in Snuggery cove, situated on the eastern side of Port San Juan. The old wharf, 600 yards northeastward of the cove, is now in ruins.

A hotel, store, telephone station (connecting with Victoria), and a post-office have been erected at the head of the cove.

Anchorage.—The port is open to SW. winds, and a heavy sea rolls in when a moderate gale is blowing from that direction; and though it is possible that a vessel with good ground tackle would ride out a gale if anchored in the most sheltered part, she should, on the first indication of such weather, weigh immediately, and, if outward bound, seek shelter in Neah bay, the entrance of which lies 10½ miles SW. by S. from Port San Juan.

There are depths of from 6 to 9 fathoms all over Port San Juan, the bottom fine muddy sand; when within ¾ mile of the head it shoals to 4 fathoms, and here in heavy gales the sea breaks; a flat extends 600 yards from the head. In the outer part of the port there is generally a swell. Good anchorage will be found about 1¼ miles from the head in 7 fathoms.

The coast.—From Port San Juan the coast trends ESE. and presents no very remarkable features; the country is thickly wooded, and the land rises to a considerable elevation. Providence cove, accessible only to boats, lies 3 miles eastward from San Juan; at 4½ miles farther eastward is a stream named Sombrio river. Jordan river is 5½ miles westward from Sherringham point; between the latter and Sombrio river depths of from 7 to 10 fathoms extend one mile from the shore; and off Jordan river the latter depth extends to the southward about 2 miles.

Eastward, 4½ miles from Sherringham point, is Otter point; the points on this side of the strait are not remarkable nor easily distinguished unless close in shore, though some of their extremes are partially bare of trees. The entrance to Sooke inlet is 3¾ miles eastward of Otter point, the intervening coast forming Sooke bay, in which there is anchorage in fine weather ½ mile offshore in 8 fathoms.

Sooke inlet, the outer entrance to which lies between Parsons and Company points, is ¾ mile wide.

On the eastern side of the entrance to the inlet there is a copper and iron mine. There are indications of coal in the district.

Navigable depths.—The bar has 14 feet on it at low water. Within the bar, the entrance between Whiffin spit and Entry ledge has 7 fathoms, but is only 70 yards across, with a sharp turn and strong tidal streams. Thence a narrow and tortuous channel, 2½ miles in length, leads to a beautiful landlocked basin, 2 miles in extent east and west, and 1 mile north and south, with a depth of from 8 to 16 fathoms all over it.

Independently, however, of strong tidal streams, and several sharp turns to be made when entering, the width of the channel seldom exceeds 100 yards and is consequently adapted only for coasting vessels or small steam vessels, unless at considerable inconvenience and loss of time.

Whiffin spit, connected with the western side of the entrance, is low and gravelly. It should be rounded close-to, as Entry ledge, making out from the eastern shore, is only 100 yards to the eastward.

Light.—A fixed white light, 18 feet above high water and visible 5 miles, is exhibited, for the convenience of fishing vessels, each year from March 1 to October 31, from a pole erected on the eastern extreme of Whiffin spit.

Beacons.—Three red perches mark the eastern edge of the channel to Sooke wharf, on the western side of the inlet, and a black perch marks the western side of the passage into Sooke basin at a point 150 yards westward of Trollope point.

Anchorage.—There is anchorage outside in 10 fathoms, ½ mile off the entrance; if necessary run inside Whiffin spit and drop anchor 200 yards beyond, in 8 fathoms; care must, however, be taken as to the depths on the bar and the state of the tide in the entrance proper, where the ebb stream at springs runs about 3 or 4 knots.

Tides and tidal streams.—It is high water, full and change, at 2 h. 0 m. During the winter months the rise of tide in Sooke inlet is said to be 10 feet, and, the diurnal inequality being large, it appears to be high water during the whole of the day. At the entrance the flood and ebb streams run 1 hour after high and low water, at the rate of 3 to 4 knots during springs.

Secretary island, 120 feet high, small, and wooded, lies about 1 mile SE. of the entrance to Sooke inlet and about ⅛ mile offshore. Between the island and the mainland there is a depth of 16 fathoms; from it Beechey head bears S. 62° E. (S. 85° E. mag.), distant 2½ miles, the shore between being bold and the water deep.

Becher bay.—This is a small rectangular indentation having its entrance between Beechey head, a bold, wooded, cliff, on the west, and cape Church on the east. Near the eastern shore of the entrance are the Church and Bedford islands. Inside the bay and about ¾ mile from its mouth are Frazer island, on the east side, and Lamb and Wolf islands, on the west side, with a channel 800 yards wide between. A number of rocks and islets lie near the main shore and the larger islands mentioned above. To anchor, stand in between Lamb and Frazer islands and come to southeastward of Bluff point with the center of Frazer island bearing S. 46° W. (S. 23° W. mag.), distant ¼ mile.

Becher bay is not recommended as an anchorage, as it affords little shelter during southwesterly winds; vessels outward bound had better wait for a fair wind in Parry bay, 3 miles northward of Race islands. Nevertheless, steamers will find good shelter behind Frazer island.

A telegraph cable, between Crescent bay and Becher bay, lands just inside the western point.

Vessels bound up the strait and intending to pass outside the Race islands should give Beechey head a berth of 2 miles.

The tides in this locality are complicated and the currents very strong.

Race islands, a group of low, bare rocks, the outermost of which lies 1 mile SSE. from Bentinck island, occupy a space about ½ mile in extent. Great Race is 300 yards in extent and 28 feet high. The bottom is foul to the southeastward of the group for a distance of ¼ mile.

Rosedale rock, with 5 feet over it, lies 800 yards S. 30° E. (S. 53° E. mag.) from Race Island lighthouse, and uneven ground with 5 to 8 fathoms extends ½ mile ESE. from the rock.

Buoy.—A steel can buoy, painted black, is moored in 10 fathoms of water, 250 yards S. 59° E. (S. 82° E. mag.) from Rosedale rock.

The tidal currents run from 5 to 7 knots per hour, and, during bad weather, heavy, dangerous overfalls and races occur.

In light winds sailing vessels should give these islands a good berth, especially when eastward of them, as the ebb stream sets in their direction. In 1860 a large vessel was drifted on them by the ebb in a calm and became a total loss.

Tides.—It is high water, full and change, at Race islands at 3 h. 0 m.; springs rise 8 feet. The ebb runs about 2½ hours after the tide begins to rise by the shore.

Light.—From a stone tower, situated on Great Race island, is exhibited, at an elevation of 118 feet above the sea, a flashing white light, showing 1 flash every 10 seconds, which should be visible 18 miles.

The tower is 105 feet high, painted black and white in alternate horizontal bands.

Approximate position: Lat. 48° 18′ N., long. 123° 32′ W.

Fog signal.—A whistle, operated by steam, gives blasts of 5 seconds' duration, separated by silent intervals of 72 seconds. In addition to the regular signal, the station will, in response to the fog signal of passing vessels, indicate, by 4 short blasts, that the northern part of the strait, as is often the case, is free from fog.

Race passage, between Race islands and Bentinck island, is about 800 yards wide, but has shoal heads of 6 and 8 fathoms nearly in mid-channel. This passage is safe for steamers, but should be avoided under ordinary circumstances by sailing vessels, on account of the strength of the currents, and of the race due to these and the irregularity of the bottom.

It may happen, however, either inward or outward bound, with a strong southeasterly wind, that it would be better to run through than to risk weathering the Great Race by less than 1½ miles. In such case keep the Bentinck island shore aboard, distant 400 yards, or just outside the kelp; for the northernmost rock of the group forming the southern side of the passage is covered at high water, and the strongest currents and eddies are formed in its neighborhood.

Race passage should not be used at low water by deep-draft vessels.

Caution.—Heavy and dangerous tide rips occur along the northern shore of Juan de Fuca strait from Beechey head as far eastward as Esquimalt.

Bentinck island, lying close off the SE. point of Vancouver island, is about 100 feet high and, like the adjacent shores, is covered with pine trees; its southern and eastern sides are fringed with kelp. Between it and the mainland is a foul channel fit only for boats; coasters acquainted with the locality find shelter at its eastern entrance. There are a few settlers' houses in the neighborhood.

Pedder bay has its entrance about 2 miles northward of Race Island light, between cape Calver and William head, where it is ¾ mile wide. The inlet runs NW. for 2 miles and narrows rapidly toward its head. Beyond ½ mile from the entrance it is fit only for small craft.

Anchorage.—Vessels of any size may anchor in the entrance, in 7 fathoms, with cape Calver bearing S. by E., distant ½ mile. The holding ground is good, but it is open to all winds from NE. round by East to South, and with a SE. gale would be neither a desirable nor a safe anchorage.

Tides and tidal streams.—The tides are very irregular in this locality. In Pedder bay (in October) the tide at high water was observed to fall about 1 foot and then to rise again. When the ebb stream had slackened in the offing, the tide rapidly fell in Pedder bay. The ebb stream coming round William head is diverted into Pedder bay and prevents the water from leaving it. Becher bay is subject to the same irregularities.

The stream in the offing runs about 2 hours after high and low water by the shore. A SW. wind frequently prevents the water from falling at all.

Parry bay, immediately northward of William head, affords good anchorage with all westerly winds. Those bound to sea and meeting with a strong wind from this quarter are recommended to return here. With a SE. wind there is ample room to weigh, which a vessel should immediately do, and if not able to round the Race islands and proceed to sea, run for Esquimalt harbor.

Albert head, the northern point of the bay, is moderately high, sloping to the sea, bare of trees at its extreme, but wooded immediately behind; a reef lies 200 yards off it.

William head somewhat resembles it, but is lower.

Anchorage.—The anchorage is in 9 fathoms at from ½ to ¾ mile off the sandy beach, with William head bearing S. by E. about the same distance.

Quarantine station.—The quarantine station for Victoria is now in Parry bay.

The wharf is 480 feet long, with depths of 25 to 30 feet alongside.

Two fixed red lights, visible 4 miles, are shown from two posts on William head; when bound for the station, proceed northward until these lights are abaft the beam, then westward until they are in line, which line defines the anchorage.

Submarine cable.—The Western Union cable connecting Albert head with Port Angeles leaves the southern shore of the head in approximately 123° 29′ 48″ west longitude.

Vessels are cautioned against anchoring in the vicinity of this cable.

Royal bay or **roads,** of which Albert head is the southern point and the entrance of Esquimalt harbor the northern limit, is a fine sheet of water 3 miles in extent, affording good anchorage with all winds which would prevent a vessel from entering that harbor.

Anchorage may be had anywhere within ¾ mile from the western shore. A good berth is 1 mile SSW. from Duntze head, with the entrance open, or the beacon on Dyke point just open of Inskip islands (in the harbor); this latter is also the leading mark for clearing the Scrogg rocks when steering in or out.

During artillery practice, from May 15 to September 15, vessels must anchor westward of a line joining Duntze head and Race Island lighthouse, or Duntze head must bear to the eastward of N. 25° E. (N. 2° E. mag.), and be not less than 1 mile distant.

Coghlan rock, on which there is a depth of 2 fathoms, lies 700 yards North (N. 23° W. mag.) from Albert head and 750 yards East (N. 67° E. mag.) from the islet at the entrance of the lagoon to the westward. It has deep water around.

Esquimalt harbor is a safe and excellent anchorage for ships of any size, and with the aid of the light on Fisgard island may be entered at all times. It has been the custom to send a boat to mark the extremity of Duntze head with a light if the night is very dark.

Constance cove, eastward of a line drawn from Duntze head to Ashe head, is the anchorage of ships of war.

There is daily communication with Nanaimo by rail. The railway terminus is situated in Thetis cove, from which there is an extension to Victoria; and a short branch runs down to a pier, which has been built out from the southern point of Thetis cove, near the Indian village, into a depth of 15 feet at low water. An electric tramway connects Esquimalt with Victoria.

The entrance, which lies NNE., distant 8½ miles from the lighthouse on Great Race island, is between Fisgard island and Duntze head, and is 600 yards wide, opening out immediately within to an extensive harbor having a general depth of 6 fathoms, and extending 1¼ miles NNW. On the eastern side are Constance cove and Plumper bay, in the former of which, built on Duntze head, is the Government naval establishment.

About 200 yards above Dyke point (northern point of Plumper bay) the water shoals to 3 fathoms, and thence to the head of the harbor is a flat with only a few feet on it at low water.

Light.—From a tower on Fisgard island (a small rocky islet, 25 feet high, almost connected with the main shore and forming the western entrance point of Esquimalt harbor), at an elevation of 67 feet above the water, is exhibited a fixed white light with a red sector, visible 10 miles.

The light shows white from N. 19° E. (N. 4° W. mag.) to N. 37° W. (N. 60° W. mag.); red from N. 37° W. (N. 60° W. mag.) through West to S. 13° W. (S. 10° E. mag.), and white from S. 13° W. (S. 10° E. mag.) to S. 28° E. (S. 51° E. mag.). The light is obscured throughout the rest of the arc.

The tower is 57 feet high, painted white, lantern red.

Signal tower.—A signal tower, called Bickford's tower, the top of which is 117 feet above high water, stands on Grant knoll, on the eastern side of the entrance to the harbor.

Scrogg rocks lie on the eastern side of the entrance, 600 yards south of Duntze head, and cover at three-quarters flood. SE. of these are the Brothers, two islands from 30 to 35 feet high.

Inskip islands kept well open of Duntze head lead clear to the westward of all dangers; but the best mark for entering is the white beacon on Dyke point, just open of the whitewashed rocks off the western end of Inskip islands, bearing N. 8° E. (N. 15° W. mag.), which leads in mid-channel. Fisgard island should be given a berth of at least 200 yards, as a rock with only 7 feet over it lies 150 yards N. 68° E. (N. 45° E. mag.) from the lighthouse.

Village rocks, a rocky patch lying 100 yards offshore, in the SE. corner of Constance cove, uncover in places at low tides. A ledge with 4 feet of water on it extends about 100 yards SSW. of the rocks.

Two heads uncover when the water stands at 5 feet 3 inches on the automatic gauge at the entrance to Dominion dock, zero of the gauge being 19 feet 6 inches above the sill of the dock.

Buoy.—A small, red platform buoy is moored westward of the rocks.

Sunken rock.—A sunken rock of small extent, with 5 feet on it at low water, lies near the southern shore of Plumper bay, with Dyke Point beacon 600 yards N. 8° W. (N. 31° W. mag.). There is a depth of 14 feet between the rock and Inskip island.

The rock is marked by a temporary buoy.

Whale rock, or White rock, with 7 feet on it at low water, lies 400 yards N. 63° W. (N. 86° W. mag.) from the outer Inskip island, or nearly midway between it and the western shore of the harbor. This rock is of small extent and not marked by kelp; there is a clear passage on either side, that to the eastward being the wider. Yew point, in line with Rodd hill, bearing S. 20° W. (S. 3° E. mag.), leads 200 yards eastward of the rock, and Yew point, in line with the lighthouse on Fisgard island, leads nearly 200 yards westward of it. When Ashe head is shut in by the Inskip islands a vessel will be clear to the northward.

Buoy.—The rock is marked by a spar buoy painted red and black in horizontal stripes, moored off its southern side.

Rock.—A rock, with 13 feet over it at low water, lies midway between Whale rock and Macarthy island, with the eastern extreme of that island bearing N. 22° W. (N. 45° W. mag.), distant 210 yards.

Patterson point—Rock.—A small rock, which dries, at low water, about 3 feet, lies about 100 yards eastward of Patterson point.

Buoy.—A small platform buoy with latticework cone is moored in 11 feet on the northern side of the rock.

Dyke point.—This point, at the head of the harbor, is marked by a white, pyramidal, wooden beacon, which is 23 feet above high water. This is a leading mark for entering or leaving the harbor.

Pilots.—Pilots for Esquimalt and Victoria are on the lookout. Pilotage is compulsory. Charges are, per foot: Sailing vessels, $3; vessels in tow, $2; steamers, $1.50. Half rates when pilot has offered himself and been refused.

Anchorage.—The most convenient anchorage is in Constance cove, on the eastern side of the harbor, immediately round Duntze head, the general depth being 6 fathoms, and the holding ground good. There is, however, safe anchorage in any part of the harbor, in not less than 4½ fathoms, as far northward as Dyke point.

Thetis cove, in Plumper bay, on the eastern side of the harbor, immediately north of Constance cove, is a snug anchorage in 4½ fathoms, with the harbor entrance just shut in by Inskip islands; but vessels proceeding above these islands must take care to avoid Whale rock.

Moorings and buoys for the use of H. B. M. ships occupy the central part of Constance cove, and along the northern shore are lesser moorings for boats and small vessels. Two hundred yards off the dock entrance are two buoys for docking purposes, and eastward of the town pier there are other buoys used as moorings for small craft.

The depth at the outer end of Dockyard jetty is 15 feet at low water.

A southerly wind, to which some parts of the harbor are open, seldom blows, and there is never sufficient swell to render the anchorage inconvenient.

Observation spot.—Duntze Head flagstaff is in lat. 48° 25′ 49″ N., long. 123° 26′ 11″ W.

Directions.—After rounding Race Island lighthouse, at a distance of 1½ miles, the lighthouse on Fisgard island will be seen; a course N. by E. direct for it will clear all dangers, but attention must be paid to the set of the tidal streams.

The ebb stream runs almost directly from Haro and neighboring straits toward the Race islands, and, unless with a commanding wind, sailing vessels should give them a wide berth, and steer NE. for 3 or 4 miles, before bearing up for the harbor. The flood sets NE., and with light winds vessels are liable to be carried to the eastward, and if far from the Vancouver island shore they may be set up Haro strait, where the water is generally too deep for anchorage; therefore, with the flood, the coast of Parry bay should be kept aboard if possible, where good anchorage may be had in moderate weather, and with all westerly winds, at less than 1 mile from the shore in 10 fathoms.

When entering the harbor under sail with a strong fair wind, take care to shorten sail in time, as the space for rounding to is somewhat limited; and it is desirable to moor if any stay is intended, as the winds are changeable.

The best time for sailing vessels to leave the harbor is early in the morning, when either a calm or a light land wind may be expected; there is little strength of tide in the harbor, or for some distance outside, and it sets fairly in and out.

Caution.—Fisgard island should not be passed within a distance of 200 yards, as a rock with 7 feet over it lies 150 yards ENE. from the lighthouse.

By night, when Fisgard Island light bears N. by E., steer for it. Keep the white sector in full view; if it becomes dim or shaded, the shore is being too closely approached, when immediately haul out to the eastward until it is again distinctly seen; the two lights (Race and Fisgard) by their bearings will show how the vessel is being affected by the tides.

The white sector is intended to guide in from seaward, and while visible clears alike the western coast between Race island and Esquimalt, and the offlying dangers, Scrogg rocks, and Brotchy ledge, between Duntze head and Trial island. The red sector will be found useful by those bound to Victoria or Esquimalt from the eastward; after rounding Trial island it will indicate a vessel's distance from the shore, and if bound to Esquimalt a West course will lead a safe distance outside Brotchy ledge until the light changes from red to white, when it may be steered for, and not before.

Entering Esquimalt harbor, Fisgard Island light should be left from 200 to 400 yards on the port hand; when it bears N. 37° W. (N. 60° W. mag.) the light changes from white to red, and shows the latter color within the harbor; and when it bears S. 34° W. (S. 11° W. mag.), at a convenient distance, a vessel may anchor in 7 fathoms, or stand into Constance cove if preferred. The Scrogg rocks, on the eastern side of the entrance of the harbor, must be avoided; they lie nearly 800 yards southeastward of Fisgard island.

Dock.—The graving dock is 450 feet long over all, and 430 feet on the blocks; 65 feet wide at the entrance, with a depth of 26½ feet over the sill at high water, ordinary spring tides. This dock is closed by a caisson which, if necessary, can be placed on the outer side of the outer invert, giving an additional length to the dock of 30 feet.

H. B. M. S. Warspite, drawing 26 feet, was docked on July 18, 1891; the depth on the sill that night was 28½ feet.

The Admiralty has the right of priority of use of the Esquimalt dock.

There is a marine railway capable of taking up a ship of 2,500 tons.

Repairs to large machinery can be effected, also to the hull of iron ships. Two tons of metal can be run at one time; cylinders of 30 inches can be cast and bored; shafting of 6 inches can be forged and turned, and a 3-inch shaft up to a length of 21 feet; pipes of any size can be brazed, masts made, and boats built.

Sheer legs lift 25 tons, small crane lifts 2 tons, and a 20-ton crane is about to be erected. The wharf is 83 feet long, with a depth of 15 feet alongside at low water.

Supplies are obtained from Victoria.

17203——8

A fresh-water service is laid on at the dock; the charge is 60 cents per 1,000 gallons.

Coal is weighed at the mines and sent down as required. Vessels of about 25 feet draft can coal alongside Thetis Island wharf.

Vessels can coal alongside Esquimalt wharf, on the eastern side of which there is a depth of 25 feet at low water; or coal can be taken on board at all times from colliers or lighters.

Telegraph.—Esquimalt is in telegraphic communication with England through Canada, by way of Nanaimo and Burrard inlet. Also through the United States, by way of Seattle.

Tides.—At Esquimalt harbor and in its vicinity there is no regular establishment. There is a large inequality in the heights of the low waters, so much so that, for about half of each fortnight, there is but one high and one low water in the lunar day, there being no apparent fall for one tide, but the water being practically at a stand for several hours together. Springs rise 7 to 10 feet, neaps 5 to 8 feet.

Winds.—The strongest and most frequent gales are from SW. and SE., which are leading winds going in, but rarely from NW. The SW. wind is a summer wind, generally fresh, and brings fair weather, unless it blows a gale. SE. winds may be looked for during the winter months, or between November and March, and generally a strong gale once a month, with rain and thick weather. The NE. wind rarely blows with much strength, and always brings fine, clear weather.

Victoria harbor, 2 miles eastward of Esquimalt, has its entrance between Ogden and McLaughlin points. Macaulay point, a remarkable projection nearly midway between the two harbors, is a bare, flat point about 30 feet high, showing as a yellow clay cliff, worn by the action of the sea and weather into a rounded knob at the extreme. The coast for 1 mile on either side of this point is fringed with sunken rocks, and is dangerous for boats in bad weather, many fatal accidents having occurred.

The entrance to the harbor is shoal, narrow, and intricate, and with SW. or SE. gales a heavy, rolling swell sets on the coast, which renders the anchorage outside unsafe. Vessels drawing 14 or 15 feet may, under ordinary circumstances, enter at high water; and ships drawing 17 feet have entered, though only at the top of spring tides.

A channel, 400 feet wide with a least depth of 13 feet, has been dredged between the wharf on the northern side of Shoal point and Laurel point.

At the entrance of the harbor, on the southern side of Shoal point, there are two wharves which are used by large vessels. The eastern wharf is 1,024 feet in length and has a depth of 29 feet alongside at low water. The western wharf is 730 feet long, and has alongside a depth of 27 feet at low water.

Brackman and Ker's wharf, on the northern side of Shoal point, has about 15 feet at its outer end.

Along the eastern side of the harbor, in front of the town, there is about 400 yards of fair wharfage, with a depth of from 10 to 16 feet at low water springs.

Pilots.—There are pilots attached to the port, who keep a good lookout for vessels off the entrance. Pilotage is compulsory to all merchant vessels, except coasters.

The charges are: Sailing vessels, $3 per foot; vessels in tow, $2; and steamers, $1.50. Half rates when services of pilot are offered but not accepted.

The United States representatives are a consul and a vice-consul.

Lights.—From a white lighthouse 30 feet high, situated on Berens island (west side of Victoria harbor), is exhibited, at an elevation of 44 feet above the sea, an intermittent white light, with a period of 20 seconds, thus: Light, 15 seconds; eclipse, 5 seconds; visible in clear weather 10 miles. It shows a red sector over Brotchy ledge, between N. 8° W. (N. 31° W. mag.) and N. 13° W. (N. 36° W. mag.).

Fog signal.—A bell is struck by machinery, giving 1 stroke every 5 seconds.

Shoal Point beacon consists of three piles, painted red, from the top of which a fixed red light is shown, visible in clear weather 3 miles.

Buoy.—A red spar buoy is moored in 9 feet of water on the western side of Shoal point.

Middle Rock beacon consists of three piles, painted black, from the top of which is shown a fixed white light, visible 3 miles.

As these two beacon lights are not constantly watched they can not be implicitly relied on.

Buoys.—The shoals on the northern and western sides of the inner harbor are marked by black buoys.

Light.—A fixed red electric light is exhibited, 40 feet above high water, from an iron arm, 4 feet in length, projecting from the northern corner of a chimney rising from a small brick house, on the extremity of Laurel point, southern side of the harbor.

The light should be visible at a distance of 1 mile from all points of approach by water.

Brotchy ledge.—About ½ mile SW. by W. from Holland point, and in the fairway to Victoria harbor coming from the eastward, lies Brotchy ledge, with 9 feet on its shoalest part; it is about 200 yards in extent within the 5-fathom curve. The tidal stream, at its maximum strength, sets toward Brotchy ledge at a rate of about 3 knots an hour.

Light.—A beacon in the form of a truncated cone, surmounted by an open steel framework, the whole painted black, has been erected on Brotchy ledge. From it is exhibited, at a height of 22 feet above the water, an intermittent white light with a period of 1 minute, thus: Light, 40 seconds; eclipse, 20 seconds.

The light is visible 9 miles.

Fog signal.—A fog bell, struck by electricity, will give one stroke every 10 seconds.

The electric fog horn formerly used is left in place; in case of accident to the bell, the use of the horn will be temporarily resumed. Should the electricity be for any cause cut off, neither alarm can be operated.

Caution.—Fisgard Island lighthouse, northern part of the Brothers, and Macaulay point in line, bearing N. 60° W. (N. 83° W. mag.), leads 200 yards northward of Brotchy ledge in 9 fathoms of water.

Fisgard Island lighthouse, just open to the southward of the Brothers, bearing N. 54° W. (N. 77° W. mag.), leads 400 yards southward of the ledge in 21 fathoms.

Anchorage.—When anchoring outside the harbor to wait for the tide, or for other reasons, do not come within a line between Ogden and Maclaughlin points; this is a good stopping place with offshore winds or fine weather, but is by no means recommended as a safe anchorage for sailing vessels during the winter months, when bad weather comes with little warning.

Directions.—The entrance to Victoria harbor being only 2 miles eastward from Esquimalt, the same precautions as regards the tides must be observed as when making for that harbor; during the daytime Victoria District church, a conspicuous white building with a spire, standing on an eminence, will be seen shortly after rounding Race islands, bearing N. 37° E. (N. 14° E. mag.); it should be kept just on the starboard bow.

At night or during bad weather it is strongly recommended not to run for this harbor, as it can only be entered at certain stages of the tide, and the anchorage outside is at such times exposed and unsafe, while Royal bay and Esquimalt harbor are always available and safe; but if it is decided to run for Victoria, it must be borne in mind that when Fisgard Island light changes from white to red a vessel will be very near the shore.

The channel is buoyed, but it is necessary for a stranger to take a pilot; when within, the port is perfectly landlocked, and vessels may lie in from 14 to 18 feet at low water, but the harbor accommodation is limited.

Tides.—For all practical purposes the tides are the same as at Esquimalt.

Victoria, the seat of the government, has a considerable foreign and coasting trade. The resident population according to the census taken in 1901 was 20,816, and the town has made great progress since 1858, when it may be said to have first sprung into existence; it now covers a large extent of ground, substantial and handsome stone and brick buildings everywhere replacing the wooden structures first erected. Victoria has excellent educational institutions, hospitals, and library, and the streets are lighted by electricity.

The provincial legislative buildings, the dome of which is a prominent object from seaward, are among the finest in Canada.

Instances have been known of shocks of earthquakes being felt at Victoria.

Between Victoria and Quatsino sound, medical assistance can only be obtained at Alberni and Clayoquot.

Supplies.—Provisions of all kinds may be procured, and water from a floating tank capable of going outside the harbor.

Coal is weighed at the mines and sent down as required, but a large quantity is not kept in store. Vessels can coal alongside the wharves in the harbor, and also from the wharves on the south side of Shoal point.

Patent slip.—There are three slips having a capacity of 500, 750, and 1,000 tons, respectively.

Repairs can be effected to large machinery. There are steam hammers, and lathes to turn shafting 10 inches diameter and 20 feet long; pipes of any size can be brazed; cylinders of any diameter up to 10 tons can be cast and bored; 12 tons of metal can be run at one time. Sheers lift 30 tons. Boilers can be made, masts and boats can be built.

Quarantine.—There is a quarantine station for persons affected with infectious diseases, and a hospital for seamen who are recommended for admission by masters of vessels that have paid sick mariners' dues.

The quarantine station is in Parry bay. The wharf is 480 feet long, with depths of 25 to 30 feet alongside.

Storm signals are displayed at the post-office.

Telegraph.—A cable crosses the strait of Georgia from Departure bay to English bay and connects the city with the mainland of British Columbia, and another crosses Juan de Fuca strait from Becher bay to Crescent bay in the State of Washington. A third cable runs from Ross bay to New Dungeness.

Victoria is connected by telephone with Saanichton, Sydney, Duncans, Chemainus, Ladysmith, Nanaimo, Vancouver, and the mainland abreast Lummi island.

Communication.—There is communication by steamer with San Francisco every five days; with Alaska every fortnight throughout the year; a weekly service to the east coast of Vancouver island; a daily service to the city of Vancouver, except on Mondays; and steamers run daily, except on Sundays, to the ports in Puget sound. There is daily communication with Nanaimo and Sydney by rail. There is a fortnightly mail service between Victoria, Port San Juan, Alberni, Ucluelet, Clayoquot, and Ahousat; and monthly between Victoria, Hesquiat, Nootka, Kyuquot, and Quatsino.

A submarine telephone cable has recently been laid across the several channels between Vancouver island and the State of Washington. The line begins at Telegraph cove and lands in the Lummi Indian reservation about 7 miles from Whatcom. Each landing is marked by a white monument sign 12 inches wide and 66 inches long, with the word CABLE in black letters. Mariners are instructed not to anchor in the vicinity of these cables.

Victoria to Burrard inlet.—The route between Victoria and Vancouver, for large vessels, is south of Trial and Discovery islands, through the main channel of Haro strait, and northward of Stuart and Waldron islands into Georgia strait.

The usual route for moderate-sized steamers is south of Trial island, westward of Chain and Chatham islands by Mayor and Baynes channels, then to the northward, passing on either side of Zero rock and Darcy shoals, through Sydney channel and Moresby passage, between Prevost and Pender islands, and through Active pass into the strait of Georgia. Weaker tidal streams are experienced by this latter route.

The coast from Victoria harbor trends in a southeasterly direction to Clover point, and is for the most part faced by white sandy cliffs, varying in height from 10 to 80 feet; a sandy beach extends along the whole way, and at 200 yards' distance in many places are rocks and foul ground. Four hundred yards eastward of Holland point, and 200 yards offshore, are the Glimpse reefs, which cover at three-quarters flood.

Beacon hill, a gentle rise of the land, 400 yards from the water's edge, and a mile eastward of the harbor, is grassy and bare of trees; its height is 140 feet.

Clover point, 2 miles eastward of the entrance to Victoria harbor, is low, bare of trees, and projecting; it is steep-to, and off it form strong tide rips, dangerous to boats in heavy weather. Ross bay to the eastward of it is open, but sometimes used by small craft if waiting for the tide.

Foul bay, nearly 1 mile to the eastward of Clover point, is of small extent and filled with rocks. Off its entrance are the Templar rocks, about 4 feet under water, and marked by kelp.

Foul point, on the eastern side of the bay, is rocky, but has not less than 4 fathoms at 200 yards distance; the land at the back of the point rises to a height of 230 feet, forming a rocky ridge or summit, known as Gonzales hill.

Trial islands, 1¾ miles eastward from Clover point, are two in number, bare and rocky, but they generally appear as one. The southern and largest island is 80 feet high. Its southern end, known as Ripple point, is steep-to, and a depth of 12 fathoms can be carried 115 yards from the shore. The northern island is low, and from it foul ground extends some distance to the northward. Strong tide rips occur near Ripple point, especially during the flood, which reaches a velocity of 6 knots during springs. Vessels should give it a good berth in thick weather on this account.

Light.—A flashing white light, giving groups of 2 flashes every 10 seconds, 84 feet above high water, and visible 15 miles, is exhibited from the lighthouse on Ripple point.

The lighthouse is a square wooden building with a square lantern rising from its roof; the building is painted white, roof and lantern red.

Fog signal.—A diaphone sounds 1 blast of about 3 seconds' duration every minute. The fog-signal building stands on a lower part of the point, southeastward of the lighthouse; it is painted white with red roof.

Inner channels.—The inner channels leading from Juan de Fuca strait into Haro strait are the Enterprise, Mouatt, Mayor, and Baynes channels, and Hecate and Plumper passages.

Strangers are advised not to use these passages.

Enterprise channel, between Trial islands and the Vancouver shore, is a narrow, tortuous, but deep channel, much used by steamers and coasters trading to Victoria harbor, as a slight saving of distance is effected and less tide experienced than by going south of the Trial islands. Its length is about 1 mile, its width in the narrowest place 100 yards, and there is not less than 24 feet in the shoalest part.

McNeil bay, on the northern side of the channel to the eastward of Foul point, is 600 yards in extent, with from 2 to 6 fathoms of water; it is open to the southward, and foul ground exists in its eastern part, but the bay is much used by small vessels waiting for the tide.

Mouatt reef, in the eastern part of the channel, nearly 400 yards offshore and about 600 yards from Little Trial island, is about 200 yards in extent, and covers at quarter flood; this reef is dangerous, as it lies just northward of the fairway. McNeil farm, just open west of Kitty islet, a bare, yellow rock 4 feet high on the eastern side of McNeil bay, bearing N. 61° W. (N. 84° W. mag.), leads 100 yards southward of Mouatt reef; and Channel point, in line with the western side of the Great Chain islet bearing N. 37° E. (N. 14° E. mag.), leads nearly 400 yards eastward of it.

Brodie rock, a patch with 3 fathoms of water over it, marked by kelp, lies nearly 1 mile N. 65° E. (N. 42° E. mag.) from the summit of Trial island.

The northern point of Little Trial island in line with Foul point, bearing West (S. 67° W. mag.), leads 300 yards northward of Brodie rock.

Foul point, seen between the Trial islands, bearing N. 75° W. (S. 82° W. mag.), leads about 500 yards southward of the rock.

Cadboro point, in line with the eastern extreme of Great Chain island, bearing N. 11° E. (N. 12° W. mag.), leads 500 yards eastward of the rock.

Gonzales point forms the SE. extremity of Vancouver island. It is low, rocky, bare of trees, and steep-to on the eastern side.

Oak bay.—From Gonzales point, the Vancouver shore trends northward, and at 1 mile from the point forms a sandy bay which affords fair anchorage.

The best anchorage is northward of Mary Todd islet in the southern part of the bay. This islet is bare and about 30 feet high; 400 yards eastward from it is Emily islet, 4 feet above high water, and the same distance southward from Emily islet lies Robson reef, which uncovers at low water.

Cadboro bay, 2 miles northward from Gonzales point, is about ½ mile in extent and open to the SE.; no sea, however, rises within it, and there is good anchorage in from 3 to 4 fathoms near the entrance. The Vancouver shore from Gonzales point to this bay is low and lightly timbered with dwarf oak and pine trees.

Thames shoal has 2 fathoms of water over it, is of small extent, and marked by kelp; it lies nearly ½ mile N. 43° E. (N. 20° E. mag.) of Gonzales point. Channel point in line with the western side of Great Chain islet, bearing N. 36° E. (N. 13° E. mag.), leads eastward of the shoal, and the highest part of Trial island in line with Gonzales point, bearing S. 30° W. (S. 7° mag.), leads westward of it.

Lee rock, which uncovers at low water springs, lies about 500 yards south of Harris island, with which it is connected by foul ground, and about 300 yards NW. of Thames shoal.

Mouatt channel leads between this rock and Thames shoal. It is about 200 yards wide. The peak on Trial island in line with Gonzales point leads midway between Thames shoal and Lee rock.

Mayor channel, eastward of Gonzales point and westward of Chain islets, is about 2 miles long in a winding direction to the northward; its breadth in the narrowest part is 600 yards, and the depths in it vary from 6 to 13 fathoms. The channel is bounded on the western side by Thames shoal, Harris island, and Fiddle reef, and abreast the latter, and on the opposite side, by Lewis reef. The tidal streams seldom run more than 3 knots through this channel, and it is the one generally used.

Shoal.—Midway between Thames shoal and Great Chain islet is a shoal having a least depth of 4 fathoms at its northern end. This shoal is about 200 yards long NNW. and SSE., and about 100 yards wide between the 5-fathom curves. It is marked by kelp in summer and autumn.

The northern end of the shoal is 750 yards S. 8° W. (S. 15° E. mag.) from Lewis Reef beacon. The channel is between this shoal and Thames shoal.

Fiddle reef, at the NW. extreme of Mayor channel, and upward of 1 mile from Gonzales point, is of small extent, and awash at high water springs.

Light.—From a square wooden tower 30 feet high, painted white, standing on a concrete pier 7 feet high, on Fiddle reef, is exhibited, at a height of 30 feet above high water, a fixed white light with two red sectors, visible 10 miles.

The light shows red over an arc of 45° 30′ between the bearings S. 9° 30′ E. (S. 32° 30′ E. mag.) and S. 36° W. (S. 13° W. mag.); red also over an arc of 48° 30′ between the bearings N. 13° 30′ E. (N. 9° 30′ W. mag.) and N. 62° E. (N. 39° E. mag.).

Caution.—It will be seen from the above that over Thames shoal to the westward and Five-fathom shoal to the northward, the light shows white.

Todd rock, 300 yards NW. of Fiddle reef, in the entrance to Oak bay, covers at two-thirds flood, and is marked by kelp.

Lewis reef, at the northeastern part of Mayor channel, lies 500 yards S. 34° E. (S. 57° E. mag.) of Fiddle reef, covers at high water, and may be approached close-to on the western side.

The passage between it and Chain islets is filled with kelp, but has not less than 2 fathoms of water.

Beacon.—A round stone tower, colored black, 10 feet in height, surmounted by a white drum, is situated on Lewis reef.

Chain islets, midway between Discovery island and the Vancouver shore, from a bare, rocky group. The largest, called Great Chain islet, is about 200 yards in extent and 30 feet above high water; it is the southwestern one of the group.

Spencer ledge, off their eastern side, at a distance of 300 yards from the easternmost high-water rock, is marked by kelp, and has 9 feet of water on its shoalest part; if going through Hecate passage it requires to be guarded against. Cadboro point, open west of Channel point, bearing N. 8° W. (N. 31° W. mag.), leads east of this ledge through Hecate passage.

Caroline reef, at the northern part of the group, and connected to it by a rocky ledge, is of small extent, and covers at one-quarter flood, but is well out of the track of vessels using any of the channels. Foul ground with depths of from 3 to 4 fathoms, marked by kelp, extends upward of 200 yards westward and northwestward from it.

Discovery island is at the junction of Haro and Fuca straits. It is wooded, about ¾ mile in extent, and its shores on all sides are bordered by rocks, extending in some places more than 400 yards off. Rudlin bay, on its southeastern side, is filled with rocks, and should not be used by any vessel.

A rock with 9 feet over it lies with Seabird point bearing N. 43° E. (N. 20° E. mag.), distant about 800 yards. Another rock with 15 feet over it lies about 75 yards northward of the first. These rocks are usually marked by kelp, and, commencing a short distance away, kelp extends, in patches, to the shore of Rudlin bay.

Light.—From a white lighthouse 47 feet high, situated 160 yards from the eastern extreme of Discovery island, is exhibited, at an elevation of 91 feet above high water, an intermittent white light, visible over an arc of 253°, from S. 20° E. (S. 43° E. mag) through West to N. 53° E. (N. 30° E. mag.), and from a distance of 15 miles.

Fog signal.—A steam horn gives blasts of 8 seconds' duration, separated by silent intervals of 1 minute.

Approximate position: Lat. 48° 25½′ N., long. 123° 13½′ W.

Chatham islands, northwest of Discovery island, and separated from it by a narrow boat pass, are of small extent, low, wooded, and almost connected with each other at low water; the tidal streams set with great strength between them.

Leading point, the southwestern extreme, is a bare, rocky islet at high water; to the eastward of it is a small boat cove.

Channel point, their western extreme, is also bare and steep-to. The tide runs strongly past it.

Strong Tide islet, the northwestern of the Chatham islands, is rocky, about 50 feet high, and wooded; its western side forms the eastern boundary of Baynes channel and is steep-to.

Refuge cove, on the eastern side of Chatham islands, is small, and has a depth of 1½ fathoms in the center; coasters or small craft entangled among these islets may find shelter in it. Alpha islet, the easternmost of the group, is bare, and 10 feet above high water; only a boat should attempt to go westward of, or inside, it.

Fulford reef, 600 yards northward of the Chatham islands, is about 200 yards in extent, and covers at three-quarters flood. Vessels using Baynes channel should keep well to the westward to avoid this reef, as the tide sets irregularly in its vicinity.

Hecate and Plumper passages.—Discovery island is separated from the Chain islets by a passage ½ mile wide in the narrowest part, forming an apparently clear and wide channel. Near the middle of the southern part lies Center rock, which has only 3 feet over it; this rock is marked by kelp, but because of the strength of the tides it is often run under and seldom seen. There is a deep passage on either side of this danger, the one to the westward being called Hecate, and the eastern one Plumper passage. The latter is wider and better adapted for large steamers, but the current sets very strongly through both of them.

During the strength of the current Center rock is marked by heavy tide rips.

Cadboro point, open west of Channel point, N. 8° W. (N. 31° W.), leads through Hecate passage in mid-channel, west of Center rock.

Cadboro point, shut in, north of Leading point, N. 16° W. (N. 39° W. mag.), leads through Plumper passage in mid-channel, east of Center rock.

Baynes channel, between Cadboro point and the Chatham islands, connecting these inner channels with Haro strait, is upward of 1 mile long and ½ mile wide; the depths in it are irregular, varying from 2¾ to 30 fathoms, and the current at springs sets through it with a velocity of 4 to 6 knots, strongest along the eastern side.

Five-fathom shoal, which lies in the middle of the channel, is not marked by kelp. It has a least depth of 3 fathoms on its southern edge, while on its northern side there is only 15 feet of water. It lies about 800 yards eastward of Jemmy Jones islet. To avoid it a vessel should keep a little on either side of mid-channel.

Jemmy Jones islet, which is bare and 15 feet above water, lies 600 yards offshore, and 900 yards S. 33° W. (S. 10° W. mag.) of Cadboro point; foul ground extends around it for upward of 200 yards in some parts, and though there is deep water between it and the shore, none except small craft should go through that passage.

A shoal of small extent with 4½ fathoms of water on it lies about 400 yards SE. by E. from the eastern extreme of Jemmy Jones islet. It is marked by kelp in summer and autumn.

Cadboro point, on Vancouver island, at the termination of the Inner channels, is nearly 3 miles NNE. from Gonzales point, and ¾ mile NNW. from the Chatham islands. It is about 50 feet high and rocky. A small islet lies just off it, also a reef which covers; when passing do not approach the islet within 400 yards.

The northern extremity of the point is marked by a conspicuous fir tree.

The coast westward from Cadboro point to Cadboro bay is low, very much broken, and there are some offlying rocks.

Directions.—Though the Inner channels are deep, they should not be used except by steamers, or by small craft, unless in case of necessity, and a knowledge of the tides is indispensable.

Coasters and small steamers, when taking advantage of them, generally proceed through Mayor channel. If using this channel, after passing Gonzales point, keep the western side of Great Chain islet in line with Channel point, N. 36° E. (N. 13° E. mag.), till Emily islet begins to show past the northern side of Harris island; then haul up for Fiddle Reef lighthouse and pass between Fiddle and Lewis reefs.

When past Lewis and Fiddle reefs, steer N. 45° E. (N. 22° E. mag.), and pass out of Baynes channel between Five-fathom shoal and Strong Tide islet.

Going through Mouatt channel, which is very narrow and seldom used, having rounded Gonzales point at a distance of 200 yards, bring the highest part of Trial island in line with Gonzales point, bearing S. 30° W. (S. 7° W. mag.), and steer so as to keep these objects in range astern until on a line between Harris and Great Chain islands. Then haul up for Fiddle Reef lighthouse as before.

The range given above, if closely held, leads clear of dangers through Baynes channel into Haro strait, but it passes close to the shoal spots of Five-fathom shoal, and, though the currents are weaker, it is not recommended.

Hecate and Plumper passages are nearly straight, and better adapted for large steamers than those west of the Chain islets. If using either of them, after passing either through Enterprise channel or southward of Trial islands, bring the leading marks on, and keep them so till northward of Center rock, when steer up in mid-channel between Chain islets and Chatham islands toward Jemmy Jones islet, and through Baynes channel into Haro strait.

Cadboro point, open west of Channel point, bearing N. 8° W. (N. 31° W. mag.), leads through Hecate passage in mid-channel, west of Center rock.

Cadboro point, shut in north of Leading point, bearing N. 16° W. (N. 39° W. mag.), leads through Plumper passage, in mid-channel, east of Center rock.

Tides and tidal currents.—The high water at full and change is irregular and much influenced by prevailing winds.

In Baynes channel, and between Discovery island and the shore, the flood stream begins at 11 h. 15 m.; or immediately after low water by the shore; it runs with great strength for 3¾ hours, after which a considerable period of slack water intervenes. The ebb runs with great strength from 4 h. 0 m. to 11 h. 0 m.

The greatest rise and fall of tide at Discovery island is 12 feet.

The tidal streams run strongly off the southern points of Trial and Discovery islands, and there are heavy tide rips formed off these points by both streams. Heavy rips occur also in the vicinity of Center rock.

Constance bank, lying in Juan de Fuca strait, nearly 6 miles SE. by S. of Fisgard lighthouse, is upward of 1 mile in extent with depths of from 9 to 14 fathoms, but a vessel should not anchor on it, as the bottom is rocky.

Middle bank, lying in the southern entrance of Haro strait, 5 miles E. by S. of Discovery island, and almost in mid-channel, is a rocky patch about 2 miles in extent each way, and the least water found on it is 10 fathoms. In bad weather there are heavy tide rips on and in the vicinity of this bank, which are dangerous to boats or small craft.

Hein (Fonte) bank, within the 10-fathom curve, is about 1½ miles in extent, and lies nearly in the middle of the eastern end of Juan de Fuca strait, and 8 miles SE. by E. from Discovery Island lighthouse. The least water found is 13 feet over a bowlder lying on hard clay and gravel toward the center of the bank, the average over the bank being from 4 to 7 fathoms. This bank should be avoided, as there may be less water than shown on the chart.

Buoy.—A nun buoy, painted in red and black horizontal stripes, is moored in 6 fathoms about 50 feet N. 16° E. (N. 7° W. mag.) from the bowlder. From the buoy Smith Island lighthouse bears S. 75° E. (N. 82° E. mag.), and New Dungeness lighthouse S. 14° W. (S. 9° E. mag.).

Smith, or Blunt, island, lies almost in the center of the eastern end of Juan de Fuca strait, about 13 miles NE. ½ E. from New Dungeness lighthouse, and 6 miles SSW. from the entrance of Rosario strait. It is about ½ mile in length, cliffy at its western end, and 50 feet high. A large kelp patch extends 1½ miles from the western extreme, which should be avoided; there are 6 fathoms on its outer edge. From the eastern end of the island, which is low, extends for a distance of ¾ mile a spit of sand, gravel, and bowlders, partially covered at high water.

On the north side of this spit there is anchorage in 5 fathoms, sandy bottom, about ½ mile from the shore, but no vessel should lie here with any appearance of bad weather.

Light.—On the summit of Smith, or Blunt, island, near the western end, is a lighthouse rising from a dwelling, both painted white, lantern black, from which is exhibited, 87 feet above high water, a flashing white light every 30 seconds, visible 15 miles.

Beacon.—A beacon, with a white, truncated, pyramidal base surmounted by a black iron spindle and cage, the whole 24 feet high, has been erected on Minor island, at the extremity of the spit extending from the eastern end of Smith island, 1 mile ENE. of Smith Island lighthouse.

Partridge bank and buoy have already been described.

McArthur bank, of small extent, with a depth of 15 to 17 fathoms, lies about 4 miles NW. by N. from Smith Island lighthouse.

Eastern bank.—This bank lies about 5 miles WSW. from Smith Island lighthouse. It is about 2 miles in extent with depths varying from 11 to 19 fathoms.

Hassler bank lies N. 38° W. (N. 61° W. mag.) of New Dungeness lighthouse, and nearly halfway between New Dungeness and Victoria. This is a 20-fathom bank, 2 miles long and ½ mile wide, with as little as 15 fathoms of water over it.

CHAPTER III.

HARO STRAIT AND THE WESTERN CHANNELS AND ISLANDS TO NANAIMO HARBOR AND DEPARTURE BAY.

VARIATION IN 1906.

East point .... 23° 45′ E. | Nanaimo .... 24° 00′ E.

Haro strait, the westernmost of the three channels leading from Fuca strait into the strait of Georgia, trends in a N. by W. direction for 18 miles; it then turns sharply to the ENE. round Turn point of Stuart island, for a farther distance of 12 miles, leaving Saturna island to the westward and Waldron and Patos island to the eastward, when it enters the strait of Georgia between Saturna and Patos islands.

It is for the most part a broad, and for its whole extent a deep, navigable ship channel; but on account of the reefs which exist in certain parts, the general absence of steady winds, the scarcity of anchorages, and, above all, the strength and varying direction of the tides, much care and vigilance is necessary in its navigation, and it is far more adapted to steam than to sailing vessels.

Besides the main channel of Haro strait thus described, there are several smaller channels and passages branching from it by which vessels may enter the strait of Georgia; thus Swanson channel leads into the strait by Active pass, and Trincomali and Stuart channels by Portier pass, or Dodd narrows.

These channels may be again entered by smaller ones; thus Sidney and Cordova channels, on the western side of Haro strait, lead by Moresby, Colburne, and Shute passages into Swanson, Satellite, and Stuart channels, and finally into the strait of Georgia. These channels are essentially adapted to steam navigation, or to coasting vessels; they afford smooth water, and many of them anchorages.

Middle bank, lying in the southern entrance to Haro strait, having a least depth of 10 fathoms, has already been described. In bad weather heavy tide rips occur in the vicinity of this bank.

Two banks, of small extent, with 7 to 8 fathoms least water, lie 3¼ miles NNE. ½ E. and 2½ miles NE. ¼ N., respectively, from Discovery Island lighthouse. There are heavy tide rips over both these banks in bad weather.

Telegraph cove is a small indentation, 100 yards wide, on the northern side of Cadboro point; it is available only for small craft.

The western side of the cove, at its entrance, is steep-to, but off the eastern point foul ground, marked by kelp, extends to the northward for a distance of 150 yards; near its outer end is a rock which uncovers at extreme low water.

Dynamite works have been established at the head of the cove, and a wharf has been built, the head of which is 90 feet long with a depth of 10 feet alongside at low water.

The tidal streams set strongly across the entrance. Springs rise 11 feet.

Vessels visiting the cove should give the eastern point a good berth, and should not head in for the wharf until the red brick chimney of the works is well open westward of the largest reservoir, bearing about SSE. ¼ E.

The submarine telephone cable connecting Victoria and Vancouver lands in Telegraph cove.

Johnstone reef, the shoalest part of which is awash at low water, lies 1,500 yards from shore, midway between Cadboro point and Gordon head. It is of small extent and there is deep water all round it.

A rock, on which is a depth of 2 fathoms, with 12 to 19 fathoms around, lies 450 yards SW. from the shoalest part of Johnstone reef.

Buoy.—A black can buoy is moored 200 yards NNE. of the shoalest part of Johnstone reef.

A rock, on which is a depth of 2 fathoms, with 12½ to 19 fathoms around, lies 600 yards W. by S. from Johnstone reef, nearly midway between the reef and the shore.

Zero rock, one of the principal dangers on the western side of the southern end of Haro strait, lies 6¼ miles NNW. from Discovery Island lighthouse; it is of small extent, steep-to on its western side, and dries 10 feet at low water.

Beacon.—Zero Rock beacon consists of a frustum of a cone in stonework, surmounted by open slatwork in the form of a triangle, point upward. The top is 28 feet above high water. The beacon is painted black.

A rocky patch, part of which nearly uncovers at low water springs, lies 700 yards N. ½ W. of Zero rock.

Discovery Island light is obscured in the direction of Zero rock and westward of it.

Little Zero rock, which dries 6 feet at low water springs, lies 1 mile WNW. ½ W. from Zero rock. It is steep-to on its eastern side and there is deep water between it and Zero rock.

A rocky patch, a part of which is awash at low water, lies 600 yards WNW. ½ W. from Little Zero rock.

Another shoal with 1½ fathoms over it lies 500 yards NW. by W. from the last-named patch. Both of these shoal spots are marked by kelp during part of the year.

Kelp reefs, ¾ mile in extent, lie on the western side, but well toward the center, of Haro strait, and southeastward of Darcy island. They are about 7 miles northward of Discovery Island lighthouse. The southern reef is awash, and the two northern ones uncover at low water springs. The reefs are marked by kelp, which extends in detached patches to Darcy island.

Beacon.—On the eastern of the two northern reefs is a stone beacon in the form of a frustum of a cone surmounted by staff and ball, the whole 20 feet high.

There is foul ground between Kelp reefs and Darcy island, and a rock with less than 6 feet over it lies midway between the two.

Unit rock lies ¾ mile eastward of the southern point of Darcy island and uncovers 2 feet at low water.

Note.—Bare island, well open north of Sidney island, bearing N. 25° W. (N. 49° W. mag.), leads eastward of Kelp reefs and Unit rock.

Cormorant bay, between Gordon and Cowichan heads, on the western side of Haro strait, is a good stopping place, easy of access under most circumstances. Off Gordon head, the southern point of the bay, are several low-lying islets, and 100 yards outside them is Gordon rock, awash at low water. The bay may be entered either to the southward or northward of the group consisting of Zero and Little Zero rocks and the shoals westward of the latter; the passage to the southward is 1½ miles wide, with a depth of 20 fathoms. There is a clear passage nearly 1 mile wide, with 20 fathoms, between Zero and Little Zero rocks. Mount Douglas, a remarkable hill, 723 feet high, with a summit bare of trees, rises immediately over the coast at the head of the bay.

Cowichan head, on the northern side of Cormorant bay, is remarkable for its conspicuous white cliffs, which reach a height of 190 feet, gradually sloping on the southern side to a rocky point and on the northern side to the sandy shore terminating in Cordova spit.

A rock with 4 fathoms over it lies about 1,600 yards offshore, midway between Gordon and Cowichan heads; from it Zero Rock beacon bears N. 88° E. (N. 64° E. mag.), distant $2\frac{1}{10}$ miles.

Two islets, 1 foot high, lie nearly midway between Gordon and Cowichan heads and about 400 yards offshore; between these islets and Cowichan head there are several patches of foul ground, and the shore here should be given a berth of at least 800 yards.

The tidal streams are not much felt in Cormorant bay when westward of Zero rock, and the holding ground is good.

This anchorage is exposed to SE. winds, but a vessel with good ground tackle will be safe. Small vessels may obtain good shelter close in under Gordon head.

Darcy island.—About 2¼ miles N. by E. from Zero Rock beacon is Darcy island. The island is low, wooded, and about ½ mile in extent. Its shores are rocky, and the height of the island, to the top of the trees, is about 150 feet.

Off the north and east sides of the island are several small islets and rocks, and from the south and east sides foul ground extends for 1½ miles to Kelp reefs.

Sidney island is an irregularly shaped island 5 miles long in a NNW. and SSE. direction and a little more than a mile wide in its widest part. The island is thickly wooded and about 250 feet high to the tops of the trees, and terminates at its NW. end in a low, sandy spit partially covered at low water. A sand spit also extends for 1 mile NNW. from the western point of the island, almost inclosing a shallow lagoon between it and the island.

The SW. side of the island is formed of earthy cliffs and banks which toward the southern end of the island rise into conspicuous white earth cliffs 120 feet high. This SW. shore, from the southern point to the second spit above mentioned, is bordered by a mud bank from 200 to 400 yards in width at low water. There is a pier on the shore ¾ mile NNW. from Whale rock.

Beacon.—A black and white beacon, pyramidal, of latticework, 50 feet high, marks the NW. end of Sidney spit; at high water this end of the spit is an island 3 feet high.

Dot rocks are three small islets lying from 400 to 1,000 yards off the southern point of Sidney island; the largest is 17 feet high.

Foul ground exists between Dot rocks and Sidney island.

Miners channel.—Halibut (Low) and Ridge (Bare) islands are two small islands lying off the eastern side of Sidney island, and between them and the latter is a good passage, ½ mile wide, with 8 fathoms least water.

A 3-fathom patch 200 yards in extent lies 500 yards NE. by N. from the eastern point of Sidney island, at the southern entrance of the channel.

This channel may prove convenient for those having passed up Haro strait eastward of Kelp reefs, and desiring to take the inner channels to Saanich, Cowichin, or through Stuart channel.

The eastern side of Sidney island affords good anchorage in 8 fathoms, out of the tide, off a bay SW. from the northern end of Ridge island; the bay is shoal as far out as a line between its entrance points.

Shoals.—A shoal, with a depth of 1¼ fathoms over it and 100 yards in extent, lies about 350 yards from the shore of Halibut island, with the western point of the island bearing N. ½ W., distant 450 yards.

Another shoal, with a depth of 3½ fathoms over it, and with deep water around, lies 600 yards SE. by E. from the above shoal. Both these dangers are marked by kelp. Kelp extends for a distance of 600 yards from the eastern point of Halibut island, at which distance there is a shoal spot with 3 fathoms on it.

A rock, awash at low water, lies nearly 600 yards ESE. from, and another which uncovers at low water 500 yards South of, the eastern point of Ridge island.

A rock, 3 feet high, lies 600 yards WNW. from the western end of Ridge island.

Jones, Domville, Hill, Comet, and Gooch islands are the principal islands of the group that lies between Sidney and Moresby islands and westward of Haro strait. They are all wooded and about 100 feet in height to the tops of the trees. The passages between them are not recommended.

There are several rocks off the SE. end of Jones island, the highest being 30 feet in height. The NW. end of Jones island is ¾ mile N. by E. from Sidney Spit beacon, and has a rock awash at low water 200 yards off it. There is a clear passage between Jones and Sidney islands.

Cod reefs.—North Cod reef is about 400 yards in extent, and covers at a quarter flood; it lies 800 yards S. 17° W. (S. 7° E. mag.) from the western end of Gooch island.

South Cod reef, also about 400 yards in extent, has 6 feet on it at low water; it lies 1,400 yards S. 17° W. (S. 7° E. mag.) from the western end of Gooch island. Both reefs are marked by kelp.

Prevost passage lies between the group of islands northward of Sidney island and the southern side of Moresby island. This passage is not much used, but is a good, deep, and navigable channel; the only known dangers show at low water and are both marked by kelp.

Cooper reef, lying ½ mile N. 10° W. (N. 34° W. mag.) from Tom point (Gooch island), is marked by kelp and uncovers at half ebb; there is a passage 1 mile wide between it and Arachne reef.

Arachne reef lies nearly in the center of Prevost passage and in a direct line between Fairfax point (SE. point of Moresby island) and Tom point (eastern end of Gooch island), and 2¼ miles S. 83° W. (S. 59° W. mag.) from Turn point, on Stuart island. The reef uncovers at three-quarters ebb. It is marked by kelp, but the kelp is frequently run under by the tide.

Mouatt point, on Pender island, kept open of Pelorus point, Moresby island, clears Cooper and Arachne reefs to the eastward, for ships navigating Haro strait.

The northern point of Portland island in line with the southern side of Moresby island, N. 48° W. (N. 72° W. mag.), leads northward of both reefs.

Moresby island, lying between Haro strait and Moresby passage, is 2¼ miles long NNW. and SSE., and a little over 1 mile wide. The island is thickly wooded except for a large clearing on its western side, and rises, near its middle, to a rather conspicuous hill 533 feet in height to the tops of the trees.

Point Fairfax, the SE. point of the island, terminates in a cluster of small rocks, the highest of which is 10 feet high.

From Reef point, the NW. extreme, a rocky ledge runs out under water for nearly 400 yards to the 3-fathom curve; several heads on this ledge dry at low water.

San Juan island, the western coast of which forms for some distance the eastern boundary of Haro strait, is 13 miles in length in a NW. and SE. direction, with an average breadth of about 4 miles. Its western coast is steep and rocky, and affords no anchorage. Mount Dallas rises abruptly 1,086 feet, but the eastern side of the island falls in a more gentle slope, and affords a considerable extent of good land available for agricultural or grazing purposes.

Toward the southern end, and visible from seaward, are some white buildings, the farming establishment of the Hudson Bay company; the SE. extreme terminates in a white clay cliff, over which rises Mount Finlayson to a height of 550 feet, remarkable as being entirely clear of trees on its southern side, while it is thickly wooded on the northern. There is a clean gravel beach under Mount Finlayson, where boats can generally land.

Henry island lies off the NW. end of San Juan, being only separated from it by a narrow channel called Mosquito passage. The island might easily be taken for a part of San Juan, the passage appearing merely as an indentation in the latter.

Kellett bluff, the SW. point of Henry island, shows as the most prominent headland on the eastern side of Haro strait, when seen from the southward.

Immediately eastward of it is Open bay, which has more the appearance of a channel than the true one, Mosquito passage. There is no shelter in the bay, or anchorage in the passage, for anything but coasters.

Mosquito passage is studded with numerous reefs, which are marked by kelp. When a mile within the passage, Westcott creek, an indentation in San Juan, branches off to the NE., and affords a haven for coasters. There is a 2-fathom channel through the passage and into this creek. The only directions necessary are to avoid the kelp patches. The tide runs strongly through it.

Morse island, a small, flat, cliffy island, lies ¼ mile NW. of McCracken point, the northern point of Henry island. Between Morse island and the point is foul ground, and vessels should not attempt this passage.

Roche harbor, between San Juan and Henry islands, is landlocked and ½ mile in extent, with depths of from 6 to 8 fathoms over the greater part of it. It must be entered from the northward by all except small craft; its entrance is somewhat confined, but not very difficult of access, and it affords good shelter when within.

The breadth of the entrance between Inman point (Henry island) and the shore of Pearl island is over 400 yards, but the navigable channel is contracted to little over 100 yards by shoal water which extends off both shores. A stranger must not count on more than 24 feet at low water when rounding in.

Pearl island, about 800 yards long east and west, and 300 yards broad, and wooded, lies in the center of the passage, forming two entrances, the eastern of which, however, is barred; off the northern side of Pearl island is a small islet (Posey) connected to it at low water.

Scout patch, a dangerous spit projecting from Inman point, has 17 feet on it; and, although there is a depth of 5 fathoms in mid-channel, great care must be exercised to avoid this patch by those drawing over 14 feet.

A good anchorage is in 6 fathoms, with the western end of Pearl island NNW., distant about ¼ mile, and the northern part of Henry island just open of it. If working in, remember that a shoal of 15 feet lies 300 yards northward from Bare islet.

The time of high water at full and change in Roche harbor is 3 h. 35 m. Springs rise 6½ feet, neaps 5¼ feet.

Roche harbor to Port Townsend.—During the strength of the flood proceed through Spieden channel, President channel (leaving Barnes island to the eastward), and Rosario strait.

With ebb tide and clear weather use Spieden and San Juan channels.

Spieden channel, between the island of that name and San Juan, has a general east and west direction. Its eastern entrance, between Green point and the NE. point of San Juan, is ⅜ mile wide, and for 2 miles the water is deep and clear of dangers. The meeting of the flood tide, however, from Haro strait, with that from Middle channel, causes heavy rips and irregular eddies. These, together with the general absence of steady winds, render the navigation always tedious and dangerous for sailing vessels. Its western entrance is encumbered with reefs and shoals with irregular soundings.

Bare islet is a rock about 15 feet high, lying in the southern part of the channel, 1 mile E. ½ S. from Morse island. Two shoal patches with 1¾ fathoms over them lie about 300 yards to the northward and northeastward, respectively, of the islet. They are marked by kelp.

Buoy.—A black can buoy marks the NW. extreme of the shoal ground.

Sentinel island stands in the western entrance of this channel. It is small, bare on its southern side, and about 150 feet high. The passage between it and Spieden island is more than 200 yards wide. Vessels using the Spieden channel are recommended to keep the Spieden island shore aboard, and to pass between it and Sentinel island. There is much less tide here than in the center of the channel or on the San Juan shore. Sentinel rock lies 400 yards westward of the island, the passage between being foul.

Center reef is a dangerous patch, awash at low water, and almost in the center of the channel. It bears from Sentinel island S. 62° W. (S. 38° W. mag.), distant nearly ½ mile. Kelp will generally be seen around the reef, but it is sometimes run under. Both the flood from Haro strait and the ebb through Spieden channel set on to the reef. When nearing it the San Juan shore should be kept aboard, avoiding the shoal 300 yards north of Bare islet.

Danger shoal is also at the western entrance. It is marked by kelp, though not always to be distinguished. It lies about 1 mile N. 12° E. (N. 12° W. mag.) from Morse island. It has only ¾ fathom of water over it.

Directions.—Vessels bound from Haro strait to the eastward through the Spieden channel should pass about ¼ mile to the northward of Morse island and then steer N. 85° E. (N. 61° E. mag.) for Green point, the eastern extreme of Spieden island, until Sentinel island bears North (N. 24° W. mag.); the dangers in the western entrance will then be passed and a straight course may be steered through, bearing in mind that less tide will be found near Spieden island shore.

Bound westward through this channel, if the passage between Spieden and Sentinel islands is not taken, the shore of Spieden island should be kept aboard to avoid the tide races. If Center reef is awash, or the kelp on it is seen, pass ¼ mile south of it and steer to pass the same distance north of Morse island. If Center reef is not seen, take care not to bring Morse island to bear to the southward of S. 68° W. (S. 44° W. mag.) until Bare islet bears S. 22° E. (S. 46° E. mag.).

Spieden island, lying between San Juan and Stuart islands, is 2¼ miles long in an east and west direction, and very narrow; its southern side is grassy and bare of trees, its summit and northern side thickly wooded; Green point, its eastern extreme, is a sloping grassy point.

There is a channel on both sides of Spieden island; but from the strength and irregularity of the tidal streams, and the hidden dangers which exist in certain parts of them, they can not be recommended for sailing vessels, nor indeed to any vessel without a pilot.

New channel, to the northward of Spieden island, though narrower than Spieden channel, is deep, more free from danger, and the navigation of it more simple. The northern shore of Spieden island is bold and steep-to, and should be kept aboard; the narrowest part of the channel is ¼ mile wide between Spieden and Cactus islands, and care should be taken not to get entangled among the reefs to the northward of the latter. The flood tide sets to the northeastward among them; but is also sets fairly through New channel, and by keeping the Spieden island shore aboard there will be no danger of being set to the northward; the ebb tide runs to the southwestward between Johns and Spieden islands.

Stuart island, lying 3 miles northwestward of the northern part of the island of San Juan, is of an irregular shape, about 3 miles long in an east and west direction, 642 feet high, and the summits of the hills partially bare of trees.

Turn point, its NW. extreme, a bold, cliffy bluff, forms the salient angle of Haro strait, where it changes its direction suddenly from N. by W. to ENE. before entering Georgia strait.

There are two anchorages in Stuart island, Reid harbor on its southern side and Prevost harbor on its northern; both are small and intricate for sailing vessels larger than coasters.

Light.—Turn Point light, fixed white and of small power, is exhibited from a white staff, 38 feet above high water.

The fog-signal house and the keeper's dwelling, each painted white with brown roofs, are situated close southeastward of the light.

Fog signal.—Turn Point fog signal is a Daboll trumpet, which during thick or foggy weather gives blasts of 3 seconds' duration, separated by silent intervals of 27 seconds.

Reid harbor.—When entering Reid harbor from the southward, beware of being drawn by the flood stream into the channel between San Juan and Stuart islands, where there are several dangers, and the tidal streams are most irregular in their direction. The SW. side of Stuart island should, therefore, be first closed.

The harbor is 1 mile NNW. from Spieden bluff (a remarkable bare, grassy point, generally of a yellow color), the western extreme of the island of the same name. Gossip islands lie in the entrance, and from them a shoal extends 300 yards NW. by W.; leave them on the starboard hand when entering. The channel is 300 yards wide, with depths of from 4 to 5 fathoms. The best anchorage is off an Indian village on the southern side about half a mile within the entrance.

Prevost harbor, on the northern side of Stuart island, 1½ miles eastward from Turn point, has James island lying in the center of it. The entrance is to the westward of this island, between it and Charles point, and is about 400 yards in breadth, the harbor extending southward for a short distance, and then taking an easterly direction. Anchor in 6 fathoms as soon as the eastern arm opens out, or if desired run up the arm into 4½ fathoms; here it is narrow, but perfectly sheltered. The passage to the eastward of James island is a blind one, but a vessel may anchor, if necessary, outside the entrance in 10 or 12 fathoms of water.

Waldron island lies in the northern entrance of San Juan (Middle) channel. As its anchorages are frequently available for vessels passing to or from Haro strait, it seems desirable that it should be described while treating of this neighborhood.

The island is thickly wooded, moderately high, and cliffy on its southern and eastern sides, but falling to the northward, where it terminates in low, sandy points. Disney point, its southern extreme, is a remarkable, high, stratified bluff.

Cowlitz bay, on the western side of Waldron island, between Disney and Sandy points, affords good anchorage with all winds, the depth of water being from 3 to 8 fathoms, and the holding ground stiff mud; it may be sometimes more desirable for sailing vessels to anchor here than to work up into Plumper sound, particularly for those coming up San Juan channel. If entering from the northward or westward, Sandy point may be passed at a distance of ⅓ mile; standing into the bay, anchor on the line between it and Disney point in 5 or 6 fathoms. If a southeaster is blowing, a vessel may stand far enough in to get smooth water under shelter of Disney point; no sea, however, to affect a vessel's safety gets up in this bay with any wind.

Mouatt reef, with a depth of only 3 feet on it, lies ½ mile N. 17° W. (N. 41° W. mag.) of Disney point, with deep water between it and the shore.

If entering from the southward, Disney point should be kept within less than ¼ mile, particularly with the ebb, for as soon as President, or Douglas, channel (the continuation of Middle channel), through which the current runs sometimes 5 knots is opened out, vessels are apt to be set down on Danger rock.

White rock is 35 feet above high water and lies WSW., 1¾ miles from Disney point. There is a reef extending 400 yards NW. by N. from it.

Danger rock, a dangerous reef with only 5 feet on it, and on which kelp is rarely seen, lies SE. by S. ⅓ mile from White rock.

Caution.—It is particularly recommended to give these rocks a wide berth, as with strong tides the water is too deep for anchorage in case of getting entangled among them in light winds.

North bay, on the NW. side of Waldron island, affords anchorage in 8 to 10 fathoms about ½ mile offshore, but is not by any means such a desirable place as Cowlitz bay, the bank being rather steep and the tidal streams stronger.

A rock with only 2 feet of water over it lies 900 yards E. by N. from Hammond point, the NE. extremity of the island; foul ground, marked by kelp, extends to the northward and eastward of the same point for a distance of ½ mile.

Skipjack and Penguin islands are small islands lying close off the northern side of Waldron island; the former is considerably the larger, and is wooded; the latter is small, grassy, and bare of trees. A reef which covers, and is marked by kelp, lies between the two, but between this reef and Skipjack island there is a narrow passage of 8 fathoms. The tides, however, set strongly between the islands, and the passage is not recommended; neither, for the same reason, is the passage between them and Waldron island.

Patos island lies on the eastern side of the northern end of Haro strait and opposite Saturna island on the western side. The passage between them is the widest, and at present the most frequented, though it is not always the best channel from Haro or San Juan channels into the strait of Georgia. Patos is 1½ miles long in an east and west direction, narrow, wedge-shaped, 70 feet high, sloping toward its western end, and covered with trees. Active cove, at its western end, is formed by a small islet connected at low water, and affords anchorage for one or two small vessels in 2 fathoms, but a strong tide rip at the point renders it difficult for a sailing vessel to enter.

The passage into the strait of Georgia between Patos and Sucia islands, although narrower than the one just mentioned, is to be preferred, especially for vessels passing through San Juan channel, or for sailing vessels with a NW. wind. The tides are not so strong, are more regular, and set more fairly through; the passage is almost free from tide rips.

Light.—Patos or Alden Point light is fixed red, of small power, shown from a white post at a height of 28 feet above high water. The fog-signal station and dwelling are a little southeastward; both are painted white, with brown roofs.

Fog signal.—A trumpet gives blasts of 2 seconds' duration separated by silent intervals of 18 seconds.

Pender, Saturna, and Tumbo islands.—These islands, lying northward of Stuart and Waldron islands, may be called the northwestern boundary of Haro strait after it turns to the ENE.

Bedwell harbor, the entrance to which is 3 miles NNE. from Turn point of Stuart island, is, on account of its narrow entrance, not a good stopping place for sailing vessels waiting for the tide, but for steamers it is a good harbor. Its narrowest part, which is at the entrance, is ¼ mile wide, but it soon opens out to ½ mile, and trends NW. for 2 miles, with depths of 5 to 10 fathoms, mud bottom.

The only danger which does not show is Drew rock, with 10 feet on it, in the center of the harbor and ⅓ mile from its head; there is, however, no necessity to go as far up as this.

The most convenient anchorage is in a bay on the northeastern shore ⅔ mile within the entrance, in 8 fathoms, midway between Hay point and Skull reef, which always shows some feet above high water.

Camp bay, between Bedwell harbor and Plumper sound, and ½ mile westward of Blunden island, offers shelter as a stopping place to small craft, when not convenient for them to work into either of these ports.

Plumper sound.—If necessary to anchor in Haro strait between Stuart island and the east point of Saturna island, Plumper sound is recommended as safe and convenient, easy of access with the wind from any quarter. The entrance lies 5 miles NE. from Turn point, and an equal distance from Saturna Island lighthouse. Blunden (Douglas) island, close to the shore of Pender island, with only a boat passage (choked with rocks and kelp) between, forms the southwestern entrance point; Monarch, or Java, head (Saturna island), a high, bold, rocky, headland, the northeastern.

For the first 2 miles the water is too deep for convenient anchorage, being generally from 25 to 50 fathoms, except on the southern side, where, if necessary, an anchor may be dropped ¼ mile from shore in from 10 to 12 fathoms.

There are no dangers at the entrance and but little tide is felt. A rocky patch, with 15 feet on it, lies about N. 56° W. (N. 80° W. mag.), distant 550 yards, from Croker point. It is of small extent and steep-to, except on its northern edge, where it shoals gradually from 8 fathoms. Between this patch and Saturna island the soundings are irregular, varying from 8 to 20 fathoms.

In coming from the southward, the western extremity of Fane island in line with the NE. extreme of Pender island clears this patch, and Lizard islet open of Elliot bluff clears its western edge.

The most convenient anchorage is off the entrance of Port Browning, on the western side of the sound, in 8 fathoms, ½ mile from the shore. Above Port Browning is Perry rock, with 6 feet on it, marked by kelp. It is 400 yards from the shore and N. 11° W. (N. 35° W. mag.), ¾ mile from Razor point, the northern point of the port.

Java reef (Seagull islet), 15 feet high, lies 600 yards off the southern shore of Java (Monarch) head. It is usually marked by kelp.

Port Browning is on the southern side of Plumper sound; it is ⅓ mile wide, but rather less at the entrance. The depth decreases from 10 fathoms at the entrance to 4 fathoms at its head, with good holding ground. The best anchorage is in the center just above Shark cove, which is a convenient creek, with 4 fathoms in it, on the southern side of the harbor, ¾ mile within the entrance; here a ship might beach and repair on a sandy spit.

Shark cove is separated from Bedwell harbor by an isthmus 150 yards wide, across which the natives transport their canoes.

Lyall harbor is on the eastern side of Plumper sound, and its southern entrance point, Elliot bluff (cliffy), bears NNE. ½ E., distant 2 miles, from the entrance to Port Browning. King islets, two low, rugged islets, with a reef extending nearly 200 yards off their western end, form the northern entrance, which is ½ mile wide. The harbor trends easterly 1¼ miles, gradually narrowing and terminating in a sandy beach with a stream of good fresh water at its head; the depths decrease regularly from 8 to 4 fathoms.

Crispin rock, with 6 feet on it, is a pinnacle, exactly in the middle of the harbor, ½ mile SE. by E. from the outer King islet; there is, however, a clear passage on either side of it 300 yards wide, and when anchoring above it drop the anchor in 5 fathoms, ½ mile from the beach at the head of the harbor.

The anchorage outside of Crispin rock is with the outer King islet bearing N. by W., distant ⅓ mile, in 7 fathoms, muddy bottom.

Boot cove, on the southern side of the harbor, has 3 fathoms of water and is a convenient spot for repairing a vessel; a small islet lies off its western entrance point.

Hope bay, on the western side of the sound, is formed between Fane islet and the two islets westward of it and the coast of Pender island. There is a wharf on the extremity of the point immediately north of the stream flowing into the bay. There are no outlying dangers in the bay, nor in the approach to the wharf.

Samuel island, between Saturna and Mayne islands, is almost connected with both, but leaving two passages by which boats or even small coasters may pass into the strait of Georgia at proper stages of tide. This island is indented on its southern side by several bays.

Winter cove is between Samuel island and the NW. point of Saturna. The depth being from 2 to 3 fathoms, it is only fit for small vessels. Coasting vessels might take the passage at slack water, or boats overtaken in the strait by bad weather might take shelter under the lee of Belle chain, and enter Plumper sound by this pass on the flood tide.

Minx reef, marked by kelp, lies fair in the western entrance to the cove.

Rock.—A rock, awash at high water, is situated about 150 yards ESE. of the extreme SE. end of Lizard island; there is foul ground between the rock and the island.

Water is easily obtainable during the winter or rainy months from streams in almost any part of Plumper sound. At the head of Lyall harbor or Port Browning, constantly in the former, a certain quantity may be procured during the driest months of summer, from June to August.

Navy channel is a continuation of the western part of Plumper sound, and leads, between Pender and Mayne islands, into Trincomali channel.

Independently, therefore, of its value as an anchorage, Plumper sound becomes a highroad for vessels bound into the strait of Georgia, or Fraser river, by Active pass, or to Nanaimo, or any of the northwestern ports of Vancouver island.

Conconi reef.—Conconi reef lies about halfway through Navy channel, 1¾ miles from Fane island, and nearly 400 yards off the northern shore, and narrows the strait at that part to ⅓ mile. It is a ledge of rocks extending in the direction of the channel for more than 200 yards, and covering at half tide; its vicinity is marked by kelp, and a patch of 2 fathoms lies nearly 400 yards westward from it. The general depth of water in the channel is from 20 to 30 fathoms.

Enterprise reef consists of two rocky patches, the westernmost of which is covered at a quarter flood. The outermost of these patches lies 1 mile NW. from Dinner point, the northern entrance point of Navy channel. A patch of 2 fathoms lies 400 yards southeastward from the westernmost rocky patch.

Enterprise reef is covered by the red sector of Portlock Point light.

Beacon.—A stone beacon, surmounted by a latticework tripod and ball, stands on the reef near its western extremity; the top of the beacon is 20 feet above high water. The stonework is painted black, the tripod and ball white.

Village bay, on the west coast of Mayne island, is an excellent anchorage with 10 fathoms in the middle of the bay. From Helen point to the anchorage the shore is bold and clear. The passage between the southern point of the bay and Enterprise reef is also free from danger.

Directions.—Vessels using Navy channel should keep rather southward of mid-channel. The shores of Pender island are bold. When passing out of the western entrance, if bound through Trincomali channel or Active pass, steer over toward Prevost island until Pelorus point (the east point of Moresby island) is open of Mouatt point (the west point of Pender island) bearing S. 19° E. (S. 43° E. mag.); then haul up to N. 19° W. (N. 43° W. mag.), keeping the marks just open, which will lead over ⅓ mile to the westward of Enterprise reef.

When Helen point, which is a low, bare, yellow point, bears N. 34° E. (N. 10° E. mag.) steer for the entrance of Active pass, or up Trincomali channel.

Tides.—The flood tide from Swanson channel runs through Navy channel to the eastward and meets the flood in Plumper sound, causing a slight ripple at the eastern entrance; its strength is upward of 3 knots.

East point is the eastern extremity of Saturna island and lies on the western side of the northern entrance of Haro strait. It is about 3 miles W. ½ S. from Alden point, the western end of Patos island, which is on the eastern side of the entrance.

Light.—Saturna or East Point light is a revolving white light, attaining its greatest brilliancy every 30 seconds. It is 125 feet above the sea and is visible 18 miles through an arc of 278°, from N. 62° E. (N. 38° E. mag.) to S. 36° E. (S. 60° E. mag.).

The lighthouse is a square wooden tower, 60 feet high, painted white, lantern red; a keeper's dwelling is attached to the tower.

Boiling reef extends northward from East point toward the buoy marking Rosenfelt reef. The inner part, showing above high water, is about ¼ mile from the lighthouse; the outer portion runs off but a little under the surface at low water.

Tumbo island, separated from Saturna island by Tumbo channel, is about 2 miles long east and west. From both ends of the island foul ground extends for a distance of 1 mile.

Tumbo reef, a ledge of foul rocky ground, over which there are very heavy tide rips and dangerous overfalls, extends 1 mile E. by N. from the eastern end of Tumbo island; it has numerous rocky patches with from 6 to 25 feet over them.

Buoy.—A large can buoy surmounted by a cage, the whole painted black, moored in 12 fathoms of water, 1¼ miles N. 27° E. (N. 3° E. mag.) from Saturna Island lighthouse, marks the extreme end of the reef.

About 400 feet inshore of the buoy is a small patch of 2 fathoms; it is marked by kelp. This is known as Rosenfelt reef.

Orcas knob, near the western shore of Orcas island, bearing S. 3° E. (S. 27° E. mag.) and well open to the eastward of the eastern point of Waldron island, leads in the fairway between Saturna and Patos islands, about 1 mile eastward of the reef.

Toe point (Patos island) in line with the northern extreme of Sucia island, bearing S. 64° E. (S. 88° E. mag.), leads nearly ¾ mile northward of the reef.

Anchorages.—Although there are harbors in Haro strait and its tributary channels, the number eligible for sailing vessels overtaken by darkness, or an adverse tide, is small.

Between Cormorant bay and the northern entrance of Haro strait, Plumper sound and Cowlitz bay are the only eligible stopping places for a sailing vessel seeking shelter.

Stuart island has two fair harbors, and Roche harbor, at the northwest end of San Juan island, is a suitable anchorage for steam vessels or small coasters, but no sailing vessel of moderate tonnage could enter either under ordinary circumstances without great loss of time, as well as risk.

Caution.—As previously mentioned, seamen are again cautioned that, when navigating the inner waters of British Columbia, it should be constantly borne in mind that many of the main channels and most of the minor passages have been only roughly examined; detached bowlders from the broken shores and pinnacles of rock are still frequently found. Whenever, therefore, a broad and clear channel is known to exist, there is no justification in using, without necessity, one of more doubtful character, even if there is some saving in distance; and a ship should always be maintained in the safest possible position in a channel, as well as when going in or out of port.

Tidal currents.—The flood current sets northward through the strait and the ebb in the opposite direction. At its northern entrance the flood sets eastward on both sides of Sucia islands, and eastward across Alden bank. Close along the SE. side of East point the current always sets NE. and only decreases in velocity at the turn of the tide in the strait. The velocity of the current in the strait is 2 to 5 knots, increasing to between 3 and 6 knots at Discovery island, between Stuart and Gooch island, at East point, and between Patos island and Sucia islands. The current has a moderate velocity between Sucia islands and Orcas island.

Heavy tide rips occur on Middle bank and to the northward of it, around Discovery island, between Henry island and Turn point on the ebb, and around Turn point. Specially heavy tide rips occur between East point and Patos island and for 2 miles northward in Georgia strait.

At its southern entrance, the flood commences at 11 h. 30 m. The currents continue to run from 1½ to 2½ hours (latter for large tides) after high and low water by the shore. To find the approximate time of slack water at East point, take the Port Townsend time of high tide for high water slack, and add 1½ hours to the time of low tide for low water slack.

Directions—Haro and Georgia straits.—After rounding Discovery island at a distance of 1 mile, steer North (N. 24° W. mag.), or for Kellett bluff (Henry island), a remarkable, steep, rocky headland. This course made good for 8 miles leads clear of all dangers to a point midway between Kelp Reefs beacon and San Juan island. In working up, when standing westward, tack when the NW. extreme of Low island comes in line with the SE. point of Sidney island, which will give Zero rock a good berth; but when approaching Kelp reefs, Bare island must be kept well open eastward of the same point to avoid them. The San Juan shore is steep close-to.

Coming from Puget sound, pass midway between Wilson point and Admiralty head, and steer N. 50° W. (N. 73° W. mag.) for 8 miles, when Partridge Bank buoy, a black can, should bear NE., distant 1¾ miles. Then bring Wilson point astern and steer N. 36° W. (N. 59° W. mag.). This course made good for 23 miles leads to the point mentioned in the last paragraph, halfway between Kelp Reefs beacon and San Juan island. Hein Bank buoy will be left 2 miles on the port, and the shore of San Juan island ½ mile on the starboard, hand.

From a point midway between Kelp Reefs beacon and San Juan island, a N. 14° W. (N. 38° W. mag.) course will pass ¾ mile from Kellett bluff and about the same distance from Turn point of Stuart island. There are no dangers off this point; but whirling eddies and tide rips, caused by the meeting of the streams from so many channels, are generally met with, particularly on the ebb. A vessel may reach this point with a fresh southerly wind, but will almost invariably lose it here, until Middle channel, eastward of San Juan, is opened out.

Rounding Turn point at a distance of ¾ mile, steer N. 64° E. (N. 40° E. mag.) for 10½ miles. Alden point should be directly ahead on this course, which leads to the northern entrance of Haro strait, between East point (Saturna island) and Alden point (Patos island). These two points are marked by lights already described. This passage is 2½ miles wide, but subject to heavy tide rips and eddies; vessels should, when possible, pass through the center of it.

Steering N. 64° E. (N. 40° E. mag.), bring Oscar knob (Orcas island), well open to the eastward of Waldron island, to bear S. 3° E. (S. 27° E. mag.); then steer for the white cliffs on the eastern end of point Roberts, keeping the ship on the above range. This course, N. 3° W. (N. 27° W. mag.), should lead through in mid-channel. Do not bear away westward until the southern end of Sucia island is shut in with the southern end of Patos island.

At night, after passing between Saturna and Patos islands, maintain a northerly course for about 2 or 3 miles, and then if the light on Georgina point, at the entrance to Active pass, is not visible, steer N. 45° W. (N. 69° W. mag.) until it is sighted; remembering that this light becomes obscured when it bears to the northward of N. 73° W. (S. 83° W. mag.), and that while it is in view all dangers on the southern shores of the strait will be avoided; be careful to keep it in sight and by no means stand to the southward of the above line of bearing.

The flood from Rosario strait, which is met with as soon as the passage between Orcas and Sucia islands is open, is apt to set a vessel toward the east point of Saturna, off which and Tumbo island there is much uneven and broken ground, with heavy tide races. This point should be given a berth of 1½ miles.

The extreme end of Tumbo reef, marked by a black buoy, lies 1$\frac{3}{10}$ miles N. 26° E. (N. 2° E. mag.) from Saturna Island lighthouse. Great care should be taken to avoid this reef.

The ebb sets to the eastward even before the strait of Georgia is well open, and a vessel finding herself not likely to weather Patos should pass between it and Sucia, where there is a good clear passage more than 1 mile in breadth; if this passage is taken, the Patos island shore should be favored. Beware of Plumper and Clements reefs; the former lies 1¼ miles S. 56° W. (S. 32° W. mag.) of the NW. bluff of Sucia island and has 10 feet on it; the latter the same distance N. 62° E. (N. 38° E. mag.) of the same bluff and has 9 feet over it.

When in Georgia strait, from NW. by W. to NW. is a fair mid-channel course. If bound for Fraser river, and having cleared Tumbo reef, a N. 36° W. (N. 60° W. mag.) course will lead to the Sand heads, a distance of nearly 20 miles. Entering the strait and having passed northward of Patos island, if the ebb current is running, a sailing vessel is very liable, unless with a commanding breeze, to be set eastward and down Rosario channel.

The northern shore of Sucia island should by all means be avoided. If Alden bank can be fetched it offers a good anchorage while waiting for a tide. Alden point, the western point of Patos island, in one with Monarch head, a bold, cliffy bluff, bearing S. 74° W. (S. 50° W. mag.), leads over the northern edge of this bank in from 6 to 9 fathoms. When mount Constitution is in line with the center of Matia island, bearing S. 3° E. (S. 27° E. mag.), 9 fathoms may be expected, and vessels should not anchor in much less than this depth, as in the shoaler parts rocky ground is found. The least water on the bank is 2¼ fathoms.

Against a head wind and ebb tide work up on the northern shore; there are no known dangers, little current when eastward of a line between Roberts point and Alden bank, and anchorage may always be had within 1 mile of the shore if necessary. Birch and Semiahmoo bays offer good anchorage and are easy of access. In working up Georgia strait the southern shore should never be approached within 2 miles until westward of Active pass, and then not within 1 mile; the currents sweep strongly along this shore, and there are several outlying reefs between East point and Active pass.

As soon as the strait is entered from the southward, Roberts point will show its eastern part as a bold, white-faced cliff, its western part as a low shingle point. Its summit is covered with trees, and it would at first sight be taken for an island in consequence of the land on its northern side falling rapidly in elevation. After passing northward of this point its low-water extreme, or the trees just within it, must not be brought to bear southward of S. 62° E. (S. 86° E. mag.) to avoid Roberts bank, which extends 5 miles off the Fraser river entrance, is steep-to, and shoals suddenly from 25 to 2 fathoms.

THE WESTERN CHANNELS AND ISLANDS OF HARO STRAIT.

The western channels of Haro strait may be used with advantage by steamers and coasters bound from the southern ports of Vancouver island to the strait of Georgia, or to the districts of Saanich, Cowitchin, Nanaimo, and the numerous intermediate harbors. Their advantage over Haro strait consists in the strength of tide being less, besides sheltered anchorage being obtainable in almost all parts; while in the latter strait the depth of water is so great that it is impossible to anchor, and sailing vessels may frequently be set back into Juan de Fuca strait, thus entailing great delay as well as risk. On the other hand, the western channels are not entirely free from danger; yet, with the assistance of the chart, and a good lookout from aloft for kelp, a precaution which should never be neglected, they may be navigated during daylight with ease and safety.

For vessels passing from the southward, and intending to take the western channels, the dangers to be avoided after passing Discovery and Chatham islands are: Johnstone reef, lying nearly 1 mile from the shore, midway between Cadboro point and Gordon head; Zero rock, which lies in the fairway; and the shoals which extend off Darcy, Sidney, and James islands.

Sidney channel lies between Darcy and Sidney islands on the east and James island and spit on the west; it is ⅜ mile wide in its narrowest part and is from 15 to 25 fathoms deep. The channel is a good navigable one.

James island is 2 miles long SSE. and NNW., ¼ mile broad, thickly wooded, and about 260 feet high to the tops of the trees.

The SE. end of the island terminates in a remarkable, white, earth cliff, extending across nearly the whole width of the island, and rising to a height of 200 feet in the center. A little to the eastward of the highest part of the cliff is a rather conspicuous notch in the otherwise smooth upper line of the cliff. The eastern shore of the island is low and sandy. A shallow bank extends for upward of 400 yards from the northern shore of the island. The NW. point of the island is low.

James spit.—An extensive sand spit extends SSE. for 1¾ miles, from the southern end of James island, with depths less than 3 fathoms. The eastern edge of the spit is steep-to. Just inside the edge are patches with only 2 to 3 feet over them at low water springs. The spit also extends to the southward and westward of the island for about 600 yards.

Shoals.—A shoal patch with 4½ fathoms lies ¾ mile S. 67° W. (S. 43° W. mag.) from the southern point of Darcy island.

Another shoal patch with 4¼ fathoms lies 800 yards N. 42° W. (N. 66° W. mag.) from the NW. point of Darcy island.

Darcy shoals are two rocky heads lying SE. and NW. of one another in mid-channel, and 1,200 and 1,600 yards, respectively, westward of the NW. point of Darcy island. The western head has 2½ fathoms, and the eastern one 3½ fathoms, over it at low water.

Buoy.—A black can buoy is moored, in 6 fathoms, to the eastward of, and close to, the eastern head. Cadboro point in line with Zero Rock beacon, S. 14° E. (S. 38° E. mag.), leads about 400 yards westward of these shoals.

Whale rock, a small rock 4 feet high, lies 700 yards from the western shore of Sidney island, and ½ mile NW. by W. ½ W. from the southern point of the island.

Shoal.—A shoal nearly 400 yards in extent, and with 6 feet least water over it, lies 600 yards westward from the elbow of the sand spit extending from the western point of Sidney island.

Buoys.—A red can buoy is moored westward of the western edge of the shoal in 7 fathoms. From the buoy Sidney Spit beacon bears N. 4° E. (N. 20° W. mag.), distant 1¾ miles.

A black can buoy marks the eastern edge of the shoal. There is no channel between these buoys.

Whale rock open of Darcy island clears the shoal.

Cordova channel, between James and Vancouver islands, is a good passage with from 8 to 18 fathoms of water, and the tidal streams are not strong. It is not, however, to be preferred to Sidney channel, neither is any distance saved by taking it.

A shoal bank extends to the southwestward, for a distance of 600 yards, from the southwestern point of James island, narrowing the navigable channel between it and the shoal water on the western side of the channel to 600 yards.

From a point a little northward of Cowichan head, the shore is low and swampy for a distance of 2 miles, terminating in Cordova spit. Shoal water extends from 200 to 400 yards off this flat.

Cordova spit, on the mainland of Vancouver island and about 2 miles north of Cowichan head, is a sandy arm extending out from shore in a northerly direction for ½ mile. It is from 2 to 4 feet above high water, and has some clumps of stunted bushes on it.

Cordova bay is formed by Cordova spit and affords good protection from all winds; the holding ground is good and the tidal currents are not felt.

On the southern shore of the bay is an Indian reservation with a small village, the church being the only conspicuous building in it.

Sidney.—The village of Sidney, situated on the eastern side of the Saanich peninsula, on the western shore of Sidney channel, is about 2 miles west of Sidney Spit beacon. The land in the vicinity is cleared and cultivated, but a conspicuous clump of fir trees remains close to the village. There is a good wharf and pier with 20 feet at low water springs, and the village is connected with Victoria by railroad; there is both telephonic and telegraphic communication.

Trains are now run from Victoria in connection with daily steamer service to Port Guichon on the mainland, laden freight cars being transported by this means.

Shoals.—From a point 200 yards south of the pier, a shoal with 6 feet least water over it extends to the southward for a distance of 400 yards. Its outer edge is marked by 2 red spar buoys.

Another shoal with from 1½ to 3 fathoms over it lies 700 yards northward of the pier and about 600 yards offshore. From the eastern extreme of the shoal the end of the pier bears S. 44° W. (S. 20° W. mag.), distant 500 yards.

A pinnacle rock with 9 feet of water over it lies 400 yards N. 80° E. (N. 56° E. mag.) from the end of the pier.

Buoy.—A pyramidal-shaped buoy, painted red, is moored 50 yards eastward of this rock.

Ships are recommended to pass to the southward of this rock in approaching and leaving Sidney.

Anchorage.—There is good anchorage ½ mile S. by E. from the pier, 600 to 800 yards from shore, in from 8 to 10 fathoms, sand and mud.

Directions.—From a point 1 mile east of Discovery Island lighthouse, steer for Zero Rock beacon and pass 600 to 800 yards west of it, and between it and Little Zero rock. Then gradually bring Zero Rock beacon in line with Cadboro point and the western fall of the trees on Chatham island, S. 15° E. (S. 39° E. mag.), being careful to avoid the shoal ½ mile north of Zero rock.

Proceed on this line until abreast of the southern point of James island, when steer in mid-channel between James and Sidney islands until past the shoal off the western spit of the latter island, the western edge of which is marked by a red can buoy; then alter course to pass as close west of Sidney Spit beacon as desired.

Or, after rounding Discovery island as before, steer N. 23° W. (N. 47° W. mag.), passing about 1 mile NE. of Zero Rock beacon. This course made good for 9¾ miles should lead 600 yards west of the western point of Darcy island and between Darcy shoals and the 4½-fathom shoal NW. of Darcy island. When past Darcy shoals, steer in mid-channel as before.

If using Baynes channel, steer so as to pass 500 yards from Cadboro point. When abreast of the point, alter course to N. 9° W. (N. 33° W. mag.), heading for left tangent of Darcy island. When Morse island shuts in with the SE. point of Darcy island, bearing N. 63° E. (N. 39° E. mag.) steer N. 23° W. (N. 47° W. mag.), giving Darcy island a berth of 600 yards, and proceed as before.

Passing out of Baynes channel, be careful to avoid Johnstone reef; it is marked by a black can buoy.

Shell island and Little group.—On the western side of the route from Sidney channel to Moresby passage, and from 1 mile to 1½ miles NW. of Sidney Spit beacon, is a group of small islets and rocks, the largest of which, Shell island, is wooded and 120 feet in height to the top of the trees.

Little group is the name given to the four most easterly of these islets; they are nearly bare and from 30 to 35 feet high. The two eastern are the largest; they are joined together at low water, covered with grass, and have one or two stunted trees on their summits. The northern of these two islets is called Dock island.

There is very foul ground, with several sunken rocks, between Little group and Coal island.

The eastern extreme of Little group is about 1,400 yards WNW. ½ W. from the NW. end of Jones island, and there is a good and deep passage between, though it is narrowed to less than 400 yards by Sunk rock and the foul ground extending NW. from the end of Jones island.

Light.—From the eastern end of Dock island an intermittent white light, automatically eclipsed at short intervals, is shown at an elevation of 40 feet above high water, visible 10 miles. It is shown from a beacon consisting of a cylindrical steel tank, standing on a steel framework, and surmounted by a pyramidal steel frame supporting the lantern, the whole painted red. The height of the structure from the ground to the top of the lantern is 24 feet. The light is unwatched.

Coal island lies close off the northeastern point of Saanich peninsula, its eastern point is a little over 1 mile WNW. from Bird islet, and there is deep water between. The island is irregular in shape, nearly 1 mile in extent, wooded, and 315 feet high to the tops of the trees.

The northern coast of the island is cliffy and steep-to.

There are several islets and rocks between it and Saanich peninsula and many sunken dangers; a narrow and tortuous channel between these is sometimes used by small local steamers.

Vessels should not approach the eastern side of Coal island inside a line joining its eastern point with the eastern point of Dock island.

Knapp and Pym islands are two, small, wooded islands situated about 800 yards NW. of Coal island; they are 163 and 124 feet high, respectively.

Rocks.—A reef, with 3 to 4 fathoms over it, extends from ¼ to ½ mile east and south of these islands, narrowing the passage between them and Coal island to less than 400 yards; this reef is marked by kelp in summer and autumn.

A rock with less than 6 feet over it lies 250 yards off the eastern shore of Pym island.

A rock which dries at low water lies nearly 200 yards off the western point of Knapp island.

A rock with 2¾ fathoms over it lies 600 yards S. 73° E. (N. 83° E. mag.) from the southern extreme of Pym island.

A rocky head, with a least depth of 3 fathoms, lies N. 28° E. (N. 4° E. mag.), distant 450 yards, from the western extreme of Coal island.

Another rocky head with a least depth of 3 fathoms lies 450 yards N. 7° W. (N. 31° W. mag.) from the western extreme of Coal island.

Piers island, which lies ½ mile NE. of the northern end of Saanich peninsula and ⅓ mile to the westward of Knapp island, is a little over ½ mile in extent, and wooded.

Colburne passage, between Piers, Knapp, and Pym islands, and Saanich peninsula, has two reefs in it which contract the passage to a width of 200 yards; these reefs are marked by two platform buoys; the channel between them carries 8 fathoms. The northern buoy is red, the southern black. This passage is used by local vessels.

The leading mark through the channel, should the buoys not be in position, is the southern tangent of cape Keppel bearing N. 70° W. (S. 86° W. mag.) and just barely open of the high coast line southward of Cowitchin harbor (Cowitchin head).

The southern shore of Pym island should not be approached nearer than 600 yards.

Shute passage, which lies between Coal, Pym, Knapp, and Piers islands on the south, and Celia reefs, off the southern side of Portland island, on the north, is an open and deep passage, ½ mile wide, leading into Satellite channel.

The only prominent danger is Celia reefs on the northern side of the channel.

Portland island, on the western side of Moresby passage and more than 1 mile distant from Moresby island, is a little over 1 mile in extent, wooded, and rising to a height of 287 feet to the tops of the trees.

Black island, 147 feet high, lies about 400 yards SW. of Portland island.

Hood island, 133 feet high, lies close to the southern end of Portland island. NE. of it are the Tortoise islands.

Celia reefs, a cluster of sunken rocks, the western rock having only 9 feet over it, lie nearly ½ mile off the southern side of Portland island.

Buoy.—The western extreme of Celia reefs is marked by a red conical buoy, moored in 8 fathoms.

Sisters islets.—These are three small rocky islets extending in a line for nearly 400 yards off the eastern point of Portland island. They are from 20 to 25 feet high, and there are a few stunted trees on their summits. They are joined together at low water and show plainly from the north or south.

Sunk rock, with 3½ fathoms over it, lies 1,050 yards WNW. ½ W. from the NW. point of Jones island and nearly in mid-channel between it and the Little group.

Between Sunk rock and Jones island is another rock with 4 fathoms over it; it lies 400 yards WNW. ½ W. from the northern point of Jones island.

Bird islet, a small bare rock, 15 feet high, lies 800 yards W. by N. from the northern extreme of Domville island. Foul ground, with several rocky heads that dry at low water, extends for more than 400 yards NNW. of the islet. It is usually marked by kelp.

Tree islet, a grass-covered ridge of rock 23 feet high, with a single small tree on it, lies ½ mile northeastward of Bird islet, and nearly ½ mile NW. of Hill island; there are several rocks between it and the latter.

Yellow islet, about 100 yards in extent and 14 feet high, its top covered with grass, lies in the middle of the western end of Prevost passage, where that passage joins Moresby passage. It is about 1 mile N. by E. from Bird islet and 1,200 yards from the northern end of Tree islet. There are two rocks, awash at low water, off its western side.

Rock.—WSW. of Yellow islet, 800 yards distant, is a rock with 3½ fathoms over it; it is marked by kelp in summer and autumn.

Directions—Sidney channel to Moresby passage.—Passing Sidney Spit beacon at a distance of 600 yards, steer to pass from 200 to 300 yards east of Little group, which course carries midway between Dock island and Sunk rock. If the weather is clear, Beaver point (the eastern point of Admiral island), just showing between the eastern point of Portland island and the Sisters islets, N. 5° W. (N. 29° W. mag.), will clear Sunk rock to the westward. After passing Little group steer toward Canoe rock beacon, but so as to pass not less than 1,200 yards westward of Yellow islet, to clear the 3½-fathom rock SW. of the islet, and head up for Moresby passage.

If intending to navigate Shute passage, from Little group steer so as to pass from 400 to 600 yards off the eastern point of Coal island, and proceed in mid-channel.

If bound through Colburne passage, steer along the northern shore of Coal island, giving it a berth of from 200 to 300 yards, taking care to avoid the reefs that extend to the southward from Knapp and Pym islands, and then in mid-channel between the buoys.

Moresby passage, between Moresby and Portland islands, is only 800 yards wide from Canoe rock to Turnbull reef. For deep-draft vessels it is further contracted to 600 yards by a 5-fathom shoal which lies 500 yards NW. by W. from Canoe rock.

Canoe rock lies 870 yards N. 62° W. (N. 86° W. mag.) from Reef point, the NW. extreme of Moresby island.

Beacon.—A stone beacon, surmounted by a staff and ball, 26 feet high, painted black, stands on Canoe rock.

Turnbull reef extends from the northern point of Portland island in a semicircle round to the Sisters islets, and 800 yards from the shore of the island. The depths range from 2 to 3 fathoms, but there are numerous heads with less than 6 feet over them. The reef is marked by kelp in summer and autumn, but the kelp is frequently run under by the tide.

A patch, with 3 fathoms least water, off the outer edge of the reef, and nearest the fairway of Moresby passage, lies nearly 1,000 yards WSW. from Canoe Rock beacon.

A patch with 2 fathoms of water over it, not quite so near the fairway, lies about 350 yards NNW. of the 3-fathom patch.

Directions.—From a position ½ mile east of the Sisters, steer so as to pass 400 to 600 yards west of Canoe rock. If of heavy draft, bring the single tree on the summit of Tree islet in one with the southwestern high-water tangent of Yellow island, bearing S. 14° E. (S. 38° E. mag.); this will lead through in 15 to 20 fathoms of water. Beaver point in one with the easternmost of the Channel islands will lead clear of the shoals. When Canoe Rock beacon is open south of Reef point all dangers are passed and the vessel is in the deep waters of Swanson channel.

Swanson channel leads from Haro strait northwestward between Admiral island on the west and Pender island on the east;

passing eastward of Prevost island it enters Active pass, between Galiano and Mayne islands, which leads into Georgia strait; northward of Active pass it connects with Trincomali channel.

Admiral island, locally known as Salt Spring island, separating Stuart from Trincomali and Swanson channels, is of considerable extent, being nearly 15 miles in length NW. and SE., and varying in breadth from 2 miles at its northern end to 6 at its southern. It has two good ports, Fulford harbor on its southeastern and Ganges harbor on its eastern side. The southern portion of the island is a peninsula formed by the indentations of Fulford harbor and Burgoyne bay (a valley separating the heads of these ports), composed of a lofty ridge of mountains over 2,000 feet in height, rising abruptly from all sides; the summit, mount Bruce, being 2,329 feet high.

Immediately northward of the valley, and over Burgoyne bay, on its western side, mount Baynes rises to an elevation of 1,953 feet, and is very remarkable, its southern face being a perpendicular precipice visible a long distance from the southward or eastward. The Otter range, of somewhat less elevation, rises northward of mount Baynes, from whence the island slopes away in a wedge shape, its northern termination, Southey point, being a sharp extreme. The island is for the most part thickly wooded, but there is a considerable extent of partially cleared land both in the valley at the head of Fulford harbor and at the northern end of the island, which has become peopled by settlers under the name of Salt Spring district, from the fact of several salt springs having been discovered.

Ganges harbor is a safe and commodious port for vessels of any description or size, and has two entrances. Its southern entrance, from Swanson channel, lies between Admiral and Prevost islands; the northern entrance is by Captain passage. When entering from the southward, Channel islets may be passed on either side, but by far the widest passage is to the northward of them; they are two small wooded islets, 1½ miles within Beaver point, and 400 yards from the shore of Admiral island.

The fair channel into the harbor, between Channel and Acland islands, is nearly ½ mile wide, the depth being 30 fathoms; having passed these islands the harbor is nearly 1½ miles wide, and the general depth for 2 miles is from 20 to 13 fathoms.

There are few dangers in the harbor, and they are easily avoided. A rocky patch with 1 fathom on it lies 550 yards NW. by W. ¾ W. from the western point of the westernmost Acland island, and the same distance offshore. There is another 1-fathom patch which is more in the track of vessels; it lies nearly 2 miles NW. ¼ W. from the southernmost Channel islet.

Buoy.—A black can buoy is moored close northward of this last rocky patch.

Horda rock.—A rock, consisting of a narrow ridge with a least depth of 2 fathoms at its western end, is situated in the northern part of Ganges harbor and southern approach to Captain passage, with Nose point bearing North, distant 1,300 yards, and the eastern extreme of Chain islands W. by N.

The eastern extremity of this danger is a pinnacle, with a depth of 3 fathoms, situated 150 yards SE. by E. from the 2-fathom rock.

Buoy.—A platform buoy with slatwork pyramid, surmounted by a latticework drum, the whole painted black, is moored in 5 fathoms, close eastward of the 3-fathom head.

Rocks.—A pinnacle rock with 2 fathoms over it at low water lies 700 yards S. 89° W. (S. 65° W. mag.) from point Liddell.

A rock with 3 fathoms over it at low water lies 1,400 yards N. 83° W. (S. 73° W. mag.) from point Liddell.

These rocks are near the Acland islands.

A rock with 2½ fathoms over it at low water lies in the approach to Glenthorne creek; it is 2,060 yards S. 49° E. (S. 73° E. mag.) from the southern point of the entrance to Long harbor.

The shoals lying 700 yards S. 64° W. (S. 40° W. mag.) and S. 82° W. (S. 58° W. mag.) from the southern point of entrance to Long harbor have 3 fathoms and 4 feet, respectively, over them at low water, the latter being well marked by kelp.

A shoal with 3 fathoms over it at low water lies to the southward and eastward of One Fathom patch. It is 2,800 yards S. 8° E. (S. 32° E. mag.) from the southern point of entrance to Long harbor.

A shoal with 1¾ fathoms over it at low water lies to the southward of the eastern end of the Chain islands. It is 2,600 yards S. 75° W. (S. 51° W. mag.) from the southern point of entrance to Long harbor.

A shoal with 5 fathoms over it at low water lies in Captain passage, 700 yards S. 79° E. (N. 77° E. mag.) from the southern point of entrance to Long harbor. This shoal is marked by tide rips with a stream of any strength.

Liddell point, the SE. extreme of Prevost island, and the northern entrance point of the harbor, has a reef, which is covered at half flood, extending 400 yards southeastward from it.

The Acland islands, two in number, lie to the northwestward of Liddell point along the shore of Prevost island, between which and them there is no ship channel.

The Chain islands are a group of 6 or 7 low narrow islets connected by reefs, extending from the head of the harbor in a SE. direction for 1½ miles. To the southward of these islands the ground is clear, but to the northward of them are scattered reefs, and vessels are not recommended to anchor on that side above the outermost island.

Anchorage.—A vessel may anchor as soon as a depth of 10 or 12 fathoms is found; a good berth is in 11 fathoms of water with Peile point and the two entrance points of Long harbor nearly in line, bearing N. 56° E. (N. 32° E. mag.), and the easternmost Chain island N. 45° W. (N. 69° W. mag.). If desirable, anchorage may be had in 6 fathoms, mud, midway between the Chain islands and the south shore, the easternmost island bearing East, or in a still snugger berth 1 mile above, off the sandy spit on Admiral island, in 4 or 5 fathoms. This latter berth is recommended for vessels of moderate size intending to make any stay.

Captain passage also leads into Ganges harbor, westward of Prevost island. With one exception, it is a clear deep passage, ½ mile wide, with depths of 30 to 40 fathoms. This exception is the 5-fathom shoal described under the head of Ganges harbor. It lies 700 yards S. 79° E. (N. 77° E. mag.) from the southern point of entrance to Long harbor. Vessels from the northward intending to enter the harbor should always use this passage.

Horda rock, already described, lies in the middle of the southern end of the passage, where it opens into Ganges harbor; it is marked by a black can buoy.

The only other known dangers, which are well inside Ganges harbor, and which are almost equally in the track of vessels working up by the southern passage, are the two shoals 700 yards S. 64° W. (S. 40° W. mag.) and S. 82° W. (S. 58° W. mag.), respectively, from the southern entrance point of Long harbor, with 3 fathoms and 4 feet over them, respectively. Entering by Captain passage, Peile point should not be shut in by the entrance points of Long harbor until the opening between Prevost and Acland islands is shut in, when these shoals will be well cleared. When working up the southern channel, do not stand so far eastward, when in the neighborhood of these patches, as to open the passage between these islands; this will also keep a vessel clear of Horda rock.

Long harbor may be considered as part of Ganges harbor. It is a long, narrow creek, its general breadth being 400 to 600 yards. Entering between two, sloping, rocky points, similar to each other, on the western side of Captain passage, it runs parallel to Ganges harbor for 2½ miles. About ½ mile inside the entrance is a high, bare islet, which must be passed on its southern side; and about 1 mile inside is another and somewhat similar island, which may be passed on either side. Below these islets the depth is from 11 to 17 fathoms; above them 4 to 6 fathoms.

Prevost island, lying in the center of Swanson channel, is moderately high, thickly wooded, and of an irregular shape. It is 3 miles long, in a NW. and SE. direction, 1¼ miles in breadth, and on its southern and western sides it is indented by several bays and creeks; its northern side is an almost straight, cliffy shore.

Light.—Portlock Point light is a fixed white light, with a red sector showing over Enterprise reef, elevated 72 feet above high water, and visible from a distance of 10 miles in clear weather.

The lighthouse, 48 feet high, is a square, pyramidal, wooden tower, with room attached, painted white, lantern red.

Fog signal.—From a small wooden tower 300 yards SSE. of the lighthouse a bell is struck once every 15 seconds.

Ellen bay, on the southeast side of Prevost island, between Liddell and Red Islet points, is ¾ mile deep by ⅓ in breadth, narrowing to 400 yards ⅓ mile from its head, and affords fair anchorage with all but southeasterly winds in 10 fathoms, mud bottom. The head of this bay is a grassy, swampy flat, only 200 yards wide, separating the bay from the creeks on the western shore. There are two bays northward of Ellen bay, but too small to afford any shelter.

The bay northeastward of Ellen bay, though small, is clear of dangers, and has a depth of 9 fathoms; it is known as Diver bay.

Annette and Glenthorne creeks, on the western, or Ganges harbor, side, are curious, narrow indentations extending into the island for 1 mile in a SE. by E. direction, and only separated from each other by a narrow stony ridge. In Glenthorne, the western one, there are 3 fathoms of water, the other has 1½ fathoms; they are snug places for small craft, or to repair a vessel.

James bay, on the NW. side of the island, and on the eastern side of Captain passage, affords fair, but very confined, anchorage in 10 fathoms for a vessel of moderate size, sheltered from southerly winds; but she must get well in, as there are 18 to 20 fathoms of water in the outer part of the bay.

Hawkins island, a small, rocky islet, with a few bushes on it, lies close off a remarkable white shell beach on the NE. side of Prevost island.

Charles rocks.—From 400 to 700 yards NW. by W. ½ W. from the NW. point of Hawkins island are the Charles rocks, three smooth-topped rocks, not marked by kelp, and uncovering toward low water.

Active pass.—From Discovery island, at the southern end of Haro strait, to the Sand heads of Fraser river, by Active Pass, between Mayne and Galiano islands, is just 40 miles, and the line is almost a straight one. By adopting this route, not only the most dangerous and inconvenient part of Haro strait is avoided, viz, its northern entrance, between the eastern point of Saturna island and Patos island (where the currents are strong and apt to set a vessel down Rosario strait or over on the eastern shore), but a distance of nearly 10 miles is saved.

From Portlock point, the eastern point of Prevost island, the western entrance of Active pass bears N. ½ E., distant 1¾ miles, and is 600 yards wide.

Helen point, the southern entrance point of the pass, is the termination of a thickly wooded slope which gradually rises to mount Parke, the highest point of the island.

Collinson point, the northern entrance point, is the southern extreme of Galiano island, and is steep-to. It lies at the foot of a steep summit, 1,090 feet high—a rugged, rocky point, easily recognized. The entrance does not become very apparent until it is approached within 1 mile.

Active pass takes an easterly direction for 1½ miles and then turns NNE. for the same distance, fairly into Georgia strait. The average width of the channel is about ⅓ mile, and its general depth about 20 fathoms.

A small flat ledge, which uncovers 6 feet at low water, extends about 170 feet from the southern shore just inside Helen point, and 260 yards N. 44° E. (N. 20° E. mag.) from the same point is a rocky head with 3 fathoms least water over it, and which is not marked by kelp. A quarter of a mile within the entrance, and very close to the northern shore, lies a long low rock which uncovers 8 feet at low water springs, and 400 yards NNE. from it and 200 yards offshore is a rocky patch with several heads with only 5 feet over them at low water. They are well marked by kelp.

Georgina shoals lie northeastward of Georgina point, the northern point of Mayne island, and extend east and west a distance of ½ mile. The western shoal, which has as little as 5 feet over it, and on which the sea occasionally breaks, lies 500 yards NE. ½ N. from Georgina point. The channel between the shore reef and the shoals has a depth of 12 fathoms.

A patch of 5 fathoms least water lies near mid-channel in the eastern entrance of the pass, 1,100 yards N. 64° W. (N. 88° W. mag.) from Georgina point. Except at slack water it is marked by tide rips. Kelp does not grow in this position.

Buoy.—The eastern edge of the reef off Gossip island, northern side of the eastern entrance to the pass, is marked by a black can buoy, moored in 9 fathoms.

Light.—From a square, white, wooden tower, 42 feet high, situated on Georgina point, is exhibited, at an elevation of 55 feet above high water, a fixed white light, visible 12 miles between the bearings N. 73° W. (S. 83° W. mag.) and N. 62° E. (N. 38° E. mag.), through South.

Fog signal.—A steam horn gives a blast of 10 seconds' duration every minute.

Otter bay.—If overtaken by night, or waiting for tide, Otter bay, on the west side of Pender island, is a good stopping place; it is

1 mile north of Mouatt point; fair anchorage is to be had in the center of the bay, in 8 fathoms.

Village bay, which is close south of Helen point, is also a good stopping place. There is good anchorage in the middle of the bay in 10 fathoms. The shore from Helen point is bold and clear of danger. The passage between the southern point of the bay and Enterprise reef is also safe.

Miners bay, on the south side of Active pass, where it takes the sharp turn to the northward, affords anchorage, if necessary; but a vessel must go close in to get 12 fathoms, and then is barely out of the whirl of the tide. With the flood current there is a strong set into the bay close south of Laura point.

At the head of the bay is a small settlement called Mayne. There is a wharf with a depth of 8 feet alongside. Supplies and water can be obtained in small quantities.

Communication may be had by steamer with Victoria, Sidney, New Westminster, and Nanaimo.

An Anglican church, which has been erected in a position from which Laura point bears N. 45° W. (N. 69° W. mag.), distant 800 yards, is a prominent object.

Sturdies bay, on the western side of the northern entrance to the pass, has foul ground in its center and is filled with kelp; there is a wharf on its NW. side with 15 feet at its outer end at low water.

Kelp grows strongly on all shoal rocky bottoms during the summer and autumn months.

Directions.—After entering Swanson channel, between Admiral and Pender islands, steer to pass ¼ to ½ mile to the eastward of Portlock point on Prevost island, and keep Pelorus point (eastern extreme of Moresby island) open of Mouatt point (the western extreme of Pender island) bearing S. 19° E. (S. 43° E. mag.), which will lead westward of Enterprise reef, and when Helen point bears N. 34° E. (N. 10° E. mag.) the reef will be cleared, and the entrance of the pass may be steered for. There is a passage inside Enterprise reef which may be taken when both kelp patches can be seen. If coming out of Navy channel, between Pender and Mayne islands, a vessel should keep over for Prevost island until Pelorus point is open of Mouatt point; these two points in line, or just touching, lead very close to Enterprise reef. On the western side of Swanson channel, the reef which lies 400 yards eastward from Liddell point must be avoided, and Red and Bright islands, off the points to the northward of it, should be given a berth of 200 yards.

Entering Active pass from the southward, make good a mid-channel course until well past Helen point; then favor the southern shore in order to be ready for the sharp turn to the northward.

When entering or passing out of the northern entrance of the pass, the point of Gossip island, on the west, and also Georgina point, on the east, should be given a good berth.

Mary Anne point (SE. extreme of Galiano island, opposite Miners bay), bearing S. 33° W. (S. 9° W. mag.), is a good line for leaving or entering the pass.

Caution.—The great strength of the tides, together with the absence of steady winds, renders Active pass unfit for sailing vessels. The best advice that can be given a stranger is to pass through in mid-channel; thorough local knowledge is necessary to take advantage of slacker currents and eddies. Any vessel having a speed of 10 knots can always get through in mid-channel against a strong tide, but, if possible, pass through at slack water. With the flood stream there is a strong set into Miners bay. Round Laura point the flood runs with great strength. During the flood there is a strong eddy off Georgina point.

Tides and tidal currents.—It is high water, full and change, at 5 h. 14 m. Springs rise 12 feet, neaps 8 feet. It is slack water in Active pass 1 h. 26 m. before high, and 1 h. 13 m. before low, water in the pass, or very nearly at high water at Port Townsend, and about half an hour after low water at that place, for which see "Tide Tables for the Pacific Coast, United States Coast Survey." The flood stream sets from south to north, or from Swanson channel into Georgia strait, and the ebb in the opposite direction. Strong contrary undercurrents and cross currents have been experienced.

At ordinary springs, in the southern entrance, the velocity of both streams is 6 to 7 knots; at other tides 3 to 5 knots. In the northern entrance, the rate at springs is 4 to 5 knots. There is sometimes a heavy tide rip, caused by the 5-fathom patch, and also by the meeting of the flood current through the pass with that in the strait.

For detailed remarks as to tides hereabout, see remarks on tides at Telegraph harbor.

Trincomali channel commences at Active pass, from the southern entrance of which its general direction is NW. for 24 miles, when it enters Dodd narrows.

This channel must be classed as a channel for steamers or coasters; it can only be used with advantage by vessels bound to the eastern ports of Vancouver island below Nanaimo, or by such as choose to enter Nanaimo itself by Dodd narrows.

The eastern side of the channel is formed by the long narrow islands Galiano and Valdes, and the western by Admiral, Kuper, and Thetis islands, and part of the eastern shore of Vancouver island. Montague harbor, on the western side of Galiano island, is a good stopping place, also Clam bay, on the eastern side of Thetis island.

Trincomali channel contracts when abreast Narrow island to less than 1 mile in width, but the shores are steep-to on both sides. On the shore of Galiano island, 1 mile ENE. from the SE. point of Narrow island, is Retreat cove, offering shelter for boats or anchorage for coasters; an island lies in the center of it.

Porlier and Gabriola passes, leading from Trincomali channel into Georgia strait, are both intricate and dangerous, and the currents are so strong and so variable in their set that they can not be said to be applicable to the general purposes of navigation, and few navigators would be justified in using them except in cases of emergency. A telegraph wire spans Gabriola pass, which admits of no masted vessel larger than a boat passing underneath it.

Benmohr rock.—This rock has a depth of 15 feet on it, and is situated with Peile point bearing S. 32° W. (S. 8° W. mag.), distant 1,300 yards. It is nearly in mid-channel and forms part of a ridge running parallel to the channel for about ¾ mile, having depths on it of 2½ to 13 fathoms.

A 5-fathom spot lies in the vicinity of Benmohr rock; it bears N. 29° E. (N. 5° E. mag.) from Peile point, distant 1,140 yards.

A 4-fathom spot lies N. 71° E. (N. 47° E. mag.), distant 1$\frac{1}{10}$ miles, from Peile point.

Buoy.—A platform buoy, surmounted by a pyramid of latticework and painted in red and black horizontal bands, is moored on the shoalest part of Benmohr rock.

Montague harbor is between the SW. side of Galiano island and Parker island, and its entrance, between Phillimore point and Julia island, is 1¾ miles NW. from the western entrance of Active pass. The entrance is only about 200 yards wide, but has deep water. This harbor, though small, is a snug and secure anchorage, with a general depth of 6 fathoms, good holding ground; several Indian lodges are built on the shores of the bay. There is a narrow passage northwestward from this harbor into Trincomali channel, the least depth in which is 3 fathoms.

Several small islands extend NW. from Parker island, namely, Sphinx, Charles, Wise, and Twin islands; the latter are two rather remarkable rocky islets about 30 feet high; between this group and Galiano island is a passage ½ mile wide with good anchorage in 10 fathoms.

A rock which uncovers at low water springs is reported to lie 400 yards N. 51° W. (N. 75° W. mag.) from Twin islands.

A small rocky head with a depth of 18 feet over it and steep-to all around lies 820 yards N. 56° W. (N. 80° W. mag.) from the western Twin island.

A depth of 12 feet exists 220 yards from the shore of Galiano island with the western Twin island bearing S. 18° E. (S. 42° E. mag.), distant 1,840 yards.

Atkins reef lies on the western side of Trincomali channel, ¼ mile from the shore of Admiral island, and in the track of vessels working up or down. It is a narrow ridge 1,300 yards long, in the direction of the channel, within the 5-fathom curve. A rocky head, 200 yards in extent, on the western part of the reef, dries 5 feet at low water, its neighborhood being marked by kelp, which, however, is rarely seen when there is any ripple on the water. This head lies 1¼ miles S. 17° W. (S. 7° E. mag.) from Twin islands, and 1 mile S. 55° E. (S. 79° E. mag.) from the SE. end of the peninsula which forms Walker hook. The SE. end of the reef terminates in a rock, awash at low water springs, situated 860 yards S. 51° E. (S. 75° E. mag.) from the above rocky head. There is a passage of 14 fathoms between the reef and Admiral island, and it may be passed at a distance of 200 yards on the outside.

Beacon.—A stone beacon surmounted by a staff and ball, the whole painted white, and showing 9 feet above high water, stands on the shoalest part of the reef.

Walker hook is formed by a peninsula or tongue of land projecting from Admiral island, 4 miles northwestward of Captain passage. On its SE. side is fair anchorage for small vessels in 6 fathoms, but a shoal patch with less than 6 feet of water on it, marked by kelp, ⅛ mile in extent, lies 400 yards eastward of the southeastern point of the peninsula; small vessels may pass between the shoal and the point in 5 fathoms, or between it and Atkins reef, which is better, and anchor in 6 fathoms, 400 yards southward of the neck of the peninsula. There is also anchorage in 10 fathoms northward of the peninsula, but vessels must not go within the northern point of the tongue of land forming the hook, as it dries a long way out.

Governor rock, a dangerous rocky patch lying almost in the center of Trincomali channel, has 4 feet on it, is about 100 yards in extent, and, though kelp grows on it, is very difficult to make out until it is quite close aboard. It lies 1⅝ miles N. 76° W. (S. 80° W. mag.) from Twin islands, and S. 45° W. (S. 21° W. mag.) from Quadra hill. This hill can not be mistaken; it rises from the center of Galiano island 746 feet, and a remarkable, white, basaltic cliff will be seen on the coast immediately southwestward of it.

Buoy.—A black platform buoy, with wooden pyramid surmounted by a ball, is moored on the eastern side of this rock.

Walker rock lies 1⅝ miles N. 49° W. (N. 73° W. mag.) from Twin islands, and 1¼ miles S. 56° W. (S. 32° W. mag.) from Quadra hill; it dries 5 feet at low water.

Beacon light.—A fixed white light, elevated 15 feet above high water, and visible 8 miles, is shown from a small wooden tower erected on the stone beacon marking the rock. Both beacon and tower are painted white.

A narrow rocky ridge, terminating in a pinnacle with 2 fathoms over it at extreme low water, extends for a distance of 450 yards to the northwestward of the beacon.

The depth over this ridge is from 1 to 7 fathoms, with deep water on either side of it.

The beacon should not be approached, when bearing S. 55° E. (S. 79° E. mag.), nearer than 600 yards.

Victoria rock.—This rock is of small extent and has a least depth of 15 feet over it at low water. It is situated with Walker Rock beacon bearing N. 68° E. (N. 44° E. mag.), distant $1\frac{3}{10}$ miles, and the southeastern extreme of Narrow island N. 29° W. (N. 53° W. mag.). The rock has deep water all round it.

Buoy.—A can buoy, painted in red and black horizontal stripes, is moored in 6 fathoms on its northeastern side.

Rock.—A small, isolated, rocky head with 18 feet over it is situated 600 yards eastward of Victoria rock, with Walker Rock beacon bearing N. 71° E. (N. 47° E. mag.), distant 1,860 yards.

Wharf.—A wharf, 450 feet in length, with a depth of 9 feet at its outer end, extends from the shore at Fernwood, situated 3 miles southeastward of Southey point.

Directions.—Mariners are advised to use the passage between Governor and Walker rocks, or the passage between the latter and Galiano island. Two rocky heads (Victoria rock and one other) exist to the northwestward of Governor rock, and these contract the western passage.

The range for a mid-channel course through the middle passage, after passing Benmohr rock, is the northeastern point of Thetis island kept just halfway between the east side of Narrow island and the west side of Hall island; these marks are very clear and well defined, and are generally seen from a long distance.

Vessels using the eastern channel, between Walker rock and Galiano island, should not haul to the northward till the SE. point of Walker hook bears to the southward of S. 35° W. (S. 11° W. mag.), in order to avoid the foul ground off the Twin islands. Mount Sutil, on the southern end of Galiano island, in line with Charles island, bearing S. 53° E. (S. 77° E. mag.), leads well inside Walker rock.

In either case, when Quadra hill bears N. 70° E. (N. 46° E. mag.) the vessel will be clear of the rocks and may steer a mid-channel course between Galiano island and the islands forming the western side of the channel.

If proceeding into Houston passage, the southeastern end of Narrow island must be given a berth of at least $\frac{1}{2}$ mile, to clear the reef extending off it.

Houston passage, between Kuper island and the northwestern end of Admiral island, leads from Trincomali into Stuart channel.

The entrance is between the northeastern shore of Admiral island and Narrow and Secretary islands. The southwestern side of Narrow island is foul, several small islets and rocks extending from 200 to 600 yards off it. A rock with only 6 feet on it lies in the entrance with the extreme southeastern end of Narrow island bearing East (N. 66° E. mag.), distant ½ mile. From the wharf at Fernwood to a point 1½ miles SE. of Southey point the shore of Admiral island is bordered by a bank with 2 to 3 fathoms on it which extends ¼ to ⅓ mile offshore, narrowing the navigable channel to ⅓ mile. The general depth of water in mid-channel is 20 fathoms, and anchorage within a moderate distance of the shore of Admiral island may be obtained in 10 or 12 fathoms of water, off Saltspring settlement, 2¼ miles SE. by E. of Southey point.

Southey point, the sharp northern extreme of Admiral island, should be given a berth of 200 yards. At ½ mile SW. of it is Grappler reef (marked by a black buoy); around Southey point Houston passage turns abruptly to the southward, and Stuart channel may be entered either by the main passage between North reef and Admiral island, or, if necessary, between North reef and Tent island. Give North reef a good berth, as a shoal ridge of rocks extends ⅓ mile off its NW. and SE. ends.

Porlier pass, between Galiano and Valdes islands, is the first outlet into the strait of Georgia northward of Active pass; the pass, though short (not exceeding 1 mile from its southern entrance until fairly in the strait), is narrow, and is rendered still more so by sunken rocks; the tides are very strong, running from 4 to 9 knots, and overfalls and whirling eddies are always to be met in the northern entrance.

Caution.—In consequence of the numerous dangers existing in Porlier pass, mariners are advised to avoid that passage.

Romulus rock, with 5 feet over it at low water, lies 800 yards S. 40° W. (S. 16° W. mag.) from Race Point lighthouse, and nearly 400 yards from the shore of Galiano island. This rock is the southeastern extremity of a rocky shoal 250 yards long in a N. by W. and S. by E. direction and about 200 yards wide. The general depths between Romulus and Black rocks are from 3 to 5 fathoms. A rocky head with 4 feet of water over it at low water exists at a distance of 800 yards S. 50° W. (S. 26° W. mag.) from Race Point lighthouse. A shoal lies southeastward of Romulus rock; it has 4 fathoms over it and is 980 yards S. 24° W. (South mag.) from Race Point lighthouse.

Beacons.—There are on Galiano island, northeastward and southeastward of Romulus rock, two pairs of white beacons for marking that rock.

Black rock, which dries 11 feet at low water, is on the northwestern side of the entrance to the pass; it lies 266 yards S. 45° E. (S. 69° E. mag.) from Native point, the southern point of Valdes island.

Virago rock is almost in the center of the pass, but rather on the western side; it only uncovers at low tides, and lies 400 yards S. 84° E. (N. 72° E. mag.) of Native point, and a little over 400 yards from Race point, the (middle) projecting point on the east side of the pass.

A rock with 10 feet on it lies 132 yards S. 5° E. (S. 29° E. mag.) from Virago rock.

Buoy.—A large spar buoy, painted black, is moored in 4½ fathoms close to the 10-foot rock.

A rock with 8 feet on it at extreme low water is situated S. 52° W. (S. 28° W. mag.) from this buoy and westward of a line drawn from the buoy to Romulus rock.

All that portion of the pass lying between the above-mentioned line and the shore of Valdes island is foul and must be avoided.

Range lights.—Two fixed white lights, which, in line and bearing S. 19° W. (S. 5° E. mag.), lead through the northern entrance to the pass, have been established on the northwestern end of Galiano island.

The front light, 21 feet above high water and visible 9 miles, is shown from a white, square tower with red lantern, 24 feet high, 50 feet inside Race point.

The rear light, 32 feet above high water and visible 11 miles, is shown from a similar tower, 31 feet high, close to the beacon on Virago point, and 400 yards S. 19° W. (S. 5° E. mag.) from the front light.

Rock.—A sunken rock lies SW. from Virago point, distant 150 yards.

Shoals.—A small rocky head, with 5 fathoms over it, lies 300 yards N. 2° E. (N. 22° W. mag.) from Race Point lighthouse.

A rock, which dries 4 feet at low water, lies about 100 yards southwestward of Race Point lighthouse.

A large rocky patch, 250 yards long north and south and about 125 yards broad, having several heads with 3 to 6 feet over them at low water, lies on the Valdes island side of the pass. The southernmost head of this shoal lies 460 yards N. 40° W. (N. 64° W. mag.) from Race Point lighthouse.

Eastward of a line drawn N. 39° E. (N. 15° E. mag.), and northward of Galiano island, lies foul ground. At the northern extremity of this foul ground is a rock, with 4 fathoms over it, 600 yards N. 13° W. (N. 37° W. mag.) from Tongue point. Kelp grows on this area.

Foul ground extends for a distance of 600 yards to the eastward, and 1 mile to the southward, of Canoe islet.

Buoy.—A can buoy, surmounted by a latticework drum and painted in black and white vertical stripes, has been established as a fairway buoy off the northern entrance to the pass. It is moored in 17 fathoms, with the south point of Canoe islet bearing N. 47° W. (N. 71° W. mag.), distant 650 yards.

Directions.—Vessels entering Porlier pass from the southward should proceed as follows:

Give South point a berth of at least 200 yards until Race Point lighthouse is just open of the high-water line of Virago point, and then steer for the lighthouse on that bearing. When the two white beacons on the point northward of South point come in line, bring South point astern bearing S. 1° 30′ E. (S. 25° 30′ E. mag.). This course should leave Virago point about 200 yards to the eastward. The buoy marking the rock southward of Virago rock should be nearly ahead. When Virago point is abeam, alter course to starboard and steer so as to pass 200 yards from Race point. When Race Point lighthouse bears S. 45° E. (S. 69° E. mag.) steer N. 45° E. (N. 21° E. mag.) until on the leading range; then keep on the range, passing about 200 yards eastward of the fairway buoy.

Great care must be taken that the current does not set the vessel out of the track laid down, especially when near the rock SW. of Virago point, the rock southward of Virago rock, or Race point.

From Georgia strait the pass is always easily recognized by the gap formed by its sloping, wooded, entrance points terminating in two low extremes, from most points of view overlapping each other. The lighthouses should be seen from a distance of several miles.

Tides and tidal streams.—The flood stream sets from Trincomali channel northward into Georgia strait, and the ebb in the contrary direction. The ebb stream commences from 1 to 1½ hours before high water by the shore, and runs for 1 hour after low water, or from 7 to 8 hours.

It is high water, full and change, at about 4 h. 0 m., but it is not very regular. At springs the streams run 4 to 9 knots with dangerous whirls and eddies.

Narrow, Secretary, and Indian islands form a chain running NW. and SE., that separates Trincomali channel and Houston passage. A reef extends 400 yards from the southeastern end of Narrow island; this point should be given a wide berth. The passages between the islands should not be used.

Hall and Reid islands and Rose islets form a similar chain; they lie near the middle of Trincomali channel, Reid island being broad off the entrance to Porlier pass.

A patch of foul ground extends to the eastward of the small islet to the southward of Reid island. A rock which dries 4 feet is situated at its eastern extreme, and bears S. 69° E. (N. 87° E. mag.) from the islet above mentioned, distant 240 yards.

Rose islets, five small rocky islets, the northernmost about 20 feet high with a few bushes on it, lie nearly ¾ mile northwestward from the NW. end of Reid island, but with no ship passage between. When bound to Clam bay from the northward, pass westward of these islets.

Kuper and Thetis islands, divided only by a boat channel at high water, lie NW. of Admiral island, from which the former is separated by Houston passage. Each of these islands is about 3 miles long NW. and SE. and about 1½ miles wide.

Clam bay, on the eastern side of Thetis and Kuper islands, opposite Porlier pass, is formed by the shores of these two islands approaching each other. The continuation of the bay separates these two islands at high water, when there is a boat channel into Telegraph harbor on their western side.

White spit, a remarkable point of broken clam shells which can be seen from a long distance, forms the southern entrance point of the bay; immediately southward of it is a considerable native lodge; a reef, having less than 1 fathom of water on it in some places, extends over 600 yards in a S. 45° E. (S. 69° E. mag.) direction from White spit. Leech island, off the northern point of the bay, is a small wooded islet.

A spot with 18 feet over it lies 320 yards N. 39° E. (N. 15° E. mag.) from the northern extreme of White spit. Vessels entering Clam bay should pass on the southern side of this danger, giving the northeastern shore of White spit a berth of 100 yards.

Center reef, with 6 feet of water on it and marked by kelp, should not be approached nearer than 250 yards; it lies almost in the center of the entrance, nearly 600 yards N. 28° W. (N. 52° W. mag.) of White spit.

Rocket shoal, on which there is a depth of only 6 feet, lies nearly in the center of the bay, with White spit extreme in line with the highest part of Indian island, bearing S. 65° E. (S. 89° E. mag.); it is 100 yards in extent, with depths of from 2 to 4 fathoms around it.

An isolated, rocky head, with a depth of 5 feet over it, lies nearly midway between Center reef and Rocket shoal, and 840 yards N. 44° W. (N. 68° W. mag.) from the northern extreme of White spit.

Directions.—The best passage into Clam bay from the southward is eastward of Narrow, Secretary, and Indian islands, and between them and Hall island; after passing Indian island steer for

White spit on a S. 69° W. (S. 45° W. mag.) bearing, and give the northeastern extreme a berth of 100 yards.

Vessels may pass between Indian and Kuper islands, keeping the Indian island shore aboard, but on account of the many dangers this passage is not recommended.

Anchorage may be had in Clam bay in 6 fathoms between Rocket shoal and the shore.

North cove is a small bay in the northern end of Thetis island, lying between Pilkey point on the east and Reef point on the west. The head of the bay is shoal, but anchorage may be had just inside a line joining the entrance points, in 7 fathoms of water. A rock with 4 feet over it at low water lies in the western side of North cove; it bears N. 77° E. (N. 53° E. mag.), distant 620 yards, from Reef point.

Ragged island, covered with trees and about 20 feet high, lies ⅓ mile NW. from Pilkey point, the northern end of Thetis island, with a passage of 10 fathoms of water between them. The rocky ledge extending from Pilkey point dries 150 yards from that point.

A rocky ledge extends northwestward from Reef point for a distance of nearly ½ mile.

White rock, about 30 yards long and 15 feet above high water, lies 1 mile northward of Reef point, the northwestern extreme of Thetis island; a bank having from 2 to 5 fathoms of water on it extends 400 yards northwestward from the rock. This rock has a whitish appearance and is readily distinguished from a vessel's deck at a distance of 2 or 3 miles. It should be given a berth of at least 500 yards in passing.

A reef with several rocky heads, on one of which there is only 3 feet of water, extends to the SE. for a distance of ½ mile from White rock toward Ragged island, rendering the passage between the two unsafe.

Buoy.—A red can buoy, surmounted by a cage, is moored in 6 fathoms N. 40° W. (N. 64° W. mag.), 500 yards distant, from White rock. There is no passage between this buoy and the rock.

Yellow Cliff anchorage.—There is fair anchorage on the western side of Valdes island, 2 miles above Porlier pass, immediately off a yellow cliff; 8 fathoms, sandy bottom, will be found with the cliff bearing N. 10° W. (N. 34° W. mag.), distant ½ mile.

It will also be known by Shingle point, a low projection with a native village on its extreme, ⅓ mile NW. by W. from the yellow cliff.

Danger reef, lying 1 mile N. by W. ½ W. from White rock, and 1½ miles NE. by E. from Yellow point, on the Vancouver shore, covers a space of ½ mile, almost in the center of the channel. A small portion of it is generally awash at high water.

Light.—A fixed white light, visible 9 miles, is shown from a square, white, wooden tower on the easternmost rock of Danger reef, at a height of 24 feet above high water. This rock is awash at high water; the western rock dries only at low water. The light is unwatched.

Foul ground extends 600 yards to the SE. from the light.

The De Courcy group of islands lies in the northern end of Trincomali channel. They form a chain 4½ miles in a NW. and SE. direction. Mak island, the northwestern of the De Courcy group, is about 1,400 yards long, about 150 feet high, and densely wooded; its SW. side is precipitous. Between the two northern and the two southern islands of the group is Ruxton passage, with a depth of 16 fathoms and ½ mile wide.

The two southern islands are separated by Whale Boat passage.

Tree island, which is wooded, lies S. 72° W. (S. 48° W. mag.) from the southern point of the southernmost island of the De Courcy group.

The passage between these two islands is nearly 400 yards wide. That between Tree island and Danger reef is 1,200 yards wide.

Mudge island lies northwestward of, and is nearly joined to, the northwestern island of the De Courcy group. It is separated from Gabriola island by False narrows and from Vancouver island by Dodd narrows. The island is densely wooded and about 350 feet high.

Boat harbor is a small indentation in the shore of Vancouver island about 4 miles north of Yellow point. Vessels waiting for slack water in Dodd narrows may anchor off the harbor in 10 to 12 fathoms.

Round island lies 1½ miles southwestward from Dodd narrows and 700 yards from the shore of Vancouver island. It is 40 feet high and wooded. A shoal, usually marked by kelp, extends northward from it for a distance of 200 yards, where there is a rock with only 6 feet on it; there is a small rocky islet 100 yards south of the island.

Abreast Round island and as far to the southward as Boat harbor the Vancouver island shore is foul and should be given a berth of more than ¼ mile. Vessels should pass to the eastward of Round island.

Shoal.—A shoal with 4 fathoms on it lies southeastward of Round island. The shoalest head lies 540 yards S. 76° E. (N. 80° E. mag.) from the islet south of Round island, and 1,800 yards S. 18° E. (S. 42° E. mag.) from the islet south of Mudge island.

Dodd narrows is at the northwestern end of Trincomali channel and connects that channel with Northumberland channel. To steam vessels of moderate length, that answer the helm quickly, this narrow pass offers no danger at or near slack water, or when going with the stream; but with the current against them, vessels should wait for slack water. The velocity of the tidal stream at its greatest rush is over 8 knots, the least depth of water 6 fathoms, and the narrowest part of the channel is 80 yards wide; but lying 20 yards off the shore of Mudge island, in the narrowest part, is a small rocky head, drying 6 feet at low water, which narrows the available channel.

Under ordinary circumstances it is considered that the passage of the narrows should not be attempted by any vessel whose length exceeds 200 feet. A vessel of greater dimensions should employ a competent pilot.

If bound through Dodd narrows from the southward, and having to wait for slack water, the most suitable place is about ¾ mile to the northward of Round island; the best anchorage is off Boat harbor, 1½ miles south of Round island. A 12-foot rock lies 140 yards off the southern shore of Mudge island. From this rock the northern tangent of Round island bears S. 31° E. (S. 55° E. mag.), distant 1,740 yards, and the small islet off the southern side of Mudge island S. 76° E. (N. 80° E. mag.), distant 800 yards. This rock is surrounded by deep water and is not marked by kelp.

Percy anchorage, on the northern side of the narrows, between Gabriola and Mudge islands, is a convenient place to wait for slack water, for those bound south.

Tides and tidal currents.—In Dodd narrows the flood sets to the northward, the ebb to the southward. It is high water, full and change, at 5 h. 0 m. Springs rise 14 feet, neaps 9 feet. Slack water occurs 1 h. and 32 m. before high water in the narrows, or 16 minutes before the higher low water at Port Townsend; and 38 minutes after low water in the narrows, or 16 minutes after the lower low water at Port Townsend. Variations in these times must be expected and allowed for.

There is, strictly speaking, no slack; the tidal streams, having become very weak, change from one direction to the opposite without any cessation of motion in the narrows as a whole. When the current is running strongly in the narrows, a well-defined curve of tide rips is always to be seen outside the narrowest part of the narrows, lying on the side toward which the stream is running; the gradual disappearance of this is the sign of a slackening stream, and the passage should not be attempted until it has entirely disappeared.

The maximum velocity of the stream may be taken as 8 to 10 knots at ordinary springs.

Directions.—When proceeding for Dodd narrows from abreast Porlier pass, the most direct route is eastward of Danger reef, between it and Tree island; this passage is ¾ mile wide with depths of from 25 to 30 fathoms. Give Danger reef a berth of at least ½ mile. Then steer a mid-channel course, leaving Round island to the westward.

When through the narrows the strength of the tide lessens, and the ship will be in Northumberland channel, a fine wide passage leading to the anchorage at Nanaimo (5 miles NW. of the narrows), Departure bay, and into Georgia strait.

Dodd narrows is not so easy to pass through from the north as from the south, as in the former case the slight bend that has to be made must be made immediately on entering the narrow part.

Vessels should pass through at slack water; no vessel without thorough local knowledge should attempt the passage against the current.

Pylades channel.—That portion of Trincomali channel lying between the De Courcy group and Valdes island is known as Pylades channel, and leads up to Gabriola pass and False narrows. It has an average width of 1 mile, and at its head, near the entrance to False narrows, there is good anchorage in 9 fathoms.

Rocks.—A rock awash at low water lies 220 yards off the eastern extreme of the southeasternmost island of the De Courcy group. The ground between this rock and the island is foul.

A rock, which dries at lowest tides, exists in the center of a kelp patch about 700 yards N. 72° 30′ E. (N. 48° 30′ E. mag.) from the opening between the two northern De Courcy islands.

Gabriola pass, between the south end of Gabriola island and the north end of Valdes island, is not recommended, unless for coasting vessels knowing the locality, or small steamers, if necessary; for it is a narrow and intricate channel, something of the same character as Dodd narrows, except that it is a much longer reach. Its direction is easterly for a little over 1 mile, its narrowest part not over 250 yards in breadth, and the shoalest water 6 fathoms.

An island nearly 1 mile long in a north and south direction lies over ½ mile eastward of the narrow eastern entrance of the pass; shoal water extends ¼ mile S. 45° E. (S. 69° E. mag.) from the southeastern end of the island; the channel from the pass into the strait of Georgia is between the southwestern side of this island and a chain of low wooded islets on the west side, off which a chain of covering rocks marked by kelp extends nearly 400 yards to the eastward.

There is also a passage in a northerly direction from the pass into the strait, between the east extreme of Gabriola and the islands off it, but it is not recommended.

Telegraph.—Overhead telegraph wires are stretched across Gabriola pass; vessels having masts over 30 feet high should not attempt to pass under the wires.

The shore end of the telegraph cable laid from point Grey (connecting Vancouver island with the mainland) is landed at Valdes island, 2½ miles SE. of Gabriola pass. Wires are thence carried to Nanaimo and Victoria.

Tides.—It is high water, full and change, in Gabriola pass at 4 h. 49 m. Springs rise 12 feet, neaps 8 feet. The tidal streams run from 5 to 6 knots.

False narrows.—When standing for Dodd narrows from the northward, be careful not to mistake for it False narrows, on the northeastern side of Mudge island; False narrows appears much wider than the real pass, but is only 200 yards wide, with but 6 feet at low water; it is fit only for boats or very small steamers, and should not be attempted by anyone not acquainted with the locality, and then only at an hour before or after low water, when most of the reefs are visible. During summer and autumn kelp grows profusely in the narrows and is an additional source of danger. Three red, wooden, spar buoys mark the channel, but they can not be depended upon.

The maximum strength of the tidal streams at springs is 3 to 4 knots.

Northumberland channel runs from Dodd and False narrows in a northwesterly direction for 3½ miles, its northern end lying between Sharp point and the western shore of Gabriola island. The water is deep, and the shore of Gabriola island consists of bold, steep cliffs, about 600 feet high. A rock which uncovers lies 100 yards off the extreme of Sharp point.

Percy anchorage is that portion of the channel lying between Mudge and Gabriola islands and westward of False narrows. Good anchorage with mud bottom may be had, in 6 to 9 fathoms, while waiting for slack water.

Tidal current.—The tidal current in Northumberland strait is unusual, as there is a constant set to the eastward during both flood and ebb. This appears to be due to the more rapid progress of the tidal wave in the strait of Georgia than in the inner channels south of Dodd narrows. The maximum velocity of this constant easterly stream is from 1 to 2 knots at springs.

Satellite channel, Sansum narrows, and Stuart channel furnish a second route from Swanson and Sidney channels to Portier pass and Dodd narrows. This, however, is not so short or so direct as the one previously described, by way of Trincomali channel.

Satellite channel, beginning between Beaver point (Admiral island) and Parkin point (Moresby island), runs in a SW. direction for 7 miles between Admiral island on the NW. and Moresby, Portland, and Piers islands and the northern end of Saanich peninsula on the SE.; it then turns NW. for 4 miles between Admiral and

Vancouver islands. It leads to Saanich inlet, Cowitchin harbor, and by Sansum narrows to Stuart channel. It is a good, deep passage with few hidden dangers; among these are Cecil rock, Shute reef, Patey rock, and Kelp reef. The general width of the channel is 1 mile, and the strength of the tide from 1 to 3 knots.

Chesil bank, with a depth of 5½ fathoms, lies about ½ mile to the northward of Portland island.

Chads island is a small island, 150 feet high, lying close to the northern shore of Portland island. There is a rock close to its western side.

Cecil rock, with 6 feet on it, lies ⅓ mile S. 42° E. (S. 64° E. mag.) from the southern point of Russell island at the entrance of Fulford harbor, and must be avoided when working up Satellite channel.

Fulford harbor penetrates the SE. side of Admiral island in a NW. direction for 2½ miles. At its entrance is Russell island, between which and Isabella point, the western point of the harbor, is the best passage in. Immediately over the northeastern side of the harbor is Reginald hill, a stony elevation between 700 and 800 feet high.

The western entrance is ⅔ mile wide with a depth of 20 fathoms until nearly up to North rock; here the harbor narrows and has a general breadth almost to its head of a little less than ½ mile; the depths decrease to 13 and 10 fathoms, and at 700 yards from the head to 5 fathoms, when the water shoals rapidly on the edge of the bank which extends about 600 yards from the shore at the head of the harbor.

North rock is a small rocky islet lying close off the north shore of the harbor. A rock which covers at a quarter flood lies 400 yards WNW. from it and more than 300 yards from the shore, so that strangers entering should keep to the westward of mid-channel until past it.

The eastern passage into the harbor between Russell island and Eleanor point, though in places not more than ¼ mile wide, is a safe channel of from 14 to 18 fathoms of water.

Louisa rock, with 1 fathom on it, is the only known danger; it lies 400 yards from the northern, or Admiral island, shore, with the west end of Russell island bearing S. 15° E. (S. 39° E. mag.), distant 800 yards, and North rock S. 88° W. (S. 64° W. mag), at the same distance; with a leading wind the Russell island shore should be kept rather aboard.

Anchorage.—There is good anchorage in 10 fathoms in the center of the harbor with Reginald hill bearing East (N. 66° E. mag.); at the head of the harbor is a considerable fresh-water stream, from which shoal water extends for 600 yards.

Village island is a small island lying 800 yards SW. from Isabella point.

Shute reef is a ledge less than 100 yards in extent, with two rocks, one of which is covered at 8 feet flood, its vicinity being marked by kelp. It lies ⅜ mile N. 89° W. (S. 67° W. mag.) from Harry point, the northern point of Piers island, and nearly 600 yards N. 39° E. (N. 15° E. mag.) from Arbutus, a small islet with two or three of the red-stemmed arbutus growing on it, and lying ½ mile westward from Piers island.

Beacon.—A stone beacon, painted black, and surmounted by a staff and ball, showing 18 feet above high water, stands on the highest part of Shute reef. The beacon should be given a berth of 200 yards.

Patey rock, just beyond the elbow in Satellite channel, is a single rock, covered at 6 feet flood, with kelp around it, and is in the way of vessels working into Saanich inlet or Cowitchin harbor. It lies nearly 2 miles N. 39° W. (N. 63° W. mag.) of Coal point (a remarkable knob point), the southern extreme of Deep cove, and ¾ mile NE. from Hatch point, the western point of Saanich inlet.

Harry point, open northward of Arbutus islet, bearing N. 79° E. (N. 55° E. mag.), leads 600 yards south of Patey rock.

The high, round summit of Moresby island, well open northward of Arbutus islet, bearing East (N. 66° E. mag.), leads 700 yards northward of the rock.

Boatswain bank, on the western side of the channel, extending ¾ mile from the Vancouver shore between Cherry and Hatch points, affords good anchorage in from 4 to 9 fathoms, sandy bottom. The outer edge of the bank is steep-to; the 10-fathom curve (defining the bank) runs ¾ mile E. by S. from Cherry point and then South for more than ¾ mile. From 300 to 600 yards inside the 10-fathom curve the water shoals rapidly from 5 to 3 fathoms, the latter depth being 800 yards from the shore.

Saanich inlet is a deep indentation running in a southerly direction for 14 miles, carrying deep water to its head, which terminates in a narrow creek within 4 miles of Esquimalt harbor. About 1½ miles inside, the inlet is crossed by a submarine cable.

The inlet forms the southeastern portion of Vancouver island into a peninsula about 20 miles in a north and south direction, and varying in breadth from 8 miles at its southern part to 3 miles at its northern. The coast line is fringed with pine forests, but in the center it is clear prairie or oak land, and much of it under cultivation; seams of coal have also been found.

Off the eastern or peninsula side of the inlet there are some good anchorages, the center being for the most part deep. Immediately southward of James point, the northwestern point of the peninsula, is Deep cove, but there is no convenient anchorage.

Norris rock, awash at half tide, lies S. 57° W. (S. 33° W. mag.) 400 yards from James point, with 6 fathoms between it and the point. Vessels rounding this point should give it a berth of ½ mile.

Union bay, 2 miles southward of James point, affords good anchorage in 8 or 9 fathoms ½ mile from the beach. A shoal bank extends 400 to 600 yards from the shore around the bay. There is a stream of fresh water in the southeastern corner of the bay.

Mill Creek bay, a fair anchorage in 7 to 9 fathoms, and the only one on the western side of Saanich inlet, is directly opposite Union bay; a bank of sand and rock, which has only from 1 to 3 fathoms of water on it and extends 400 yards from the western shore, lines the bay.

A rock with only 6 to 9 feet on it lies almost in the center of the bay, a short distance outside the 3-fathom curve, and 800 yards S. 49° W. (S. 25° W. mag.) from Ford point.

Tanner rock lies 250 yards to the southward of Camp point and about 150 yards from the western shore of the inlet.

Tozier rock.—A rock drying 2 feet at low water, now known as Tozier rock, lies 500 yards N. 48° E. (N. 24° E. mag.) from the extreme of Village point, a point on the western shore nearly 2¾ miles northward of Turn point on the western side of the entrance to Squally reach. Village point is marked by the buildings of an Indian village. Another rock is situated 300 yards N. 81° W. (S. 75° W. mag.) from Tozier rock.

Cole bay, 1½ miles southward from Union bay, and immediately under mount Newton, is small, but capable of affording shelter to a few vessels of moderate size.

White rocks.—Off the northern point of Cole bay are two small bare islets known as White rocks; the outer one is 3 feet high.

Shoal.—A narrow, rocky shoal, with three heads on it of 1¾, 3¼, and 3½ fathoms, running nearly north and south for 800 yards, lies off Cole bay. The northern head, which has 1¾ fathoms on it, lies 400 yards S. 70° W. (S. 46° W. mag.) from the outer White rock. The southernmost head, with 3½ fathoms on it, lies 750 yards S. 32° W. (S. 8° W. mag.) from the outer White rock.

Approaching Cole bay from the northward, vessels should give White rocks a berth of not less than ½ mile, and should not turn into the bay for the anchorage until Village point bears West (S. 66° W. mag.) Village point, on the western shore of Saanich inlet, is marked by the buildings of an Indian village, and is easily recognized. Anchor in the center of the bay in 8 fathoms, with White rocks bearing West (S. 66° W. mag.).

Both Union and Cole bays are open to SW. winds, but gales rarely blow from that quarter, nor from the proximity of the opposite shore, distant scarcely 3 miles, could much sea get up.

Tod creek is 2 miles southward of Cole bay. Senanus island, a small wooded islet, 150 feet high, lies off its entrance; foul ground extends nearly 200 yards off the northwestern side of the island; on the other sides the water is deep. A small islet, and a rock lying 200 yards north of it, lies in the entrance to the southeastern part of the creek. A short distance inside, it narrows rapidly and winds to the southward and southeastward for ¾ mile, with a breadth of less than 200 yards, carrying 6 fathoms nearly to its head.

There is anchorage in the outer part of the creek in 15 fathoms.

Squally reach—Finlayson arm.—From Willis point, the western point of Tod creek, the next 3 miles of the inlet, known as Squally reach, trends to the SW., the width of the arm here being ¾ mile, with no bottom at 100 fathoms. Finlayson arm, its continuation, trends to the southward for 3 miles, and terminates Saanich inlet.

Beacon rock, which covers at ¾ flood, lies 200 yards S. 62° W. (S. 38° W. mag.) from Elbow point, Finlayson arm. A small islet, named Dinner, with deep water on either side, lies near the head of this arm; good anchorage in 9 fathoms may be had 300 yards SSW. of the islet. Six hundred yards south of the islet the arm terminates in a flat, which dries at low water. Immediately over the head of the inlet, on the eastern side, Leading peak rises to an elevation of 1,346 feet.

Cowitchin harbor is 4 miles westward from cape Keppel, the southern extreme of Admiral island; Separation point (the western point of entrance to Sansum narrows), its northern entrance point, is somewhat remarkable, being the termination of a high, stony ridge. Cowitchin harbor extends westward from this point for 2 miles, and the general depth in it is 30 fathoms, which shoals suddenly as the flat is approached; this dries off for more than ½ mile from the head of the harbor.

But for the large tract of good land contained in Cowitchin valley, the port would scarcely be deserving of notice, and it is more of a bay than a harbor. In its NW. end is a considerable river, the Quamitchan, which flows through the fertile valley, and is navigable for small boats or canoes for several miles. There is a settlement and post-office here, off which is a long pier (on the south side of the harbor). Coming from the southeastward the entrance is easily distinguished by the pier and lumber yard, just inside the point on the southern side.

The only anchorage is about 400 yards northwestward of the pier; a vessel must approach the shore cautiously and anchor, as soon as 12 fathoms is obtained, little more than 200 yards from the shore.

Snug creek is a convenient anchorage for small craft or coasters, and a moderate-sized vessel can obtain anchorage and shelter in it. It extends from Cowitchin harbor, on the western side of the ridge that terminates in Separation point, in a northerly direction for nearly 1 mile, and is ¼ mile wide.

Nearly in the middle of the entrance is a rock which uncovers at low water; it is about 20 feet in extent, has 1½ fathoms around it, and is marked by kelp. The western point of entrance can be passed close-to as it is steep-to, and has 10 fathoms within 100 yards of it. When ½ mile, or less, inside the point, anchor in the center of the creek in 6 fathoms.

Buoy.—A red spar buoy is moored on the west side of the rock.

Sansum narrows takes a general northerly direction between Vancouver and Admiral islands for a distance of 6 miles, when it leads into Stuart channel; the average breadth of the narrows is about ½ mile, but at its narrowest part, abreast Bold bluff, it is contracted to ⅓ mile. The high land on both sides renders the wind generally very unsteady; from this cause, as well as from the somewhat confined nature of the channel and the depth of water, which prevents anchoring, the narrows can not be recommended except for steamers or coasting vessels. There are but few dangers to be avoided, and the strength of the tides has seldom been found to exceed 3 knots, generally much less.

Kelp reef, with 9 feet of water on it, lies on the Admiral island side of the entrance to Sansum narrows; it is 400 yards S. 45° W. (S. 21° W. mag.) from a small islet close to the coast and 1,800 yards S. 79° E. (N. 77° E. mag.) from Separation point.

Buoy.—A red and black can buoy painted in horizontal stripes is moored in 15 feet of water on the reef.

Another rocky patch extends nearly 200 yards offshore from the eastern side of the narrows, and is 1,800 yards N. 25° E. (N. 1° E. mag.) from Separation point.

Burial islet, a small island once used as an Indian burying place, lies on the eastern side of the narrows, 1½ miles above Separation point; pass outside it as close as convenient to the kelp.

Bold bluff, a smooth headland of bare rock, is steep-to; the channel here is scarcely ⅓ mile across. Rocky ground marked by kelp extends 200 yards off Kelp point on the western side, almost opposite to Bold bluff; northward from these points the narrows increases in breadth to nearly 1 mile.

A sunken rock lies 800 yards NW. of Bold bluff and 150 yards from shore; it is marked by kelp.

Burgoyne bay, the entrance to which is ½ mile northeastward from Bold bluff, is a narrow and rather deep indentation terminating in a sandy head; there is no bottom in the bay under 30 fathoms until within 400 yards of its head, when the water shoals suddenly from 10 to 4 fathoms. Anchorage may be had if necessary.

Maple bay.—From Grave point the narrows takes a northwesterly direction 1 mile to Maple bay. Bowlder, the southern entrance point is remarkable from a large bowlder standing at its low-water extreme. Although an inviting-looking bay, the water is too deep for comfortable anchorage, being generally 40 fathoms, and 16 fathoms within 200 yards of a smooth, sandy beach at its western end.

Birdseye cove, which takes a southerly direction for nearly 1 mile from Bowlder point, affords fair anchorage at its entrance in about the center of the cove, in 13 fathoms, mud bottom, with the bowlder bearing N. 62° E. (N. 38° E. mag.). The cove at this part is not more than $\frac{1}{3}$ mile across; 400 yards southward from this anchorage, shoal water, with 2 to 3 fathoms, extends 150 yards from each side of the cove, which is here only 500 yards wide; coasters may go up mid-channel into 4 or 5 fathoms near the head.

Tides.—The rise at springs in Maple bay is 12 feet.

Stuart channel.—Sansum narrows extends $1\frac{1}{2}$ miles northward from Maple bay, when it leads into Stuart channel, the westernmost of the ship passages which lie on the eastern side of Vancouver island.

The western side of Stuart channel is formed by the shores of Vancouver island; its eastern by the coasts of Admiral, Kuper, and Thetis islands; it extends in a general NW. direction for nearly 13 miles, when it joins Trincomali channel between Yellow point (Vancouver) and Reef point (Thetis island). The general breadth of the channel is about 2 miles; the depth varies in the southern part from 60 to 140 fathoms, in the northern portion from 20 to 55 fathoms; the principal dangers are North and Escape reefs.

On the western or Vancouver island shore there are some good harbors, viz, Osborn bay, Chemainus bay, Oyster harbor; on the eastern side there are two anchorages, Telegraph and Preedy harbors, on the western side of Thetis and Kuper islands.

Osborn bay, the southernmost anchorage on the western side, may be known by the Shoal islands, a low, wooded group extending over 3 miles in a NW. direction, connected at low water by reefs and mud banks, and which form the northern side of the bay; the southeasternmost of these islands lies N. 33° W. (N. 57° W. mag.), a little over 2 miles from the northwestern entrance point of Sansum narrows; it can be recognized by the lighthouse standing on it. The bay affords good anchorage, sheltered from the prevailing winds from the westward and southward. The best anchorage is with the southeasternmost Shoal island in one with Southey point, and the southern point of entrance bearing S. 60° E. (S. 84° E. mag.).

Crofton is the name of a settlement growing up around the smelting works at the head of the bay, where there are wharves.

Light.—A fixed white light 33 feet above high water, and visible 10 miles, is shown from a small, square, wooden tower, built on an open frame 12 feet high, the whole painted white, on the southeasternmost of the Shoal islands. The light, which is unwatched, is maintained by the Britannia Smelting Company, limited.

The coast trends NW. for 4 miles from Osborn bay to Chemainus bay, and is faced by the Shoal islands and adjacent reefs and mud flats for nearly the whole distance; drying mud banks and shoal water extend 700 yards northwestward of the Shoal islands.

Vessels should keep well outside a line joining the black buoy off the southeastern end of the Shoal islands and Bare Point lighthouse, bearing N. 50° W. (N. 74° W. mag.).

The northern point of the largest Shoal island has a remarkable, flat, sandy spit, on which is built an Indian village; there are no passages between the small islands north of this, and the bank dries off 400 yards at low water.

Rocks—Buoy.—A rocky ledge, awash at low water, lies 600 yards northward of the southeasternmost Shoal island. A black can buoy is moored in 7 fathoms close northeastward of the ledge. Between this ledge and the island lies a rock awash at high water.

Chemainus bay.—Bare point, which forms the eastern entrance to the bay, will be readily recognized by the lighthouse near its extremity. The bay extends in a southerly direction for ¾ mile and is ⅓ mile in breadth; it is sheltered from all but northerly winds. There is a large settlement of the same name on the west side of the bay, with stores, post-office, and railroad station; there are also a timber yard and a sawmill from which spars may be obtained. A plentiful supply of fresh provisions and good water may be had. There is direct communication by rail and telegraph with Victoria and Nanaimo.

Light.—On the extremity of Bare point a fixed white light is exhibited, at an elevation of 36 feet above high water, from a lantern on the roof of the keeper's dwelling, the whole 30 feet high and painted white; the light is visible 11 miles, from N. 49° W. (N. 73° W. mag.), through West and South, to N. 58° E. (N. 34° E. mag.).

Bird rock, a rocky ledge uncovering at half tide, extends 200 yards from the shore northwestward of the western entrance point, and is ½ mile W. by N. from Bare point.

Rocks.—A rock, with 11 feet over it at low water, is situated on the western side of the entrance, with Bare Point lighthouse bearing S. 82° E. (N. 74° E. mag.), distant 550 yards, and the NE. extremity of the wharf S. 8° E. (S. 32° E. mag.).

A narrow ridge, on which are several detached rocky heads, with 12 to 18 feet over them at low water, extends westward from the entrance of the harbor for about 800 yards and parallel to the coast. From the eastern end of this ridge, which has a depth of 12 feet over it, Bird rock bears S. 5° W. (S. 19° E. mag.), distant 440 yards, and Bare Point lighthouse S. 58° E. (S. 82° E. mag.).

A rocky patch, with a depth of 18 feet over it at low water, lies 640 yards N. 69° E. (N. 45° E. mag.) from Bare Point lighthouse.

Anchorage.—There is a depth of 3 to 4 fathoms at low water alongside the wharves; the anchorage is in from 10 to 20 fathoms. At a distance of 400 yards from the head of the bay the water shoals suddenly from 5 fathoms.

Vesuvius bay is a small bight on the western side of Admiral island immediately opposite Osborn bay and ½ mile southeastward of Dock point, which is foul for a distance of 200 yards. Off the southern point of the bay are two small islets. There is a wharf, store, and post-office. Anchorage may be had in 10 fathoms.

The larger bay, 1 mile south of Vesuvius bay, has deep water, but shoals at its head; if necessary, anchorage may be had, in 9 fathoms, 300 yards from the shore, but it is not recommended.

North reef is a sandstone ledge extending in a NW. and SE. direction, as do all the reefs in this channel. It lies ½ mile S. 6° W. (S. 18° E. mag.) from the southern point of Tent island. It is just awash at high water and therefore easily avoided. Shoal ground extends 400 yards NW. and 500 yards SE. from the beacon. At the SE. end of this foul ground is a rock, with 12 feet on it, bearing S. 40° E. (S. 64° E. mag.) from the beacon, and 500 yards distant. On the NE. and SW. sides there is deep water close up to the beacon.

Beacon.—A pyramidal, wooden beacon, 19 feet square at the base, surmounted by a staff carrying a latticework ball 6 feet in diameter, the whole painted white, and showing 40 feet above high water, has been erected on North reef.

Tent island, narrow and ⅝ mile long, lies off the southern extreme of Kuper island; 200 yards off its southern end are two remarkable worn, sandstone rocks 8 to 10 feet above water; the breadth of the passage between them and North reef is ⅓ mile. Eastward, nearly 400 yards from the southeastern end of Tent island, is a rock which uncovers 2 feet; this rock forms part of a reef with 15 feet on it. In passing eastward of Tent island, its eastern shore should be given a berth of ½ mile, as some rocky ledges extend off it. There is no ship passage between Tent and Kuper islands, there being only 1 fathom at low water.

Houston passage.—The western portion of Houston passage runs between North reef and Tent and Kuper islands on the west, and Admiral island on the east; it is 1¼ miles wide and has from 16 to 30 fathoms of water. The eastern end has been already described under Trincomali channel.

Note.—The ebb stream sets to the northward through this passage.

Idol islet lies 1¼ miles E. by S. from the SE. end of Tent island and 500 yards from the shore of Admiral island; with the islet bearing West (S. 66° W. mag.), and midway between it and the shore, there is anchorage in 10 fathoms.

Grappler reef, on the eastern side of Houston passage, is 200 yards in extent and uncovers at very low water. It lies ¼ mile off the NW. end of Admiral island, and there is a depth of 5 fathoms between it and the shore of the island. Passing through Houston passage, the eastern point of Sansum narrows, abreast Arbutus point, kept well open of the points of Admiral island to the northward of it, bearing S. 15° E. (S. 39° E. mag.), leads 400 yards westward of the reef, and when the southern point of Secretary islands is open of Southey point and bearing N. 58° E. (N. 34° E. mag.), it is cleared to the northward.

A black can buoy, in 7 fathoms, lies on the SW. extreme of the reef.

Escape reef, 2 miles NW. by N. from North reef, is a dangerous patch, nearly ⅓ mile in extent, in a NW. and SE. direction, which covers at a quarter flood, and has no kelp to mark its position. It lies nearly ½ mile from the west shore of Kuper island, 1¼ miles WNW. ¼ W. from Josling (its south) point, and a little more than ¼ mile SSW. from Upright cliff, Kuper island; there is a deep channel ⅓ mile wide between it and Kuper island.

Yellow point, just open westward of Scott island, off Preedy harbor, bearing N. 24° W. (N. 48° W. mag.), leads 600 yards westward of the reef. Sandstone rocks off the southeast point of Tent island kept open of that island also lead westward of it and the rock NW. of it.

Rock.—A rock, with a depth of 12 feet over it and steep-to all around, is situated in the approach to Telegraph harbor, with the beacon on Escape reef bearing S. 46° E. (S. 70° E. mag.), distant 1,300 yards, and Active point N. 40° E. (N. 16° E. mag.).

Beacon.—A white, pyramidal, wooden beacon, surmounted by a staff and drum, showing 20 feet above high water, stands on Escape reef.

Alarm rock is scarcely in the track of vessels working up Stuart channel. It lies 200 yards S. 34° W. (S. 10° W. mag.) of the SE. point of Hudson island, the southeasternmost of the group of islands which lie off the western sides of Kuper and Thetis islands, facing Preedy and Telegraph harbors. It just covers at high water, and is connected by a ledge with Hudson island.

False reef lies 700 yards N. 50° W. (N. 74° W. mag.) of Scott island, the northwesternmost of the group just mentioned, and a long ¼ mile S. 62° W. (S. 38° W. mag.) of Crescent point, the NW. point of Preedy harbor.

This reef is nearly 400 yards in extent within the 5-fathom curve, the shoalest portion, awash at low water, being situated on the southeastern part of the reef.

Buoy.—A can buoy, painted in red and black horizontal stripes, is moored in 14 fathoms about 150 yards to the southward of the reef.

A rocky patch, composed of rock, large stones, and sand, lies off the western side of Reef point. It has several heads with 6 feet of water over them at low water, and is connected with the shore. The outermost head, with 6 feet of water over it, lies 500 yards southward of Reef point and 360 yards from the shore abreast of it.

Telegraph harbor, on the west side of Kuper island, is a snug anchorage, and its entrance is between Hudson island and Active point, which are ½ mile apart. Entering from the southward, Escape reef and the rock NW. of it must be avoided. If passing inside the reef, the shore of the island should be kept aboard within a quarter of a mile; if outside or westward of it, then keep Yellow point (north point of Kulleet bay) just open westward of Scott island, off Preedy harbor, bearing N. 24° W. (N. 48° W. mag.), until Upright cliff of Kuper island bears East (N. 66° E. mag.), when a vessel will be northward of the reef and the rock NW. of it, and may steer for the entrance of the harbor.

Anchorage.—There is good anchorage in 8 fathoms, with the NW. end of Hudson island bearing West (S. 66° W. mag.), and Active point S. 17° E. (S. 41° E. mag.), or 400 yards farther in, in 8 fathoms. Above this, the harbor contracts to a narrow creek extending 1 mile NNW., where coasters may find anchorage in 2 to 3 fathoms; the continuation of this creek to the eastward separates Kuper from Thetis island, which at low water are connected. The wharf on the eastern shore has a depth of 9 feet alongside the end.

Rocks.—A rock, with 5 feet over it, is situated off the west coast of Kuper island. It lies 320 yards S. 19° W. (S. 5° E. mag.) from Active point. The 10-fathom curve extends to a distance of about 200 yards outside this rock.

A rock, with 4 feet over it at low water, lies inside the harbor, and 200 yards from the point to the northward of Active point. It is 1,160 yards N. 3° W. (N. 27° W. mag.) from Active point and 980 yards N. 55° E. (N. 31° E. mag.) from the SE. point of Hudson island. The white flagstaff in line with the head of the wharf leads well clear of this danger.

Tides.—At Telegraph harbor a series of observations, extending over a period of nearly eight months, was made in 1904 by Commander J. F. Parry, H. B. M. surveying vessel Egeria. High water, full and change, was found to be at 4 h. 44 m.; springs rise 12 feet, neaps 8 feet; neap range irregular. The tides were marked by their regularity during the whole period of observation, the wind and the changes of atmospheric pressure having practically no effect.

During the lunar day there are two high and two low waters which are generally unequal in height, the diurnal inequality being most marked in the low-water heights and during the greatest tides; the greatest inequality during the period under observation was 8 feet 7 inches.

When the moon is at its extreme north or south declination, and at its greatest parallax, about the time of full or new moon, the range of the tide is considerably increased.

The larger tide occurs during the daytime when the sun is north of the equator, and during the night when it has south declination.

Preedy harbor is separated from the one just described by a group of small islands and reefs; its entrance is to the northward of them between Scott island and Crescent point of Thetis island, and is ⅓ mile in breadth. When entering, the Thetis island shore should be kept aboard to avoid False reef.

Shoal water extends for 300 yards off the northern sides of Scott and Dayman islands.

Anchorage will be found in 7 fathoms, with Crescent point bearing N. 45° W. (N. 69° W. mag.), distant nearly ½ mile, and the east point of Dayman island bearing S. 34° W. (S. 10° W. mag.).

Oyster harbor is 4 miles NW. from Chemainus bay; the harbor extends in the same direction for 4 miles and is nearly 1 mile wide at the entrance, narrowing gradually within.

Bowlder point, the southern entrance point, having a large bowlder at its extremity, is conspicuous. On the northern side of the entrance is Coffin islet, which will be recognized by the lighthouse standing on it. Foul ground extends eastward of Coffin point and beyond the lighthouse for a distance of about 500 yards from the latter. A head, with 6 feet over it at low water springs, lies 260 yards N. 85° E. (N. 61° E. mag.), and another 380 yards N. 88° E. (N. 64° E. mag.), from Coffin Islet lighthouse.

In passing give Coffin islet a berth of ½ mile.

The bight between Coffin and Sharpe points is known as Evening cove. From the point in this cove 600 yards north of Sharpe point a reef with depths of 2 and 3 fathoms extends in an ESE. direction for a distance of ½ mile. The extremity lies 520 yards S. 50° W. (S. 26° W. mag.) from Coffin Islet lighthouse.

About 1 mile inside Sharpe point and on the NE. side of the harbor are the Twin islands, from which a reef, covering at half flood, extends southwestward for nearly 300 yards. A reef which dries extends from the opposite shore for nearly 500 yards, the space between the reefs being only 750 yards wide.

From the western end of the western Twin island, a ridge extends in the direction of the coal wharf on the opposite shore. The 3-fathom curve lies 260 yards, and the 5-fathom curve 380 yards, from the end of the island. Vessels should be careful in this vicinity.

Above the wharves the harbor is narrowed by the Long islands to a width of ¼ mile. A narrow channel with 5 to 3½ fathoms runs parallel to the islands, the 3-fathom curve being 1½ miles from the head of the harbor.

Ladysmith, founded in 1900, is situated on the SW. shore just above Hail point; it is in railroad communication with Victoria and Nanaimo, and also in connection with the telegraph and telephonic systems of Vancouver and the mainland. There are three wharves on the SW. side at Hail point where coal can be shipped; lengths 800 feet, 540 feet, and 300 feet, respectively; depths alongside 33, 29, and 32 feet. Fresh provisions may be obtained, and water from the coaling wharves, but the supply is uncertain during summer.

A good anchorage for large vessels is about a mile inside the entrance in 9 fathoms, mud bottom, with the SE. end of Long island bearing NW. by N. and east extreme of Twin islands NNE; good anchorage may also be had in 6 fathoms, mud bottom, nearly ¾ mile farther up the harbor, with the SE. end of Long island bearing N. 15° W. (N. 39° W. mag.), and the NW. extreme of Twin islands N. 45° E. (N. 21° E. mag.).

Tides.—It is high water, full and change, in Oyster harbor at 4 h. 44 m.; springs rise 10 feet, neaps 8 feet. The characteristics of the tides at this place are the same as those of Telegraph harbor.

Light.—A fixed white light, elevated 29 feet above high water and visible 10 miles, is shown from a square, wooden tower, painted white, on the center of Coffin island. The light is unwatched.

Beacons.—A black beacon, showing 10 feet at high water, surmounted by white drum, has been erected on the drying flat which extends 500 yards from the southwestern shore of the harbor.

A red beacon, showing 10 feet at high water, surmounted by a white cone, stands on the reef which dries at high tide, situated off the southwestern side of Twin islands.

Kulleet bay is 2½ miles northward of the entrance of Oyster harbor, and about the same distance westward of Reef point, the NW. point of Thetis island.

Anchorage may be had in 8 fathoms ½ mile from its head, on a bank which projects from the southern shore, with Deer point at the northern entrance of the bay bearing N. 65° E. (N. 21° E. mag.), and the southern trend of the coast bearing S. 83° E. (S. 57° E. mag.). It is open and can not be recommended, unless in fine weather or with offshore winds. No dangers, so far as is known, interfere in working into the bay.

Yellow point, bare and grassy at its extreme, is the western point of the northern entrance to Stuart channel.

A rock, nearly awash at low water springs, with 10 fathoms 100 yards eastward of it, lies about 400 yards eastward of the point, and nearly 1⅜ miles N. 83° W. (S. 73° W. mag.) from the center of White rock.

Directions.—Passing through Stuart channel, a mid-channel course clears all dangers. Bound northward for Dodd narrows, there is a clear passage about 1 mile wide between the Vancouver shore and White rock and Danger reef. White rock, in line with the NE. tangent of Thetis island, bearing S. 45° E. (S. 69° E. mag.), leads clear of Danger reef.

Bound southward from Dodd narrows through Stuart channel, steer midway between Round island and the islands eastward of it; when abreast Round island, steer for Rugged peak, the westernmost peak on Thetis island, bearing S. 28° E. (S. 52° E. mag.). This course leads in deep water and ½ mile SW. of Danger reef. When the lighthouse on Danger reef is in line with Tree island, change course to South (S. 24° E. mag.), and pass fairly into Stuart channel between Yellow and Reef points.

There is a clear passage between Danger reef and White rock; it is ½ mile wide.

CHAPTER IV.

SAN JUAN (MIDDLE) CHANNEL—LOPEZ SOUND—ORCAS, WEST AND EAST CHANNELS.

VARIATION IN 1906.

Cattle point	23° 30′ E.	Alden point	23° 45′ E.

San Juan (Middle) channel is the central of the three passages leading from Juan de Fuca strait into Georgia strait, and is bounded by San Juan island on the west and the islands of Lopez, Shaw, and Orcas on the east. Although a deep navigable ship channel, and eligible for steamers of the largest size, the southern entrance is somewhat confined, and subject to strong tides, with a general absence of steady winds; the wide straits of Rosario and Haro, on either side of it, are therefore far to be preferred for sailing vessels.

The general direction of the channel is northerly for 5 miles, when it trends to the NW. for 7 miles to its junction with President (Douglas) channel. The southern entrance lies between the southeastern point of San Juan and Cattle point, the southwestern point of Lopez island; for 1½ miles its direction is northward, and the breadth of the passage for this distance varies from ¾ mile to 800 yards; abreast Goose island, on the western side, it does not exceed the latter breadth. When entering, the danger to be avoided on the western side is Salmon bank, extending southerly from San Juan, and on the eastern, White (Whale) rocks, always out of water. The currents in this entrance run from 3 to 7 knots an hour, with eddies and confused rips; when within the entrance there is far less current, and Griffin bay, offering good anchorage, is easily reached.

Light.—On Cattle point a fixed white light is exhibited at an elevation of 100 feet above high water. The lighthouse consists of a wooden framework over a sentry box, the whole painted white.

Salmon bank extends 1½ miles south from Cattle point, the southeastern extreme of San Juan island, a bare point about 50 feet high sloping from Mount Finlayson, and the least depth of water found on it is 9 feet, with rocky patches, marked in summer by kelp; depths varying from 4 to 9 fathoms extend for a farther distance of ¾ mile in the same direction.

Buoy.—A black spar buoy, moored in 7 fathoms, marks the southern edge of the bank.

White (Whale) rocks, on the eastern side of the entrance, are two black rocks, 200 yards apart, and 3 or 4 feet above high water; a patch, on which kelp grows, with one fathom on it, extends 400 yards to the southward of them, otherwise they are steep-to, but it is not recommended to pass them nearer than ¼ mile, as the tides set strongly over them.

Long, Hall, and Charles islands, 20 to 25 feet high, lie off the southern shore of Lopez island and eastward of the entrance to Middle channel.

Goose island, small and low, lies about ½ mile northward of Cattle point and close to the western shore of the channel. Abreast of it, near the eastern shore, is another small island; the channel here is only 800 yards wide.

Shark reef, immediately within San Juan channel, and ½ mile northward of White cliff, consists of two rocks awash at low water, extending a little over 200 yards offshore. There are no dangers on the coast of the island for 2 miles northward of this reef, but large vessels working up should not approach nearer than ¼ mile.

Directions.—Entering San Juan channel from the westward, Cattle point should be given a berth of at least 1⅝ miles. Mount Erie, a remarkable summit on Fidalgo island 1,250 feet high, in line with Iceberg (Jennis) point, bearing N. 82° E. (N. 58° E. mag.), leads 1¼ miles south of Salmon bank in 13 fathoms; when the entrance to the channel is open, bearing North (N. 24° W. mag.) or when Goose island, a small islet on the western side of the entrance, is in line with Orcas knob, bearing N. 5° W. (N. 29° W. mag.), a vessel will be well to the eastward of the bank, and may steer in for the passage. Orcas knob is a remarkable, conical hill, with a bare, stony summit, 1,104 feet above the sea, rising over the western side of Orcas island.

The bottom in the channel is rocky and irregular, varying in depth from 18 to 60 fathoms, causing overfalls and eddies which are apt to turn a ship off her course, necessitating quick use of the helm; there are no positive dangers after passing Salmon bank; between this bank and Cattle point there is a passage carrying 3½ fathoms, ¼ mile in breadth; 5 fathoms will be found within 200 yards of the point. The westernmost Whale rock, seen in the center of the channel between Charles island and the north side of Mackaye harbor, leads through the middle of this narrow channel, which, however, is not recommended.

Griffin bay is immediately within the southern entrance of Middle channel. Although spacious, yet from the great depth of water there is but a limited portion of the bay available for anchorage, and this is in the southern angle, immediately off the remarkable prairie land between two forests of pine trees.

With all westerly or southerly winds Griffin bay affords good shelter; but with those from North or NE. it is considerably exposed, and landing is difficult in consequence of the long flat which extends off the beach. These winds, however, are not of frequent occurrence.

The western and southern shores of the bay are foul for a distance of 800 yards in some parts and should not be approached nearer than ½ mile.

Harbor rock, which dries 6 feet at low water, lies 250 yards northward of the southern entrance point of Griffin bay. A sunken rock lies halfway between it and the point, which latter should be given a berth of 600 yards.

North Pacific rock, which covers at a quarter flood, lies ⅓ mile N. 18° E. (N. 6° W. mag.) from the pier on the beach at San Juan.

Half-tide reef, awash at high water, lies 800 yards from the western shore and ⅓ mile SE. from Low point.

Hope reef, awash at low water, is 600 yards to the southward of Half-tide reef.

Anchorage.—The best anchorage is in 9 fathoms, mud bottom, with the southernmost of the white cliffs on Lopez island kept well open of Harbor rock, bearing S. 84° E. (N. 72° E. mag.), and the black, rocky extreme of Low point just open northward of Half-tide rock, bearing N. 45° W. (N. 69° W. mag.). From this position the water shoals rapidly toward the shore, and 300 yards nearer in there is only 3 fathoms; strangers should drop an anchor directly 12 fathoms is obtained.

North bay, in the NW. angle of Griffin bay, immediately under Park hill (a bare grassy eminence about 180 feet high), affords good anchorage in from 4 to 10 fathoms, mud bottom, with all winds but those from SE., to which it is somewhat exposed. The bottom here is more regular than in Griffin bay, and altogether it is perhaps a snugger anchorage.

Anchor in from 6 to 9 fathoms, mud bottom, with the eastern point of Dinner island bearing S. 5° E. (S. 29° E. mag.), distant 800 yards.

The village of Argyle lies on the shore of North bay; there is a small wharf making out into 9 feet of water.

Dinner island is a small island lying about 1 mile WSW. from Pear point and 400 yards from the western entrance point of North bay. There is shoal water between the island and the point; foul ground extends 400 yards to the southward of Dinner island.

New reef, in the entrance to North bay, has 10 feet over it, and is marked by kelp. A spar buoy painted in black and red horizontal stripes is moored close to the western side of the reef, in 18 feet of water, with the northern extreme of Dinner island bearing

N. 77° W. (S. 79° W. mag.), distant 1,200 yards. The buoy should be given a berth of not less than 100 yards.

Old reef, with 6 feet over it, and marked by kelp, lies ½ mile S. 38° E. (S. 62° E. mag.) from the eastern point of Dinner island.

Tides and tidal streams.—The range at the southern entrance of Middle channel, at full and change, is 12 feet; but little current is felt at the anchorages. With the flood an eddy, of about 1 knot an hour, sets southward in Griffin bay, and with the ebb in the opposite direction.

Fisherman bay is a small, shallow cove on the western shore of Lopez island. At its entrance, which is about 4 miles from the entrance to San Juan channel, is the settlement of Lopez, where there is a post-office. A wharf extends into 11 feet of water.

Turn island lies nearly 5 miles to the northward of the southern entrance to San Juan channel. Its eastern point, a cliffy bluff, makes as the extreme of the peninsula which forms the northern side of Griffin bay. The island should be passed at a distance of over ¼ mile, particularly going northward with the flood; there is a channel for boats or small craft between it and the peninsula.

Turn rock lies nearly ¼ mile NE. from the island, and covers at high water; it is marked by an iron spindle, surmounted by a white cage. The tide sets with great strength over this rock, and those passing up or down the channel are recommended to give it a good berth.

Opposite Turn island and on the eastern side of the channel is the entrance to Upright channel leading northeastward between Lopez and Shaw islands to East and Lopez sounds.

Friday harbor, on the eastern shore of San Juan island, about 1 mile westward from Turn rock, is a small cove about 1 mile long. Brown island, wooded and about ½ mile long, occupies the center of the bight. The harbor is rather confined, but offers good anchorage, and is easily entered by steamers or small craft.

The entrance westward of Brown island is the wider, being 600 yards across, but it is narrowed by a rocky patch, nearly in mid-channel, with 2½ fathoms over it, lying 300 yards westward of the northwestern extreme of the island; there is shoal water between this rock and the island. Using this entrance, favor the western shore. Using the eastern entrance, which is 300 yards wide, favor the eastern point of entrance to avoid the shoal extending southeastward of Brown island.

Friday harbor is a small settlement and post-office on the western shore of the cove.

Anchor in 6 to 7 fathoms off the wharves.

Reid rock.—After rounding Turn island, San Juan channel trends to the northwestward, and Reid rock, the least water on which is 12 feet, lies right in the fairway; it is surrounded by thick kelp, which, however, is sometimes run under by the tide. The rock lies $1\frac{3}{10}$ miles N. 52° W. (N. 76° W. mag.) from Turn Rock beacon. The passage on the north side of the rock is recommended for vessels bound up or down San Juan channel, as, having to give Turn rock a good berth, it is the more direct one.

After passing Reid rock there are no known dangers which are not visible. From Caution point, 1 mile above the rock, on the western side, the channel gradually increases in breadth, and varies but little from a NW. direction, the depth of water increasing to 60 and 70 fathoms.

Buoy.—A nun buoy, painted in red and black horizontal stripes, marks Reid rock.

Parks harbor, immediately eastward of George point on Shaw island, about 2 miles northward of Turn island, is about ½ mile long and ¼ mile wide. It affords good anchorage for small vessels in 6 to 8 fathoms, soft bottom. The entrance is clear and there are no dangers.

Rocky bay, on the western side of San Juan channel, 4 miles from Caution point, does not afford much shelter, and vessels are not recommended to use it unless in case of necessity. The small island, O'Neal, lies in the center of it. There is a depth of 14 fathoms between the island and San Juan, but the bottom is rocky. A reef of rocks, on which the sea generally breaks, extends 300 yards off the San Juan shore, bearing S. 59° W. (S. 35° W. mag.) of O'Neal island.

Wasp islands.—Between Neck point, the western end of Shaw island, and Steep point, the southwestern point of Orcas island, are a number of islands, rocks, and sunken ledges, between and among which are several passages leading between Shaw and Orcas islands, and communicating with the harbors which deeply indent the coast of the latter island.

The passages in general use are North and Pole passages, close under the Orcas island shore. The currents have considerable velocity, and these passages are navigated only by small vessels with local knowledge.

Yellow island, the westernmost of the group, is rather remarkable from its color, and from being grassy and bare of trees, the remainder of the group being wooded. From its western shore a sandy spit extends 200 yards, having at its extreme a rock which dries at low water and is surrounded by kelp.

Jones island lies in the northern entrance of San Juan channel, nearly ½ mile from Orcas island, being separated from the latter by Spring passage. The island is less than 1 mile in extent, mostly wooded, but its western points are bare and grassy.

Spring passage is a safe deep-water channel, and saves some distance to a steamer passing up or down San Juan channel by President channel.

Some rocky patches extend 200 yards off the eastern side of Jones island, and a rock which covers at 2 feet flood lies the same distance north of a small cove on the northeastern side of the island; a rocky patch, with 5 fathoms of water on it, lies 400 yards off the west side of Orcas island; therefore it is desirable to pass through in mid-channel.

Caution.—Passing up or down San Juan channel, the NE. end of San Juan should be avoided, as the tides are strong, and a sailing vessel is apt to be drawn into the strong tide rips and overfalls in the eastern entrance of Spieden channel.

Flattop island, in the northern entrance of San Juan channel, 2 miles NW. by N. from Jones island, is ⅓ mile long, wooded, and about 120 feet high. Gull rock, 200 yards in extent, bare, and 25 feet high, lies 400 yards off its NW. side.

President (Douglas) channel may be said to be the continuation of San Juan channel, and leads into Haro strait, between Orcas and Waldron islands. There are other passages leading into Haro strait, viz, westward of Flattop island, between it and Spieden and Stuart islands, and eastward of Flattop, between it and Waldron island. In the former, the confused tides and eddies are liable to entangle sailing vessels among the Spieden and neighboring groups of small islands and rocks; amongst the latter, White rock, with its offlying dangers, offers serious impediments to the safe navigation of the same class of vessels.

The channel is about 5 miles long, with a least width of 1¼ miles. The depths are generally great and the passage is free from all dangers. The currents range from 2 to 5 knots in velocity and the rips and eddies are heavy, especially off the entrance points, point Hammond (Waldron island) and point Doughty (bill of Orcas).

The northern and western shores of Orcas island are particularly steep and thickly wooded. Mount Constitution, 2,409 feet high, in the eastern part of the island, and Orcas knob, 1,060 feet high, conical and bare on the summit, in the western part of the island, are prominent and easily recognized from northward and southward.

If necessary, temporary anchorage may be had, in 12 fathoms, in the bay about 800 yards southward of Doughty point (bill of Orcas).

Directions.—The channel westward of Flattop island is less than 1 mile in breadth at its narrowest part. Green point of Spieden island is steep-to; a tide rip is generally met with off it. After passing Flattop island the channel course is N. 11° W. (N. 35° W. mag.) until Skipjack island is open of Sandy point (Waldron island), bearing N. 37° E. (N. 13° E. mag.), when a course may be shaped either up or down Haro strait; with the ebb, be careful not to get set into the channel between Spieden and Stuart islands.

The channel eastward of Flattop island, between it and White rock, is about the same breadth as the one just described, but Danger rock, with 8 feet of water on it, which lies ¼ mile S. 33° E. (S. 57° E. mag.) of the center of White rock, must be carefully avoided.

After passing Flattop island, keep its eastern side just touching the western point of Jones island, bearing S. 24° E. (S. 48° E. mag.), and it will lead nearly ¾ mile westward of Danger rock; when Skipjack island opens out northward of Sandy point, bearing N. 37° E. (N. 13° E. mag.), all the dangers are cleared.

If passing between White rock and Disney point, the latter should be kept well aboard if the ebb is running, or a vessel is liable to be set on the rock. The western bluff of Sucia should by no means be shut in by the SE. tangent of Waldron island until Java (Monarch) head is well shut in with Sandy point, the latter bearing N. 17° W. (N. 41° W. mag.); steer through with these marks on, and when White rock is in line with the west side of Flattop island, bearing S. 29° W. (S. 5° W. mag.), a vessel will be clear of all dangers, and may steer either up or down Haro strait, giving Sandy point a berth of ½ mile.

If entering Haro strait westward of Waldron island, be careful to give the northeastern point a berth of 1 mile, to avoid the sunken rock lying nearly ½ mile eastward of it.

If intending to take the passage between Patos and Sucia islands, either up or down, an excellent mark for clearing Plumper and Clements reefs (dangerous patches lying westward and northward from Sucia) is to keep the remarkable round summit of Stuart island (650 feet high) just open northward of Skipjack island, bearing S. 62° W. (S. 38° W. mag.); this leads well clear of both reefs, and the same marks would lead across Alden bank in 5 fathoms of water.

If taking the passage from San Juan or President channels, keep the white-faced cliffs of Roberts point well open westward of Patos island, the cliffs bearing N. 5° W. (N. 29° W. mag.), until the marks before described are on, when steer through the passage. If the ebb stream is running, it is better to keep the Patos island shore aboard; 16 fathoms water will be found on the Sucia shore, but it is not recommended to anchor unless positively necessary.

Standing to the northeastward, when the northern end of Clark island is open of the eastern end of Matia, the former bearing S. 45° E. (S. 69° E. mag.), a vessel will be eastward of Clements reef.

Tides.—Sailing vessels working through President channel should beware of getting too close over on the Waldron island shore, near Disney point, as with calms or light winds they would run the risk of being set by the ebb onto Danger rock, on which the kelp is seldom seen. Both flood and ebb set fairly through San Juan and President channels, at the rate of 2 to 5 knots.

The ebb tide, coming down between East point and Patos island, strikes the north point of Waldron island, and one part of it, together with the stream between Patos and Sucia islands, passes down President and San Juan channels. The other part sets between Skipjack and Waldron islands; thence southerly through the groups in the neighborhood of Stuart island into Haro strait, as well as down San Juan channel. The ebb stream continues to run down through the whole of the passages in the archipelago for 2¼ hours after it is low water by the shore, and the water has begun to rise.

Sucia island is of a horseshoe shape, remarkably indented on its eastern side by bays and inlets; the largest of these, Echo bay (Sucia harbor), affords fair anchorage. The island is from 200 to 300 feet high, thickly covered with pines, and its western side a series of steep wooded bluffs.

Plumper reef, or West bank, is 1 mile in extent inside the 10-fathom curve in an ESE. and WNW. direction; the shoalest point, with 10 feet over it, lies 1¼ miles S. 57° W. (S. 33° W. mag.) from Lawson bluff, the highest western point of Sucia island. There are depths of 3½ fathoms ½ mile southeastward of this shoalest point, and a depth of 5½ fathoms ⅝ mile north of the western end of the bank. There is a deep passage between the reef and Sucia island, but it is not recommended.

Clements reef, on which there is a depth of 9 feet, lies 1½ miles N. 65° E. (N. 41° E. mag.) of Lawson bluff. Some rocky patches covering at high water, and marked by kelp, lie between Clements reef and Ewing island, and it is not safe to pass between them. There is a deep channel of more than 1 mile in breadth between Sucia and Matia islands.

Buoy.—A red nun buoy is moored in 13 fathoms ¼ mile NE. of Clements reef.

Directions.—Entering Sucia harbor from the northward, steer for the northern point of Clark island open of Puffin islet, bearing S. 37° E. (S. 61° E. mag.), which leads between Alden bank and Clements reef; when the SE. end of Ewing island bears S. 57° W. (S. 33° W. mag.), alter course to about S. 23° W. (S. 1° E. mag.). Give the point of the island a berth of at least 600 yards to avoid some rocky patches which extend 400 yards southeastward of it. When the harbor is well open steer up the center N. 70° W. (S. 86° W. mag.); it is better to keep the southern or Wall island shore rather aboard, as it is quite steep, and there are some reefs extending 200 yards off the north shore. When the west point of Ewing is just shut in by the east point of Sucia, anchor in the center in 7 or 8 fathoms, mud bottom. If intending to make any stay it is desirable to moor, as the harbor is small for a large vessel; it affords good shelter from westerly winds; with those from SE. some swell sets in but never sufficient to render the anchorage unsafe.

If entering from President channel, Flattop island open of point Doughty, bearing S. 54° W. (S. 30° W. mag.), leads westward of Parker reef. The SE. points of Sucia may be passed at 200 yards; they are a series of narrow islands the sides of which are as steep as a wall, with narrow deep passages between them; steer in, keeping the northernmost of these islands aboard, to avoid the reefs on the northern side of the harbor. A steamer may pass in between the north and middle Wall islands; this passage, though less than 200 yards wide, has 12 and 15 fathoms of water in it, and the wall-like sides of the islands are steep-to.

If bound to Sucia harbor from Rosario strait, pass on either side of Barnes, Clark, and Matia islands as convenient; if northward of the latter, as soon as the harbor is open steer for it, keeping the southern side aboard as before directed, or passing between north and middle Wall islands; if southward of Matia island, then do not stand so far to the westward as to shut in the north part of Sinclair island with Lawrence point, in order to avoid Parker reef.

Parker reef lies in the passage between Sucia and Orcas islands and ⅜ mile from the latter; at low water it uncovers ¼ mile of rock and sand, but its eastern end always shows its rocky summit, which is just awash at high water. This summit lies 2¼ miles N. 77° E. (N. 53° E. mag.) from Doughty point (Orcas bill). A shoal head with 2½ fathoms least water lies 1,200 yards N. 77° W. (S. 79° W. mag.), and another with 2¾ fathoms least water lies 600 yards N. 88° W. (S. 68° W. mag.) from the shoalest point of Parker reef. There is a passage on both sides of the reef; the one to the southward is ½ mile wide, with a depth of from 6 to 8 fathoms, but it is not recommended, as the points of Orcas island at this part run off shoal.

Tilly point, the southern extreme of Pender island, open north of Skipjack island, bearing N. 89° W. (S. 67° W. mag.), leads north of Parker reef.

A part of the ebb stream setting down between Sucia and Matia islands runs to the westward strongly over Parker reef, and through the channels on both sides of it; the flood sets in the contrary direction.

Matia island, a little more than 1 mile eastward of Sucia, is about 1 mile in extent, east and west; on its southern side are several boat coves. Close off its eastern extreme is Puffin islet, off which a flat rock extends for 300 yards.

Lopez island, the southernmost island on the eastern side of Middle channel, is 9 miles long, north and south, 3 miles wide, and thickly wooded, but differs from all the other islands of the archipelago in being much lower and almost flat, except at its northern and southern extremes, where elevations of a few hundred feet occur. Its southern side is much indented by bays and creeks, which, however, from their exposed position and rocky nature, can not be reckoned on as anchorages.

Mackaye harbor, on the south coast of Lopez island, 2 miles eastward of the entrance to Middle channel, is entered between Iceberg (Jennis) point on the south and Long and Charles islands on the north; from the latter it takes an easterly direction for 1 mile and then trends southward for a short distance, terminating in a low sandy beach. In the entrance there are depths of from 8 to 12 fathoms, muddy bottom, but with the prevailing southwesterly winds the anchorage is a good deal exposed; with northerly or easterly winds there would be fair anchorage. Coasters or small vessels drawing 12 feet may get shelter in the southern bight; Jennis point should be passed at about 600 yards distance; the anchorage is 1½ miles from it.

With southwesterly winds the coast and islands on the eastern side of Middle channel entrance, between Whale rocks and Jennis point, should be avoided, as then a considerable sea sets in; and when passing the coast between Jennis point and cape Colville it is desirable to keep 1 mile offshore, as some straggling rocks exist, which will be treated of under the head of Rosario strait.

Careen creek, on the west side of Lopez island, is 4 miles from the southern entrance of Middle channel, and its entrance lies 2 miles ESE. ½ E. from Turn island. The western entrance point is a low sandy spit, close round which there is 3 fathoms of water, and on it a vessel might, in perfect shelter, be beached and repaired with much facility; the creek terminates in a large salt lagoon known as Fishermans bay.

Upright channel, separating Lopez from Shaw island, is a deep passage leading from Middle channel to the sounds Orcas and Lopez, and by several passages into Rosario strait. The narrowest part, between Flat point and Canoe island, is scarcely 400 yards wide between the shoals.

Flat point is a low shingle or sandy point, with grass and small bushes on it; it is steep-to, and may be passed at less than 200 yards.

Canoe island.—The shore of Canoe island is fringed by kelp, close outside of which a vessel may pass; a rock marked by kelp lies 200 yards S. 23° W. (S. 1° E. mag.) off its southern point; shoal water extends 200 yards southward of the island. The tides in

Upright channel are seldom over 3 knots, and the channel is in all respects safe.

Rock.—A sunken rock marked by kelp lies 300 yards S. 53° E. (S. 77° E. mag.) from the southern point of Shaw island, the western point of entrance to Upright channel.

Anchorage may be had in 6 or 7 fathoms in Indian cove, westward of Canoe island, with Flat point in line with the SW. point of Canoe island; the only precaution necessary is to avoid the rock off the southern point of the island.

Shoal bay extends in a southerly direction for 1 mile to its head, which is separated from False bay, in Lopez sound, by a low neck of land. Although apparently a considerable sheet of water, the anchorage for large vessels is much limited by a shoal which extends more than halfway across from just within Upright point to the head of the bay, leaving the greater half, on the western side, with no more than from 2 to 3 fathoms at low water.

Anchorage.—The best anchorage for large vessels is in 8 fathoms, with Upright point in line with the east point of Shaw island bearing N. 51° W. (N. 75° W. mag.) and the east point of Shoal bay S. 33° E. (S. 57° E. mag.); 200 yards inside this position there is 4 fathoms; the holding ground is good. Vessels desiring to proceed up the bay after rounding Upright point, which may be passed close-to, must steer for the east point of the bay, until within 200 yards of it, and then keep along the eastern cliffy shore at the same distance, when not less than 5 fathoms will be found until within ¼ mile from the head, where there is anchorage in 4 fathoms; the space between the eastern side of the shoal and the eastern shore of the bay is nearly 400 yards.

Lopez sound, on the eastern side of Lopez island, extends south for 7½ miles. Its eastern side is formed partly by Lopez and partly by Decatur and Blakely islands, lying parallel with it; and between these islands, as well as northward of the latter, are passages leading into Rosario strait. The average breadth of the sound is nearly 1½ miles, and there is a convenient depth of water for anchorage in almost every part of it.

Middle bank, on which there is not less than 3 fathoms, is ½ mile in extent north and south, 400 yards east and west, and lies almost in the center of the sound, its north end being a quarter of a mile south from the south end of Frost island. Between Middle bank and Houston island there is anchorage in any part of the sound in from 5 to 7 fathoms, mud bottom.

Just abreast Lopez (Maury) passage (between the southern end of Decatur and the NE. point of Lopez), the water deepens to 13 to 15 fathoms, and this depth is maintained for 1½ miles, or as far as

Crown islet, a small, steep, rocky islet on the eastern side, within 1 mile of the head of the sound.

Tidal streams.—There is but little tide felt in Lopez sound, unless in the immediate neighborhood of the narrow passages from Rosario strait.

Entrance shoal, with 2 fathoms on it and marked by kelp, lies 1¼ miles N. 88° E. (N. 64° E. mag.) from Upright point and ½ mile from the shore of Blakely island; there is deep water on either side if it.

False bay (also called Swifts bay) is on the west side of the sound, 1 mile from Shoal bay. A shoal, of 2 fathoms, extends from the center of False bay, and connects with the small island, Arbutus, lying in its entrance, and renders it unfit for anchorage except for small vessels; but vessels may anchor in 8 fathoms southward of Arbutus, between it and Frost island.

Half-tide rock, covering at half flood and not marked by kelp, is in the track of vessels entering. It lies 800 yards northward of Arbutus island. It is better to pass eastward of it; when it is not visible. Upright point kept just open of Separation point, bearing N. 53° W. (N. 77° W. mag.), until the clay cliff of Gravel spit is in line with the east point of Arbutus island, bearing S. 12° W. (S. 12° E. mag.), will lead clear of it.

Frost island, ½ mile long north and south, lies close off Gravel spit on the west side of the sound; it is wooded, and its western side a steep cliff, between which and the spit end there is a narrow channel with a depth of 5 fathoms.

Black and Crown islets.—The Black islets are a ridge of steep, rocky islets, lying within and across the entrance of Lopez (Maury) pass; at 400 yards S. 34° W. (S. 10° W. mag.) of the southernmost and largest of these islets (Ram islet) is a rock which covers at quarter flood. There is a passage of 8 and 9 fathoms on either side of Crown islet, and anchorage above it in 5 or 6 fathoms, but vessels should not proceed far above, as at a distance of ⅓ mile it shoals to 1 and 2 fathoms, and dries for a considerable distance from the head of the sound; there is also good anchorage in 5 fathoms in the bight westward of Crown islet.

Passing up the sound between Crown islet and the western shore a rocky patch of 2 fathoms must be avoided; it lies ¼ mile N. 53° W. (N. 77° W. mag.) of Crown islet, and 800 yards from the western shore of the sound; there are 12 fathoms close to it, and deep water in the passage on either side of it.

Lopez (Maury) passage, between Decatur island and the NE. point of Lopez,, is the southernmost entrance to the sound from Rosario strait. It is scarcely 400 yards at the entrance, with a depth of 12 fathoms; the Black islets lie across the western entrance, and it is necessary to keep to the southward, between them and Lopez.

Light.—A fixed white light, elevated 25 feet above high water, is shown from a white post on the southern end of Decatur island.

Thatcher pass, between Blakely and Decatur islands, is the widest and most convenient passage into Lopez sound from Rosario strait; it is 1½ miles in length, and its narrowest part 800 yards wide, with a general depth of from 20 to 25 fathoms.

The currents in Thatcher pass run from 2 to 4 knots.

Lawson rock, lying almost in the center of the eastern entrance, is awash at low water. It lies 800 yards N. 11° W. (N. 35° W. mag.) of Fauntleroy point, the southeastern entrance point. There is a good passage on either side of the rock, but that to the southward is the best.

Buoy.—The southern edge of Lawson rock is marked by a can buoy, painted red and black in horizontal stripes.

Directions.—Entering Thatcher pass from the southward, if the flood is running, the southern shore should be kept pretty close aboard, as until well within the passage it sets up toward Lawson rock.

When the passage between Decatur and James islands is shut in by Fauntleroy point, a vessel will be just westward of or inside the rock.

Vessels entering by Thatcher pass, and drawing over 18 feet, to avoid Middle bank, should keep the southern shore aboard within 400 yards. White rock in line with the south point of Blakely island leads over the tail of the shoal in 20 feet.

The flood tide sets from Rosario strait through Thatcher pass both up and down the sound; a slight stream of flood also enters the sound from the northward.

Obstruction island lies in the center of the channel, between the northern point of Blakely and the SE. point of Orcas island, and the passages on either side of it form safe and convenient communication, by Upright channel, between San Juan channel and Rosario strait; they likewise lead from Rosario strait to Orcas and Lopez sounds. These passes are better adapted to steam than sailing vessels, although there should be no difficulty with a leading wind and fair tides. Small vessels should find no difficulty if the tides are properly taken advantage of.

Lights.—A fixed white light is exhibited from a post on the NE. point, and a fixed red light from a post on the SW. extreme, of Obstruction island; both posts are painted white.

North Obstruction pass is about 1¼ miles long, its average breadth 400 yards, the narrowest part (less than 400 yards) occurring just after making the bend; the general depth is from 8 to

14 fathoms. In consequence of the bend in this channel it has the appearance of a bay when seen from either entrance. The east end of Obstruction island should not be approached nearer than 200 yards, as shelving rocks extend a short distance off it; the best course for a steamer is to keep in mid-channel.

South Obstruction pass, though narrower than the northern pass, is the better of the two, as it is not more than ¾ mile in length, and is straight ENE. and WSW. Its narrowest part is 200 yards wide; the depth is much the same as in the northern pass. On the south side of the eastern entrance two rocks lie off Blakely island, the inner being always above high water; the other, a long black rock, is nearly ¼ mile offshore, just awash at high water; and marked by an iron spindle surmounted by a white barrel.

Entering from Rosario strait, the pass should be brought well open, bearing S. 68° W. (S. 44° W. mag.) before approaching it nearer than ½ mile; in like manner when passing into Rosario strait, if the black rock is not seen, a N. 68° E. (N. 44° E. mag.) course should be maintained until at that distance from the entrance. When the west point of Burrows island opens eastward of the east point of Blakely island, bearing S. 21° E. (S. 45° E. mag.), a vessel will be ½ mile eastward of any dangers. The south side of the pass appears like a round wooded island, in consequence of the land falling abruptly behind it, where there are two lagoons.

Tidal streams.—The flood stream in both passes sets westward from Rosario strait, and the ebb eastward; the latter runs for nearly 2 hours after it is low water by the shore; the velocity varies from 2 to 5 knots.

Shaw island is much of the same character as Lopez, though considerably smaller, being about 3 miles in extent; between it and Orcas island lies the Wasp group, among which are several passages leading to Orcas and Lopez sounds, and into Rosario strait.

Wasp islands, five in number, besides some smaller islets and rocks, lie on the eastern side of San Juan channel, between Shaw and Orcas islands. Wasp islands have been referred to under San Juan channel.

Yellow island, the westernmost of the group, rather remarkable from its color, is grassy and nearly bare of trees, the remainder of the group being wooded; from its west end a sandy spit extends 200 yards, having at its extreme a rock which dries at low water, and around which kelp grows. This point should be avoided when passing up or down San Juan channel.

A rock with 1¼ fathoms over it lies 300 yards N. 21° W. (N. 45° W. mag.) from the NW. point, and a rock with the same depth over it lies the same distance S. 2° W. (S. 22° E. mag.) from the southern point of the island.

Brown and Reef islands lie northward of Yellow island; off the western side of the latter (Reef) a reef extends more than 200 yards and several rocks surrounded by kelp extend over 200 yards off the western side of Brown island. A depth of 4 fathoms is reported to lie between Brown and Reef islands. A rock with 2 fathoms over it lies 400 yards eastward of the northern point of Reef island.

Wasp passage leads through this group to Orcas sound and Rosario strait. With the assistance of the chart, a steam vessel would find but little difficulty in passing through it, though the passage by Upright channel is to be preferred.

Crane island, on the northern side of Wasp passage, is wooded and much larger than any other of the Wasp group. The northern shore of the island is foul, shoals extending out in places to more than 200 yards. A sunken rock with 5 feet over it lies 250 yards off the shore and 700 yards N. 72° W. (S. 84° W. mag.) from Pole Pass light.

Pole passage, northward of Crane island, is so narrow (150 feet) that the two islands seem to be joined; this channel is fit for boats only.

Light.—A fixed red light is shown from a pile on the northern shore of Pole passage.

Bell island, wooded and of small extent, lies about ¼ mile eastward of Crane island.

Passage rock, dry at low water, lies 300 yards eastward of Bell island; it is marked by a black can buoy moored in 5½ fathoms close eastward of the rock.

Cliff island lies about 500 yards SW. of Crane island. Nob islet, a remarkable, round islet, with two or three bushes on its summit, lies just westward of Cliff island.

Directions.—Passing between Brown and Reef islands, where the channel is nearly ¼ mile wide, with a general depth of 9 fathoms, and a patch of 4 fathoms nearly in mid-channel, Bird rock (awash at high water) may be passed on either side; the wider passage is eastward of it, between it and Crane island, where the channel is ¼ mile across, and has a depth of 15 fathoms.

Passing eastward of Bird rock, care must be taken to avoid the 2¾-fathom patch that lies 200 yards SSE. of Bird rock and 400 yards westward of Crane island.

After passing Bird rock steer westward of Crane island, between it and Cliff island, and thence between Crane island and the northern shore of Shaw island.

Approaching the eastern end of Crane island, the channel narrows to 200 yards. The Shaw island side must be kept aboard to avoid Passage rock. Nob islet, just touching the northern end of Cliff island and just open southward of the southern side of Crane island, leads 200 yards south of Passage rock.

When Orcas knob is just over the narrow passage between Double islands and the west shore of West sound, bearing N. 10° W. (N. 34° W. mag.), vessels are eastward of Passage rock and may steer up West sound or eastward for East sound or Rosario strait. Passing out of West sound the same marks are equally good; steer down just westward of Broken point (a remarkable, cliffy peninsula on the north side of Shaw island) until the islands above mentioned touch, when steer for them, giving the south side of Crane island a moderate berth, and passing out of Wasp channel as before directed for entering it.

If desired, a vessel may pass into Wasp channel to the southward of Yellow island, between it and Low island (a small islet), thence northward of Nob island, as before directed, between Crane and Cliff islands.

There is another passage into Wasp channel southward of Cliff island, between it and Neck point, the remarkable western extreme of Shaw island. The breadth between them is a little over 200 yards, but there is a patch of 4 fathoms, with kelp on it, in the center of the passage. If taking this channel, avoid a reef lying S. 62° W. (S. 38° W. mag.) and extending more than ¼ mile from the SW. end of Cliff island; this reef is sometimes covered, and is the only danger known that is not visible.

These two latter passages are the shortest into Wasp channel for vessels from the southward. The eye will be found the best guide; a good lookout is necessary and to steamers there are no difficulties.

Tidal streams.—The flood stream sets westward in the eastern entrance of Wasp channel, but in the western entrance the flood from the San Juan channel partially sets eastward, and causes some ripplings among the islands, which may be mistaken for shoal water.

North passage.—This clear, deep channel, leading to Deer harbor, the westernmost port of Orcas island, is between Steep point and Reef island. It is nearly ¼ mile wide, and the danger to avoid is the reef off the western side of the latter island. A patch of 2 fathoms lies nearly 200 yards W. by S. from the NW. point of Brown island.

Orcas island is the most extensive in Haro archipelago, and contains the finest harbors. It is mountainous and in most parts thickly wooded, although in the valleys there is a considerable portion of land available for agricultural purposes, and partially clear of timber. Its southern side is singularly indented by deep sounds, which in some places almost divide the island; this is particularly the case in the East sound, separated only from Georgia strait by a low neck of land 1 mile across. On the eastern side of this sound mount

Constitution rises to an elevation of 2,420 feet, wooded to its summit. On the west side is the Turtle back, a long wooded range 1,600 feet high, and west of it, rising immediately over the sea, is the singular bare-top cone known as Orcas knob, a remarkable object when seen either from the north or south.

Deer harbor and West and East sounds are on the southern side of the island; on the western and northern sides there is no convenient anchorage. A vessel might drop an anchor, if necessary, southward of Doughty point (a remarkable, projecting, bare point, with a knob on its extreme), where 12 fathoms will be found within 200 yards of the shore; a small vessel might also anchor in 4½ fathoms just inside Freeman islet, a small islet in the bay ⅜ mile southward of Doughty point.

The northern coast is precipitous, except between Doughty point and Thompson point, a distance of 2½ miles; here occurs the low land at the head of East sound, and the points are shelving, with large bowlders extending some distance off. Immediately off this part of the coast is Parker reef.

Thompson point is bare and cliffy; from it the coast forms a slight curve southeastward to Lawrence point, distant 6 miles.

Lawrence point, the sloping termination of the high range of mount Constitution, is the eastern extreme of Orcas island; on its northern side it is a steep and almost perpendicular cliff, and from it the coast turns abruptly to the southwestward, forming the western side of Rosario strait; 4 miles southward from the point is the entrance to the northern Obstruction pass.

Deer harbor, the westernmost of the three ports of Orcas island, is conveniently entered from the Middle channel by North passage, between Reef and Brown islands. The harbor is 1 mile long in a north and south direction, and about the same breadth at its southern end; it narrows, however, rapidly, and terminates in a shoal creek and fresh-water streams fed from a lake. Fawn islet lies off the steep, cliffy shore of the west side of the harbor.

Between Fawn islet and the western shore is a passage 200 yards wide with 9 fathoms. A reef extends from the north side of Crane island; if working up the harbor, do not stand so far eastward as to shut in the east end of Cliff island behind the west end of Crane island; this will lead more than 200 yards clear of the reef. Care must be taken to avoid the 2-fathom rock, 400 yards east of the north point of Reef island.

Anchorage.—A convenient berth is in 7 fathoms, mud, halfway between Fawn islet and the eastern shore; or a snug anchorage, in 5 fathoms, will be found ¼ mile northward of the islet.

There is a small settlement and a post-office on the eastern side of the harbor.

West sound may be entered from San Juan channel, either by the Wasp or Upright passages already described, or from Rosario strait by either of the Obstruction passes. Having entered by Wasp passage, cleared Passage rock, and being off Broken point, West sound will be open, with Orcas knob immediately over the head of it. The sound is about ¾ mile broad with depths of from 10 to 16 fathoms.

Anchorage may be had in any part above Double islands, which lie close off its western shore, ½ mile northward of Broken point; but the snuggest anchorage, and the best for vessels intending to make any stay, is either in White Beach bay, on the eastern shore, or in Massacre bay, at the head of the sound.

White Beach bay is on the eastern side of the sound, 2 miles above Broken point. A small islet, Sheep islet, lies in the middle of the bay, nearly connected with the shore at low water.

On the northern shore of the bay is a small settlement and post-office.

Anchorage.—There is good anchorage in 9 fathoms of water, with Sheep islet bearing N. 62° E. (N. 38° mag.) and Haida point, the northern point of the bay, N. 34° W. (N. 58° W. mag.), distant ¼ mile.

Massacre bay is between Haida and Indian points. Harbor rock, with 4 feet over it, is almost in the center of the bay, between the two entrance points, and nearly 600 yards east of Indian point; it may be passed on either side in a depth of 9 fathoms. If to the eastward, Haida point should be kept within 300 yards; if to the westward, the eastern cliffy part of Broken point and the eastern side of Double islands kept in line astern, bearing S. 17° E. (S. 41° E. mag.), leads westward of the rock. When Indian point bears S. 23° W. (S. 1° E. mag.) good anchorage will be found in the center of the bay in 8 fathoms, mud bottom.

Harney channel, between Orcas and Shaw islands, connects the West and East sounds of Orcas. It commences at Broken point and takes an easterly direction for 3 miles, when it enters Upright channel between Foster and Hankin points; the former is a low, sloping, green point, the southern termination of the peninsula which separates the two sounds; the latter is the eastern, bluff, wooded point of Shaw island. The depth of water in this channel varies from 20 to 30 fathoms, and its average breadth is ½ mile, though it narrows for a short distance about its middle to ¼ mile.

The north side of Harney channel is a series of small bays with shingle beach, and there is a deep cove ⅔ mile west of Foster point; just westward of this cove, and NNW. from Hankin point, is a rocky patch which lies more than 200 yards offshore, and covers at half flood.

On the northern shore, near the entrance to West sound, there is a settlement, called Orcas, and a post-office. A wharf extends into 12 feet of water. A rock with 15 feet over it lies 125 yards off the wharf.

From the eastern end a telephone cable crosses the channel.

Camp cove is immediately eastward of Foster point; it is a convenient cove for boats, or a small vessel might anchor there in 6 fathoms; there is a good stream of fresh water running into it.

High Water (Shag) rock lies more than 200 yards from the shore, ½ mile northeastward of Foster point; it is awash at high water, and there is a depth of 8 fathoms between it and the shore; it is marked by a spindle surmounted by a white barrel.

Blind bay is on the southern shore, midway between Broken and Hankin points. A small round islet, partially wooded, lies in the middle of the entrance, and a reef of rocks, covering at high water, extends from its western point, almost choking the entrance on that side, but leaving a narrow passage close to the islet; a rock covering at one-quarter flood also lies off the eastern side of the islet, leaving a channel of 5 fathoms almost equally narrow on that side, so that the bay is only eligible for coasters, which should keep the island close aboard when entering; the eastern side is the best.

Anchorage in 4 or 5 fathoms may be had with the islet bearing North (N. 24° W. mag.), distant 400 yards.

Griswold, a small settlement and post-office, is situated at the head of the bay.

East sound.—Entering this sound by Upright channel or through Wasp passage and Harney channel, when abreast Upright point, its entrance will be easily made out. If by the Obstruction passes, as soon as a vessel is at their western entrance, the whole length of the sound will be open to the northwestward; conical hills, over 1,000 feet high, rise on both sides of the entrance, which is between Diamond and Stockade points. The general depth of water in the sound is 15 fathoms. The sound is 6 miles long and about 1 mile wide, except at Cascade bay, where it is ½ mile wide only.

Stockade (Buck) bay, on the eastern side of the entrance to the sound, nearly 1 mile northward of Stockade point (the northwestern entrance point of north Obstruction pass), affords anchorage in 8 fathoms about 600 yards from the shore; with a strong SW. wind some swell sets into this anchorage; there is a good stream of fresh water running into the bay.

Green bank, on the western side, immediately opposite Stockade bay, is a bank of sand extending halfway across the sound; on it there are depths of from 5 to 9 fathoms, with one patch of 4 fathoms, and a vessel might anchor on it if necessary, as being more convenient than the deep water immediately off it. The best anchorage is in 6 fathoms ½ mile northward of Diamond point, with a small green islet, which lies just off a white shell beach, bearing N. 67° W. (S. 89° W. mag.), distant about 800 yards.

Cascade bay, on the eastern side of the sound, 2 miles NW. of Stockade bay, is formed by a small hook of land extending southward. Anchorage may be had at 300 yards from the beach in 10 fathoms; but it would not be a desirable place with a southeasterly wind.

A large stream falls by a cascade into the bay, and it would be a convenient place at which to water a ship.

Fishing and Ship bays.—Fishing bay, the westernmost of the two bays at the head of the sound, has good anchorage in 10 fathoms, with Arbutus point, the cliffy extreme of the jutting peninsula that divides the two bays, bearing N. 68° E. (N. 44° E. mag.), midway between it and the west side of the sound.

Ship bay, eastward of Arbutus point, runs off shoal for 400 yards, or nearly to the extreme of the point; but it affords good shelter, perhaps better than Fishing bay. There is good anchorage in 9 fathoms, mud bottom, with Arbutus point bearing N. 55° W. (N. 79° W. mag.), distant 600 yards.

CHAPTER V.

ROSARIO STRAIT AND SHORES OF GEORGIA STRAIT.

VARIATION IN 1906.

Smith island.................23° 20′ E. | Sand heads.................23° 50′ E.

Rosario strait is the easternmost of the principal channels leading from Juan de Fuca strait into that of Georgia. Its southern entrance is between Lopez and Fidalgo islands, and thence its general direction is from North to NNW. for 25 miles, when it enters Georgia strait. It western shores are formed by Lopez, Decatur, Blakely, and Orcas islands; its eastern by Fidalgo, Cypress, Sinclair, and Lummi islands, and the mainland.

Rosario strait has several smaller channels which branch eastward, and lead between islands to United States ports in Bellingham bay, or, by a more circuitous route, into Georgia strait; among the principal of these channels are Guemes, Bellingham, and Lummi. The greatest breadth of the strait is 5 miles at its southern entrance; the least is about its middle, between Blakely and Cypress islands, where it is less than 1½ miles; the depth varies from 25 to 45 fathoms, occasionally deeper.

The principal dangers are the Bird and Belle rocks, which lie almost in the center of the strait, 4 miles within the southern entrance. There are several anchorages available for vessels delayed by the tides or other causes: Davis bay, on the eastern side of Lopez island, 3 miles within the southern entrance; Burrows bay, immediately opposite it, under mount Erie on the west side of Fidalgo island; Ship harbor or Guemes channel; and Strawberry bay, on the western side of Cypress island, are the principal.

Those entering Juan de Fuca strait, and bound to any of the ports of Puget sound, or up Rosario strait, either by day or night, should make New Dungeness light, which is 69 miles from the light at Tatoosh island, and Smith, or Blunt, Island light.

Tidal streams.—The streams in Rosario strait are strong, from 3 to 7 knots in the narrower parts.

Submarine cable.—A submarine cable is laid across Rosario strait from Lawrence point, Orcas island, to Lummi island.

Smith, or **Blunt, island** lies almost in the center of the eastern end of Juan de Fuca strait, 13 miles N. 52° E. (N. 29° E. mag.) from New Dungeness, and 6 miles southward of the entrance of

Rosario strait. It is about ½ mile in length, cliffy at its western end, and 50 feet high; a large kelp patch extends 1½ miles from the western extreme, which should be avoided; there is 6 fathoms on its outer edge. From the eastern end of the island, which is low, a sand spit extends ¾ mile ENE., partially covered at high water; on the north side of this spit there is anchorage in 5 fathoms, sandy bottom, about ½ mile from the shore, but no vessel should lie here with any appearance of bad weather.

Beacon.—A beacon has been erected on Minor island, at the extremity of the spit extending from the eastern end of Smith, or Blunt, island.

Light.—On the summit of Smith, or Blunt, island, near the west end, is a lighthouse painted white, with a black lantern, from which, at an elevation of 87 feet above the sea, is exhibited a flashing white light every 30 seconds, visible in clear weather from a distance of 15 miles.

Tidal stream.—The ebb stream here, as in the narrower straits, runs from 2 to 2½ hours after low water.

Directions.—Vessels from sea bound up Rosario strait should steer so as to pass 3 miles southward of Race rocks. When the light bears North (N. 23° W. mag.) steer N. 86° E. (N. 63° E. mag.) for 17 miles; Dungeness light should then bear South (S. 23° E. mag.), distant 5 miles, and Smith Island light N. 73° E. (N. 50° E. mag.), distant 11 miles. From this position steer N. 54° E. (N. 31° E. mag.), passing 3 miles NW. of Smith island and about 1 mile SE. of Davidson rock, off point Colville. At night Burrows Island light should be sighted before Smith island is abeam. After passing Smith island do not bring Burrows Island light to the eastward of N. 44° E. (N. 21° E. mag.) till Smith Island light bears S. 25° W. (S. 2° W. mag.). When on this latter bearing steer N. 25° E. (N. 2° E. mag.), keeping Smith Island light astern This leads fairly into the strait and nearly a mile westward of Burrows island.

If intending to pass southward of Smith island, from the position 5 miles northward of Dungeness light, steer N. 80° E. (N. 57° E. mag.), passing midway between Smith island and Partridge bank. When Partridge point bears S. 7° E. (S. 30° E. mag.), or, at night, Burrows Island light bears N. 16° E. (N. 7° W. mag.), haul up to N. 12° E. (N. 11° W. mag.); this course should lead, as before, nearly 1 mile westward of Burrows island. At night, be careful not to get into the red sector of Burrows Island light, which covers Lawson reef and Dennis rock.

Coming from Puget sound steer for Smith Island light on a N. 18° W. (N. 41° W. mag.) bearing, passing ½ mile outside the bell buoy off Partridge point. When on line between the bell buoy and the black buoy on Partridge bank, change course to N. 12° E. (N.

11° W. mag.), which will lead to a point nearly 1 mile west of Burrows island. At night steer for Smith Island light as before, until Dungeness light bears S. 74° W. (S. 51° W. mag.); then haul up to N. 12° E. (N. 11° W. mag.). On this last course, Burrows Island light should be made a little on the starboard bow.

Those from the southern parts of Vancouver island, bound up Rosario strait, should pass northward of Smith island, avoiding Salmon bank, with 9 feet over it, off the southern end of San Juan, and Davidson rock, off Colville island. Mount Erie (on Fidalgo island) in line with Iceberg, or Jennis, point, bearing N. 82° E. (N. 58° E. mag.), leads 1½ miles south of the former, and it is not recommended to pass the southern side of Lopez island at less than 1 mile distant, which will insure clearing the latter; moreover, the coast is rocky, and the flood stream sets onto it. There are several indentations, with sandy beaches, on the south side of Lopez, which, although offering shelter for boats, are not recommended as anchorages for vessels.

Watmough head (cape Colville), the southeastern extreme of Lopez island, is the western entrance point of Rosario strait; Watmough hill, flat-topped, and about 450 feet high, rises immediately over it.

Colville (Southwest) island, small, bare of trees, and about 40 feet high, lies 1 mile SW. from the cape; close to the cape, and appearing from most points of view a part of it, is Castle island, a high precipitous rock. Entering the strait, Colville island should be given a berth of 1 mile.

Davidson rock, on which is only a depth of 4 feet at low water, occasionally uncovering at low springs, lies a little more than 600 yards S. 67° E. (N. 89° E. mag.) from the east end of Southwest island and nearly 1 mile S. 23° W. (S. 1° E. mag.) of Watmough head; kelp grows about the rock, but the patch is so small that it is difficult to make out. Kellett island, or cape St. Mary, kept open of the extreme of Watmough head, bearing North (N. 24° W. mag.), leads ½ mile to the eastward of the rock, and Eagle point (San Juan) kept open of the south end of Lopez island, bearing N. 64° W. (N. 88° W. mag.), leads 1 mile southward of it.

Buoy.—A black can buoy is moored in 4¼ fathoms immediately eastward of the rock.

A shoal with a least depth of 5¾ fathoms lies 2 miles S. 83° E. (N. 73° E. mag.) from Davidson rock and nearly midway between that rock and Lawson reef.

Kellett island is a small flat-topped islet covered with grass, lying immediately northward of, and close to, the low extreme of Watmough head.

Cape St. Mary, the next point northward of Watmough head, and a little more than 1 mile from it, forms the southern point of Davis bay.

Kellett, or Hulah, ledge, with 1 fathom of water on it, and marked by kelp, lies 600 yards N. 58° E. (N. 34° E. mag.) from cape St. Mary; there is a deep passage between it and the cape. Vessels passing outside it should give the cape a berth of over ½ mile.

Shoal bight (Davis bay).—Shoal bight affords good and convenient anchorage in a moderate depth of water. After rounding Hulah ledge, a vessel may stand to the westward into the bay and anchor in 6 fathoms, mud bottom, at little more than ½ mile from the shore, with cape St. Mary bearing S. 11° E. (S. 35° E. mag.); inside this the water shoals rather suddenly to 2½ and 3 fathoms. A kelp patch, on which there is shoal water, lies 1 mile N. 11° E. (N. 13° W. mag.) from the cape. There is anchorage in from 4 to 8 fathoms anywhere within 1 mile of the east shore of Lopez and Decatur islands, from a little northward of cape St. Mary, as far north as the white cliff of Decatur island, avoiding the kelp patches just mentioned, or while Bird rock bears anything to the northward of S. 67° E. (N. 89° E. mag.), and little tide will be felt. With Lopez (Maury) pass open, bearing N. 67° W. (S. 89° W. mag.), there is good anchorage at from ½ to 1 mile from the shore, in from 6 to 8 fathoms.

Deception pass.—From Partridge point the shore of Whidbey island runs NNE. for 12 miles to Deception pass, which is a narrow channel separating Fidalgo from Whidbey island, and communicating with the waters of Puget sound and Admiralty inlet; but it is only eligible for such small vessels or steamers as are well acquainted with the locality. The tides set through it with great velocity. The pass has been described already under the head of Saratoga passage. Deception island lies in the entrance; its SW. side is shoal.

Light.—A fixed white light is exhibited from the SW. extremity of Fidalgo island.

Lawson reef, on which there is only a depth of 3 fathoms at low water, is a ledge of small extent lying 1$\frac{6}{10}$ miles S. 84° W. (S. 60° W. mag.) from the west point of Deception island at the entrance to Deception pass.

Buoy.—A bell buoy, painted red and black in horizontal stripes, marks the eastern side of the reef.

Allan island is ¾ mile in extent and 230 feet high. Its southern face is bare.

Burrows island, separated from Allan island by a channel ¼ mile wide, is 640 feet high, has a notably flat top, is wooded, and may be seen from the strait of Fuca.

Light.—A fixed white light with a red sector, elevated 57 feet above the water, visible 13 miles, is exhibited from an octagonal lantern with a black roof, surmounting a square, white, two-story, wooden tower, 27 feet high, on the western point of Burrows island. The tower is attached to the western front of the white fog-signal building. Approximate position: Lat. 48° 28′ 34″ N., long. 122° 42′ 36″ W.

The red sector extends from N. 48° W. (N. 72° W. mag.) to N. 10° E. (N. 14° W. mag.), and covers Lawson reef, Dennis shoal, and other dangers lying to the southward of the light station. The light is obscured to the eastward of N. 2° W. (N. 26° W. mag.) and S. 21° W. (S. 3° E. mag.).

Fog signal.—A Daboll trumpet gives blasts of 4 seconds' duration separated by silent intervals alternately of 7 and 25 seconds.

Burrows bay, on the eastern side of the entrance to Rosario strait, is well marked by mount Erie, a remarkable conical hill, rising 1,300 feet immediately over it, at 1 mile from the coast. The bay is sheltered from westerly and southwesterly winds by Burrows and Allan islands, and affords good anchorage to vessels wind or tide bound.

Light.—A fixed white light is exhibited from the end of the wharf in Burrows bay.

Williamson rock, 22 feet above high water, lies in the southern entrance of the bay ½ mile southward of Allan island.

Dennis rock.—There is a deep channel ½ mile wide between Williamson rock and Allan island, but those taking it, or working up westward of the latter island, must avoid Dennis rock, which has 2 feet on it at low water and rarely uncovers. It lies nearly 1,200 yards NW. by N. from Williamson rock, and the same distance westward from the south end of Allan island.

Anchorage may be had in 6 fathoms, with the passage between Burrows and Allan islands open, bearing West (S. 66° W. mag.), ½ mile from Young island; but the most sheltered anchorage is in 12 fathoms at the head of the bay, ½ mile from the eastern shore of Burrows island, with the passage shut in, and Young island bearing SW. ½ S.; if, however, only a temporary anchorage is desired, the former will be found the most convenient.

The eastern shore of the bay is shoal for 600 yards off the beach. About 700 yards NE. from Langley point, the southern point of the bay, is a small, bare rock; and nearly 1 mile NE. by N. from the same point is a bowlder, awash at low water, and lying nearly 800 yards offshore.

Directions.—The best entrance, which is 1 mile wide, is eastward of Williamson rock, between it and Langley point.

Those from the northward may enter Burrows bay by the passage north of Burrows island, or by that between the latter and Allan island; they are about equal in breadth, a little over 400 yards wide at their narrowest part, and run nearly east and west; the latter is the straightest.

Bird rock, lying almost in the center of Rosario strait, nearly 4 miles N. 26° E. (N. 2° E. mag.) of Watmough head, consists of three detached rocks close together, the southernmost being the largest and 30 feet high. There is deep water close to it, but on account of the strong tides, sailing vessels working up or down, particularly during light winds, should give it a berth of ½ mile. There is an equally good passage on either side of the rock; that to the eastward is the wider (2 miles across); to the westward it is 1 mile wide, with somewhat less tide. By taking the latter channel with a leading wind, strangers will more easily avoid Belle rock; passing Bird rock at a convenient distance, steer just outside, or to the eastward of James island, until the passage between Guemes and Fidalgo islands is open.

Belle rock, the most serious danger in Rosario strait, uncovers only near low water, and the tidal streams set over it from 2 to 5 knots. It lies 1,200 yards N. 43° E. (N. 19° E. mag.) from Bird rock, and in the passage between them are depths of 8 to 20 fathoms. Seamen, however, are recommended not to pass between them except in cases of necessity.

Belle rock is easily avoided by day; if passing to the eastward of it, keep Lawrence point (the eastern point of Orcas island) in line with Tide point (the western extreme of Cypress island), bearing North (N. 24° W. mag.), which will lead ½ mile clear of it; when the passage between Guemes and Fidalgo islands is just open, a vessel will be more than 1 mile to the northward of it.

If taking the channel westward of Bird rock, keep that rock well eastward of cape Colville until Guemes channel is open. The great danger of Belle rock to a sailing vessel is being left with a light wind in the center of the strait, as the water is too deep to expect an anchor to hold in so strong a tideway.

Buoy.—A black can buoy, with the words BELLE ROCK on it, is moored in 9 fathoms NNW. of Belle rock. This buoy has occasionally broken adrift.

James island, almost divided in the center, is a remarkable saddle island with a double summit, 250 feet high, lying close off the east side of Decatur island.

White and Black rocks are ¾ mile apart, and lie off the southeastern shore of Blakely island. White rock, the southernmost, is 16 feet above high water, and a little more than ¼ mile from the shore at the eastern entrance of Thatcher pass. Black rock, 14 feet high, lies ¾ mile N. 57° E. (N. 33° E. mag.) of White rock, and ½ mile from Blakely island. There is a deep channel between these rocks, as also between them and Blakely island.

Beacon.—An iron spindle, surmounted by a barrel painted black and white in horizontal stripes, stands on the highest part of Black rock.

Cypress island, northwestward of Fidalgo, forms a portion of the eastern side of Rosario strait. It is 4 miles long by about 2 in breadth and 1,525 feet high; it is thickly wooded with pine and white cedar trees; on its northern extreme, a remarkable, bare, rocky cone rises immediately over the sea to 720 feet. A reef of bowlder stones, some of which uncover, with kelp growing about them, extends ½ mile off Reef point, the SW. point of the island; the outer bowlder covers at half flood.

Between Cypress and Blakely islands is the narrowest part of Rosario strait, being 1⅓ miles across, and here the tidal streams during springs occasionally run between 6 and 7 knots.

Strawberry bay, on the western side of Cypress island, will be known by the small island of the same name, which lies immediately off it, 1¼ miles NNW. from Reef point, and protects the bay from the westward.

Indifferent anchorage may be had in 7 fathoms nearly out of the current, but at certain times of the tide it is difficult of entrance for sailing vessels.

There is a belt of flat marsh land in Strawberry bay, through which several streams of good water run from the mountains.

Rock islet, a small round islet covered with trees, lying nearly 400 yards northward of the north end of Cypress island, has its shores strewn with large bowlders. There is a passage of 8 fathoms of water between it and Cypress island; but the ebb stream sets with great strength to the southward, and, indeed, close round the western points of the latter island.

Cypress reef, lying northwestward of Rock islet, is a dangerous, rocky patch, the southern part uncovering at half ebb, with kelp growing about it; from the southern point it extends northward for upward of 600 yards with depths of 9 to 15 feet.

Buckeye shoal, of small extent, with a least depth of 4 fathoms over it, lies 1,800 yards N. 40° W. (N. 64° W. mag.) from Rock islet.

The SE. end of James island, well open of Tide point (the western point of Cypress island), bearing S. 12° W. (S. 12° E. mag.), leads westward of Cypress reef and Buckeye shoal.

Sinclair island, thickly wooded and comparatively low, lies to the northeastward of Cypress island, with a deep passage of nearly 1 mile in breadth between them, leading to Bellingham channel. Shelving rocks project a short distance off its western shores.

Bowlder reef (Panama reef), an extensive and dangerous shoal, extends nearly ½ mile in a northwestern direction from the NW. side of Sinclair island, some parts of it uncovering at half tide; a large bowlder stands on the inner part of the reef. Great quantities of kelp grow in the neighborhood, but it is sometimes run under by the tide or concealed by the rips; there is 6 fathoms of water close to the edge of the kelp. By keeping Cypress cone open to the westward of Rock islet, or the strait between Cypress and Blakely islands well open, vessels will clear it in passing up and down; and Vendovi and Barnes islands in line leads clear to the northward and eastward of it.

Buoy.—A red nun buoy is moored northward of the reef in 12 fathoms of water.

Lydia shoal, of small extent, with a least depth of 3¾ fathoms, lies on the western side of Rosario strait and in the approach to Obstruction passes. The shoal is 1 mile N. 81° E. (N. 57° E. mag.) from Obstruction Passes light.

The Peapods are two small rocky islets, bare of trees, lying ½ mile from the western shore of Rosario strait, and from 1¼ to nearly 2 miles southward from Lawrence point. They are ¾ mile apart in a NE. and SW. direction, the northernmost being the larger and higher. A little to the westward of a line drawn between them is a third rock which just covers at high water. There is a passage 20 fathoms deep between them and Orcas island.

The eastern side of Orcas island between the Peapod islets and Obstruction passes, falls back in a bight, where there is considerably less current than in the main portion of the strait, and, if necessary, vessels may anchor within ½ mile of the shore in about 16 fathoms of water.

Light.—A fixed white light is shown from the northern Peapod rock at a height of 25 feet.

Lawrence point, the eastern extreme of Orcas, is a long sloping point; immediately on its north side it rises abruptly in almost perpendicular cliffs, and trends to the westward, falling back for 3 miles in a somewhat deep bight, which is rocky, has deep water, and is unsheltered.

To the northward, Rosario strait lies between Orcas and Lummi islands, the direct channel being along the western shore of the latter. Anchorage may be had, if necessary, on the eastern side of the strait, within 1 mile of the shore, in 15 fathoms, between Sandy and Whitehorn points, northward of Lummi island.

Tides.—After passing northward of Lawrence point, the ebb tide sets to the eastward between Orcas and the small islands to the northward of it, as well as to the SE. through the northern entrance of the strait. When in the vicinity of Alden bank, or about 8 miles above

Lawrence point, the strength of the tide sensibly decreases, and while vessels are eastward of a line between this bank and Roberts point they will be entirely out of the strong tides of the archipelago and the strait of Georgia. It is recommended with the ebb tide to work up on this shore.

Lummi island is 8 miles long and very narrow. On its southwestern side it is high and precipitous, a remarkable mountain rising about 1,500 feet abruptly from the sea; a small, high, double, rocky islet, Lummi rock, lies close off the shore, 3 miles from its southern point; foul ground extends from its northwestern point in a NW. direction for more than ½ mile; and at about 1,600 yards SW. of Carter point lies Viti rocks. A reef extends 600 yards from this rock in a southeasterly direction.

Rock—Buoy.—A rock with a depth of 12 feet over it lies about ¾ mile N. 39° W. (N. 63° W. mag.) from Migley point. This rock is marked by a nun buoy, red and black horizontal stripes, moored in 6 fathoms.

Lummi bay, on the mainland, opposite Migley point, is almost entirely filled with flats, which dry at low water. The land at the head of the bay is marshy, being the delta of the river Lummi. Sandy point, the northern entrance point of the bay, is low and grassy with a few bushes on it.

Clark and Barnes islands are two small wooded islands 2 miles NW. of Lawrence point; two smaller islets, the Sisters, bare of trees, and a high rock, lie immediately southward of Clark island. There is a passage 1½ miles in breadth between these islands and Orcas with a depth of 45 fathoms; there is also a narrow channel with a depth of 20 fathoms between Clark and Barnes islands, which a vessel may take if necessary.

The currents set strongly about the Sisters, and the best and most direct channel is between Clark and Lummi islands. When taking this channel the north point of Lummi island should not be approached within 1 mile, as shoal and broken ground extends for some distance off it; Sinclair island kept just open westward of the NW. point of Lummi leads to the westward of this foul ground in 15 fathoms of water, and when the east end of Matia island, or Puffin islet close off it, is in line with the NW. point of Orcas island (Bill of Orcas) bearing S. 68° W. (S. 44° W. mag.), a vessel will be northward of it.

Matia island, 3 miles NW. from Clark island, is 1 mile in length east and west, moderately high and wooded, and has some coves on its southern side affording shelter for boats; close off its east point is Puffin islet, and lying a short distance eastward of the islet is a flat rock which covers. Those bound through Rosario strait are recommended to pass eastward of Matia.

Alden bank, 3 miles in extent north and south and 1 mile east and west, lies in the center of the northern entrance of Rosario strait; its southern limit is 2 miles north of Matia island, and there is a channel 3 miles in breadth between it and the eastern shore.

The depth of water on this bank varies from 2¼ to 7 fathoms; the bottom is in some parts rocky, with patches of kelp growing on it; in other parts it is sandy, and offers a convenient anchorage for vessels becalmed or waiting for tide. It frequently happens that a vessel, having passed to the northward between East point and Patos island, meets the ebb tide and is carried to the eastward; in such a case it would be desirable to anchor in 7 or 8 fathoms on Alden bank, and thus avoid being set down Rosario strait.

The shoalest part, 16 to 17 feet, covering a considerable area, lies about 3 miles north of Matia island.

Buoy.—A can buoy, painted red and black in horizontal stripes, is moored near the shoalest part of the bank, and should be given a berth of 1 mile.

The position of the bank is well indicated by numerous fish traps and weirs, which are visible for some distance.

Vessels passing up or down are recommended to pass on the eastern side of the bank; mount Constitution on Orcas island kept just open eastward of Puffin islet, bearing S. 9° W. (S. 15° E. mag.), leads over the eastern edge of the bank in 13 fathoms; and the low, west point of Patos island in line with Monarch head (Saturna island), bearing S. 74° W. (S. 50° W. mag.), leads over the northern edge in 7 fathoms.

Directions.—Standing into Rosario strait, pass ¾ to 1 mile westward of Burrows island and bring Burrows Island light to bear S. 16° E. (S. 40° E. mag.). Then steer N. 16° W. (N. 40° W. mag.), keeping Burrows Island light astern. This course leads midway between Strawberry and Blakely islands. When Obstruction Pass Rocks beacon bears West (S. 66° W. mag.), or, if at night, Obstruction Passes light bears N. 71° W. (S. 85° W. mag.), change to N. 20° E. (N. 4° W. mag.); pass about ¼ to ½ mile eastward of North Peapod (marked by a white light). When abreast of Lawrence point—at night, when East Point light is made northward of Lawrence point—bring Cypress cone to bear S. 8° E. (S. 32° E. mag.) and keep it on this bearing astern, passing nearly midway between Village point and the Sisters. Steer N. 8° W. (N. 32° W. mag.) until Monarch head (Saturna island) is just open north of Patos island, or East Point light bears S. 77° W. (S. 53° W. mag.), when a course may be laid up Georgia strait in safety.

Bellingham channel, between Guemes and Cypress islands, is about 3½ miles long and ¾ mile wide in its narrowest part, between East point and Guemes island. Abreast the northern end of Guemes island, which is a steep bluff called Clark point and on the western side of the channel, are several small, high, wooded islets, called the Cone islets. Should the wind be light and the tide flood, pass close to Clark point to avoid being set past Sinclair island.

Guemes channel, south of Guemes island, leads into Padilla bay and eastward of the island to Bellingham bay. At the western entrance, on the southern shore, is Ship harbor.

Shannon point—Buoy.—Shannon point, the southern point at the western entrance, is low and rounding; a rocky shoal, marked by a red nun buoy at its northern extremity, extends 200 yards northward from the point.

City of Seattle rock.—This rock has 9 feet of water over it, and lies about 200 yards from the southern shore of the channel, about 2 miles eastward of Shannon point.

Anacortes is a small town at the eastern end of Guemes channel, on the south shore, at its juncture with Padilla bay. The main industry is the canning of salmon; some lumber is exported. There are several wharves with depths alongside varying from 12 to 20 feet. Water and a limited amount of supplies can be obtained. Communication is by daily steamers, rail, and telegraph. Anchorage may be had off the wharves in 10 to 12 fathoms.

Padilla bay, between the NE. side of Fidalgo island, Guemes island, and the mainland, is largely filled with flats, the greater portion of which dries at low water. Entrance to the bay may be had either by Guemes channel or from Bellingham bay, eastward of Guemes island. William point, the northern point of the bay, is about 100 feet high and wooded; owing to the low land behind it, it generally appears as an island.

From William point, flats and shoals forming the eastern side of the northern channel extend southward to Saddlebag, Dot, and Hat islands, which lie about 1 mile eastward of the eastern point of Guemes island.

Huckleberry island, small and low, lies nearly in mid-channel between Guemes and Saddlebag islands.

Fidalgo bay lies westward of March point; it is shoal nearly to its mouth.

Lights.—Fixed white lights are shown from March and William points.

Bellingham bay.—The general direction of this bay is north and south; it is 4 miles wide and 14 miles long, including the broad flats at either end. The depths over the greater portion of the bay vary from 6 to 15 fathoms. The holding ground is not good, and in southeasterly weather vessels frequently drag.

In the southeastern part is Samish bay, with flats that dry for a long distance at low water. Chuckanut bay, on the eastern side, is a small cove affording shelter to small vessels.

In the northeastern corner of the bay is situated the town of Bellingham. There are coal mines in the vicinity, but the supply of coal is small and its quality poor. Provisions and water can be obtained; repairs to wooden vessels, and limited repairs to machinery, can be made. Communication is by steamers and by rail.

The depths at the wharves vary from 12 to 27 feet.

Vendovi island, about ½ mile in extent and 330 feet high, lies in the middle of the approach to Bellingham bay and 1½ miles south of Lummi island. Nearly midway between Vendovi and the northwestern end of Guemes island is a shoal with 4¼ to 5½ fathoms; this should be avoided by deep-draft vessels.

Eliza island, abreast the southeastern end of Lummi island, is 2¼ miles SSE. of point Frances. Between these two runs a shoal bar with depths of from 4½ fathoms to 8 feet.

Buoys.—A can buoy, red and black horizontal stripes, is moored close southward of the 8-foot spot. When passing to the northward of this buoy give it a berth of ½ mile.

A red spar buoy marks the end of the spit extending from Frances point.

Starr rock, with 6 feet over it, lies about 250 yards offshore a little northward of the sawmill wharf in the southern portion of Bellingham.

Buoy.—Starr rock is marked by a red nun buoy moored close westward of the rock; vessels should not pass eastward of the buoy.

Hale passage, between Lummi island and the mainland, is about 6 miles long with an average width of ¾ mile. There is a bar across the NW. end of the passage with 13 feet of water over it. Toward the SE. end the spit westward of Frances point is marked by a red nun buoy.

Submarine cable.—A submarine cable is laid between Lummi island and the mainland across Hale passage.

Light.—A fixed white light is exhibited, at an elevation of 27 feet, from a white post on Lummi point on the eastern side of Lummi island, 1½ miles southeastward of point Migley.

The passage is available for a draft of about 15 feet at high water; it is used mainly by vessels with local knowledge.

Directions.—The usual route is through Bellingham channel and northward of Vendovi island; a mid-channel course is all that is required, but deep-draft vessels must be careful not to set onto the bank between Guemes and Vendovi islands, on which there is a shoal of 4¼ fathoms. Yellow bluff on the SW. shore of Guemes island should be given a wide berth to clear the foul ground extending off it.

With strong flood tide and clear weather, vessels bound to Bellingham bay from the south use Guemes channel instead of Bellingham channel, and, rounding the SE. point of Guemes island at a distance of ¼ mile, proceed between Huckleberry and Saddlebag islands; then steer northwestward toward Vendovi island, to avoid the bank extending southward from William point; when abreast of the latter point alter course into the bay.

From the northward, vessels pass between Viti rocks and Carter point, the SE. point of Lummi island.

Small vessels use Hale passage, crossing the bar at its northwestern end, on which there is a least depth of 13 feet at low water, and proceeding in mid-channel pass close southward of the red spar buoy off Frances point into Bellingham bay.

Whitehorn point is a remarkable, bold bluff about 150 feet high, its face showing as a steep, white, clay cliff. It is the southern point of Birch bay, and is 9 miles NNW. of the northern point of Lummi island.

Anchorage may be had, if necessary, on the eastern side of Rosario strait, within 1 mile of the shore, in 15 fathoms, between Sandy and Whitehorn points, northward of Lummi island.

Birch bay is between Whitehorn point and Birch point (South bluff); the latter, which is a moderately high, rounding point, forms the north entrance point of the bay; some large bowlder stones stand a short distance off it, and it should not be rounded at a less distance than ½ mile. The bay is nearly 2 miles in breadth at a distance of 1 mile inside the entrance points; the head of the bay dries off a considerable distance at low water, and the 3-fathom curve extends 1½ miles offshore in the center of the bay. The holding ground is good, and with SE. gales it affords excellent shelter. A good berth is in 4 fathoms, with Whitehorn point bearing S. 23° W. (S. 1° E. mag.), distant 1 mile; the water shoals gradually from 14 fathoms at 1 mile off to 6 fathoms between the entrance points; inside this line, 4 fathoms only will be found for a farther distance of 1 mile toward the head of the bay.

Semiahmoo bay, between Birch point (South bluff) and Kwomais point (North bluff), affords good anchorage in from 6 to 8 fathoms water, at about 1½ to 2 miles distance outside Drayton harbor entrance; a good berth is in 6 fathoms, mud bottom, with Birch point bearing S. 12° W. (S. 12° E. mag.) and Tongue point bearing S. 78° E. (N. 78° E. mag.). This is always good anchorage, unless with a heavy SW. gale, when vessels might take shelter in Drayton harbor, with which it is connected by a narrow channel.

Fishing stakes fringe the shore; some extend into 11 fathoms and are marked by a white light. The southeastern side of the harbor is shoal for a distance of ¼ to ½ mile.

The edge of this shoal is marked by a red buoy moored about ⅓ mile SW. by S. from Semiahmoo light.

Light.—To the westward of Tongue point, Semiahmoo bay, a fixed red light, elevated 42 feet above high water and visible 11¾ miles, is exhibited from a white, pile structure, with brown roof, erected in 3 feet of water in a position about ⅜ mile westward of Tongue point. the light is obscured between the bearings NNE. and WNW.

Fog signal.—A trumpet worked by compressed air gives blasts of 3 seconds' duration separated by silent intervals alternately of 4 and 20 seconds.

Drayton harbor, 3½ miles NE. by N. from Birch point, is formed by a low, narrow spit over 1 mile long. The spit is covered with grass and drift timber, and a few pines grow on it.

The basin inclosed by the spit is about 2 miles in diameter, but flats, which uncover at low water, occupy a large area in the southern and eastern parts of the harbor. The entrance is about ¾ mile wide, but the navigable channel is contracted to a width of 300 yards by flats, which extend from the eastern shore and dry at low water. Blaine is situated on the eastern shore, from which several wharves extend to the edge of the flats. Several sawmills and other buildings, constituting the town of Semiahmoo, are on the end of the sand spit.

Lumber and salmon are the principal exports. Provisions and water can be obtained, but little coal. Communication is by rail and steamer; there are telegraph and telephone facilities.

The depths in the channel vary from 4½ to 12 fathoms; inside are depths of 4 to 7 fathoms, mud bottom. Springs rise 13 feet.

Directions.—Outside of Tongue spit a bank extends a considerable distance; do not approach the spit within ¾ mile until its extreme point bears S. 69° E. (N. 87° E. mag.), when it may be steered for and passed close-to. The channel is narrow, and no one unacquainted with the locality should enter without a pilot.

Boundary bay is an extensive sheet of water between Roberts point on the west and Kwomais point (North bluff) on the east. The bay extends in a northerly direction for nearly 5 miles, and is only separated from the southern bank of Fraser river by a low delta 3 miles across, intersected by streams and swamps; it is very shallow and dries off for a distance of 3 miles at low water; the edge of the bank in 3 fathoms of water extends 4½ miles off the whole of the northern shore of the bay.

Vessels should never stand so far to the northward as to bring the white bluff of Roberts point to bear to the southward of S. 79° W. (S. 55° W. mag.), which line of bearing leads more than ½ mile outside the shoal edge of the bank; the general depth of water outside this line is from 7 to 15 fathoms, good holding ground, but this anchorage is exposed to all southerly winds, which send in a considerable sea.

Fishing stakes fringe the shore; some extend into 11 fathoms, and are marked by a white light.

Mud bay.—The NE. part of Boundary bay is a mud flat, dry at low water. Pile beacons have been erected to mark shallow channels through the banks. The beacons consist of three piles braced together, and are painted as buoys for similar positions would be colored. The three principal channels are Big slue, the Serpentine, and Nicomeckl river. These have a common outlet immediately west of Blackie spit at the mouth of Nicomeckl river.

To reach the outermost pile vessels should round Roberts point at a distance of 2 miles and steer about NNE. until the white cliff on the east side of Roberts point, the vessel, and four trees on Blackie spit are in line; then steer with the trees ahead and the white cliff astern; this gives a depth of 2¼ to 2½ fathoms at high water. Then run along the west side of Blackie spit, 100 yards from shore, to the outermost black beacon.

The three channels are marked by thirty black, eight red, and one black and red banded, piles, the last named marking the junction of the Big slue and Serpentine.

Big slue dries completely, the Serpentine varies in depth from 2 to 6 feet, and Nicomeckl river from 1½ to 4 feet at low water springs.

Roberts point is the termination of a remarkable promontory which stretches southward from the delta of Fraser river; the eastern point of the promontory is a remarkable, white cliff, 200 feet high, its summit crowned with trees; from it the land gradually falls westward and terminates in Roberts spit, a low shingle point, back of which is a small space of level, clear land.

From the spit the coast trends northward with bluff shores of moderate height for 3½ miles, when it merges into the swampy delta of the Fraser. From most points of view, and particularly from the southward, Roberts point presents the appearance of an island; shoal water and rocky, irregular bottom, on which kelp grows in summer, extends for more than 1 mile SE. from the point, and it is recommended to give it a berth of 2 miles.

Boundary mark.—There is a granite monument, 25 feet high, erected on the summit of Boundary bluff, which is only just visible from the anchorage on account of the trees; it marks the boundary between the British and United States possessions, or the forty-ninth parallel of north latitude.

Anchorage will be found on either side of the promontory; to the eastward in 9 fathoms, sandy bottom, with the extreme of the white cliff bearing West (S. 66° W. mag.), distant 1½ miles, and

Roberts spit, the western termination of the promontory, just shut in by the white cliff. To the westward of the spit there is fair anchorage in 8 fathoms, good holding ground, with the spit extreme distant 1 mile, bearing S. 39° E. (S. 63° E. mag.), and Boundary bluff, or the monument on its summit, N. 23° E. (N. 1° W. mag.); here the edge of the bank is distant ¼ mile, and vessels should not anchor any farther to the northward, as Roberts bank trends rapidly to the westward.

Directions.—Vessels should feel their way by the lead cautiously into this anchorage; the bank is very steep outside, and shoals suddenly within.

Ships should not lie at this anchorage with strong southerly or westerly winds, but should shift round to the eastern one, or to Semiahmoo bay, and give the southern face of Roberts point a berth of 2 miles in rounding it; neither of the anchorages at Roberts point can be considered as more than stopping places, and during winter vessels should be prepared to weigh at short warning.

Roberts bank, formed by the alluvial deposits of Fraser river, extends from Roberts spit NW. by W. for 9½ miles, to the Sand heads, and at this point is 5 miles from the shore; it then takes a northerly direction for a farther distance of 12 miles, joining Grey point. The portion of the bank northward of Fraser river is named Sturgeon bank; it is steep-to, there being depths of from 60 to 70 fathoms at 1 mile from its edge, shoaling suddenly to 20, and then to 2 fathoms.

Two black beacons, 12 feet above high water, mark the edge of Roberts bank, but these are liable to be washed away.

Georgia strait.—Having passed out of Juan de Fuca strait by either of the channels before described, when northwestward of a line drawn between East point (Saturna island) and Whitehorn point (mainland) a vessel may be considered in Georgia strait.

Caution—Buoys and beacons.—In consequence of the steepness of the shores and rapidity of tidal streams, buoys and beacons in Georgia strait are liable to be swept away, and should not therefore be implicitly relied on.

General remarks.—To those bound from sea, or from any of the southern ports of Vancouver island, to Georgia strait, Haro channel is preferable, while to reach the same destination from Admiralty inlet or Puget sound, Rosario strait is the most direct and desirable. Having traversed either channel, the promontory of Roberts point will be seen, appearing as an island.

The dangers to be avoided when working through Georgia strait are, on the northern shore, Roberts and Sturgeon banks; and on the southern, the neighborhood of East point and Tumbo island and the coasts of Saturna and Mayne islands, until beyond the entrance of

Active pass. A chain of reefs and rocky islets lies parallel with this shore, in places extending nearly 1 mile off, and the bottom is rocky and irregular, with strong currents.

Extending 1 mile eastward from the east end of Tumbo island is a ledge of foul, rocky ground, over which there are very heavy tide rips and dangerous overfalls.

Buoy.—A large can buoy surmounted by a cage, the whole painted black, moored in 12 fathoms of water 1¼ miles N. 27° E. (N. 3° E. mag.) from Saturna Island lighthouse, marks the extreme of the reef. About 400 feet inshore of the buoy is a small patch of 2 fathoms, marked by kelp, and known as Rosenfelt reef.

At ¾ mile N. 62° E. (N. 38° E. mag.) from Race point is a rocky patch of 5 fathoms, about 400 yards in extent; and at about 200 yards to the northwestward of this patch there is a rock with only 14 feet of water on it, possibly a shoal head of the 5-fathom patch. This rock lies ¾ mile N. 43° E. (N. 19° E. mag.) from Race point. Orcas knob kept well open to the eastward of the east point of Waldron island, bearing S. 3° E. (S. 27° E. mag.), leads in the fairway between Saturna and Patos islands, 1¼ miles eastward of the rock; and Toe point (Patos island), in line with the north extreme of Sucia island, bearing S. 64° E. (S. 88° E. mag.), leads nearly ¾ mile to the northward of it.

A rock lies 300 yards S. 56° E. (S. 80° E. mag.) of Edith point, Mayne island. The least depth on it is 2 feet, with irregular soundings around.

Caution.—As before observed, vessels should when possible pass midway between Saturna and Patos islands; they should on no account give the east point of Tumbo island a berth of less than 1½ miles, and are recommended not to approach the northern shores of the islands lying between Haro strait and Active pass within a distance of 2 miles, and they are strongly urged to adhere strictly to this advice.

The light on Georgina point, at the entrance to Active pass, becomes obscured when bearing to the northward of N. 73° W. (S. 83° W. mag.), and it should be borne in mind that during the night while this light is in sight all the dangers off the northern shores of the above islands will be avoided.

It should also be remembered that the ebb sets to the SW., through Active pass, and that tide races occur in its northern entrance. Roberts bank is easily avoided. The extreme of Roberts spit, or the tangent of the high trees immediately within it, should not be brought to bear to the southward of S. 67° E. (N. 89° E. mag.). If the weather is thick, when 50 fathoms is struck, vessels will be getting very near the edge.

The tides, although not nearly so strong as in the Haro archipelago, yet run with considerable strength (3 knots), particularly during the freshets of summer, when the Fraser river discharges an immense volume of fresh water, which takes a southerly direction over the banks almost straight for the entrance to Active pass. This peculiar milky-colored water is frequently carried quite across the strait, and is sometimes seen in the inner channels along the shores of Vancouver island; at other times it reaches the center of the channel only, forming a remarkable and most striking contrast with the deep-blue waters of the strait of Georgia.

Below the mouth of the Fraser, the tide is rather the stronger on the southern shore. On the northern side, within the line between Roberts and Sandy points, scarcely any tide is felt; during the ebb vessels will gain by working up on that shore, where good anchorage can also be found, if necessary.

Allowance must be made for the tide; this is not difficult after having once entered the strait of Georgia by daylight and noted which tide is running. In the center of the strait above Saturna and Patos islands the strength of the tide varies from 1 to 3 knots, seldom more, unless close to the island shores, which are swept by the rapid currents out of Gabriola, Porlier, and Active passes. Above the mouth of the Fraser there is still less current and plenty of sea room, the breadth of the strait being nearly 15 miles.

Fraser river, in point of magnitude and commercial importance, is second only to Columbia river on the northwest coast of the United States. In its freedom from risk of life and shipwreck it possesses infinite advantages over any other river on the coast, and the cause of this immunity from the dangers and inconveniences to which all great rivers emptying on an exposed coast are subject is sufficiently obvious. A sheltered strait, scarcely 15 miles across, receives its waters, and the neighboring island (Vancouver) serves as a natural breakwater, preventing the possibility of any sea arising which would prove dangerous to vessels even of the smallest class, unless they ground.

The river, with its numerous tributaries, has its rise in the Rocky mountains, between 400 and 500 miles from the coast in a northerly direction, whence it forces its way in torrents and rapids through one of the many great parallel valleys which intersect this region, confined by gigantic mountains, with large tracts of country rich in agricultural resources on either side of them, until it reaches the town of Hope, which is about 80 miles, by the windings of the river, in an easterly direction from its entrance.

Above the city of Lytton, which stands at the fork or confluence of Fraser and Thompson rivers, 55 miles above Hope, many rich deltas occur, or, as they are termed by the miners, bars, and among these, known as the wet diggings, gold was first discovered in British Columbia.

Midway between Langley and Hope, Harrison river falls into the Fraser, and by it and a long chain of lakes extending in a general NW. direction a comparatively easy route has been established, by which the upper Fraser is reached at a point just below Bridge river, in the heart of the gold regions. Considerable attention has been attracted to the sulphur springs (temperature 164° F.) of Harrison river.

Navigable depths.—The old channel, southward of the Sand Head lighthouse, is entirely closed. The entrance to the present channel is 1¾ miles northwestward of the lighthouse, and as dams and training walls have been erected, it is considered probable that the direction of and depth in the channel will be maintained. As changes may occur, the following information and directions should be used with caution:

The least depth to be passed over between Georgia strait and New Westminster is about 12 feet at low water and 22 feet at high water springs, situated southward of English's cannery, about 5½ miles within the entrance.

Vessels of 14 feet draft can proceed as high as Langley with ease, provided they have, or are assisted by, steam power, and are acquainted with the existing deep-water channel, which, it should be remembered, is subject to change. It must be remembered, however, that the tidal streams of Georgia strait sweep across the channel of the entrance, and to those in a large ship it is recommended to enter or leave with the last quarter of the flood.

Steamers of light draft reach Hope, and even the town of Yale, 15 miles above it, during from 6 to 9 months of the year. In June, July, and August the melting of the snow causes so rapid a downward stream that vessels even of high steam power are rarely able to stem it, and during these months numbers of large trees are brought down from the flooded banks, which offer another serious obstruction to navigation. Between Hope and Langley, the latter 30 miles from the river's mouth, there is always a considerable strength of current, from 4 to 7 knots, at times more; but at Langley the river becomes a broad, deep, and placid stream, and except during the three summer months the influence of the flood stream is generally felt, and vessels of any draft may conveniently anchor. The depth is 10 fathoms; the current not above 3 knots.

Pilots can be obtained at Skunk cove, Burrard inlet, or at Victoria.

Lights.—A lightvessel, moored near the Sand heads, at the main entrance to Fraser river, shows two fixed white lights, one at each of her two mastheads. These lights are 29 feet apart, 56 feet above the water, and visible 13 miles.

The vessel is of wood with two masts and no bowsprit. She is painted red, with the words SAND HEADS in white on the forward bulwarks; her bottom is coppered, and her upper works are painted light gray.

Approximate position: Lat. 49° 06′ 55″ N., long. 123° 18′ 08″ W.

Fog signal.—In thick or foggy weather a bell is struck by machinery once every 10 seconds.

River entrance lights.—From a square, white, wooden tower standing on piles, erected on the sands on the south side of the river, and situated with Garry Point lighthouse bearing N. 65° E. (N. 41° E. mag.), distant $3\frac{1}{10}$ miles, is exhibited a fixed light, white from October 1 to June 30, red from July 1 to September 30; it is unwatched.

A light similar in every respect is shown from a square, white, wooden tower, erected on the southwestern end of a dam constructed on the northern side of the river, and situated with Garry Point lighthouse bearing S. 83° E. (N. 73° E. mag.), distant $1\frac{6}{10}$ miles; it is unwatched.

These lights are 22 feet above high water and visible 9 miles in clear weather. They are moved without notice whenever necessary on account of scouring of the channel.

Garry point—Fishing light.—The northern entrance point of the Fraser river is low. From the platform of the tide-gauge house, 300 yards westward of the point, is exhibited, for the benefit of fishing vessels, a fixed red light, 22 feet above water and visible 6 miles.

Rise and fall of the river.—The river is at its lowest stage during the months of January, February, and March. In April it commences to rise from the melting of the snow, and is perhaps 2 feet above its lowest level; the flood stream is strong enough to swing a ship at New Westminster up to the end of this month. In May the water rises rapidly; the river is at its highest about the end of June, and remains up with trifling fluctuations until the end of July or middle of August. During these six weeks the banks are overflowed, and extensive plains above Langley covered for a space of several miles, the strength of the stream between Langley and Hope being from 4 to 7 knots, and in the narrow parts even more. The usual rise of the river at Langley due to these floods is about 14 feet, but it has been known to reach 25 feet.

From the middle to the end of August the waters begin to subside, and in September the stream is not inconveniently strong. September, October, and November are favorable months for the river navigation, as the water is then sufficiently high to reach Hope, and the strength of the current considerably abated. The shallow stern-wheel steamers have reached Hope as late as December; between this month and April, owing to the shoalness of the water and the great quantity of ice formed, navigation, even by these vessels, drawing only 18 inches, is attended with great difficulty and rarely practicable at all. The snags or drift trees which become embedded in the river also form a serious obstacle to navigation at this season.

In April the steamers commence again to run; in June, July, and August the rapidity of the current is the great obstacle, but these high-pressure vessels, commanding a speed of 11 and 12 knots, frequently accomplish the voyage, though at much risk.

Buoys and beacons.—A black beacon with ball lies 4⅜ miles S. 66° W. (S. 42° W. mag.), and a similar beacon with drum 5¼ miles S. 25° W. (S. 1° W. mag), from Garry Point lighthouse, marking the edge of Roberts bank.

A bell buoy, painted red, is moored in 15 fathoms near the extreme western edge of Roberts bank; it lies 1 mile S. 2° W. (S. 22° E. mag.) from Fraser River lightship.

The channel into the river is shown by red buoys on the south side and black buoys on the north. A steel conical buoy, painted in black and white checkers, is moored off Steveston to mark the bar on the northern side of the main channel. A white beacon is placed on the east side of Westham island, on the south bank of the river, 2¼ miles within Garry point; and a small spar buoy marks the south side of the channel (Woodward slough) eastward of the beacon.

The beacons in this river are liable to be washed away. The buoys are shifted when there is any alteration in the channel.

Tide gauges are placed on the northern side of the entrance channel 300 yards westward of Garry point, and on the east side of Annacis island, nearly 1 mile from the north end.

Tides.—It is high water, full and change, at Fraser river entrance at 5 h. 0 m.; springs rise 7 to 10 feet.

The time of high water is about 2 to 3 hours later at New Westminster than at the entrance of the river, and the rise and fall due to tidal causes at springs is 6 feet, and at Langley scarcely perceptible. There are nearly always two tides in the lunar day.

The state of the weather in Georgia strait, the rains, and the amount of water in the river, affect the tides. Vessels will seldom swing to the flood stream until October, the change of tide at other times being shown by a decrease in strength of the ebb or down stream. In September the ebb has been observed to run 3 or 4 knots and the flood 1½ knots, the water being quite fresh.

Ice.—The river is very seldom frozen over at New Westminster, but loose pieces of ice come down the river in the early spring.

Directions.—Coming from the northward, Passage island at the entrance of Howe sound, kept in line, or just open eastward of a remarkable peak on Anvil island within the sound, bearing N. 3° E. (N. 21° W. mag.), leads 1½ miles clear of the edge of Sturgeon bank.

The lightship moored off the Heads enables a vessel to pick up the entrance to the channel. Owing to the frequent changes in the channels of the Fraser river, pilots must be employed; written directions can not be given.

Bridge.—A bridge spans the river about 200 yards to the northward of Brownsville jetty. It has a swinging section to allow the passage of vessels up and down the river.

A fixed red light is exhibited at the hinge, and another at the movable end of each span, the latter being obscured when the span is shut, but visible immediately over the light at the hinge when the span is open for vessels to pass. A fixed green light, visible downstream only, is exhibited at the south end of the south opening, and a fixed green light, visible upstream only, at the north end of the north opening.

Vessels must always pass through the opening which is on their starboard hand, between the green and red lights, and only when the span is completely open, that is, when the movable end of the span appears in line with the hinge, or at night when the two red lights are seen to be vertical.

Steveston, situated on the north bank of the Fraser river, about ½ mile eastward of Garry point, extends along the bank of the river about 1 mile. There are extensive canneries and wharves; large vessels can lie alongside the latter at all stages of the tide. Steveston is the center of the canning industry of the Fraser river.

Port Guichon, on the mainland, on the south bank of the river at the northern entrance to Canoe pass, is the terminal on the mainland of the Victoria terminal railroad, which connects with the Great Northern railroad.

A daily steamer runs from Sidney, Vancouver island, to Port Guichon, connection being made at both places with the Victoria terminal railroad. Laden freight cars are transported by this steamer.

New Westminster stands on the north or right bank of Fraser river, just above the junction of North fork, and 15 miles in a general northeasterly direction from the entrance proper. It occupies a commanding and well-chosen position, being within an easy distance of the entrance and having great facilities for wharfage along its water front, a good depth of water, and excellent anchorage.

Vessels moor abreast New Westminster in mid-channel, where the depth is 6½ to 7 fathoms, sand and mud bottom.

17203——15

The town is connected with Vancouver city by electric tramway, and with the Canadian Pacific railroad by a branch line; it is connected with Seattle by the Great Northern railroad, the terminus being on the opposite side of the river at Brownsville.

In 1901 the population of New Westminster was 6,499.

Supplies of all descriptions are readily obtained, and salmon in abundance in the season. There are not many facilities for repairs to shipping and machinery.

Coal can be obtained. About 500 tons are usually kept in stock, but any quantity can be procured at short notice. Vessels can coal from barges, or they can go alongside a wharf, which extends into a depth of 20 feet at low water.

Pitt river.—At 5 miles eastward of New Westminster is the entrance to Pitt river, which trends in a general northeasterly direction for 11 miles, terminating in a remarkable lake inclosed between almost perpendicular mountains, and navigable (for those that can pass the railway bridge) to the head of the lake, a total distance of 28 miles, by vessels of 14 feet draft, the depth in places being far too great for anchorage. A large tract of low grass land lies on both sides of the entrance of the river, which, however, is generally overflowed, or partially so, during 6 weeks of summer.

Derby or New Langley.—The landing place at Fort Langley, is 12 miles above New Westminster in an easterly direction, on the south or opposite side of the river; the channel between is deep, and there are no impediments to navigation. This spot was first selected as the capital, and as a town site it is unobjectionable, having a considerable tract of good cleared land in its neighborhood, and all the requirements of a commercial port; the depth of water here is 10 fathoms. Vessels may proceed with ease 7 miles beyond Langley; the navigation then becomes somewhat intricate, and the current too rapid for any vessels but steamers of light draft and great power.

North arm is another entrance to the Fraser, navigable for vessels of light draft at high water, and is generally used by the natives proceeding to or from Burrard inlet. Its junction with the main stream occurs immediately below New Westminster, whence it runs in a westerly direction, and enters Georgia strait through Sturgeon bank, about 5 miles northward of the Sand heads; two low, partially wooded islands (Sea and Iona islands) lie in its entrance, and split the channel into three arms.

In many parts of North arm the water is deep, in holes, and the bottom irregular, the depth in some places being not more than 2 feet. It can only be considered a boat channel.

Beacon lights.—Two small, square, wooden towers, painted white, erected on piles, are situated in the north fork of North arm,

Fraser river entrance, at distances respectively of 1 mile S. 32° E. (S. 56° E. mag.) and $2\frac{4}{10}$ miles S. 50° E. (S. 74° E. mag.) from point No Point. A fixed white light (dioptric, unwatched), 20 feet above high water, visible 9 miles, is exhibited from each of these towers.

Canoe pass is also an outlet of the Fraser, the entrance from Georgia strait being to the southward of the main channel. Westham island separates the pass from the river, the junction being about 3 miles above Pelly point. The channel across Roberts bank is intricate and winding, and is marked by pile beacons and spar buoys; it can be used only by small vessels at high water.

Burrard inlet is the first great harbor which indents the shores of British Columbia north of the forty-ninth parallel. Its entrance is between Grey point on the south and Atkinson point on the north.

Grey point, a long wooded promontory terminating in a rounded bluff, is very conspicuous from the southward, while Bowen island, which lies at the entrance of Howe sound, and may also be said to form the northern boundary of the inlet, is very remarkable; its high, round, and almost bare summit, mount Gardner, reaching an elevation of 2,479 feet, is easily recognized from any point of view. Passage island, small, but prominent, lies in the eastern passage of Howe sound, midway between Bowen island and Atkinson point, and is an excellent mark from the southward.

Leading peak, Anvil island, in line with or just open westward of Passage island, bearing N. 3° E. (N. 21° W. mag.), leads clear of Sturgeon bank. At night Atkinson Point light should not be brought to bear westward of N. 23° E. (N. 1° W. mag.).

Burrard inlet differs from most of the great sounds of this coast in being comparatively easy of access to steam vessels of any size or class, and in the convenient depth of water for anchorage which may be found in almost every part of it; its close proximity to Fraser river, with the great facilities for constructing roads between the two places, and its having become the terminus of the Canadian Pacific railroad, add considerably to its importance. It is divided into three distinct harbors, viz, English bay or the outer anchorage; Vancouver, above the First narrows; and Port Moody, at the head of the eastern arm of the inlet.

Light.—From a square white wooden lighthouse, situated on Atkinson point, is exhibited, at an elevation of 96 feet above high water, a revolving white light, attaining its greatest brilliancy every minute, visible in clear weather 14 miles. The light is obscured when bearing southward of S. 85° E. (N. 71° E. mag.).

Fog signal.—A horn gives a blast of 8 seconds' duration at intervals of 1 minute.

Pilots.—A small pilot vessel usually cruises between Grey and Atkinson points, or will be at anchor near Spanish bank, or in Skunk cove, ½ mile eastward of Atkinson point.

English bay is more than 3 miles in breadth at the entrance between Grey and Atkinson points, which bear from each other north and south, and has the same breadth for nearly its entire length, or almost 4 miles.

The head of English bay on the south shore terminates in a shoal arm named False creek; on the north shore it leads by First narrows to Burrard inlet. The great volume of water which discharges itself from the upper parts of the inlet through these narrows has scoured out a deep channel on the north side of the outer anchorage.

Spanish bank, which extends in a northerly direction from Grey point for ¾ mile and then curves easterly, joining the south shore of the inlet at the distance of 2 miles within the point, contracts the entrance in some measure. This bank is composed of hard sand, and is dry at low water; its edge is steep-to. When covered its existence would not be suspected; there is no ripple on it unless with strong westerly winds, and then only near low water.

Beacon and buoy.—A red pile beacon with drum, which shows 10 feet above water, stands on the northern edge of the bank. This beacon dries at low water.

A red bell buoy is moored in 10 fathoms of water westward of the bank; it lies 1¼ miles N. 3° W. (N. 27° W. mag.) from Grey point.

Anchorage.—There is good anchorage in English bay in 6 fathoms, stiff mud bottom, at about ½ mile from the south shore of the bay (off Indian huts), with the extreme of Coal peninsula bearing N. 40° E. (N. 16° E. mag.), and the lighthouse on point Atkinson bearing N. 47° W. (N. 71° W. mag.). This anchorage is well protected from westerly winds by Spanish bank, and is also out of the influence of the current. Anchorage may also be had farther to the eastward if desired; a remarkable high rock (Siwash rock) stands close off the west end of Coal peninsula, and when this rock is just shut in by the point, bearing N. 10° E. (N. 14° W. mag.), a vessel will be far enough in.

If intending to pass above the narrows, attend to the tides; a stranger will do well to anchor in English bay before proceeding farther up.

The telegraph cable, connecting Vancouver island with the mainland, is landed on the eastern side of English bay at a position marked by a small, white hut; vessels should anchor well clear of the cable, which extends in a W. by N. direction from the hut for 1$\frac{1}{10}$ miles, and then WSW., passing 700 yards north of the beacon on Spanish bank.

Tides.—In English bay it is high water, full and change, at 5 h. 30 m.; springs rise 13 feet, neaps 11 feet. During the winter months from September to March there is what is locally called a "short run out" during the day, and a "long run out" at night. The water is consequently high during the day and low at night. The duration of the short run out is from 3 to 4 hours, that of the long 7 to 9 hours. This is entirely reversed during the summer months, when it is high water during the night and low water during the day. The tides are very complicated and can not be depended on, except at full and change of the moon.

The First narrows, or Lions gate, lies between the bluff of Coal peninsula and the northern side of the inlet, where the breadth of the channel is not more than 200 yards, with a depth of 6 to 12 fathoms. The entrance is not easily made out by a stranger until close in.

Directions.—A flat composed of shingle and bowlders, covering with the early flood, extends from 200 to 600 yards off the north shore, so that Prospect point must be kept pretty close aboard, rather less than 200 yards.

In a sailing ship a knowledge of the locality is necessary, as well as a commanding breeze, and the narrows should never be attempted with the full strength of the stream; and you must be quick and careful with the helm. Even for a steam vessel the strength of the streams in First narrows necessitates unusual care.

The narrow part of the channel is ½ mile in length, when it gradually opens out from 400 yards to ½ mile, which is the breadth abreast Brockton point. When past the narrowest part, the south shore should be kept aboard within 250 yards until abreast Brockton point. A spar buoy, painted red, is moored in 3 fathoms, at the edge of the bank on the south side of First narrows, with Brockton Point lighthouse bearing S. 63° E. (S. 87° E. mag.), distant 800 yards.

There are five pile beacons situated near the edge of the drying flat on the north side of the narrows. Two of these, the third and fourth from seaward, are substantial structures marking the shore ends of the water pipes which cross the narrows from these points. The other beacons, maintained as aids to navigation, are surmounted, the eastern one by an inverted white triangle, and the western one by a white square.

Two white masts, each 20 feet high and surmounted by a drum, stand on the shore southward of Parthia shoal, and show the east and west limits of the shoal.

Parthia shoal lies in mid-channel northwestward of Brockton point. Within the 5-fathom curve it is 600 yards long, east and west, and 200 yards broad, and the least water is 3½ fathoms near the east end. A second bank of 25 feet, with 7 fathoms between, lies 200 yards northeastward of Parthia shoal. The passage for large vessels is southward of the shoals with the chimney of the sugar refinery in line with Brockton point, S. 52° E. (S 76° E. mag.), passing Brockton point at a distance of 200 yards.

Lights—Prospect point.—A fixed white light, 28 feet above high water, visible for 10 miles through an arc of 226° between N. 87° 30′ E. (N. 63° 30′ E. mag.) and N. 46° 30′ W. (N. 70° 30′ W. mag.), obscured over the dangers on the south side of the channel, is exhibited from a square lantern surmounting a square wooden building situated under the bluff of Prospect point. The house is painted white, with red roof and lantern.

Fog signal.—A bell is struck once every 20 seconds.

Brockton point.—A light is shown from a wooden building painted brown and yellow with a red roof. The light is 42 feet above high water, and shows fixed white with a red sector over an arc of 24° between N. 49° W. (N. 73° W. mag.) and N. 73° W. (S. 83° W. mag.), and should be visible 8 miles. The red sector covers Burnaby shoal.

Fog signal.—A fog-bell tower stands on the northern extreme of Brockton point. The bell is struck by machinery once every 20 seconds.

Tidal streams.—At high water, the flood stream in the First narrows terminates 4 minutes before high water at Vancouver, the duration of slack water being 10 minutes.

At low water the ebb stream terminates 23 minutes after low water at Vancouver, the duration of slack being 14 minutes.

Slack water occurs 54 minutes after high water and 50 minutes after low water at the Sand heads.

The strength of the tidal stream in the narrowest part of First narrows is from 4 to 8 knots.

When the tidal streams are running with any strength there are eddies in First narrows, and it is necessary to exercise caution, especially with heavy-draft vessels, in passing through. A stranger should not enter the narrows unacquainted with the state of the tide.

Vancouver harbor, just inside First narrows, is a bight in the southern shore of Burrard inlet, formed by the land falling back from Brockton point. It is a fine and secure harbor, capable of accommodating a large number of vessels, and with anchorage depths of from 6 to 10 fathoms over a considerable area, well out of any strength of the tidal streams. The holding ground is good.

Burnaby shoal, the only danger, lies at the entrance to the harbor between 400 and 600 yards southeastward of Brockton point. It is about 200 yards in extent with 9 feet least water over it; kelp grows on it in the season, but is often run under by the current.

Buoy.—A red spar buoy is moored on the NE. edge of the shoal, with the lighthouse on Brockton point bearing N. 64° W. (N. 88° W. mag.), distant 600 yards.

The northwestern side of the Indian sheds on the southern side of First narrows in line with the north extreme of Brockton point, bearing N. 74° W. (S. 82° W. mag.), clears the shoal to the northward.

The spire of the Roman Catholic cathedral in Vancouver city in line with the center of the Canadian Pacific Railroad station, bearing S. 17° W. (S. 7° E. mag.), clears it to the eastward.

The Congregational Church tower in line with the NW. corner of the Canadian Pacific Railroad wharf, S. 6° W. (S. 18° E. mag.), leads between Burnaby shoal and the bank extending 200 yards east of Brockton point in 3½ fathoms.

Time signal.—A time gun is established near the floating pontoon on the south side of Brockton point. It is fired daily at 9 h. 0 m. Pacific standard (one hundred and twentieth meridian) mean time, corresponding to 17 h. 0 m. Greenwich mean time, by electricity from McGill college observatory, Montreal.

Compass beacons.—Two beacons 1,000 feet apart, painted in red and white horizontal bands and surmounted each by a white triangular topmark with black center line, stand near the Siwash Indian mission, on the north side of Burrard inlet, to enable seamen to ascertain the error of their compasses. These beacons in line bear N. 29° E. (N. 5° E. mag.).

Vancouver, situated on the southern side of Vancouver harbor, is rapidly increasing in size; it is the terminus of the Canadian Pacific railroad, and trains leave twice daily for Montreal. There are several prominent buildings in the city, and spires and towers of several of the churches are conspicuous from the anchorage. The Roman Catholic cathedral has two spires, the taller of the two being the most conspicuous spire in the city; the Presbyterian church also has a conspicuous spire; the Congregational church has a short, square tower on its NE. angle; the Methodist church is a tall building with a crenelated roof and a small triangular spire on its east end; the Wesleyan church has a large, square tower surmounted by a short spire, and is very conspicuous. The courthouse has a large dome surmounted by a figure representing Justice.

Substantial wharves with 22 to 25 feet alongside occupy a large portion of the water front.

At Hastings sawmill there are several piers, with a depth of 25 feet alongside the largest.

A patent slip, capable of taking a ship of 1,500 tons, is situated at Cedar cove, 1 mile eastward of Hastings sawmill.

The population of Vancouver city in 1901 was 26,133.

The United States is represented by a consul and a vice-consul.

Supplies.—Supplies of all kinds can be obtained. Good water is obtainable through pipes laid to all the wharves; the supply is brought from the mountains some 20 miles distant and is remarkable for its purity.

Coal is obtained from Nanaimo and Union, on Vancouver island; the amount kept in stock is uncertain.

Communication.—Trains leave twice daily for Montreal and other towns on the Canadian Pacific railroad, and there is also direct communication by rail with Seattle, Tacoma, Portland, San Francisco, and other places in the United States.

There is an electric tramway to New Westminster.

Steamers run daily to Victoria and Nanaimo, on Vancouver island, and there is regular communication with Japan, China, Hawaiian islands, New Zealand, Australia, San Francisco, and the ports in Puget sound.

There is telegraphic communication with all parts of the world.

Towing.—There are powerful tugs available for towing vessels between Juan de Fuca strait and Burrard inlet.

Anchorage.—The best anchorage in Vancouver harbor is in the SW. corner, between Brockton point and the Canadian Pacific Railroad wharf, in 6 to 8 fathoms.

Tides.—The higher high water at Vancouver occurs 2 h. 52 m. and the lower high water 1 h. 42 m. after that at Port Townsend.

The higher low water occurs 2 h. 11 m. and the lower low water 2 h. 30 m. after that at Port Townsend.

For time of high water add 29 minutes to the time of high water at the Sand heads; for low water add 28 minutes to the time of low water at the Sand heads.

At point Atkinson high and low water are about ¾ hour earlier, and at Port Moody ¼ hour later than at Vancouver.

The tide has the peculiarity of rising to nearly the same level at the higher high waters, whether it be at springs or neaps, whereas the level of the low waters varies in the usual manner. In summer the higher tides occur at night and in winter during the day.

Tide tables are published by the department of marine and fisheries of Canada and by the Coast and Geodetic Survey of the United States.

Tidal streams.—The streams, both flood and ebb, in First and Second narrows, turn at high and low water by the shore.

Hastings, a small village situated on the south side of the inlet, is 3 miles eastward from Vancouver, and is connected with New Westminster by a road 9 miles long. It is much frequented during the summer months.

Second narrows.—The Second narrows is similar to the First; a bank of the same description, but more extensive, is caused by the deposit brought down from the high mountains by the numerous streams which flow into the inlet on the north side. This bank is dry at low water, and the breadth of the deep channel, at the narrowest part and for ½ mile on either side of it, varies from 300 to 400 yards, with a depth of from 10 to 20 fathoms. The channel, however, is straight, and the tides, which run from 3 to 7 knots, set fairly through it. The only directions necessary are to keep the southern shore close aboard, and steer from point to point without going far into the bights which indent the coast on either side of the narrowest part. The great strength of the tide ceases when ½ mile from the narrowest part of the narrows.

Telegraph.—A submarine telegraph cable crosses Second narrows in the narrowest part, marked by three painted wooden posts placed on the mud flat; and the outer of these, being on the southern edge of the flat, is a good guide for the deep-water channel.

Port Moody.—The entrance to this snug harbor is 4 miles eastward from the Second narrows, at the head of the eastern arm of the inlet. It is 3 miles in length, and varies in breadth from ⅓ to ½ mile, except at its entrance, where it is only 400 yards across; there are no known dangers, and there is a uniform depth of water, with good holding ground. The port takes an ENE. direction for nearly 2 miles, and then ESE. for 1 mile, terminating in a muddy flat at its head, which reaches within 3 miles of the banks of Pitt river, and about 4 miles from the site of the military camp at New Westminster, on the Fraser.

Anchorage.—The best anchorage is in the widest part of the harbor just before reaching the arm which turns ESE., in from 5 to 6 fathoms. Abreast the turning point, and on the north shore, a bank dries off for nearly 400 yards at low water.

North arm, 3 miles eastward of Second narrows, branches in a general northerly direction for 11 miles. It is entirely different in its character from other portions of the inlet. The depth varies from 50 to 110 fathoms, and it is inclosed on both sides by rugged mountains rising from 2,000 to 5,000 feet almost perpendicularly, down the steep sides of which the melting snow in summer forces its way in foaming cascades, rendering the surface water in the inlet below nearly fresh.

There is scarcely sufficient level land in this arm to pitch a tent, nor is there any anchorage except in Bedwell bay, a narrow creek 2 miles within the entrance, on the eastern shore, where 7 to 9 fathoms are found near its head. North arm is nearly 1 mile wide at the entrance, but 1 mile within it is contracted to a little over 400 yards, when it shortly opens out again, and maintains an average breadth of ¾ mile as far as Croker island.

Tupper rock, in the approach to Bedwell bay, is of small extent with deep water around, and having 10 feet over it at low water. The rock lies 600 yards N. 61° E. (N. 37° E. mag.) from Jug island, and is very dangerous to vessels entering Bedwell bay.

Croker island is 1 mile from the head of the arm, and on both sides of it there are deep but narrow channels; that to the eastward is the wider. The head terminates in a delta of swampy rushes, through which some rapid streams find their way into the inlet from a deep and narrow gorge in a northerly direction.

SOUTHERN SHORE OF GEORGIA STRAIT.

Gabriola reefs, a dangerous cluster of rocks covering a space of nearly 1½ miles, some of which cover at half flood and others having only a few feet water over them, lie 2 miles off the eastern point of Gabriola island. Nanoose, or Notch, hill just open of Berry point (the NE. point of Gabriola island), bearing N. 72° W. (S. 84° W. mag.), leads 1 mile northward of them.

Thrasher rock, lying about 400 yards seaward from the northern end of the Gabriola reefs, is a detached rock which dries 1½ feet in the kelp which marks the neighborhood.

A rocky head with 30 feet over it lies 400 yards NE. from the beacon; there is 11 fathoms within 200 yards of the rock on its eastern side. The passage between Gabriola reefs and Gabriola island is not recommended until it has been examined.

Berry point bearing N. 72° W. (S. 84° W. mag.) (well open of Flattop islands), leads about 1 mile northward of Gabriola reefs and Thrasher rock. The entrance points of Portier pass just touching on a S. 2° E. (S. 26° E. mag.) bearing, leads more than 1½ miles eastward of the reefs.

Beacon.—A stone beacon, surmounted by a staff and ball, painted black, and showing 22 feet above water, stands on Thrasher rock.

Caution.—Westward of Flattop islands the shore of Gabriola is bold until near Berry point and Entrance island, when it should not be approached within a long ½ mile; foul ground extends for some distance eastward from the point of the island.

Lock bay, near Berry point, is not recommended as an anchorage, owing to its great depth.

Temporary anchorage may be found midway between Flattop islands and Lock bay in 10 fathoms, mud and sand.

The whole of the north side of Gabriola island is thickly wooded.

Entrance island, ½ mile NE. from Berry point, is rocky, 30 feet high, formed of sandstone, and bare of trees, but has some vegetation on it. Vessels passing up the strait bound for Nanaimo should round this island; there is a passage between it and Berry point, named Forwood channel, a little more than 400 yards in breadth, which is used by local steamers, but as there is a rock nearly in its middle this channel should not be attempted by strangers. The southern and western sides of Entrance island must be avoided, as reefs and broken ground extend 400 yards off them.

Rocky shoals, with depths of 7 and 8 fathoms, extend 1¾ miles east of Entrance island.

Light.—From a square, white, lighthouse situated on Entrance island is exhibited, at 65 feet above high water, a fixed white light, with red sector between N. 67° W. (S. 89° W. mag.) and N. 59° 30′ W. (N. 83° 30′ W. mag.), over Gabriola reefs. It is obscured by land when bearing northward of N. 59° 30′ W. (N. 83° 30′ W. mag.). The light should be seen in clear weather from a distance of 14 miles.

[The lighting apparatus at this station having been damaged by fire, a fixed white light of the 7th order is temporarily shown.]

Fog signal.—A steam horn gives blasts of 8 seconds with silent intervals of 45 seconds.

Fairway channel, between the NW. end of Gabriola island and Lighthouse, or Snake, island, is the most direct passage for vessels entering Nanaimo from the southward or eastward. A line of small islets on a rocky ledge, uncovering at low water, extends parallel to the island on both sides at distances of 40 and 75 yards.

The Gabriola side of the channel is foul for a distance of 200 to 500 yards from the shore.

Lighthouse (Snake) island is a smooth-topped, grassy, sandstone island, 400 yards long north and south, about 39 feet high, and 3 miles W. ½ N. from Entrance island.

A shoal about 300 yards long north and south, on which lie submerged rocks, with depths of 1¼ to 2¼ fathoms between, is situated SE. of the island. From the south end of the island the northern end of the reef is 500 yards S. 75° E. (N. 81° E. mag.), and the southern end S. 46° E. (S. 70° E. mag.); the shoal is marked by kelp, and there is a 21-fathom channel between it and the island.

Buoy.—The southern end of the shoal is marked by a red conical buoy, moored in 9 fathoms 800 yards S. 35° E. (S. 59° E. mag.) from the south end of Lighthouse island.

Directions.—Having entered Georgia strait between East point (Saturna island) and Patos island, a N. 45° W. (N. 69° W. mag.) course for 38 miles will lead nearly 3 miles outside Gabriola reefs. Entrance island should be rounded at a distance of not less than ½ mile; then steer to pass about 600 yards south of the red conical buoy marking Lighthouse Island ledge. When proceeding through Fairway channel, if northward of mid-channel, keep a lookout for kelp on the ledge. When Lighthouse island bears N. 22° W. (N. 46° W. mag.), steer S. 25° W. (S. 1° W. mag.), which leads to the entrance of Nanaimo harbor, distant a little over 2 miles.

Strangers should be careful not to mistake Northumberland channel for the entrance; the former lies in a southerly direction from Lighthouse island, between the high, cliffy, west coast of Gabriola island and Sharp (Jack) point, a remarkable, narrow projection on the mainland, off which at the distance of nearly 200 yards is a rock which uncovers.

Shoal water extends to the northward of Sharp point for a distance of 300 yards. When approaching Nanaimo harbor from Dodd narrows, or from the eastward, this point should be given a wide berth, especially in thick weather, as the tides set past it occasionally with considerable strength.

Having passed between Lighthouse and Gabriola islands, there is a good working space of 1½ miles in breadth, between Gabriola on the east and Newcastle and Protection islands on the west, but the water is too deep for anchorage. The shores of the latter islands should not be approached within ¼ mile, as shoal rocky ledges extend off them. A shoal, about 200 yards in extent with 3 fathoms over it, lies 1,100 yards S. 80° E. (N. 76° E. mag.) from McKay point, the NE. point of Newcastle island. Having brought Gallows point (the southern extreme of Protection island) to bear S. 73° W. (S. 49° W. mag.), the town will come in view.

Vessels of heavy draft may find anchorage in the bight of the mud bank to the westward of Sharp point, in 24 fathoms, mud bottom, with the extreme of the point bearing S. 88° E. (N. 68° E. mag.), distant 900 yards; but they will swing nearly into the fairway of the entrance. Small vessels may anchor on the same bearing, distant 1,100 yards, in 13 fathoms.

Nanaimo harbor.—The entrance to the harbor lies between Gallows point on the north and a mud bank on the south. A rocky ledge extends for nearly 200 yards from the eastern side of the point, and is marked in summer by kelp. At the southern extreme of the point mine refuse has been dumped, extending to the low-water line of the rocky ledge, and forming a prominent object from seaward.

The south side of the entrance, and of the harbor itself, is the northern edge of the mud bank which completely fills the large bay to the southward, through which the Nanaimo and Chase rivers reach the sea. The bank does not quite dry at its northern edge at lowest water, but carries from 2 to 3 feet of water and is then steep-to.

General description.—After rounding Gallows point the harbor opens out to the northward.

The western side is occupied by the town of Nanaimo, built on land sloping from the water to a height of 230 feet, and fronted at the southern end by a loading wharf 785 feet long, near the northern end of which is a ballast wharf.

Farther northward, at the foot of a steep, grassy slope, are the wharves for the local ferry and trading steamers. Along the summit of this slope are several prominent buildings, the southernmost being the old blockhouse of the Hudson Bay Company, an octagonal tower with black roof, which has been reerected here as a landmark. The post-office, a large, gray, stone building with a flagstaff, is on the right of the road leading up from the steamer wharf; northward of it, and on the road that runs along the summit, is the courthouse, a large, gray, stone building with a square tower at each of its front angles.

There are several church spires in the town, the most conspicuous being that of St. Paul's (Episcopal), situated near the post-office, and the high, pointed steeple of the Wesleyan church, situated some distance farther back.

At the northern end of the grassy slope the shore turns sharply to the NW., forming the mouth of Millstone creek, where two sawmills face the water. The mouth of this creek is fronted by a drying mud-bank delta, extending outward from the bridge crossing the creek to a distance of about 400 yards.

Beyond Millstone creek the land is lower and flatter, and the houses more scattered; this district is known as the Newcastle town site, and terminates with the jail, a high, prominent building, painted gray and surrounded by fencing painted white, which is just beyond the town limits.

A drying mud flat, from 100 to 200 yards in width, fronts the shore from Millstone creek to the end of the strait leading to Departure bay; two piers are built over it, each with a floating boathouse at its extremity, the southern one being owned privately. the other belonging to the jail.

There is a small fishing village 300 yards beyond the jail, with floating houses between piles; farther on is an Indian village. This part of the coast forms the western shore of the narrow strait between Newcastle island and the mainland. This is known as Newcastle Island passage.

Protection island, which forms the eastern side of the harbor, is divided from Newcastle island by a strait about 200 yards wide, which dries about 5 feet at lowest water.

The northern and western shores are for the most part rocky, with drying ledges extending from 70 to 170 yards from high-water mark. The northern extreme is a flat, partially-cleared point with a few farm buildings, from which the western shore trends to the southward and then to the eastward, forming a good-sized bay which shoals to a mud flat at its head.

The coast-line here becomes steeper, and the rocky ledges fronting it are covered with a tolerably deep deposit of small coal and mine refuse.

Near the southern end of the island is a loading wharf 665 feet long connected with the mine by two railroads. There are chutes for discharging coal at any stage of the tide; on the southern chute is a flagstaff.

The southeastern part of the island is cleared of trees and occupied by houses and other buildings in connection with the coal mine.

From Gallows point the eastern shore of the island trends to the northward with a succession of indentations to Batchelor point, where it turns to the westward and faces Newcastle island. The portion as far as Batchelor point is fronted with rocky ledges which in places extend 100 yards from the shore. Two rocks, one of which dries 2 feet and the other awash at low water, lie about 100 yards outside the low-water line of the largest bay.

Protection island is, with the exception of its northern and southern ends, thickly wooded; the tops of the trees are 200 feet above high water.

Newcastle island.—The coast line of this island is rocky, and nearly steep-to on its western side. The southern termination is a flat, grassy point with a reef of rocks extending 200 yards from high-water mark. To the eastward of this is a square-headed inlet of shoal water, from which the land turns in a second, flat, grassy point, and trends to the NE., forming the northern side of the strait separating it from Protection island.

From the harbor side Newcastle island appears completely wooded with the exception of the two points above mentioned, to the eastward of which is a small landing pier and a few farmhouses. The island slopes gently from the sea, and has the appearance of being flat; the tops of the trees are about 370 feet above high water.

Sharp point, locally known as Jack point, which has been mentioned before in connection with the approach to the harbor, is the termination of a long, rocky, wooded peninsula, and is about 12 feet above high water, backed by higher ground covered with trees. The western side of this peninsula runs nearly north and south, and has a few indentations.

There is a small cove about 200 yards inside Sharp point, with a rather prominent white cottage, and a few farm buildings at the back of it; 1 mile farther south is a similar white cottage with outhouse, standing on a slight eminence cleared of trees.

Two hundred yards to the northward of the latter cottage is a small boat passage, severing the narrow neck at that point, which has about 5 feet at high water, but is dry at low water.

Dangers—Buoys and beacons.—The dangers off Sharp point have been already alluded to. Within the harbor there are two dangerous shoals, Middle bank and Satellite reef, also four rocks, Beacon rock, Nicol rock, Carpenter rock, and Passage rock.

Middle bank, which occupies the middle of the harbor, is composed of rock covered with mud and bowlders, some of which are said to have been visible in years of extreme range of tide, but which have at ordinary lowest water from 2 to 3 feet of water over them. The shoal inside the 3-fathom curve is 400 yards long in a nearly north and south direction and is nearly 150 yards wide.

It is marked at its northern end by a black pile beacon carrying a fixed white light at a height of 10 feet above high water; at its southern extremity by a platform buoy carrying a latticework pyramid surmounted by a ball, the whole painted red; and on its western edge by two small red spar buoys.

Satellite reef, a rock which dries 4 feet, with shoal water extending from it to the NE. and SE. for a distance of 250 yards, lies to the northward of Middle bank with a ship channel between.

It is marked by a platform buoy carrying a latticework pyramid surmounted by a ball, the whole painted red.

There are two small 3-fathom patches lying off the SW. limit of Satellite reef; they are unmarked.

Beacon rock, which lies 200 yards from the shore, north of the steamer wharves, consists of two small closely adjoining patches of rock which dry 4 feet at lowest water.

A circular beacon of masonry, surmounted by a staff and topmark of latticework, 22 feet high, the upper part painted white, the lower part black, stands on the southern rock.

Nicol rock.—A circular shoal, about 50 yards across and a like distance from the ballast dock, lies 300 yards SE. from Beacon rock. It has been dredged to a depth of 2¾ fathoms.

Carpenter rock, which lies 200 yards offshore near the southern mouth of Millstone creek, is a small rocky head with 2 feet over it at lowest water.

It is marked by a platform buoy carrying a black lattice pyramid surmounted by a white ball.

Millstone Creek bank.—The eastern edge of the bank is marked by a black platform buoy with lattice pyramid surmounted by a triangle.

Passage rock, which lies off the eastern extreme of the mud bank extending from the western shore of Newcastle Island passage, is a small bowlder with 5 feet over it at lowest water. The channel between it and Newcastle island is only about 50 feet wide.

It is marked by a platform buoy carrying a lattice pyramid, surmounted by a drum, the whole painted black.

South side of harbor.—The northern extreme of the mud bank opposite Gallows point is marked by a platform buoy carrying a lattice pyramid, surmounted by an inverted lattice triangle, the whole painted black.

Two similar buoys, except that the topmarks are diamonds, mark the northern edge of the mud bank up to the loading wharf.

Gallows point.—The edge of the shoal water off this point is marked by a platform buoy, carrying a lattice pyramid, surmounted by a lattice ball, the whole painted red.

There are hauling-off buoys moored off the loading wharves on either side of the harbor.

Lights.—A fixed red light, 18 feet above high water, visible 3 miles, is shown from a square, white, wooden tower erected on piles, on the southern side of the entrance to the harbor, in a position from which the flagstaff on the loading wharf north of Gallows point bears N. 16° W. (N. 40° W. mag.), distant 500 yards.

A fixed white light, as previously mentioned, is shown from the pile beacon to the northward of Middle bank.

A fixed red light is shown from the northern end of the steamer wharf, and a fixed green light from the southern end.

Fog signal.—A fog bell, operated by machinery, giving 1 stroke every 5 seconds, surmounts a square, white, wooden building, located on Gallows point. The bell is 20 feet above high water.

Nanaimo contained, in 1901, 6,130 inhabitants, a large proportion of whom were employed in the coal mines, which form the leading industry of the place. The surrounding country possesses great agricultural capabilities, and is being largely opened up by the Western Fuel company, as well as by other private enterprises.

The town is situated about 73 miles by rail from Victoria, with which place there is a daily service. It is distant about 33 miles from Vancouver; a ferry steamer runs there and back daily in connection with the Canadian Pacific railroad. There is telegraph and telephone connection with Victoria and Vancouver.

Trade.—The value of the imports for the year ending June, 1903, was $157,150; the exports for the same period, consisting chiefly of coal, iron, copper ore, and salt fish, reached the value of $1,106,150.

The number of foreign vessels that cleared from the port in the same time was 177, with a gross tonnage of 149,020 tons, while the local vessels numbered 1,478, with a gross tonnage of 341,000 tons.

The greater part of the foreign steamers come from the United States, for which country there is a consular agency in the town.

Coal.—The extensive colliery of Nanaimo is the oldest of those now working in the province of British Columbia. There are two pits, or shafts, one at Nanaimo and the other at Departure bay; these shafts are connected underground.

The coal lies in seams from 600 to 700 feet below the surface, and the workings extended, in 1899, under the sea for 3 miles to the northward, and for more than 1 mile to the southward and eastward from the Protection Island shaft. The output in 1899 amounted to 600,000 tons.

The wharf accommodation is excellent; three steamers of 6,000 tons capacity can lie alongside at the same time and could be loaded simultaneously with 10,000 tons in 24 working hours, by giving previous notice. The coal is discharged by chutes, the height of which can be adjusted to the state of the tide.

About 8,000 tons is usually kept in stock. The price, in 1901, of the best seam coal was $3.50 per ton.

There are depths of from 20 to 29 feet alongside the Nanaimo wharf. Alongside the Protection Island wharf there are depths of from 30 to 34 feet, except near its southern end, where there is only 22 feet. A rock with only 17 feet lies just outside the line of the dock and 45 feet from its extremity.

Supplies of almost every kind, and both fresh and preserved provisions, can be obtained. Fresh water, of excellent quality, is laid on from the corporation mains.

Repairs.—There are not at present facilities for making large repairs to a vessel, nor is there any dock or patent slip, but minor repairs could be undertaken in the town.

Hospital.—Seamen are either admitted to the Nanaimo hospital, where the charges are $10 per week, or transferred to the marine hospital at Victoria.

Shipping office.—The shipping office for seamen is at the custom-house.

Wharves.—Besides the two coal wharves already described, there is also a ballast wharf, 315 feet long, which lies to the northwestward of the Nanaimo wharf, with a least depth of 16 feet (the site of Nicol rock) just off it. Westward of the ballast dock there are two smaller wharves, the southern having 5 feet least water alongside, the other, used by the ferry steamers to Vancouver and Comox, 240 feet long, with 8 feet alongside.

Storm signals are shown from the post-office.

Quarantine.—The quarantine station for Nanaimo is the same as that for Victoria, viz, at William head (Parry bay), where all vessels entering must report themselves.

Tides.—The tides at Nanaimo are similar in character to those of Port Townsend. It is high water, full and change, at 5 h. 0 m.; springs rise 14 feet, neaps 9 feet.

By observations taken at Nanaimo for a period of 6 weeks in 1899, the following results were obtained:

Higher high water and lower high water occur 1 h. 22 m. after Port Townsend.

Higher low water occurs 1h. 56 m. after Port Townsend.

Lower low water occurs 1 h. 53 m. after Port Townsend.

To find the range of any tide multiply the corresponding range at Port Townsend by 1.23.

The extreme range of tide observed during the above period was 13 feet 6 inches.

Directions.—After passing or rounding Sharp point at a distance of not less than 400 yards, steer to pass midway between Nos. 1 and 2 buoys, off Gallows point. From this position there are two channels by which the anchorage situated off the northern steamer wharf may be reached; that passing to the northward of Middle bank, with a least depth of 36 feet at low water, is called the North channel; the other passing to the southward of Middle bank and past the Nanaimo loading wharf, with a least depth of 25 feet, is called the South channel, of which that portion lying between the mud banks and Middle bank is being dredged to 30 feet at low water.

The usual route for vessels entering to load at the Nanaimo coal wharf is to enter by the North channel and leave by the South, thus making a complete circuit of Middle bank. This brings the vessel with head to the prevailing SE. wind when alongside the coal wharf, and when leaving, laden with coal, the route out of the harbor is more direct than by the other channel.

Vessels going alongside the Protection island wharf usually secure with stern to the southeastward and then slue round when leaving.

The best anchorage is in 30 feet with Beacon rock bearing S. 75° W. (S. 51° W. mag.), distant 250 yards.

Anchorage may also be found, in 27 feet, WNW. of Satellite rock, distant about 400 yards.

Caution.—When approaching or leaving Nanaimo harbor by Middle or Inner channels, care must be taken to avoid the 3-fathom shoal lying 1,100 yards eastward of Newcastle island.

Departure bay.—From Nanaimo, the long, narrow channel between Newcastle island and the mainland leads in a northerly direction to Departure bay. It is 1½ miles long, and about 200 yards wide, except abreast Passage rock, where the navigable channel is only 50 yards across.

Vessels of 15 feet draft with masts less than 100 feet high (because of the telephone wire crossing the passage near its northern end) may enter Departure bay by this channel at suitable stages of the tide, but large vessels must enter northward of Newcastle island.

The flood stream sets to the northward, the ebb to the southward, but neither stream attains great velocity.

Excellent facilities for beaching a vessel exist in Departure bay.

The telegraph cable making connections with the mainland is landed just inside the Black rocks.

The northern entrance to Departure bay is between Bowlder (Nares) point, the steep, cliffy north point of Newcastle island, and

Jesse island, a small island to the northward of it, and lies 2 miles WSW. of Lighthouse island. It is 600 yards wide with depths of 13 to 21 fathoms. Very little less than 20 fathoms will be found in any part of the bay, and it is not nearly so sheltered as Nanaimo harbor. When coming from the northward care must be taken to avoid the reef which makes out 600 yards from Horswell bluff, the north entrance point of the bay. Fresh water can be obtained.

Coal.—There are several wharves in the southern corner of the bay and one on the NW. side of Newcastle island, near a shaft to a coal mine which has been recently sunk. The wharf is 300 feet long and has 36 feet of water alongside. Coal is shipped here.

Brandon islands (Double island) lies west of Jesse island and near the northern shore of the bay.

Black rocks, halfway between the eastern end of Double island and the shore, generally show four heads, but at low water appear as one rock. There is a small rock with 6 feet over it 50 yards west of the westernmost Black rock, with 4 fathoms close-to.

Buoys.—The reef extending to the eastward of Horswell bluff is marked by a red can buoy; it is moored in 6 fathoms.

A red platform buoy with pyramid and ball marks the reef extending off Newcastle island on the SE. side of the bay.

A mooring buoy is anchored in 22 fathoms south of the western Brandon island.

A white beacon stands on the small islet west of the Brandon islands.

Horswell rock.—An isolated bowlder, of small extent, with 2 feet of water over it at extreme low water, lies on the 5-fathom curve about 200 yards offshore, with Horswell bluff N. 13° E. (N. 11° W. mag.) and the west end of Jesse island S. 67° W. (S. 43° W. mag.).

Horswell reef extends to the northward and to the eastward of Horswell bluff. The reef uncovers in places at low water for a distance of 300 yards, and the 5-fathom curve is about 600 yards from the bluff. A red can buoy moored in 6 fathoms, 700 yards eastward of the bluff, marks the reef.

Directions.—No directions are necessary for entering the bay, but care must be taken in anchoring, as the shores of the bay shoal very abruptly from deep water to 3 fathoms. A stranger should take a pilot from the pilot station at Rocky Point cove, Gabriola island, or in Nanaimo harbor.

The passage between Double island and Black rocks is safe. That northward of and between Black rocks and the shore is also used; the Black rocks side must be favored in order to avoid the shoal making out from the shore, hauling a little to the northward after passing the easternmost rock to avoid the shoal extending eastward from it.

Middle channel, over 1 mile wide, lies between Lighthouse (Snake) and Five Finger islands; it has an average depth of 80 fathoms. Passing through the center of it a South course leads between Protection island and Sharp point for Nanaimo harbor.

Tides.—It is high water, full and change, at Departure bay at 5 h. 0 m.; springs rise 14 feet, neaps 9 feet. The general characteristics of the tides have been found to agree closely with those of Telegraph harbor.

Five Finger island is a bare rugged islet 48 feet high, of about the same dimensions as Lighthouse island, but of trap formation, instead of sandstone; the five hummocks on it resemble knuckles more than fingers.

A 3-fathom patch lies with the summit of this island bearing N. 87° E. (N. 63° E. mag.) distant 620 yards.

West rocks.—Eight hundred yards SW. from Five Finger island are three smaller islets of similar character and formation, with some rocks about them, which uncover. These islets and rocks occupy a space of ½ mile in a NW. and SE. direction; there is a passage 600 yards wide between them and Five Finger island with irregular rocky bottom, the depths varying from 9 to 35 fathoms.

As several 3-fathom patches have been found in this passage it is not recommended.

Foul ground, terminating in a rock with 11 feet over it, extends N. 39° W. (N. 63° W. mag.) nearly 500 yards from the largest islet of the group. A 3-fathom patch lies with the same islet bearing N. 80° W. (S. 76° W. mag.), distant 440 yards. The south side of the group is clear of offlying dangers.

Inner (Horswell) channel, 800 yards in breadth, lies between the above islets and the shore of Vancouver island, and being more direct, is convenient for steamers or small craft bound to or from the northward; the mid-channel course through it is about NNW. and SSE. Almost in the center of this channel is Clarke rock, which dries 4 feet at low water.

Buoy.—A black platform buoy with pyramid is moored close on the east side of Clarke rock.

Hammond bay lies 1¼ miles northward of Horswell bluff; temporary anchorage may be had in this bay in 7 to 9 fathoms; but a heavy swell prevails there in all seasons.

Shoals.—In the NW. entrance to Inner channel and off the entrance to Hammond bay are two patches with 5 fathoms over them at low water. The northern patch is 1,040 yards N. 13° W. (N. 37° W. mag.) and the southern one 700 yards N. 12° 30′ E. (N. 11° 30′ W. mag.) from Lagoon head.

Caution.—When approaching or leaving Nanaimo harbor by either Middle or Inner channels, be careful to avoid the 3-fathom shoal 1,100 yards eastward of Newcastle island.

Northumberland channel, before mentioned as lying between Sharp point and the western shore of Gabriola island, runs in a SSE. direction for 1⅓ miles, and then ESE. for 2 miles, when it enters Dodd and False narrows, the former on the south side of Mudge island, the latter on the north; a rock which uncovers extends 100 yards off the extreme of Sharp point. False narrows is shoal with no ship passage, but there is excellent anchorage in Percy bay at the western entrance, in from 7 to 10 fathoms, where vessels may lie to await the tide through Dodd narrows.

A submarine electric cable crosses Northumberland channel ¾ mile westward of Dodd narrows.

Dodd narrows has been already described from the southward; it communicates with the inner channels leading to the southern ports, and saves a distance of 20 miles in the passage from Nanaimo to Victoria or Esquimalt, and is consequently frequented by boats, small vessels, and sometimes by steam vessels of considerable size acquainted with the locality. Strangers are not recommended to use it. Coming down Northumberland channel, look out for the narrow entrance on the south side, and when it bears SSE. steer for it; the tidal streams run at their strongest 8 knots, and there is a very short interval of slack water; the breadth in the narrowest part is 65 yards. The tides in Dodd narrows are about 1 hour earlier than at Nanaimo, therefore a vessel intending to pass down should be at the narrows 1 hour before high water at that place, if going through with the first of the ebb; or at 2 hours before low water if with the last of it.

CHAPTER VI.

THE STRAIT OF GEORGIA, FROM NANAIMO HARBOR AND BURRARD INLET TO CAPE MUDGE AND BUTE INLET.

VARIATION IN 1906.

Burrard inlet	24° 10′ E.	Cape Mudge	24° 45′ E.
Bute inlet, entrance	25° 00′ E.		

Georgia strait, as already observed, commences at the northern end of the Haro archipelago and extends in a general NW. direction to cape Mudge, a distance of 110 miles. There are many harbors, both on the Vancouver and continental shores; and several islands, some of considerable size, form other channels, all of which are navigable.

The average width of the main strait westward of Nanaimo is about 9 miles, diminishing at its narrowest part, between Lasqueti and the Ballenas islands, to 5 miles. The general depth of water is great, frequently over 200 fathoms. The tides are not strong, and between Nanaimo and cape Mudge there are few dangers in the way of ships navigating the strait.

The smaller channels on the continental shore are Malaspina strait and Sabine channel, the former lying between the continent and Texada island, the other separating Texada from Lasqueti island.

On the Vancouver shore is Ballenas channel, lying westward of the islands of the same name; also Lambert channel and Baynes sound, the former between Hornby and Denman islands, and the latter dividing Denman island from Vancouver island.

Tides and tidal streams.—The meeting of the tides takes place between cape Mudge and cape Lazo; that is to say, the flood entering by Juan de Fuca strait meets that entering by the north end of Vancouver island within 20 miles of the former cape, generally much nearer, but varying according to the phases of the moon and the state of the winds; and at the point of meeting a considerable race occurs, which would be dangerous to boats; there is generally such a race at the entrance of Discovery passage. It is high water, full and change, at cape Mudge and cape Lazo at about 5 h. 0 m.; and the range during ordinary springs is from 12 to 14 feet. At the entrance of the passage during springs the tidal streams attain a velocity of 4 to 6 knots an hour, the flood, or easterly stream, being the stronger.

Winds.—The prevailing summer wind is from NW., or the same as on the outside coast, and between May and September it blows strong and steady, commencing about 9 a. m. and dying away toward sunset. The winds do not generally extend much below point Roberts; in the Haro archipelago they become variable and baffling, while in the main channels of Rosario and Haro, the westerly wind entering the strait of Fuca is deflected to SW., and vessels running up these channels with a fair wind will almost always find it ahead on entering the strait of Georgia. During winter there is a good deal of moderate, calm, and gloomy weather, but gales from SE. and SW. are frequent.

Nanoose harbor, 8 miles westward from Nanaimo, is easily recognized by Nanoose, or Notch, hill, a remarkable hill 625 feet high, immediately over its north side, showing as a double or notch peak from the southward; the harbor trends 3 miles west. The entrance between Maude island and Blunden point is ¾ mile wide, and the width of the harbor varies between 600 yards and over 1 mile. The head of the harbor is low and swampy.

Leaving Nanaimo harbor, and passing out by either channel (Middle channel to be preferred), or being at from ½ to 1 mile northward from Five Finger island, a West course, or straight for Nanoose hill, leads for the entrance of the harbor, distant 7 miles.

Winchelsea and Ada islands, a group of small wooded islands, lie off the north point of Nanoose harbor. Shoal ground extends for nearly ½ mile SE. of the Winchelsea group.

Maude island, small, wooded, and about 100 feet high, is the southernmost of the group, and lies ¾ mile east from the north point of the harbor. When working in stand pretty close to it and to Blunden point, but when inside the latter, a sand bank dries for a considerable distance off at low water, and the south shore should not be approached within 600 yards.

Edgell banks lie ENE. of Maude island; they have a general depth of 15 fathoms. But a shoal spot with only 4½ fathoms lies near their western extreme. This head is situated with the eastern extreme of Maude island bearing S. 70° W. (S. 46° W. mag.), distant 1,200 yards.

A detached head with 3 fathoms over it, not marked by kelp, lies 600 yards N. 76° E. (N. 52° E. mag.) from Wallis point, the northern entrance point of Nanoose harbor. Another unmarked spot with 4 fathoms lies 1,200 yards from the point on the same bearing.

North rock.—From the north side of the entrance, just inside Wallis point, a shoal runs off for a distance of 400 yards, terminating in North rock, with only 5 feet on it; the rock lies S. 31° W. (S. 7° W. mag.) from Wallis point, distant 600 yards.

Entrance rock.—Westward of Blunden point the southern shore is shoal for a distance of nearly 2 miles, the shoal extending off nearly 600 yards from the shore. Near the western end of this shoal bank is a group of rocks; the largest, showing 5 feet above high water, is known as Entrance rock; it lies S. 47° W. (S. 23° W. mag.), distant $1\frac{1}{10}$ miles, from Wallis point.

Imperieuse rock, with a depth of 6 feet on it at low water, is situated in the narrow part of the entrance to Nanoose harbor; it lies nearly 400 yards N. 8° E. (N. 16° W. mag.) from Entrance rock. The shoal extends 100 yards to the eastward of the rock, terminating in a $2\frac{1}{2}$-fathom spot.

A 4-fathom spot of small extent lies 500 yards S. 89° E. (N. 67° E. mag.) from Imperieuse rock.

The channel between Imperieuse rock and the northern shore is little more than 300 yards wide.

Directions.—When midway between Maude island and Blunden point, the fair course in is West (S. 66° W. mag.). When the east point of Southey island is shut in by the north entrance point, North rock will be passed, and the north shore should be kept rather aboard. Entrance rock should in no case be passed nearer than 500 yards, and if working in, beware of the North rock, and the sand bank already mentioned as extending off the south shore, and which stretches also $\frac{1}{4}$ mile westward from Entrance rock.

No convenient anchorage in less than 18 fathoms will be found, until well up toward the head. When Nanoose hill bears N. 24° E. (North mag.) anchor in 12 fathoms in the center of the harbor, or as near to either shore as desired. It is a spacious anchorage, and well sheltered from all winds.

There is a convenient nook with a steep shingle beach, where a vessel might be laid for repairs if necessary, on the north side, 1 mile from the head.

Communication—Supplies.—Skirting the southern shore of the harbor will be found the main road between Nanaimo and Comox and Alberni. The nearest post and telegraph office is at Nanoose, about $2\frac{1}{2}$ miles along the main road from the head of the harbor toward Alberni.

Meat and vegetables can be obtained from the ranches in the vicinity. In summer good water can be obtained from a stream emptying into the harbor just eastward of the old wharf near the Indian village. In winter nearly all the ravines have good water.

Tides.—It is high water, full and change, at 5 h. 4 m.; springs rise 14 feet, neaps rise 9 feet.

The coast for 6 miles westward of Nanoose harbor is fringed with numerous small islands and reefs, the latter generally marked by kelp. The outermost of them, Winchelsea and Yeo islands, already mentioned, extend from 1 to 2 miles from the land.

During westerly and southerly winds small vessels with local knowledge may find shelter in Schooner cove, which is 1½ miles westward of Nanoose harbor. The bottom is rocky, and a heavy swell prevails with other winds. There is a rock awash nearly in the center of the entrance, but nearer to the northern point.

Vessels should not attempt to pass between the Winchelsea islands and the northern entrance point of Nanoose harbor, as the existing survey is very inadequate. The tidal streams run irregularly amongst these islands.

Grey rock, awash at high water springs, lies 400 yards east of the eastern end of the Winchelsea group.

Rudder reef, awash at lowest water, lies ¼ mile S. 27° E. (S. 51° E. mag.) from Grey rock, and has very little kelp on it. This reef must be avoided by those bound westward from Nanoose harbor, and the SE. end of the Winchelsea islands should be given a berth of at least ½ mile.

Yeo and Gerald islands lie westward of the Winchelsea islands, and are smaller. Foul ground with several heads uncovering extends a distance of 550 yards to the westward of the west extreme of southern Yeo. A patch having 4 feet over it lies 200 yards from the SE. extreme of Gerald island.

Ballenas islands, two in number, are larger than those of the groups just described, and lie 2¼ miles offshore. The northernmost is 250 feet high; it has only two or three trees on it, and its summit terminates in a sharp bare nipple. The southernmost is 175 feet high and wooded.

They have the appearance of being one island seen from all points, being only separated by a narrow passage, which at the eastern entrance is less than 200 yards wide, but opens out within, and forms a sheltered cove with anchorage for small vessels in 8 fathoms, close to its southern sandy beach; on the west side this channel is almost closed, and there is no passage into it. The islands are steep and bold on all sides except a rocky shoal with 4 fathoms lying 450 yards off the SE. extreme of the southern island, and are conspicuous after passing westward of Nanaimo.

Light.—A fixed white light elevated 100 feet above high water, visible from a distance of 16 miles, is exhibited from a white, square, wooden tower, 38 feet high, erected on the SE. part of the eastern island.

The light may be obscured at intervals by trees when bearing from S. 51° E. (S. 75° E. mag.) through South to S. 45° W. (S. 21° W. mag.).

Fog signal.—A hand fog horn is sounded at the lighthouse when a vessel's fog signals are heard.

Ballenas channel, southward of the islands of the same name, is a safe, clear passage, 1¼ miles in width at its narrowest part (abreast Gerald island).

To steamers, coasters, or vessels with a fair wind, Ballenas channel is recommended. Large sailing vessels with a head wind would find it an advantage to make long boards, and pass northward of the islands through the main strait.

A rock with 15 feet of water over it, and 20 to 40 fathoms close around, is situated on the southern side of the channel, with Ballenas lighthouse bearing N. 1° W. (N. 25° W. mag.), distant 1$\frac{1}{10}$ miles. No kelp has been seen on this rock.

A rocky shoal with 24 feet over it lies 500 yards off the SE. extreme of the southern Ballenas island, with the lighthouse bearing N. 61° W. (N. 85° W. mag.); depths of 10 fathoms exist between the shoal and the island and 20 to 40 fathoms close-to on the outside. No kelp has been seen on the shoal.

Cottam reef has 2½ fathoms on it, and is generally marked by kelp; it lies on the southern side of the channel, and 1¾ miles S. 49° W. (S. 25° W. mag.) from the highest part of north Ballenas island. The northernmost of the Winchelsea islands kept open of Yeo islands bearing S. 61° E. (S. 85° E. mag.) leads well northward of the reef.

Dorcas rock.—This rock has a least depth of 4 feet over it, and lies 750 yards N. 30° W. (N. 54° W. mag.) from Dorcas point. The rock is 100 yards in extent and marked by kelp.

Buoy.—A black spar buoy is moored in 4 fathoms about 200 feet northward of the shoalest part of the rock.

Northwest bay, 5 miles westward from Nanoose, is much exposed to NW. winds and the water in it is very deep; a considerable stream flows into the bay at its western entrance.

Mistaken island, low, wooded, and ½ mile long, lies close off its northern entrance point, and 2½ miles southwestward from the north Ballenas island.

The coast.—From Northwest bay the land trends, with a slight indentation, nearly WNW. for 19 miles to Denman and Hornby islands, and to the southern entrances of Baynes sound and Lambert channel. This stretch of coast presents no remarkable feature, wooded bluffs, of moderate height, terminating in sandy or shingle points, off which for a very short distance the water is shoal.

The land between Nanoose and Comox district, a distance of 24 miles, is undulating and of a moderate height from the seacoast to the base of the mountain ranges, a distance of about 4 miles, and, although generally densely wooded near to the sea, is lightly timbered a short distance inland, with some patches of prairie land.

Qualicum river empties 30 miles westward from Nanaimo and 5 miles eastward from the southern entrance of Baynes sound. It is a small stream, only noticeable as affording shelter to canoes or boats within its entrance, and as being the terminus of the trail between the headwaters of Barkley sound and the eastern coast of the island, a distance of only 13 miles in a direct line.

Horn lake, from which this stream has its source, is 5½ miles SW. of the river entrance.

Buoy.—A black can buoy is moored in 5 fathoms about ⅓ mile northward of the river entrance.

Qualicum bay is a slight indentation of the coast, immediately westward of the river, where very fair anchorage will be found in 8 or 10 fathoms, at ¾ mile from the shore, with the east point of Hornby island bearing N. 18° E. (N. 6° W. mag.); the holding ground is good, and northerly winds, which would make it a lee shore, seldom blow with any strength. From NW. winds it is in a great measure sheltered by the islands, but with those from SE. a considerable sea will get up, though there would be plenty of room, and with good ground tackle no danger of drifting.

The mountain ranges westward of Nanaimo are of considerable height, and very striking in their general features and varied outlines; most conspicuous among them, and midway between Barkley sound and the east coast, rises mount Arrowsmith to a height of 5,976 feet, its remarkable summit terminating in three sharp, well-defined peaks, rarely free from snow.

General directions.—Ships may approach the coast between Qualicum bay and Yellow island to a distance of 1 mile, and convenient anchorage can be found off it. The only thing to be noticed is that as the entrance of Baynes sound is approached the water shoals very rapidly inside the 10-fathom curve; it will, therefore, be prudent to anchor in not less than 15 fathoms. The bottom is soft and the holding ground should be good. At night, or in thick weather, if the lights or the land of Yellow island can not be seen, ships should close the Vancouver island shore and anchor.

Denman and Hornby islands lie immediately off the coast 34 miles westward from Nanaimo. The former island is 10 miles long in a NW. direction, or parallel with the coast, and has an average width of 2 miles. Its highest elevation is 535 feet to the tops of the trees.

Hornby island is about 4 miles across in all directions; on its western side the land rises precipitously in terraces to a height of 1,090 feet, and then slopes away to the eastward. Both the islands are thickly wooded and contain a considerable quantity of good land occupied here and there by settlers with well-stocked farms. Denman island is separated from Vancouver island by Baynes sound, and Hornby from Denman by Lambert channel.

Baynes sound is a narrow sheet of water 15 miles long and accessible to ships of the largest size. It is important as containing the shipping place of the Union Collieries company of Cumberland; it is constantly visited by H. B. M. ships for gun and musketry practice. There are several good anchorages and few dangers. At the northern end is the mouth of the Courtenay river, one of the largest streams in Vancouver island, and in this neighborhood there is a large extent of good farming land cleared and cultivated.

Yellow island lies close off the SE. point of Denman island and forms the eastern entrance point of Baynes sound. It is small, bare, about 50 feet high, and rises steeply from the water. Ships may approach it from the southward and eastward with safety. Its yellow appearance and the white buildings of the lighthouses on it render it conspicuous.

There is no passage, except for boats, between Yellow and Denman islands; it dries nearly across at lowest tides.

Lights.—On Yellow island stand two light towers, 28 and 18 feet high, respectively, painted white, with red lanterns, and about the center of the island a large white house, the residence of the light-keeper.

From the eastern and higher tower there is shown, at an elevation of 71 feet above high water, a fixed white light of low power, visible in all directions, except where obscured by land, at a distance of 13 miles.

From the western tower, at an elevation of 48 feet above high water, a fixed white light is shown only in the direction of the entrance of Baynes sound.

The two lights, or towers, in one, bearing S. 82° E. (N. 74° E. mag.), lead through the entrance into Baynes sound in not less than 7 fathoms of water.

It is important to keep the towers exactly in line, as they are only 290 feet apart.

Buoys and beacons.—In addition to the two leading lights the following aids to navigation are maintained in the southern entrance of Baynes sound:

A beacon, painted black, with white latticework topmark consisting of two circular disks placed at right angles, stands in 6 feet of water near the northern extreme of the spit which dries off Maple point. This beacon shows 15 feet above high water.

A red conical buoy surmounted by a red triangle, R. B. No. 1, lies in 5 fathoms off the extreme of the rocky ledge which dries for 600 yards from Reef point.

Another red conical buoy, R. B. No. 2, lies in 8 fathoms and marks the outer edge of the foul ground 1,200 yards to the westward.

Maple point is low, and from the extremity of its trees, which are maples and contrast strongly with the prevailing pines, it extends in a westerly direction in the form of a narrow tongue of sand covered with grass. A solitary clump of high bushes stands near the center of this tongue. South of it is Deep bay, a good, sheltered anchorage for all classes of vessels.

A spit of sand and shingle dries off Maple point to the northward for ⅓ mile; its western side is steep, but shoal water extends to the eastward from the spit for a full ½ mile, and neither Maple point nor the shore line for 2 miles to the eastward of it should be approached by ships within ¾ mile, as the bank off it shoals very rapidly from 10 to 2 fathoms. The spit off Maple point is marked by a pile beacon, previously described, situated about 200 yards NE. of its extreme drying point. The line of shoal water extends for a distance of 600 yards eastward from the beacon straight toward Yellow island and then trends ESE. for ¾ mile.

The shore of Denman island for a distance of 2¾ miles forms the northern side of the entrance of Baynes sound, and is composed of steep slopes and cliffs of earth, fringed at the foot by a rocky reef strewn with bowlders, which gradually increases in width until at Reef point, 2 miles from Yellow island, it projects as a shelving rocky ledge for 500 yards into the channel in a southerly direction. Care is necessary in this locality, as the tidal streams, during the larger tides, run with a velocity of 2 to 3 knots, and the navigable width of the channel is reduced to 500 yards.

Reef point is a steep earth cliff of a red color, situated 2 miles W. by N. from Yellow island.

The fringing reef continues along to the westward from Reef point and shoal water extends off it, the outer edge being marked, 1,300 yards west of Reef point, by the red buoy, R. B. No. 2, previously mentioned, which lies 600 yards offshore. From here the coast of Denman island takes a NW. direction, and the fringing bowlder reef closes with the shore line with deep water close outside it.

Directions for approaching and entering Baynes sound by the southern entrance:

By night.—Approach Yellow island on a N. 55° W. (N. 79° W. mag.) bearing, and steer to come on to the line of lights in one at a distance of ¾ mile westward of the lower light. Keep the lights in line astern, attending carefully to the steering, until the second red buoy is passed, and the light on Denman island bears N. 40° W. (N. 64° W. mag.). The lead will prove of assistance, as a bank with depths of less than 10 fathoms extends beyond the second buoy, and must be crossed. When deep water is obtained on the western side of this bank a ship will be clear of the shoal water which extends off Denman island. Then steer for the light on this bearing until abreast Ship point. When Ship point is abeam alter course to N. 47° W. (N. 71° W. mag.); this course leads in mid-channel between Base Flat reef and Denman island. When the light bears East (N. 66° E. mag.) haul gradually to the northward and pass up mid-channel.

By day.—A good line of approach is the right tangent of Ship peninsula in line with the extreme of the trees on Denman island, bearing N. 63° W. (N. 87° W. mag.). When Yellow island is abeam steer to come on the line of the lighthouses at a distance of ¾ mile west of Yellow island, and keep them astern until the second buoy is passed.

Deep bay.—From Maple point the land recedes to the southward for ¾ mile, forming a sheltered bay in which there is convenient anchorage for vessels of any class. Short ships will find room close to the southward of the grassy tongue of land which projects westward from Maple point, a good line of approach being the extreme of trees on Maple point in line with the clear slope of a hill near the southern end of Denman island, bearing N. 62° E. (N. 38° E. mag.), until the solitary clump of bushes west of Maple point comes in line with the summit of Hornby island, or with the beacon off Maple point, bearing N. 28° E. (N. 4° E. mag.).

Larger ships are recommended to anchor farther southwestward on the same line, that is, with the extreme of trees on Maple point in line with the clear slope on Denman island, bearing N. 62° E. (N. 38° E. mag.), the end of the tongue of Maple point bearing N. 28° E. (N. 4° E. mag.), and the extreme of Ship peninsula bearing N. 44° W. (N. 68° W. mag.), in 13 to 15 fathoms at lowest water.

The tongue of Maple point is steep-to at its western end and on its southern side.

To clear the western edge of the drying spit off Maple point, Reef pont should bear to the eastward of N. 13° E. (N. 11° W. mag.).

At the head of Deep bay the shores are low and swampy, with shoal water extending some distance off, and flats of sand, mud, and shingle uncovering for 700 yards from the high-water line. From here to Ship peninsula, a distance of 2¾ miles, the same character prevails; at a distance of 1½ miles the shore recedes, forming a bight which entirely dries at low water; it is fronted by detached drying reefs of a dangerous character. This part of the sound should not be approached by vessels nearer than 1 mile from the shore.

Ship peninsula, the land of which is rendered conspicuous by high, dark trees, is connected by low, flat land, partly cleared, with the main island, and extends in a NW. and SE. direction for 1 mile. Its southeastern point is very foul and should on no account be approached by ships. Its northwestern extremity, known as Ship point, forms the eastern point of Fanny bay, where there is good anchorage for vessels.

Fanny bay.—This anchorage is limited by the drying flats which extend off the northern side of Ship peninsula and the southern side of Base flat, which is the delta of a small river called Baynes river.

To enter Fanny bay from the southward pass Ship point at a distance of 600 yards and steer S. 84° W. (S. 60° W. mag.) until the extreme of Ship peninsula is in line with the extreme of Denman island bearing S. 63° E. (S. 87° E. mag.), when anchor with the beacon on the edge of Base flat showing just outside Village point (Denman island), bearing N. 20° W. (N. 44° W. mag.), in 12 fathoms of water.

Base flat—Beacon.—Base flat is low and surrounded with a drifting bank of semicircular form, composed of sand and shingle, extending 500 yards from the shore. A beacon, exactly similar in appearance to that off Maple point, stands on the outer edge of the bank, but the form of the shoal is such that it runs nearly parallel to the general direction of the sound for quite ½ mile to the southward of the beacon, and in approaching Fanny bay from the northward, with the intention of entering, ships should not turn in for the anchorage until the wharf on Denman island bears to the westward of North (N. 24° W. mag.).

Light.—A fixed white light, 23 feet above high water, visible 7 miles, is exhibited from a tower erected on the reef off the western side of Denman island, about 1¼ miles southward of Village point and 250 feet from the shore.

The tower is a square wooden building with sloping sides, surmounted by a square wooden lantern, the whole painted white. It is 27 feet high and stands on a 12-foot concrete foundation; a bridge connects the tower with the shore.

Beacon.—A beacon, consisting of a pole and latticework drum, painted white, stands on the outer edge of the reef 200 feet S. 69° W. (S. 45° W. mag.) from the lighthouse.

Village point—Buoy.—Village point, on Denman island, is 3 miles north of Fanny bay. A sand spit, with rocky ledges uncovering, extends 300 yards from the shore, its western edge being marked by a red conical buoy. Northward of the sand spit is good anchorage for vessels of all classes.

Union bay.—On the western side of Baynes sound, 11 miles from Yellow island, is the shipping place for the coal brought from the mines of the Union Collieries company, situated near the town of Cumberland. A railroad 14 miles in length connects the mines with the wharves, alongside which there are depths of 30 to 36 feet, the bottom having been dredged to these depths to a distance of about

100 feet from the wharf. Ships can load alongside directly from the trucks, or from lighters if available. The output of the mines is about 1,000 tons per diem, and this amount can be delivered to ships. There are coke manufactories capable of producing 100 tons a day, and it is shipped to Victoria in specially adapted railroad trucks.

Good water is piped to the wharves, and a limited supply of fresh provisions can be obtained from Cumberland. There is anchorage off the wharves, in 10 or 11 fathoms, near a mooring buoy used for hauling off.

A drying spit of mud and stones extends off Union point, which is situated immediately to the northward of the wharves.

Beacon.—A beacon, consisting of a single black pile with circular white disk of latticework, showing 10 feet above high water, standing in 18 feet of water, marks the edge of this mud bank.

Henry bay.—The NW. end of Denman island terminates in a narrow, sandy extreme, running to the westward from the end of the trees, called Beak point. On its southern side is Henry bay, a safe and convenient anchorage.

From Beak point a series of sandy islets, standing on a drying flat, extends for 1½ miles in a northwesterly direction. The largest of the islets, Sandy island, has a conspicuous clump of trees; the others are bare. These islets are used as sites for targets in connection with the gun practice of H. B. M. ships.

Three red spar buoys, to mark the prize-firing base, are moored in the sound to the westward of Sandy island, on a NW. by N. and SE. by S. line of bearing, and about 1,200 yards from the edge of the drying flat.

Kelp bar.—From the northernmost islet, which nearly covers at highest tides, the drying flat extends to the northwestward for ¾ mile. A shallow ridge, forming a barrier impassable for ships at low water, and about a mile broad between the 5-fathom curves, connects the flat with the main shore eastward of Goose spit at Comox. This ridge is locally known as Kelp bar, and is composed of sand interspersed with patches of rocks and bowlders. Great quantities of kelp grow on it during summer. The edges of Kelp bar are steep, shoaling rapidly from upward of 20 fathoms.

Navigable depths.—There is a depth of 10 feet on the crossing at low water of a tide which falls to zero at Port Townsend.

To find the depths on the bar at high or low water of any tide: Multiply the height of the tide as given in the tide tables for Port Townsend by 1.36 and add 10 feet to the result.

Buoys and beacons.—Two red spar buoys have been placed, at a distance of 1,000 yards apart, to mark the best crossing over the bar. These replace the beacons which formerly led over the bar. In addition, there are four white planks nailed diagonally on trees close to the shore, at a distance of 2 miles from the inner buoy, which, when on the line of crossing, appear as two St. Andrew's crosses, one vertically above the other.

A red bell buoy is moored on the eastern side of the bar, in 25 fathoms, 1,100 yards from the outer buoy. From the buoy Goose Spit beacon bears S. 88° W. (S. 64° W. mag.), distant 2¾ miles, and the highest tree on Sandy island S. 4° E. (S. 28° E. mag.).

Port Augusta occupies the head of Baynes sound and is a well-protected anchorage for all classes of vessels, but is limited in extent by the extensive mud flats making off from the shores of the bay. The Courtenay river flows into it on the western side.

The anchorage is situated to the northward of Goose spit, a remarkable, elbow-shaped tongue of low land which projects to the southward and westward from White bluff.

The small village of Comox occupies the northern shore, and is the shipping place for the surrounding agricultural district. There is a long wooden pier with 12 to 14 feet of water alongside its outer end at lowest water.

Communication.—There are roads connecting Comox with Nanaimo, Cumberland, Courtenay, and the surrounding district. A steamer from Victoria calls weekly. There is a post-office and telegraphic communication.

Supplies of fresh provisions are procurable in small quantities at Comox; they can be obtained from Cumberland on due notice.

Goose spit—Beacon.—Goose spit forms the northern point of the entrance and is marked, near its SW. extreme, by a beacon of pyramidal form, 32 feet high, painted black and white, and surmounted by an inverted triangular topmark. The spit is low and grassy, with one or two sand hillocks and clumps of trees, and contains the naval rifle range, the buildings of which are conspicuous.

Grassy point—Beacon.—Grassy point, the southern entrance point of Port Augusta, is low and swampy, the delta of a small river. Off it, at low water, mud and shingle flats uncover for 400 yards, their eastern extreme being marked by a black pile beacon, showing 12 feet above high water, with a white ball topmark of latticework, standing in 2½ fathoms. The line of drying flats extends for ½ mile in a WNW. direction, and in a SSE. direction for ¾ mile from the beacon.

Directions.—Entering Port Augusta, round Goose spit at a distance of 300 yards and anchor as convenient. A good line for anchoring on is the Musketry pier end in line with the north extreme of the range house bearing S. 71° E. (N. 83° E. mag.).

Caution.—Some local magnetic disturbance has been observed here, about 2½° in excess of the variation, but it does not appear to extend beyond the port.

The end of the Musketry pier in line with the south extreme of the Range house will keep a ship from 100 to 200 yards clear of the bank which extends entirely along the north side of the anchorage.

Tides.—At Port Augusta the higher high waters occur 1 h. 30 m., and the lower high waters at 1 h. 5 m., after those at Port Townsend. The higher and lower low waters occur 1 h. 57 m. and 1 h. 47 m., respectively, after those at Port Townsend. The ratio of ranges is 1.36.

Courtenay river drains Puntluch lake, and is joined by several large streams having their sources in the mountains, the principal being the Brown and Tsolum rivers, the latter joining the Courtenay at the village of that name about 4 miles from Comox. The valley of the Tsolum has a considerable extent of grass country lightly timbered.

Lambert channel, between Denman and Hornby islands, is a safe passage 6 miles long in a general NW. direction. It is 1¼ miles wide at its southern entrance between Norris rock and Yellow island. The chart is sufficient guide for vessels to pass through in mid-channel.

Norris rock, 10 feet high, is 400 yards long at low water, but is a mere patch at high water. It lies 1½ miles N. 63° E. (N. 39° E. mag.) from Yellow island and ¾ mile from Norman point, the south point of Hornby island. From the latter, reefs and foul ground extend for nearly 800 yards toward Norris rock, leaving a narrow passage of 8 fathoms between; this passage is not recommended.

Three-quarters of a mile NW. of Norman point a reef of rocks, 600 yards in length, drying 14 feet, lies about 300 yards from the shore-line of Hornby island; just inside is a pier at which the steamer from Victoria calls weekly. There is 6 feet alongside the end of the pier at lowest water. Norris rock bearing S. 66° E. (East mag.) clears the reef.

Buoy.—A black spar buoy is moored in 3 fathoms close to the southern extremity of the reef, with the end of the pier bearing N. 59° E. (N. 35° E. mag.), distant 300 yards.

Shingle spit, on Hornby island, 2 miles NW. of Norman point, extends into the channel for 300 yards and foul ground extends 300 yards farther. This shoal dries nearly its whole length at low water of the larger tides.

In passing Shingle spit, the eastern extreme of Denman island should not be brought to bear southward of S. 36° E. (S. 60° E. mag.) until the clump of trees near the end of the spit bears N. 63° E. (N. 39° E. mag.).

Anchorage.—Shelter and good holding ground will be found to the northward of Shingle spit, but to the southward the depths are irregular and it can not be recommended.

Phipps point, the west point of Hornby island, may be approached from the westward to ½ mile, but from Phipps point drying reefs and shoal water extend to the northward, and off Bowlder point, 1¼ miles NE. from Phipps point, the ledge extends for more than ¾ mile from the shore in a NW. direction, and the 5-fathom curve for ¼ mile beyond this. The northeastern shore of Hornby island presents no dangers and can be approached with safety.

St. John point.—The eastern end of Hornby island terminates in a comparatively low, lightly wooded point, with a small rocky islet, 20 feet high, situated 500 yards eastward of it. There is a boat passage between the island and the point.

Rocky ledges which cover near high water, extend in a SE. direction from the islet for 800 yards, and caution is necessary in rounding this point at high water as these reefs do not always break. Yellow Island light bearing S. 65° W. (S. 41° W. mag.), or Norris rock seen in the gap between Yellow island and Boyle point, just clears the shoal water extending from these dangers.

Tribune bay, on the SE. side of Hornby island, affords good anchorage with all but easterly or southeasterly winds, to which it is exposed. It is easy to enter or to leave, and conveniently situated as a stopping place for vessels bound either way, being 35 miles westward of Nanaimo, and 40 miles eastward of cape Mudge and the entrance of Discovery passage.

The entrance of Tribune bay is 1 mile west of St. John point; its eastern shores are bold and cliffy, its western low and shelving, with shallow water, and reefs extending a considerable distance off them.

Nash bank, the outermost of these dangers, is a 1-fathom rocky patch, which must be carefully avoided. It extends nearly 1 mile SE. by E. from Dunlop point. There is no passage between it and Dunlop point.

To clear Nash bank, Yellow island should be seen to the southward of Norris rock, bearing S. 64° W. (S. 40° W. mag.).

Denman island—East shore.—The eastern side of Denman island is fringed with reef, and should not be approached to less than a depth of 10 fathoms. At a point 5 miles NW. from its SE. point (Boyle point) and 1¾ miles from Phipps point, Hornby island, the drying reef extends 700 yards from the shore-line, and near its edge is a solitary bowlder that dries 9 feet; the 5-fathom curve is ½ mile offshore. Northward of this the shore becomes higher and is thickly wooded to the water's edge. In places landslides have occurred and formed conspicuous cliffs of white clay. The extremity of the trees on Shingle spit in line with the SE. extreme of Denman island bearing S. 25° E. (S. 49° E. mag.) will keep a vessel clear of danger.

To the northward of Beak point and eastward of the line of islets, several bowlders cover and uncover and are dangerous to boats when the water is high. These can all be avoided by keeping the distant extreme of Denman island in sight open of Komas bluff. The outer and largest of these bowlders is Palliser rock; it lies in 6 feet at lowest water, 1,200 yards NNE. from the center of the clump of trees on Sandy island. Palliser rock dries 13½ feet.

Light-draft boats may find a passage between Sandy island and Beak point when the water is high. The eastern side of the bank is rocky.

Cape Lazo.—This salient headland lies 15 miles NW. from the eastern end of Hornby island; it is about 200 feet high and flat-topped, falling abruptly to the sea in cliffs of yellow clay of about 100 feet. Extensive ledges with large bowlders dry off, and shoal water extends for 1½ miles to the SE. and 1 mile to the eastward from the cape. Ships should give the cape a berth of at least 2 miles, and, rounding it with the intention of entering Baynes sound by the northern passage, should not alter course for the bar until White bluff, near Comox, bears westward of S. 63° W. (S. 39° W. mag.), when they may steer for the bell buoy.

Oyster bay.—From cape Lazo the coast trends NW., is moderately high, and slightly indented with bowlder beaches, which makes boat landing dangerous unless it is very calm weather. At the distance of 15 miles is Kuhushan point, the southern extreme of a large but not very deep indentation named Oyster bay; it is a very low point. The trees, which might in thick weather be taken for the outer part of the point, begin 300 yards within it. Shelter point, nearly 4 miles NW. ½ N. from Kuhushan, is its northern extreme.

A reef, which affords considerable protection from NW. winds, extends ½ mile eastward from Shelter point. The entrance to Discovery passage is 4 miles northwestward from Oyster bay.

Anchorage.—There is fair anchorage in 10 or 12 fathoms in this bay for those awaiting wind or tide. A good berth is a little more than ½ mile from the shore with Mitlenatch island bearing N. 76° E. (N. 51° E. mag.), and the highest part of cape Mudge just open of the low extreme of Shelter point bearing N. 9° W. (N. 34° W. mag.).

Cape Mudge, the southern point of Quadra island (formerly Valdes island), and forming the eastern side of the entrance to Discovery passage, is flat and wooded, and terminates in a broad, whitish-yellow earth cliff, covered here and there with vegetation, and facing to the SE. The cliff is 230 feet high at its highest part and decreases gradually in height to the westward until it joins the shore-line at the entrance to Discovery passage.

A bowlder beach extends in a semicircular form from it to the eastward, and at the distance of 2 miles in this direction the depth is not more than 5 fathoms. The edge of this shoal water is fringed with kelp during summer, and is generally well defined by a tidal line, and sometimes heavy tide rips, which it is recommended not to stand into. The first of the flood sets strongly over the reef. Between cape Mudge and Willow point the tide rips at flood are dangerous to small craft in blowing weather. The low western part of cape Mudge should not be brought to bear westward of N. 45° W. (N. 70° W. mag.) when entering or leaving Discovery passage.

Light.—A fixed white light, 32 feet above high water, visible 10 miles between the bearings S. 24° E. (S. 49° E. mag.) and N. 49° W. (N. 74° W. mag.) through East and North, is exhibited from the western extremity of cape Mudge.

The lighthouse is a square wooden building, 30 feet high, painted white, with red roof and lantern.

Sisters islets are two small black rocks 17 feet above high water, SW. by W. from the west point of Lasqueti, with Stevens passage, a deep-water channel over 1 mile wide between them and Flat islands. The Sisters should not be approached too close in calm or light winds, as the tide sets straight past them.

Light.—A white intermittent light, every 30 seconds, light 20 seconds, eclipse 10 seconds, 46 feet above high water, visible 12 miles, is exhibited from a square tower, 36 feet high, with red lantern, surmounting a white rectangular dwelling, erected on the eastern and largest islet.

Fog signal.—A bell suspended at the NE. corner of the building is struck once every 30 seconds.

Rocks.—A rock with 10 feet over it lies 200 yards ENE. from Sisters Rocks lighthouse. Another, which dries 1 foot at extreme low water, lies 350 yards SW. ½ W. from the lighthouse.

Caution.—When standing westward toward the Denman island shore, Lambert channel should not be opened out between the SE. end of the island and Shingle spit, nor should cape Lazo be approached nearer than 2 miles.

NORTHERN SHORE OF THE STRAIT OF GEORGIA.

Howe sound, immediately adjoining Burrard inlet on the north, is an extensive sheet of water, penetrating the continent in a NNE. direction for 24 miles, the general depth being very great, while there are but few anchorages. It is almost entirely hemmed in by rugged and precipitous mountains rising abruptly from the water's edge to elevations of from 4,000 to 6,000 feet.

The entrance to the sound, between Atkinson point, the north point of Burrard inlet, and Gower point, is nearly 12 miles wide, and this width is maintained for over 10 miles, when it gradually narrows, the upper part of the sound having a general width of under 2 miles.

In the entrance and lower part of the sound are two large islands, Bowen and Gambier, and several smaller ones.

A river of considerable size, the Squamish, flows into the head of the sound, off the mouth of which a mud and sand flat dries out for nearly ¾ mile. There is a small settlement and post-office at the eastern mouth of the river, and a wharf extends in a SW. by S. direction to the edge of the drying bank.

Bowen island, the largest and easternmost, lying at the entrance, is remarkable, mount Gardner, rising to 2,479 feet, being round, smooth, and partially bare, unmistakably pointing out the entrance from any direction; the island is 7 miles in length in a northerly direction, and more than 3 miles in width.

Queen Charlotte channel, the easternmost passage into Howe sound, is between Bowen island and Atkinson point; Passage island, only ½ mile long, but very prominent from the southward, stands in the center of the channel, and on both sides of it is a deep-water passage; that to the west, 1½ miles in width, is the better. A tide rip is frequently met with off Atkinson point caused by the meeting of the ebb streams from the sound and Burrard inlet.

A rock with 1¼ fathoms over it at low water, and 12 to 15 fathoms close alongside, is situated midway between Bird island and the point immediately opposite on the mainland, known as Copper point.

Snug cove.—At 1¾ miles northward of Passage island, and on the eastern shore, is White Cliff point, and opposite, on the Bowen island coast, distant 1½ miles, is a double-headed cove. Snug cove, the southern of these, though narrow, affords excellent anchorage to small craft in 9 fathoms, sheltered from all winds.

Deep cove, the northern, is larger, but with a SE. wind, when anchorage would be most required, a swell would set in. After passing White Cliff point the width of the channel increases to 2¼ miles, and 3 miles to the northward is Bowyer island.

White rock is a small but remarkable islet 36 feet high about 4 miles northward of Bowyer island; some rocks which cover at high water extend ¼ mile north and south from it.

Center island lies midway between it and the south point of Anvil island.

Directions.—Vessels bound to Port Graves, which is the principal anchorage in the sound, should pass westward of Bowyer island between it and Hood point, the northern point of Bowen island. The latter is a rather remarkable, low, flat, peninsula point, with a small, high, cliffy island lying off it, connected at low water; both island and point are bold. From Hood point, Hope point bears N. 72° W.

(S. 84° W. mag.), and after rounding it a N. 23° E. (N. 1° W. mag.) course leads into the harbor.

Bound up the sound by Queen Charlotte channel, a North (N. 24° W. mag.) course leads in mid-channel; pass eastward of White rock, Center island, and Anvil island, through Montagu channel.

Anvil island is 3 miles long, and the summit, Leading peak, 2,746 feet high, is very remarkable, resembling the horn of an anvil pointed upward. From almost all parts of Georgia strait this peak appears as a most prominent object.

Anchorage.—The sound carries its depth to the head, and shoals from 100 fathoms suddenly to 2 fathoms; the latter depth is close to the mud at the head of the sound, which is so soft, that, supposing a vessel to anchor, she would be certain to drag on shore with any wind up the sound.

Anchorage may be obtained off a waterfall on the eastern side of the sound in 20 fathoms, about 400 yards from the shore and 1 mile from the entrance of the Squamish river, with Watts inner point bearing S. 58° W. (S. 34° W. mag.).

This can only be considered a temporary anchorage; the wind blows off the mountains in squalls during the winter months, and a vessel would inevitably drag her anchors.

Collingwood channel, to the westward of Bowen island, between it and the group of smaller islands which stud the center of the sound, is the most direct route to Port Graves. At the entrance both shores are steep-to and bold; the channel takes a northerly direction, and is for 4 miles about 1 mile wide, the general depth varying from 50 to 100 fathoms.

A rock which uncovers at very low spring tides lies 1⅜ miles S. 46° W. (S. 22° W. mag.) of Hutt island, and 1 mile S. 39° E. (S. 63° E. mag.) of Cotton point, Keats island.

Worlcombe island is the outermost of the small islands, ½ mile long east and west, and very narrow.

Passage rock, which lies almost midway between Worlcombe and Pasley islands, and covers at half tide, lies 700 yards N. 45° W. (N. 69° W. mag.) of the eastern point of Worlcombe island, and when working in or out, vessels should not stand so far to the westward, between Worlcombe and Pasley islands, as to shut in the western points of White and Ragged islands behind the low eastern point of Pasley island.

White island, 1½ miles northward of Worlcombe, is small and round with some white quartz veins showing through the foliage.

Ragged island is a short distance farther to the northward, and has four or five very remarkable bare white rocks lying off its eastern end.

Keats island forms the western side of the channel; it is 3 miles long, moderately high, with a bare cliffy summit near its center.

Barfleur passage lies to the westward of the central group of small islands, between them and Keats island; it is a safe ship channel, but not quite so wide as Collingwood channel.

Working in, it is better not to approach nearer than ¼ mile to Popham island and the two smaller ones north of it, which form the eastern side of the passage. The passages between the small islands are not recommended.

A rock, on which the sea breaks at low water, lies 300 yards westward from the second of these islands.

Shoal channel, the westernmost entrance to Howe sound, is convenient for those coming from the westward, and leads to Plumper cove, a snug anchorage on the NW. side of Keats island.

The southern point of Keats island, which forms the eastern point of entrance to the channel, has, lying close off it, Home island, a small but prominent and thickly-wooded island. From a short distance northward from this island a bar of sand and shingle extends quite across the channel to the steep cliffs of the mainland; the depth of water on it varies from 7 to 18 feet. When entering, keep rather over to the mainland side and about 400 yards from it.

Observation point in line with the north end of south Shelter island, or just showing to the westward of it, bearing N. 47° E. (N. 23° E. mag.), leads over the bar in 2¼ fathoms; but vessels drawing more than 8 feet are recommended not to attempt Shoal channel at low water.

Two rocks, both drying 3 feet at low water springs, and lying N. ¾ E. and S. ¾ W., distant nearly 200 yards, from each other, lie near Steep Cliff point.

From the northern rock the extremity of the wharf at Gibson's landing bears N. 63° W. (N. 87° W. mag.), distant 580 yards.

Beacon.—A stone beacon, painted black, surmounted by a wooden staff and latticework ball, painted white, showing 15 feet above high water, is erected on the northern rock.

A rocky spit extends in a southerly direction for 300 yards from the shore under the hill marked "Conspicuous cone" on the chart. The extreme of the spit is a rock awash at lowest tides. From the rock the summit of south Shelter island bears S. 18° E. (S. 42° E. mag.), distant 1,600 yards.

Plumper cove.—Immediately after crossing the bar of Shoal channel the water deepens to 20 fathoms, and two small islets, partially wooded, and almost joined at low water, will be seen 1 mile NE.; between them and the shore of Keats island is Plumper cove, which is perfectly sheltered from all winds, as, however hard it may be blowing outside, it is generally calm here. If wishing to enter, pass round the north end of the islets.

Anchor in 8 fathoms in the center of the cove. There is room to lie at single anchor, but it is recommended to moor, dropping the outer anchor in 10 fathoms when the north end of the islets bears N. 66° W. (West mag.), and running up the center of the cove, drop the inner one in 6 fathoms; there is only room for one large vessel, but several small ones could find shelter.

It is high water, full and change, in Plumper cove at 0 h. 0 m.; springs rise 12 feet.

Thornborough channel is a continuation of Shoal channel. Its direction after passing Plumper cove is north, and at the distance of 6 miles is Woolridge island. The wider channel lies westward of this island, but there is over 100 fathoms of water through Latona passage to the eastward of it, and a width of ¼ mile. Passing Woolridge island, the arm turns to the northeastward and, northward of Anvil island, leads to the head of the sound. The depth of water is very great in every part, and there is no anchorage above.

Gambier island, immediately northward of Bowen island and separated from it by Collingwood channel, is almost square-shaped and 6 miles in extent either way. On its western side rise two remarkable cone-shaped mountains over 3,000 feet in elevation. The southern face of the island is indented by three deep bays or inlets, but only in the easternmost is convenient anchorage found. Close off the SW. point of the island are the Twins, two small islets; they are the only part of its coast which may not be approached very close.

Ramilles channel separates Gambier and Anvil islands; like the rest of the sound, it is very deep.

Port Graves, the easternmost of the three bays on the south side of Gambier island, is the principal anchorage in Howe sound. It is about 8 miles from the entrance and may be reached with great facility by any of the channels already described; its entrance will not, however, be very apparent to strangers until closing Hope point, which forms its eastern side.

The direction of the port, as also of the two deep bays westward of it, is NNE. and it runs more than 1½ miles in that direction; the width is not quite ½ mile.

Hutt island, scarcely ½ mile long, but very high and remarkable, lies close off the NW. side of Bowen island, and is a good guide to the port when entering by either of the western channels; from it Hope point bears N. 13° E. (N. 11° W. mag.), distant 1½ miles; keep the Hope point shore aboard on the starboard hand.

Directions.—On the western shore, ¾ mile inside the entrance, a shingle spit extends out for a short distance, which should be given a good berth, as shoal water extends 100 yards off it; when past this spit there is anchorage anywhere in 10 fathoms, but ½ mile or more inside it, in 7 fathoms, is the best berth. When entering by Shoal channel, and bound for Port Graves, after passing Plumper cove steer N. 69° E. (N. 45° E. mag.) until near Hope point, and see the harbor open, in order not to mistake either of the western bays for it.

It is high water, full and change, in Port Graves at noon; springs rise 12 feet.

The coast from Gower point trends about WNW. for 18 miles to the entrance to Malaspina strait.

Rock point.—The point next westward of Gower point is named Rock point; a bowlder reef extends ½ mile from shore just eastward of the point.

Buoy.—A red spar buoy is moored in 6 fathoms to mark the reef off Rock point.

White islets are two bare rocks, 15 feet high, with deep water close to them, which lie 1½ miles offshore and 6 miles westward of Gower point. They always show white and are remarkable.

Seechelt light.—A fixed white light, 36 feet above high water, visible 6 miles, is shown from a small, white, wooden tower, standing on a black, wooden framework, erected on the western White islet. The light is unwatched.

Halibut bank, situated about 5 miles south of White islets, consists of two portions lying NW. and SE. of each other, 1 mile apart between their shoalest spots.

The northwestern portion is 1 mile in length, north and south, and ¾ mile wide; it has a least depth of 12 fathoms, the bottom being hard sand and stone.

The southeastern portion is ¾ mile in length, NW. and SE., with 15 fathoms least water.

Trail bay lies about 4 miles NNW. from White islets. There is a very marked drop in the land at the head of this bay, across which, by a portage of ½ mile, the natives carry their canoes into Seechelt arm, one of the many arms of Jervis inlet.

Anchorage may be had off the village in Trail bay, abreast a bluff in the NE. corner, in about 15 fathoms. The Indians (Seechelt) are under the care of the Roman Catholic mission, and their chapel is a conspicuous object from seaward.

Trail islands, four in number, lie a little more than ½ mile off the western end of this bay, and if necessary small vessels may drop an anchor inside them in 12 or 13 fathoms. There is a rock which dries at low water NW. from the western Trail island and 400 yards off the mainland coast.

Texada island is 27 miles in length, with an average width of 4 miles. Throughout its whole length stretches a ridge of rugged trap mountains, wooded generally to the summit; at the southern end mount Shepherd reaches a height of 2,906 feet; toward the northern end the range decreases in elevation, but there is scarcely an acre of land fit for cultivation throughout the island. Its shores are steep and bold on all sides, and the land rises abruptly, except at the northern extreme; good limestone is found at the northern end of the island.

A reef extends 400 yards off the northern end of the island; near the end of the reef is a rock that dries 4 feet.

Buoy.—A black spar buoy is moored in 6 fathoms of water off the end of the reef.

Gillies bay, the only anchorage, and that merely a stopping place, is on the SW. side, 2 miles north of the Mouatt islets, a small group lying nearly 1 mile from shore. The bay is easily recognized by a remarkable white patch on its northern point, which is seen for many miles, and shows as two distinct white spots; an anchor may be dropped at ¼ mile from the beach in 12 fathoms.

Upwood point, the SE. extreme of Texada island, is rugged and precipitous; stunted pines grow in the crevices of the bare trap rock; the land behind is more thickly wooded. Almost immediately over it rises mount Dick, a very remarkable hump-shaped hill, 1,136 feet high. A rock which covers lies 400 yards off the point.

Sturt bay is a small inlet situated on the NE. coast of Texada island, about 3 miles from its northern end.

It is about 700 yards in length, but at the entrance has a width of only 200 yards between the 5-fathom curves.

There is a wharf 114 feet long on the eastern side of the bay, and another 90 feet long at the head of the bay.

Van Anda cove is the bight next eastward of Sturt bay. At the head of the cove is a wharf, and a settlement is building up in connection with the development of copper mines. The approach to the wharf is free from outlying dangers.

The extremity of the spit extending from the eastern point of the cove is marked by a small beacon in 9 feet of water.

Lasqueti island is 9 miles long, with an average width of over 2 miles; mount Tremeton is a singular turret-shaped summit, 1,056 feet high, rising nearly in its center. On its southern side are several boat coves.

Tucker bay, on the north side of Lasqueti, is a very fair anchorage. Entering from the westward it will be readily known by a group of small wooded islands which form its eastern side; its western point (West point) is sloping, somewhat remarkable, and partially bare of trees. The water shoals rather suddenly from 30 to 16 fathoms.

The anchorage is in 14 fathoms, with the outermost and westernmost of the small islands bearing N. 46° E. (N. 22° E. mag.), and West point N. 50° W. (N. 74° W. mag.), which will be within ¼ mile of the shore. With a strong NW. wind and flood tide the bay, though safe, would not be a comfortable anchorage; from the eastward sailing vessels would find some difficulty in reaching it in consequence of the prevailing NW. winds and the narrowness of the channel at that end.

Small vessels may anchor in the SE. corner, inside the small island on the south shore, in 6 or 7 fathoms, sheltered from almost any wind.

Tides.—It is high water, full and change, at 7 h. 30 m.; springs rise 16 feet.

Sangster island, ½ mile long, lies 1 mile SW. from Young point, the SE. extreme of Lasqueti. There is a deep passage of 70 fathoms between the two, but a rocky ledge with shoal water on it extends off the NW. point of Sangster island.

Seal rocks, which cover at half tide, lie a little more than 1 mile N. 61° W. (N. 85° W. mag.) of the western point of Sangster island, and it is not recommended to pass between the island and the rocks.

Jenkins island lies 3 miles westward of Sangster, and close to the southern shore of Lasqueti.

Sea Egg rocks, 12 feet high, lie 600 yards off the west end of Jenkins island.

False bay, in the west end of Lasqueti island, is a deep bight, but is not recommended as an anchorage, though small vessels would find shelter in its northwestern corner in 7 fathoms.

Stevens passage, between the Sisters islets and Lasqueti, is upward of 1 mile wide. Flat islands, on its eastern side, should be given a berth of ¼ mile, as should also Bare islands, a small group lying off the northwestern end of Lasqueti.

Sabine channel, between Texada and Lasqueti islands, is a good ship passage 9 miles long in a NW. and SE. direction, with very deep water; it is 3 miles wide at its western end, but several high conical islands (the two largest being Jedidiah and Jervis islands) lying off the NE. side of Lasqueti contract the width at the eastern end to ¾ mile in some parts. There is also a narrow but deep channel, Bull passage, to the SW. of these islands, running along the Lasqueti shore.

The tidal streams through Sabine channel run 2 knots an hour, the flood running NW., the ebb SE.

Malaspina strait is a wide navigable channel, separating Texada island from the mainland. Its general direction is NW. for 30 miles, when it again enters Georgia strait between the north end of Texada and Harwood islands; its southern entrance lies between Upwood point and the western of the Thormanby islands, and is 4 miles in width. The Texada shore is steep-to, and almost straight for its whole length, fronted by narrow shingle or bowlder beaches.

Thormanby islands, two in number, about 550 feet high, almost joined, and upward of 2 miles in extent, form the SE. entrance point of Malaspina strait. Lying close to the mainland, these islands appear as part of it, terminating at their NW. point in a steep clay cliff, off which, at low water, dries a bowlder point. Shoal water extends from this point NW. for about 800 yards, and a bank with less than 10 fathoms on it extends from the northern side of the western island for 1 mile.

From the north point of the eastern island, Tattenham ledge extends ½ mile NW.; this ledge uncovers at the inner part, and has 4 fathoms of water on the outer.

On the outer part of the ledge, 700 yards NNW. from the point, is a rock which dries at low water springs.

Buoy.—A platform buoy surmounted by a latticework pyramid, the whole painted black, is moored in 4½ fathoms off the northern end of Tattenham ledge.

Welcome pass, separating Thormanby islands from the main, is a deep but narrow channel about 1 mile long. A detached rock which uncovers at lowest tides lies at the southern entrance to the pass and 400 yards from East Thormanby island; there is a depth of 18 fathoms close to the rock on the channel side. The mainland shore of the pass is steep-to and can be approached to a distance of 100 yards.

A rock which dries 9 feet, with deep water around, lies off the southern end of East Thormanby island; it is situated 1,150 yards N. 73° E. (N. 49° E. mag.) from Bare islet.

Merry island, lying about midway between the southern end of East Thormanby and the mainland, is about 250 feet high; there are several rocks off the south and east sides of the island, which should be given a berth of ½ mile.

Welcome point is the rounded point east of Merry island; off it a shoal extends for 600 yards. This shoal is marked by a red spar buoy moored in 6 fathoms.

Light.—From a wooden lantern surmounting a rectangular wooden building, the whole painted white, erected on the SE. point of Merry island, is shown a fixed white light, 57 feet above high water and visible 6 miles.

Buccaneer bay, formed by the junction of the two Thormanby islands, on their northern side, extends in a southerly direction for over 1 mile and affords good and sheltered anchorage at its head in 15 fathoms.

Caution must be observed when entering, as shoal water extends for fully ½ mile from the northern shore of both islands on both sides of the entrance.

Tattenham ledge, the northern edge of which is marked by a black buoy, will be avoided by keeping the outer of the Surry islands in line with Wolf point and the center of the beach at the head of the bay bearing S. 8° E. (S. 32° E. mag.).

Secret cove.—At 1 mile northward of the entrance to Buccaneer bay is the entrance to Secret cove, formed between Turnagain island and the shore of the mainland. The channel in, between George point (the SE. end of Turnagain island) and Entrance island to the eastward, is 100 yards wide with depths of from 7 to 11 fathoms in it. One hundred yards S. 57° W. (S. 33° W. mag.) from the west end of Entrance island is a rocky patch which covers at three-quarters flood; it will be cleared by keeping White rock (2 feet high) inside the harbor on its west shore, just open of the NW. points of Entrance island, bearing N. 54° E. (N. 30° E. mag.).

When past Entrance island, anchorage may be taken up as convenient in 7 to 9 fathoms, midway between that island and Echo island.

Bjerre shoal.—Three miles northwestward from the entrance to Secret cove and 1,800 yards from the eastern shore of the strait is Bjerre shoal, rocky, 140 yards in extent, with 12 feet over it at low water.

Rocky patch.—From Secret cove the coast, which trends NW., is steep-to for 4 miles, at which distance a rocky patch of considerable extent lies 1 mile S. 33° E. (S. 57° E. mag.) from Francis point, and extends nearly the same distance parallel to the shore. The least water found on the patch was 7 fathoms, but less may probably exist.

Bargain harbor is a small harbor with depths of 5 and 6 fathoms in it. The entrance lies between the Whitestone islands (lying about 600 yards SE. from Francis point) and the islets off the shore to the eastward, the largest of which are Flat (the southern) and Green islets. By keeping in mid-channel the harbor may be safely entered.

Pender harbor is the only anchorage with a moderate depth of water to be found in the neighborhood of Jervis inlet, but its entrance is so encumbered by islands as to render it difficult of access to any but steam or coasting vessels.

When coming from Jervis inlet by Agamemnon channel, the passage between Channel islets and Pearson island to the SW. and Norman point to the NE. is the most convenient, but coming from any other direction it would be better to use either the one between Pearson island and Channel islets, or that between the former island and Martin island; the latter is to be preferred.

A pinnacle rock, with 4 to 8 fathoms close around, which dries at extreme low water, lies with the west extreme of Martin island S. 1° E. (S. 25° E. mag.), distant 667 yards; and the north extreme of Pearson island N. 58° W. (N. 82° W. mag.).

One hundred yards NE. of Martin island is a large rock, awash at high water. There is also a rock, which dries just after high water, on the edge of the shoal extending 70 yards NW. from Williams island.

Williams and Charles islands lie immediately across the entrance forming three channels; that to the northward between Williams island and the main (Henry point) is not 200 yards in width, but it is the best and has a depth of 20 fathoms.

A rock, which covers at three-quarters flood, lies more than 100 yards N. 2° E. (N. 22° W. mag.) from the east point of Charles island.

Skardon islands, two in number, lie 500 yards eastward from Williams island; pass on either side of them and steer up the harbor, which is over ¼ mile in width, and the depth will soon decrease to 12 fathoms. One mile within the entrance, a peninsula extends southward from the northern shore; pass between its southern point and Mary island.

A rock with only 4 feet of water on it at low water, with 7 and 8 fathoms between it and the shore, lies 85 yards from the northern shore of the harbor in a position from which the eastern extreme of Mary island bears S. 19° 30′ E. (S. 44° E. mag.) and the northern extreme of west Skardon island S. 82° 30′ W. (S. 58° W. mag.).

Anchorage.—Anchor in Gerrans bay, ¼ mile southward of the peninsula, in 6 or 7 fathoms; there is also good anchorage in Garden bay, just eastward of the peninsula, and abreast an Indian village, in 5 or 6 fathoms. The latter is the more suitable for a large ship.

A very narrow pass leads from the eastern end of the harbor into Gunboat bay, an extension of the inlet eastward, but it carries only 1½ fathoms, and the tidal stream sets strongly through.

Tides.—It is high water, full and change, in Pender harbor at 6 h. 0 m.; springs rise 12 to 14 feet.

Jervis inlet is one of the most considerable of those numerous and remarkable arms of the sea which indent the continent of America from the parallel of Juan de Fuca strait as far as lat. 60° N.; it extends by winding reaches in a northerly direction for more than 40 miles, while its width rarely exceeds 1½ miles, and in most places is even less.

It is hemmed in on all sides by mountains of the most rugged and stupendous character, rising from its almost perpendicular shores to heights of 5,000 to 8,000 feet. The hardy pine, which flourishes where no other tree can find soil to sustain life, holds but a feeble and uncertain tenure here; and it is not uncommon to see whole mountain sides denuded by the blasts of winter, or the still more certain destruction of the avalanche which accompanies the thaw of summer.

Nelson island, in the middle of the entrance to Jervis inlet, is 10 miles long in a northeasterly direction, and about 4 or 5 miles wide; its shores are much broken and indented by several bays, in none of which, however, can anchorage be obtained in consequence of the great depth. The island is mountainous, ranging from 500 to 1,500 feet in height. Cape Cockburn, its SW. point, is of white granite, about 80 or 90 feet high, covered with a few dwarf pines; a rock lies 200 yards south from it.

Captain island, NE. of Nelson island, and separated from it by a narrow passage, is about 1 mile in extent, rocky, and steep-to.

Nelson rock.—When entering by the eastern passage, Agamemnon channel, or passing along the southern shore of Nelson island, avoid Nelson rock, which dries about 6 feet at low water and is 100 yards in extent in a NE. and SW. direction; it lies 1 mile S. 85° W. (S. 61° W. mag.) from Fearney point, is steep-to, and vessels are recommended to pass outside, or southward, of it.

Beacon.—A pyramidal stone beacon, surmounted by a staff and drum, the whole painted black and showing 26 feet above high water, stands on the NE. end of Nelson rock.

Rocks, with depths of 3 and 4 fathoms, are reported to lie SE. by E., distant 1¾ and 2¼ miles, respectively, from cape Cockburn, the SW. point of Nelson island, and about ½ mile offshore.

Agamemnon channel, the southern entrance to Jervis inlet, runs between Nelson island and the main in a general northerly direction for 9 miles, then joins the main channel of the inlet; its average width is little more than ½ mile; the tides run from 1 to 3 knots; the depth of water varies from 50 to 100 fathoms, and it affords no anchorage.

The western entrance to Jervis inlet is between Alexander point, the SW. extreme of Hardy island, on the east, and Scotch Fir point on the west. The points are not remarkable, but the opening is easily made out; it is nearly 2 miles in width, and takes for a short distance a northerly direction and then turns eastward. Scotch Fir point is rocky, and has two small islets lying close westward of it, which, like the point itself, are covered with stunted pines. Hardy island lies close to and is nearly connected with Nelson island; Blind bay, between them, is useless, and its entrance choked by small islands.

Thunder bay, formed on the western side 1½ miles above Scotch Fir point, is one of the few places in Jervis inlet where a vessel may drop an anchor, and being near the entrance is likely to prove convenient. The bay is about ½ mile deep, with a sandy beach at its head, off which 17 fathoms will be found; immediately outside it there are 30 fathoms, and the lead then drops suddenly to a great depth.

Hotham sound, a wide opening, trends north, terminating at the distance of 7 miles in a double-headed bay; the water in every part of it is too deep for anchorage.

One Tree islet, off the east side of the inlet, at the entrance to Prince of Wales reach, 1¼ miles east from Captain island, is small, and has a single tree on its summit, which is very conspicuous; its height is about 50 feet. A rock awash at low water lies 200 yards off its east side; just inside it, on the east shore, is a bight where a coasting vessel may drop an anchor.

Prince of Wales reach.—Dark cove, on the west side of Jervis inlet, inside the Sydney islets, is 2 miles NE. from Captain island, and 12 miles from the entrance. The cove is only about 400 yards in extent, but affords a snug anchorage in 15 fathoms; a vessel of considerable size could moor within it. There is a clear deep passage 200 yards wide into this cove on both sides of Sydney islets.

Vancouver bay, on the east side of the inlet, 19 miles from the entrance, is about ½ mile in extent. From its head, which is low, a considerable valley extends to the eastward, but the shores on both sides are craggy and precipitous, and the bay is too deep to afford anchorage, there being 60 fathoms within 200 yards of the bank which extends a short distance from its head.

Princess Royal reach.—Deserted bay, also on the east side of Jervis inlet, at the termination of Princess Royal reach, and about 37 miles from the entrance, is small, and affords an indifferent anchorage in its eastern part near the head in about 16 fathoms, exposed to westerly and southwesterly winds. A valley extends from the head of the bay to the NE., through which a trail runs to the Lilooet lakes on the Fraser river, and is much frequented by the natives in the summer season.

Queens reach.—The head of Jervis inlet terminates in a patch of low swampy land, through which flow some small streams, and a bank dries off about 200 yards; it does not afford any anchorage, there being 25 fathoms within 100 yards of the outer edge of the bank. A remarkable peak, mount Victoria, rises 2 miles north of the water's edge to a height of 7,452 feet, and is a very conspicuous object on approaching the head of the inlet.

At the head of Jervis inlet there is a valley by which the Indians go to Clahoose (Desolation sound) in 2 days.

17208——18

Princess Louisa inlet, on the east side of Jervis inlet, 5 miles below the head, is narrow, and about 4 miles long in a NE. direction; it is connected to the main inlet by a narrow gorge, which at low tide becomes almost a waterfall, rendering it impossible for boats to enter except at high water; inside, like Jervis inlet, it is deep, and the mountains on both sides rise to 7,000 and 8,000 feet.

Seechelt arm, the entrance to which is 1 mile east of Agamemnon channel, is an extensive arm of the sea, penetrating the land for 17 miles in a southeasterly direction and only separated from the strait of Georgia by a low neck of land, 1,100 yards wide. On the east side of the arm, at distances of 7 and 11 miles from its entrance, are two smaller branches, Narrows arm and Salmon arm, extending to the northeastward for upward of 10 miles.

The arm, at 3 miles within its entrance, contracts in breadth to less than ½ mile, and is partially choked up with rocks and small islands, which, preventing in a great measure the free ingress and egress of the tide, cause most furious and dangerous rapids, the roar of which may be heard for several miles. These rapids prevent any vessel, or even boat, from entering the arm, except for a short time after high and low water, when the tide slackens for a very limited period; it would, however, be hazardous for any vessel, except a very small one, to attempt to enter at any time, although there is a passage with from 4 to 7 fathoms between the islands and the southwestern or peninsula shore.

The shores of the arm, except near its south part or head, are high and rocky, and in the summer season the natives catch great quantities of salmon there.

Tides and tidal streams.—It is high water at full and change in Jervis inlet at 6 h. 0 m.; the rise and fall being about 14 feet; within the Seechelt arm the rise and fall seldom exceeds 6 or 7 feet.

The tidal streams are, except near the entrance of Seechelt arm, weak and irregular and influenced by winds.

Harwood island, off the north entrance to Malaspina strait, 1½ miles from the continental shore and about 3 miles north from point Marshall, is 2½ miles long in a northerly direction, 1½ miles wide, from 150 to 200 feet high, flat, and thickly wooded. It is bordered by a sandy beach, and at its north point is a low grassy spit. There is deep water between the island and the shore.

Rebecca islet, lying midway between point Marshall and Harwood island, is of small extent, and 5 feet above high water.

Bare islet, 1 mile west from the south end of Harwood island, is a bare, yellow, cliffy rock, about 400 yards in extent, and 30 feet above high water.

The coast.—Westward from Jervis inlet, the north shore of Malaspina strait, takes a westerly direction for 11 miles, terminating at Grief point; for a considerable distance inland it is low, and bordered by a sandy beach.

From Grief point the north or continental shore of Georgia strait trends NW. for nearly 20 miles almost straight to Sarah point, the SE. entrance point of Desolation sound. Throughout the whole distance the coast does not rise more than 500 or 600 feet, and is but slightly indented. There is a fresh-water stream, Powell river, of considerable size 4 miles north of Grief point, communicating, at about 2 miles from the shore, with Powell lake, which extends some 20 miles northward toward the head of Toba inlet. There are some remarkable falls on the Powell river only 100 yards from the sea.

At 1 mile farther westward a vessel may anchor in fine weather for night or tide at a distance of 600 or 800 yards offshore near the coast abreast Harwood island in 12 to 13 fathoms. Anchorage must be taken up with caution as flats extend a considerable distance offshore. When anchoring do not shut in the north shore of Savary island.

Navigating along this coast between Grief and Sarah points, a vessel will avoid danger by keeping a mid-channel course between Harwood and Savary islands and the mainland. When past Hurtado point, steer more westward, and pass southward or westward of the White, Double, and Powell islets.

Sliammon and Lund are settlements on the mainland, the former NE. of Harwood island, the latter, at which there is a post-office, in approximately lat. 49° 59′ N., long. 124° 46′ W.

At Sliammon the beach dries off for a distance of 400 yards southward of the village. Vessels anchoring off Sliammon should keep Dinner rock open of the point westward of the village. The church of the Roman Catholic mission is conspicuous from seaward.

Atrevida reef and buoy.—At a point on the coast 2½ miles NW. of Sliammon a reef extends for ½ mile off the shore. Dinner rock shut in with Hurtado point clears the reef.

A red spar buoy is moored in 5½ fathoms off the edge of the reef.

Dinner rock, 35 feet high, lies ¼ mile offshore 2¾ miles northwestward from Atrevida reef and 1½ miles southeastward of Hurtado point.

Savary island, nearly 6 miles NW. from Harwood island and 1 mile from the continental shore, is 4 miles long in a west direction, and less than 1 mile wide. A sandy beach with huge scattered bowlders surrounds it, and extends a considerable distance off its north and west sides, which should not be approached nearer than ¼ mile; these bowlders extend a greater distance from the south side of the island, which side, therefore, should not be closed nearer than ¾ mile. The height of the island varies from 80 to 120 feet, and the south side is faced by some remarkable, white, sandy cliffs, very conspicuous from the SE.; its eastern extreme is a granite cliff, steep-to. There are several clear grassy patches on the island, but the soil is poor and sandy. A sandy bar or ledge, with 1 to 2 fathoms of water over it, extends from its west point to Hernando island.

A reef extending about 1,000 yards NW. and SE., with a breadth of 500 yards, the bowlders on which dry at low water, is reported, with the SE. extreme of Savary island about N. 30° E. (N. 5° E. mag.), distant 3 miles. The position is doubtful. All the water inside a line from Bare island toward the west point of Savary island is said to be foul.

Mystery rock, 2¾ miles S. 27° E. (S. 52° E. mag.) from the east end of Savary island, is a patch which uncovers 4 feet at low water. From the rock, shoal patches of from 1 to 3 fathoms extend toward the east end of Savary island. When navigating this locality observe great caution. By keeping Grief point just open to the northward of the north extreme of Harwood island this danger will be avoided.

The ground between Harwood and Savary islands is said to be foul; the passage between these islands should not be attempted.

Hurtado point, on the mainland abreast Savary island, is about 250 feet high, bold, and cliffy. There is 37 fathoms of water in mid-channel between it and the island.

Ragged islands, lying close to and parallel with the continental shore, are a rocky group of small islands 2½ miles long and 600 yards wide; their SE. part is about 2½ miles NW. from Hurtado point, and some rocks extend 800 yards from their NW. extreme.

White islet, 1 mile SW. from Ragged islands, is a very remarkable, bare, white, granite rock, about 70 feet high. A rock which uncovers at low water lies 200 yards eastward from it.

Double islets, ½ mile west from the NW. part of the Ragged group, are small, and about 90 feet high, with a single tree on each of their summits.

Powell islets, 1 mile NW. from Double islets, are two in number, small, about 90 feet high, and covered with a few stunted bushes and trees; the westernmost islet is steep-to on its north and west sides.

Sarah point, 20 miles NW. of Malaspina strait, may be called the NE. entrance point of Georgia strait. It is a rounded, rocky point, sloping gradually to the sea from a height of about 750 feet, at a short distance within it. The coast here turns sharply round to the eastward into Malaspina inlet.

Mitlenatch island lies 16 miles NNW. from cape Lazo and is ½ mile in extent, 200 feet high, bare and peaked. Between it and the Vancouver island shore, distant nearly 6 miles, is the fair channel to cape Mudge and Discovery passage. Shoal water extends about ½ mile northward of Mitlenatch island.

Sentry shoal, within the limits of the 10-fathom curve, extends 1½ miles NNW. and SSE., the least depth found being 5 fathoms, from which the summit of Mitlenatch island bears N. 5° W. (N. 30° W. mag.), distant $2\frac{1}{10}$ miles.

Hernando island, 2 miles NW. from Savary island, is about 2 miles in extent, flat, thickly wooded, and from 120 to 170 feet high. A ledge composed of sand and huge bowlders extends ⅜ mile from its SE. point, and there is only a depth of 1¼ fathoms in the channel between it and Savary island; this is known as False passage. From the west side some rocks extend off upward of 400 yards in many places, and it should not be approached nearer than ½ mile in passing.

A dangerous rock, which dries at low spring tides, lies 150 yards off Hidalgo point, and there is no passage between.

Stag bay, on the north side of Hernando, affords anchorage in 12 to 15 fathoms at a distance of about 400 yards offshore, and is useful as a stopping place for vessels bound to Bute inlet or Desolation sound. There is a small fresh-water stream in the east part of the bay.

Tongue point, the NW. extreme of Hernando and of Stag bay, is a low, sharp, sandy point or spit, covered with a few trees. Vessels should anchor at about ¾ mile from this point, with the east part of Twins islands bearing N. 12° E. (N. 13° W. mag.).

Baker passage, to the northward of Hernando island and leading from the strait of Georgia to the entrance of Desolation sound, is about 3 miles long in an easterly direction, and 1 mile wide in the narrowest part, being bounded on the north side by Cortes and Twins islands.

A bowlder ledge extends ¾ mile SW. from Reef point; the bowlders cover at three-quarters flood. The outer extremity of the ledge is marked by a red can buoy.

To avoid the ledge off Reef point (the south extreme of Cortes island), when entering Baker passage, bring Tongue point on a N. 69° E. (N. 44° E. mag.) bearing, and steer for it, passing about 200 yards off; then keep midway between Hernando and the Twins.

Tides.—It is high water, full and change, in Baker passage at 6 h. 0 m.; springs rise 12 to 14 feet.

Twin islands, about 1½ miles north from Hernando, are two rocky islands connected by a sandy beach at low water, covering an extent 2 miles long in a northwesterly direction, and about 1 mile broad. The northernmost Twin is 490 feet high, rising to an almost bare summit in the center; the southern one is about 300 feet, and on both of them are numerous indications of iron and copper ores.

None but small craft should go north of these islands. Some small islets lie a short distance off their north side.

Center rock, which covers at a quarter flood, is in the middle of the passage between Twin and Cortes islands.

Blind creek, on the east side of Cortes island, 1½ miles north of Twin islands, is a basin of about 800 yards in extent, with from 7 to 9 fathoms of water; there is, however, in the entrance, a rock which covers at a quarter flood, rendering the place useless as an anchorage.

Three islets, lying ½ mile off the entrance of Blind creek, are three bare white rocks about 60 feet high, almost connected at low water; there is a depth of 27 fathoms 400 yards eastward from them.

A rocky ledge, which dries, at its extremes, 1 foot at low water, lies 300 yards eastward of the northern islet.

Lewis channel, off the entrances to Desolation sound between Cortes and Redonda islands, runs nearly straight upward of 12 miles NNW., and varies in breadth from 1 mile to 600 yards; its shores are generally rocky, low in the southern part, but rising gradually to the NW.

Turn point, the SW. entrance point of this channel and the east extreme of Cortes island, is about 100 feet high, rocky, and covered with a few stunted trees; and close inshore northward of the point are two islands forming a small boat cove.

At 6 miles from the south entrance to Lewis channel, Teakerne arm penetrates Redonda island 4 miles in an easterly direction, but is too deep to afford anchorage, except for small craft near its head, and close to the south side of entrance.

Tidal streams.—In Lewis channel the streams are weak and irregular, seldom exceeding 2 knots, and are influenced by the winds.

Squirrel cove, on the west side of Lewis channel, 4½ miles from Turn point, is a small landlocked basin with 6 to 7 fathoms of water, with room for a vessel of considerable size to lie at single anchor. It is entered by a narrow passage about 130 feet wide, with 5 fathoms of water, on the west side of the island (Protection island) in the entrance, which protects the cove from the southward. The shores are moderately high, and, though much broken, very picturesque and fertile in appearance. To the northward of, and connected at high water with, the cove, is a long narrow lagoon, stretching to the NW. nearly across Cortes island.

Squirrel cove can only be entered by steamers, or sailing vessels with a fair wind, and the chart is the best guide.

Tides.—It is high water, full and change, in Squirrel cove at 5 h. 0 m.; springs rise 12 feet.

Bowlder point, the SE. entrance point, is low, and may be easily known by a large bowlder on its west side; a rock, which covers, lies nearly 200 yards south from it, but the point may be rounded at a distance of 400 yards.

Northward from Squirrel cove the west side of Lewis channel becomes more rocky, and gradually increases in height; it takes a northeasterly direction for 1 mile to Junction point, and then trends to the NW. for 7 miles, the channel ending at Bullock bluff, the north extreme of Cortes island.

At 3½ miles from Junction point the depths in the channel shoal to 27 and 30 fathoms, and a vessel may anchor in about 18 fathoms 200 yards from the west shore. Vancouver's ship anchored here in 1792 while exploring this part of the coast.

Malaspina inlet, 1½ miles east from Sarah point, penetrates the continent 8 miles in a southeasterly direction; it has one good harbor, and several arms, at the head of some of which there is anchorage. The inlet at its entrance between Georgina point and Zephine head, the west point of Gifford peninsula, is 800 yards wide, which is its general width until abreast Scott point on the northern side, a distance of 2 miles, when it is contracted to 400 yards; this portion of the inlet, however, is so studded with islands and rocks as to considerably narrow the navigable channel. The depths in it vary from 30 to 6 fathoms.

At Scott point the inlet for ¾ mile takes an easterly direction, and then between Hillingdon point and the north end of Coode peninsula widens out to 1 mile and again turns to the southeastward for 2¼ miles, and, under the name of Okeover arm, continues in the same direction for a farther distance of 2½ miles, the width gradually decreasing to 700 yards. To the eastward of Coode peninsula the water becomes very deep, but at the beginning of Okeover arm it shoals to 40 fathoms, and gradually to 5 and 6 fathoms at nearly 400 yards from its head.

Freke anchorage, in 12 or 14 fathoms, is at the head of Okeover arm, about 600 yards from the edge of the flat that extends 400 yards from the head of the arm, just above Lucy rock, which lies very close to the southwestern shore.

Josephine islands, about ¾ mile within the entrance of Malaspina inlet, with a passage on both sides, are two in number and almost joining each other; the northwestern one is very small, the other is about 300 yards long in the direction of the inlet, and not more than 100 yards wide. The passage between them and the southwestern shore is 200 yards in width, and is to be preferred.

Cavendish rock, awash, and marked by kelp, lies 300 yards S. 78° E. (N. 77° E. mag.) from the SE. end of Josephine islands, and is a danger that must be avoided when passing eastward of those islands.

Cross islet, distant 300 yards from the eastern shore of the inlet, and 550 yards SE. from Josephine islands, lies on the eastern side of the channel; it is small, not more than 100 yards in extent.

Rosetta rock, the principal danger in entering Malaspina inlet, is awash, and lies nearly 200 yards S. 35° W. (S. 10° W. mag.) from Cross islet.

The southwestern point of Josephine islands in line with the extreme of the land near Zephine head leads nearly on the rock.

Thorp island lies close to the western shore of the inlet, 500 yards S. 7° W. (S. 18° E. mag.) from Josephine islands; a rock awash lies about 100 yards southeastward from it.

Neville islet is very small and lies close to the eastern shore nearly ½ mile SE. from Cross islet.

Cochrane islands, a group of several small islets extending 700 yards in a NNW. and SSE. direction, lie 400 yards from the west shore of the inlet, and SW. from Neville islet. These islands should not be approached too closely, and there is a patch with 3 fathoms on it about 200 yards from their western end.

A shoal patch, with 4 fathoms least water, lies toward the western side of the inlet and 400 yards southward from Scott point.

Grace harbor, on the eastern side of Malaspina inlet, about 2¼ miles from Zephine head, has its entrance between Scott and Moss points, which are about 200 yards apart in an easterly direction. The harbor extends about 1 mile NE., and is divided at the head by a jutting point into Barlands and Carberry bays. At 400 yards within the entrance points a small island lies nearly in the middle of the channel; there is a passage on both sides of it, but the western one is only suitable for boats. At 800 yards above the island the harbor for a short distance contracts to 100 yards, and then opens to the width of 500 yards.

Lion rock, surrounded by kelp, lies 400 yards SSE. from Selina point, the south extreme of Gifford peninsula, and 400 yards eastward of Coode peninsula.

Trevenon bay, one of the arms of Malaspina inlet and 2¼ miles from its entrance, runs parallel to the inlet for 1¼ miles, and at its head is only separated from Penrose bay by a narrow neck of land 600 yards broad. Off the SE. extremity of Coode peninsula, distant 200 yards, is Boundary rock. The entrance to Trevenon bay is ½ mile SE. from Scott point; the average width is less than ¼ mile, the depth varying from 25 fathoms to 4 fathoms at 400 yards from the head. Off the NW. entrance point of the bay lies the small island Alton, about 200 yards from the shore.

Lancelot arm branches off at Selina point northward and extends in that direction for 3 miles; its head is only divided from Portage cove (Desolation sound) by a low neck of land not much more than 100 yards across, forming Gifford peninsula, triangular in shape, rising abruptly over Portage cove to a height of 1,000 feet, and having part of the eastern shore of Malaspina inlet for its base, where it is not more than half the height. The arm maintains an average width of 1,200 yards until near its head, where it is only 500 yards wide. In the southern part of Lancelot arm the water is very deep, but at about ¾ mile from Selina point until ½ mile from the head the depths vary from 30 to 37 fathoms, and then shoal to 17 fathoms and gradually to 11 fathoms.

Vessels of moderate size may anchor in Wootton bay, about 200 yards from the head of Lancelot arm in 12 fathoms of water.

Isabel bay, about 1¼ miles from Selina point, on the west shore of Lancelot arm, is about 400 yards in extent, and affords anchorage for coasters in from 10 to 12 fathoms. Mary and Polly islands lie in the entrance.

Thors cove, on the eastern shore of Lancelot arm, 1½ miles north of Hillingdon point, the eastern entrance point of the arm, extends in an easterly direction for 600 yards with from 12 to 5 fathoms. A coaster might drop an anchor in this cove in about 10 fathoms. Two hundred yards off Sebastian point, the northern entrance point of Thors cove, is Thynne island.

Theodosia arm has its entrance at about 1 mile from the head of Lancelot arm, and extends in a NE. direction for 1½ miles with a moderate depth of water and a width of 600 yards, but the entrance to it is so very narrow and choked with rocks as to render it for all practical purposes useless.

Directions.—Having entered Malaspina inlet midway between Georgina point and Zephine head, keep over toward Holland point until the channel on the southern side of Josephine islands opens out, and then steer boldly through it with Cochrane islands nearly ahead; the course will be S. 38° E. (S. 63° E. mag.). Keep the extreme of the land near Zephine head about midway between the south side of Josephine islands and the south shore, if anything rather nearer the latter, which will lead between Rosetta rock and the rock off Thorp island; when Neville islet bears S. 76° E. (N. 79° E. mag.) steer toward it for a short distance, to avoid the 3-fathom patch off Cochrane islands, until the NW. Cochrane island bears South, when alter course to round Scott point, distant 200 yards, and steer up the harbor in mid-channel, passing eastward of the small island lying 400 yards within the entrance. A shoal patch on which the least water is 4 fathoms, lies 400 yards southward from Scott point.

The best anchorage is in about 10 fathoms, 300 yards northward of the small island, abreast Kakaekae village.

Tides.—The tidal streams at the entrance of Malaspina inlet run about 2 knots. It is high water, full and change, at 5 h. 0 m.; springs rise 12 feet and neaps 9 feet.

Kinghorn island, off the south entrance to Desolation sound, is about 2 miles in circumference and from 400 to 500 feet high; it is cliffy and steep-to on the SW. side.

Station island, about 250 yards in extent and 270 feet high, lies 450 yards NE. from the north point of Kinghorn island; two small islets lie between.

A rock lies 800 yards, and another 1,100 yards, westward from Station island; both these rocks dry 1 to 2 feet at low water springs.

A rocky patch with 2 fathoms over it lies about 400 yards southward of the western rock.

Mink island, nearly midway between Redonda island and the main, is ¾ mile long, ⅓ mile wide, and 700 feet high. A short distance from its NE. end are Broken islands.

Desolation sound, between the SE. shore of the western Redonda island and Mink island, has too great a depth for anchorage. At ½ mile NE. from Mink island is Otter island, only separated from the main by a very narrow passage.

Deep bay.—Bold head, the western entrance point of Deep bay, lies 1 mile SE. from the south point of Otter island; three small islets lie SW. from it, the outer one, Grey islet, being distant 800 yards. The entrance to Deep bay is about 600 yards wide, which width it maintains to its head, a distance of nearly 1 mile, with a general NE. direction.

The anchorage space is confined, but small vessels can anchor in a cove at its NW. corner in 10 fathoms. When entering from the northward pass between Otter and Broken islands and westward of Grey islet; from the westward the channel is clear.

To the northward of Otter island there are small islands lying in pairs, Morgan and Melville islands being to the westward, and Mary and Eveleigh islands to the eastward. Melville and Mary are the northernmost, the former, which is 450 feet high, being the largest of the group, and the latter the smallest. At ½ mile N. 54° W. (N. 79° W. mag.) from the south end of Morgan island there is a rock which is just awash at high water.

Prideaux haven, situated 3 miles northeastward from Mink island in the NE. part of Desolation sound, affords good and sheltered anchorage. The entrance between the east shore of Eveleigh island and the Oriel rocks is 85 yards wide, with a depth of 4 fathoms. The anchorage is in the western part of the haven in 7 to 9 fathoms. Melanie cove, the eastern part of the haven, is entered by a narrow channel about 100 yards wide, opening out inside to 200 yards in width with 4 to 6 fathoms.

It is high water, full and change, in Prideaux haven, at 5 h. 0 m.; springs rise 12 feet.

Laura cove, just NE. of Prideaux haven, and connected with it by a narrow, shallow passage south of Copplestone island, has its entrance between that island and Edward point. Small vessels will find snug anchorage in the cove.

Homfray channel, a continuation northward of Desolation sound, is 15 miles in length and curves gradually to the northward and westward to the mouth of Toba inlet; it has deep water throughout.

Waddington channel, leading from Desolation sound northwestward between the two Redonda islands, is about 1 mile wide at its southern entrance, gradually narrowing to about 200 yards at its northern.

At ¾ mile SW. of Marylebone point (the SW. entrance point of Waddington channel) there is a remarkable white patch.

Pendrell sound.—At 3 miles NW. from Horace point, the southeastern entrance point of Waddington channel, Pendrell sound branches off to the northward; it extends 6 miles, with an average width of ¾ mile, and nearly divides east Redonda island into two parts; it has no anchorage.

Walsh cove, between the Gorges islands and the western shore of Waddington channel, affords anchorage in 12 to 14 fathoms in mid-channel. The cove must be entered from the southward, the northern entrance being closed by rocks and shoals.

Toba inlet extends in a general northeasterly direction for 18 miles from the northern end of Homfray channel. At its entrance lie Channel and Double islands, each 400 feet high, leaving a channel of over 1 mile in width between them; the inlet is here nearly 2 miles wide, gradually narrowing to 1 mile wide at its head. A fair berth is in about 20 fathoms, off the flats, in the NW. corner of the head of the inlet. Care must be observed when coming to an anchor, as the water shoals rapidly alongside the flats; the water being of a milky color affords no guide as to its depth. There is a small village (Clahoose Indians) on the banks of the eastern of the two streams which flow into the head of the inlet.

Sutil channel.—This extensive channel, which leads from the western part of Georgia strait to the entrances of Toba and Bute inlets, is bounded on the east side by Cortes, and on the west by Quadra (Valdes) and Read islands. It is 15 miles long in a northerly direction, and at its entrance is 6 miles wide, decreasing to 1 mile wide in the northern part.

There are several good anchorages on both shores, two of which, Drew harbor on the west and Carrington bay on the east shore of the channel, are easy of access to all vessels, and useful as stopping places.

The tidal streams in Sutil channel are weak, seldom exceeding 2 knots; the flood stream sets to the northward from Georgia strait; it is high water, full and change, at 6 h. 0 m., and the rise and fall is 12 feet.

Cortes island.—The west side of the island, which forms the eastern boundary of Sutil channel, is for the most part low, and indented by several bays and creeks, in many of which good anchorage may be found.

Reef point, its southern extreme, has a ledge composed of sand and bowlders extending ¾ mile from it in a SW. direction which covers at three-quarters flood; off its outer edge are 6 fathoms. The northern side of Texada island well open south of Savary and Hernando islands bearing S. 56° E. (S. 81° E. mag.) will lead south of the ledge.

Buoy.—The outer extremity is marked by a red can buoy; the outer edge of the reef is just inside this buoy.

From Reef point the west coast of Cortes island trends in a northerly direction for 3½ miles, is flat, from 80 to 150 feet high, and bordered by a sandy beach extending upward of 400 yards off in some parts; it afterwards turns in a westerly direction, becoming rocky and broken, with a few islets a short distance off it in some places.

Manson bay is on Cortes island, in the angle formed where the coast begins to turn westward. There is a post-office here.

Gorge harbor, the entrance to which is on the west side of Cortes island, 4½ miles north from Reef point, is 2 miles long in an east and west direction, and 1 mile broad at the widest part, affording good anchorage in 9 to 12 fathoms. The entrance to it is through a narrow gorge nearly ½ mile long, with steep cliffs about 150 feet high on the western and a bold, abrupt shore on the eastern side, and is less than 40 yards wide in some places, with 6 fathoms in the shoalest part; the tidal streams set through it at from 3 to 4 knots. At the inner edge of the Gorge is Tide islet, 20 feet high, lying nearly in the middle of the channel; the passage is to the westward of it. There are several small islands inside the harbor, and the shores are rocky, varying in height from 100 to 300 feet.

Guide islets, just south of the entrance, are useful in indicating it, being two small, bare, yellow-topped islets about 20 feet high, and conspicuous from the southward. They are steep-to, and there is a clear passage on either side of them into Gorge harbor.

Bee islets, within the harbor, 600 yards NW. from the entrance, are two small bare rocks about 200 yards apart, and 6 feet above high water.

Brown island, in the middle of the harbor, about 600 yards NE. from the entrance, is nearly 1 mile in circumference, and thickly timbered. It is about 150 feet high, and the shores are rocky.

A rock, which dries 9 feet at low water springs, extends 200 yards from the north extreme of the island.

Ring island, about 200 yards east from Brown, and 70 feet high, is wooded, but much smaller; New rock, which covers at a quarter flood, lies nearly 200 yards east from it and should be avoided.

There are two small islands, Stove and Pill, each 30 feet high, and 600 yards apart, lying close to the shore in the northern part of the harbor. Neck islet, 20 feet high, lies off a small cove in the SE. corner of the harbor.

Anchorage.—The best and most convenient anchorage in Gorge harbor is in the west part, about ½ mile from the entrance, in 12 fathoms.

There is also good anchorage between Ring island and the NE. part of the harbor in from 7 to 9 fathoms.

Directions.—Entering Gorge harbor, which can only be done in a steam vessel, after passing Guide islets, steer boldly up the Gorge or entrance, and pass between Tide islet and the west shore, the passage east of the islet being shoal, when haul to the NW., pass on either side of the Bee islets, and anchor in from 10 to 12 fathoms, muddy bottom, 200 to 400 yards westward from them. Proceeding to the eastern part, after passing Tide islet, keep to the northward, and rounding the west side of Brown island at 200 yards distance, and passing at least 300 yards north of it and Ring island, anchor midway between the latter and the NE. end of the harbor in 7 to 10 fathoms. If requiring to water, this anchorage is more convenient; but to avoid New rock do not go to the southward of Ring island.

Mary island, on the east side of Sutil channel about 3 miles NW. from Reef point, is of a round shape, about 6 miles in circumference, and from 90 to 120 feet high; its shores are bordered by a sandy beach strewn with huge bowlders.

Bowlder reef, extending upward of 1 mile south from its south point, is a ledge about 400 yards wide, which covers at high water.

When passing west of Mary island keep the north side of Texada island open south of Savary and Hernando islands, bearing S. 56° E. (S. 81° E. mag.) until Camp island opens west of Mary island, bearing North (N. 25° W. mag.), which will clear Bowlder reef on the south and west sides.

Shark spit.—From the north part of Mary island Shark spit extends in a northeasterly direction to within 200 yards of Cortes island. In this passage there is 8 fathoms of water, but nearly in the center there is a small rock which dries at low water. This rock is marked by an iron spindle with drum on top and painted white. The passage is between the rock and the sand spit, and is not more than 300 feet wide; it should not be attempted by a stranger. The end of Shark spit is marked by a pile beacon surmounted by a drum, the whole painted white, and showing 10 feet above high water. This beacon should not be approached nearer than 160 feet. The rise of tide here is 14 feet.

Whaleton bay, on Cortes island, a little over 1 mile NW. from Shark spit, has a post-office and wharf. In the middle of the entrance is a dangerous rock, marked by a red spar buoy moored on the north side of the rock in 5¼ fathoms.

There is a small rock awash about 150 yards from the NW. shore of the bay, about 400 yards inside the north entrance point.

A rock near the head of the bay, dry at high water, is marked by a spindle and drum, the whole painted white. When the mail steamer is expected at night a light is shown from this beacon. There is good anchorage for small vessels northward of this rock in 5 fathoms.

Camp island, off the west extreme of Cortes island, and 7 miles from Reef point, is of small extent, 100 to 200 feet high, and wooded.

Plunger pass, between Camp and Cortes islands, is about 600 yards wide, and deep.

Center islet, 400 yards NW. from Camp island, is bare, and about 12 feet above high water.

Carrington bay, on the NW. side of Cortes, about 3 miles from Center islet, is 1 mile deep in an easterly direction, about 600 yards wide, and affords anchorage at 600 yards from its head in from 7 to 11 fathoms. At the entrance shoal water extends for 300 yards from the southern shore. Along its north side are some small islets, and a rock which uncovers at low water. Vessels should keep in mid-channel till Jane island is abeam; the southern shore may then be approached. Off the northern shore several patches of 4 fathoms exist; the bottom in Carrington bay is very uneven. At the head of the bay is a large salt-water lagoon.

Von Donop creek, the entrance of which is 5½ miles from Center islet, is long and narrow, penetrating Cortes island in a southeasterly direction for upward of 3 miles. There is good anchorage in 5 to 6 fathoms near its head, but the entrance being only 30 yards wide in some places, with 3½ fathoms in one spot, it should not be used as a stopping place; Carrington bay is much more convenient and easy of access.

Quadra island.—From cape Mudge, the south extreme of Quadra island and the SW. entrance point of Sutil channel, a bank extends in a southeasterly direction for nearly 2 miles, and until well inside the channel the cape should not be approached within that distance. The coast of Quadra island turns sharply round the cape NNW., trending in a straight direction for 5½ miles, and is bordered the whole distance by a beach extending off upward of 200 yards in many parts. The land is flat and heavily timbered, but appears very fertile.

Drew harbor, on the east side of Quadra island, 6 miles from cape Mudge, is about 1 mile deep, 600 to 800 yards wide, and rendered perfectly secure and landlocked by Rebecca spit, a narrow strip of land 6 to 8 feet high and thinly wooded, which forms its eastern boundary; its shores are low and bordered by a sandy beach. The anchorage, in 9 to 15 fathoms, sandy bottom, at ½ mile from its head, is the best in Sutil channel.

Heriot islet, lying NW. of the entrance, is about 250 feet high, rocky, of small extent, and separated from Quadra island by a narrow boat pass. In the bay to the southward of it (Heriot bay) is fair anchorage, and fresh water may be procured; the depths, however, in the entrance to it are irregular.

If intending to anchor in Drew harbor, round the north part of Rebecca spit at a distance of about 200 yards, proceed up the harbor in mid-channel, and anchor about ½ mile from its head in 15 to 9 fathoms. The east side of Rebecca spit should not be approached nearer than 400 yards.

Hyacinthe bay, on Quadra island, 1½ miles NW. of Drew harbor, is of small extent, with some 16 to 20 fathoms of water, but affords no anchorage; a small rock 4 feet above high water lies in the middle of the entrance.

Open bay, ½ mile north from Hyacinthe bay, and separated from it by a rocky point, is ½ mile in extent, with 10 to 12 fathoms of water; but as the bottom is rocky, and the bay open to the SE., a vessel should not anchor there.

Breton islets, 40 feet high and extending upward of 1 mile SE. from the northern part of Open bay, are small, and from the outer one, which is wooded, a reef extends 600 yards, covering at a quarter flood.

Hoskyn inlet, formed between Read island on the east and Quadra and Maurelle islands on the west, is 7 miles long in a northerly direction, with an average breadth of ⅜ mile; the shores are broken and rocky, with some small islands off the south entrance and along the east side, and there is no anchorage within it, except for small craft. This inlet contracts at its northern end to a narrow boat passage leading into Drew pass; it is choked with rocks and dries at low water, connecting Read and Maurelle islands. On the western side of the inlet a narrow pass northwestward of a chain of small islands, between them and the south point of Maurelle island, and known as Surge narrows, leads into Okisollo channel.

Village bay, on the west side of this inlet, just within the entrance, is about 1 mile deep and ⅓ mile wide, with from 12 to 24 fathoms of water, but affords no good anchorage; there is a large village at its head.

A reef, with less than 10 feet over it at low water, lies nearly in the middle of the entrance to the bay; from the reef Bold point bears N. 62° E. (N. 37° E. mag.) and the southern end of Dunsterville island S. 44° E. (S. 69° E. mag.). A pinnacle rock, with only 6 feet of water over it at low water, lies 50 yards southward of the reef.

When entering or leaving Village bay keep the northern shore aboard.

Read island, bordering the west side of the northern part of Sutil channel, is 9 miles long in a northerly direction, and from 1 to 3 miles broad; its southern part is low, but rises gradually to the northward to 1,608 feet; the shores are rocky, steep-to, and much indented, especially on the east side near the middle. Viner point, its south extreme, 7 miles north from cape Mudge, is bare and about 40 feet above high water. The east side of Read island to the northward of the Penn islands is rocky.

Burdwood bay, on the east side of Read island, 2 miles from Viner point, is about 1 mile wide, 400 to 600 yards deep, and contains several small islets. There is 12 fathoms of water at a short distance offshore, in its north and south parts, where a vessel may stop in fine weather, but the bay is open to the south and east. There is a post-office in the NW. corner of the bay.

Evans bay, the next inlet on the east side of Read island, to the northward of Burdwood bay, is about 3 miles long in a northerly direction, 1½ miles wide at the entrance, and branches off in two narrow arms near its head; its shores are rocky and much broken, and there is no anchorage except in Bird cove, on the west shore, where small craft may find shelter. Frederic point, the NE. point of entrance to the bay, is steep-to, and may be approached to within 200 yards.

Hill island, just outside the entrance to Evans bay, is of small extent, but conspicuous, its summit being 490 feet high; the coast is rocky.

Penn islands, four in number, near the middle of Sutil channel, northward of Evans bay, cover an extent about 1¼ miles long and 1 mile wide; they are rocky, covered with stunted trees, and their greatest elevation is about 270 feet. Do not venture among them.

A rock awash lies 80 yards N. 79° E. (N. 54° E. mag.) from the north point of the eastern island.

Directions.—Entering Sutil channel from Georgia strait, pass ½ mile on either side of Mitlenatch island; when past Mitlenatch island keep it on a S. 33° E. (S. 58° E. mag.) bearing, and steer N. 33° W. (N. 58° W. mag.) till the south part of Mary island bears N. 57° E. (N. 32° E. mag.); a vessel will then be clear of

Bowlder reef. Thence, steering about N. 11° W. (N. 36° W. mag.), and passing about ¼ mile westward of Center islet, steer up mid-channel, eastward of Penn islands.

A vessel may beat through this channel, but till past the dangers in the southern part it would not be prudent to near the SW. sides of Cortes and Mary islands within 1½ miles when standing eastward; and when standing toward cape Mudge do not approach it within 2 miles, or bring Mitlenatch to the eastward of S. 49° E. (S. 74° E. mag.), until the cape bears S. 69° W. (S. 44° W. mag.), when a vessel may stand to within ½ mile of the Quadra island shore. If intending to anchor, Drew harbor and Carrington bay are easy of access for any class of vessel and are but little out of the regular track.

Calm channel, north of Lewis and Sutil channels, leading from them to Bute inlet, is 9 miles long in a general northerly direction, and about 1 mile broad; its shores rise abruptly to a great height and the tidal streams are weak except in the NW. part.

Calm channel is not well adapted for any vessels except steamers, as there is generally but little wind, and no anchorage.

A channel known as Hole in the Wall, leads between Maurelle and Sonora islands, southwestward from the western part of Calm channel into Okisollo channel, and thence into Discovery passage. Both these channels are encumbered by rocks and rapids and should not be attempted. Small local steamers, however, sometimes use them.

Tides.—It is high water, full and change, in Calm channel at 7 h. 0 m.; springs rise 14 feet. In Surge narrows at 6 h. 0 m.; springs rise 12 feet, and the streams run from 7 to 9 knots.

Rendezvous islands, three in number, which lie on its west side near the southern part, cover an extent 3 miles long in a NW. direction, and about ½ mile wide; the SE. island is 350 feet, the middle 300 feet, and the NW. 601 feet, high.

Drew pass is a deep passage between the Rendezvous islands and the northern part of Read island; and between the middle and easternmost islands is a small spot with from 7 to 15 fathoms of water, where small craft may anchor.

It is high water, full and change, at Rendezvous islands at 7 h. 0 m.; springs rise 14 feet.

Raza island, lying at the northern entrance to Sutil channel, is 3 miles long north and south, and 2 miles wide east and west, and 3,020 feet high; a portion of its southern side, which forms the northern side of Calm channel, is cliffy.

North passage, on the west side of Raza island, communicates with Ramsay arm, which indents the continent in a northerly direction for 7 miles and has deep water.

Deer passage, between Raza and Redonda islands, 4 miles long and 1½ miles wide, connects Sutil channel with Pryce channel, which leads to Toba inlet.

Stuart island, at the northern termination of Calm channel, and in the entrance of Bute inlet, is about 4 miles in extent, of an undulating surface, rising in some parts to 800 and 1,000 feet. Its coast is rocky, and the tidal streams set strongly round its north and west sides, but there is a clear passage into Bute inlet eastward of it, nearly 1 mile wide, in which very little stream is felt.

Bute inlet.—This extensive arm of the sea, which penetrates the continent for nearly 40 miles in a winding course to the northward, presents many similar features to Jervis inlet, the general breadth varying from 1 to 2 miles, and the shores on both sides rising abruptly and almost precipitously in many places to stupendous mountains from 5,000 to 8,000 feet high, whose summits are generally covered with snow all the year round. At the head are two extensive valleys, one penetrating NW. and the other SE., from which flow streams; the one to the westward, is called by the natives Homalko river.

Off these rivers some sandbanks extend a short distance, affording indifferent anchorages near their outer edges; but the soundings everywhere else in the inlet are very deep. The water for some distance from the head is nearly fresh, and of a milky-white appearance; in the summer months there is a constant outset, varying in strength from 1 to 2 knots.

Tides.—In Bute inlet it is high water at 6 h. 0 m., and the rise and fall varies from 12 to 14 feet.

Arran rapids, at the entrance of Bute inlet on the west side, between Stuart island and the continent, is 200 yards wide in the narrowest part. The streams rush through with great strength, 7 to 9 knots (the flood from the westward), and it is very hazardous for a vessel to go through.

Orford bay, on the east side of the inlet, 19 miles from the entrance, is of small extent, with 35 fathoms close to the edge of the bank which extends from the head. A small vessel may use it as a stopping place.

A rock, which dries 7 feet, lies about 150 yards from the western shore of the inlet, $2\frac{9}{10}$ miles south from Boyd point.

Waddington harbor, at the head of the inlet, being in fact its termination, is about 2 miles in extent, and affords very indifferent anchorage off the edge of the banks, extending from the Homalko and Southgate rivers and off its east shore; these banks are reported to frequently change. Except in the vicinity of the rivers the land rises almost precipitously to 4,000 and 5,000 feet, is most sterile and rocky, covered with stunted pines. The best anchorage is near the northern part, and about ½ mile offshore, in 15 fathoms, but is exposed to the SW., and strong winds from this quarter would make the anchorage unpleasant, if not unsafe.

It is high water, full and change, in Waddington harbor at 6 h. 0 m.; springs rise 13 feet.

Homalko river enters Waddington harbor on the NW. side, and is a stream of considerable extent, winding from the NW. through a large valley. At the entrance is a bar with only 1 to 2 feet of water over it at low tide, but within, the water deepens to 1 and 3 fathoms; the breadth varies from 50 to 200 yards, and the river is navigable for boats and small steamers several miles. The shores for 2 miles from the entrance are low and swampy, covered with willows, but farther up on the western side the land rises 4 or 5 feet above high water, and appears very fertile, though heavily timbered; the opposite side is steep and rocky; in summer months the current runs 5 knots out of the river.

From the sources of the Homalko river there is a route to the gold-mining regions in the far north of British Columbia.

Directions.—To navigate Bute inlet but few directions are required; if intending to anchor in Waddington harbor, when nearing it, steer for its northern part, anchoring at about ¾ mile off the head in 15 fathoms, and about 600 yards from the high northeastern shore; the anchor should be dropped immediately 15 fathoms are obtained, as the bottom shoals rapidly.

Sailing vessels entering or leaving the inlet should keep close to the eastern shore, or the ebb may take them through the Arran rapids to the westward.

Cardero channel, communicating by Nodales channel with Discovery passage and Johnstone strait, winds in a general east and west direction for 19 miles, with an average width of 1 mile in the eastern part, but only ½ mile in the western; its shores are generally rocky and mountainous, and the channel is studded with numerous small islands and it is not without dangers, the water in most parts, however, being very deep.

Stuart island lies across the eastern entrance of Cardero channel, almost blocking it, but leaving passages both to the northward and southward; the former, Arran rapids, owing to its narrowness and the strength of the tide, which rushes through it at the rate of from 7 to 9 knots, is not navigable except at great risk; the latter, ½ mile wide, is also not recommended, as at its northern end the tide runs directly at right angles to a vessel's course at the rate of from 6 to 7 knots.

At 2½ miles within the entrance the Dent islands cause further obstruction by contracting the channel to 600 yards, which narrow passage is full of dangerous rapids, overfalls, and whirlpools, with the probability of the existence of sunken rocks; therefore it can not be considered safe or prudent to enter or leave Cardero channel by its eastern entrance, and it is advised to carefully avoid that part of it which is eastward of Dent islands.

A sunken rock lies about ¼ mile S. 69° W. (S. 44° W. mag.) from the southern projection of Steep point, western side of Stuart island.

A sunken rock lies 350 yards WNW. of Henry point on the northern side of the channel 1¼ miles westward of Dent islands.

A rock, which nearly dries, lies 50 yards offshore, ½ mile westward from Johns point, and southward of Chaune (Channe) island.

There is no passage northward of the small island lying S. 70° E. (N. 85° E. mag.), distant 1,400 yards from Greene point; rocks which dry at low water lie between that island and the islands ¼ mile eastward of it. Southward of these rocks there are rapids, which are stated to be dangerous at any time of tide.

Anchorages.—Cardero channel has but few places that afford anchorage. Bickley bay on the north side of east Thurlow island, and nearly opposite the Phillips arm, is about 600 yards in extent with from 16 to 21 fathoms of water, and near its head 6 fathoms. Vessels may also anchor in 15 fathoms in Crawford anchorage inside the Erasmus islands on the south side of the channel, 2½ miles westward from Bickley bay.

There are a post-office, wharf, and stores at Shoal bay at the north end of east Thurlow island, eastward of Godwin point.

Mayne passage, which branches off to the southward from Cardero channel 3½ miles eastward of Loughborough inlet, separates the two Thurlow islands and communicates with Johnstone strait; it is apparently a clear channel, but has not been surveyed. Anchorage may be had in the northern part of the passage in from 9 to 15 fathoms.

Caution.—When bound from Bute inlet to the northwestward, vessels should proceed to the eastward of Read and Quadra islands by the Calm and Sutil channels, round cape Mudge, and through Discovery passage, and not attempt to shorten the distance by using Cardero channel.

Tidal streams.—The streams in Cardero channel run at the rate of from 1 to 2 knots in the western part, increasing to 3 and 4 knots eastward of Nodales channel; between Dent island and the eastern entrance to the inlet they run with great rapidity, especially in the narrow passage between Dent and Sonora islands which, as before observed, is full of whirlpools and overfalls.

Frederick arm branches northward from Cardero channel, opposite Hall point, the north extreme of Sonora island, and extends about 3 miles in that direction, shoaling gradually toward its head, where a stream enters the inlet flowing from a sheet of water, extending some distance to the northeastward, and known as the Estero basin.

The flats usually found extending a considerable distance from the shore at the head of most of the numerous inlets or fiords, and which are invariably steep-to, only extend a very short distance offshore at the head of Frederick arm, and are not so steep-to, and it therefore appears to afford a better anchorage than any of the other inlets on the mainland, being only exposed to the southward. Anchorage may be had at a reasonable distance from the shore.

Phillips arm, lying immediately westward of Frederick arm, extends about 5 miles in a northerly direction, shoaling gradually off the flats at its head.

Loughborough inlet penetrates the continent for 17 miles in a northerly direction; it has much the same characteristics as most of the arms that indent the NW. coast of North America, being almost hemmed in by precipitous mountains rising abruptly from the shore, and having great depth of water with but few anchorages. At the entrance between Styles and Grismond points, at its junction with Cardero and Chancellor channels, the inlet is about 1,600 yards wide, which is the average width to within about 1 mile from the head, when it opens out to 1¾ miles.

From the entrance the inlet extends NNE. for 6 miles as far as Cosby point, which projects from the west side; its direction for 7 miles is then northerly, turning at Towry head into Cooper reach, which takes a gentle curve toward the NE. for 4 miles to the head, terminating in Fraser and McBride bays, which are separated by Pan point jutting out in the center. The latter bay affords anchorage in about 25 fathoms at 600 yards from the shore; in the former the water is very deep until close in.

Sidney bay, 2½ miles SSW. from Cosby point on the west shore, and 4 miles NNE. from Styles point, extends about ¾ mile to the westward and is about 200 yards wide, affording anchorage for coasters near its head in 16 fathoms.

Beaver creek, on the west shore of Loughborough inlet, 3½ miles within the entrance, extends 2 miles in a southwesterly direction, is from 200 to 600 yards wide, and shoals gradually toward its head, where good and sheltered anchorage may be obtained in 7 fathoms; anchorage may also be obtained in about 15 fathoms in mid-channel westward of Goat islands. The channel is southward of Goat islands, which lie ½ mile within the entrance, and are connected to the north shore by a flat which dries at low water. Good water may be obtained from a stream at the head of the creek.

Tides.—The tidal streams in Loughborough inlet are not strong, seldom exceeding a rate of from 1 to 2 knots an hour. It is high water, full and change, in Beaver creek at 3 h. 0 m.; springs rise 16 feet.

CHAPTER VII.

FROM THE STRAIT OF GEORGIA TO CAPE SCOTT AND THE SCOTT ISLANDS.

VARIATION IN 1906.

Cape Mudge .... 24° 45′ E. Cape Scott .... 25° 40′ E.

Cape Caution .... 26° 00′ E.

Discovery passage, formed between the west sides of Quadra and Sonora islands and the Vancouver island coast, is the only safe navigable channel from the strait of Georgia to the northwestward.

The general direction is NNW. and SSE., and its length 23½ miles from cape Mudge, the SE. entrance point, to Chatham point where it joins Johnstone strait. The average width is a little more than 1 mile, but at Seymour narrows, halfway between cape Mudge and Chatham point, it contracts to 700 yards; through the narrows the tidal streams run with great velocity.

Southward of the narrows the shores are of moderate height, that on the eastward or Quadra island side being the more broken and hilly. Northward of the narrows the shores become steep and mountainous, attaining a considerable elevation, especially on the western side, where the Mount Menzies range rises to a height of 4,070 feet, and on which the snow often remains until June. The whole country is covered with dense pine forests which, nearly everywhere, come close down to the water's edge.

The navigation of Discovery passage and Johnstone strait by steamers, which alone in these days use the route, is very simple, it being only necessary to steer in mid-channel, the chief difficulty presented being the strong tidal streams in Seymour narrows and in the vicinity of Helmcken island.

Tides and tidal streams.—The tidal wave takes about 3 hours to traverse Discovery passage, it being high water, full and change, at Chatham point at 2 h. 0 m., at Seymour narrows at 3 h. 30 m., and at cape Mudge at 5 h. 0 m.

Southward of Seymour narrows the streams run from 4 to 6 knots at springs, and turn at high and low water by the shore, the flood setting to the southeastward and the ebb to the northwestward. Off cape Mudge, and between it and Willow point, there is a heavy tide race on the flood which during strong easterly and southeasterly winds becomes dangerous to small vessels.

Northward of the narrows the streams are comparatively slack, running at from 1 to 3 knots, and turning at from 1½ to 2 hours after high and low water by the shore.

The tides and streams in Seymour narrows will be presently described.

Cape Mudge, the southern point of Quadra island, and forming the eastern side of the entrance to Discovery passage, is flat and wooded, and terminates in a broad whitish-yellow earth cliff, covered here and there with vegetation, and facing to the SE. The cliff is 230 feet high at its highest part and decreases gradually in height to the westward until it joins the shore-line at the entrance to Discovery passage.

A bowlder beach at the foot of the cliff dries out for a distance of 800 yards, and a stony reef extends off it to the eastward, there being patches of 4 and 5 fathoms at a distance of 1½ miles from the southern extremity of the cape; the edge of this reef is fringed with kelp during the summer.

The flood stream sets strongly to the northeastward over this reef, causing a dangerous race off it, often extending across the passage to Willow point, as already mentioned.

Light.—A square wooden lighthouse, painted white, with red roof and lantern, stands near the western extremity of the cape. From it is exhibited, at a height of 82 feet above high water, a fixed white light, visible from the bearing S. 24° E. (S. 49° E. mag.), through East and North, to N. 49° W. (N. 74° W. mag.), from a distance of 10 miles in clear weather.

Willow point, the southwestern point of Discovery passage, 1¾ miles SSW. from cape Mudge, is low and covered with willow bushes; a shallow ledge extends off it to a distance of 500 yards. When passing this point do not approach it within ½ mile.

Directions.—When making the entrance to Discovery passage, cape Mudge, with its whitish-yellow cliff, is easily recognized, and to enter it will only be necessary to steer in mid-channel between it and Willow point, being careful to guard against being set over toward Cape Mudge reef, if the flood or south-going stream is running.

The flood stream from the strait of Georgia sets northward up the Sutil channel, and vessels making for Discovery passage must guard against being set in that direction; this should be particularly borne in mind in thick or foggy weather, when the Vancouver island shore should be kept well aboard.

By day Cape Mudge lighthouse should not be brought to bear westward of N. 45° W. (N. 70° W. mag.), and by night the light must be kept in sight.

Orange point, on the western side of the passage, in line with the lighthouse N. 35° W. (N. 60° W. mag.), is a good guide when entering.

Quathiaski cove.—From cape Mudge the shore of Quadra island, consisting of a sand and shingle beach, curves slightly inward in a NNW. direction for 3 miles to Quathiaski cove, the Indian village of Yaculta being situated about halfway.

The cove is a small indentation and is only suitable for quite small vessels. Grouse island divides the cove into two parts; the southern channel is clear, and there is room in the southeastern part of the cove, where there is a small pier and a store, for a small vessel to be moored.

Grouse island is 400 yards long and 99 feet high; a ledge extends off its SE. point for 150 yards, which must be guarded against when entering.

The tidal streams set slightly through the cove, but sweep strongly past the entrance.

At Quathiaski cove the shore line becomes rocky and rugged and the land is more hilly and broken.

Gowlland harbor, about 5 miles NW. of cape Mudge, is 2½ miles long in a NNW. and SSE. direction and from ¼ to ⅔ mile wide. There are several islets and rocks in the harbor, and the southern end forms a fine landlocked anchorage, affording room for several moderate-sized vessels.

Gowlland island, 1 mile long, ⅓ mile wide, and 400 feet high to the tops of the trees, rugged and densely wooded, forms the outer side of the harbor.

Steep island, 200 yards from the western side of Gowlland island, is 800 yards long, steep, narrow, and 78 feet high toward its southern end, the tops of the trees being 165 feet above high water. The SW. side of the island is cliffy.

May island, forming the northwestern point of the harbor, lies 800 yards to the northwestward of Steep island; it is about 200 yards in extent, rugged, wooded, and 240 feet high to the tops of the trees.

Entrance bank, composed of sand, extending 1,000 yards SE. from May island, contracts the navigable channel into the harbor to 150 yards in width, between Entrance rock, off its SE. extremity, and the Vigilant islets off the NW. end of Gowlland island.

Entrance rock, with less than 6 feet over it at low water springs, lies 250 yards north from the east Vigilant islet; depths of less than 3 fathoms extend for 100 yards SE. of the rock.

A patch, with 4 fathoms least water, lies 200 yards NW. from the west Vigilant islet.

Spoil rock, with 3¾ fathoms least water, lies nearly in the fairway just within the entrance, and nearly 200 yards N. 87° E. (N. 62° E. mag.) from the east Vigilant islet.

Kelp grows on this rock in summer.

Tides and tidal streams.—It is high water, full and change, in Gowlland harbor at 4 h. 0 m.; springs rise 11 feet and neaps 7 feet. At neaps there is practically no range between the smaller tides of the day; the difference between two successive low waters amounts at times to as much as 9 feet.

The tidal streams run swiftly between Steep and Gowlland islands and across the entrance to the harbor; caution is therefore necessary when entering; no stream is felt inside the harbor.

Directions.—To enter the harbor pass midway between May and Steep islands and steer for the entrance, keeping the top of Mouse island within the harbor, just open northward of Vigilant islets, which will clear the 4-fathom patch. Pass within 100 yards of Vigilant islets to avoid Entrance bank and rock, and round Spoil rock to the northward, bringing the top of Mouse island in line with the north point of Doe island S. 56° E. (S. 81° E. mag.), which leads eastward of it, and proceed up the harbor, anchoring as convenient at the southern end in from 9 to 10 fathoms, mud.

With the north-going stream an eddy will be found setting to the southward close westward of Vigilant islets.

There is a boat channel into the harbor at the south end of Gowlland island.

The coast.—From Gowlland harbor a range of high, precipitous cliffs 200 to 230 feet in height, with traces of copper ore, continues for about ¾ mile, when the abrupt, rocky character of the coast is resumed, which changes to a bowlder and shingle beach about 1¼ miles farther north, and continues as far as Maud island at the entrance to Seymour narrows.

Maud island, nearly circular in shape and about ½ mile across, forms the SE. point of entrance to Seymour narrows. The island is wooded, its height being 300 feet to the tops of the trees.

Yellow islet lies 800 yards east from the east side of Maud island, and 300 yards from the shore; it is small, bare, and 51 feet high.

Willow point to the Narrows.—From Willow point, already described, a low coast trends NNW. for 5½ miles to the mouth of the Campbell river, a fine stream navigable by canoes for some miles. The coast is bordered by a shingle and bowlder beach and is wooded close down to the water's edge, except for a mile southward of Campbell river, where it consists of a low and bare sandy spit confining the river. To the southward of the spit is an Indian cemetery.

Yaculta bank.—Three miles NNW. from Willow point, and abreast of the village of Yaculta, the 10-fathom curve extends to ¾ mile from the western shore, forming Yaculta bank, on which the average depths are about 6 to 9 fathoms, and which is about ¾ mile in extent NNW. and SSE.

A rocky patch, with 4¼ fathoms least water, and 400 yards in extent, lies on this bank with the center of Yaculta village bearing E. ½ N., distant 1$\frac{3}{10}$ miles. Kelp grows on this patch during summer.

When passing Yaculta bank, Steep island open of, or the west point of Gowlland island in line with, the point NW. of Quathiaski cove, bearing N. 20° W. (N. 45° W. mag.), leads eastward of it.

Orange point, 1½ miles NW. from Campbell river, is low and has low earthy cliffs of a reddish color. A bowlder bank, marked by kelp in summer, extends 200 yards off the shore from the northern part of the point.

Duncan bay.—From Orange point the coast curves to the SW. for ½ mile and again to the NW. forming Duncan bay, where good anchorage, easy of access, may be obtained in from 10 to 15 fathoms, sand, well out of the tide and sheltered from all but northwesterly winds. There is a creek with sand and mud flats at the head of the bay.

Tides.—It is high water, full and change, at about 4 h. 0 m.; springs rise 13 feet, neaps 7 feet.

Warspite rock.—One and one-half miles NW. from Orange point is Middle point, which is low, shelving, and rocky.. Warspite rock, a dangerous pinnacle with 4 feet least water and with deep water between it and the shore, lies 300 yards N. 81° E. (N. 56° E. mag.) from Middle point. It is steep-to on its northern and eastern sides; kelp grows on it during the summer, but when the tidal streams are strong the kelp is run under.

Race point, 1½ miles NW. from Middle point, is a bold rocky bluff, 65 feet high, bare of trees, and steep-to.

From Race point the coast bends sharply to the westward, toward Menzies bay.

The tidal streams run past the point with great velocity, causing heavy overfalls and eddies with the south-going or flood stream, extending for some distance to the eastward; with fresh easterly and southeasterly winds this race becomes very dangerous for boats.

Menzies bay, whose mouth is 1½ miles to the westward of Race point, is a deep bight in the western shore, the upper part of which, inside Defender shoal, affords excellent and secure anchorage in from 6 to 7 fathoms, mud and sand, entirely out of the stream of tide.

Defender shoal, composed of sand, occupies the center of the bay, and is of considerable extent; it dries, near the middle, 4 feet at springs, and near the highest part of the bank is a small pole beacon; this shoal has extended of late years.

The entrance to the upper part of the bay, between the north shore and the northern end of Defender shoal, is nearly 200 yards wide between the 3-fathom curves and carries 5 fathoms of water.

A convenient anchorage, when only waiting for the turn of the stream in Seymour narrows, is off Trout river in the southern part of the bay, in from 5 to 6 fathoms, where there is no inconvenience from the tide or swirls.

Stephenson point, the northern point of the bay, has foul ground extending nearly 200 yards SE. from it, marked by kelp in summer. Six hundred yards NE. from Stephenson point is Wilfred point, at the south entrance to Seymour narrows; between these points is Nymphe cove, where there is good fresh water.

Directions.—When entering Menzies bay, if the stream is running strongly, get into slack water about the middle of the bay, and giving Stephenson point a good berth, keep close along the northern shore until abreast a conspicuous green ravine with a large gray bowlder, when the narrowest part is reached and the vessel should not be more than 100 yards from the shore, which is steep-to. When this ravine is passed, haul out and anchor as convenient.

Tides and tidal streams.—It is high water, full and change, in Menzies bay at 3 h. 30 m.; springs rise 11½ feet, neaps 6½ feet.

There is a large diurnal inequality in the times of high and low water, sometimes amounting to 4 hours, and also in the heights of the low waters, which latter amounts at times to as much as 9 feet. There is also a diurnal inequality in the heights of the high waters of, at times, as much as 4 feet.

When a strong flood or south-going stream is running in the narrows, the volume of water rushes past Wilfred point and striking on a point midway between Race and Huntingford points, the stronger stream goes toward the former, the other follows the coast to Huntingford point, where it is deflected and lost in the middle of the bay.

With a strong ebb, the edge of the stream from Race point strikes on Stephenson point, but without much force, that part running westward being lost almost immediately. There is no swirl to speak of inside a concave line drawn between Race and Stephenson points.

Seymour narrows, 11 miles NW. by N. from cape Mudge, is a narrow strait nearly 2 miles long and 700 yards wide in its narrowest part; the passage is, however, contracted to under 400 yards by Ripple rock lying in mid-channel at the southern end of the pass. The shores on both sides are high, rugged, and steep-to.

Ripple rock, a dangerous shoal with two heads lying north and south of each other, nearly 200 yards apart, the northern head with 2 fathoms least water being the shoalest, lies nearly in the center of the Narrows, but a little nearer the western shore. The 2-fathom head lies 500 yards West (S. 65° W. mag.) from the nearest part of Maud island and 600 yards N. 43° E. (N. 18° E. mag.) from the eastern extreme of Wilfred point. The position of the rock is indicated by the tide race and eddies over it, except for a short time at slack water. There is a depth of 4 fathoms on the southern head.

Tides and tidal streams.—It is high water, full and change, in Seymour narrows at about 3 h. 30 m. The streams run with great velocity, the flood or south-going stream attaining a rate of 12 knots at some spring tides, and the ebb of 10 knots. The strength of the flood stream is well maintained until near Race point, off which it sometimes runs 9 or 10 knots at springs, causing strong eddies SE. of Maud island and toward Menzies bay.

The time of the turn of the stream depends greatly on the range of the preceding tide. At springs, and in general after the greater range tides, the stream turns at about 20 minutes after high and low water by the shore. At neaps, and after the smaller range tides, at from 1 to 2½ hours after the same.

Owing to the large diurnal inequality in the times of high and low water in the Narrows, the turn of the stream is more conveniently referred to the time of the tide at Sitka, for which place tide tables are published by the United States Coast Survey.

To find the standard times (120th meridian) of slack water, to the time of high or low water as given for Sitka, add 4 h. 50 m. at springs and after the greater range tides; in the former case, it gives the slack before the north-going stream. At neaps and after the smaller tides the slack occurs as much as from 6 to 6½ hours after Sitka.

The duration of slack water is about 15 minutes at springs.

During the strength of either stream the eddies in the Narrows are very heavy, and no large vessels should attempt the passage.

With fresh northerly or southerly winds the races and eddies become very dangerous for boats and small vessels.

Directions.—It is recommended to enter the Narrows only at or near slack water and to keep the eastern shore aboard to avoid Ripple rock, remembering, if going north with a north-going stream, that the stream sets obliquely over toward the rock as Maud island is rounded.

The strictest attention to steering is essential at all times.

Duncan and Menzies bays on the south, and Plumper bay on the north, are convenient anchorages while waiting for slack water.

Discovery passage—Northern portion.—Northward of Seymour narrows the shores of Discovery passage become mountainous and rugged on the eastern side; near the Narrows, mount Seymour rises to a height of 2,040 feet, and at the north end of the passage, on the same side, is mount Discovery 2,115 feet high. On the western side the Mount Menzies range, with many spurs and deep valleys between, rises to a height of 4,070 feet.

The passage is a broad channel of deep water free of dangers except at its northern end off Chatham point, where it turns into Johnstone strait. On the eastern side, close north of the Narrows, is Plumper bay with good anchorage, and separated from it by the peninsula of Separation head is Deep Water bay. Five miles farther north is the entrance to Kanish bay, a deep bight with numerous islets and rocks, and separated from it by Granite point is the entrance to Okisollo channel.

On the western side, Elk bay, 9 miles from the Narrows, affords fair anchorage, and close south of Chatham point is Otter cove, a small but snug anchorage.

Plumper bay, immediately north of Seymour narrows on the Quadra island shore, ½ mile deep and a little more in width, affords good anchorage, easy of access, well sheltered, and out of the tide, in from 8 to 15 fathoms, mud and sand. A rocky patch of small extent, with 6 fathoms least water, lies 400 yards from the southern and 600 yards from the eastern shore of the bay, which should be avoided when anchoring, and 200 yards offshore in the SE. part of the bay, just inside the 3-fathom curve, is a rock with 6 feet over it.

Plumper bay is a convenient stopping place when waiting for the turn of the stream in the narrows. If anchored far out in the bay the tidal streams and eddies are sometimes strong, causing a vessel to surge on her cables. No directions are necessary for entering the bay.

Deep Water bay is too deep to afford any anchorage, except for quite a small vessel, which might anchor close inshore in the SE. corner of the bay, in from 10 to 12 fathoms.

Kanish bay, 2 miles deep and 1½ miles across its mouth, contains numerous islets and rocks with deep water between, and affords no anchorage.

Okisollo channel, the entrance to which lies immediately north of Granite point, the northern point of Kanish bay, separates Quadra island from Sonora island and joins Hoskyn inlet at Surge narrows. Seven miles from Granite point, an arm, locally known as Hole in the Wall, branches off to the NE. and joins Calm channel 2 miles below Stuart island.

Tides.—It is high water, full and change, in Surge narrows at 6 h. 0 m.; springs rise 12 feet.

Throughout this channel the tidal stream runs strongly, especially through Surge narrows and at the SW. end of the Hole in Wall, where they attain a rate of from 7 to 9 knots. These passages are unsurveyed and should not be attempted.

Elk bay, on the west side of Discovery passage, 9 miles from Seymour narrows, is 1¼ miles wide between Elk and Otter points and ½ mile deep; it affords fair anchorage in 15 fathoms, mud and sand, ¼ mile from the shore at the head of the bay, and out of any strength of tide. The anchorage is open to the north and east.

There is foul ground in the shallow bay north of Elk point, and a rock, which is awash at high water, lies 200 yards offshore.

Tides.—It is high water, full and change, in Elk bay at about 2 h. 30 m.; springs rise 15 feet, neaps 7 feet.

Otter cove, close south of Chatham point, is a small but snug anchorage sheltered from all winds. Limestone island, 26 feet high, lies in the entrance; 100 yards east from it is Snag rock with 2 fathoms least water. Five hundred yards north of Limestone island are the two Rocky islets, 14 and 11 feet high, joined together at low water.

To enter, pass midway between Limestone island and Rocky islets, and anchor midway between the former and the head of the cove, in from 6 to 12 fathoms, mud and sand; a vessel of any size should moor.

Tides.—It is high water, full and change, at 2 h. 0 m.; springs rise 13 feet, neaps range 7½ feet.

Chatham point, a low, wooded, rocky point, nearly 24 miles from cape Mudge, is the NW. extremity of Discovery passage and is the turning point into Johnstone strait.

Foul ground extends for 800 yards north and west from the east extreme of Chatham point. The point should not be approached nearer than ½ mile.

Beaver rock, with 5 feet least water, lies 400 yards N. 9° W. (N. 34° W. mag.) from the east extreme of Chatham point.

Directions.—A mid-channel course both north and south of Seymour narrows is all that is required.

When passing Yaculta bank, Steep island open of, or the west point of Gowlland island in line with, the point NW. of Quathiaski cove bearing N. 20° W. (N. 45° W. mag.), leads eastward of it.

Chatham point should be rounded at a distance of at least ½ mile.

Nodales channel, the southern end of which is opposite Chatham point, is 8 miles long in a northeasterly direction between east Thurlow and Sonora islands, and leads into Cardero channel. It has an average width of about 1 mile, and has deep water throughout.

Hemming bay is on the west side of Nodales channel, 4 miles from Chatham point; the water in it is deep. A small rock with a depth of 6 feet over it, and not marked by kelp, lies nearly in the middle of the bay, 800 yards westward from the northern Lee islet.

Hardinge island, 300 feet high, about ¾ mile long and ¼ mile wide, is about 1 mile NW. from the entrance to Cameleon harbor, with a passage on both sides. Young passage, to the southward, is ¼ mile wide, and Burgess passage, to the northward, ½ mile wide; there is deep water in both.

Maycock rock.—Three-quarters of a mile N. 68° W. (S. 87° W. mag.) from the south entrance point of Cameleon harbor, and 1,200 yards N. 76° W. (S. 79° W. mag.) from Bruce point, is Maycock rock, with 1 fathom on it. The shore, for ½ mile to the eastward of this rock, has foul ground, marked with kelp, extending off it for 200 yards.

Cameleon harbor on the SE. shore of Nodales channel (Sonora island) is about 1 mile deep in a southeasterly direction, and has an average width of 600 yards. The entrance, between Bruce point on the north shore and a small islet off the south shore, is less than 400 yards wide, and caution must be observed in rounding Bruce point in order to avoid Douglas rock, lying 100 yards off it. It is advisable to keep well outside the kelp when entering.

Anchorage, sheltered from all winds, in from 8 to 10 fathoms, may be obtained at 400 yards from the head. The lead should be kept going quickly in approaching the head as the flat which extends nearly 200 yards from it is steep-to.

It is high water, full and change, in Cameleon harbor at 3 h. 0 m.; springs rise 16 feet, neaps 11½ feet.

Johnstone strait, which separates the north side of Vancouver island from the mainland, is comprised between Chatham point and Beaver cove, a distance of about 55 miles in a WNW. and ESE. direction, and has a varying breadth of from 1 to 2 miles.

The southern shore is a continuous series of high and steep mountain ranges rising abruptly from the water's edge and attaining elevations of from 3,000 to 5,000 feet, some of the higher peaks retaining snow all the year round. The ranges are divided here and there by the valleys of some considerable streams.

The northern shore is also high and mountainous for the most part, but is not so rugged as the southern, neither do the mountains overlooking the strait attain to so great a height, and it is broken by several channels and inlets.

The shores on both sides are densely wooded except the higher peaks.

There are no anchorages whatever along the southern shore, but there are several on the northern, Vere cove, Blinkinsop and Forward bays, ports Neville and Harvey.

Tides and tidal streams.—It is high water, full and change, at the western end of the strait at 0 h. 30 m.; at Blinkinsop bay at 1 h. 5 m.; at Verde cove at 1 h. 20 m., and at Chatham point at 2 h. 0 m.

Springs rise 16 feet at the western end, and from 13 to 14 feet at Chatham point.

The streams turn everywhere at about 2 hours after high and low water by the shore. Westward of Hardwicke island the streams are not strong, seldom exceeding 3 knots an hour. In the vicinity of Helmcken island they run strongly at from 3 to 6 knots, and in the eastern part of the strait at from 2 to 4 knots.

In the neighborhood of Helmcken island there are several heavy tide rips and races, also off Ripple point and Knox bay and in the vicinity of the Pender islands, which, in blowing weather, and at certain times of the tide, are dangerous to boats and small vessels. Just westward of Chatham point occur overfalls and whirls.

Ripple point.—From Chatham point the strait takes a general westerly direction for 6 miles to Ripple point on the south shore, where the northern peak of the Halifax range rises very steeply from the water's edge to a height of 2,243 feet; the coast between is steep-to and indented by two small bays with streams at their heads.

The north shore of the strait is here formed by the south coast of east Thurlow island, which is high and mountainous, rising to two principal peaks, mount Brougham and mount Eldon, 2,262 feet and 2,022 feet high, respectively; the latter, situated near the west coast of the island, is remarkable, isolated, and square-topped.

Turn island, a little over ½ mile in length east and west, and 200 feet high to the tops of the trees, lies off the south point of east Thurlow island, from which it is separated by a narrow channel.

Siwash rock, with 6 feet least water, lies 300 yards SSE. from the SW. point of Turn island.

A rock, with 1¼ fathoms least water, lies 1 mile to the westward of Siwash rock and about 200 yards from the north shore of the strait.

Pender islands, a group of several islets and rocks, lie on the north side of the strait off the coast of east Thurlow island, westward of Turn island. They are mostly wooded, the largest being a little over ½ mile in length and 325 feet high to the tops of the trees. They should not be approached nearer than 400 yards; the tidal streams run strongly between them.

Mayne passage, the name given to the channel separating the two Thurlow islands, branches off to the NE. abreast of Ripple point and joins Cardero channel. It is apparently a clear channel, but has not been surveyed.

Knox bay, 1¾ miles NW. from Ripple point, is a deep bay on the south side of west Thurlow island; the water is too deep to afford any convenient anchorage. Between it and Ripple point are some heavy tide rips in blowing weather.

From Ripple point the strait curves slightly to the southward for 8 miles to Race passage. The north shore is formed by west Thurlow island and both shores are steep-to and free from dangers. Bear river enters the strait on the south shore 4¼ miles west from Ripple point.

Vere cove.—Tyhee point, the SW. extreme of west Thurlow island, lies 8 miles west from Ripple point; immediately north of it is Vere cove, about 400 yards wide at the entrance, gradually narrowing to 200 yards at the head, where there is a beach of bowlders and shingle with a small stream. The shores are steep and thickly wooded. Dorothy rock, which covers near high water, is close to the south shore of the entrance.

The cove is easy of access and the holding ground is good in 17 fathoms.

It is high water, full and change, in Vere cove at about 1 h. 20 m.

Eden point, the west extreme of west Thurlow island, is bold and steep-to and forms the southern point of entrance to Chancellor channel.

Hardwicke island, forming the northern shore of the strait for 7 miles westward from Eden point, from which it is separated by Chancellor channel, is high and mountainous, rising toward the center to a height of 2,626 feet in mount Royston, remarkable and bold with a steep face to the southward. The south shore of the island is steep-to, except near its SW. point where Earl ledge extends off for 700 yards, uncovering at low water, over and around which the streams boil and eddy.

York island, high, round, wooded, and about ½ mile in diameter, lies a little over ¼ mile off the west end of Hardwicke island; it is 348 feet high to the tops of the trees. Nearly 400 yards south of it are two small rocks, the highest being 16 feet in height.

Clarence island, ⅓ mile NW. of York island, is 300 yards in extent and 197 feet high to the tops of the trees.

Fanny islet, a low flat rock, 3 feet high and about 100 yards in length, and on which there is a little vegetation, lies 400 yards NW. from Clarence island.

Foul ground exists between these islands and between York and Hardwicke islands.

Camp point, sloping gradually to the water's edge on the southern shore of the strait, 1½ miles west from Vere cove, is broad and rounded, and bordered by a rocky shingle beach.

Twelve hundred yards eastward of the point and 100 yards offshore is a rocky ledge awash at high water.

Ripple shoal consists of four pinnacle rocks on a shoal about ¾ mile long, east and west. The shoalest head, near the middle of the shoal, has 10 feet of water over it at low water, and lies 1,100 yards N. 36° E. (N. 11° E. mag.) from the nearest part of Camp point, with Tyhee point bearing S. 80° E. (N. 75° E. mag.), distant 1$\frac{1}{10}$ miles.

Kelp grows on the reef in the summer, but it is generally run under by the streams which run strongly over the reef, causing rips and eddies.

It has been found impossible to maintain a buoy on this shoal.

Salmon river, of considerable size, flows into the strait on the south side through an extensive valley separating the Prince of Wales range from the Newcastle range; it is 5 miles westward from Camp point. The mouth of the river at high water appears like a large bay, but it dries out at low water to between the entrance points, the edge of the bank dropping suddenly to deep water.

The Indian village of Khusan is situated on the right bank of the river ½ mile from the mouth.

The shore between Camp point and Salmon river is abrupt and cliffy, the sides of the mountain rising steeply from the water.

Port Khusan (Hkusam).—A small islet, 24 feet high, lies 1¼ miles east of Salmon river and 200 yards offshore; between the river and the islet is a small indentation called Port Khusan where there is a post-office; a small local steamer calls weekly during the summer.

The ground is foul between the port and the islet, and a rock, with less than 6 feet of water over it, lies 200 yards offshore near the center of the port.

Helmcken island, lying in mid-strait, 3 miles westward of west Thurlow island, is 1½ miles long in an east and west direction and about ½ mile wide; it is thickly wooded, the tops of the trees being 250 feet above high water. The coast-line is rugged and much indented, especially on the northern side, close to which are several islets.

Helmcken island divides the strait into two channels, each over ½ mile wide and clear of danger, either of which can be used as convenient; that to the south of the island is known as Race passage, the one to the north as Current passage.

Speaker rock, which dries 8 feet, lies 650 yards N. 47° E. (N. 22° E. mag.) from the east point of Helmcken island.

Two rocks, with less than 6 feet of water over them, lie 300 yards eastward of the south point of the island and nearly 200 yards offshore.

Tidal streams.—The streams run strongly through both Race and Current passages, and over Earl ledge and Ripple shoal, attaining a rate of 6 knots at springs; the eddies and swirls are many and often violent, and in blowing weather cause dangerous races for boats and small vessels.

Directions.—Either Race or Current passage may be used as convenient, the stream running equally strong in both passages.

Race passage is the one generally used, vessels proceeding between Camp point and Ripple shoal keeping the middle summit of the Halifax range, or Bear point, in line with the south extreme of west Thurlow island, S. 78° E. (N. 77° E. mag.), being careful, if proceeding westward with a strong west-going stream, not to be set over toward Ripple shoal.

If intending to pass northward of Ripple shoal, proceed by way of Current passage; if going west with a west-going stream, be careful, as before, to avoid being set toward the shoal, and after rounding Helmcken island of the set over Earl ledge; the west end of Helmcken island is steep-to.

If going east with an east-going stream, after rounding Earl ledge be careful not to be set upon the west end of Helmcken island. Camp point in line with the south extreme of Helmcken island S. 74° E. (N. 81° E. mag.) leads well south of Earl ledge.

Chancellor channel, which is 8 miles long and connects with Cardero channel, lies along the north shore of west Thurlow island, and has its entrance between Eden point and the south shore of Hardwicke island, where it is ½ mile wide; the channel widens gradually from the entrance to a general width of a little under 1 mile. A kelp patch is shown on the chart nearly in mid-channel, ¾ mile east of Darcy point, 3¼ miles from the entrance. The depth of water over the patch is not known, and it should be avoided.

Wellbore channel separates the NE. side of Hardwicke island from the mainland, and leads from Chancellor channel northwestward into Sunderland channel; the entrance from Chancellor channel is nearly 3 miles NE. of Eden point.

The channel is 4 miles long and has an average width of about ⅓ mile, though at Carterer point it contracts to under 400 yards. Bulkeley island lies in the SE. entrance, off the eastern end of Hardwicke island, and there are some small islets and rocks off Carterer point; the entrance to Forward harbor is on the eastern shore near the NW. end of the channel. The water throughout is deep, and in navigating it a mid-channel course is all that is required.

Tidal streams.—The tidal streams in Wellbore channel run with great velocity, often attaining at springs a rate of over 7 knots an hour.

Forward harbor, on the eastern side of Wellbore channel, the entrance to which, between Louisa and Horace points, is only a little over 200 yards wide, extends nearly 3 miles in an easterly direction, and, though the entrance is narrow, its freedom from obstruction renders it easily accessible to vessels of moderate size. Its shores are steep-to, but, the water being of moderate depth over its whole extent (12 to 15 fathoms), anchorage may be taken up in any part of it, if requisite. At its head a flat dries out 500 yards at low water, and two small streams flow into it.

For ½ mile within the entrance the passage is from 200 to 400 yards wide, with depths of 8 to 12 fathoms, but at that distance, the harbor opens and varies from 700 to 1,000 yards in width.

Anchorage may, as already mentioned, be taken up anywhere, but a good position is in Douglas bay, on the north shore, just round Mills point, in from 6 to 10 fathoms.

It is high water, full and change, in Forward harbor at 3 h. 0 m.; springs rise 16 feet, neaps 11½ feet.

Bessborough bay, an open indentation on the north shore of Wellbore channel, ½ mile NW. of the entrance to Forward harbor, affords no anchorage, owing to the great depth of water in it.

Sunderland channel.—The entrance, which is subject to heavy tide rips, lies between Fanny islet and the shore near Blinkinsop bay. Sunderland channel is a clear navigable channel extending over 6 miles in a NE. direction to the entrance to Topaze harbor, and 2 miles farther to Wellbore channel. It is 1 mile wide at the entrance with an average width of 1½ miles. Seymour and Poyntz islands lie in mid-channel, the latter near the junction of Sunderland channel with Wellbore channel. The waters of the channel are deep and free of dangers.

Tidal streams.—The tidal streams in Sunderland channel are not strong, attaining a velocity of only from ½ to 1½ knots an hour.

Topaze harbor, a continuation of Sunderland channel, is, from its entrance (1,400 yards wide) between Murray island on the east and the shore under Geneste cone (1,400 feet high) on the west, nearly 5 miles long in an easterly direction, and nearly 1 mile wide, gradually narrowing, however, at its head to ½ mile in width. Over the whole of this harbor there is an uniform depth of from 12 to 14 fathoms until within ½ mile of its head. On the north side, 1½ miles within the entrance, is Jackson bay, a narrow bight extending 1½ miles in a northerly direction, but shoal at nearly a mile from its head.

At the head of Topaze harbor are mounts Drummond and Berkeley, 3,273 and 3,987 feet high, respectively.

Anchorage may be obtained, well sheltered, in either Jackson bay or at the head of the harbor, in 10 fathoms.

Blinkinsop bay, 1½ miles northward of Fanny islet and 26 miles from Chatham point, affords good and convenient anchorage, well sheltered and with good holding ground, for any class of vessel. The bay is 1½ miles deep in a northerly direction and ½ mile wide at its entrance between point George and point Tuna; the head of the bay dries out for ¾ mile. The western shore of the bay is high, mount Hardy rising close over it to a height of 2,074 feet; the eastern side of the bay is of moderate height, sloping gradually to point Tuna.

A small islet, Block islet, 49 feet high, lies near the shore in the NE. part of the bay.

Point Tuna, the eastern point of entrance, has foul ground extending from it for nearly 200 yards to the SW., a rock, with 5 feet least water, lying 100 yards SW. from the extremity of the point; and a rock, awash at low water, lies between it and the point and 70 yards from the latter. Tuna point should be given a berth of at least 300 yards.

From point George, the western point of entrance, a bowlder beach dries out to the eastward for nearly 200 yards at low tides, a large bowlder, which dries about 7 feet, lying 150 yards east from the point. Foul ground, on which kelp grows in summer, extends for 400 yards east of point George.

Blink rock, with a least depth of 10 feet over it, lies in the eastern part of the bay 300 yards from the nearest point of coast, with the west extreme of point Tuna bearing S. 14° E. (S. 39° E. mag.), distant 500 yards, and Block islet N. 55° E. (N. 30° E. mag.).

Elf shoal, a rocky ledge 100 yards in length NE. and SW., with 3¼ fathoms over it, lies 300 yards North (N. 25° W. mag.) from Blink rock, with Block islet bearing N. 72° E. (N. 47° E. mag.), distant 800 yards. This shoal and Blink rock are marked by kelp in summer.

Tides.—It is high water, full and change, at 1 h. 5 m.; springs rise 15½ feet, neaps 10 feet.

Directions.—Enter in mid-channel, pass to the westward of Blink rock and Elf shoal, and anchor as convenient in from 6 to 10 fathoms, mud.

Jesse island, about 200 yards in extent and 42 feet high, on which are a few pine trees, their tops being 132 feet above high water, lies ½ mile SW. of Blinkinsop bay and 300 yards offshore; it is steep-to.

Port Neville, the entrance to which is 3 miles from Blinkinsop bay, trends in a NNE. direction for 7 miles, varying from ¼ to 1 mile in breadth.

The port affords spacious and secure anchorage, but the entrance channel, 1¼ miles long, being narrow, shallow, and obstructed by Channel rock, it should not be used except by those locally acquainted with it; with Blinkinsop bay and Port Harvey near at hand, it is not required.

The entrance is between Milly island, 272 feet high and wooded, lying off the western point of entrance, and Ransom point. The water shoals quite suddenly at the entrance from 4 to 5 fathoms. The channel is little more than 400 yards wide at its narrowest part, with an average depth of from 4 to 5 fathoms, narrowing and shoaling abreast of Channel rock to 15 feet at low water, after which it deepens gradually to from 6 to 12 fathoms in the port.

The best channel is on the west side of Channel rock, that to the eastward of the rock having a depth of only 12 feet at low water.

Channel rock, with only 4 feet of water over it, is very dangerous; it lies in mid-channel 700 yards S. 63° W. (S. 38° W. mag.) from Bowlder point.

The streams run in the entrance channel at a rate of from 2 to 3 knots.

Kelp grows right across the channel near the entrance during the summer months.

Bowlder point, the NE. point of the channel, is a low, earthy bluff; a shoal extends from it northward and eastward for over ¼ mile.

Robbers Nob is a remarkable knob of rock at the extremity of a low, grassy point on the NW. side of the port, a little over 1 mile distant from Bowlder point.

There is a post-office in Port Neville and a mail once a week.

Directions.—Entering Port Neville after rounding Milly island, which may be approached close-to, proceed up mid-channel until Robbers Nob comes in line with Bowlder point bearing N. 52° E. (N. 27° E. mag.), when keep well over to the western side of the channel to avoid Channel rock. When Bowlder point bears N. 80° E. (N. 55° E. mag.), vessels will be clear to the westward of the rock, and may then steer for Robbers Nob, avoiding a patch of 3 feet which skirts the western shore abreast Bowlder point, after passing which steer into the port and anchor in 7 fathoms, about ½ mile S. 79° W. (S. 54° W. mag.) of Robbers Nob. If necessary, vessels may anchor in the entrance about ½ mile north of Milly island, in 4½ and 5 fathoms.

The coast from Port Neville to the Broken islands at the entrance to Port Harvey, a distance of 8 miles, is nearly straight, steep, and rugged.

Mount Nelson, overlooking the coast and 3 miles westward from Milly island, rises abruptly to a height of 2,170 feet.

Stimpson reef, 4 miles westward from Milly island, is a rocky ledge, which dries 9 feet at low water springs, lying 500 yards offshore; it is steep-to on its outer side.

Broken islands, situated off the east side of the entrance to Port Harvey and Havannah channel, are a group of small islets and rocks with foul ground among them and between them and Domville point.

The southern islet is the largest, being from 400 to 600 yards in diameter and 208 feet high to the tops of the trees.

There is deep water close to the group on its southern and western sides.

Port Harvey, the entrance to which, and also to Havannah channel, is immediately west of the Broken islands, indents the coast in a northerly direction for nearly 4 miles, with a breadth varying from 400 yards to ¾ mile; it affords good and well-sheltered anchorage in 7 to 9 fathoms, muddy bottom, at ½ mile from its head. Several small islets, the Mist islets, lie off the eastern shore of the harbor, which is much indented; the anchorage is above them. From the head of the harbor low, swampy ground extends northeastward for ¼ mile, and to the NW. is a narrow gorge which partly fills at high water and joins Clio channel.

Tides.—It is high water, full and change, in Port Harvey at 0 h. 55 m.; springs rise 16 feet, neaps 9 feet.

Havannah channel, the entrance of which is 1½ miles north of Broken islands, runs in a northeasterly direction from the east side of Port Harvey, connecting it with Call creek. Its length is about 4 miles, and its breadth varies from ½ to 1 mile; the shores are high and much broken, and the depths in mid-channel vary from 9 to 50 fathoms. There are several islands within it which lie mostly in mid-channel. Hull island, the largest, is ¾ mile long and ½ mile broad.

Boughey bay, in the SE. part of Havannah channel, is about 1 mile deep in a southerly direction and ½ mile broad; there is good anchorage ½ mile from the head of the bay, in 10 to 14 fathoms, good holding ground.

Browning rock, in the north part of Havannah channel, about ¼ mile north of Hull island, has only 12 feet over it, and lies nearly in the fairway of the channel north of Hull island; the passage is northwestward of the rock.

The channel southward of Mistake island and eastward of Hull island is apparently deep and free from dangers.

Caution.—As the soundings are uneven and the bottom rocky west and NW. of Hull island, great care should be used in navigating this channel in that neighborhood.

Call creek, the eastern termination of the inlet leading from Havannah channel, is of considerable extent, its length in a northeasterly direction being 12 miles, and its breadth varying from ½ to 1¼ miles; the shores on either side are high and precipitous, rising abruptly to mountains from 1,000 to 4,700 feet in height. The head terminates in a low swamp and a valley extends NE. from it.

There is no anchorage whatever except near its entrance, on the north side among the Warren islands, where from 6 to 14 fathoms will be found. These islands, four in number and small, are ½ mile from the entrance; they are parallel to the shore and from 200 to 400 yards off it. A vessel may anchor between the two southern islands in from 6 to 10 fathoms.

The anchorages in Boughey bay, Havannah channel, and among the Warren islands on the shore of Call creek, are secure; but the passages to them, though probably deep, have not been sufficiently examined to give directions for entering them.

In 1902, the United States revenue cutter Grant anchored in Boughey bay during a heavy SE. gale. Lily islet and the Bockett islands were left to the northward, a mid-channel course being followed to the anchorage, in 14 fathoms at nearly high water. No indications of obstructions or dangers were observed.

Chatham channel, the east part of which commences at Root point, the NW. extreme of Havannah channel, is about 5 miles long and trends NW., connecting these waters with Knight inlet. The southern half of the channel is under 400 yards in breadth and has 4 fathoms of water in mid-channel; the northern part widens out to over ½ mile and has deep water. It is not recommended to use this channel until it has been more closely surveyed.

The coast.—Westward from Port Harvey to Blakeney passage, a distance of 15 miles, the northern side of the strait is formed by the southern coast of Cracroft island, an irregular shaped island 18 miles in length, and separated from the mainland only by the narrow strait of Chatham channel. With the exception of mount Thomas, rounded and 1,770 feet high, situated toward its eastern end, the portion of the island overlooking the strait is comparatively low.

The general trend of the coast is more or less straight from the entrance to Port Harvey to the Sophia islets, 2 miles east of Blakeney passage, with the exception of the two indentations of Forward bay and Boat harbor.

Escape reef.—Two miles westward from the entrance to Port Harvey and ½ mile from the shore is Escape reef, consisting of two rocky heads lying ESE. and WNW. of each other and nearly 400 yards apart. The eastern rock has only 4 feet over it, and lies 2 miles S. 87° W. (S. 62° W. mag.) from the outer Broken island and ½ mile from the nearest shore. The western rock has 12 feet least water. Both rocks are marked by kelp in summer. There is deep water between the reef and the shore.

The reef lies in the track of vessels bound to Port Harvey from the westward; to clear it, keep Bockett point, on the north side of Havannah channel, in line with Domville point, bearing N. 65° E. (N. 40° E. mag.).

Forward bay, 3 miles westward from Port Harvey, is a broad but slight indentation of the coast, affording fair anchorage in from 15 to 16 fathoms. A bank dries out from the head of the bay for a distance of 400 yards, the best anchorage being off the edge of this bank.

In the SW. corner of the bay are two small islets, 35 feet and 10 feet high.

Between Forward bay and Boat harbor there are a number of rocks, but these are close to the shore.

Boat harbor, 6 miles westward from Forward bay, is a small cove formed by a slight indentation of the coast and by an islet,

179 feet high, lying 300 yards offshore. It affords good shelter for boats.

A rock, awash at high water, lies 300 yards south of the islet.

Growler cove.—Two miles westward from Boat harbor the coast of Cracroft island is indented in an irregular manner, forming, a mile farther westward, Growler cove, a small narrow inlet running in an easterly direction for nearly a mile.

The entrance to the inner part of the cove is under 200 yards in width, but it widens slightly inside, affording a landlocked but limited anchorage in from 5 to 8 fathoms, mud. A flat dries out from the head of the cove for about 200 yards. Close off the southern shore of the cove is a rock which dries 12 feet, and two others off the northern shore dry 7 and 8 feet.

Sophia islets, consisting of two principal and several smaller islets and rocks, lie ½ mile to the southward and eastward of the entrance to Growler cove. The western of the two principal islets is the larger, and is about 200 yards in diameter and 85 feet high. The southern and western sides of the group are steep-to.

Baron reef, a shoal with two heads, lies about 500 yards offshore and ¾ mile to the westward of Growler cove. The eastern head, with a depth of 1½ fathoms over it, is situated 1,250 yards N. 50° W. (N. 75° W. mag.) from the south point of Sophia islet; the western head, 550 yards West (S. 65° W. mag.) from the eastern head, has 2 fathoms least water.

Two miles westward from Growler cove is Cracroft point, the western termination of Cracroft island, and forming the eastern point of entrance to Blakeney passage.

Blakeney passage, between the western extremes of Cracroft and Harbledown islands, and the eastern end of Hanson island, is a deep channel varying from 1 mile to ½ mile in breadth and connects Johnstone strait and Blackfish sound.

The tidal streams run through it at a rate of from 3 to 5 knots. There is a strong race off Cracroft point with both east- and west-going streams. The east-going streams meeting from each side of Hanson island cause a strong race near mid-channel at the entrance to Johnstone strait.

Baronet passage, a long narrow channel, extends to the eastward out of Blakeney passage and separates Harbledown and Cracroft islands.

Hanson island, which forms the northern shore of the western end of Johnstone strait, is 3½ miles long in an east and west direction, 1¾ miles broad, and 600 feet high. The southern and eastern shores are regular and steep-to, but the northern and western shores are much broken and indented with many islets and rocks.

Several rocks, drying from 9 to 12 feet at low water, lie 600 yards off its SW. point.

Plumper islands, consisting of many islands, islets, and rocks, separated by narrow and tortuous channels, extend for upward of 1 mile off the NW. end of Hanson island.

These islands, with the west end of Hanson island, form the NE. side of Weynton passage.

The southern shore of Johnstone strait westward from Salmon river to Blinkhorn island, near its western end, is steep-to throughout its length, the lower spurs of the high mountain ranges rising nearly everywhere abruptly from the water. There are but two indentations of any size, one opposite the entrance to Port Harvey, where the Adams river flows into the strait, the other, called Robson bight, at the mouth of the Tsitika river opposite Boat harbor. Both have deep water up to the edge of the bank at the mouth of the rivers, and are useless as anchorages.

Blinkhorn island, a small islet 189 feet high to the top of the trees, and connected with the mainland of Vancouver island at low water by a shingle beach, lies 4 miles W. ½ S. from Cracroft point.

Bauza cove, 1 mile westward of Blinkhorn island, is of small extent; it affords anchorage for a small vessel, in from 15 to 16 fathoms, close off the bank, which dries out for 300 yards from its head.

A small islet, 22 feet high, and rock lie off the entrance to the cove, and one or two islets and rocks close off the western point of entrance.

Directions.—The navigation of Johnstone strait is perfectly easy, it being only necessary to keep in mid-channel, except in the vicinity of Helmcken island, for which directions have already been given.

Broughton strait, connecting Johnstone strait with Queen Charlotte sound, lies between Vancouver island and Malcolm island. It is 15 miles in length and varies in breadth from 1 to 4 miles. There are several islands in the eastern part of the strait, of which the principal are Cormorant island and the Pearse islands.

The high mountain ranges which rise abruptly from the southern shore throughout the whole course of Johnstone strait, in one almost continuous chain, recede considerably from the shore-line on entering Broughton strait, and become detached into more or less isolated groups, leaving the land near the coast comparatively low.

Nimpkish river, of considerable size, flowing out of lake Nimpkish, enters the strait opposite Cormorant island.

The islands forming the northern shores of the strait are comparatively low. Both shores are densely wooded.

The direct and main channel through the strait lies along the southern shore, southward of Cormorant island and the Pearse islands, and is a little under ½ mile in width in its narrowest parts.

There are two good anchorages near the main channel, Alert bay on the south side of Cormorant island, and Port McNeill on the Vancouver island shore.

Tides and tidal streams.—It is high water, full and change, over the strait in general, at 0 h. 30 m.; springs rise 16 feet.

In the main channel the streams do not exceed a rate of 3 knots at springs, but in Race and Weynton passages they run from 4 to 5 knots, and there are considerable eddies and swirls with strong races off the points during the strength of the stream.

The streams turn at from 1½ to 2 hours after high and low water by the shore.

Beaver cove, at the southeastern end of Broughton strait and 1 mile westward of Bauza cove, extends in a southerly direction for upward of 1 mile, dividing into two arms, and is ½ mile wide near the entrance; it is too deep for convenient anchorage, except at the head of the western arm, where a small vessel could find room to anchor in 15 fathoms 300 yards off the bank.

A small stream runs in at the head of the cove.

Mount Holdsworth, 2,957 feet high, with an abrupt fall on its southern side, rises to the SW. of Beaver cove and is remarkable from the eastward.

Nimpkish river.—From Beaver cove the coast trends in a westerly direction for 5 miles to the mouth of the Nimpkish river and is rocky and comparatively low.

The river, which is the outlet from lake Nimpkish, a sheet of water of considerable size, after a winding course of about 5 miles, flows into the strait at the head of a bight in the coast opposite Cormorant island. The river is full of rapids and only navigable for canoes except for a short distance inside its mouth.

Nimpkish bank extends off the mouth of the river for over 1 mile and dries in several places at low tide.

There is a narrow boat channel into the river carrying from 5 to 6 feet.

Green islet, situated near the northern edge of Nimpkish bank and 1,800 yards from the mouth of the river, is a small islet, 4 feet high, barely 100 yards in extent, and is covered with coarse grass.

A bank of bowlders and gravel dries out for 800 yards ESE.

Alert rock, with 3¼ fathoms least water, lies on the southern side of the main channel 1,100 yards N. 15° W. (N. 40° W. mag.) from Green islet, with deep water close-to on its northern side.

Deer point, just open northward of Broad point, N. 85° W. (S. 70° W. mag.), will clear Alert rock to the northward.

Kish rock, with 5 feet least water, lies 800 yards N. 35° W. (N. 60° W. mag.) from Green islet.

From the mouth of the Nimpkish river the coast trends to the northward for nearly 1 mile and then to the westward for 4 miles to the entrance to Port McNeill.

Port McNeill, on the south side of Broughton strait, about 10 miles west of Beaver cove, runs in a westerly direction for 2 miles, is ¾ mile broad, and affords good, well-sheltered anchorage in from 6 to 9 fathoms. The water shoals gradually, a bank of mud, sand, and gravel drying out for over ½ mile from its head.

The shores of the port are low and consist in general of shingle and bowlder beaches, and are thickly wooded.

Eel reef, a rocky ledge, 135 yards in extent, and which dries 10 feet, lies in the southern part of Port McNeill nearly 1 mile within the entrance, with Ledge point bearing N. 37° E. (N. 12° E. mag.), distant 1,600 yards.

Neill ledge—Buoy.—From Ledge point, the northern point of entrance to Port McNeill, a rocky shoal extends to the east for 1¼ miles within the 5-fathom curve, on which are several heads with less than 3 fathoms over them. The shoalest part of the ledge, where there is a rock with only 6 feet of water, lies 1,600 yards S. 82° E. (N. 73° E. mag.) from Ledge point. Kelp grows on the ledge during the summer.

A red spar buoy is moored, in 6 fathoms, off the NE. side of the ledge.

Neill rock, an outlying head to the northward of the ledge, with 3¾ fathoms least water over it, lies 1 mile N. 70° W. (S. 85° W. mag.) from the west end of Haddington island.

Directions.—Coming from the eastward no directions are required for Port McNeill. From the westward, keep Yellow bluff, Cormorant island, in line with, or open of, the north point of Haddington island, bearing S. 68° E, (N. 87° E. mag.) until past Neill rock; round the red spar buoy at not less than 400 yards distant, and do not haul up for the anchorage until Yellow bluff is well open south of Haddington island.

The tidal streams set obliquely across the ledge to the ESE. and WNW.; there is no stream in the anchorage.

The coast.—From Ledge point the coast trends west for 3 miles to the western end of the strait, which is there just under 1 mile wide. From thence to False head, a distance of 5 miles, the general direction of the coast, which is low and wooded, is WNW.; it consists of bowlder and shingle beaches with rocky points and ledges between.

Just outside the western entrance to the strait a small river, the Klucksiwi, enters the sea.

False head is low and has a ledge of bowlders extending from it to a distance of 300 yards.

The water deepens gradually offshore, at 1 mile east of False head the 10-fathom curve extending 1 mile from the shore, which in this neighborhood should not be approached within $\frac{1}{2}$ mile.

Pearse islands, lying in the middle of the strait at its eastern end, are low and thickly wooded. On the eastern side of the group are several rocks and small islets extending to more than 1 mile SE. from the NE. island; the largest of a cluster of three, the most southeasterly of these islets, called Stephenson islet, is 27 feet high and lies $1\frac{1}{10}$ miles S. 85° E. (N. 70° E. mag.) from the eastern extreme of the largest and most southern of the Pearse islands. Several rocky ledges, some of which dry at low water, extend 800 yards east from Stephenson islet. The tidal streams set over and across these ledges, and they must be carefully guarded against by vessels using Weynton passage.

Pearse reefs, lying between 700 and 1,200 yards from the northern side of the Pearse islands, consist of three rocks in line, ESE. and WNW., extending over a distance of 1,600 yards. The middle rock dries 10 feet and lies 800 yards N. 38° E. (N. 13° E. mag.) from the west extreme of the northern Pearse island.

The western rock, which dries 4 feet, lies 1,000 yards from the middle rock; the eastern rock, with 13 feet of water, lies 500 yards from the middle rock.

Stubbs island, lying midway between the Plumper islands and the eastern end of Malcolm island, is small, nearly bare, and 72 feet high; it is steep-to all round.

Weynton passage, between the western sides of Hanson and the Plumper islands and the Pearse islands, is nearly 1 mile wide, with deep water throughout, and may be used by vessels wishing to proceed to Malcolm island or into Blackfish sound.

The tidal streams are strong, from 3 to 5 knots, and vessels must take care not to be set toward the rocks eastward of Stephenson islet.

The only direction needed is to keep in mid-channel. Stubbs island may be passed on either side. While passing the rocks east of Stephenson islet, Donegal head, the east extreme of Malcolm island, should not be opened west of Stubbs island.

Race passage, between the Pearse islands and Cormorant island, is $\frac{3}{8}$ mile wide, but the channel is narrowed by Gordon rock, situated in mid-channel.

Gordon rock only dries at low water springs. Kelp grows on it during summer, but it is frequently run under by the tide.

The tidal streams run strongly and obliquely through the passage at a rate of from 3 to 5 knots.

The channel is west of Gordon rock, but it is not recommended.

Cormorant island, lying west of the Pearse islands and abreast of the mouth of the Nimpkish river, is 2¼ miles long in an ESE. and WNW. direction, from ½ to 1 mile wide, wooded, and 400 feet high to the tops of the trees.

Its shores consist of bowlder and shingle beaches.

Alert bay, on the south side of Cormorant island, ¾ mile wide and ⅓ mile deep, affords good, well-sheltered, and convenient anchorage in from 4 to 8 fathoms, sand and mud bottom.

A salmon cannery, post-office, and an Indian village stand on the eastern shore of the bay; off the cannery is a pier with a depth of 10 feet at its extremity.

Round the northern shore of the bay are the church and establishments of the Church Missionary Society's mission, including a sawmill and small pier; fresh water is laid on to the end of the latter.

Yellow bluff.—The SW. point of the bay consists of a yellow earth bluff, but it is much overgrown with vegetation and is not very conspicuous.

A ledge of bowlders, fringed with kelp in summer, extends for 200 yards southward from Yellow bluff.

Tides.—It is high water, full and change, in Alert bay at 0 h. 30 m.; springs rise 16 feet, neaps 9 feet.

Leonard rock, a rocky patch on which kelp grows in summer, with 2½ fathoms least water, lies 1¼ miles N. 86° W. (S. 69° W. mag.) from the north extreme of Cormorant island and 1½ miles East (N. 65° E. mag.) from the NE. point of Haddington island; there is deep water between the rock and Cormorant island.

Cormorant channel, leading from the west end of Cormorant island along the south shore of Malcolm island to Blackfish sound, is a wide channel clear of danger, except for the Pearse reef already described.

A patch of kelp, suspected of indicating a shoal, has been reported as lying in the approach to Mitchell bay. From the patch the SE. extreme of Malcolm island (Donegal head) bears N. 57° E. (N. 32° E. mag.) and Stubbs island S. 59° E. (S. 84° E. mag.), distant 2,200 yards.

Haddington island, lying in the middle of Broughton strait, about 2 miles westward from Cormorant island, is ½ mile in extent, wooded, 316 feet high to the tops of the trees, and steep-to on all sides. On the SE. side of the island are some conspicuous but deserted stone quarries.

There is a passage on either side of the island; that to the northward between the island and Haddington reefs is 600 yards wide with 20 fathoms least water; that to the southwestward between the island and Neill ledge is a little over ½ mile wide with not less than 7 fathoms.

Haddington reefs, a bowlder patch 1,200 yards in extent, ENE. and WSW., marked by kelp in summer, on which are several heads with less than 6 feet of water over them, and which are joined to Dickenson point, on the south side of Malcolm island, by a shallow bank, lie to the northeastward of Haddington island with a deep channel between.

At the SW. extremity of this patch is a rock with 3 feet least water, situated with the north point of Haddington island bearing S. 51° W. (S. 26° W. mag.), distant 700 yards; it is steep-to on its southern side.

Malcolm island, which forms the north side of Broughton strait, is of irregular shape, 13 miles long, east and west, with an average breadth of 2 miles. The island is comparatively low, undulating, with rounded hills, and densely wooded, its greatest height, near the middle of the island, being about 600 feet to the tops of the trees.

The shores of the island consist almost entirely of shingle and sand beaches.

Donegal head, its eastern point, is a conspicuous, white, earth cliff, 100 feet high, bordered by a shingle beach. A bank extends off the head to a distance of 800 yards within the 5-fathom curve. The tidal streams run strongly over and off this bank.

Rock.—A patch of kelp, probably indicating a rock, lies in the approach to Mitchell bay in a position from which Stubbs island bears S. 59° E. (S. 84° E. mag.), distant 2,200 yards, and the southern extremity of Donegal head N. 57° E. (N. 32° E. mag.).

Dickenson point, on the south side of the island, has a bowlder bank, with depths of 3 to 4 fathoms over it, extending from it to Haddington reefs, which have been already described.

Mitchell and Rough bays are on the south side of the island, the latter bay, 1½ miles to the westward of Dickenson point, affording good anchorage, in from 6 to 8 fathoms, 500 yards from the mud flat that dries out 600 yards from the head of the bay. There is a settlement and a pier on the east shore of Rough bay.

Light.—A fixed white light, 38 feet above high water, visible 11 miles, is exhibited from a tower erected at the extremity of the low gravel spit making out from Pulteney (Graeme) point, the SW. point of Malcolm island.

The light is visible over an arc of 230° from N. 80° W. (S. 75° W. mag.) to S. 30° E. (S. 55° E. mag.). The tower is a square wooden building with square wooden lantern rising from the middle of the roof. The house is painted white with red roof.

Fog signal.—A hand fog horn will be sounded in answer to the fog signals of vessels.

Trinity bay, on the north side of the island, between Lizard and Bowlder points, is an open bay 2½ miles wide and ¾ mile deep. A broad bank of sand and gravel extends seaward from the shores of the bay, the 10-fathom curve being in one place nearly 1½ miles from its head, when the depths increase to 20 and 50 fathoms.

Anchorage may be had on this bank, but it is quite exposed to all winds except those from the southward and eastward.

A fringe of kelp grows, in summer, along nearly the whole of the western and northern sides of the island at from 200 to 400 yards from the shore, being especially thick on the western side.

Kelp patch.—Off the western extreme of Malcolm island, a bank extends WNW. for 2 miles inside the 10-fathom curve. On this bank, 1¼ miles NW. by W. from the point, is a shoal patch on which are depths of 3½ fathoms; this patch is marked by kelp in summer.

Directions for Broughton strait.—Coming from the eastward proceed in mid-channel till Gordon point, the SE. point of Cormorant island, bears N. 45° E. (N. 20° E. mag.); then haul up to N. 45° W. (N. 70° W. mag.), steering for the eastern edge of Yellow bluff. This course leads fair between Nimpkish bank and Cormorant island. When the north extreme of Blinkhorn island, open of Cormorant island, bears S. 70° E. (N. 85° E. mag.), steer N. 70° W. (S. 85° W. mag.). This range leads in the channel between the bank and the island and clear of Alert rock. Deer point, just open northward of Broad point, N. 84° W. (S. 71° W. mag.) clears Alert rock to the northward. When the western extreme of Cormorant island is abeam steer to pass 200 yards north of Haddington island. In daytime bring the SW. extreme of Malcolm island, at night the light on Pulteney (Graeme) point to bear N. 75° W. (S. 80° W. mag.) and steer for it on this bearing, which will lead between Haddington island and reefs, and to the northward of Neill rock. Yellow bluff just open to the northward of Haddington island leads well clear of Neill rock. When past Neill rock proceed in mid-channel. When ¾ mile West (S. 65° W. mag.) of Pulteney (Graeme) point, a N. 45° W. (N. 70° W. mag.) course will lead between the bank extending off the western extreme of Malcolm island and that along the shore of Vancouver island. Pulteney Point light bearing S. 58° E. (S. 83° E. mag.) leads between these banks.

Queen Charlotte sound, the seaward entrance to which, between cape Commerell on Vancouver island and cape Caution on the mainland, is 20 miles wide, is an extensive arm of the sea connecting the inner waters north of Vancouver island with the Pacific. The sound extends in an ESE. direction and is 50 miles long to the entrance to Knight inlet, at its eastern end, with an average width of from 10 to 15 miles, being bounded on the north by the shores of the mainland, and on the south by the north shore of Vancouver island. In the western half of the sound are numerous rocks and islands through which are two good broad channels, Goletas and New channels. The eastern half is much more open, though there are several rocks and islands at the eastern end at the entrances to Knight inlet and Fife sound. The waters of the sound are deep, and there are but two places, Beaver harbor and Port Alexander, where a vessel of any size can find good anchorage, though there are several secure anchorages for small vessels. The western part of the sound with the exception of Goletas channel, which is protected by Nahwhitti bar, is open to the Pacific and there is frequently a heavy swell.

The southern shore of the sound, as far west as the eastern end of Goletas channel, will be first described, then the eastern end with the many inlets leading therefrom, followed by the northern shore from east to west, and lastly the channels leading to the Pacific.

Broughton strait enters this sound at its SE. part. From thence to Thomas point the coast of Vancouver trends WNW. for 9 miles, and is low; it is bordered the whole distance by a beach composed of sand and bowlders, and foul ground marked by kelp extends off it, from ¼ to ½ mile.

If intending to enter Beaver harbor from the eastward, do not approach this shore within 1 mile till near Thomas point; and, as but very few soundings have been obtained in this part of Queen Charlotte sound, if beating to windward, great caution ought to be observed when standing to the southward.

Beaver harbor, on the southern side of Queen Charlotte sound, is 9 miles westward of Broughton strait. The harbor is formed by several islands and islets lying across the mouth of a bay and affords a well protected anchorage, within the islands, in from 8 to 12 fathoms; the shores of the harbor are comparatively low and are wooded. Thomas point, the SE. point of the harbor, is low, and a rocky ledge off it dries out to 200 yards from the point. Thomas point should be given a berth of at least 600 yards.

The shore-line extends westward from Thomas point for 1½ miles and then turns to the northward. Two-thirds of a mile west from Thomas point the land is cleared, and there is an Indian village and trading station on the site of the old Fort Rupert of the Hudson Bay Company. A bank of sand and shingle extends along the south shore of the bay, drying out to from 400 to 800 yards.

Deer island, 1,200 yards north from Thomas point, is about 1¼ miles in circumference, wooded and about 230 feet high to the tops of the trees. Eagle islet, 90 feet high, lies close off its SE. side, and two rocks, 16 and 15 feet high, lie close south of Eagle islet.

A sunken reef extends off the NW. side of Deer island for 800 yards, to the 5-fathom curve, and between it and Twin rocks.

Peel and Round islands, Charlie islets, and Twin rocks.—Twelve hundred yards NW. from Deer island is Peel island, ¾ mile long ENE. and WSW., ⅓ mile wide, wooded, and 200 feet high.

Half a mile NE. from the north point of Deer island is Round island, small but conspicuous, and 150 feet high. A rock with 5 feet of water over it lies 300 yards east of it.

Six hundred yards north of Peel island are the two Charlie islets, bare and 20 to 30 feet high. Midway between Round island and Peel island are the Twin rocks, 15 feet high. There is foul ground between them and Deer island and the reef off it.

Cattle islands lie in the middle of the harbor; they are small, wooded, and joined together at low water by reefs; the southern and largest island is 216 feet high to the tops of the trees. Three hundred yards NW. from the north extreme of the Cattle islands is a rock with 2¾ fathoms least water over it.

Shell islet lies 300 yards south of the Cattle islands; it is small, has a few bushes on it, and is 25 feet high. Rocky ledges which uncover extend from all sides of it for about 100 yards, and 200 yards off its south side is a reef which covers at high water. A rock with 1¾ fathoms least water lies 200 yards SW. from the west end of Shell islet.

Cormorant rock, lies 600 yards from the west shore of the harbor and 800 yards WNW. from Shell islet; it covers at high water and has 5 to 6 fathoms close to it. One-third of the way between this rock and the south end of the Cattle islands, is a patch with 3½ fathoms least water.

Herald rock, with 2 fathoms least water over it, lies in Dædalus passage, 200 yards from the west shore of the harbor abreast of the northern end of Peel island.

Directions.—Beaver harbor is easy of access for steamers. The best anchorage is nearly midway between the Cattle islands and the west shore of the harbor, but nearer the former, in from 8 to 12 fathoms, mud.

There are two entrances, one from the eastward between Thomas point and Deer island, and Dædalus passage, from the northward, between Peel island and the western shore of the bay.

To enter the former, steer to pass 600 yards north of Thomas point, thence to pass 200 yards south of the reef south of Shell islet, and the 1¾-fathom rock, and proceed between Shell islet and Cormorant rock, passing either side of the 3½-fathom patch, to the anchorage west of the Cattle islands.

Dædalus passage is only 400 yards wide between the west end of Peel island and the west shore of the bay, but the water is deep throughout. The only direction needed is to keep in mid-channel, avoiding Herald rock, and steer for the anchorage.

Tides.—It is high water, full and change, in Beaver harbor, at 0 h. 10 m.; springs rise 14 feet, neaps 10 feet.

Hardy bay, westward of Beaver harbor, separated from it by Dillon point, indents the coast in a southerly direction for 4 miles; it terminates in a narrow creek 1¼ miles long and 400 to 800 yards broad, with a sand bank extending off its head for ¾ mile. The shores of the bay are rugged, and off the west side, near the head, are some outlying rocks. There is a wharf, with 27 feet of water at its outer end, 600 yards to the northeastward of the entrance to the narrow creek or inner harbor.

There is no anchorage except in the small creek at the head, which is difficult of access and should not be used by a stranger.

Masterman islands, off the NE. point of the bay, about ¾ mile from the shore, are small, wooded, and four in number; foul ground exists between them and the shore.

The eastern shores of Queen Charlotte sound consist of an archipelago (Broughton archipelago of Vancouver) 12 miles in length, extending from Hanson island on the south to the entrance to Fife sound on the north. Between the numerous islands, islets, and rocks which form this archipelago are many narrow channels leading to the entrances of extensive inlets, in which the water is of great depth, and the shores, in many places, rise in almost sheer precipices to a height of from 5,000 to 6,000 feet, and farther inland to stupendous peaks, clad in perpetual snow. Down the barren, rugged sides of these mountains rush numberless cataracts, caused by the melting snow. These inlets are intensely dreary and gloomy, owing to their overshadowing by the lofty and precipitous mountains, the frequent mist and rain, and the almost entire absence of life.

Baronet passage.—From Blakeney passage along the north shore of Cracroft island, between it and Harbledown island, is a narrow channel 6 miles long, known as Baronet passage. At this distance it splits into several small passages, lying between many small islands, islets, and rocks, the navigation of which must be undertaken with great caution.

Kelp rocks lie just within the entrance to Baronet passage, on the north shore, and extend over 400 yards offshore in some places, two of them uncovering at low water 11 and 7 feet, respectively; they leave a channel 300 yards wide along the south shore in which is a depth of from 10 to 20 fathoms. From here the passage is clear as far as Channel island, 4 miles from the entrance, and maintains a uniform depth of 8 fathoms. The channel on either side of Channel island is less than 200 yards wide, that to the northward being the deeper. Shoal spots extend both off the east and the west ends of the island.

Steamer passage, between the islands above mentioned as lying 6 miles from the entrance to Baronet passage, is 200 yards wide, with depths of 10 to 15 fathoms in it. Great care must be observed when passing through Steamer passage, as a dangerous rock, awash at low water, lies a little over 400 yards north of it.

Clio channel, the continuation of Baronet passage, to the NE. along the north side of Cracroft island, between it and Turnour island, and communicating with Knight inlet, is 7 miles long. Negro rock (awash at low water) lies in the fairway ½ mile S. 80° W. (S. 55° W. mag.) from Sambo head, on Cracroft island, and 5 miles northeastward from Steamer passage; to avoid this rock the SE. shore of Turnour island should be kept aboard about 500 yards distant.

Lagoon cove, a small sheltered nook on the NE. side of Double island, 2 miles SE. of the junction of Clio channel with Knight inlet, affords anchorage for a small vessel in 10 fathoms. When entering, pass in mid-channel between the north shore of Double islands and a small round island northward of them, but do so with caution. From the head of Lagoon cove a chain of narrow salt-water lagoons connects the cove with Port Harvey.

Harbledown island, forming the northern shore of Baronet passage, is 6½ miles long, in an east and west direction, and 3 miles across at its broadest part, its highest elevation (over Baronet passage) being 1,240 feet.

Parson bay, on the west side of Harbledown island, is 1½ miles deep and ¾ mile wide, shoaling gradually from 30 fathoms just inside the entrance to 12 fathoms at its head. Anchorage may be obtained in the SE. corner, well sheltered from all but westerly winds blowing down Blackfish sound, in which direction it is open.

A rocky patch, Harris shoal, with a depth of 6 fathoms over it, lies in the entrance to the bay with Red point, the west point of Harbledown island, bearing N. 40° W. (N. 65° W. mag.), distant 1,200 yards.

Compton island, ¾ mile long east and west, is 364 feet high, and is separated from Harbledown island by White Beach passage. Berry island, NE. of Compton island, is nearly 1 mile long and forms the east side of Farewell harbor. Lewis island is separated from Berry island by Village passage; it is 2¼ miles long and forms the north side of Farewell harbor, and the entrance to Knight inlet lies along its northern shore.

Blackfish sound, between the north shore of Hanson island and Swanson island, has an average width of 1½ miles, and leads from Queen Charlotte sound into Parson bay and Blakeney passage to the SE., and to Farewell harbor and White Beach passage to the northward.

Swanson island, forming the north shore of Blackfish sound, is 2½ miles long, east and west, and 1 mile wide, with regular bold shores, and only one or two small indentations. Harbor cone, at its east end, is 522 feet high. Numerous small islets and reefs extend off the north shore of the island for nearly 1 mile.

Farewell harbor, a snug anchorage for a small vessel, is ½ mile across in every direction. Its approaches, however, both from the northward and southward, are only 100 yards wide, that to the northward from the main entrance to Knight inlet being obstructed by the Twilight reefs and several islets lying ½ mile outside it. Entering through North passage, Charles point (the west entrance point) kept touching Maggy point (the southern point of North passage, on the eastern shore), bearing South (S. 25° E. mag.), clears the Twilight reefs, passing eastward of them.

The southern entrance, named West passage, between Punt rock and Apples island (lying close to the shore of Swanson island) and the Star islands lying off the NW. shore of Compton island, leads out of Blackfish sound and must be approached with caution, as a rock, awash at low water, lies nearly 200 yards WSW. from the south end of the western Star islet, leaving a passage to the east of Punt rock only 100 yards wide.

Twilight rock, which uncovers at low water, lies 1,400 yards N. 9° W. (N. 34° W. mag.) from Charles point, and 400 yards N. 60° W. (N. 85 W. mag.) from it is Chick reef, 200 yards in extent, and drying 4 feet. To the westward of the above dangers is a group of small islets and reefs extending along the whole of the north shore of Swanson island nearly 1 mile from it.

The southern entrance should only be used by a small vessel, and should be approached on a NE. by E. bearing, passing about 200 yards southeastward of Bare rock (10 feet high) off the south side of Swanson island, ¼ mile outside the entrance. The channel between Punt rock and the rock, awash at low water, lying 200 yards WSW. of the Star islands, is under 200 yards in width, but presents no difficulty approached as described.

The best anchorage is toward the eastern part of the harbor midway between Kamux island and the north shore of Compton island in 9 fathoms, with the west side of the former bearing NNE.

If it can be clearly made out, the north extreme of Kamux island open a little north of the NW. Star island, bearing N. 70° E. (N.

45° E. mag.) will clear the shoal ground extending SW. of the Star islands.

Tides.—It is high water, full and change, in Farewell harbor at 0 h. 35 m.; springs rise 15 feet, neaps 8 feet.

Village channel, between Lewis and Berry islands, is a narrow but apparently clear channel 250 yards wide, leading out from the NE. part of Farewell harbor, north of Carey group, to Native anchorage and Elliot passage.

White Beach passage, between Compton island and the NW. point of Harbledown island, is a narrow pass, only 80 yards across, leading into Indian passage; it is not recommended. A rock is reported to lie 600 yards S. 9° E. (S. 34° E. mag.) from the east point of Berry island.

Village island, 3 miles long and 787 feet high, is situated 2 miles eastward of Lewis island, and is bounded on the north by Knight inlet and separated from Turnour island on the SE. by Canoe passage. The space between Lewis island and Village island is occupied by the Indian islands. Elliot passage leads into Knight inlet, between the easternmost of these islands and Village island. Kelp has been reported as growing to the southward of the Indian islands.

At the SW. end of Village island is Mamalilaculla village, and at the mouth of a small bay to the southeastward of it, at the entrance to Canoe passage, is Native anchorage, with from 7 to 8 fathoms. Hail islands, two small islets, lie to the southward of it, and Chart and Cecil islets to the southwestward. Kelp patches lie 700 yards W. by S. from Cecil island and also NE. of that island.

Carey group is a chain of several small islands lying to the southward of the Indian islands, and stretching across from Berry island to Turnour island, a distance of 3 miles.

Turnour island is 9 miles long east and west, and at its center 3 miles wide, narrowing toward its extremities; at its eastern end it is 1,580 feet high. It is separated from Harbledown island on the south by Beware passage; Clio channel runs along its SE. side, separating it from Cracroft island, and Knight inlet along its NW. side, the two latter channels joining at Batt bluff, its NE. point.

Beware passage, lying between the NE. shore of Harbledown island and the SW. shore of Turnour island, leads from Native anchorage eastward into Clio channel. Vessels can not pass through it into Clio channel, owing to a barrier of islets and rocks across it at 1 mile from its junction with that channel; it is only available for boats. An Indian village (Karlukwees) is situated on Turnour island at the eastern entrance to Beware passage.

Canoe passage is a narrow pass leading from Native anchorage along the SE. shore of Village island, between it and Turnour island At 2 miles up it is completely closed at low water by a stony barrier which dries across, and it is only available for canoes at high water.

Knight inlet.—The main entrance to this inlet, which is one of the most extensive of the sea canals of British Columbia, lies northward of Swanson, Lewis, and Village islands, and between them and Midsummer island and several smaller islands and rocks. The entrance may be easily recognized by White Cliff islands, a chain of small islets of a whitish color, situated on the northern side of the passage into the inlet, and which lie 4 miles E. by N. from Donegal head, the east extreme of Malcolm island. The entrance, between Wedge island on the north and the NW. shore of Swanson island on the south, is 700 yards wide, and thence the course is northward of Chick and Twilight reefs and Clock rock, and southward of Jumble island to the entrance proper to the inlet, between Warr bluff, the western point of Village island on the south, and Slope point, the south point of Gilford island on the north, 5½ miles from Wedge island. Chick and Twilight reefs, which have already been mentioned in the account of Farewell harbor, lie 1¼ miles, and Clock rock 5 miles, from Wedge island.

The inlet, between Warr bluff and Slope point, is ¾ mile wide; it trends in a general easterly direction for 33 miles, and then turns suddenly to the northward for 26½ miles to its termination, with an average width throughout of 1½ miles. The shores of the inlet are generally bold, and are formed by high mountains rising precipitously from the water's edge; down the sides of these rush many cataracts.

The water is everywhere deep, except at a spot about 7 miles eastward of Sargeaunt passage, where a rocky ridge was found to extend across the inlet, and on which there are heavy overfalls, but no less depth than 23 fathoms was obtained.

There are but few places that afford anchorage; Port Elizabeth on the north shore and Cutter creek and Glendale cove on the south are the only three that may be considered generally available, though anchorage can be obtained at the head of the inlet, on the western shore, in 23 fathoms, with Dutchman head bearing East and Hatchet point SE. by S. At 11½ miles east of Slope point, Tribune channel branches off to the northward.

On the southern side, Knight inlet is connected with Johnstone strait by two passages, viz, Clio channel and Baronet passage and Chatham and Havannah channels.

Tidal streams.—The tidal streams at the entrance to Knight inlet run at the rate of from 1 to 3 knots.

Wedge island, a small round island 400 yards in extent, lies 700 yards north of the NW. shore of Swanson island, the channel into

Knight inlet lying between them; it may be boldly steered for, passing in mid-channel between Wedge island and the small islets lying close to the shore of Swanson island. Surge rocks are a small group of rocky islets lying 600 yards NE. from Wedge island.

White Cliff islands.—From Wedge island a line of small islets, named White Cliff islands, extends over 1 mile in a northerly direction with patches of shoal water between them and for ½ mile westward of Wedge island. A rock awash at high water lies nearly 200 yards northwestward of the northern islet. A rock with 6 feet of water over it lies ½ mile WNW. ½ W. from the west extreme of Wedge island.

These islands, by their color, as indicated by their name, are very conspicuous, and would be most useful for a stranger to identify the entrance to the main channel of the inlet.

Midsummer island, separating Knight inlet from Spring passage, is 650 feet high, 3 miles long, and 1 mile wide. Owl island, 1 mile in length and about ½ mile broad, lies off the west end of Midsummer island, with a narrow passage (Providence passage) between them. Passage islet is a small round islet about midway between Surge rocks and Owl island. Northward of the White Cliff islands another channel leads into Knight inlet on either side of Passage islet.

Twilight reefs, which uncover only 4 feet at low water springs, lie about 1½ miles east of the main entrance to Knight inlet, and from 200 to 250 yards northward of a group of small islets on the south side of the channel. To clear them keep Coast cone (a conical hill on the NW. shore of Village island), in line with the southern shore of Jumble island, bearing East (N. 65° E. mag.).

Jumble island is ½ mile long (east and west), and lies 2 miles east from Wedge island. Off its west side is Night islet, and off its east point lie the three small Bush islets. When within 400 yards of Night islet stand southeastward to pass at that distance southward of it, Jumble island, and the Bush islets.

Indian islands lie on the south side of Knight inlet, between Lewis and Village islands. Between them are several small channels leading to Native anchorage, but only the easternmost, Elliot passage, is navigable, and that only by small vessels.

Live kelp has been seen in Elliot passage and great care should be exercised in its use.

Clock rock, which covers at half flood, lies 500 yards north of the easternmost of the Indian islands, and is especially dangerous to vessels going through Elliot passage. To clear it keep the coast of Village island aboard and 400 yards distant.

Passing up or down Knight inlet, Clock rock may be safely cleared by keeping Leading point (on the north shore), in line with

Ripple bluff (the north extreme of Village island), bearing East (N. 65° E. mag.).

Ridge islands lie on the north side of Knight inlet between the east end of Midsummer island and the SW. shore of Gilford island, at the entrance (from Knight inlet) of Spring passage.

A rock which dries 8 feet at low water lies 600 yards from the shore of Gilford island; it is, however, out of the fairway of vessels passing up and down Knight inlet, but should be carefully avoided by those passing through Spring passage. Chop bay is a small bight on the north side of Knight inlet opposite Ripple bluff.

Tide rip.—Between Ripple bluff and Leading point, on the opposite shore, the tidal streams run at a rate of from 2 to 3 knots an hour. Heavy tide rips occur in this locality.

Lady islands consist of two islands with deep water on both sides of them, and are 3 miles eastward of Leading point; the largest is 1 mile long, but narrow, with several small islets lying off its west extreme.

Port Elizabeth.—Northwestward of the Lady islands a large bight branches off NW., curving round to the SW. It opens out at its head, forming a sheltered anchorage named Port Elizabeth, about 1 mile in extent, but it is, however, somewhat contracted by two small islands lying in the middle.

Duck cove, SW. of these small islands, forms the termination of the port; a flat dries off its head nearly ½ mile.

Anchorage may be taken up as convenient in the southern part of the port in from 9 to 4 fathoms, the latter depth being found south of the eastern island, midway between it and the shore.

Minstrel island lies to the eastward of Turnour island, at the junction of Clio and Chatham channels with Knight inlet. Between the south side of Minstrel island and the opposite shore of Cracroft island a deep bight is formed, in the center of which is Double island, two small islets connected at low water with each other and also with the shore to the eastward, forming to the northward Lagoon cove.

Chatham channel, on the south side of the inlet, 3½ miles eastward of the Lady islands, has its entrance between White Nob point (Minstrel island) and Littleton point, where it is over 1 mile wide. Thence the channel takes a southeasterly direction, and gradually contracting in width and shoaling, it, at 5 miles from the entrance, joins the head of Havannah channel.

Cutter creek, a narrow bight on the east shore of Chatham channel, 1¼ miles deep in a NE. direction and ¼ mile wide, terminates in marshy land bordered by a sand flat which dries out for nearly 400 yards. It affords good anchorage to a small vessel in 6 fathoms, but caution must be observed when entering, as a small islet (Block islet) lies in mid-channel at the entrance, leaving a passage less than 200 yards wide on each side of it; that to the south of the islet should be used.

Shewell island, lying on the north side of Knight inlet, 2 miles from the entrance to Chatham channel, is 1¼ miles long (NE. and SW.) and 280 feet high; it lies at the southern entrance to Tribune channel, which it divides into Clapp and Nickoll passages.

Viscount island, forming the eastern side of the southern entrance to Tribune channel, is 1,950 feet high, 3 miles long north and south, and 1 mile wide.

Sargeaunt (Pumish) passage, 1 mile east of Nickoll passage, 2¾ miles long, is a narrow pass on the east side of Viscount island, separating it from the mainland, and communicating with Tribune channel.

It is high water, full and change, in Sargeaunt passage at 1 h. 0 m.; springs rise 15½ feet, neaps 12 feet.

Tsakonu cove, on the south side of the inlet, round Protection point, is probably too deep for anchorage.

Hoeya sound, on the north shore of the inlet, 7 miles from Protection point, is a bight ½ mile wide, indenting the coast in an easterly direction. There are depths of over 40 fathoms over the greater part of the sound, but it shoals suddenly to 5 fathoms at 300 yards from its head.

Prominent point, on the south shore of Knight inlet, opposite the entrance to Hoeya sound, has a rocky ridge of less water than in the center of the inlet extending northward from it, on which there are heavy overfalls; the least depth obtained during the survey was 23 fathoms.

Glendale (Kiokh) cove, on the south shore of the inlet, 40 miles from the entrance and immediately eastward of Macdonald point, takes a southerly direction for 1¾ miles, and is ¾ mile wide at its entrance. It dries about half its length, but the water in the remaining part is deep.

A river flows into the head of Glendale cove from a sheet of water 1 mile distant, named Tom Browne lake, about 5 miles long, which extends nearly to the head of Topaze harbor.

Anchorage may, with care, be taken up in the SE. corner in 23 fathoms, but the bank is very steep-to.

Glacier.—On the east shore, at 14 miles from the head, over a gully, under Glacier peak, there is a remarkable glacier a short distance from the sea. Anchorage was tried for, but no bottom was obtained, at 200 yards from the shore with 40 fathoms of line.

Wahshihlas bay is a small bay, ½ mile deep, on the west shore of the inlet, 4½ miles from its head. Anchorage may, with care, be found in 30 fathoms, close to the south shore of the bay near its head, securing the vessel's stern to the trees by a hawser.

Knight inlet widens slightly at its head but maintains its great depth close up to the mud flat, which extends about ½ mile from the shore of the marshy ground at the foot of the valley in which the inlet terminates. Anchorage may be had on the western shore, in 23 fathoms, with Dutchman head bearing East and Hatch point SE. by S.

Mount Blair, immediately over the head of the inlet, attains an altitude of 6,550 feet.

In the valley, near a stream, is Tsauwati village, frequented during the summer months by large numbers of Indians for the purpose of making fish oil.

Fire islands, at the entrance of the inlet, consisting of one large and four small islets, lie close to the west end of Owl island.

Escape, Canoe, and House islands.—From the west end of Midsummer island several small islands extend in a northwesterly direction for 1¼ miles, with rocks between some of them. The largest, Escape island, lies close off the shore of Midsummer island. House island, the NW. islet of the group, is merely a round rock, but reefs extend over 400 yards east and west from it.

Sedge, Start, and High islands are the southern and largest of numerous small islands and rocks lying off the SW. end of Bonwick island. Several patches of rock lie off and between them, but a clear passage, ½ mile wide, exists between Sedge islands and House island, leading into Retreat passage.

Green rock, 25 feet high, lies 1$\frac{1}{10}$ miles east of House island, another small rock lying 300 yards westward of it.

Spring passage, leading from Retreat passage into Knight inlet, is about ½ mile wide, but at the western end the channel is contracted by Broken islands to a width of 600 yards, the passage being to the northward of these islands. Ridge islands lie across the eastern entrance of the passage.

Retreat passage, an entrance to which lies between House and Sedge islands, extends in a northeasterly direction, between Bonwick and Gilford islands. Along the shore of Bonwick island, which is steep-to, it is a clear navigable passage; but the eastern shore is skirted by several small islands, islets, and rocks, between which a vessel should not pass.

Seabreeze island is the largest and most southern of the islands on the eastern shore of Retreat passage. Whale rock, 3 feet high, lies 800 yards NE. of Seabreeze island, nearly midway between it and Yellow rock at the entrance to Health bay.

Health bay, a bight 1 mile deep in a SE. direction, may be safely entered by passing in mid-channel between the south end of Sail island (which lies off the entrance) and Yellow rock, 500 yards south of it, or midway between the latter and the shore, when convenient anchorage in 9 to 10 fathoms may be obtained. A narrow passage in the NE. corner of the bay communicates with a lagoon.

Grebe cove, a narrow bight on the west shore, extends 1 mile in a westerly direction, shoaling gradually from 18 fathoms off its entrance to 6 fathoms at its head.

Camp bay, opposite Grebe cove, is too small, and has too great a depth of water, for anchoring in.

Fox islands.—The north end of Retreat passage opens out into a space about 2 miles across. In the middle of this space, extending right across from the north end of Bonwick island to the south shore of Baker island, are the Fox islands. There is a clear channel east of the Fox islands up to the entrance of Cramer passage, passing midway between the eastern islet of the chain and Solitary island.

Cramer passage, between the SE. shore of Baker island and NW. shore of Gilford island, leading from Retreat passage northeastward into Fife sound and to Shoal harbor, is a deep navigable channel, 400 yards wide at its southern entrance. A rock on which the steamship Coquitham struck in the southern entrance to Cramer passage is situated about midway between Islet point and Steep islet. This danger is shown on the chart as a rock with less than 6 feet over it.

Shoal harbor, on the east shore of Cramer passage, is a narrow inlet 1¼ miles long east and west, to which access is gained by a channel 150 yards across from shore to shore, in some parts less than 40 yards wide between the 3-fathom curves, and in which there is a depth of only 3¾ fathoms. It is only safely available for small coasting vessels, and with local knowledge.

It is high water, full and change, in Shoal harbor at 1 h. 0 m.; springs rise 15 feet, neaps 10 feet.

At the northern entrance, 300 yards from the west shore, is a sand patch, about 400 yards in extent, with from 9 to 16 fathoms on it. A sunken rock lies 250 yards west from Powell point, the NE. entrance point of the passage.

Bonwick island is 3 miles long NE. and SW., and 2 miles across, its highest part being about 770 feet high. Off its SW. end, north of Sedge, Start, and High islands, it is skirted by numerous small islets and rocks, between which, near the shore of Bonwick island, sheltered anchorage may be found.

Fog islands are a small group lying off the shore of Bonwick island, on the south side of the entrance to Arrow passage. Evening rocks and the ledges extending westward from Cove island, lie ½ mile southward of them.

Dusky cove, the anchorage above referred to, affords anchorage in 6 to 8 fathoms, about 200 yards eastward of Cove island, the largest of the islets. It is entered by a passage 200 yards wide between ledges of rock (which extend in patches ½ mile westward from Cove island) and a chain of islets to the southward. Care must be observed, when entering, to avoid the reefs, which may be cleared by keeping the north point of the small Leading island at the head of the cove in line with the north extreme of South island, bearing S. 82° E. (N. 73° E. mag.).

The westernmost of the reefs above mentioned (Evening rocks) covers at 6 feet rise, and Ledge rock, the outer of the islets on the south side of the channel, is only 3 feet above high water. Trap and South islands lie eastward of Ledge rock, the former being 25 feet high.

It is high water, full and change, in Dusky cove at 1 h. 0 m.; springs rise 13 feet.

Horse rock, awash at low water, is a dangerous rock lying off the north side of the entrance to Arrow passage, 1,600 yards N. 72° W. (S. 83° W. mag.) from the westernmost Fog island, and 600 yards southward from the Coach islands.

Arrow passage, between Bonwick island to the SE., and Hudson and Mars islands on the NW., is a navigable channel. Having passed Horse rock, the passage may be boldly passed through in mid-channel, and if necessary, passing westward of Fox islands, and rounding the northern islet of that group at 300 yards, pass between it and Steep island and enter Cramer passage.

The Coach islands are several small islands lying on the north side of the entrance to Arrow passage; they extend over a distance of ¾ mile from the SW. end of Hudson island. This island, on the north side of Arrow passage, NE. of the Coach islands, is 1 mile long and 700 yards broad. Mars island, 2¼ miles long and ¾ mile wide, lies close to, and northeastward of, Hudson island. Spiller passage, between it and Hudson island, leads out NW. among the islets on the SW. side of Eden island and into Trainer and Philips passages.

Scrub, Kate, and Triangle islands, with some other small islets, extend 1¼ miles from the western end of Hudson island, Scrub island being the smallest and westernmost of the group.

Sunday harbor is a small but sheltered anchorage affording refuge for small vessels. The western entrance is between Scrub island and Huston island (a small islet lying 400 yards north of Scrub island). Half a mile in, the channel contracts to less than 100 yards between Narrows island and Island point, between which is a ridge with 4½ fathoms on it, deepening again to 7 fathoms. There is a shoal passage out to the eastward leading into Spiller passage.

Crib island, forming the NW. shore of Sunday harbor, is 1¼ miles long and ½ mile wide at its broadest part.

Anchorage should be taken up in mid-channel as convenient, but at not more than 600 yards from the Narrows, in 5 fathoms, with Bush point bearing N. 29° E. (N. 4° E. mag.), and the north point of Kate island shut in with Island point.

It is high water, full and change, in Sunday harbor, at 1 h. 0 m.; springs rise 13 feet.

Eden island, forming the southeastern shore of the entrance to Fife sound, is about 4 miles long east and west and 1½ miles broad, and has some smaller islands and rocks off its western end. Its SW. shore is a little more than ½ mile northward of Crib island, and the passage between them is divided, by a group of islets lying in the center, into two passages, that to the northward named Trainer, and that to the southward Philips passage.

Marsden islands are a group of five islets lying eastward of the two passages; southward of them, toward Spiller passage, are several other islets and rocks, but NW. and north of them there is a clear channel to the NE. leading into Joe cove (Eden island) and Misty passage, and thence northward through Blunden and Old passages, on either side of Insect island, into Fife sound, south of the Benjamin group. These passages are, however, very narrow and shoal in places, and are not navigable except by small coasters.

Tracey island, 1½ miles long and ¾ mile wide in its broadest part, lies between the eastern ends of Eden and Mars islands. Between it and Eden island is Misty passage.

Monday anchorage.—Between Tracey island and Mars island is Monday anchorage, a sheltered position affording secure anchorage midway between the shores of the above islands in about 8 fathoms.

Baker island, forming part of the southern shore of Fife sound and the northern side of Cramer passage, is situated eastward of Eden island, the triangular-shaped island named Insect island lying between them. It is 1,385 feet high, 4½ miles long east and west, and 1¼ miles broad.

Fife sound, bounded on the north by Broughton island, and on the south by Eden, Insect, and Baker islands, and the Benjamin group lying to the northward of them, and leading from Queen Charlotte sound to Sutlej and Tribune channels and Kingcome inlet, extends in a general ENE. and east direction for 8 miles, when the Burdwood group divides it into two channels (Raleigh and Hornet passages) leading into Tribune channel; it has an average breadth of over 1 mile.

Fife sound, between Pearse peninsula and the Burdwood group, at 8 miles from its entrance, turns suddenly to the westward and joins

Penphrase passage, which connects it with Sutlej channel and Kingcome inlet.

The entrance from Queen Charlotte sound, between Duff island (south shore) and the entrance to Cullen harbor (north shore), may be boldly steered for, passing at about ½ mile SE. of Gore rock (4 feet high), which lies about 1 mile westward of the entrance.

Foster island, the southern summit of which forms a remarkable cone 251 feet high, lies about 5 miles SW. by W. from the entrance to Fife sound, and 2¾ miles NE. from Lizard point, the northern point of Malcolm island; off its southern side are the Twin islets, 40 and 35 feet high. Two hundred yards south of the southern Twin islet are two rocky heads awash at high water.

Shoals.—A rocky shoal with 3 fathoms least water over it lies 1,300 yards N. 80° W. (S. 75° W. mag.) from the western extreme of Foster island. Three hundred yards NNE. from the northern point of the island is a patch of 4½ fathoms, and 800 yards E. by N. from the same point is a shoal with 5¼ fathoms least water over it. SE. by E., 800 yards from the last-mentioned shoal, is a shoal with 8 fathoms over it. All these shoals are marked by kelp in the summer and autumn.

Penfold island, 38 feet high, covered with trees, and small, lies 1½ miles southeastward of Foster island; off its western end are two rocks, 1 to 2 feet above high water.

The channel between Foster and Penfold island, on the NE., and Malcolm island is named George passage.

Holford islands, lying 2 miles NE. by N. from Foster island, consist of two small islands, covered with trees, the tops of which are from 160 to 200 feet above the water. From the western island a reef, which uncovers 3 feet at low water, extends ⅓ mile northwestward, and the islands in this direction should be given a berth of 1 mile. Salmon channel is between Foster island and Holford islands, in which a mid-channel course should be kept.

Cullen harbor, on the south side of Broughton island, at the entrance to Fife sound, extends about 1,400 yards in a northerly direction. Its entrance, between Nelly island and the shore westward of Gordon point, is less than 200 yards wide, and when entering care should be taken to keep exactly in mid-channel. Inside the harbor opens out to 600 yards wide, with depths of from 4 to 8 fathoms.

At the head of the harbor, on the western side, a narrow boat passage, through which the tide runs with great strength, leads into Booker lagoon, an extensive sheet of water about 1¼ miles in extent, with depths varying from 12 to more than 45 fathoms. This lagoon has an outlet into Queen Charlotte sound to the westward of Long island, which forms the western side of Cullen harbor.

Anchorage may be had, well sheltered, in 5 fathoms, sandy bottom, at 300 yards S. by W. from Davidson island at the head of the harbor.

Tides.—It is high water, full and change, in Cullen harbor at 0 h. 0 m.; springs rise 16 feet, neaps 11½ feet.

Deep harbor, on the northern side of Fife sound, 7 miles within the entrance, is formed by a narrow inlet which indents the coast in an easterly direction, forming on its southern side Pearse peninsula. At its entrance is Jumper island, 400 yards eastward of which, and just north of two small islets, is a reef, leaving a clear passage in along the north shore 400 yards wide. The depths in the harbor vary from 14 to 37 fathoms; but anchorage may be found off a small bight on the southern shore, in 18 fathoms, at 600 yards southwestward of the narrow entrance to the bight which forms the head of the harbor.

Benjamin group, consisting of three islands and several smaller islets and rocks, lies off the south shore of Fife inlet, opposite Deep harbor. Indian passage, the narrow channel lying between them and the south shore, has a shoal patch of 1½ fathoms in it, and, though otherwise apparently clear of danger, should not be attempted.

Ragged island, lying 1½ miles eastward of Gull rock (at the eastern extreme of the Benjamin group), has a rocky patch extending 300 yards from its NW. side.

Pym rock, which uncovers 2 feet at low water and is steep-to, is a dangerous patch lying in the way of vessels entering Cramer passage.

Viner sound, on the southeastern shore of Fife sound, about 3 miles NE. of Ragged island, gradually narrows from 1 mile at the entrance to 400 yards wide at the head, from which a bank, drying at low water, extends ½ mile. Anchorage may be had in 10 fathoms at about ¾ mile from its head, abreast an old Indian village.

It is high water, full and change, in Viner sound, at 1 h. 0 m.; springs rise 15 feet, neaps 10 feet.

Burdwood group, consisting of six large and several small islands, lies off the entrance to Viner sound. The largest, which is the northwestern one, is 700 feet high. Vessels should not pass between them.

Simoom sound, the entrance to which is 1¼ miles NW. from the Burdwood group, between Deep Sea bluff on the east and Pollard point on the west, extends 1½ miles NE. and then turns suddenly to WNW., which direction it maintains for nearly 2 miles as far as Curtis point. Here the width decreases from ½ mile to 400 yards, and the inlet bends to the west, expanding to a width of ½ mile at its head, which is only separated by a narrow neck of land, from

120 to 150 feet wide, from Shawl bay, an indentation on the eastern side of Sutlej channel, and forms Wishart peninsula.

The width of Simoom sound at the entrance is ⅓ mile, and on the eastern side, 1 mile from Deep Sea bluff, is the small islet Louisa. The water is deep, but where the sound turns to the westward it shoals to 40 and gradually to 20 fathoms, and southwestward of Curtis point, in O'Brien bay, decreases to 11 fathoms.

Raleigh passage, northward of the Burdwood group, connects Tribune channel with Fife sound and Sutlej channel; there is also a passage to the southward of the group called Hornet passage. There is deep water in both these passages, but the former is wider and the more direct.

Evangeline rock, which dries at low water, lies about 300 yards N. 43° W. (N. 68° W. mag.) from White point on the NW. side of the island.

Tribune channel extends in an ENE. direction for 10 miles; it then takes a southeasterly direction for 5 miles to the entrance of Thompson sound; thence it turns to the SW. for 7 miles, communicating with Knight inlet.

Kwatsi bay, on the northern shore of Tribune channel, about 8 miles eastward of the Burdwood group, indents the coast for about 2 miles in a northerly direction. The water in the southern part is very deep, but shoals at ½ mile from the head of the bay to 28 fathoms, and gradually to 13 fathoms.

Wahkana bay, on the southern shore, opposite to Kwatsi bay, indents the shore of Gilford island in a westerly direction for nearly 2 miles, varying from 400 to 800 yards in width; the depth at about 1 mile within the entrance is 32 fathoms, and near the head 18 fathoms.

Bond sound, which indents the northern shore, extends 3 miles, and has an average width of nearly 1 mile. Owing to the great depth of water, it affords no anchorage, there being 30 fathoms close alongside the mud bank at its head, through which some streams enter the sound.

Thompson sound, 5 miles southeastward of Bond sound, extends in a NE. direction for 5 miles, its entrance being on the eastern shore opposite Trafford point, where Tribune channel turns to the southward. At the head of the sound is Sackville island, and the Kakweiken river flows into the sound northward of it. Between Sackville island and the mud flat off the river the depths shoal, but rather steeply; anchorage, however, might with ease be picked up in the NE. corner, in 12 fathoms.

Humphry rock, with 3 fathoms of water on it, lies nearly in the center of the southern part of Tribune channel, abreast Bamber point, the western salient point of Viscount island, and 2 miles to the northward of the NE. point of Shewell island.

Gilford island, the largest of the islands forming the archipelago on the eastern shore of Queen Charlotte sound, is 18½ miles long in a NE. and SW. direction, and 11 miles wide at its NE. end, gradually decreasing to 2 miles near its SW. extreme (Bare hill). Gilford island is considerably elevated, the highest parts being near the NE. end, where mount Read rises to a height of 4,800 feet; mount James, near the center, is 2,676 feet high. The SW. part of the island, however, is not so lofty, the hills over Bare Hill point being not more than 925 feet high; but round its eastern, southern, and northern shores mountains ranging from 2,600 to 1,500 feet high rise almost precipitously from the coast.

Broughton island, which forms the NW. shore of Fife sound, and the southern and western shores of Sutlej channel, is 15 miles long in an east and west direction, and 6 miles wide at its western end, gradually tapering to 1 mile wide at its eastern extreme. The island is much indented, the largest inlet, Greenway sound, nearly separating the island into two parts; and a canoe passage also leads from Greenway sound to Carter bay, at the western point of the island, thus detaching the northern part of Broughton island, which is, therefore, really another island. The hills on Broughton island are not so lofty as those of the mainland contiguous to it, the highest peaks being mount Browne, 1,745 feet on the northern shore of Greenway sound, and Quoin, or Stoney mountain, 1,500 feet high over the entrance to Deep harbor, the remaining hills varying from 600 to 1,000 feet in height.

Dobbin bay and Cockatrice bay, on the southern side of the island, afford no anchorage.

Polkinghorne islands lie off the coast at the entrance to Wells pass; the largest island, 190 feet high, is over 1 mile in length in a NW. and SE. direction, but only about 400 yards wide, and is distant from Broughton island 1½ miles. Foul ground extends for some distance from the eastern side of this group, and it should not be approached within a distance of ½ mile.

Vincent island lies ½ mile north of the west extreme of the largest of the Polkinghorne islands, some smaller islands lying between them.

Percy island lies ¼ mile NW. of Vincent island, and has several islets and rocks skirting its NW. shore and bordering on Wells pass.

Dickson island, at the western extreme of Broughton island, is ½ mile NE. of Percy island and forms the southern shore of Carter bay; its southern shore is skirted by islets and rocks, some of which extend across to Percy island.

Caution.—Vessels passing between the Polkinghorne islands, Vincent, and Percy islands should do so with great caution, and should not attempt to pass between the latter island and Dickson island.

Carter bay is formed between Dickson and Broughton islands, on the eastern shore of Wells pass; the water in it is deep.

Wells pass is the entrance to Sutlej channel from Queen Charlotte sound. From the entrance between Boyles point and Percy island, the pass extends 5 miles in a NE. direction to its junction with Patrick passage, Grappler sound, and Drury inlet. The width at the southern part, between Dickson island and Popplewell point, is only ½ mile wide, widening gradually to 1 mile at the northern end.

Ommaney islet, about 120 feet high, is the westernmost of the islets lying in Wells pass; its south and SE. sides are surrounded by kelp to a distance of about 400 yards among which are rocks drying at low water. The passage into Wells pass is westward of Ommaney islet, which narrows the navigable channel to a width of 800 yards. When entering Wells pass and approaching Ommaney islet, keep the highest peak of Numas islands (lying well off the entrance) just open of Boyles point until Ommaney islet is well shut in under Dickson island; whence steer to pass in mid-channel between the islet and James point.

Sutlej channel from its entrance (Wells pass) takes a NE. direction for nearly 5 miles, varying from ¾ to 1 mile in breadth. At that distance it turns to the eastward through Patrick passage between Atkinson and Kinnaird islands, and thence southeastward for 5 miles to the entrance to Greenway sound, whence it takes a general easterly direction through Pasley and Sharp passages (on either side of Stackhouse island) to its junction with Penphrase passage and Kingcome inlet. It is a deep channel throughout, and there is no known impediment to safe navigation by maintaining a mid-channel course.

Tracey harbor, on the eastern shore of Sutlej channel (Broughton island), nearly 3 miles within Wells pass, is at its entrance between Lambert island (on the north) and Mauve islet, 800 yards wide, but it soon narrows to from 500 to 300 yards, maintaining that width for a little over 1 mile in an easterly direction; the harbor then opens out and forms two bights at its head, Napier bay, the northern, being 500 yards broad. The only known danger is the reef skirting Star rock (which lies on the north shore about halfway through the narrow portion of the harbor).

Anchorage, completely sheltered, may be obtained in from 6 to 7 fathoms in Napier bay, or abreast Freshwater cove, at about 400 yards SE. of Star rock, in 10 fathoms, mud bottom.

Tides.—It is high water, full and change, in Tracey harbor at 0 h. 0 m.; springs rise 16 feet, neaps rise 11½ feet.

Lambert island, on the north side of the entrance to Tracy harbor, is 500 yards long, 400 yards wide, and 350 feet high; immediately to the eastward of it is Wolf cove, extending 800 yards in a northeasterly direction with a width of 400 yards at the entrance, gradually narrowing to 200 yards; it, however, affords no anchorage.

Atkinson island, 715 feet high, lies close off the NW. shore of Broughton island, at 2 miles northward of the entrance to Tracey harbor; some islets extend off its SW. point. Do not attempt to pass between it and Broughton island.

Surgeon islands, a group of small islets close together, lie ½ mile westward of Atkinson island at the entrance to Patrick passage.

Kinnaird island, 680 feet high and 1¼ miles long, lies on the east side of Grappler sound, with Dunsany passage on the east and Patrick passage on the south.

Greenway sound, on the southern shore of Sutlej channel, 5 miles eastward of Patrick passage, has deep water throughout its entire extent, and affords no anchorage; inside its entrance are Cecil and Maude islets, 180 and 150 feet high.

Cypress harbor, in Sharp passage, 2½ miles eastward of the entrance to Greenway sound, extends about 1 mile south; the upper half, however, is both narrow and shallow. The entrance between Donald head (on the eastern side) and Woods point is 400 yards wide, but the navigable channel is only a little over 200 yards wide; the harbor then opens, and is from 400 to 800 yards across, the depths varying from 19 fathoms in mid-channel to 6 fathoms abreast Berry cove.

Fox rock, awash at high water, lies in the entrance, and is the outer part of a reef which extends 200 yards eastward from Woods point.

Anchorage.—Good anchorage may be obtained on the west side 800 yards from Woods point in 6 fathoms, mud bottom, off Berry cove, at 200 yards NE. by E. from Tree islet. The land southward of the anchorage, between the head of Berry cove and Roffey point, is fringed with large cypress trees. A stream of fresh water flows into Berry cove.

Tides.—It is high water, full and change, in Cypress harbor at 0 h. 0 m.; springs rise 16 feet, neaps 11½ feet.

Stackhouse island, 690 feet high, is about ½ mile in extent, and lies in the middle of Sutlej channel abreast the entrance to Cypress harbor. Sharp passage to the southward of it, and Pasley passage to the northward, are each ½ mile wide.

Rocks.—A rock is situated in Sharp passage in a position from which the northern end of Moore point bears N. 73° E. (N. 48° E., mag.), distant 1,400 yards, and the eastern extremity of Stackhouse island N. 15° E. (N. 10° W. mag.).

An uncharted rock, with 9 feet over it at low water, is reported to exist, where the chart shows 31 to 40 fathoms, in Pasley passage.

Magin islands, three small islands from 120 to 180 feet high, lie 1 mile northward of Stackhouse island, and ½ mile from the west shore.

A small rock, awash at high water, lies nearly midway between the islands and the shore.

Tides.—The tides in Sutlej channel run at the rate of from 1 to 3 knots.

Kingcome inlet takes a northeasterly direction for 6 miles to the entrance to Wakeman sound (on the north shore), whence it trends eastward for a farther distance of 12 miles to its head, maintaining an average width of 1 mile.

The inlet, at its entrance, is 2 miles wide, but the navigable channel between the Magin islands (lying off the western shore) and Bradley point (the western point of Gregory island) is contracted to 1¼ miles in width. Its termination on the northern shore is a low marshy plain, dotted with patches of scrub and stunted trees, and bordered by a flat of soft mud and sand 1¼ miles wide, which extends ¼ mile from the shore. This flat is steep-to.

The northern shores of this inlet are bordered by snow-clad peaks of 5,000 to 6,000 feet in height, which are conspicuous from Queen Charlotte sound; the southern shore is not quite so lofty, the range varying from 3,000 to 4,000 feet. Kingcome mountains, 5,600 feet high, rise over the head of this inlet, being 2 miles inland in an easterly direction.

A rock, with less than 6 feet of water, and marked by kelp, lies in Moore bay, northern side of Gregory island, Kingcome inlet, situated at a distance of about 1,600 yards S. 20° W. (S. 5° E. mag.) from Thomas point.

Anchorage.—Kingcome inlet, in regard to the great depth of water, presents the same features as most of the chasm-like fiords on this coast. Anchorage, however, may be obtained in 18 fathoms, off a small cove, near two small bights, at 1½ miles south of the head of the inlet.

Wakeman sound, on the northern shore of Kingcome inlet, branches off to the northward at 6 miles from the entrance, in which direction it extends for a distance of 5 miles, terminating in a low marshy plain, dotted with patches of scrub and stunted trees, through which several streams flow, bringing down from the high ranges inland the melting snow, and causing the water for 1 mile from the head of the sound to be perfectly fresh at low water, and of a dull, milky color. At its head is an Indian village. The water is too deep for anchorage.

Belleisle sound, on the south shore of Kingcome inlet, at 3 miles SE. from the entrance to Wakeman sound, has its entrance through a narrow pass which lies south of the small Edmond islands. The inlet takes a SSE. direction for about 1 mile and then suddenly turns to the WSW. for a farther distance of 3 miles; it, however, from its great depth of water, affords no anchorage.

Penphrase passage, connecting Sutlej channel and Kingcome inlet with Fife sound and Tribune channel, is about 2¼ miles long SE. and NW. The west entrance between Hayes and Vigis points is 1 mile wide, but the width of the passage decreases to 500 yards abreast Trivett island.

Rocks.—About 200 yards east from Trivett island is a shoal patch of 3 fathoms.

In Penphrase passage, a rock, which uncovers at low water, is situated at a distance of 1,800 yards South (S. 25° E. mag.) from Vigis point.

A rock, which dries at low water, is reported to exist in a position about 300 yards from the southern coast of the Wishart peninsula and N. 6° W. (N. 31° W. mag.) from the 3-fathom patch lying 200 yards east of Trivett island. This position is, however, doubtful.

Shoal ground extends 200 yards off the bluff nearly midway between Steep and Vigis points, Wishart peninsula.

Nicholls island lies just inside the west entrance on the south side of the channel. A rock, awash at low water, lies 300 yards westward of the west point of Nicholls island.

Drury inlet.—Between Pandora head and the shore to the southward is the entrance to Drury inlet, which is here only 200 yards wide, with a depth of 15 fathoms in it; just outside (eastward) the entrance is Morris island, which should be passed on the northern side, and the northern shore should be closed to avoid a reef (marked by kelp in the season) lying on the southern shore, halfway between Morris island and the narrowest part of the entrance. The inlet extends in a westerly direction for 12 miles to its head, near which another and narrower arm (Actæon sound) extends to the northeastward for a distance of 4 miles.

Over the greater part of Drury inlet the depth is less than 25 fathoms, and it is nowhere so deep as most of these inland channels; in width it varies from 200 yards to 1 mile, the latter being its width throughout the greater part of the inlet; but at one place, Stuart narrows, 1¼ miles within the entrance, two islets (each connected to the shore by reefs) leave a passage of only 300 yards between them, and this is further obstructed by a dangerous rock, which uncovers

5 feet at low water, lying directly in the fairway between the two islets. Through these narrows the tidal streams during springs attain a velocity of 5 knots an hour.

Passing up Drury inlet, the shores of which have an average height of less than 1,000 feet, at 1 mile from Stuart narrows, Leche island is seen lying in mid-channel, and may be passed on either side; here the inlet opens out to the southward, forming Richmond bay, in which are several islets. At a little over 1 mile westward of Leche island is Ligar island, 150 feet high, having at 200 yards east of its southern point a dangerous sunken rock, uncovering 5 feet at low water springs.

Voak rock, another dangerous rock, awash at low water spring tides, lies 600 yards N. 10° W. (N. 35° W. mag.) from Ligar island, with deep water between.

Sir Everard islands, on the south shore, 1½ miles westward of Ligar island, form a chain extending in a NNW. direction, with rocks between them, a clear channel lying between them and Hooper island to the northward.

Blount rock, 3 feet above high water, lies close to the southern shore ½ mile to the westward of Sir Everard islands.

Jennis bay, on the northern shore, abreast the Sir Everard islands, would afford anchorage for a small vessel; when entering, pass eastward of Hooper island lying at the entrance, and anchor in the center of the bay in 7 to 10 fathoms.

Center rock, a dangerous sunken rock, uncovering 8 feet at low water springs, lies in the middle of Drury inlet, 1$\frac{1}{10}$ miles WNW. of the northern of the Sir Everard islands; it is steep-to around, and vessels will clear it by keeping at 400 yards from either shore.

Muirhead islands.—At 2¼ miles westward of Center rock the inlet becomes studded with small islands having deep channels between them and extending over a distance of 2 miles. The easternmost of these is Wilson island, 105 feet high; Keith island, 105 feet high, lies 400 yards westward of it, and the Muirhead islands, three in number, extending 1 mile in an east and west direction, are situated 200 yards westward of the latter. The west Muirhead island is the largest and 255 feet high.

Between this group and the southern shore the space is occupied by numerous small islands, but there is a clear channel along the northern side of the group; westward of these, however, the water shoals rapidly, there being only 2 to 3 fathoms in Sutherland bay at the head of Drury inlet.

A densely wooded valley extends across the peninsula in a SW. direction to the outer coast of Queen Charlotte sound.

Actæon sound, which branches off from the northern side of Drury inlet abreast the west Muirhead island, is so blocked at its entrance by islets and rocks as to render it only available to boats.

Grappler sound.—West of Patrick passage, between Kinnaird island and Pandora head, is the entrance to another inlet which continues in a northerly direction for 4 miles, and is known as Grappler sound. From it several smaller bights branch off on both sides, those on the east communicating with Hopetown and Kenneth passages, south and north of Watson island. The depths in the sound range from 20 to 30 fathoms, but are shoaler in Claydon and Carriden bays on the western shore. At the entrance to the former a reef lies nearly in mid-channel, and a reef extends 300 yards from Linlithgow point, on the northern shore of the entrance to the latter.

Buckingham, Hammersley, and Hanbury islands lie on the northern side of Kinnaird island at the entrance to Hopetown passage, the first being the largest and 300 feet high.

Dunsany passage, leading from Grappler sound to the entrance to Hopetown passage and southeastward into Sutlej channel, east of Kinnaird island, is apparently clear of dangers, with the exception of a reef, which covers at high water springs, lying off the northern shore at the entrance to Hopetown passage.

Hopetown passage can only be used by boats, which can pass the barrier of rocks (that extend right across the passage at 1¾ miles from the entrance) at high water, and can thence proceed into Mackenzie sound.

Kenneth passage, leading from the head of Grappler sound round the northern side of Watson island, is 3½ miles long, and communicates with Mackenzie sound at its junction with Hopetown passage. About 1 mile from its entrance (which is only a little over 200 yards broad) from Grappler sound it widens considerably, a bight, named Turnbull cove, extending 1 mile in a NW. direction; but ½ mile farther eastward the passage contracts to 600 yards between Alexander and Jessie points, and thence several islands, islets, and rocks obstruct the passage, rendering its navigation dangerous.

Mackenzie sound, from the east point of Watson island, extends 3 miles eastward, gradually narrowing toward its head at the foot of mount Stephens (5,665 feet high), where it becomes a mere chasm, and shoaling in the same direction from 25 to 10 fathoms.

Boyles point, the western entrance point of Wells pass and the southern point of the peninsula formed by Drury inlet, has three small islets lying close off it, the outer of which is only 4 feet above high water. Over and on each side of the point are undulating hills about 500 feet high, rising gradually inland to mount Wynyard (about 1,200 feet high).

Lewis rocks, a small cluster 4 to 30 feet above high water, lie 1 mile west from Boyles point, with rocks awash and foul ground extending 1,400 yards southward from them.

Numas islands, the largest of which is 1¼ miles long east and west, lie 4 miles SW. from Boyles point; the largest is 434 feet high, and off its western extreme is Staples islet, 24 feet high. These form an excellent landmark.

Labouchere channel, between Numas islands and the Lewis rocks, is over 2 miles wide. The tidal streams run at the rate of from 1 to 3 knots through this channel.

Rayner group consists of four or five small islands, 120 to 150 feet high, lying close to the shore eastward of Blunden harbor. The southern edge of the group is fringed with sunken rocks, and they should not be approached in that direction nearer than ½ mile. Masses of kelp surround these islands in the season and skirt the shore toward Blunden harbor.

Gillot rock, 2 feet above high water, is the easternmost of the dangers lying to the southward of the Rayner group.

Black rock, 7 feet above high water springs, is the westernmost of the dangers in the vicinity of Rayner group.

Blunden harbor, on the northern shore of Queen Charlotte sound, about 12 miles to the westward of Wells pass, is formed between Robinson and Edgell islands and the mainland; there are several islands and islets within the harbor. Robinson island, which forms the southern side of the harbor, is 1 mile long east and west, and about ¼ mile broad; it is densely wooded and about 260 feet in height to the tops of the trees. Edgell island, which forms the eastern side of the harbor, is about 700 yards in extent, wooded, and about 290 feet high; it is only separated from the mainland at high water. The entrance to the harbor is between these two islands and is 250 yards wide.

Burgess island, a small island 28 feet in height, lies nearly 200 yards off the southern side of Robinson island and 650 yards southwestward from Shelf point, its eastern extreme. A shoal patch, marked by kelp, with 2 fathoms least water and general depths of from 2½ to 5 fathoms, lies NE. of Burgess island; the least depth is on its eastern edge and is 400 yards ENE. from the island.

Barren rock, 7 feet high, lies on the eastern side of the entrance 400 yards south of Edgell island; foul ground extends to the northward and westward of it to a distance of 100 yards, and two rocks which dry 2 and 9 feet at low water lie, respectively, 50 and 100 yards north of the rock.

A shoal with 3¾ fathoms over it lies 350 yards SW. ½ S. from Barren rock.

Siwiti rock.—A rocky patch, 100 yards in extent north and south, and marked by kelp, lies SSW. of Barren rock; Siwiti rock, its shoalest head, with only 6 feet of water over it at low water, is on the SE. side of the patch and 366 yards S. 26° W. (South mag.) from Barren rock.

A rock, with 5 feet over it at low water, lies 66 yards offshore 150 yards N. 7° E. (N. 19° W. mag.) from Shelf point.

Just within the entrance the harbor divides into two arms, one to the west, the other to the north. There is good anchorage in the western arm; the northern arm, after a short distance, becomes very shallow and is choked with islets and rocks, between which a boat passage leads to the rapids at the entrance to Bradley lagoon; these rapids are only navigable by canoes and at slack water.

Bonwick islands.—The two principal islands in the harbor are the north and south Bonwick islands, which at low water are joined together and to the mainland on the NW. side of the harbor by a mud flat with scattered bowlders; an Indian village is situated on the NW. shore of the harbor northwestward of the islands. Moore rock, drying 5 feet at low water, lies 150 yards WNW. of the western extreme of south Bonwick island. The channel leading to the inner anchorage, in the western arm, is contracted, between the south Bonwick island and Bartlett point, on Robinson island, to under 100 yards by rocks which lie off either shore.

Rocks.—A rocky ledge, with 8 feet over it, lies 50 yards off the southern side of south Bonwick island with the western extreme of Bartlett point bearing S. 14° E. (S. 40° E. mag.); 100 yards NE. by E. from this ledge is a rock which dries 3 feet at low water and which is 240 yards NNE. from Bartlett point. On the southern side of the channel, N. 50° E. (N. 24° E. mag.) from the western extreme of Bartlett point, is a rock which dries 2 feet at low water, and 300 yards N. 79° E. (N. 53° E. mag.) from the same point is a rock with 8 feet over it at low water. In the southern part of the inner anchorage, over 100 yards from the nearest point of Robinson island and S. 86° W. (S. 60° W. mag.), 450 yards from Bartlett point, is a rock with 4 feet over it at low water.

The ledge off the southern side of south Bonwick island, the rock with 8 feet over it, northeastward of Bartlett point, and the last-described rock, are not marked by kelp.

Anchorages.—There are two anchorages, the outer immediately inside and to the northward of the entrance, in 7 to 10 fathoms, mud, and the inner to the westward of Bartlett point, in 4 fathoms, soft mud bottom; they afford good, sheltered anchorage for moderate-sized vessels.

Tides.—It is high water, full and change, at 0 h. 22 m.; springs rise 16½ feet, neaps 11½ feet.

Directions.—On entering, keep Charles point (the SW. point of Edgell island) slightly open of Shelf point until well inside Siwiti rock, when alter course to pass Shelf point at a distance of about

150 yards, and steer in mid-channel for the center of north Bonwick island to the outer anchorage. If proceeding to the inner anchorage, when Gregory island, 31 feet high and bare of trees, at the western end of the inner harbor, is in line with the southern point of south Bonwick island, steer in on that line until the north tangent of south Bonwick island bears N. 33° W. (N. 59° W. mag.), when a mid-channel course, S. 67° W. (S. 41° W. mag.), between the last-named island and Bartlett point will lead into the inner anchorage. When Bartlett point is in line with the point next east of it, haul up to N. 74° W. (S. 80° W. mag.), and anchor as convenient.

During the summer and autumn months kelp grows only on some of the dangers in Blunden harbor, and it can not be depended upon in the same degree as in other parts of the coast.

Nankivell islands, a small group extending from the shore in a southeasterly direction for nearly ½ mile, lie 1½ miles to the westward of the entrance to Blunden harbor. The largest island of the group is wooded and about 85 feet in height to the tops of the trees; the other islets of the group are small, barren rocks. There is foul ground round the islands; a rock with 4 feet over it lies SE. by E., 240 yards, and a rocky head, with 3 fathoms least water, ESE., 650 yards, from the SE. islet. Vessels should not approach within ½ mile of the SE. islet.

Browning islands, a small group, the largest being 500 yards long and about 200 feet high, are 2½ miles west from the entrance to Blunder harbor. A dangerous rock, which dries 10 feet at low water springs, lies 600 yards SE. from the eastern extreme of the largest of the Browning islands; these islands should be given a berth of 1 mile in passing.

Stuart point, 1¾ miles NW. by W. from the Browning islands, has a cluster of rocky islets and rocks, from 2 to 4 feet high, extending for a distance of 300 yards off it; a bay extends to the eastward to a considerable depth between the point and the Browning islands, in the center of which is a patch with 2 fathoms on it, which is marked by kelp.

From Stuart point the coast trends in a W. by N. direction for about 1¾ miles, to the point running down from Leading hill, 517 feet high, the southern summit of the coast range south of Shelter bay; this line of coast is very rugged.

Jeannette islands, two in number and thickly wooded, lie off the point from Leading hill, before mentioned; the eastern is the largest, being about 700 yards long in an east and west direction and 500 yards wide, the tops of the trees being 249 feet above high water. Two small wooded islets 50 and 60 feet in height lie close to the eastward of the eastern Jeannette island, and several small rocky islets lie inshore of them and off Leading Hill point.

Robertson island, which is about 500 yards long, has trees on it, the tops of which are about 179 feet high; it lies north from the larger of the Jeannette islands, and is separated from them by a channel 200 yards wide which should not be used.

The main track for ships to seaward in this neighborhood is called the North channel, and the eastern end of it passes between the Jeannette islands and the Millar group, and to the northward of Ghost (Round) island.

From Leading Hill point the coast runs in to the northward, forming a bay which is guarded by Robertson island. This bay, which is open to the westward, is useless except for small craft, having several patches of foul ground in it. From the head of the bay the coast trends northwestward for 2¼ miles to the Wallace islands, and has several small bights and a few rocks and islets lying close along the shore. The hills near the coast are densely wooded, have no distinctive features, and attain a height of 718 feet about midway between Leading hill and the Wallace islands; Leading hill can sometimes be distinguished plainly when approaching from the westward.

Shelter bay trends easterly for nearly 2 miles, forming two bights at its head. The entrance between the Wallace islands and the shore to the northward is 800 yards wide, but the bay is encumbered with rocks in its most sheltered part, and could only be made use of as an anchorage by those possessing local knowledge. In a small bay north of Wallace islands there is good landing for boats, and there is also good landing for boats in southeasterly winds, in a bight 600 yards NW. of the point forming the NW. entrance to Shelter bay.

Annie rocks, two bare rocky islets, lie about 700 yards off the coast nearly midway between Shelter bay and the Southgate group; the highest is 28 feet in height. Foul ground extends nearly 200 yards both east and west of the islets. A rock, with 2 feet on it, lies on the eastern end of a rocky shoal, 200 yards in length, 300 yards SSW. from the highest Annie islet. A rocky shoal, about 400 yards in extent in an ESE. and WNW. direction, lies with its western end 500 yards ESE. of the highest Annie islet; in its eastern part are two heads, the northern awash and the southern with 8 feet over it at low water.

Southgate group consists of several islands, islets, and rocks, lying close off the mainland about 2½ miles westward of Shelter bay, which extend parallel to the shore in a general northerly direction for 2 miles. The principal islands are, Southgate, the northern and largest of the group, and Knight island, near the middle of the group; both are thickly wooded. The entrance to the anchorage is between these two islands.

Southgate island, of irregular shape, is nearly 1,600 yards in length, north and south, 600 yards wide toward its northern end, and 235 feet in height to the tops of the trees in the northern part of the island. A chain of several islets and rocks extends in a southerly direction for over 400 yards from the southern end of the island; the outer and largest of these islets is Stevens islet, thickly wooded, and 145 feet high; a rock, 3 feet high and steep-to, lies close off the southern side of, and a rock which dries 8 feet at low water lies nearly 200 yards WNW. from, Stevens islet.

Several small islets lie close off the northern point of the island; a rock with 4 feet over it at low water lies 150 yards NW. from the northern of these islets.

Knight island is about 900 yards in extent and 190 feet in height to the tops of the trees; it is situated 400 yards southeastward from the nearest point of Southgate island, but the channel between is narrowed to 150 yards by a rocky ledge extending northward from Knight island. Guard islet, small, bare, and 12 feet high, lies 100 yards north from the NE. point of the island, and several rocks, the northern of which dries 11 feet at low water, extend to 150 yards north from it, where there is a head of 2 fathoms least water which is steep-to on its northern and western sides.

West 350 yards from Guard islet and nearly 100 yards offshore is a rock which dries 12 feet at low water, and extending northward from it, for 250 yards, is a narrow rocky ledge of a general depth of 4 fathoms, but with two heads of 2 fathoms least water, the northern of which is 150 yards north from the rock.

A rock, with 6 feet over it at low water, and a 3-fathom head lying close to it, are situated 200 yards off the SW. side of Knight island.

Tinson islands are a chain of four islands situated about 600 yards south of Knight island; the three eastern islands are joined together at low water. The islands are all wooded; the middle island is the largest and highest, being 257 feet in height to the tops of the trees. A shoal, with 5 fathoms least water, lies 750 yards WSW. from the western island, and a rocky ledge, with 2 to 5 fathoms on it, extends 200 yards SE. from the eastern island.

Between the Tinson islands and Knight island are scattered a number of wooded and rocky islets and rocks, the passages between which can only be used by small boats.

Approach rock, a small bare rock 2 feet high with foul ground close round it, marked by kelp, is situated 200 yards east from the east Tinson island.

Simpson rock, a bare rock 5 feet high, with several rocks that dry at low water extending 100 yards NW. from it, is situated 420 yards S. ¾ E. from east Tinson island.

South, 440 yards, from Simpson rock is a narrow rocky shoal, 100 yards in extent north and south, the southern head of which is awash at low water; SE. ¾ E., 420 yards, from Simpson rock is another rock with 5 feet least water over it.

Arm islands form a chain of narrow wooded islands lying close off and parallel to the mainland at about 100 yards distance to the eastward of Knight and Tinson islands, the northwestern part of the chain being between those islands and the mainland. The largest island is nearly 1,200 yards long and 173 feet high to the tops of the trees. Foul ground, marked by kelp, extends for nearly 200 yards to the southward of the SE. end of these islands; there are several islets and rocks on the outer edge of this ground, the highest being 7 feet in height.

A line of small wooded islets lies nearly midway between the northwestern end of the Arm islands and Knight and Tinson islands. Tide rock, 2 feet high, is one of the northern of these islets and lies 266 yards NE. ¾ N. from the SE. extreme of Knight island.

The mainland abreast the Southgate group is hilly and thickly wooded. Conspicuous cone, a remarkable conical summit, 605 feet in height to the tops of the trees, is situated northward of the anchorage and is easily distinguished. Coast hill, the northern summit of a flat-topped hill to the southeastward of the anchorage, is 795 feet high; it is the highest part of the coast in the vicinity.

Tides.—It is high water, full and change, at 0 h. 22 m.; springs rise 16½ feet, neaps rise 11½ feet, neap range is irregular.

Tidal streams.—The streams turn at high and low water by the shore, but do not exceed a rate of 1 knot an hour.

Anchorage.—The anchorage, situated between Knight island and the mainland, affords complete protection from all directions and is suitable for moderate-sized vessels; the holding ground is good stiff mud. The best position for anchoring is in 12 fathoms with Guard islet bearing NW. by W. ¼ W.

Directions.—In entering bring Conspicuous cone on a N. 36° E. (N. 10° E. mag.) bearing and showing just inside the eastern extreme of Southgate island; steer in on this bearing until the NE. extreme of Knight island is abeam, when alter course as necessary for the anchorage.

The anchorage can also be entered from the southward, but the channel between Tide rock and a rock, which dries 5 feet, lying 66 yards off the eastern side of Knight island, though deep is only about 60 yards wide and is not recommended.

Elizabeth island, a bare rock 22 feet high and about 100 yards long north and south, is situated about 600 yards NW. of Southgate island; a small rock 9 feet high lies close to its SE. extreme, and a rocky head, drying 15 feet at low water, lies to the northward about 100 yards distant.

A small shoal with 2 fathoms least water on its northern end, lies SW ½ W. 400 yards from Elizabeth island.

Woods rock is a rock, with 4 feet over it at low water, lying on the western edge of a small 3-fathom shoal; from it Elizabeth island bears S. 82° E. (N. 72° E. mag.), distant 1,300 yards. Another rock, having 3 fathoms over it at low water, lies 300 yards NNE. of Woods rock.

A large patch of foul ground, marked by kelp, and nearly 300 yards long in a NW. and SE. direction, lies with its center about 850 yards N. ½ W. from Elizabeth island; three rocky heads, drying 2 feet at low water, are situated in its western part and several rocks with less than 6 feet over them in the eastern part.

A small rock, drying 4 feet at low water, is on the western edge of a small shoal with Elizabeth island bearing SW. by W., distant 700 yards.

Harris island is a bare rock 39 feet high and about 150 yards in extent, lying 1,800 yards WSW. ¾ W. from Stevens islet of the Southgate group; two rocks, drying 1 and 3 feet, lie 100 yards off its eastern side and a rock with 4 fathoms over it lies SSE. ½ E. 260 yards from the summit of the island.

Dickenson islet, a bare rocky islet, 17 feet high, lies 1,480 yards NW. from Harris island; a rock with 3 fathoms over it lies 300 yards off its eastern side.

Rogers islets are two bare rocky islets, the western being the larger and 51 feet in height. Foul ground extends off their SE. sides for 500 yards, a rock, drying 1 foot, being on the SE. extreme of it, and another head, awash at low water, lying nearly midway between it and the western islet.

Emily islands.—Lying to the NE. and about ¾ mile from the Rogers islets are the Emily islands, a group of about 6 small, wooded islands, the trees on the highest being about 180 feet above high water; they extend about ½ mile in an east and west direction. These islands have no offlying dangers and possess no special features.

Eliza islands are two islands lying to the NE. of the Emily group, the northern being considerably the larger. They are both densely wooded, the larger island being 204 feet in height to the tops of the trees; on the eastern side of the larger island are some conspicuous white marks in the cliffs.

A reef, which has 3 heads that dry 6 feet at low water, lies to the NW. of the larger island less than 200 yards distant.

Nearly midway between the Eliza islands and Branham island are two rocky heads with 5 feet of water over them at low water, lying close together.

Frederick islet is a small islet 90 feet high, lying ½ mile eastward of Eliza island. From Frederick islet, toward Elizabeth rock, there are several rocky patches.

Town rock, 6 feet high, lies ½ mile eastward of Frederick islet.

Murray labyrinth is the name given to the many channels which lie between a group of several islands, islets, and rocks, lying off the SE. coast of Branham island and 2 miles north from the Southgate group.

Branham island, 3½ miles long east and west and 2½ miles broad, lies off the coast of the mainland, and together with the Fox islands forms the southern shore of Slingsby channel. Skull cove, indenting the SE. coast of the island, affords good shelter for boats. The western shore of Branham island is almost equally divided by Miles inlet, running in a NE. direction, which at the entrance between Cust and McEwan points is about 600 yards across and which gradually narrows to 60 yards at about 1,800 yards from the entrance, where it branches off at right angles in a NW. and SE. direction and leads up to large lagoons; the inner arms of the inlet afford good anchorage and protection for small craft.

The hills on the coast of Branham island to the south of Miles inlet are small; the summits are nearly bare, the sides being covered with stunted trees; Nina hill, 275 feet high, is situated over Cust point.

There are several rocky islets and rocks lying close off the south and SW. shores of Branham island.

Schooner passage, between the eastern shore of Branham island and the mainland, is a narrow pass having an average width of 200 yards, and extending in a northerly direction for a distance of 2½ miles; it is, however, at one place obstructed by a rock lying in mid-channel, which leaves a passage only 80 yards wide between it and the shore of Branham island. Schooner passage communicates with Slingsby channel, at 1 mile southward of the Nakwakto rapids.

The tidal streams in Schooner passage run at the rate of from 2 to 5 knots.

Mayor islands are situated from 600 to 800 yards off the SW. extreme of Branham island; there are three islands, the largest being wooded, and 155 feet high to the tops of the trees; the trees give this island a wall-like effect which renders it somewhat conspicuous. The two other islands are bare and rocky, 9 and 10 feet high, and lie close to the eastward of the larger one.

Foul ground extends for 1,200 yards NW. from the largest Mayor island, having at its western end two rocks, 150 yards apart, with 4 feet over them at low water, the western one lying NW. ¼ N. 1,100 yards from the western end of the largest Mayor island. A rock, awash at low water, lies 500 yards E. ¼ S. from the last-mentioned rock. Foul ground also extends to the northeastward of the islands, a rock, awash at low water, lying 300 yards E. ¼ S. from the northern Mayor island. The southern side of the Mayor islands is free from dangers.

White island, small, bare, and 57 feet high, lies 1,700 yards SW. by W. ¾ W. from McEwan point, the western extreme of Branham island; two small rocks, the outer of which is awash at high water, lie close-to on its eastern side.

Morphy rock, drying 9 feet at low water, lies between White island and the western shore of Branham island, 535 yards SW. from McEwan point; it is situated in the center of a shoal about 600 yards long in a NW. and SE. direction.

A rocky head, with 6 feet over it at low water, lies S. by W. ¼ W. 700 yards from McEwan point, and an isolated 2-fathom rock lies 400 yards SW. ¾ S. from it, nearly midway between White island and Cust point, and 1,200 yards distant from the former.

Fox islands.—The Fox islands, three in number, lying to the westward of the Branham island, are only separated from that island and each other by very narrow passages. They form the southern shore of the outer part of the entrance to Slingsby channel and extend over a distance of more than 1½ miles in an east and west direction; they are all thickly wooded, the summit of the western island, which is situated in the north part of that island, being 370 feet high.

The western extreme of the western Fox island is called Dalkeith point, and, with the exception of a small islet 11 feet high close off it, appears to have no offlying dangers.

A group of rocks, the highest of which dries 8 feet, lies about 200 yards off the western shore of the west Fox island from 400 to 600 yards northward of Dalkeith point.

A patch with 7 fathoms over it lies 1,200 yards SSE. from Dalkeith point.

The bay formed between Branham island and the Fox islands has islets and rocks skirting its shores.

Lascelles point is the southern termination of the mainland on the northern side of Slingsby channel. A cluster of small islets, the highest of which is 12 feet high, lies close offshore 300 yards to the westward of the point. A small wooded summit, 165 feet high, stands immediately over the point. The seaward entrance to Slingsby channel, between Dalkeith and Lascelles points, is nearly 1,200 yards wide.

Buccleugh point lies 1,200 yards NW. by W. ¼ W. from Lascelles point, the coast being very rugged between them.

Bremner island, 56 feet high and covered with coarse grass, lies 1,800 yards WNW. of Buccleugh point; a small rocky islet, 6 feet high, lies close to it on its eastern side.

From Buccleugh point the coast trends in a general NW. direction for 6 miles to cape Caution, forming two broad bays, but slightly indenting the coast, and separated by Rayner point 1¾ miles SE. by E. from cape Caution.

Cape Caution, the northern entrance point of Queen Charlotte sound, is of moderate height and level, the tops of the trees being about 200 feet above the sea; the shore is white and of granite formation.

Slingsby channel, on the northern shore of Queen Charlotte sound, 7 miles southeastward of cape Caution, leading to Seymour and Belize inlets, the entrance to which is between Dalkeith and Lascelles points, is 5 miles in length east and west, with an average breadth of 600 yards, between Outer narrows and Nakwakto rapids.

It is high water, full and change, in Slingsby channel at 0 h. 30 m.; springs rise 11 feet, neaps range 5 feet.

Outer narrows.—At ¾ mile within the entrance the channel contracts to only 200 yards in width, with no bottom at 40 fathoms. With the wind blowing in, i. e., between West and South, the sea breaks across the entrance, and in the narrowest part, even during calms, the water is much agitated.

Tidal streams.—In the narrows the flood stream runs 2½ hours after high water by the shore; at springs the velocity is from 5 to 9 knots, at neaps from 4 to 6 knots, the change of stream occurring after only about 15 minutes slack water. The ebb stream runs 2½ hours after low water by the shore, attaining, at springs, a velocity of 10 knots, and at neaps from 5 to 7 knots.

Nakwakto rapids, at the eastern end of Slingsby channel (communicating with Seymour inlet), is 400 yards wide, but in the center of the rapids is Turret islet, 80 feet high, against which the tide rushes with great fury. The channel westward of Turret islet has a rock in it with only 2 fathoms of water on it; that to the eastward has depths of from 6 to 11 fathoms.

The flood stream commences 2½ hours after low water by the shore in Slingsby channel (see above), and runs (with a velocity at springs of 12 to 15 knots) from 2 to 2¾ hours after high water, or until it is high water at Seymour inlet; after an interval of 10 minutes slack water the ebb commences and runs until 2 to 3 hours after low water in Slingsby channel, attended by very heavy and dangerous overfalls, and attaining a velocity at springs of 20 knots.

Directions.—Steam vessels may enter Slingsby channel from the westward through the Outer narrows in fine weather, at or near slack water, and proceed to Treadwell bay, 4 miles within the entrance on the northern shore, where anchorage will be found in from 9 to 15 fathoms, avoiding the shoal of 2½ fathoms situated southward of the center of the bay.

If it be necessary to proceed through Nakwakto rapids, the turn of the stream should be most carefully watched, so that the vessel may with certainty make the passage during the only 10 minutes of slack water, for at no other time would it be possible to do so with any degree of safety.

The narrows, however, should only be used by a vessel in emergency, and after acquiring some practical knowledge by passing through at slack water in a boat. It is also imperative that the tides should be previously watched from Treadwell bay.

Small canoes pass from Slingsby channel into Seymour inlet at half tide through a very narrow passage on the northern shore inside the small island forming the northern point of the narrows.

Treadwell bay, on the northern shore of Slingsby channel, is formed by the channel widening to 1,700 yards and forming a bight in which lie the Anchor islands (a group consisting of several islands), leaving a sheltered space 500 yards in extent between the northern coast of the largest island and the shore. The largest Anchor island is ½ mile long east and west, and 220 feet high. The depth of water in the bay varies from 7 to 12 fathoms, but near the center, rather over to the southern side, there is a shoal spot with from 4 to 2½ fathoms on it. The bay affords shelter free from tidal streams. Large ships should moor.

Entering Treadwell bay, give the southeastern Anchor islands (Current point) a berth of 300 yards, and having rounded them, keep the shore of the mainland aboard.

Anchor as convenient in 10 to 12 fathoms northward of the 2½-fathom patch, before mentioned.

It is high water, full and change, in Treadwell bay at 0 h. 30 m.; springs rise 11 feet, neaps 5 feet.

Caution rock, which uncovers 6 feet at low water springs, is a dangerous rock lying in the fairway southeastward of the Anchor islands, and 300 yards from the southern shore of Slingsby channel. To avoid it, keep the southern shore aboard at less than 200 yards distance.

Schooner passage, north entrance.—One mile southward of the Nakwakto rapids is the northern entrance to Schooner passage; it may be approached on either side of Buttress island (210 feet high), which lies on the southern shore of Slingsby channel, fronting the passage.

Nugent sound.—From Nakwakto rapids a branch ½ mile wide trends SE. about 1 mile; here it divides into two, one branch continuing SE., and the other (Nugent sound) east for 11 miles. Nugent sound in some places is only 400 yards across, but it has deep water throughout, and is navigable, though there is no anchorage in it.

Seymour inlet.—The other branch, from Margaret point at the entrance to Nugent sound, trends SE. for 6 miles, with deep water in mid-channel. On the northern shore is Charlotte bay, and on the southern Ellis bay, both, however, unavailable as an anchorage. At the above distance, on the northern shore, is the entrance to Seymour inlet, several islets lying just within it. A narrow pass of shallower water, with depths of 4 to 10 fathoms, continues for 3 miles SE.

Wawatle bay lies between the entrances to these two arms and extends 1 mile east, with depths of from 23 to 18 fathoms.

Seymour inlet, from its entrance to the head of Salmon arm, is 25 miles long, varying from ¾ to 1½ miles in width, and maintains a depth of over 40 fathoms throughout to within 400 to 600 yards of the shore at its head. There are several indentations on both shores, the largest being Maunsell bay on the northern shore; none, however, afford an anchorage.

At 3 miles eastward of Maunsell bay is Eclipse narrows, where the tidal streams run with great strength, and no bottom could be obtained at 12 fathoms; this narrows leads to Salmon arm and Frederick sound, the latter extending 5 miles SSE., the former 3 miles ENE.

Salmon arm terminates at the foot of Perpendicular mountain, 5,000 feet high. Taaltz, an Indian winter village, is situated on the shore at its head.

The continuation of Seymour inlet northward of Eclipse narrows is 6 miles long, a river flowing into it at its head, on which is situated a winter village of the Wawatle Indians.

Belize inlet.—From Nakwakto rapids another branch, 600 yards wide, takes a NW. direction for 3 miles to Mignon point, where it suddenly turns eastward for 24 miles, with an average width of ½ mile, and with deep water throughout; it lies between high ranges, 3,000 to 4,000 feet high. From the head of Belize inlet to Maunsell bay, on the northern side of Seymour inlet, there is, according to Indian reports, a portage about 2½ miles long.

Lassiter bay, at the head of the continuation of the inlet, between Harvell and Mignon points in a westerly direction, forms two small bights, with some islets and rocks in it, but the water is inconveniently deep for anchorage.

Mereworth sound.—At 5 miles eastward of Mignon point, on the northern shore, is the entrance to Mereworth sound, another similar inlet branching off to the northward, in which direction it continues for 4 miles and then suddenly turning to the eastward for 6 miles, maintaining deep water throughout. Flat rock, Square and Round islands, lie on the western shore at the entrance to Mereworth sound, with deep water around.

Strachan bay, at 1½ miles from the entrance to Mereworth sound, on the western shore, is the entrance to a small inlet which takes a westerly direction for 1½ miles and has depths of 40 to 16 fathoms. Village bay, on the opposite shore, abreast Strachan bay, is a small bay with two islets off its northern point, and depths of 19 to 22 fathoms in it. Westerman bay is a small bight 1½ miles long in a northerly direction with from 30 to 20 fathoms water in it, except at its head, where it suddenly shoals to 3½ fathoms at 800 yards from the shore. The entrance to Westerman bay is 2 miles westward of the entrance to Mereworth sound.

Alison sound.—At about 10 miles eastward from the entrance to Mereworth sound, on the northern shore of Belize inlet, is the entrance to Alison sound, another narrow branch which, like Mereworth sound, first takes a northerly direction (for 3 miles) and then suddenly turns eastward for 3 miles, finally turning again to the northward for a further distance of 2 miles, to its head. At about 2 miles from the entrance Alison sound is only about 350 yards wide; here, in the middle of the passage, is a small islet (Obstruction islet) having a passage on either side of it 150 yards wide, with a depth of 10 fathoms in it.

North channel.—There are three channels by which vessels may enter or leave the eastern waters of Queen Charlotte sound: North channel, along the mainland coast, southward of the various islands and rocks already described; Goletas channel, along the northern shore of Vancouver island; and New channel, north of Goletas channel, and separated from North channel by several groups of islands, which will now be described.

Ghost (Round) island, which lies at the eastern end of North channel, 1,200 yards SSW. of the largest Jeannette island, is small and wooded, the trees giving it a rounded appearance; it is 83 feet in height to the tops of the trees. The island forms a good mark, as it always stands out clearly when approaching it from the SE. or NW.

Two rocky heads, drying 2 and 4 feet at low water, lie, respectively, S. 86° E. (N. 68° E. mag.) 300 yards, and N. 49° E. (N. 23° E. mag.) 200 yards, from the summit of the island, and foul ground extends for 600 yards SE. of it, being marked by kelp.

Vessels should give Round island a berth of at least 600 yards.

Millar group.—The Millar group, situated southwestward of Ghost island, consists of a chain of nearly thirty islands and islets of all sizes, varying from 800 yards long to mere rocky islets; they extend in a NW. and SE. direction for nearly 2 miles, and are all wooded, with the exception of the smallest rocks, their heights, to the tops of the trees, varying from 190 feet downward.

David rock, awash at low water, is on the southern end of a small rocky 3-fathom patch and lies 780 yards N. 53° W. (N. 79° W.

mag.) from the western islet of the Millar group; there are soundings of from 12 to 22 fathoms close round the patch. Vessels should not pass between David and Wentworth rocks, as several dangers obstruct the passage.

An isolated rock, which dries 16 feet, lies 680 yards S. 13° E. (S. 39° E. mag.) from Ghost island, between that island and the Millar group.

Vessels should not pass between the Millar group and Ghost island.

A rock, with 13 feet over it, lies 300 yards N. 75° W. (S. 79° W. mag.) from the SW. Millar islet.

Mary rock, a dangerous rock which dries 16 feet at low water springs, is the eastern of two heads of a rocky shoal situated 1,400 yards S. 33° E. (S. 59° E. mag.) from the SE. extreme of the SE. Millar island; the western head dries 3 feet at low water. The shoal is 200 yards long in a SE. and NW. direction, with depths of 17 fathoms close-to; a small patch, the western edge of which is awash at low water, lies 300 yards N. 65° E. (N. 39° E. mag.) from Mary rock.

Vessels passing through the North channel from the southeastward should approach it with Ghost island bearing N. 55° W. (N. 81° W. mag.) and not bring the island to bear northward of that bearing until the SE. end of the Millar group bears West (S. 64° W. mag.), when alter course for mid-channel between Ghost island and Jeannette island.

Wentworth island, a bare, rocky islet 10 feet high, stands in the center of a rocky shoal extending nearly ½ mile in a SE. and NW. direction, and having 3-fathom heads at the extreme ends; this shoal is marked by kelp. Another 3-fathom head, with from 11 to 15 fathoms close round it, lies 1,300 yards S. 41° E. (S. 67° E. mag.) from Wentworth island.

Vessels are advised to give Wentworth island a berth of ½ mile; do not pass between Wentworth island and David rock.

Ripple passage, lying between the Millar and Deserters groups, should not be used by vessels, as it has several dangerous rocks in it, and the tidal streams, which sometimes run with a strength of 4 knots, cause heavy eddies and tide rips in the passage.

Several small rocky islets are scattered in Ripple passage, of which the two Richard islets are the nearest to the Millar group, and lie 1,750 yards W. ¾ S. from the SE. extreme of the SE. island of that group; the islets, small and bare, are 150 yards apart, ESE. and WNW.; the eastern islet is 16 feet in height, the western one 11 feet.

Foul ground, marked by kelp, extends to the SE. of the Richard islets for 700 yards, a rocky head, with 4 feet over it at low water, lying S. 61° E. (S. 87° E. mag.), 500 yards, from the eastern islet.

An isolated rocky head, with 4 fathoms least water over it and deep water close round it, lies 1,200 yards N. 41° W. (N. 67° W. mag.) from the western Richard islet.

Barry island, a bare rock 41 feet high, lies S. 39° E. (S. 65° E. mag.), distant 1 mile, from the eastern Richard islet, and has no dangers near it.

Twin islets are two bare rocks, 10 and 16 feet high, lying close together; from the southeastern and highest, the SE. Richard islet bears N. 68° E. (N. 42° E. mag.), distant 1,400 yards. The islets are steep-to all round, excepting for a 3-fathom rocky ledge extending 400 yards southeastward from the eastern islet.

Echo islands lie about 1,400 yards to the SW. of Barry island. There are four islands, which extend in a chain NW. and SE. for 1,200 yards; they are well wooded and vary from 125 to 208 feet in height to the tops of the trees.

George rock, 1 foot high, lies 500 yards N. 53° W. (N. 79° W. mag.) from the NW. extreme of the NW. Echo island with two rocky heads, drying 5 and 6 feet at low water, lying midway between.

A 3-fathom patch, with deep water all round, lies 300 yards off the SE. Echo island.

Deserters group consists of a number of islands, islets, and rocks, divided by Shelter pass from the Walker group, a similar collection of islands lying farther NW. The largest island is nearly 2 miles long in a NW. and SE. direction, about 700 yards wide, well wooded, and has several summits, the highest, at the NW. end of the island, being 343 feet in height to the tops of the trees. The southeastern extreme of the island is called Castle point, and two wooded islands, 160 and 120 feet high, lie 500 yards north of it.

An island, 1¼ miles long, wooded, and 257 feet high, lies parallel to the large island on its SW. side, being separated by only a very narrow gutter-like passage, only navigable for boats; an Indian village is situated on the northeastern shore of this passage, but is inhabited only during the fishing season.

A number of small islands and rocks of this group extend to the SW. from the last-described island for a distance of about 1,600 yards, to Race island and White rock.

Race island, the western island of the Deserters group, is nearly round in shape, 300 yards in extent, wooded, and 244 feet high to the tops of the trees.

White rock, 14 feet high, lies 550 yards SSE. from the southern end of Race island.

Macleod island, the northern island of the group, is separated from the largest island by a narrow channel about 200 yards broad, which should only be used by boats. The island is about 1,400 yards long in a NW. and SE. direction, and between 400 and 600 yards broad; it is well wooded and 270 feet in height; several small islands extend off its NW. extreme for about 800 yards, and two small wooded islets, 103 and 24 feet high, lie about 300 yards off its NE. point.

Ellinor rock, with 6 feet over it at low water and from 8 to 18 fathoms close round it, is situated with the NW. Twin islet bearing ESE. ¾ E. and distant 2,060 yards.

Shelter pass, between the Deserters and Walker groups, has a clear channel about 400 yards wide on its western side, but it is not recommended.

Walker group.—The Walker group is a similar group of islands, islets, and rocks to the Deserters, and covers an extent of nearly 3 miles in a NW. by N. and SE. by S. direction.

Staples island, the southern island of the group, is about 1¼ miles long in a north and south direction and nearly 1 mile across at its greatest width; it is heavily timbered and has several summits, the highest of which, 303 feet high, is situated above its northern shore. The eastern coast of Staples island, off which are several conspicuous islets, is the western side of Shelter pass. Staples and Kent islands are separated by a very narrow passage, and by a cluster of wooded islands and islets with narrow channels between.

Kent island, which is the NW. island of the Walker group, is over 1½ miles long in a NW. and SE. direction and about ½ mile wide in its center. It is densely wooded and has several summits, the highest being 324 feet high, but none can be recommended for use as marks, the vegetation, in certain lights, quite obscuring their individuality; the rounded summit, 304 feet high, at the NW. end of the island, over Tommy point, sometimes shows up distinctly.

The western coasts of Kent and Staples islands are steep-to and clear of danger.

The eastern shore of Kent island has several rocky patches of 2 and 3 fathoms, all marked by kelp, lying off it at a distance of about 300 yards.

Philcox island is the northernmost island of any size in the Walker group and lies 300 yards to the eastward of the NW. end of Kent island; it is densely wooded and 115 feet in height to the tops of the trees. A chain of small islands stretches to the SE. from Philcox island for a distance of nearly ½ mile, and between these islands and Kent island, and in a small cove in the latter, good protection and anchorage will be found for small craft.

Green islet is a low islet, covered with grass and 18 feet high, situated 500 yards WSW. of Tommy point; it has 3 rocky heads, drying at low water, within 150 yards of its SE. side; with this exception it is steep-to.

Joan islet, 9 feet high, is a bare islet lying 600 yards northward of Tommy point; a small rock close-to on its southern side dries 5 feet at low water.

Ragged rock, 2 feet high, is the highest point of a rocky shoal, 300 yards long, lying N. by W. about 800 yards from Philcox island; the shoal is steep-to on its north and east sides; from the rock, Tommy point bears SW. ¼ W. distant 1,100 yards. A separate rocky head, with 4 feet of water over it at low water, lies 200 yards S. ¼ W. from Ragged rock.

A rock, drying 2 feet at low water, is the highest part of a small shoal lying 560 yards NW. ¼ W. from Tommy point, and 500 yards in a NNW. direction from this latter rock are two separate shoals, each having rocky heads with 4 feet over them at low water.

Schooner passage lies between the Walker group and the Hedley islands and has a navigable breadth of about 800 yards; the best water is obtained by keeping on the eastern side of the passage.

Hedley islands are a cluster of small wooded islands, covering an extent of over 1 mile in a NW. by N. and SE. by S. direction with a maximum breadth of about 800 yards; the tops of the trees on the largest island are 220 feet above high water.

A rock which dries 10 feet at low water is the highest part of a shoal patch 300 yards in extent, lying 700 yards ESE. ¾ E. from the SE. Hedley islet; there are soundings of from 13 to 23 fathoms close round the shoal.

The east and west coasts of the Hedley islands are steep-to and have no offlying dangers.

Malpas rock, drying 3 feet at low water, consists of 2 heads lying 500 yards NW. of the NW. Hedley island. A detached rock, with 4 feet over it at low water, lies 460 yards WNW. ¼ W. from Malpas rock, with depths of from 18 to 20 fathoms close round it.

Redfern island, ¾ mile long east and west, a little over 600 yards in width, wooded, and 264 feet in height, lies SW. of the Hedley group, its NE. shore being 600 yards distant from the SW. island of that group, with 3 small islets lying between. North, 350 yards, from the NW. point of the island are 3 small islets close together, the highest 131 feet in height, and 200 yards from them is Jane rock, 10 feet in height.

Cecil rock, drying 3 feet at low water and marked by kelp, lies 400 yards NW. ½ N. from Jane rock; a rock with 5 feet over it at low water lies 150 yards W. ¾ S. from Cecil rock.

Sussex reefs.—From the southern side of Redfern island a chain of rocks, some above water, extend in an ESE. direction to a distance of 1,600 yards. Barge rock, the southernmost, is 11 feet high and lies 700 yards south from the eastern point of Redfern island, and between them are two other rocks 11 and 6 feet high. ESE. ¾ E., 600 yards, from Barge rock is a rock which dries 4 feet at low water, and a rock which has 5 feet of water over it, and which is the eastern danger of the reef, lies 900 yards SE. by E. ¾ E. from Barge rock.

Buckle group, consisting of Herbert and Bright islands, Prosser rock, and several other islets and rocks, is situated about 2¾ miles northwestward from the Hedley islands with a clear channel between them marked by Prosser rock on its NW. side and Cecil and Malpas rocks on the SE.

Prosser rock is 3 feet high and has a rock, drying 3 feet, 100 yards SE. by E. ¾ E., and a 2-fathom head lying 300 yards E. ¾ N. from it.

Herbert island has some trees on it, and is 108 feet in height to their tops; it has no dangers close to it.

Bright island is nearly bare, only a few small trees being on it; it is 72 feet in height and has a small detached islet close-to on its eastern side; foul ground, marked by kelp, extends 300 yards off its ESE. extreme.

Almost midway between Herbert and Bright islands are three rocky islets, the highest being 15 feet high.

A large shoal about 600 yards long in an east and west direction and having five heads that are uncovered at low water, lies 1,200 yards NW. ¾ W. from Herbert island; there are depths of from 20 to 30 fathoms close round the shoal.

A shoal with 5 fathoms least water over it, lies NNW. ¾ W., distant $1\frac{4}{10}$ miles, from Herbert island.

Storm islands, lying about 4¼ miles SW. of the entrance to Slingsby channel, consist of a chain of islands extending in an ESE. and WNW. direction for 1¾ miles with an average width of ¼ mile; they are wooded and the tops of the trees vary from 160 to 190 feet in height. None of the islands possess any conspicuous marks; the western islet of the group is a bare rock 4 feet high. On the northern side of the second large island from the eastward is an Indian fishing station, consisting of some huts which are only used at certain seasons; good water may be found to the eastward of the huts. Protection can be found here for small boats only. A rock drying 5 feet at low water lies 200 yards to the eastward of the SE. extreme of the group.

Reid and Naiad islets.—About 800 yards to the SE. of the Storm islands are the four Reid islets, the highest islet having some trees on its summit; it is very precipitous and 135 feet high; the eastern islet, 99 feet high, is bare and has a peaked summit. The Naiad islets consist of a cluster of bare rocky islets lying 800 yards northward from the Reid islets; they almost touch each other, and the highest, 49 feet high, is on the western side.

A rocky head, with 12 feet over it, marked by kelp, and with deep water all round, lies SE. by E. $\frac{1}{4}$ E., distant 1,240 yards, from the highest Reid islet.

A shoal with 3 fathoms over it lies 560 yards E. $\frac{3}{4}$ S. from the same islet.

South rock, which dries 4 feet at low water, is a small head with 21 to 24 fathoms close-to, and lies about $1\frac{7}{10}$ miles SE. by E. $\frac{1}{4}$ E. from the highest Reid islet.

Middle rock, drying 6 feet at low water, is the highest part of a 10-fathom shoal and is on its SE. side. The shoal is about 500 yards long in an ESE. and WNW. direction and about 400 yards wide; a 4-fathom head is near its western extreme. From Middle rock the highest Naiad islet bears W. $\frac{3}{4}$ N., distant $1\frac{7}{10}$ miles.

North rock is a small rocky head which dries 13 feet at low water, and has depths of from 6 to 7 fathoms close-to on its northern side; from it the highest Naiad islet bears West (S. 64° W. mag.), distant $2\frac{3}{10}$ miles.

Sealed passage, lying between the Storm islands on the north, and Pine and Tree islands on the south, is about 2 miles in width; until it has been completely surveyed its passage should not be attempted. Blind reef, on which the sea breaks in heavy weather, is reported to extend nearly across Sealed passage and to close it to navigation. No indications of such an extensive reef were seen by H. B. M. S. Egeria during her survey in the vicinity, in 1903; the only danger found was an isolated 2-fathom rocky head, marked by kelp, lying nearly in the center of the passage, from which the highest Reid islet bears NE. $\frac{1}{4}$ N., distant $1\frac{3}{10}$ miles.

Pine island, situated about $3\frac{1}{4}$ miles NW. $\frac{3}{4}$ W. from Bright island, is 1,200 yards long in a NW. and SE. direction and about 700 yards wide; its coasts are nearly everywhere precipitous. The island is wooded, the tops of the trees being 200 feet high; at the western end of the island there is a distinct summit, the tops of the trees being 180 feet above high water.

Tree islands, three and close together, lie about 1,200 yards to the north of Pine island; the two southern islands are wooded, the tops of the trees being 115 feet high, while the northern island has a single tree only on it, the land being 50 feet high.

A 2-fathom rock, marked by kelp, lies 560 yards south from the northern Tree island.

Vessels should not pass between Pine island and the Tree islands until the channel has been examined.

Sunken rock, drying 3 feet at low water, is an isolated head with 22 fathoms close-to, and lies nearly midway between the Buckle group and the Tree islands; from it Bright island bears SE. by S., distant a little more than $1\frac{3}{8}$ miles.

General remarks.—North channel may be described as extending from seaward into Queen Charlotte sound, past Bremner island, to the passage between the Jeannette islands and the Millar group; passing on its way between White and Mayor islands on the NE., and North rock on the SW., then southwestward of Rogers, Dickenson, and Harris islands, and thence to the eastward of Wentworth island.

There is usually a westerly swell rolling in from seaward which immediately after a SE. blow of any strength is considerably increased; this swell is broken on reaching the islands between the Millar and Gordon groups, and is not felt to the eastward of those islands.

The density of the vegetation in this vicinity renders it difficult to distinguish ranges of hills and their summits, which, even when familiar objects, can not be always clearly recognized.

Directions.—Entering from seaward, after passing Bremner island, enter North channel about midway between the Storm islands and Dalkeith point, and bring the wooded Mayor island on a S. 80° E. (N. 74° E. mag.) bearing; proceed on this course until White island bears N. 16° E. (N. 10° W. mag.), when alter course to S. 38° E. (S. 64° E. mag.), and steer on this line, passing North rock at ½ mile, and Dickenson island at about 800 yards; when Harris island is abeam, distant ½ mile, alter course to S. 57° E. (S. 83° E. mag.), passing the dangers off Simpson rock at a distance of 750 yards; and when Wentworth island is abeam, distant ½ mile, steer S. 48° E. (S. 74° E. mag.), which course will lead between the Jeannette and Ghost islands into the clear water of the eastern part of the sound.

Jeannette island just open eastward of Harris island, bearing S. 48° E. (S. 74° E. mag.), leads nearly ½ mile eastward of North rock.

Vessels passing through North channel from the southeastward should approach it with Ghost island bearing N. 55° W. (N. 81° W. mag.) and not bring the island to bear northward of that bearing until the eastern end of the Millar group bears West (S. 64° W. mag.), when alter course for mid-channel between Round island and Jeannette island.

The tidal streams reach a velocity of 2 to 5 knots in that portion of the channel between Jeannette and Millar groups.

Goletas channel, which runs along the northern shore of Vancouver island, is 22 miles long ESE. and WNW., with a breadth varying from 1 to 2½ miles. Its shores are high, rugged, and steep-to, except in the western part, and may be generally approached to about ¼ mile; the northern side is composed of a chain of islands, lying parallel to the shore of Vancouver island, the principal of which are Nigei and Hope islands; between the islands are several navigable passages.

There are four anchorages in the channel, viz, Shushartie bay on the southern side; Port Alexander, Shadwell passage, and Bull harbor on the northern side; and all, with the exception of the latter, are accessible to sailing vessels.

Duval point, on the southern side at the eastern entrance of the channel is 15 miles west of Broughton strait.

Navigable depths.—The depths throughout the channel to the western entrance are deep, varying from 190 to 80 fathoms, but there the bottom suddenly rises from 40 to 7 and 9, and in one part to less than 3 fathoms, forming Nahwhitti bar, stretching completely across the channel, and in a great measure preventing any heavy sea rising inside it during westerly gales.

Tides and tidal streams.—It is high water, full and change, in the Goletas channel at 0 h. 0 m., and the rise and fall varies from 12 to 14 feet. The tidal streams in the eastern part of the channel run from 1 to 3 knots, but near the western entrance, in the vicinity of the Nahwhitti bar, they are much stronger (2 to 5½ knots), turning shortly after high and low water by the shore.

Shushartie bay.—From Duval point the southern shore of Goletas channel trends westward 15 miles to Shushartie bay. This bay is about ½ mile in extent, and its shores are high, except at the head, from which a sand bank extends more than 400 yards. Halstead islet, a small bare rock, lies close off the east point of the bay. There is a very limited but fairly sheltered anchorage just inside the NE. point of the bay, in about 13 fathoms, 200 yards offshore, but from the steepness of the bank it should only be considered as a stopping place.

Dillon rock, which uncovers 10 feet at low water, lies 300 yards WNW. from Halstead islet, and is in the way of vessels entering from the eastward.

Directions.—If entering Shushartie bay from the eastward, and Dillon rock be covered, do not steer in for the anchorage till the easternmost peak of the Shushartie saddle (a remarkable double-topped mountain, 1,900 feet high, situated south of the bay), is seen in the center of the bay bearing S. 15° W. (S. 10° E. mag.), when proceed in with that mark on, which leads westward of Dillon rock; when the NE. point of the bay bears S. 83° E. (N. 72° E. mag.), the vessel will be south of it, and should steer for the eastern shore.

Entering from the westward keep the western shore aboard till Halstead island bears S. 83° E. (N. 72° E. mag.), when steer in as before directed.

Anchor immediately 14 fathoms is obtained, as the bank is steep, with the extremes of the bay bearing N. 70° E. (N. 45° E. mag.) and N. 31° W. (N. 56° W. mag.).

Shingle point, 2 miles west of Shushartie bay, is low; a beach runs off it a short distance; westward of this point it is difficult to land, except in fair weather.

Cape Commerell, 22 miles west of Duval point, is the northernmost point of Vancouver island, and the southern point of the western entrance to Goletas channel. The cape is low and some rocks extend off it for nearly 400 yards; eastward of it the coast forms a large bay 3 miles wide and about 1 mile deep, with from 2½ to 6 fathoms, rocky bottom, and not in any way adapted for anchoring. The shoal part of Nahwhitti bar, on which there is as little as 1¾ fathoms, extends northwestward from the eastern point of this bay; it is marked by kelp and named Tatnall reefs. Weser islet, 25 feet high, lies in the western part of the bay, distant ¼ mile from the shore.

Gordon group consists of a number of small islands extending in an ESE. and WNW. direction for 5 miles, and bordering the northern part of the eastern entrance of Goletas channel. They are high, wooded, and, in general, steep-to. Their eastern extreme is 2 miles NNE. of Duval point.

Doyle island, the eastern island of the group, is 430 feet in height to the tops of the trees, and has several small islets and rocks extending off its eastern end, the most eastern of which is a rock, which dries 8 feet at low water and which lies 750 yards SE. from the SE. side of Doyle island. Miles cone, the southwestern summit of the island, is a remarkable conical hill 380 feet high.

Heard island, about ½ mile in extent and 397 feet high to the tops of trees, is 1½ miles NW. from Doyle island, with a chain of several islets between. NE. by N., 300 yards, from the eastern point of the island is a rock with less than 6 feet of water over it at low water.

Bell island, the next island westward of Heard island, is 1⅓ miles long east and west, from 400 to 1,000 yards wide, and 386 feet in height toward its western end; three small islands lie close off its SE. side, and 600 yards off the northern side are the Crane islets. The eastern end of Bell island is 350 yards distant from the western side of Heard island, the channel between being choked by rocks, but between the eastern side of the islands lying SE. of Bell island and the western side of Heard island is a deep channel, 200 yards in width, leading to a secure but limited anchorage for small vessels in from 12 to 15 fathoms, mud bottom, inside the islands.

Hurst island, the western island of the group, is irregular in shape, 1¾ miles long ESE. and WNW., and rises to a height of 562 feet in Meeson cone, a well-defined conical hill near its center; it is only separated from Bell island by a narrow pass little more than 100 yards wide. Off the NE. part of the island several rocky islets and rocks extend to a distance of 800 yards, between which is the entrance to a good boat harbor on the northern side of the island. Boyle island lies ½ mile NE. from the NE. point of the island.

Duncan island, 1 mile south of the Gordon group, with Blyth island about 400 yards off its western side, is about 1 mile in circumference and 300 feet high.

Noble islets, the eastern one covered with coarse herbage and about 40 feet high, the western with a few stunted bushes and about 68 feet in height, lie 1½ miles WNW. from Duncan island, between which and the group it is not advisable for a large vessel to go.

Blyth islet, 20 feet high, lies 300 yards west of Blyth island; and Mouatt rock, with 6 feet over it, lies 500 yards north of Blyth islet.

Balaklava island, 2½ miles long NNW. and SSE., and from ½ mile to 1 mile wide, and with three peaks, lies between the Gordon group and Nigei island, forming Christie and Browning passages. Close off the southern side of the island are several small islands, the Lucan islands, 200 yards south from the southeastern of which are two rocks, 6 and 7 feet high, close together and joined at low water; 300 yards south from Nolan point, the southern point of the island, are two rocks which dry 8 and 4 feet at low water. The northern side of the island is fringed with rocky ledges which, off Raglan point, the NW. point of the island, extend 500 yards. A rock, which dries 3 feet at low water, lies 400 yards off the middle of the northern side of the island.

Light.—On Scarlett point, Balaklava island, is exhibited a fixed red light, elevated 90 feet above high water and visible in clear weather from a distance of 10 miles. The light is shown from a white lantern, 37 feet above the ground, surmounting the red roof of a rectangular wooden structure, painted white.

A hand fog horn will be used to answer signals from vessels during thick or foggy weather.

Cardigan rocks, 4 to 12 feet high, lie ½ mile NNW. from Raglan point, with Croker rock, drying 2 feet, 300 yards ENE. from them.

George rock, with less than 6 feet of water over it, lies 400 yards off the eastern side of Balaklava island and 1,250 yards southward of Scarlett point, its NE. point.

Christie passage, between Hurst island and Balaklava island, is a clear and deep channel ½ mile wide, the only dangers being George rock, already described, on the western side of the channel, and a rock, awash at low water, lying 150 yards from the NW. point of Hurst island. The tidal streams run from 1 to 3 knots through it, the flood to the southward.

If intending to go through this passage from Goletas channel, a large vessel should enter it westward of the Noble islets.

Browning passage, west of Balaklava island, between it and Nigei island, runs in a NNW. direction. Its length is about 3 miles, its breadth in the narrowest part 400 yards, and a rock, which covers at three-quarters flood, lies on the western side of the channel about 150 yards from Nigei island. A reef and foul ground, marked by kelp, extends 300 yards from Balaklava island just opposite the above-mentioned rock, and this is the narrowest part of the channel, which is deep. The tidal streams are weak in this channel.

Nigei island, the largest of the islands on the northern side of Goletas channel, is nearly 8 miles long and 3½ miles broad. Mount Lemon, a remarkable peak of conical shape, 1,265 feet high, rises near its SW. part, and Magin saddle, consisting of two peaks, 700 and 800 feet high, is situated at less than 1 mile from the western extreme of the island.

The southern side of Nigei island is high, steep-to, and cliffy; at 4½ miles west from Boxer point is a small cove which would afford shelter to small craft from westerly winds.

Willes island, 208 feet high, lies close off the western extreme of the island with a narrow boat channel between; 400 yards SSE. from it is a small, low islet, named Slave island.

Port Alexander, on the western side of Browning channel, in Nigei island, trends NNW. for 1½ miles, with a general breadth of fair wind, and affords good anchorage in 12 to 13 fathoms at ½ mile from the entrance, and another close off Boxer point on the western side of the entrance.

This port is easy of access to steamers and sailing vessels with a fair wind, and affords good anchorage in 12 to 13 fathoms at ½ mile from its head, well sheltered from all except southeasterly winds.

Bate passage, between Nigei island on the SE. and Hope and Vansittart islands on the NW., is a straight, clear channel ½ mile wide, and can be safely used by any vessel. Entering from the northward it can be easily recognized by mount Lemon showing prominently over the entrance on a S. by W. bearing.

Vansittart island, situated ½ mile from the NW. shore of Nigei island, at the northern end of Bate passage and separating it from Shadwell passage, is 1 mile long and ¾ mile wide, wooded, and 260 feet high; NW. of it are some rocks and small islets extending 1,200 yards off it; and ½ mile from the northern point are two wooded islets 70 feet high, named Nicolas islands. A sunken rock lies 450 yards NW. of the northern Nicolas island.

Shadwell passage, between Vansittart and Hope islands, is about 1½ miles long in a northerly direction and leads out of Bate passage; there is generally a heavy swell in the northern part and the tidal streams are strong.

A vessel may anchor from 400 to 600 yards NNW. of Center island, sheltered from all except northerly winds, if occasion require. The channel is not recommended.

Center island, small and 20 feet high, lies at the southern end of the passage toward mid-channel but nearer the western shore; the passage is eastward of it. Suwanee rock, drying 4 feet at low water, lies 200 yards W. by N. of the island.

One Tree islet, 800 yards west of Vansittart island, is small, about 40 feet high, and has a single tree on its summit, which is very conspicuous when seen from the northward; between it and Vansittart island are rocks and foul ground. Breaker reef, the outer of the dangers extending NW. from Vansittart island, lies ¾ mile N. ½ E. from One Tree islet.

Cape James, the NW. extreme of Shadwell passage and NE. point of Hope island, is a rocky bluff 90 feet high; some rocks extend off it to the southward for a short distance. The cape should at all times be given a berth of at least ½ mile.

Tidal streams.—The flood stream runs to the southward through Shadwell passage at the rate of about 4½ knots, while the ebb, in the northern part, sets 2 knots in the contrary direction; southward of Center island, however, it runs as strong as the flood. Tide rips exist between Center and Vansittart islands.

Hope island, the westernmost of the group which forms the northern side of Goletas channel, is 6 miles long, east and west, and its greatest breadth is 3¾ miles; the sea breaks heavily along its northern and western sides. From Mexicana point, the western extreme of the island, a reef, drying at low water, extends to the westward for nearly 600 yards. From the SW. point of the island, 1,200 yards southeastward from Mexicana point, foul ground extends to the WSW. for 800 yards, a rock, drying 4 feet at low water, lying 666 yards west from the point. In a small bay at the eastern end of the island, guarded by Village island, 190 feet high, is the Indian village of Nahwhitti.

Bull harbor, on the southern side of Hope island, is 2 miles from the western entrance of Goletas channel at Nahwhitti bar, and though small, affords a secure and landlocked anchorage for small vessels.

The entrance to the harbor is between two high and steep, cliffy bluffs, that on the eastern side being the highest, where the cliff rises almost perpendicularly to a height of 130 feet, with deep water close into its base. Just within the entrance is Indian island, of small extent, wooded, and 145 feet high to the tops of the trees; the channel up the harbor is to the eastward of it. Beyond the island the harbor opens out to 300 yards in width, and affords secure but limited anchorage in 4 fathoms, mud and sand. A flat of mud and sand dries out from the head of the harbor for a distance of 800 yards.

Tides.—It is high water, full and change, at about 0 h. 0 m.; springs rise 14 feet.

Directions.—To enter, steer in mid-channel between the bluffs, pass eastward of Indian island in mid-channel, and anchor north of it as convenient.

Nahwhitti bar.—The 20-fathom curve to seaward lies 6 miles westward from the western end of Hope island, and thence the water shoals very gradually eastward to 6 and 7 fathoms between the western end of Hope island and the mainland of Vancouver island, and is there called Nahwhitti bar; it then deepens again very suddenly to 40 fathoms. The bar is composed of rock overlaid with sand and gravel.

One mile south of the southern coast of Hope island the bar is 1¼ miles wide between the 10-fathom curves with from 6½ to 7 fathoms least water. Southward of this and toward the Vancouver island shore the area between the 10-fathom curves widens considerably, and there are several shoal spots.

Tatnall reefs, lying on the southern part of Nahwhitti bar and extending 1¾ miles from the south shore, consist of a group of several shoal patches of 2½ and 3 fathoms of water, with one head of 1¾ fathoms, occupying a considerable area within the 5-fathom curve. The outer head, of 3 fathoms least water, lies 1¼ miles N. 59° E. (N. 34° E. mag.) from Weser islet.

Tidal streams.—The tidal streams set fairly in and out over the bar in the direction of Goletas channel, and run with a velocity of from 2 to 5½ knots, turning at high and low water by the shore.

There is nearly always a swell on the bar, and in bad weather, with a strong ebb stream and westerly winds, there is a very heavy and breaking sea on it, dangerous to small vessels. In heavy westerly gales the sea breaks right across the bar, and it is dangerous to attempt it.

Directions.—The only conspicuous and remarkable object in the neighborhood is mount Lemon, on Nigei island, a high, conical, and wooded peak 1,265 feet in height. Coming from the westward, approach the bar with mount Lemon showing nearly midway between Hope island and the Vancouver island shore, but a little nearer to Hope island; this will lead 1½ miles north of cape Commerell. Steer in over the bar, midway between Tatnall reefs and Hope island, bringing mount Lemon nothing to the south of midway between Hope island and Shingle point, the northern point of Vancouver island. If mount Lemon is obscured, the points of land on the southern side of Goletas channel (Shingle point and the point

1 mile eastward of it) must be kept open of one another, which will lead well north of Tatnall reefs.

For the remainder of Goletas channel no directions are required; it is a deep and perfectly clear channel, and a mid-channel course is all that is necessary.

If obliged to anchor for the night, or tide, Shushartie bay, though small, is easy of access, the only danger being Dillon rock off its eastern point. Port Alexander, at the eastern end of Nigei island, is also, with a fair wind, easy of access to sailing vessels.

New channel, northward of Goletas channel, and between Nigei island and the Gordon group on the south, and the Deserters, Walker, and Buckle groups on the north, is about 12 miles long, and has a breadth varying from 1¼ to 3 miles.

The waters of the channel are in general very deep, though in the eastern part of the channel are several rocks which must be guarded against.

Crane islets, three small bare islets, the southwestern islet being the largest and 34 feet high, lie on the southern side of the channel 600 yards off the northern side of Bell island.

A rock with 2¾ fathoms least water over it lies 300 yards N. by E. from the SW. Crane islet.

Boyle island, a narrow crescent-shaped island, 400 yards long ENE. and WSW., and 135 feet high to the tops of the trees, lies ¼ mile NE. of Hurst island. The NW. side of the island is a cliff, from which it slopes evenly to the SE.

Grey rock.—Foul ground extends for ½ mile in a NW. direction from Boyle island, with several patches of rock which dry at low water. Grey rock, the NW. danger, dries 14 feet at low water, and lies 900 yards NW. by N. from the SW. point of Boyle island. The Crane islets just touching the northern side of the Gordon group, S. 45° E. (S. 70° E. mag.), leads nearly ½ mile north of it.

Davey rock, on the northern side of the channel, is a dangerous pinnacle rock with 4¾ fathoms over it and from 20 to 40 fathoms close round it, lying 1,100 yards S. 55° W. (S. 30° W. mag.) from White rock; no kelp grows on this rock. An isolated 8-fathom patch lies 500 yards SSW. from Davey rock.

Alexander rock, awash at low water, is the head of a rocky patch 300 yards in extent NNW. and SSE. and lies 1,850 yards N. 84° W. (S. 71° W. mag.) from Race island.

In line between Davey and Alexander rocks and 900 yards from the former, is Roach rock with 5½ fathoms least water over it; it is the western end of a rocky patch 266 yards in extent, within the 10-fathom curve.

Nye rock consists of 3 rocky heads which dry 13 feet at low water, and are in the center of a rocky patch of less than 5 fathoms of water, 400 yards in extent ESE. and WNW.; it lies 2¼ miles N. 60° W. (N. 85° W. mag.) from White rock, and in a line between Alexander rock and the eastern end of Redfern island. There is a deep-water channel between Nye and Alexander rocks into Schooner passage, but a vessel should not go between Nye rock and the eastern end of Sussex reefs.

Directions.—The only directions required for New channel is to keep a mid-channel course, passing not more than ½ mile northward of the Crane islets to keep well clear of Davey rock.

The coast from cape Commerell, the northern point of Vancouver island, takes a WSW. direction for 16 miles, to cape Scott. It is rather low, but rises at a distance inland to hills 800 and 1,000 feet high; it is indented by several bays, which, however, are too open to afford any shelter, except from southerly winds; foul ground extends off in some places more than 1 mile.

Hecate rock, lying 1⅜ miles west from cape Commerell, and ½ mile offshore, dries 12 feet at low water and the sea breaks heavily over it. Lemon point (Nigei island) just open of or touching Shingle point (Vancouver island), bearing S. 77° E. (N. 78° E. mag.), leads 1 mile northward of it.

Cape Scott, the extreme NW. point of Vancouver island, is a small promontory about 500 feet high, connected to the island by a low sandy neck about 200 yards wide; some rocks extend west from it for more than ½ mile.

There is a bay on both sides of the neck, which would afford anchorage to boats or small craft, but in fine weather only; close to its SW. extreme is a small creek among the rocks, difficult of access, but, once within it, boats may get shelter in southerly gales; unless acquainted with the locality, it would, however, be hardly prudent to venture it in bad weather.

Caution.—When navigating between cape Commerell and cape Scott, do not approach the shore within 1½ miles.

Tidal streams.— At cape Scott the flood stream comes from the southward, and rounding the cape sets into Goletas channel, its strength varying from 1 to 3 knots.

Scott channel, between cape Scott and Cox island, is 5¼ miles wide. It is a safe navigable channel for any class of vessel, the only known dangers in it being the rocks extending nearly 1 mile west from cape Scott. There are some heavy tide rips near its east and west sides, but a large vessel may beat through with safety, tacking when upward of 1 mile from cape Scott, or ½ mile from Cox island.

Scott islands, five in number, with some adjacent smaller islets, extend nearly 25 miles west from cape Scott. There are wide passages between the western islands, but as no soundings have been obtained in them, and strong tide rips and overfalls have invariably been observed there, a vessel should not pass through them unless compelled to do so.

Cox island, 1,047 feet high, the easternmost and largest of the group, is about 2½ miles in extent, with iron-bound rocky shores and several offlying dangers.

Lanz island, separted from Cox island by a passage ¼ mile wide, is upward of 2 miles long and 1 mile broad; its shores, like those of Cox island, are rocky, and it rises near the center 1,177 feet above the sea; both the islands are wooded.

Good anchorage, during winds from SE. to SW., may be had on the NW. side of Cox island, in from 8 to 12 fathoms, about ¼ mile from the beach; also, off the NE. side of Lanz island, in about 10 fathoms, and at the same distance from the shore.

East Haycock, a small islet 80 feet high, is 2½ miles WSW. from Lanz island; it is covered with a few stunted trees. Some small islets extend a short distance north of it. West Haycock, 5 miles WNW. from East Haycock, is small and rocky, about 180 feet high. Some small islets extend upward of 1 mile west of it, foul ground existing around them for ½ mile.

Triangle island, the westernmost of the group, 25 miles W. by N. from cape Scott, is 680 feet high, about 1 mile in extent, and differs from the other islands in being very precipitous and bare of trees, and has a remarkable gap in its summit; a ledge or reef extends 1 mile northward of it, and 1¼ miles eastward of it are two rocky islets 20 and 40 feet high.

In the bight on the eastern side of the island, fair anchorage, during southerly winds, can be obtained in 13 fathoms, at about 600 yards from the head of the bight.

Caution.—When navigating near Scott islands, it is recommended to give them a good offing, especially in a sailing vessel, as the tidal streams set very strongly through the passages between them.

CHAPTER VIII.

WEST COAST OF VANCOUVER ISLAND, FROM THE STRAIT OF JUAN DE FUCA TO CAPE SCOTT.

VARIATION IN 1906.

Cape Beale ....24° 00′ E.	Cape Cook ....25° 00′ E.

General description.—The outer or western coast of Vancouver island is comprised between Bonilla point, at the entrance of Juan de Fuca strait, and cape Scott, the NW. extreme of the island, a distance of upward of 200 miles. Its general direction is NW. and SE., but the coast is broken into deep inlets, the principal of which are Barkley, Clayoquot, Nootka, Kyuquot, and Quatsino sounds.

The coast is mostly low and rocky, but rises immediately to mountains of considerable height. It is fringed by numerous rocks and hidden dangers, especially near the entrances of the sounds, and the exercise of great caution and vigilance will be necessary on the part of the navigator to avoid them, even with the best charts.

Caution.—On no occasion, therefore, except where otherwise stated in the following pages, should a stranger attempt to enter any of the harbors or anchorages during night or thick weather, but rather keep a good offing until circumstances are favorable; and when about to make the coast, it can not be too strongly impressed on the mariner to take every opportunity of ascertaining his vessel's position by astronomical observations, as fogs and thick weather come on very suddenly at all times of the year, more especially in summer and autumn months. The use of the lead is strictly enjoined.

Tides and tidal streams.—All along the outer or western coast of Vancouver island it may be said to be high water at full and change when the moon crosses the meridian, viz., at midnight and noon, the tide showing considerable regularity as compared with the inner waters, the greatest rise and fall being everywhere about 12 feet.

The flood stream appears to set along the coast to the NW., and the ebb to the SE., except near the entrance to Juan de Fuca strait and for some distance westward of it; neither are of great strength, except in the vicinity of Scott islands.

Soundings.—At the entrance of Fuca strait the 100-fathom curve extends 40 miles offshore; it then runs in nearly a straight direction, gradually nearing the coast, and abreast cape Cook or

Woody point the depth of 100 fathoms will be obtained within 4 miles of the shore; to the NW. of Woody point the 100-fathom curve does not extend more than 10 miles offshore, and to the southward and westward of the Scott islands even less.

The bottom, when under 100 fathoms, appears to be generally composed of sand and gravel, and does not differ in one part from another sufficiently to afford any guide for ascertaining a vessel's exact position on the coast; the bank, however, extends far enough offshore to the SE. of cape Cook to enable the mariner making the coast in thick weather, by sounding in time, to get due notice of his approach to the land, as the curve of 100 fathoms does not come within 18 miles of it, and the bank shoals very gradually.

Climate and winds.—The seasons, wet and dry, generally take the following course: After the gales with rain, which usually occur about the time of the equinox, fine clear weather sets in, and continues until about the middle of November. At this period rain begins to fall continuously for days, and gales of wind are frequent on the coast.

The barometer ranges from 29.50 to 30.10 and falls rapidly on the approach of a southerly gale. Rising gradually to 30.20 and 30.50, a northerly wind springs up, and three days of fine clear weather with hoarfrost generally follow. After the third day the barometer slowly falls, and again the gale with rain springs up, to be succeeded after a few days by a rising barometer and frosty weather, which, as the season advances, occasionally becomes intense, and is accompanied by hail and snow; the latter seldom lasts for any length of time. The summer is dry, with a most scorching sun. Little or no rain falls from the middle of April until the equinox. The prevailing winds during these summer months are from SW. to NW., blowing freshly during the day; the nights are calm and clear. Northerly winds occasionally prevail, and in the southern parts of the island are hot and dry.

Natives.—The west coast of the island is very thinly populated, the highest estimate of the natives not exceeding 4,000, divided into a number of very small tribes. As a rule they are harmless and inoffensive, though in a few cases the crews of vessels wrecked on their coasts have been plundered and ill treated. They are addicted to pilfering, especially in the vicinity of Nootka sound, and ought to be carefully watched.

The tribes speak different dialects, and the Chinook jargon, which is used at Victoria in transactions with the settlers and natives, will not be generally understood on the west coast.

Supplies.—The natives live principally on fish, potatoes, and berries. Salmon, halibut, rock cod, herring, and hoolican, the latter somewhat resembling a sardine, are found in great abundance.

Telephonic communication has been established between Victoria, Vancouver island, and the following stations on the northern side of Juan de Fuca strait: Port San Juan, at the mouth of Gordon river; Carmanah lighthouse; and Cape Beale lighthouse.

Messages will be transmitted from the stations at fixed tariff rates.

The coast from Port San Juan trends 10 miles in a westerly direction to Bonilla point, rising gradually to elevations from 1,000 to 2,000 feet. Bonilla point, the northern entrance point of Juan de Fuca strait, is 12 miles north from cape Flattery; the point slopes gradually to the sea, and a reef extends ½ mile from it. This point should be given a berth of not less than 1½ miles; a conspicuous house stands ½ mile eastward.

Carmanah light is a flashing white light every minute, showing 3 flashes with intervals of 15 seconds between their points of greatest brilliancy, followed by an interval of 30 seconds, during the greater part of which the light is eclipsed. It is elevated 173 feet above high water, and should be visible in clear weather from a distance of 19 miles.

The lighthouse, 46 feet high, is a wooden structure, and, with the dwelling attached, is painted white, lantern red.

Fog signal is a horn, worked by steam and compressed air, giving 1 blast of 6 seconds' duration every 30 seconds.

The fog-signal station, constructed of wood, and painted white, with red roof, is situated immediately in front of, and a little below, the lighthouse. It faces S. ½ W.; the horns (which are in duplicate) are 125 feet above high water.

A signal station in addition to the fog horn, for the purpose of enabling passing steam vessels to communicate during fogs, is established at Carmanah lighthouse. This signal consists of a steam whistle, and passing vessels may communicate by whistle sounds, using the Morse or Continental telegraphic codes.

The signal and rescue station at Carmanah lighthouse, with which vessels may communicate by means of the International code of signals, is under the following rules and regulations:

Vessels exhibiting their distinctive numbers will have their names transmitted to Victoria, for publication only, free of charge.

Dispatches to or from vessels within signaling distance, by flags of the International code, will be duly delivered as addressed, at tariff rates.

Dispatches will be charged for at the regular telephone rates, but no charge will be made for signaling between the flag station and vessels at sea.

Dispatches may be delivered in cipher, by special request, otherwise they will be transmitted in ordinary language.

A depot of provisions and other necessaries for shipwrecked persons is maintained at the lighthouse.

Nitinat lake, the entrance to which is narrow and shoal, is 7 miles westward of Bonilla point. The lake is of considerable size extending to the northward. There are 1 to 2 fathoms in the entrance, and the sea generally breaks heavily across it in bad weather.

Four miles to the westward of the entrance is a remarkable waterfall, called by the natives Tsusiat, which may be seen at a good distance, even in thick weather, when it would help to identify a vessel's position, being the only waterfall on this part of the coast.

Clo-oose.—In the small cove lying between the outlet of the lake and the mouth of Chuckwear river is the village and Methodist mission of Clo-oose. The village is connected with the Government telegraph line to Victoria and by telephone wth Carmanah lighthouse. Shipwrecked mariners may obtain shelter and assistance here.

A reef, ¾ mile long NW. and SE., with a rock 4 feet high in its center, lies ¾ mile south of the outlet of Chuckwear river.

Light.—A lighthouse and fog-alarm station is in process of construction on Pachena (Beeghadoss) point, about 6 miles SE. of cape Beale.

Pending the completion of the station, a fixed white light, 100 feet above the sea, and visible 6 miles, will be shown at the station.

Pachena bay, 20 miles westward of Bonilla point, is nearly 2 miles deep in a northerly direction and ½ mile wide, with from 5 to 6 fathoms of water, but as it is open to the southward, and there is usually a heavy swell setting into it, no vessel should anchor there. At its head, on the west side, is a stream where boats can get in and find shelter in bad weather.

Seabird islet, off the entrance of the bay, is bare, about 10 feet above water, and of small extent. The two rocks off the islet lie S. 48° E. (S. 72° E. mag.) nearly ½ mile, and S. 39° W. (S. 15° W. mag.) ½ mile. The latter is awash at high water. There is no safe passage inshore of Seabird islet, and it should not be approached within 1½ miles.

Barkley sound, an extensive arm of the sea, 30 miles westward of the entrance of Juan de Fuca strait, is upward of 14 miles wide at its entrance, and though encumbered by numerous islands it maintains this breadth for nearly 12 miles inland, when it separates into several narrow islets or canals, the principal of which, the Alberni canal, extends 23 miles in a northerly direction, its head reaching within 14 miles of the eastern or inner coast of Vancouver island. Off the entrance, and in the southern parts of the sound, are innumerable rocks and islands, with several navigable channels between them, which, however, ought to be used with great caution by a stranger. The shores are low, except in the northern part and among the canals, where they become high, rugged, and mountainous.

Cape Beale, the SE. entrance point of Barkley sound and of the Eastern channel, is 30 miles NW. ⅜ N. from Cape Flattery lighthouse on Tatoosh island. It is a bold rocky point 120 feet high (the tops of the trees being 300 feet above high water) and some rocks extend off it from 400 to 800 yards.

Rescue station.—The lighthouse is in telegraphic communication with the lighthouses at Carmanah, San Juan, and Victoria; it is also a rescue station for shipwrecked persons.

Light.—Situated on a small islet at the extremity of cape Beale is a square lighthouse, painted white with red lantern, 42 feet in height, from which is exhibited, at an elevation of 178 feet above the sea, a revolving white light every 30 seconds, and should be visible in clear weather 19 miles. A red sector is shown over Channel and Western reefs, between the bearings S. 66° E. (East mag.) and S. 2° W. (S. 22° E. mag.).

Caution.—The light should not be brought to bear southward of S. 72° E. (N. 84° E. mag.), to avoid the foul ground which extends off the entrances to Barkley sound.

Tides.—It is high water, full and change, in Barkley sound at 0 h. 0 m., and the rise and fall is about 12 feet.

Eastern channel of Barkley sound is 12 miles long in a NE. direction, and its breadth varies from 1 to 1½ miles. Its shores are low and rugged, except in the northern part, where they become high. There are several dangers within it, viz., the rocks off cape Beale, Channel rocks at the southern part, and Fog rock off the eastern side of Tzaartoos island.

Bamfield creek.—At 4 miles from cape Beale, on the east side of Eastern channel, is the entrance to two creeks, the southern of which extends 1¼ miles in a southerly direction, with a breadth of from 200 to 400 yards; there is room for a vessel to moor at a short distance from its head in 6 fathoms. A narrow passage, 30 yards wide, with 6 feet at low water, runs from the head to an inner basin, which is 1 mile long, and has from 2 to 4 fathoms.

On the western side of the creek, 600 yards north of Burlo island, a narrow ledge of rock, with 3 to 4 feet over it, projects nearly into the middle of the passage. The track or trail leading to Cape Beale lighthouse begins on the western side of the head of the inner basin, and is shown by a board nailed to the trunk of a large tree and marked TO CAPE BEALE LIGHTHOUSE.

Grappler creek, the northern arm, extends ¾ mile southeastward from the entrance of Bamfield creek, being about 40 yards wide, with from 8 to 10 fathoms, after which it takes a northerly direction for 1 mile and becomes very shoal. Both these creeks afford good sheltered anchorage to small craft.

Telegraph.—The Pacific cable from Fanning island lands at Bamfield creek, with communication thence by cable to Alberni.

A large building of the Pacific Cable board stands on the point separating Bamfield and Grappler creeks. Vessels are warned not to anchor near the cable.

Kelp bay, 5¾ miles from cape Beale, is ⅜ mile wide, ¼ mile deep, and affords a fairly well sheltered anchorage in from 6 to 14 fathoms. Its shores are low, and a rock which covers at one-third flood lies 200 yards NE. of its southern entrance point, and there is a small islet at its northern point which shows a conspicuous white mark; foul ground, marked by kelp, exists in the northern part of the bay.

If intending to anchor in this bay, give the entrance points a berth of 400 yards and anchor in its southern part in 6 or 14 fathoms, with the entrance points bearing W. by S. and NE. by N. This anchorage is easy of access, but the bottom is irregular.

Mark islet, 8 miles from cape Beale, and 200 yards off the eastern side of the channel, is small, wooded, and conspicuous from the entrance of Middle channel; the shore between it and Kelp bay is nearly straight and may be approached to a distance of 400 yards.

Numukamis bay, 9 miles from cape Beale, at the NE. part of Eastern channel, is 3 miles wide and 1½ miles deep; its shores rise gradually to mountains from 1,000 to 2,000 feet high. From the center of its head Sarita valley extends eastward, a stream of considerable size flowing from it into the bay. In the center of the bay are San José and Reef islets, of small extent and low; from the SW. side of the latter islets a reef extends 200 yards.

There is no anchorage except in Christie bay, in its SE. corner, where there are from 10 to 6 fathoms at a distance of 300 yards from the shore. The shores of Numukamis bay are steep-to, except off Sarita valley, where a sand bank extends ½ mile.

Poett nook, in the southern part of Numukamis bay, about 1 mile within its SW. point, is a landlocked basin, about 600 yards long and 400 yards wide, with 7 fathoms of water. The entrance to it is nearly straight, 200 yards long, and 150 feet wide, with 7 fathoms in the shoalest part.

A small ledge extends a short distance off the western point of entrance.

Turn island, at the NE. point of the Eastern channel, and dividing it from the Alberni canal, is small and wooded, and separated by a narrow boat pass from the eastern shore. One-third of a mile south of it is a narrow creek, 600 yards long and 100 yards wide, with from 9 to 12 fathoms, available for small craft.

Deer islands, which form the western side of Eastern channel, extend NE. and SW. for 10 miles, with a breadth varying from 1 to 2 miles. They are low, and of inconsiderable size, except the northern (Tzaartoos island), which is 1,026 feet high in parts, and of considerable extent. There is only one navigable passage through them, Satellite pass, between Helby and Hill islands.

Ship islet, at the SW. point of Eastern channel, 2 miles NNW. from cape Beale, is 100 feet high and rocky. It shows from the eastward or westward as two hummocks, the northern one the larger and covered with grass, with two or three dead tree stumps on it.

King island, the southernmost of the Deer islands, is from 300 to 400 feet high, about 1 mile long and ½ mile broad; its shores are very rugged and broken, with rocks extending from 200 to 400 yards off. This island is separated from Ship islet by a passage ½ mile wide, but there is a rock in the middle of it, which is awash at high water.

Channel rocks, on the western side of the channel, 600 yards SE. of King island, and 1 mile east of Ship islet, are about 200 yards in extent, and cover at half flood; there are 10 to 12 fathoms 200 yards to the eastward, and the sea generally breaks over them; they must be carefully avoided.

Leading mark.—Turn island, at the northeastern point of the Eastern channel, shut in by Leading bluff of Tzaartoos island bearing N. 44° E. (N. 20° E. mag.), leads east of the Channel rocks, and west of the rocks off cape Beale.

Diana island, 350 to 400 feet high, separated from King island by a passage full of rocks, is about 1½ miles long, and ¾ mile broad; its shores are rocky. Taylor islet, 50 feet high, lies 600 yards SW. ½ W. from its southern point.

Todd rock.—At 400 yards from the eastern side of Diana island is Todd rock, which covers at high water, with 3 fathoms just eastward of it.

Helby island, the next island northward of Diana, has off its northern side Entrance anchorage, a small but well-sheltered anchorage in from 6 to 9 fathoms, easy of access from either the Eastern or Middle channels, and very convenient as a stopping place for vessels entering or leaving Barkley sound.

Self point, at the eastern end of Helby island, appears like an islet and is conspicuous at night, the neck joining it to Helby island being very low.

Wizard islet, to the northeastward of the anchorage, is small, about 8 feet high, and bare. It is about 800 yards from Helby island, and those intending to anchor should do so about 200 yards SW. of the islet in 6 fathoms.

Hill island, ⅔ mile north of Helby island, is small, with a summit of moderate height at its southern end. At ¼ mile SSW. of it is a patch of 3½ fathoms, marked by kelp, and there are several small islets and rocks off its east and west sides.

Robbers island, separated from Hill island by a passage full of rocks, is 2 miles long and 1 mile broad at its widest part. It is low and steep-to on the eastern side, and between it and Tzaartoos island is a small landlocked basin of 5 to 7 fathoms of water, but almost inaccessible in consequence of the many rocks at its entrance.

Tzaartoos or Copper island, the northernmost of the Deer islands, is 4½ miles long in a NE. direction and 1½ miles broad. It is higher than the other islands, rising in many parts to 800 and its summit to 1,026 feet; its eastern side, except in the vicinity of Sproat bay, is steep-to. Limestone of a fine quality is to be found in its northern part, and there are indications of copper and iron ores.

Sproat bay, on the eastern side of Tzaartoos island, is about ½ mile wide and 400 yards deep. In its center are two small islets, and between them and the southern side of the bay a vessel may anchor in from 11 to 15 fathoms.

Leading bluff, situated just south of the bay, is a steep point 405 feet high, conspicuous from the entrance of Eastern channel.

Fog rock, lying about 400 yards east of Sproat bay, is of small extent, with only 9 feet of water over it, and steep-to around. This danger is in the track of vessels using Sproat bay, and requires caution to avoid it, not being marked by kelp in the spring.

The eastern side of Hill island open of Leading bluff bearing S. 62° W. (S. 38° W. mag.) leads SE. of Fog rock, and the western side of Nob point well open east of Limestone point N. 21° E. (N. 3° W. mag.) leads well eastward of it.

Nob point, the SW. entrance point of Alberni canal, and NW. point of Eastern channel, is about ½ mile northward of Tzaartoos island, and nearly 13 miles from cape Beale. It is a remarkable, cliffy, projecting point 475 feet high, steep-to on its southern and eastern sides.

Alberni canal, at the NE. part of Barkley sound, winds in a northerly direction for 23 miles, with a breadth varying from 400 yards to 1 mile, and terminates in a fine capacious anchorage at its head; the shores on either side are rocky and rugged, rising abruptly from the sea to mountains 2,000 and 3,000 feet high; at the head, however, the land becomes low and fertile, a large extent being fit for cultivation. The town of Alberni is at the head of the inlet and has a church and post and telegraph offices. In 1901 the population of the town was 502.

San Mateo bay, on the eastern side of the canal, 1½ miles north of Turn island, is ¾ mile wide, and 1 mile deep; its shores are high.

A rock, part of which dries 3 to 4 feet at low water, with depths of 3 to 6 feet extending 50 yards southward, deepening to 7 fathoms between it and the south shore of the bay, with deep water near in other directions, is situated near the head of San Mateo bay, with Banton island center bearing NW. by N., distant 450 yards.

Mutine point, midway between Mateo bay and Turn island, is rocky. A sunken rock, with a depth of 8 feet on it at low water, and 7 to 8 fathoms close around, lies about 200 yards offshore, northward of Mutine point, with Turn island (northern point) bearing SW., distant 1,150 yards. A berth of 400 yards should be given in passing.

Just south of this point is Crickitt bay, not recommended. Ritherdon bay is reported to be a good anchorage, on clay bottom, but it is deep; at the head of the bay a small flat dries at low water.

Uchucklesit harbor, on the western side of Alberni canal, 2 miles within Nob point, is 3 miles long in a northwesterly direction, and its average breadth is about ½ mile; the northern shore is high, rising gradually to mountains of 2,000 and 3,000 feet, but the southern shores and heads are low. There are two secure anchorages, Green cove at the entrance, and Snug basin at the head, with from 9 to 15 fathoms of water. Limestone of a very fine quality is to be procured at the head of the harbor.

Blunden rock, on the SW. side of the harbor, 1,400 yards NW. from Steep bluff and 200 yards offshore, covers at three-quarters flood; it is marked by a stake with a horizontal topmark.

Green cove, just within the entrance, on the eastern side of the harbor, affords a snug, well-sheltered anchorage, in from 9 to 14 fathoms. Harbor island, off its west side, and completely landlocking the anchorage in that direction, is of small extent, with passages on either side into the anchorage. A rock lies 100 yards off its SE. point.

This anchorage is convenient as a stopping place for vessels bound to or from Stamp harbor at the head of Alberni canal.

Steamer passage, on the southern side of Harbor island, is 400 yards long, and about 150 yards wide in the narrowest part, with not less than 9 fathoms. A rock, which dries about 6 feet at low water, lies 100 yards off the SE. point of Harbor island.

Ship passage, east of Harbor island, is 800 yards long, and 400 yards wide, with from 11 to 20 fathoms, and available for sailing ships unable to enter or leave Green cove by Steamer passage.

Snug basin, on the northern side of the head of Uchucklesit harbor, ½ mile long in a northerly direction, and about 400 yards broad, is well adapted for refitting or repairing a ship, and affords anchorage in 12 to 14 fathoms; but the entrance, though deep, is only 150 feet wide.

Water.—On the northern shore, 1 mile from Green cove, is a large stream of fresh water, with a bank extending a short distance off it.

Nahmint bay, on the western side of Alberni canal, 10 miles within its entrance, is about ½ mile in extent, with from 19 to 20 fathoms water, and may be used as a stopping place, if working down the canal; a large stream disembogues at its head.

First narrows, 13 miles from the entrance of the canal, is 500 yards wide at low water, with 26 fathoms in mid-channel. Shoal water extends off the mouth of the Owatchet river, and also from the western shore off the mouth of a small stream which enters the canal about 600 yards above Owatchet river, where a sand spit, which dries at low water, extends out for about 100 yards; a ship should keep in mid-channel.

Second narrows, 18 miles from the entrance, is 400 yards wide at low water, steep-to on the eastern side; the western side dries out 200 yards at low water. The depth in mid-channel is 40 fathoms, and in going through a vessel ought to keep well over on the eastern side.

Stamp harbor, at the head of Alberni canal, is a capacious and secure anchorage, 2 miles in length and varying in breadth from 800 yards to 1 mile. Its western shore is high and rocky, but the eastern side and head are low and fertile, with a quantity of clear level land.

Somass river, a stream of considerable size, flows into the head of the harbor and is navigable for canoes several miles; it has its source in a chain of extensive lakes in the interior of Vancouver island, and the quantity of water discharged from it is so great that there is a constant current out of the canal, often exceeding 1 knot in strength. A deep-water wharf, with a depth of 24 feet at low water, has been erected at the town site on the eastern side of the harbor; a good road connects this town site with Alberni. The town Alberni is a settlement about 1½ miles up the river.

Navigable depths.—Steam vessels not more than 150 feet in length and of 10 feet draft can reach the town wharf at high water, where there is a depth of 13 feet at low water.

There are four rough wooden pile beacons marking the entrance into Somass river, the two inner ones being surmounted by a white cask; the innermost beacon is composed of three piles, the others are single piles. The least depth at the entrance is 3 feet; the channel deepens to 9 feet within.

Observatory islet, in the center of the harbor, is a small bare rock about 6 feet above high water; some rocks extend 100 yards NE. of it.

Sheep islet, in the NW. part of the harbor, and 1,200 yards from Observatory islet, is wooded and connected to the head of the harbor at low water by a sand bank.

Anchorage.—The anchorage in the harbor is excellent between Observatory islet and the old wharf, in depths of from 12 to 7 fathoms.

Supplies.—Game is plentiful, and there is excellent fishing in the river and lakes. Fresh beef, vegetables, and fruit are fairly plentiful.

Communication.—A steamer runs weekly to and from Victoria.

Tides.—It is high water, full and change, in Stamp harbor at 0 h. 0 m.; springs rise 12 feet.

Directions for Barkley sound.—Entering Barkley sound through Eastern channel, cape Beale may be easily recognized from the southward by the lighthouse and by the islands westward of it. When approaching or rounding the cape do not come nearer than ½ mile, to avoid the rocks off it; bring Leading bluff (Tzaartoos island) to bear N. 44° E. (N. 20° E. mag.), and steer up the Eastern channel with that mark on, which will lead clear of the rocks off the west side of cape Beale, and east of Channel rocks.

When the northern point of Ship islet is in line with the southern point of King island bearing S. 82° W. (S. 58° W. mag.), the vessel will be well north of Channel rocks, and may then steer up mid-channel about NE.; on nearing Leading bluff, keep the east side of Hill island open south of it bearing S. 62° W. (S. 38° W. mag.), to pass east of Fog rock, until the west side of Nob point comes open east of Limestone point bearing N. 21° E. (N. 3° W. mag.), when steer up in mid-channel.

If bound to Stamp harbor, after entering Alberni canal keep in mid-channel, except when passing through the Second narrows, and anchor on the eastern side of the harbor NNE. of Observatory island.

After entering Alberni canal, a strong southerly wind will generally be experienced, blowing home to the head; it, however, usually falls a little during the night.

If beating into the Eastern channel (which should only be done by small or quick-working vessels), when standing toward cape Beale, tack before the passage between Turn island and the main comes open of Leading bluff, bearing NE. Ship islet may be approached to ¼ mile; when nearing King island, or the Channel rocks, tack when Turn island becomes shut in with Leading bluff. As a rule, in standing toward the east shore, do not approach within 400 yards, and after passing the Channel rocks keep outside of the lines of Deer islands. On nearing Leading bluff use the above-mentioned precautions for clearing Fog rock; when standing into Numukamis bay give Reef and San José islands a berth of about 400 yards, after which the shore on either side may be approached to about 200 yards, except near the center of Numukamis bay, which should not be approached closer than ½ mile.

Anchorages.—If necessary to anchor, Entrance anchorage in the Deer group, just north of Helby island, is recommended, being easy of access from either Eastern or Middle channels. Kelp, Sproat, Christie, and Nahmint bays, also Green cove, are easy of access and may be used as stopping places.

Middle channel, the largest passage into Barkley sound, is upward of 12 miles long NE., and 3 miles wide in the narrowest part, being bounded on either side by numerous small islands and rocks. The depths within it vary from 30 to 54 fathoms, and off its entrance are three dangers, viz., Western reef, Channel reef, and Danger rock, which only break in heavy weather and require great caution to avoid. In southerly or southwesterly gales there is generally a very heavy sea in this channel.

Leading marks.—Swiss Boy island just open west of Entrance island bearing N. 44° E. (N. 20° E. mag.), leads ½ mile east of Danger rock; Mark islet open north of Ragged islet bearing N. 68° E. (N. 44° E. mag.) leads ¾ mile west of it, and the same distance east of Channel reef; and Sail rock in sight west of Storm island bearing N. 41° W. (N. 65° W. mag.) leads south of it and Channel reef.

Danger rock, in the SE. part of the entrance of Middle channel, 3½ miles N. 62° W. (N. 86° W. mag.) from cape Beale, and 2½ miles S. 86° W. (S. 62° W. mag.) from Ship islet, is of small extent. There are from 22 to 40 fathoms at a distance of 400 yards around it.

Channel reef lies near the center of the entrance to Middle channel, 3½ miles N. 76° W. (S. 80° W. mag.), from Ship islet, and 1½ miles N. 43° W. (N. 67° W. mag.) from Danger rock. It is about 200 yards in extent, and uncovers at low water.

Western reef lies in the SW. part of the entrance to Middle channel, 5½ miles N. 76° W. (S. 80° W. mag.) from Ship islet and 1 mile south of the Broken group. It is about 200 yards in extent, awash at low water, and should not be approached within ½ mile.

Entrance island, at the SE. part of Middle channel and nearly 1 mile NW. from Ship islet, is of small extent and wooded, the tops of the trees being 350 feet above high water. It is steep-to and cliffy on the southern and western sides; ¼ mile NE. of it is Leach islet and some offlying rocks.

Hecate passage, leading into Middle channel between Entrance island and Danger rock, is 2 miles wide and is the best way to enter Middle channel in thick weather, or from the southward or eastward.

Shark pass, between Entrance and Ship islands, is ¾ mile wide, and may be used by steamers or sailing vessels with a fair wind.

Dodger cove.—Between Diana and King islands are two small islands (Hains and Seppings) connected to each other by a reef. Dodger cove, on the eastern side of Middle channel, is situated between these islands and Diana island, and is a narrow creek about ¾ mile long and 200 yards wide; a rock which covers at three-quarters flood lies nearly in mid-channel in the entrance and 200 yards N. by E. from Seppings island. It affords good shelter to coasters or small craft at its head, in from 2½ to 3 fathoms of water, but it should not be attempted by a stranger, as the entrance along the southern side of Diana island is rather intricate. There are several rocks and small islets off the SE. end of the creek where it joins Eastern channel.

Dodger cove is frequented between January and July, especially in bad weather, by the vessels engaged in the seal fishery.

Satellite pass, 3 miles from Entrance island, lies between Helby and Hill islands, connecting the Eastern and Middle channels. It is about 1 mile long and ½ mile wide; the depths in the middle vary from 9 to 22 fathoms, but 600 yards SSW. of Hill island on the north side of the pass is a shoal patch of 3½ fathoms, marked by kelp; Leading bluff open of the east side of Hill island bearing N. 57° E. (N. 33° E. mag.) leads to the SE. of this shoal. Do not attempt to pass between Ragged island and Helby island.

If bound to Alberni canal, after having entered Middle channel, proceed through this pass into the Eastern channel and on to the canal through the latter, keeping about 300 yards north of Ragged, Helby, and Wizard islands.

Village rocks, lying on the eastern side of Middle channel, 6 miles from Entrance island, and ⅓ mile from the NW. point of Robbers island, are 400 yards in extent, nearly awash at low water, and the sea usually breaks on them in heavy weather; they should not be approached within ¼ mile.

Chain islands, on the eastern side of Middle channel, are a chain of small islets and rocks nearly 4 miles long in a NE. direction. They lie parallel to the western side of Tzaartoos island, being separated from it by a passage ¾ mile wide, but filled with rocks, and through which no vessels should attempt to pass.

Swiss Boy island, the southernmost of this group, is small and cliffy. Bull rock, 400 yards NW. of it, is of small extent, and has less than 2 fathoms on it, and breaks in bad weather.

Caution.—Do not approach the western side of Chain islands within ½ mile, except when rounding their northern part.

Junction passage, at the NE. part of Middle channel, connecting it with Alberni canal and Eastern channel, lies north of the Chain and Tzaartoos islands. It is 2 miles long in an easterly direction and about ⅓ mile wide.

On the north side of the passage is Rainy bay, about 1½ miles in extent, but there are several rocks and small islets within it, the shores are rugged and broken, and the water too deep to afford anchorage. Ecoole village is situated on Seddall island NW. ¾ W. from Nob point; the wharf can only be used by very small craft.

Northward of this bay, and connected to it by a very narrow boat pass, is Useless arm, a large sheet of water with from 9 to 20 fathoms, and not accessible to vessels.

Broken group, which forms the boundary of Middle channel along the western side, is composed of a number of small islands and rocks, covering a space upward of 6 miles long and 4 miles wide. They are comparatively low and the principal ones are wooded, the largest being about 1 mile in extent; there are several passages through them, and a good anchorage (Island harbor) in their NE. part, but as a rule no stranger should venture among them or approach within ½ mile, as the depths are irregular, and other rocks may exist besides those known. No detailed description of the various islands and rocks can be given, but the principal and outlying dangers will be enumerated.

Redonda, the southern island of this group, lies 4½ miles NW. by W. ⅜ W. from Ship islet. It is small, wooded, of a round shape, and about 290 feet in height; a rock which dries 3 to 4 feet at low water lies 600 yards S. by W. from its SW. point, and ½ mile east of it is a reef which covers at half flood. Between Redonda island and Channel reef is a passage 1 mile wide, with from 19 to 33 fathoms, but it should not be attempted by a stranger.

Village island, the largest of the group, is 1¼ miles NE. of Redonda, and upward of 1 mile in extent; the eastern side is bold and cliffy. On its NE. side is a village of considerable size, where landing may be effected in almost any weather. Off its western side are several small islets and rocks inclosing Port Effingham, a good and safe anchorage.

Coaster channel, which runs in a westerly direction through Broken group, north of Village island, is about 4 miles long and from ½ mile to 1 mile wide, but as there are several rocks in it, this channel should not be attempted by strangers.

A sunken rock lies 600 yards N. 19° W. (N. 43° W. mag.) of the northern end of Grassy island.

Port Effingham, on the western side of Village island, has an inner landlocked basin, with good holding ground in from 7 to 9 fathoms, formed by an islet and several rocks extending across the bay. The entrance, which is southward of the islet, is very narrow and great care is necessary in entering. There is good fresh water at a small stream in the inner anchorage. It is much used by sealing schooners in preference to Dodger cove. A rock, with a depth of 7 feet on it and marked by kelp, lies on the northern side of the entrance to the outer part of the port; it is situated 350 yards south from the rock 40 feet high, the western rock of the chain extending westward from the NW. point of Village island.

Rocks.—Two rocks, about 6 and 7 feet high, respectively, lie to the southwestward of Howell island; the former is situated with Redonda island summit bearing N. 86° E. (N. 62° E. mag.), distant nearly 1 mile; the other rock is about 650 yards N. 71° E. (N. 47° E. mag.) from it. A shoal apparently extends for about 400 yards SSW. of the outer rock.

A rocky patch, with a depth of 5 fathoms over it, lies to the southwestward of Storm island, with the western extreme of Combe rock bearing N. 51° E. (N. 27° E. mag.), distant 1 mile.

A rock, with a depth of 4 fathoms over it, lies off the western edge of the group with Puffin islet summit bearing N. 54° E. (N. 30° E. mag.), distant 800 yards.

A rock, awash at low water springs, lies eastward of Owens island, with Puffin islet summit bearing N. 32° W. (N. 56° W. mag.), distant 1,150 yards.

Village reef, ½ mile NE. of Village island, is small, and 4 feet above high water.

Island harbor, 5 miles from the entrance to **Middle channel,** is a good, well-sheltered anchorage, about ½ mile in extent, with 10 to 14 fathoms, formed by several rocks and islands in the NE. part of Broken group; Puzzle and Gibraltar islands are on the north, and Protection, Keith, and Mullins islands on the south and west. There are two passages into it from Middle channel, Harbor entrance between Gibraltar and Protection islands, and South entrance south of the latter island and between it and Elbow rocks.

Protection island, 250 to 300 feet high, is ¾ mile long, narrow, and its coast rugged and broken. Observation islet, 30 feet high, and another small islet south of it, lie 100 yards from the middle of the southern side of Protection island.

Elbow rocks, which cover at two-thirds flood, lie 300 yards NE. from Elbow island, between it and Protection island, and are steep-to on all sides.

Pinnace rock, 600 yards east of Elbow island, almost in the fairway of the South entrance, only breaks in heavy weather, and is dangerous.

Channel rock, in the middle of Harbor entrance, 800 yards from its eastern end, is of small extent, with 9 feet on it at low water.

No one should attempt to enter this harbor without the chart, unless thoroughly acquainted with the place.

The best anchorage is near the center of the harbor, about 400 yards NW. of the NW. end of Protection island, in from 10 to 12 fathoms, protected from the northward and from the westward by Puzzle, Leith, and Mullins islands.

It is high water at full and change in Island harbor at 0 h. 0 m.; springs rise 12 feet.

Maud rock, awash at low water, lies 300 yards S. 80° W. (S. 56° W. mag.) from the western extreme of Mullins island.

A shoal with a depth of 9 feet over it extends for 250 yards ESE. from the rock, 10 feet high, which lies 350 yards eastward from the eastern point of Turtle island.

A ledge extends eastward from the NE. point of Marchant island with a depth of 9 feet at 250 yards from the island.

Nettle island, the NE. island of Broken group, is nearly 1 mile in extent, steep-to off its northern side, but east and west of it islets and rocks extend ½ mile.

Sechart channel, north of Broken group, connects Western and Middle channels. It is a winding channel 5 miles long and about ½ mile wide. A rock that uncovers at low water springs lies 500 yards S. 60° W. (S. 36° W. mag.) from Sechart village and 300 yards N. 14° W. (N. 38° W. mag.) from the westernmost of the Hundred islands.

Capstan island, 3 miles from the eastern entrance and nearly in the middle of this channel, is small, and the southernmost of a number of small islands named the Hundred islands, extending nearly 1 mile from the northern shore; a rock lies 100 yards south of it. Northwestward of these islets is the extensive village, Sechart, off which a vessel may anchor ¼ mile from the shore in 14 fathoms.

Eastward of Canoe island, in the approach to Anderson's wharf, rocks extend from the eastern shore of the passage to nearly mid-channel. Anderson's wharf is 200 feet long and has a depth of 18 feet of water at the outer end.

Northward of Sechart channel the western side of Middle channel is bounded by two narrow islands about 2 miles in length and separated from the mainland by a narrow boat pass; they should not be approached nearer than ½ mile.

Swale rock, at ½ mile east of the eastern point of Nettle island, is a small bare rock 8 feet above high water, which is very conspicuous from the Middle channel, and marks the eastern entrance of Sechart channel.

Light.—A fixed white light, 25 feet above high water, and visible 10 miles from all points of approach, is exhibited from the top of a small wooden tower standing on a wooden framework foundation on the eastern end of Swale rock. The tower and foundation are painted white.

Peacock channel, through the NW. part of Broken group, is about 3 miles long and nearly 1 mile wide.

A rock, with 4 feet over it, lies nearly in the center of the channel, midway between Dodd and Pender islands, with the south point of the latter bearing N. 43° E. (N. 19° E. mag.), distant 900 yards. Galley rock, on the east side of the channel, 1¾ miles within the western entrance, and 400 yards WNW. from the west extreme of Jarvis island, uncovers at low water.

Bird islets, two small, bare, conspicuous rocks, lie almost in the center of the north part of Middle channel, 9 miles from the entrance; the southern islet is 35 feet, and the northern 30 feet above high water; some rocks, which cover, extend 200 yards northward and westward of them.

Effingham inlet, the entrance to which is in the NW. part of Middle channel, is narrow, and about 8 miles long in a curved direction to the northward, terminating in a low swamp; its shores on both sides are high and rocky, the western being indented by several bays. The depths in it vary from 35 to more than 70 fathoms, and there is no anchorage; off its south entrance point are some small islets and rocks extending 1 mile to the eastward. Twin islets, George islet, and several sunken rocks lie off the entrance to the inlet.

A sunken rock lies 700 yards N. 70° E. (N. 46° E. mag.) of the north end of Webster island, and nearly 200 yards distant from the eastern shore of Effingham inlet.

Vernon bay, 1 mile east of Effingham inlet, at the head of Middle channel, is upward of 1 mile in extent, open to the southward, and too deep to afford anchorage; its shores are high and rocky. At 600 yards SSE. from Palmer point, the SW. extreme of Vernon bay, is Edward rock, 3 feet above high water, and 400 yards off the eastern shore of the bay, just within the entrance, is a reef awash at high water.

Directions.—Entering Barkley sound by the Middle channel with a fair wind, and coming from the west or SW., keep well clear of the western part of the sound and 3 miles south of Broken group. Steer toward Ship islet on an East (N. 66° E. mag.) bearing until Mark islet comes open north of Ragged islet bearing N. 68° E. (N. 44° E. mag.), when haul into the Middle channel with that mark on, which will lead midway between Channel reef and Danger rock; when Ship islet bears S. 66° E. (East mag.) the vessel will be north of these reefs, and may then steer up in mid-channel. If bound to Alberni inlet, a sailing vessel should proceed through Satellite pass into the Eastern channel. Should it be necessary to go through Junction passage, give the Chain islands a berth of nearly ½ mile to avoid the rocks off them, and proceed in mid-channel through the passage into Alberni inlet.

Unless intending to go through Satellite pass, do not approach the Deer islands within ½ mile.

If entering Middle channel from the eastward or in thick weather, and not able to see the marks for clearing the reefs, keep well out until Entrance island bears N. 24° E. (North mag.), when steer through Hecate passage so as to pass ¼ mile west of the island, which will lead well eastward of all danger; then proceed as above directed.

Beating into Middle channel, when south of Danger rock and Channel reef, keep Sail rock open south of Storm island, the southernmost of the group, bearing N. 41° W. (N. 65° W. mag.) until Mark islet comes nearly in line with the SE. point of Hill island N. 71° E. (N. 47° E. mag.), when, if standing to the westward, tack; in standing to the eastward avoid shutting in the passage between Hill island and Ragged islet, which should be kept open with the SE. edge of Hill island bearing N. 62° E. (N. 38° E. mag.); tacking when these latter marks are on will lead between Danger and Channel reefs, and clear of them; when Ship islet bears S. 66° E. (East mag.) vessels will be northward of them, and may stand over to within about ½ mile of the Deer islands and 1 mile of Broken group. If bound to Alberni inlet, when able to lie through the Satellite pass do so, keeping nearer to its southern shore, and beat up to the former through the Eastern channel. Vessels should not attempt to beat through Middle channel unless the weather be clear and the marks well made out.

Vessels may go between Entrance island and Danger rock, to the northward of the latter and Channel reef, by keeping Seabird islet at the entrance of Pachena bay well shut in by cape Beale, bearing S. 47° E. (S. 71° E. mag.).

Western channel, leading into Barkley sound westward of Broken group, between it and Great bank, is about 4 miles long, and from 1 to 2 miles broad.

Sail rock, lying off the SW. part of Broken group, is a bare rock like a sail, rising 82 feet above the sea, and very conspicuous; northward of it are some low islets (Green islets) and rocks extending from Hawkins island, the SW. island of the Broken group; and on the eastern side of Western channel foul ground projects in some places ½ mile off. Drum rocks extend 800 yards westward from Quoin island and are 25 feet high.

Black rock, at the SW. part of Western channel, 3½ miles S. 84° W. (S. 60° W. mag.) from Sail rock, is about 23 feet high; some rocks which break extend 400 yards east of it.

Great Bear islet, 38 feet high, lies 1½ miles NE. from Black rock; about 100 yards off its eastern end there is a rock awash.

Channel rock at the southern extreme of the Great bank, on the western side of the Western channel, is 15 feet above high water, bare, and steep-to on its eastern side. From Channel rock a reef upon which the sea breaks at low water extends 350 yards N. by E.

Great bank is, within the 10-fathom curve, 2⅓ miles long, and its greatest breadth is 1½ miles; on the shoalest parts, near the NE. and SW. ends, are from 3 to 4 fathoms, over which in heavy gales the sea breaks.

Shag rock, 8 feet above high water, on the eastern side of the channel, 2¾ miles N. by E. from Sail rock, and midway between Round and Hankin islands, is small and bare, and foul ground exists 200 yards from it.

Round island, near the middle of the north part of the channel, 3¼ miles N. ¾ E. from Sail rock, is small, and 161 feet high.

Gowlland, Table, and Castle islets, at the northern termination of Western channel, are small, but steep-to on their southern sides. At 400 yards NNW. of Table islet is a small rock, 6 feet high; a rock with 8 feet over it lies 250 yards off the SE. side of the island, with the southern end bearing S. 85° W. (S. 61° W. mag.); ½ mile ENE. from it is a patch 600 yards in extent, with from 4 to 7 fathoms. A rock, which dries 9 feet, lies about 150 yards eastward of, and a rock, awash at low water, lies 200 yards north of, Gowlland islet. The best passage into Toquart harbor appears to be eastward of these islets.

Directions.—Western channel, though wide, should only be used by steam vessels, or sailing vessels with a fair wind, and not then unless bound to Toquart harbor, in the northwestern part of Barkley sound. When entering, give Sail and Black rocks a berth of ½ mile, and steer up in mid-channel, passing ½ mile west of Round island.

Keeping Castle islet well open westward of Round island, bearing N. 24° E. (North mag.) will lead between the reefs.

Hand island, the northwestern island of the Broken group, is small and rugged; foul ground exists off its eastern and western sides, which should not be approached within 600 yards.

Lyall point, at the northwestern extreme of Sechart channel on the mainland, is a low, sharp point, with a sandy beach round it; there is a depth of 18 fathoms within 200 yards of it.

Mayne bay, northward of Lyall point, in the NW. part of the sound, is 2 miles long and 1 mile deep. Its shores, except near the northern part, are low and steep-to; there is no anchorage except in its SE. corner, where there is a limited area with 14 fathoms about 400 yards offshore.

The Sisters, a group of small islets, extend for ½ mile southward from the NW. point of the bay.

Stopper islands, lying ½ mile off Mayne bay, are about 1½ miles in extent, wooded, and 200 feet high; rocks extend from 400 to 600 yards off their east and west sides. Larkins island lies close off the western side of the southern island; a reef awash at high water extends 500 yards from its northern end. Richard rock, 800 yards eastward of Stopper islands, is steep-to on the eastern side. Do not pass between this rock and the islands. Hermit islet, 600 yards north of Stopper islands, at the NW. point of David channel, is low; 400 yards NW. by N. from it is a small wooded islet, about 50 feet high to the tops of the trees; a rock lies close to its SW. side.

St. Ines island lies to the southward of Stopper islands, 1⅛ miles west of Lyall point. David island lies about ¾ mile SW. of St. Ines island and ½ mile off the Vancouver shore. Forbes island is 1 mile SW. of David island and ½ mile offshore.

David channel, leading from the Western channel into Toquart harbor, eastward of the Stopper islands, has its southern entrance between Lyall point and St. Ines island.

Toquart harbor, in the NW. corner of Barkley sound, is about 1½ miles in extent and well sheltered from all winds by Stopper islands. Its shores are low and steep-to, except at the head, where Black patch, a shoal with 9 feet on its outer part, extends out nearly ½ mile in the direction of Image island.

Image island, lying 600 yards offshore in the NE. part of the harbor, is small, and NW. of it is an excellent anchorage in from 11 to 12 fathoms. A rock lies close to its NW. end, and a reef near its southern point.

Pipestem inlet, extending upward of 5 miles ENE. from Toquart harbor, has depths of 19 to 37 fathoms, but affords no anchorage whatever; its shores are rocky and rise abruptly to 1,000 and 2,000 feet above the sea; at its head is a small patch of swampy ground, with some fresh-water streams flowing through it.

Entering Toquart harbor by David channel, between Mayne bay and Stopper islands, after passing Lyall point, steer well into Mayne bay, to avoid Richard rock; when Hermit islet comes well open of the Stopper islands, steer for the harbor, passing midway between the Sisters and Stopper islands, and eastward of Hermit islet; anchor in 14 fathoms, with Image island bearing NE. by E. and Hermit islet SSE., or proceed farther northward and anchor in 11 or 12 fathoms NNW. of Image island.

Village passage leads into the harbor westward of Stopper islands; it is upward of 1 mile long, and 600 yards wide in its narrowest part, and is clear in mid-channel; some rocks, awash at high water, lie on its eastern side, extending from the northern end of Larkins island.

For 2½ miles from the Stopper islands a chain of small islands lies parallel to the coast at a distance of about ¾ mile, with from 5 to 11 fathoms between them and the shore. Forbes island, the southernmost of them, is moderately high, steep-to on its southern side; nearly 1 mile SW. of it, and extending from the opposite shore, are a number of rocks above high water.

Ugly channel, an entrance to the sound eastward of Shelter islands, is bounded on both sides by rocks and reefs, and, though probably deep, it has not been sufficiently examined to recommend its being used by a stranger.

Starlight reefs, at its SE. part, are a cluster of rocks about 1,400 yards in extent, the highest 18 feet in height; in bad weather the sea breaks heavily over them. Lookout island, on the western side of Ugly channel, is well wooded, of small extent, and about 168 feet high; a rock 25 feet high is situated 600 yards east of it, and 1,000 yards north of it is a rock 6 feet in height.

Six hundred yards south of Lookout island is Humphries reef, a patch of rocks 400 yards in extent, between which and the Starlight reefs the entrance to the channel is 1,800 yards wide.

Ship channel, a continuation of Ugly channel, between the Vancouver coast and Great bank, southward of Forbes island, leads also into the Ucluelet arm from the northward, and is 4 miles long NE. and SW. and ¾ mile broad in its narrowest part.

Double islands, at its SE. part, are of small extent, and steep-to on the western side; from the southern and eastern sides foul ground extends upward of ½ mile, the outer part of which, where there are several rocks that uncover, is known as Sykes reefs; a rock about 12 feet high is situated 600 yards S. by W. from the western extreme of the large island. Kelp islet, 1,200 yards NNW. of Double islands, on the opposite side of the channel and 400 yards from the mainland, is low and bare; kelp extends 400 yards south of it.

Heddington reef, ½ mile in extent, lies nearly midway between Double islands and Black rock. On its eastern edge are two heads which dry 6 and 10 feet, respectively, the latter and southern rock is 1,600 yards N. 24° E. (North mag.) from Black rock.

Ucluelet arm, just within the SW. part of Barkley sound, extends 5½ miles NW. by N. Its southern shore is low and the northern shore rises gradually to a flat-topped range of considerable height, the SE. shoulder of which, mount Ozzard, 2,270 feet high, is conspicuous from the SE.

The depths in this arm vary from 4 to 8 fathoms, and there is secure and well-sheltered anchorage between Sutton rock and Channel island. Care should be taken when entering this arm, as there are several sunken rocks near the shore.

There are stores and a post-office at Ucluelet.

Shelter islands, upward of ½ mile SSE. of the entrance, are small islets and rocks about 1 mile long and 600 yards wide, which completely shelter the arm from the sea. Center reef, 600 yards westward of their northern part, is of small extent, and about 3 feet above high water. Alpha passage, between Center reef and Shelter islands, is 400 yards wide at its narrowest part, with depths of from

' fathoms. There is, however, said to be a sunken rock in ʔe, and it should, therefore, not be used.

channel, westward of Center reef, appears to be the ŋger to use if entering the Ucluelet arm from seaward, ather, when there is a long swell from seaward roll- ce often appears to be an unbroken line of surf.

ıarked by kelp, with a depth of 5 fathoms on it, phitrite point bearing N. 70° W. (S. 86° W. ds.

..arked by kelp, with a depth of 3¼ fathoms on it, .. the islet (50 feet) on the SW. side of Round island .. 70° W. (S. 86° W. mag.), distant 350 yards.

.. rock, which dries 2 to 3 feet, with 4 fathoms close-to on its northern side, lies about 100 yards from the northern coast of Round island, with Native islet bearing N. 11° W. (N. 35° W. mag.), distant 1,150 yards.

A small pinnacle rock, with a depth of 5 feet on it, with 4½ to 5 fathoms between it and the shore, and 6¼ fathoms close eastward, marked by seaweed, but not by kelp, lies nearly 100 yards from the southern entrance point of Stewart bay, with Native islet bearing N. 27° W. (N. 51° W. mag.), distant 950 yards.

A rock with a depth of 5 feet on it and 3½ fathoms close-to on its northern side, lies, on the southern side of the arm, with Native islet bearing N. 4° W. (N. 28° W. mag.), distant 850 yards.

Round island, at the northern part of this channel, is the south entrance point to the Ucluelet arm; it is high and connected by a sandy beach at low water to the mainland; the eastern side is steep-to, and may be approached to within 200 yards; on the opposite side of the entrance rocks awash at high water extend 200 yards off the eastern shore.

Leading point, on the western side of Ucluelet arm, is bold, steep-to, and may be approached to within a distance of 50 yards; between it and Round island is a narrow creek, with 2 fathoms of water, but the entrance is blocked up by kelp. At Leading point the breadth of the inlet contracts to 200 yards.

Stewart bay, on the northern side, ½ mile within the entrance, is 400 yards deep and ½ mile wide. In its center is a rock, awash at high water, and the bay is too shallow to afford anchorage except to a coaster; there is a native village of considerable size in its western part, off which some small rocks extend about 100 yards.

A rock, with 2¾ fathoms on it, lies with wharf in bay on southern side of entrance bearing S. 31° W. (S. 7° W. mag.), distant 600 yards, and Native islet N. 29° W. (N. 53° W. mag.).

A rock, with 3 feet of water, marked by kelp and eelgrass, lies nearly 150 yards off the first point NW. of the Indian village abreast

Leading point. There are $2\frac{1}{2}$ fathoms close around, and the depth increases quickly to 7 fathoms in the fairway.

Channel islet, in the middle of the arm about 2 miles within the entrance, and 1 mile past Leading point, is small. There is a clear passage north of the islet with 7 fathoms, but with only 2 fathoms on its southern side; at 400 yards N. 32° W. (N. 56° W. mag.) from the islet lies a small rock above high water, steep-to on all sides, except the SE., from which a shoal with $2\frac{1}{2}$ fathoms of water extends 200 yards. To the westward of Channel islet the arm becomes wider, affording good anchorage in 4 to 7 fathoms, over a space 1 mile long and $\frac{1}{2}$ mile wide.

Sutton rock consists of two rocks, each of small extent, lying 93 yards apart in a NW. and SE. direction. The southern rock, 600 yards S. 38° E. (S. 62° E. mag.) from Channel island, has 7 feet on it, the northern one 10 feet. A spar buoy colored red and black in horizontal stripes is moored on the shoalest of the rocks.

A little more than 200 yards ENE. of Sutton rock, and 30 feet from low-water mark, is a narrow rocky ledge 40 feet in length, which dries 2 feet.

Amphitrite point—Light.—A fixed white light, 60 feet above high water and visible 13 miles from all points of approach by water, is exhibited from the top of a small, square, wooden tower built on a wooden framework, situated on the extremity of Amphitrite point, on the western side of the entrance to Ucluelet arm. The tower is painted white; the light is unwatched.

Whistling buoy.—A whistling buoy, painted red, is moored on the southern side of Carolina channel in 25 fathoms of water. From the buoy the lighthouse bears N. 7° E. (N. 17° W. mag.), distant $\frac{3}{4}$ mile.

Directions.—Several channels lead into Ucluelet arm, with apparently deep water through them, but there are so many rocks and dangers in their vicinity that great vigilance is recommended, and it would hardly be advisable to enter without a pilot; should it, however, be necessary to do so, steer for Amphitrite Point lighthouse until the whistling buoy is picked up. Pass close westward of the buoy and steer a N. 43° E. (N. 19° E. mag.) course for the summit of Round island. When about 400 yards from that island haul to the eastward and round it at a distance of 300 yards. Steer up the arm, keeping well over to the western shore; pass Leading point within 200 yards to avoid the rocks abreast of it on the northern side, and anchor midway between Sutton rock and Channel islet, in 6 to 9 fathoms; or proceed farther westward, where a more extended anchorage will be found, taking care to pass north of Channel islet.

Channel islet kept open between the sides of the inlet bearing N. 42° W. (N. 66° W. mag.) leads to the entrance of Ucluelet arm from off the entrance of the Western channel, to the northward of the Shelter islands, and between the Great Bear and Sykes reef to the eastward and Black rocks, Starlight and Heddington reefs to the westward; but as this channel has not been closely examined, it should be used with great caution.

Entering the arm from the northward through Ship channel, keep about ½ mile off the western shore, and passing about 400 yards northward of Shelter islands, steer up the arm as before directed.

The coast from Amphitrite point takes a NW. by W. direction to point Cox; it is low and indented by two large sandy bays, which afford no shelter; at a distance of 4 miles from it are depths of from 20 to 27 fathoms.

Wreck bay, 4 miles westward of Amphitrite point, is nearly 3 miles wide, and 1 mile deep, with the small islet Florencia in the center; there are several rocks in the bay and it is totally unfit for anchorage.

Long bay, 8 miles westward of Amphitrite point, is 7 miles wide and upward of 1 mile deep, with from 8 to 11 fathoms between the entrance points; there are several rocks in it, and no vessel should anchor here; at its SE. point, just within the reefs, good shelter for boats will be found in all weathers. Schooner cove, in the NW. part of the bay, is of small extent, with 2 fathoms of water; it would afford good shelter to a coaster or small vessel. Portland point, the NW. extreme of Long bay, is high and abrupt, with some small rocks and islets around it, at a distance of ½ mile. Gowlland rocks, 1½ miles west from Portland point, are of small extent, bare, and from 10 to 15 feet above high water; they should not be approached nearer than 1 mile.

Caution.—When navigating between Barkley and Clayoquot sounds, do not approach the shore within 2 miles.

Clayoquot sound comprises a number of inlets, covering an area 30 miles long and 16 miles broad. The entrance to it is fringed by numerous dangerous rocks, which require caution to avoid; it lies between Cox and Rafael points, bearing from each other NW. ½ W. and SE. ½ E., distant 17 miles.

There are several channels into the inner waters of this sound, but with the exception of Ship channel they should not be attempted by a stranger.

Tides.—It is high water, full and change, in Clayoquot sound at 0 h. 0 m., the rise and fall being about 12 feet.

Cox point, at the SE. extreme of Clayoquot sound, is rocky, and Vargas cone, a remarkable summit, 432 feet high, rises just within the point, and is very conspicuous from the westward.

Templar channel is a winding passage about 4 miles long in a northerly direction, with an average breadth of ½ mile. The soundings vary from 8 to 10 fathoms, in its entrance, to 3¼ fathoms in its shoalest part near the north end, and a shoal bank lies in the middle abreast Wakennenish island; in heavy weather the sea breaks across the channel. No vessel drawing more than 12 feet should attempt to enter the sound by this channel, and not even then without a pilot, as it is very intricate, and no directions can be given.

False bay, just northward of Cox point, is about ½ mile in extent, open to the SW., and unfit for anchorage; its shores are low and sandy.

Lennard islands, on the western side of the entrance, are 1¾ miles NW. by W. from Cox point. The largest and most easterly of the islands is wooded, the other islands are rocks 10 to 12 feet in height; a reef extends for some distance from the SE. point of Lennard island.

Light.—A flashing white light, every 11¼ seconds, elevated 115 feet above high water, and visible in clear weather from a distance of 16 miles, is shown from a white, wooden, octagonal lighthouse, with red lantern, standing 500 yards from the eastern extremity of Lennard island.

The light may be obscured by trees on the eastern part of the island.

Fog signal.—A diaphone, operated by compressed air, gives 1 blast of 4 seconds' duration every 45 seconds.

The building is white and about 300 feet southeastward of the lighthouse.

Village island is ½ mile north from Lennard islands.

Rock.—In the fairway of the channel is a rock with 4 feet of water over it.

Buoy.—A black can buoy with T. C. in white letters is moored in 4 fathoms on the SE. side of the rock.

Wakennenish island, on the western side of the channel, 1 mile from Lennard island, is about 200 feet high; at its southern point is Echachets, a large Indian village, generally occupied by the natives during the summer fishing season.

Stubbs island, ½ mile NNE. from Wakennenish island, and between which and Round island to the eastward the channel is but little over 250 yards wide, has a sand bank extending 1 mile northeastward of it, the extreme of which is marked by a black platform buoy in 17 feet. There is a village and post-office on the north side of the island.

A wharf, 230 feet long, with a depth of 18 feet alongside at low water, extends from the NE. point of Stubbs island.

A sand spit also extends for ¾ mile NNE. from Round island.

Directions.—Local vessels pass from 300 to 400 yards to the eastward of Lennard and Village islands; from Village island abeam they keep to the eastward to clear the 4-foot rock in the fairway, marked by a black can buoy; when Echachets point is seen northward of the high rock abreast of it the danger is passed, and a course is then shaped along Wakennenish island, avoiding the dangers on its SE. side.

The anchorage is on the east side of Wakennenish island, or just northward of a line joining Stubbs and Round islands, in from 5 to 6 fathoms of water.

Broken channel, between Wakennenish and Vargas islands westward of the former, is upward of 2 miles long, and ½ mile wide in its narrowest part, with from 6 to 15 fathoms of water; several rocks lie off its entrance and on both sides; the tidal streams run through from 2 to 5 knots, and no one should use it without a pilot.

McKay reef, lying off the entrance, 4 miles WNW. from Cox point, is of small extent, 5 to 10 feet above high water, and the sea generally breaks heavily over it. Passage rock, which covers at high water, lies ⅜ mile NNE. of McKay reef.

Vargas island, on the western side of Broken channel, is 4½ miles long and 4½ miles wide at its broadest part, and its surface is low and undulating; on the eastern side near the middle is Kelsemart, a native village.

Blunden island, westward of Open bay on the SW. side of the island, is ¾ mile in extent and wooded; numerous reefs are scattered about this locality.

Rugged group, a chain of islets and rocks, from 8 to 50 feet in height, extending in an ESE. and WNW. direction for 3 miles, fringes the south side of Vargas island.

Ship channel, westward of Vargas island, between it and a number of small islands and rocks, is the only passage into Clayoquot sound which should be attempted by a stranger; it is 5 miles long and from ¾ to 1½ miles wide. The depths in the south part vary from 20 to 22 fathoms, decreasing to 5½ fathoms in the shoalest part near the north end; the tidal streams set through it from 1 to 2 knots.

Bare island is small, 40 feet high in the center, and forms a good mark for identifying Ship channel; it is 1 mile SW. from Blunden island and 9 miles westward from Cox point; a rock on which the sea breaks lies ½ mile SE. by E. from it; and a shoal spit extends to the WNW. a distance of about 800 yards.

Plover reefs, on the eastern side of the channel ½ mile north from Bare island, are of considerable extent, stretching 1 mile from the western side of Blunden island; some parts are 6 feet above high water, and there are only 5 fathoms at 400 yards west of them.

Sea Otter rock, 2 miles NW. by W. from Bare islet, is very small, 6 feet above high water, and there are 5 fathoms close-to, off its east side. A rock upon which the sea sometimes breaks lies about ½ mile NE. of Sea Otter rock, and broken water has also been observed ¼ mile north of it.

Shark reefs, some of which cover, others 6 and 10 feet above high water, lie 2 miles NE. by E. ½ E. from Sea Otter rock; they are about 600 yards in extent, and should not be approached nearer than 400 yards on their south and east sides. Lawrence islands, on the west side of the channel, about 500 yards NE. of Shark reefs, and 2¾ miles from Sea Otter rock. are small, low, and wooded, but steep-to on the east side.

Bartlett island, ½ mile NW. of Lawrence islands, is low and wooded; its shores are much broken, and a number of rocks extend for ¼ to ½ mile on all sides of it, and the island should not be approached within the latter distance. Twin islets, the easternmost of the islets NE. of Bartlett island and 4 miles from Sea Otter rock, are low, but wooded, and connected at low water; kelp extends 200 yards south of them.

Hecate passage, NE. of and connecting Ship channel with the inner waters of Clayoquot sound, is 3 miles long and upward of 1 mile wide; there are several rocks on both its shores, and North bank, of sand, lies in its center, but to the southward of this bank along the north coast of Vargas is a clear passage with not less than 5½ fathoms.

Buoy.—The southern extreme of North bank is marked by a black platform buoy, with slatwork pyramid surmounted by a drum, moored in 5 fathoms.

Half-tide rock, 400 yards from the NW. point of Vargas island, is of small extent, and covers at half flood. Hobbs islet open west of Burgess islet bearing S. 38° W. (S. 14° W. mag.) leads 400 yards NW. of it; and the Twins in line with the north Whaler island bearing N. 77° W. (S. 79° W. mag.) leads 400 yards north of it, and south of North bank.

Two rocks, about 200 yards apart, the northwestern of which dries about 1 foot and the other is awash at low water, lie at the eastern end of Hecate passage and nearly in the middle of the channel. The northwestern rock is situated 400 yards S. 4° E. (S. 28° E. mag.) from the SE. extreme of the island forming the south side of Deep pass.

Buoy.—A red platform buoy, with slatwork pyramid surmounted by a ball, moored in 5 fathoms, marks the northwestern rock.

Cat Face mountains, fronting Ship channel, are a remarkable flat-topped range 3,370 feet high, with some patches of cliff and white bare rock in about the middle of their southern side. They are very conspicuous from seaward.

Deep pass, between two islands at the NE. part of Hecate passage, is about 600 yards long and 300 yards wide, with 9 fathoms of water, and is the best channel leading from Hecate passage into the inner waters. The tidal streams set at the rate of from 2 to 3 knots through it.

Hecate bay, 2 miles NE. from Deep pass, on the western shore, is 1,200 yards wide and 600 yards deep, with from 9 to 10 fathoms; it is one of the best anchorages within the sound, being easy of access and well sheltered. There is a stream of fresh water in the middle of the bay, very convenient for watering.

Cypress bay, 4 miles NE. from Deep pass, is nearly 2 miles in extent, with from 12 to 26 fathoms over it. On the east and west sides the shores are low, but are high on the north. Mussel rock lies 800 yards off the eastern shore of the bay and ½ mile N. 8° W. (N. 32° W. mag.) from the eastern extreme. It is of small extent and covers at three-quarters flood. Calm creek, in the NE. part of Cypress bay, is 1,200 yards long in that direction, with from 4 to 6 fathoms, but, the entrance to it being narrow, with only 2 fathoms of water, it is useless for anchorage, except to small craft.

There is good anchorage in Cypress bay in 12 fathoms near its northern part, at ½ mile from the shore; and though it is open to the southward, no sea rises.

Meares island, within the eastern part of Clayoquot sound, is 6 miles in extent in a northerly and 7 miles in an easterly direction. The coast, except on the northern side, is high and rugged, and there are several mountains on the eastern and western sides upward of 2,000 feet above the sea; one on the latter side, named Lone cone, an isolated conical mountain, is 2,325 feet high, and very conspicuous from seaward near the entrance of Ship channel. Disappointment inlet runs nearly through the island from south to north, and there are several other bights and bays.

Clayoquot.—The large Indian village of Clayoquot is situated at the SW. extreme of Meares island and fronts Village channel.

Deception channel, a continuation of Broken channel, between Meares and Vargas islands, is about 3 miles north and south, and ½ mile wide, with irregular depths of from 5 to 20 fathoms.

There are several rocks in its NW. part; and a large sand bank, which partly dries at low water, extends from Vargas island along its western side for nearly 2 miles, reducing the deep part of the passage to about 600 yards. The tidal stream sets at from 2 to 5 knots through this channel, and a stranger should not attempt its navigation. Local steam vessels and those having local knowledge use it, keeping close along the eastern shore.

Buoy.—A black platform buoy has been moored in a depth of 21 feet off the end of the spit extending from the SW. point of Meares island, to mark the turn from Deception channel to Village channel leading to Clayoquot village, and to Templar channel and Browning passage.

Small vessels anchor in Village channel off Clayoquot village; larger vessels may anchor off Kelsemart, Vargas island.

Stockham island.—The island next eastward of Clayoquot village, and on the western side of the entrance to Disappointment inlet, is known as Stockham island, on the southern side of which is a narrow channel connecting Village channel and Browning passage.

A rock which dries 2 feet at low water lies 200 feet to northward of the rock on the edge of the sand bank which forms the southern side of this channel, and shoal water extends about the same distance from the shore of Stockham island abreast of this rock.

The safest course is in mid-channel between Stockham island and the rock on the sand bank above mentioned.

There is a wharf and store at the western end of Stockham island.

Ritchie bay, on the NW. side of Meares island, 2 miles eastward of Deep pass is 1 mile wide and ½ mile deep and affords good anchorage in 5½ to 10 fathoms 400 yards off its eastern side. The shores of the bay are rocky. Yellow bank, which lies almost athwart the entrance of this bay, is about ¾ mile in extent and has 3 feet on the shoalest part.

If wishing to anchor in Ritchie bay, and coming from Deep pass, proceed eastward to pass about 200 yards northward of Robert point, and keeping the same distance off the southern shore steer into the bay, anchoring in 5 or 7 fathoms about 400 yards from its eastern side, with the extremes bearing N. 24° E. (North mag.) and S. 76° W. (S. 52° W. mag.); entering from the northward, steer midway between Saranac island and the northern point of the bay.

Saranac island, near the northern part of Ritchie bay, is wooded, and steep-to on the eastern side; some small islets extend 600 yards off its western side and there is a narrow but deep passage between it and Yellow bank.

Bedwell sound, the entrance to which is 1½ miles east from Cypress bay, is 7 miles long and 1 mile broad till within 2 miles of its head, when it contracts to 600 yards; the shores are high and rugged, rising on the eastern side to sharp jagged peaks from 2,000 to 4,400 feet above the sea. At its head is a small patch of low swampy land, and a valley from which Bear river, a stream of considerable size, flows into the sound. The depths in the sound vary from 35 to 45 fathoms, and there is no anchorage whatever within it.

Race narrows, east of the entrance of Bedwell sound, and between the NE. part of Meares island and the mainland, is 1½ miles long, and about 400 yards wide in the narrowest part; the tidal streams set through it at 3 to 4 knots, the flood from the westward, and there is 10 fathoms in the shoalest part of mid-channel, Ripple islets, off the eastern entrance to Race narrows, are about 20 feet high, small, and covered with bushes; there are some strong tide rips around them.

Warn bay, to the eastward of Race narrows and 1 mile from the NE. part of Meares island, is upward of 2 miles long and about ¾ mile wide; the shores on both sides are high, but low at the head, whence issue several streams, and a sand bank dries out upward of 200 yards. The depths in the bay are irregular, varying from 50 to 8 fathoms, but a vessel may anchor about 600 yards offshore near the western side of the head of the bay in 14 to 16 fathoms.

Fortune channel, between the eastern side of Meares island and the main, is 5 miles long, north and south, and varies in breadth from 600 yards to 1¼ miles; its shores are high, and there are several offlying rocks on its western side near the middle. The eastern shore of the channel from Warn bay to Deception pass is rocky and indented by several small bays which afford no anchorage.

Mosquito harbor, on the eastern side of Meares island, is narrow and about 2 miles long; there are several rocks and small islets off its entrance, but it affords good anchorage inside in from 4 to 7 fathoms; the entrance is 300 yards wide, with from 4 to 7 fathoms, and the harbor is easily entered by a steamer.

Hankin rock lies 500 yards SW. of Plover point, and in the track of vessels entering Mosquito harbor; it is marked by kelp and there are 23 fathoms midway between it and the point. The rock is marked by a platform buoy, with pyramidal slatwork top painted in red and black horizontal stripes.

Wood islands, in the middle of the entrance, nearly ½ mile west of Plover point, are small, and some rocks lie a short distance off their southern part, but there is a clear passage into the harbor on either side of them, with from 4 to 7 fathoms of water.

Blackberry islets, in the center of the harbor and ¾ mile from the entrance, are small, but steep-to, there being 4 fathoms within 200 yards of them.

When entering Mosquito harbor, round Plover point 200 yards distant to avoid Hankin rock, and keep midway between Wood islands and the eastern shore, anchoring in about 7 fathoms, ⅓ of a mile south of the Blackberry islets; a vessel may enter westward of the Wood islands by keeping midway between them and the shore.

Deception pass, at the southern extreme of Fortune channel and connecting it with Tofino inlet and Browning passage, is a winding channel about 1½ miles long and 400 yards wide; the depths vary from 10 to 20 fathoms, and the tidal streams set with considerable strength through it. On its west side is a narrow creek ½ mile long with from 8 to 9 fathoms, and in the middle of the pass is a small islet.

Tofino inlet, in the eastern part of Clayoquot sound, is about 10 miles long and varies in breadth from ½ to 1½ miles; its shores are high and rocky, indented on the west side by some large creeks. The depths vary from 22 to 68 fathoms, and there is no anchorage, except near the entrance on the west side.

Island cove, on the west side of the inlet, 1 mile from the entrance and NW. of Warne island, is of small extent, with from 8 to 10 fathoms in the middle, and completely landlocked; a small island lies off the entrance, with a clear passage 200 yards wide on either side of it into the cove.

Gunner harbor, on the west side of the inlet, just north of Warne island, is 1½ miles long, but narrow; a small islet lies in its center, about ½ mile north of the entrance, and between the two islands a vessel may find good anchorage in about 10 fathoms; the harbor becomes shoal toward the head.

Tranquil creek, on the west side of the inlet, 4½ miles NE. from Warne island, is narrow, and upward of 1 mile long; its shores are high and rocky, and the creek is too deep for anchorage.

Between Tranquil creek and Warne island, along the west shore, are several small rocky islets, extending from 400 to 600 yards off.

Deer creek, at the head of the inlet, 1 mile long and ¼ mile broad, has an inconvenient depth for anchorage, there being from 22 to 29 fathoms inside it.

Browning passage, on the southern side of Meares island, connecting Tofino inlet with Templar channel, is 5 miles long in a NW. and SE. direction and less than ½ mile broad. At its eastern end the channel is but little over 200 yards wide, and off the western entrance there are several rocks, and no stranger, except with a small vessel, should attempt it. The depths in it vary from 4 to 12 fathoms, and the tidal streams set through at a rate of 2 to 4 knots, the flood stream from the westward.

A rock, with a depth of 8 feet on it, is situated 150 yards NE. of the three small wooded islets at the eastern end of Browning passage.

The passage southward of the islets is the one used and is clear of danger.

A black spar buoy is moored in 5 fathoms on the north side of the passage, 1,400 yards NW. ½ W. from Ginnard point, to show the extent of the shoal ground on that side of the channel.

A dangerous shoal, with from 3 to 4 feet of water over it, extends from the southern shore of the passage ⅜ mile westward of Ginnard point. The northern end of the shoal is situated with the house on Ginnard point bearing S. 83° E. (N. 73° E. mag.), distant 1,200 yards. It is usually marked by kelp. A red spar buoy is moored in 5 fathoms off the northern edge of the shoal.

A rock, with a depth of 3 feet over it, is situated nearly in mid-channel, at the southern end of the narrows at the western end of Browning passage, with the NE. point of Low peninsula bearing S. 80° W. (S. 56° W. mag.), distant about 700 yards. It is marked by a spar buoy painted in red and black horizontal stripes.

The buoy may be passed on either hand, but the channel to the eastward of the rock is the one that should be used.

A rock, with a depth of 2½ fathoms over it, extends 200 feet from the middle of the northeastern shore of the middle island on the western side of the narrows at the western end of Browning passage. The narrows is here little more than 100 yards wide.

North channel, to the northwestward of Ship channel, and separated from it by a number of small islands and rocks, lies along the SE. side of Flores island in an easterly direction. It is 4 miles long, ¼ mile wide in the narrowest part, and the depths in it vary from 7 to 17 fathoms; both sides of the channel are bordered by innumerable rocks, and a stranger is not recommended to use it, as it has not been closely examined; the sea generally breaks heavily along both sides of its outer part.

Flores island, in the western part of Clayoquot sound, between North channel and Sydney inlet, is nearly 7 miles in extent; it is low on the south and east sides, but high on the north and west, rising in some places to 3,000 feet; the shores are rugged and broken, and there are several offlying rocks along its south and west sides; as a rule its outer part should not be approached nearer than 2 miles.

North arm, between the eastern side of Flores island and the main, is about 8 miles long in a northerly direction, and nearly 1 mile broad. Its western shores are high, but decrease gradually to the southward; the depths are very great in the north part, but they shoal rapidly to the southward, where a vessel may anchor in from 5 to 8 fathoms abreast Base point, the SE. point of the island.

The Indian village of Ahousat, where there is a store and post-office, is situated ½ mile northward of Base point. There is good anchorage off the village in 6 fathoms.

Matilda creek, on the west side of North arm, the entrance to which is 2 miles northward from Base point, is 1¼ miles long in a southerly direction, very narrow, with from 5 to 25 fathoms, but useless as an anchorage.

Herbert arm, the entrance to which is on the eastern side of North arm, about 2 miles from the southern entrance of the latter, is 9 miles long in a NNE. direction, and its average breadth is about 1 mile. The shores are mountainous and much broken.

Bawden bay, on the southern side of the entrance to Herbert arm, and about 1½ miles NE. from Base point, is of small extent and affords anchorage in 15 fathoms, near the center; enter it in mid-channel.

Cone island, lying at the entrance of this arm, is steep-to on the southern and western sides, but the passage into Herbert arm, north of it, is blocked up by rocks and small islets.

White Pine cove, on the eastern side of Herbert arm, nearly 3 miles from the entrance, is small, with a bank extending from the head; a small vessel may anchor close to the edge of this bank in about 10 fathoms; care, however, should be taken to avoid Sutlej reef, a shoal of 3 fathoms lying near the middle of the entrance to the bay, but toward the southern side, at about 1,400 yards from the head of the cove.

Directions.—Entering Clayoquot sound by Ship channel (which latter will easily be recognized, if the weather be clear, by Bare island, Sea Otter rock, and the remarkable summit Lone cone on Meares island), round either Bare island or Sea Otter rock at the distance of ¾ mile, and steer up the channel with the SE. point of Lawrence island and the Twins islets in line with the north summit of the Cat Face mountains bearing N. 48° E. (N. 24° E. mag.). Keep the above-mentioned mark on till within ½ mile of the Shark reefs, when haul more to the eastward toward Hobbs and Burgess islands, off the NW. end of Vargas island, which islands may be passed at a distance of 600 yards. If going on through Hecate passage, to clear Half-tide rock, keep Hobbs islet open west of Burgess islet bearing S. 37° W. (S. 13° W. mag.) until the Twins come in line with the north Whaler island bearing N. 77° W. (S. 79° W. mag.), when steer up the passage with that mark on astern, which will lead north of Half-tide rock and south of North bank. When past the latter, if going farther up the sound, proceed through Deep pass.

During heavy southwesterly gales the sea is said to break right across Ship channel, between Lawrence and Hobbs islands.

Caution.—Although there are several apparently deep channels into Clayoquot sound, they are, with the exception of Ship channel, so tortuous and so filled with rocks that no stranger should attempt to enter by any except the latter, and not by it unless having the latest chart of the sound.

Intending to navigate the inner waters of the sound, which can only be done by a steamer or small craft, the chart will be found the best guide.

Sydney inlet, westward of Clayoquot sound, is 10 miles long in a northerly direction, and varies in breadth from ½ to 1 mile. Its entrance is 3½ miles north of Rafael point, between the western side of Flores island and the mainland of Vancouver; at 4 miles from the head are two small branches about 2 miles in length, one extending north, the other SW.; the shores are high and rugged, rising abruptly from the sea to 2,000 and 3,000 feet. The depth in the entrance is 15 fathoms, increasing gradually toward the head.

Refuge cove, just west of Sharp point, and separated from Sydney inlet by a narrow peninsula, extends 1½ miles in a northerly direction, is from 200 to 600 yards wide, and affords good anchorage in 4 to 5 fathoms at from ¾ to 1 mile within the entrance, well sheltered and secure from all winds.

The entrance is narrow, and at 400 yards inside Sharp point and about 200 yards from the eastern shore is a rock having only 9 feet on it at low water. This rock lies slightly eastward of the fairway, but a good lookout is necessary, as it is not always marked by kelp.

Canoe reef, lying just WSW. from the entrance and ¾ mile S. 80° W. (S. 56° W. mag.) from Sharp point, is 2 feet above high water, but steep-to on the south and west sides.

Breakers are reported in rough weather with the southern extreme of Sharp point bearing N. 15° W. (N. 39° W. mag.), distant 300 yards.

Directions.—Entering Refuge cove from seaward, bring the entrance or Sharp point to bear N. 5° W. (N. 29° W. mag.), and steer for it, so as to pass 200 yards west of the point; then keep in mid-channel, or rather nearer the western shore, to avoid the 9-foot rock, and having passed this keep close to the eastern shore and proceed up the harbor; anchor in 4½ or 5 fathoms, about 1 mile within the entrance.

A sailing vessel, if embayed near this part of the coast, could find safety and shelter in Refuge cove.

Shelter arm branches off from the eastern side of Sydney inlet 4 miles from the entrance, and extends in an easterly direction along the northern side of Flores island for 4 miles to Rocky pass, whence it winds in a northeasterly direction for 4 miles farther, and terminates in a narrow creek.

The shores of Shelter arm are high, precipitous, and steep-to; the tidal streams run from 1 to 2 knots through it, the flood stream from the westward.

Steamer cove, the only anchorage (indifferent) in it, is just 2 miles within the entrance on the northern side of Flores island; it is a small bight where a vessel may anchor in 17 to 19 fathoms, passing on either side of the islet at its entrance.

Rocky pass, between Flores and Obstruction islands, connects North arm with Shelter arm, and is used by coasting vessels in rough weather. There is a sunken rock at the western end of the pass, and one in the middle of the pass that is visible at low water; both are generally marked by kelp. There is a rocky islet at the western end, and two close together at the eastern entrance. It is desirable to have slack water when using this pass; vessels pass to the southward of the rocky islets, and about midway between them and the southern shore.

The strength of the tidal stream seldom exceeds 4 knots.

Hesquiat harbor, 8 miles northwestward of the western part of Clayoquot sound, lies on the eastern side of Estevan point. It is 4 miles long in a northerly direction, and upward of 2 miles wide at the entrance, opening out a little inside, but on nearing the head it contracts to less than 1 mile. The depths within the harbor vary from 4 to 8 fathoms, and there is a good and secure anchorage in 7 or 8 fathoms at ½ mile from the head.

Hesquiat is a large Indian village, and has a Roman Catholic mission establishment. The store is about 1 mile northward of the village on the western shore. The anchorage used by the sealers is off the store; that off the village is too rocky.

The bar.—Across the entrance, between Hesquiat bluff and Estevan point, is a bar or ledge, from about ½ mile to 1 mile wide, with from 3 to 5 fathoms of water over it, which in a great measure prevents the sea from setting home into the harbor. Kelp grows more or less all over the anchorage in a depth of 5 fathoms.

Hesquiat bluff, on the eastern side of the entrance to the outer part of the harbor, is a remarkable, low, wooded point, with a shingle beach around it; a reef, which covers at a quarter flood, lies ½ mile SW. from it.

The shores of the harbor are mostly low and wooded. On the western side of the bay near Estevan point are several indications of coal, and the land is apparently fertile.

Boat basin is a small cove with 4 fathoms at the head of Hesquiat harbor on the eastern side; there is a large fresh-water stream there, and vessels may obtain wood and water with great facility.

Tides.—It is high water, full and change, in Hesquiat harbor at 0 h. 0 m.; springs rise 12 feet.

Directions.—Hesquiat harbor is easy of access to sailing vessels, even with a foul wind. The notch of Leading mountain in line with East Entrance point to the upper part of the harbor, bearing N. 1° E. (N. 24° W. mag.), leads over the bar in 4½ fathoms at low water. Entering either from the east or west give the outer shores of the harbor a berth of more than ½ mile till past the bar; anchor in 7 or 8 fathoms near the center of the harbor, about ½ mile from its head.

In strong southerly or southwesterly gales the sea breaks heavily over the bar, but the anchorage is always safe, and landing is at all times practicable in Boat basin.

Estevan point, 13 miles WNW. from Rafael point, is a low, wooded, and projecting point, bordered by a sandy beach, strewed with huge bowlders. A ledge extends nearly 1 mile off its western side. Hole in the Wall, the southwestern part of the point, may be easily known by a remarkable gap in the trees at its extreme, which is conspicuous from the SW.

When rounding the western part of Estevan point, it would not be prudent to approach the shore within 2 miles.

From this point the coast takes a northerly direction for 8 miles to Escalante point at the entrance of Nootka sound, and is low; foul ground extends off it for some distance.

Sunday rock lies 1¾ miles distant from the shore and nearly 3 miles N. 64° W. (N. 89° W. mag.) from Hole in the Wall, the pitch of the point; within the ledge good shelter will be found for boats in all weathers.

Nootka sound, called King George sound by the celebrated navigator, Capt. James Cook, in 1778, is a large sheet of water upward of 6 miles in extent, containing several islands, and from its northern side three narrow arms penetrate the land for distances of 18, 7 and 14 miles, respectively. Its entrance is 5 miles wide between Maquinna and Escalante points, which bear NW. by W. and SE. by E. from each other; at the entrance the shores are low, and have several offlying dangers, but inside the sound they become high, rugged, and precipitous.

In fine weather the natives will be met with in canoes in considerable numbers on the banks, fishing for halibut, which are very plentiful along this coast.

There are four anchorages in the sound, two of which, Friendly cove and Plumper harbor on the eastern side of Nootka island, are small, though easy of access to steam vessels; the former is 1 mile and the latter 7 miles within the entrance; the others in the Tlupana arm, though well sheltered, are more inconvenient, being 13 and 16 miles from the entrance.

Aspect.—From seaward the appearance of the land near the entrance of the sound offers to the navigator many striking features which in fine weather render it almost impossible to be mistaken; the low land of Estevan and Maquinna points at the entrance, with the breakers off them, the Nootka cone at the eastern point of Nootka island, and, if coming from the southward and westward, Conuma peak, a remarkable steeple-shaped mountain, 4,889 feet high, 20 miles NE. from the entrance, are conspicuous features.

Tides.—It is high water, full and change, in Nootka sound at 0 h. 0m., and the rise and fall is about 12 feet; the tidal streams are everywhere inconsiderable.

Escalante point, the eastern entrance point of the sound, is low and rocky; some small islets and rocks, generally above high water, extend off it in a westerly direction for upward of 1 mile, but they are steep-to on their outer edge. At their outer end is a rock only uncovering at low water.

From Escalante point to Burdwood point, at the narrowest part of the entrance on the eastern side, the coast, which still keeps a northerly direction for 3 miles, is bordered by several offlying rocks, and should not be approached within 1½ miles until close to the latter point.

Maquinna point, the western entrance point of the sound, is low and wooded, and at its extreme is a remarkable bare-topped conical rock about 60 or 70 feet high; some rocks extend 600 yards off it in a southeasterly direction, and the coast from it to the eastward nearly as far as the entrance of Friendly cove is foul, and the shore should not be approached nearer than ¾ mile till near the latter place.

Bajo reef, 6 miles S. 84° W. (S. 59° W. mag.) from Maquinna point and 2¾ miles distant from the shore, is about 400 yards in extent, and the sea only breaks on it in heavy weather. This reef is the only known hidden danger outside the sound, and is dangerous to vessels entering it from the westward. Yuquot point, the SE. extreme of Nootka island, kept open east of Maquinna point bearing N. 70° E. (N. 45° E. mag.), leads 1½ miles SE. of it; and Bight cone (a remarkable hill on the southern side of Nootka island) kept well open west of Bajo point bearing N. 14° E. (N. 11° W. mag.), leads 1¾ miles west of the reef.

Friendly cove, at the eastern extreme of Nootka island, just within the narrowest part of the entrance to the sound and about 2½ miles ENE. of Maquinna point, is about 400 yards in extent and sheltered from the sea by several small rocky islets on its SE. side. The entrance, 200 yards wide, is from the eastward. The shores on both sides of the cove are rocky and about 60 feet high on the northern side, but at the head is a small space of clear, cultivated, flat land, where is situated the Indian village of Nootka. There is a church and store at the northern end of the village.

Anchorage in Friendly cove, in from 5 to 9 fathoms, is of small extent, affording only room for one vessel of moderate size to lie moored in the middle, though several small ones would find shelter.

Directions.—If desiring to anchor in Friendly cove, round Observatory islet, the eastern entrance point, close-to, and if in a large vessel moor with anchors SW. and NE., letting go the first immediately on entering the cove. Sailing vessels, unless with a fair wind, would find some difficulty in entering; and if unable to shoot in, it would be preferable to proceed farther up the sound to Plumper harbor.

Supplies.—Fresh water in quantity can not be procured at Friendly cove, or nearer than Marvinas bay; but fish and deer may generally be obtained from the natives.

Marvinas bay.—The western shore of Nootka sound from Friendly cove trends in a northerly direction for about 6 miles to the entrance of the Kendrick arm and Tahsis canal; it is rocky, and near the southern part some islets lie parallel to it, extending for nearly 2 miles, distant about 600 yards from the shore. There are two small creeks with entrances too narrow for a vessel to enter; the northernmost of them, named by the Spaniards Boca del Infierno, lies abreast the northern part of the above-mentioned islands and 1¾ miles from Friendly cove. Marvinas bay, 4 miles north from Friendly cove, on the eastern side of Nootka island, is of small extent and open to the southward; it only affords anchorage to a coaster.

Water.—There are large fresh-water streams at the head of Marvinas bay, and just south of it, convenient for watering.

Kendrick arm, at the NW. end of Nootka sound, between Nootka and Narrow islands, is about 5 miles long in a northerly direction, and ½ mile wide, connected at the northern part by a narrow boat pass to the Tahsis canal; on the western side, 2 miles from its entrance, is Plumper harbor, easy of access, and well sheltered. Northward of this harbor the shores of the arm on both sides are rocky, terminating in two narrow creeks at the head, useless for purposes of navigation.

Plumper harbor, on the western side of Kendrick arm, and 6 miles from Friendly cove, is a small bay indenting the eastern side of Nootka island, about 600 yards in extent and affording good anchorage in 12 fathoms. It is protected on the eastern side by two small wooded islets from 30 to 40 feet high, Pass island and Bold island, the latter being the most northerly; on the western side the shore is rather swampy, and there are several fresh-water streams.

Anchorage.—There is a clear passage into the harbor between the two islets, or to the northward of the northern one, which may be rounded at the distance of 200 yards, and there is room for a vessel to lie at single anchor inside; it is the best anchorage in the sound, the only drawback being its distance from the entrance. Foul ground extends for a short distance from the NW. side of Pass island.

Tahsis canal, the entrance to which is at the NW. part of Nootka sound, about 6 miles from Friendly cove, is a long, narrow arm of the sea, nearly straight, and 14 miles long in a northerly direction; the shores are mountainous, rocky, and steep-to, and there is no anchorage in it. In many parts this canal is only 400 yards wide, but it becomes gradually broader at the head, where is a large stream, and also a considerable village, to which the natives resort during the summer season for salmon, which are caught here in great numbers.

At 10½ miles from the entrance of the canal on the western side, and separating the northern point of Nootka island from the main of Vancouver island, are the Tahsis narrows, 200 yards wide, with 28 fathoms in the center; they connect Esperanza inlet with the Tahsis canal; the tidal streams run weakly through them, the flood from the westward.

At the entrance of Tahsis canal is a small island (Canal island) with a clear passage about 200 yards wide on either side of it.

Bligh island, lying in the center of Nootka sound, is the largest island in it, being about 4½ miles long in a northerly direction, and 2 miles wide in the northern part; its shores are rocky and indented by creeks on the southern side. Its south extreme is a long, narrow point about 3 miles NE. of the entrance to the sound, and off its western side are a number of islands extending upward of 1 mile from it, all steep-to on their outer edges, but among which no vessel should venture. The south part of the island is rather low, but it rises in the north and west parts to 1,030 and 1,200 feet.

Resolution cove, at the SE. point of this island, just within the entrance of the Zuciarte channel, is only deserving of notice as the spot where Captain Cook refitted his ships in April, 1778; it is only a slight bend in the coast, with a deep and rocky bottom, and inconvenient for anchorage, being also open to the southward.

Junction island, lying about midway between the southern point of Narrow island and western side of Bligh island, is about ½ mile long and 250 feet high; a small islet lies close off its NW. side and another on the opposite side. The channel lies to the west and north of Junction island, and no vessel should pass between the latter and Bligh island.

Zuciarte channel, between the eastern shore of Nootka sound and Bligh island is about 5 miles long in a northeasterly direction and upward of ½ mile wide in the narrowest part; its shores are high, and the depths within the channel vary from 80 to 100 fathoms.

Guaquina, or Muchalat, arm, extends 17 miles in an easterly direction from the NE. part of Nootka sound, and varies in breadth from ¼ to upward of 1 mile. It is bounded on both sides by mountains from 2,000 to 4,000 feet high, and presents similar features to the inlets before described along this coast, terminating in low land at the head, through which a small stream flows into the inlet; there is no anchorage whatever within this arm except for coasters.

One and a half miles within the entrance is Gore island, which is narrow and about 3 miles long in an easterly direction; there is a clear, deep passage on either side of it, the southern one being less than 200 yards wide at the eastern end. The island rises in the center to 1,200 feet, sloping gradually to each end; its shores are rocky.

A rock, awash at low water, lies about 200 yards from the southern shore of the arm, with the western end of Gore island bearing N. 8° W. (N. 33° W. mag.), distant 1,200 yards.

On the north side of this arm, 14 miles within the entrance, is an extensive valley, through which flows a large stream, named the Gold river, indications of that metal having been discovered there; the land in the vicinity of this stream is lightly timbered and very fertile; a small vessel may enter it at high water.

The Muchalat Indians have a village at the mouth of Gold river.

Tlupana arm, the entrance to which is in the northern part of Nootka sound, is about 7 miles long in a northerly direction, branching off at the head in two smaller arms extending to the NNW. and ENE., the former about 3 miles, the latter 2 miles, long, and each terminating in low land. Its shores are high and rocky, and the depths in it vary from 80 to 100 fathoms; there are two anchorages, one at Deserted creek on the western side, and the other at Head bay, the termination of the northwestern branch.

The mountains at the northern part of this arm are the highest in the sound, many being from 4,000 to 5,000 feet above the sea; Conuma peak, rising 7 miles NE. from the head, is 4,889 feet high, and of a steeple shape.

Deserted creek, on the western side of the arm, 3 miles within the entrance, is 2 miles long in a NW. direction and about 400 or 500 yards wide; a vessel may anchor in 12 to 14 fathoms at ⅓ mile from its head. Island bay, a small cove on its NE. side, just within the entrance, has an islet in the center, to the westward of which is room for a vessel to anchor in 12 fathoms.

At the southern extreme of the promontory separating the two branches at the head of Tlupana arm is Perpendicular bluff, a remarkable precipice of considerable height.

Head bay, the termination of the western branch of the Tlupana arm, is nearly 1 mile long in a NW. direction, about 800 yards wide, and affords anchorage in from 14 to 16 fathoms at the distance of 600 to 800 yards from its head. At the entrance on the northern side are three small islets about 3 or 4 feet above high water, the inner one connected to the shore by a beach at low water; between these islets and Perpendicular bluff is a small bay, where a vessel may anchor in from 16 to 18 fathoms.

Directions.—Entering Nootka sound from the southward, after rounding Estevan point, steer about North for the entrance, which will be easily made out by the rocks off Escalante and Maquinna points; keep about 2 miles off the eastern shore till past Escalante point, when steer up mid-channel into the sound. If bound to Friendly cove haul over to the western side of entrance for Yuquot point, which may be approached within a distance of 200 yards, and rounding it, anchor or moor, as most convenient, in Friendly cove in from 5 to 9 fathoms.

If bound to Plumper harbor, after passing Yuquot point keep about ½ mile from the eastern side of Nootka island for 5 miles to the entrance of Kendrick arm, when steer up the latter in mid-channel till abreast Plumper harbor, which may be entered by passing between Bold and Pass islets on its eastern side, or going to the northward of the former; anchor in 11 to 12 fathoms near the center of the harbor.

Should it be desired to anchor in any of the anchorages within the Tlupana arm, steer as before directed till within ½ mile of the entrance to the Kendrick arm, when haul to the NE.; pass to the westward of Junction and Bligh islands and steer up the Tlupana arm, in mid-channel or close-to on either shore. Deserted creek and Head bay may be entered without difficulty.

Entering Nootka sound from the westward, on nearing Bajo point do not approach the south shore of Nootka island within 4 miles, or shut in Bight cone with Bajo point bearing N. 14° E. (N. 11° W. mag.), until Yuquot point opens east of Maquinna point bearing N. 70° E. (N. 45° E. mag.), which will clear the Bajo reef; a vessel may then steer for the entrance of the sound, about E. by N., not approaching the shore between Maquinna and Yuquot points nearer than 1 mile, until abreast the latter, after which proceed up the sound as before directed.

If beating into Nootka sound, when standing to the westward, keep Yuquot point open east of Maquinna point bearing N. 70° E. (N. 45° E. mag.), which will keep a vessel well clear to the southward of Bajo reef; in standing to the eastward do not approach Escalante point within 1½ miles, nor bring Burdwood point to bear northward of N. 36° E. (N. 11° E. mag.) until abreast it; when standing toward Maquinna and Yuquot points on the west side, avoid bringing the latter to bear to the eastward of N. 47° E. (N. 22° E. mag.) until abreast it.

Nootka sound is easier of access than any other place on the whole of the west coast of Vancouver island, the entrance being nearly 2 miles wide in the narrowest part; and by attending to the above directions any sailing vessel may beat in or out of the sound. If the night be clear, and provided with a chart, it may be entered without risk by bringing the entrance to bear N. 47° E. (N. 22° E. mag.), and in a steamer but little difficulty would be experienced in picking up the anchorages of Friendly cove and Plumper harbor.

Nootka island, which bounds the western side of Nootka sound, is of considerable extent, being 15 miles long in a northerly and 20 miles wide in a westerly direction. Its southern, or outer shore, is low, rising gradually inland 1,500 and 2,900 feet above the sea, and has a beautiful and fertile appearance; it is bordered by a sandy beach nearly the whole distance, and the sea breaks heavily along it.

Bajo point, 6 miles westward from Maquinna point, is low and rocky. A ledge named the Inner Bajo reef extends 1¼ miles from it in a southerly direction; and the Bajo reef lies 2¾ miles south from it.

Westward of Bajo point the coast takes a NW. direction for 10 miles to Ferrer point, and is slightly indented. Bight cone, a remarkable summit, 540 feet high, rises 3 miles N. 4° W. (N. 29° W. mag.) from Bajo point, and is about 1 mile inland.

When navigating along the southern side of Nootka island west of the Bajo reef, it would not be prudent to approach the shore within 2 miles until near Ferrer point, though there are no known outlying dangers.

Nuchatlitz inlet, on the NW. side of Nootka island, about 18 miles NW. from the entrance to Nootka sound, is 6 miles long in an easterly direction and 3 miles wide at its entrance, narrowing toward the head; its shores are high and rocky and much broken into creeks and small bays; off the entrance and within are several dangers. The depths in the inlet vary from 5 to 17 fathoms, and there are two good anchorages, Port Langford on the northern side and Mary basin at the head; but, owing to the dangers off the entrance of the inlet, they are both rather difficult of access.

Caution.—None but small vessels should attempt to beat into this inlet, as there is generally a heavy sea at the entrance, and no stranger should attempt to enter unless the leading mark is easily distinguished.

Ferrer point, the southern entrance point of the inlet, is low and rocky; there is a depth of 14 fathoms at 400 yards from it, and ½ mile eastward of the point is Northwest cone, a very remarkable conical hill, 350 feet high, which proves a very useful guide to this locality from the westward.

Danger rock, lying in the southern part of the entrance, upward of 1 mile N. 27° W. (N. 52° W. mag.) from Ferrer point, is the worst danger, as it is of very small extent, and the sea only breaks on it in heavy weather; it is steep-to on all sides, there being 11 fathoms close to it. The best passage into the inlet is between this rock and Ferrer point.

Leading mark.—Mark hill, at the head of the inlet, in line with the northern part of Fitz island, bearing N. 74° E. (N. 49° E. mag.), or Bare rock, which is often more easily distinguished than Mark hill, in line with the center of Fitz island, leads south of this rock, midway between it and Ferrer point, and through the fairway into the inlet.

Nuchatlitz reef, in the center of the entrance and ⅓ mile north of Danger rock, is about ¾ mile long in an east and west direction, and 200 yards wide. The sea generally breaks on this reef, and at its eastern extremity is a small rock awash at high water; there is a passage between it and Danger rock, and also apparently northward of it, but neither should be attempted by a stranger, as no leading marks can be given for them.

South reef, nearly 400 yards in extent and covering at three-quarters flood, lies just within the entrance on the southern side, 1 mile N. 58° E. (N. 33° E. mag.) from Ferrer point, and about 600 yards distant from the shore.

Mark hill, in line with the northern summit of Fitz island, bearing N. 74° E. (N. 49° E. mag.), leads 400 yards north of this reef.

Louie creek, just inside South reef, is shoal, and nearly 1 mile in extent; there are several rocks off its entrance, and no vessel should enter it; to the eastward of the creek the southern shore of Nuchatlitz inlet is rocky.

Fitz island, in the center of the inlet, and 3 miles from the entrance, is of small extent, low, rugged, and covered with a few stunted pine trees, the tops of which are about 100 feet above the sea. At ½ mile WNW. of it is Bare island, small and 20 feet high; between it and Fitz island foul ground exists. Bare rock, of small extent, and 12 feet above high water, lies ¾ mile WSW. of Fitz island.

Mary basin, the termination of the inlet, is of considerable extent, and completely landlocked by Lord island, which lies across the inlet at the SW. part of the basin. The depths inside the basin vary from 5 to 9 fathoms, and the entrance on the northern side of Lord island appears clear of danger, but it has not been sufficiently examined to recommend its use by a stranger.

Eastward of Mary basin, and connected to it by a narrow pass 50 yards wide, with from 7 to 9 fathoms, is Inner basin, a sheet of water upward of 3 miles long in an easterly direction, with from 20 to 39 fathoms, and apparently useless as an anchorage.

Port Langford, on the northern side of Nuchatlitz inlet, 2 miles within the entrance, is about 1¾ miles long in a northerly direction, and varies in breadth from ¼ to ½ mile. The depths in it vary from 5 to 8 fathoms, and it affords a secure and well-sheltered anchorage in about 6 fathoms, muddy bottom, at ½ mile from the head. The eastern shore of the port is high, rising to mount Rosa 2,553 feet above the water, but the western shore is much lower; both are rocky.

Colwood islet, at the SW. extreme of the entrance, is small, and bare, 20 feet high, and nearly ½ mile offshore; between it and the shore, and to the westward skirting the northern entrance point of Nuchatlitz inlet, are innumerable rocks and small islets, among which no vessel should venture.

Belmont point, the eastern entrance point into Port Langford, is ¾ mile N. 76° E. (N. 51° E. mag.) from Colwood islet; it is low, and a rock uncovers at 200 yards west of it.

Directions.—Entering Nuchatlitz inlet from the southward, bring Ferrer point on a N. 13° E. (N. 12° W. mag.) bearing, and steer to pass ½ mile west of it; and when Mark hill comes in line with the northern part of Fitz island N. 74° E. (N. 49° E. mag.), or Bare rock in line with the center of the island, haul in for the entrance on that mark, which will lead in clear of Danger rock and South reef. When Ferrer point bears SSW., a vessel will be inside the rock, and may steer for the entrance to Port Langford; pass midway between Colwood islet and Belmont point, and proceed up the port in mid-channel, anchoring in 5 or 6 fathoms, at ½ mile from the head.

Approaching the port from the westward, keep an offing of 4 or 5 miles till Ferrer point bears S. 65° E. (East mag.), when steer for it on that bearing till the leading mark for the channel (Mark hill in line with the northern part of Fitz island N. 74° E. (N. 49° E. mag.), comes on, when proceed as before directed to the anchorage in Port Langford.

Intending to enter Mary basin (which is not, however, recommended), when past Ferrer point keep the leading mark on till abreast Louie creek, then steer a little to the eastward, passing about 200 yards southward of Bare rock and Fitz island; when past the latter steer N. 86° E. (N. 61° E. mag.) until the western point of Lord island bears N. 35° E. (N. 10° E. mag.), which will clear the shoal extending ½ mile to the southward from Benson point, and then, on approaching Lord island, close the north shore a little and enter Mary basin to the westward of the island and the small islet NW. of it; when abreast the latter haul more to the eastward and anchor in from 5 to 6 fathoms near the middle of the basin.

Tides.—It is high water, full and change, in Nuchatlitz inlet at 0 h. 0 m.; springs rise about 12 feet.

Esperanza inlet, the entrance to which lies between the NW. side of Nootka island and the mainland of Vancouver island, 122 miles NW. from the lighthouse on Tatoosh island, is about 16 miles long in a winding northeasterly direction, with an average breadth of about 1 mile, narrowing at the head, and connected by a narrow pass (Tahsis narrows) to the Tahsis canal in Nootka sound.

The entrance, though wide, contains several dangers; inside the shores rise on both sides to mountains of considerable height. The southern shore is indented by three bays of moderate extent, which, however, afford no anchorage; and from the northern one three arms of considerable length penetrate the Vancouver shore for several miles. Port Eliza, the western arm, has the only anchorage in the inlet.

Middle channel, the widest and best into Esperanza inlet, is 3 miles long in a NE. direction, and upward of 1 mile wide in the narrowest part. Its entrance lies 3 miles NW. from Ferrer point, between Blind reef, Needle rock, and a number of small islets extending off the western side of Nootka island on the east, and Middle reef and Black rock on the west; a part of the former is always above water.

Blind reef, at the SE. extreme of the channel, 3 miles N. 27° W. (N. 52° W. mag.) from Ferrer point, is about 400 yards in extent, and the sea only breaks on it in bad weather; 300 yards northward of it is a small rock, and at a distance of 400 yards from its southern and western sides are depths of 13 to 19 fathoms.

Pin rock, of small extent, awash at low water, lies ⅜ mile ESE. from Blind reef.

Needle rock, which is of small extent, lies ⅜ mile NNE. of Blind reef, and has from 14 to 15 fathoms at 400 yards westward of it.

Middle reef, at the SW. entrance point of Middle channel, is about 600 yards long in a northeasterly direction and 200 yards wide. The sea generally breaks on this reef, and at its southern extreme is a small rock 4 feet above high water; there are from 5 to 20 fathoms at a distance of 200 yards on all sides of it; its southern part lies 4 miles N. 40° W. (N. 65° W. mag.) from Ferrer point.

A patch, which occasionally breaks in heavy weather, lies 700 yards NE. from the northern end of Middle reef.

Leading hill, in line with Black rock, bearing N. 13° E. (N. 12° W. mag.), leads through the fairway of Middle channel ⅜ mile westward of Blind reef, 1 mile westward of Needle rock, and ¼ mile eastward of Middle reef.

North channel leads into Esperanza inlet west of Middle reef, between it and the dangers off the southern side of Catala island. It is about ⅓ mile wide and upward of 2 miles long.

Black rock, in line with Double island, bearing N. 43° E. (N. 18° E. mag.), leads in through the fairway of North channel clear of Middle reef.

Catala island, 5½ miles NNW. ½ W. from Ferrer point, on the western side of the entrance to Esperanza inlet, is about 1¾ miles long in a WNW. and ESE. direction and 1 mile wide in its broadest part. It is wooded and from 150 to 200 feet high; its shores are rocky, and several dangers exist at a considerable distance off it on all sides; its northern side is separated from the Vancouver shore by a passage ½ mile wide, known as Rolling roadstead, and a vessel may find a tolerably secure anchorage there in from 4 to 6 fathoms, though generally a swell prevails in it.

The Twins, two small islets connected with each other at low water, lie off the southern point of Catala island, and foul ground extends nearly 1½ miles SSW. from them. Low rock, 6 feet above high water, is 1⅛ miles SSW. from the western Twin islet, and 500 yards southward from it is a patch over which the sea occasionally breaks in heavy weather.

Black rock, which lies 800 yards SSE. from the eastern point of Catala, is a small bare rock 20 feet above high water; foul ground exists between it and Catala, and also 200 yards southward of it; do not approach its eastern side nearer than 400 yards, nor attempt to pass westward of it.

Entrance reef, about 600 yards northward of the eastern point of Catala island, at the eastern part of Rolling roadstead, is of small extent, and covers at half flood.

Arnold rock, ¼ mile NNE. from Entrance reef, and about 400 yards distant from the opposite shore, is awash at high water; midway between these rocks is 6½ fathoms, and in the roadstead from 4 to 6 fathoms. The outer rocks off the NW. part of Catala island, open northward of the low grassy point at the northern side of the latter, bearing N. 77° W. (S. 78° W. mag.), leads into Rolling roadstead, midway between Arnold rock and Entrance reef.

Half a mile inshore, and overlooking the NE. part of Rolling roadstead, is Leading hill, 1,104 feet above the sea; it is of conical shape and conspicuous from the entrance to Middle channel.

Double island lies ½ mile from the northern shore at the inner and narrowest part of the entrance to Esperanza inlet. It is of small extent, and wooded; a number of rocks exist between it and the shore. It should not be approached too closely, as rocks extend to a distance of about 300 yards from its eastern side.

Flower islet, on the opposite shore, at the northwestern extremity of Rosa island, 1 mile SE. from Double island and ½ mile from the NW. point of Nootka island, is small and bare, and is the northernmost of the islets off Nootka island between the entrances of Nuchatlitz and Esperanza inlets. At 400 yards WSW. from it is a small rock 2 feet above high water.

Eastward of Flower islet the southern shore of Esperanza inlet takes a winding irregular outline to the ENE., is everywhere steep-to, and rises gradually to mountains 2,000 and 3,000 feet high.

There are three bays, all too deep for anchorage; in the western one which is just within the entrance, are several small islets.

Center island, ¼ mile off the southern shore, and about 1½ miles NE. of Flower islet, is about ¾ mile long in an east and west direction, and of moderate height; its shores are rocky.

Hecate channel, near the head of the inlet, is 4¾ miles long in a winding direction to the southeastward, and its average breadth is about 1,200 yards. The western end is 10 miles from the entrance of Esperanza inlet; and the eastern (Tahsis narrows) is about 200 yards wide, with 28 fathoms, connecting this channel with the Tahsis canal in Nootka sound; the shores are high and rocky.

Port Eliza, the entrance to which is on the northern side of Esperanza inlet, 1 mile NE. of Double island, is a narrow arm 5¼ miles long in a NNW. direction, its breadth varying from 400 to 800 yards; the shores are high, and there are some rocks and small islands in the entrance and along the eastern shore. There is good anchorage in from 14 to 15 fathoms at ½ mile from the head, and also in Queens cove, which is upward of 1 mile within the entrance on the east side.

The head terminates in a small patch of low swampy land, through which flow two fresh-water streams, and off it a bank dries 200 yards at low water.

The passage into Port Eliza is through Birthday channel, eastward of Harbor island, and is 300 yards wide in the narrowest part.

Harbor island, in the center of the entrance, is about 800 yards in extent, wooded, and of moderate height. Between Harbor island and the western shore lies False channel, which has irregular soundings, and in its southern part are two rocks which cover at half flood.

Fairway island, on the eastern side of Birthday channel, and 800 yards eastward from Harbor island, is of small extent and covered with a few stunted trees; some rocks extend a short distance off on both sides of it, and 300 yards ENE. of it is a group of rocks 6 feet in height.

Channel reef, ½ mile north of Harbor island, in the middle of Port Eliza, is about 200 yards in extent, and covers at three-quarters flood.

Queens cove, on the eastern side of the port, about 1½ miles from the entrance, is ½ mile long and 400 yards wide, but at the entrance the width is contracted to 100 yards by a small island, which at low water is connected to the eastern side of the cove. The channel lies to the westward of the island.

The cove affords room for a large vessel to lie moored in the center in from 6 to 7 fathoms. Its shores are high and rocky, and it is completely landlocked, but is easy of access for a steamer; a large sailing vessel would, however, most likely be obliged to warp in; there is a fresh-water stream of considerable size on the west side of its head, very convenient for watering.

Espinosa arm, the entrance to which is 2 miles NE. of Port Eliza, is 8 miles long in a northerly direction, and its average breadth is ½ mile. The water within it is deep, and it affords no anchorage; at the entrance on the western side are some small islets, and a rock which uncovers. This inlet presents similar features to the other inlets along the coast, being bounded by high, rocky, rugged shores, and terminating in low land at the head. At 4 miles within the entrance, on the eastern side, is a narrow branch or fork extending 3 miles northeasterly to its head, which is separated by a narrow neck 600 yards wide from the Zeballos arm, forming a peninsula of considerable size to the southward. The entrance to this narrow branch is choked up with rocks.

Zeballos arm, the entrance to which lies 10 miles within the inlet, at the west end of Hecate channel, is about 6 miles long in a winding direction to the NW., and about ¾ mile wide; similar to Espinosa arm, it offers no anchorage whatever, and is of no use to the navigator.

Directions.—A stranger entering Esperanza inlet from the southward, through the Middle channel, and intending to anchor in Port Eliza, should pass Ferrer point at a distance of about 3 miles, and keep on a northerly course till nearing the entrance to Middle channel, when steer to bring Leading hill in line with Black rock bearing N. 13° E. (N. 12° W. mag.), which will lead through the fairway, and clear of the dangers on both sides of the channel. When the southern point of Catala island bears N. 44° W. (N. 69° W. mag.), a vessel will be inside the dangers at the entrance, and should steer about NE. for the entrance to Port Eliza.

When entering the port, steer through Birthday channel, passing 200 yards east of Harbor island; when past the eastern point of the latter, keep about N. by W. for the entrance to Queens cove, or farther over to the eastern shore, to avoid Channel reef; when entering the cove, pass west of the island at its entrance and moor.

If going to the head of Port Eliza, keep on as before directed till about 200 yards distant from the entrance to Queens cove, when haul sharply to the westward, keeping about 200 yards from the northern shore, till Fairway island comes in line with the east point of Harbor island bearing S. 32° E. (S. 57° E. mag.), when the vessel will be past Channel reef, and may steer up the port in mid-channel, anchoring near the center, about 800 to 1,000 yards from the head, in 15 or 16 fathoms.

No large sailing vessel should attempt to enter Port Eliza unless with a steady fair wind.

Entering Esperanza inlet from the westward, keep an offing of 2½ or 3 miles from Catala island (if Kyuquot hill be made out, by keeping it open west of Tatchu point N. 31° W. (N. 56° W. mag.), a vessel will be well clear of any dangers off Catala island), till Double island comes in line with Black rock bearing N. 43° E. (N. 18° E. mag.), and enter the inlet through the North channel with this mark on, which will lead in. When the Twins islets bear N. 32° W. (N. 57° W. mag.), haul more to the eastward, passing ¼ mile outside Mid and Black rocks, and steer for Port Eliza as before directed.

If bound to Rolling roadstead, enter by either channel as before directed, and, after passing Black rock, haul up to N. 12° E. (N. 13° W. mag.), giving Black rock on this course a berth of ¼ mile. When the outer of the islets off the northwestern part of Catala island comes open north of the low grassy point on its northern side bearing N 77° W. (S. 78° W. mag.), haul in for the roadstead on that mark, which will lead between Arnold and Entrance reefs. Anchor in 6 fathoms, with the extremes of Catala island bearing West (S. 65° W. mag.) and S. 10° E. (S. 35° E. mag.).

If the weather be clear and the marks can be made out, North and Middle channels are equally good, the latter being wide enough for a vessel to beat through, though it would be hazardous for a stranger to attempt, as no turning marks can be given.

Generally a heavy swell prevails off the entrance to Nuchatlitz and Esperanza inlets, and no sailing vessel should attempt to enter or leave either of them, unless with a steady fair, or leading, wind.

Tides.—It is high water, full and change, in Esperanza inlet, at 0 h. 0 m.; springs rise 12 feet.

The coast, westward of Catala island to Tatchu point, takes a westerly direction for upward of 3 miles, is indented by two small sandy bays and bordered by a number of rocks, some of which extend nearly 2 miles offshore. Tatchu point is cliffy; some rocks lie a short distance to the southward of it, and there is a native village of considerable size ½ mile east of it. Eliza dome, a remarkable mountain, 2,819 feet above the sea, rises 1½ miles NE. of the point, and is very conspicuous from seaward.

From Tatchu point the coast turns NW. for 7 miles to the entrance of Kyuquot sound and is indented by several small bays, in some parts of which boats may find shelter.

Barrier islands.—At 2 miles westward of Tatchu point is the commencement of a chain of small islands and reefs bordering the coast of Vancouver island for nearly 20 miles in a northwesterly direction to the entrance of Ououkinsh inlet. They extend in some parts as far as 5 miles offshore, and through them are two known navigable channels, the Kyuquot and Halibut, leading to anchorages; the former channel leads into Kyuquot sound, and the latter into Clanninick harbor; but as a rule no stranger should venture in the channels among these islands without a pilot, unless the weather be clear.

In thick weather do not stand nearer the Barrier islands than into a depth of 40 fathoms.

Highest island, one of the Barrier group, lying 2 miles SW. of Union island, is a remarkable bare rock 98 feet high, and useful in identifying the Kyuquot channel.

Kyuquot sound, the eastern entrance to which is 12 miles from Esperanza inlet, is a large broken sheet of water penetrating from the coast to a distance of 14 or 15 miles inland in two large arms, and several smaller ones.

Union island, 1,484 feet high, lying in the entrance, forms on either side of it a channel into the sound, only the eastern one being fit for large vessels; there are several islands within, mostly small; its shores are mostly rocky and very much broken, rising to high mountains, 2,000 and 4,000 feet above the sea.

There are three anchorages, Narrowgut and Easy creeks and Fair harbor, the two latter being of considerable size, but 13 and 10 miles, respectively, from the entrance; the former, very small, is 5 miles within the sound.

Kyuquot channel leads into the sound through the Barrier islands and southeastward of Union island. It is nearly straight, about 5 miles long in an NE. direction, and about ¾ mile wide.

East Entrance reef, one of the Barrier group lying at the SE. extreme of the channel, is about 400 yards in extent and 4 feet above high water; no vessel should stand east of it, nor, when entering the channel, round the reef nearer than ½ mile.

Rugged point, the eastern entrance point to Kyuquot sound, is upward of 2 miles NE. of East Entrance reef; it is rugged and rocky, but steep-to on the western side; between it and East Entrance reef are a number of rocks, among which no vessel should venture. The eastern side of the channel northward of this point is slightly indented and steep-to, to the termination of the channel.

West rocks, on the NW. side of Kyuquot channel and 2¼ miles NNW. ¼ W. from East Entrance reef, are two in number, the higher being 50 feet above high water; some rocks which cover at quarter flood extend ½ mile SSE. from them, with 20 fathoms close to their outer edge. When navigating the channel do not approach West rocks within ⅜ mile.

White Cliff head, the southern extreme of Union island is 1 mile NE. by E. of West rocks, and abreast Rugged point; it is about 70 feet high, faced to the southward by a remarkable white cliff. Half a mile north of the head is Kyuquot hill, remarkable, 740 feet high, bare of trees on its eastern side, and very conspicuous from seaward.

Chatchannel point, the NW. extreme of Kyuquot channel and the eastern point of Union island, is a low rocky point with a remarkable knob just inside it; a rock which covers at a quarter flood lies 400 yards east of it, and the point should not be rounded nearer than ½ mile.

Leading island, at the NE. end of Kyuquot channel, and nearly 8½ miles from White Cliff head, is about 1¼ miles long in an east and west direction, ¼ mile wide, and rises near the center to a hill 489 feet high, which, when kept midway between White Cliff head and Rugged point N. 42° E. (N. 17° E. mag.), leads into the sound through the fairway of Kyuquot channel.

Blind entrance leads into Kyuquot sound NW. of Union island, forming a narrow tortuous channel with some rocks in the outer part; it should not be entered by a stranger, and though coasters often enter the sound by this channel, no directions can be given for navigating it.

Narrowgut creek, in the SE. part of the sound, about 1½ miles from the termination of the Kyuquot channel, is 1¼ miles long in an easterly direction, but is less than 200 yards wide just inside the entrance. The depths in it vary from 16 to 8 fathoms, and there is only just room for a small vessel to moor; the shores are high, and the creek easy of access to a steam vessel. A stream of considerable size runs into the head of the creek, from which a bank extends 600 yards.

Shingle point, at the entrance to the creek on the northern side, is bordered by a sandy beach, and has 9 fathoms close-to.

Deep inlet, at 1½ miles north from Narrowgut creek, is about 3 miles long in an easterly direction, but affords no anchorage; on its northern side, at the entrance, is a remarkable high precipice.

Hohoae island, nearly in the center of the sound, ¼ mile NE. of Union island, is about 2 miles long in a northeasterly direction, upward of 1 mile wide, and about 600 feet high; its shores are rocky. On its eastern side is Dixie cove, where a small craft may anchor in 6 fathoms completely landlocked.

Pinnace channel, between Hohoae island and the eastern shore of the sound, is about 3 miles long in a northerly direction and ½ mile wide.

Tahsish arm, in the northern part of the sound, has its entrance 5 miles from the termination of Kyuquot channel. It is 6 miles long in a winding direction to the NE., and its shores, except at the head, are high and rugged; the head terminates in low swampy land, through which flows a considerable stream, off which a bank dries 200 yards; there is a small village at the mouth of the stream;

on the eastern side, 2 miles below the head, is a similar stream, off which a bank extends about 400 yards.

Fair harbor, on the eastern side of Tahsish arm, is 2½ miles in length in an east and west direction, from 600 to 800 yards wide, and affords anchorage near either end in from 13 to 11 fathoms; its shores, generally, are high and steep-to; at its head a bank dries off for 200 yards. The western end of the harbor is formed by a low, narrow neck about 200 yards wide at low water, connecting an island to the mainland of Vancouver, and separating the harbor from Pinnace channel.

The entrance lies on the eastern side of this island, is nearly 1 mile long, and from 200 to 400 yards wide, with some small islets on its eastern side, the depths in it being very irregular, varying from 5 to 20 fathoms; when entering keep the western shore pretty close aboard, but take care to avoid a rock which lies on that shore about halfway in. A patch of 9 feet lies abreast it, and therefore considerable caution must be observed. This harbor can be entered by steam vessels, or sailing vessels with a fair wind.

Some rocks, the outer one of which covers, lie 600 yards westward from the entrance to Fair harbor, about 200 yards distant from the shore.

Moketas island, in the northern part of the sound, between the entrance to the Tahsish and Kokshittle arms, is about 2 miles long, 1 mile wide, rocky, and about 400 feet high, its eastern and western sides being steep-to. At 200 yards from its northern shore, near the middle is a sunken rock, and off its southern side lie Channel rocks, a small patch about 3 feet above high water; they, however, are steep-to.

The passage between Moketas island and the northern shore of the sound is 600 yards wide in the narrowest part, with from 14 to 38 fathoms in mid-channel; if using it, keep well over to the northern side.

Kokshittle arm, the entrance of which is in the NW. part of the sound, about 6 miles from Kyuquot channel, is upward of 8 miles long in a northerly direction, and about 1 mile wide at the entrance, narrowing gradually toward the head; its shores are rocky, and of a broken outline, with several small islets off them. The depths in it vary from 20 to 80 fathoms, shoaling gradually toward the head. A very good anchorage, the best in the sound, is on its western side at 4 miles from the entrance. The head of the arm terminates in low swampy land, through which flows a small stream, and a bank extends off about 400 yards.

Just within the entrance, on the eastern side, is a small cove with 4 fathoms in the center, available for small craft.

Easy creek, the anchorage before referred to, on the western side of Kokshittle arm, and 13 miles from the entrance of the sound, is about 2 miles long in a NW. and SE. direction, turning sharply round from its entrance and running in this direction parallel to the inlet, being separated from it by a narrow rocky peninsula. It is 800 yards wide at the entrance, narrowing gradually to the head; the depths in it vary from 12 to 20 fathoms, and there is good anchorage from ½ mile within the entrance to the head. The shores are rocky, of moderate height, steep-to on the northern side, but from the west a sand bank dries off in some parts nearly 200 yards. The best anchorage is 1 mile within the entrance, in from 13 to 16 fathoms, between 200 and 400 yards from the eastern shore. When entering keep near the northern shore to clear a rock off the southern entrance point; afterwards favor the eastern shore.

On the opposite side of the arm, abreast Easy creek, is a village and a stream of considerable size, off which a bank dries out about 400 yards.

Chamiss bay, on the western side of Kyuquot sound, about 1 mile from the northern part of Blind entrance, is nearly ½ mile in extent, but affords no anchorage, the water being too deep.

Directions.—No sailing vessel should attempt to enter Kyuquot sound, unless with a steady fair, or leading, wind, as generally a heavy swell prevails outside, which in a light wind would render the position critical; and no stranger should attempt to venture in, unless the weather is clear, and the leading mark for the channel can be easily made out.

Entering the sound by the Kyuquot channel, which is the only one a stranger should use, keep a good offing till the entrance of the channel is made out (White Cliff head and Kyuquot hill at the southern end of Union island, which have been before described, are very conspicuous, and will identify the channel), when bring the summit of Leading island midway between Chatchannel and Rugged points bearing N. 42° E. (N. 17° E. mag.), and steer up the channel with that mark on; when nearing Chatchannel point, give it a berth of ½ mile to avoid the rock which lies off it. If bound to Narrowgut creek, pass south of Leading island, and keeping about 200 yards from the south shore, enter the creek in mid-channel, and moor when inside.

If bound to Fair harbor, proceed as before directed till near Leading island; pass to the westward of this island, and proceed to the northward through Pinnace channel, keeping about 200 or 300 yards from either shore, to the entrance of Tahsish arm. On nearing Fair harbor keep from 400 to 600 yards from the eastern side of the arm till the entrance bears SE., when steer for it on that bearing, keeping close over to the western shore till inside, and anchor in the middle, about ½ mile from the eastern end, in 11 fathoms.

Bound to Easy creek, pass westward of Leading, Hohoae, and Moketas islands; enter the Kokshittle arm in mid-channel, and proceed up it for a distance of 4 miles, which will bring a vessel abreast the creek, which may be entered in mid-channel; anchor in from 13 to 16 fathoms, about 1 mile within the entrance, and from 200 to 400 yards from the shore.

Tides.—It is high water, full and change, in Kyuquot sound at 0 h. 0 m.; springs rise 12 feet.

Clanninick harbor, on the Vancouver shore, 3 miles westward of Kyuquot sound, is about 1 mile long in a NW. direction, ⅓ mile wide, and affords good anchorage, in from 7 to 10 fathoms, at ½ mile from the head, from which a sand bank extends 400 yards. Its shores are mostly low and there are some rocks on either side of the entrance.

The harbor is protected by Village, Table, and other islands of the Barrier group. Halibut channel is the only channel through them which should be attempted by a stranger; Blind entrance and Schooner entrance are sometimes used by the local trade.

Halibut channel, through the Barrier group to Clanninick harbor, lies west of Table and Village islands, and east of Lookout island. It is about 3 miles long in a northeasterly direction and ½ mile wide in the narrowest part; the depths in it vary from 16 to 6 fathoms, being somewhat irregular.

A dangerous sunken rock, marked by kelp, and which occasionally breaks, lies 600 yards N. 6° W. (N. 31° W. mag.) from Trap bluff, Table island.

Table island, on the eastern side of the channel, is the largest of the Barrier group, being nearly ½ mile in extent, and about 150 feet high to the tops of the trees; some rocks, mostly above water, extend ½ mile from its southern and western sides, the outer one being 50 feet high, with 15 fathoms 400 yards west of it. Trap bluff, on the west side of the island, is conspicuous.

Half a mile east of Table island is an anchorage with from 4 to 6 fathoms, tolerably sheltered from seaward by some islands, and much used by coasters in summer months; Schooner entrance, the entrance to it, is rather intricate, and no stranger, or any except a small vessel, should attempt to enter.

Village island (locally known as Kyuquot), on the SE. side of Halibut channel, just NE. of Table island, is small and about 150 feet high to the tops of the trees; on its eastern side is Kyuquot, a large native village, where there are a church, post-office, and store; off it a bank dries nearly 600 yards. Eastward of this island, among the Barrier islands, is a small cove (Barter cove), with from 1 to 4½ fathoms; it is well sheltered in all weathers, and much frequented by sealing vessels and coasters; the entrance to it is very narrow, being obstructed by a rock that dries 6 feet, but leaves a clear channel of 4 fathoms.

Four hundred yards north of Village island is a rock awash at high water springs, but there is a depth of 5 to 6 fathoms 200 yards off its western side.

Lookout island, at the southern entrance of Halibut channel, lies nearly 1 mile westward of Table island; it is small, has a few trees, and is about 150 feet high; its eastern side may be approached to 400 yards, but ¼ mile W. by S. from it are some rocks, on which the sea always breaks.

Granite island, which forms the south side of Clanninick harbor, is about ½ mile in extent, and joined by a sandy beach at low water to the Vancouver shore.

Chief rock, 600 yards SE. from its eastern point, is a very dangerous rock, which lies at the termination of Halibut channel, and only uncovers at low water springs.

Louise rock, a sunken rock with less than 6 feet over it, lies with Channel rock bearing S. 42° E. (S. 67° E. mag.), distant 1,220 yards.

A rock which breaks lies 400 yards WNW. from the SW. extreme of Granite island.

Directions.—Bound into Clanninick harbor by Halibut channel (which is the only passage by which a stranger can enter it), keep about 2 miles off the Barrier islands till Lookout island bears N. 10° W. (N. 35° W. mag.), when steer for the entrance of the channel, passing about 400 yards east of Lookout island. Pass Trap bluff at not less than ½ mile, so as to avoid the dangerous rock northward of it. On nearing Granite island alter course to the eastward and steer for Channel rock, 8 feet above high water, on a N. 87° E. (N. 62° E. mag.) bearing. When nearing this rock alter course to the northward and steer for the small rock, 4 feet above water, at the eastern side of the entrance to the harbor, which may be passed on either side.

Anchor in from 7 to 10 fathoms, with the extremes of the harbor bearing S. 65° E. (East mag.) and S. 9° E. (S. 34° E. mag.).

As before noticed, no stranger should attempt to enter this harbor without a pilot, unless from absolute necessity, and, if in a sailing vessel, only with a steady fair wind.

Ououkinsh inlet, 10 miles NW. from Kyuquot sound, is 7 miles long in a northeasterly direction, and 1,600 yards wide at the entrance, narrowing gradually toward the head; the shores within are high, rising from 2,000 to upward of 3,000 feet.

The depths in the inlet vary from 40 to 60 fathoms, and there is only one indifferent anchorage, Battle bay, just within the entrance on the west side. The entrance lies west of the Barrier islands, and the depths in it vary from 40 to 48 fathoms.

Fairway rock, awash at low water, is situated in the approach to Ououkinsh inlet, with Clara islet N. 71° E. (N. 46° E. mag.), distant 1 mile.

Clara islet, at the SE. extreme of the entrance, is small, bare, and 20 feet above high water; no vessel should go eastward of it, or approach it within ¼ mile. This island is the westernmost of the Barrier islands, and lies 21½ miles NW. ¾ W. from Tatchu point, where they may be said to commence.

Bunsby islands, on the SE. side of the entrance, close inshore, are about 2 miles in extent, and from 250 to 300 feet high; the passages between them and the shore are choked up with rocks, but their west side is steep-to; Gays passage, between the two larger islands, is used by the coasting steamers. Pinnacle point and Green head at the SW. extreme of the group are remarkable. Northeastward of these islands is Malksope inlet, 4 miles long in a northeasterly direction, but the entrance is intricate, and there is no anchorage within it.

Cuttle group, lying east of the SW. entrance point of Ououkinsh inlet, and 1½ miles north from Clara islet, comprises a number of small islets and rocks, some of the former being wooded. Nearly 1 mile SW. from them is a rock on which the sea breaks in fine weather. On the Vancouver shore, just north of them, is Low cone, a remarkable summit 356 feet high, and useful in identifying the entrance.

Do not go to the westward of these islets, or approach their eastern side nearer than 400 yards.

Sulivan reefs are a very dangerous patch of rocks lying nearly 3 miles outside the entrance of Ououkinsh inlet, 2½ miles W. by N. from Clara islet, and nearly 4 miles S. ¾ W. from Hat island in Nasparti inlet; they are about ½ mile in extent east and west, and the sea only breaks occasionally on them; there are from 10 to 11 fathoms close around them.

Solander island, off cape Cook, just visible south of the extremity of Brooks peninsula, N. 70° W. (S. 85° W. mag.), leads 1½ miles south of Sulivan reefs; and Hat island, in the entrance of Nasparti inlet, in line with a summit on the western shore of the inlet bearing N. 22° E. (N. 3° W. mag.), leads over 1 mile westward of them.

Battle bay, just within the entrance of Ououkinsh inlet, on the western side, is upward of 1 mile wide and ½ mile deep, with several islets and sunken rocks inside it near the middle; near the northern part there is anchorage in from 6 to 9 fathoms which may be used in fine weather.

A rock, with a depth of 9 feet on it, lies with the summit of the southern Skirmish islet bearing N. 73° E. (N. 48° E. mag.), distant 550 yards, and a rock, with a depth of 6 feet on it at low water, lies 100 yards S. 82° E. (N. 73° E. mag.) from the northern point of the islet on the western shore of Battle bay.

Directions.—If intending to enter Ououkinsh inlet and anchor in Battle bay, keep an offing of 4 to 5 miles from the main till Clara islet, at the western extreme of the Barrier islands, is made out, when steer for it on a N. 70° E. (N. 45° E. mag.) bearing, passing about ½ mile NW. of the islet, being careful to avoid Fairway rock, awash at low water, situated 1 mile S. 71° W. (S. 46° W. mag.) of Clara islet. When abreast the islet steer for the center of the entrance about NE.; round the Skirmish islets, which lie in the middle of Battle bay, at a distance of 400 yards and anchor in 7 fathoms midway between them and the northern side of the bay.

It is not recommended to use this anchorage, unless embayed, as it affords but indifferent shelter in southerly gales, and no sailing vessel should attempt to enter unless with a steady fair wind.

Tides.—It is high water, full and change, in Ououkinsh inlet at 0 h. 0 m.; springs rise 12 feet.

Nasparti inlet, 8½ miles westward of Ououkinsh inlet, on the eastern side of Brooks peninsula, and in the head of an open bight or bay, is about 4 miles long in a NE. direction and about ½ mile wide at the entrance, decreasing in some places to less than 600 yards. Its shores are high and rocky, indented by some slight bays; there is a fresh-water stream at the head, from which a bank extends about 600 yards. The depths vary from 13 to 30 fathoms, and there is a secure though rather limited anchorage, in from 13 to 16 fathoms, at ½ mile from the head. Outside the entrance are several dangers.

Haystacks, off the eastern side of the entrance, and 1⅜ miles NNE. from Sulivan reefs, are two bare, sharp-topped, cliffy rocks, 65 feet high, and about 400 yards apart; at 400 yards from their western side are from 25 to 26 fathoms; northward of them rocks and foul ground exist.

East rock, 600 yards from the eastern entrance point, is of small extent, has 17 fathoms at 200 yards westward of it, and covers at half flood; the Haystacks, open west of Yule islet, bearing SE. by S., leads from 400 to 600 yards westward of it.

Yule islet, about 40 feet high, lies midway between the Haystacks and East rock.

Mile Rock breaker lies 1¾ miles from the western shore of the entrance to the inlet, and 2 miles NW. from Sulivan reefs. It is very dangerous, as it is of small extent; the sea breaks on it with any swell; the depths around it are irregular.

Hat island, in the entrance of the inlet, in line with a summit on the western side bearing N. 22° E. (N. 3° W. mag.), leads over 800 yards east of it, and well clear of the Sulivan reefs, into the inlet. Do not stand westward of this danger.

Mile rock, nearly 1 mile NNE. of the above-mentioned danger, is a small bare rock, 12 feet above high water; there are 29 fathoms 200 yards east of it. A ledge extends fully 200 yards from its northern side.

Hat island, 70 feet high, lying in the center of the inlet just within the entrance, is small, and has a few stunted trees on the summit; from the southward it is very conspicuous, and appears somewhat like a hat. It is steep-to on the northern side, but nearly midway between it and the western shore is a shoal patch of 2½ fathoms, marked by kelp; also two rocks marked by kelp lie in the fairway SSE. of Hat island. The inner rock lies about 200 yards from the island; the outer rock with 8 fathoms over it lies 450 yards S. 2° E. (S. 27° E. mag.) from the eastern extreme of the island.

Directions.—Nasparti inlet should not be used by a stranger unless from necessity, as in thick or cloudy weather it might be difficult to make out the leading marks, and no one should attempt to enter unless they are well made out, especially as the sea breaks on the outlying dangers only in heavy weather, and they are seldom seen. A sailing vessel should, in passing the entrance of this and Ououkinsh inlet, keep Solander island open south of the land east of cape Cook bearing N. 66° W. (S. 89° W. mag.).

If entering Nasparti inlet, keep Solander island (off cape Cook) in line with the land eastward of it bearing N. 69° W. (S. 86° W. mag.) until Hat island comes in line with a summit on the western side of the inlet bearing N. 22° E. (N. 3° W. mag.), when steer in for the entrance on that bearing, which will lead 800 yards east of Mile Rock breaker, well clear of the Sulivan reefs, and ½ mile west of East rock; pass east of Hat island and the shoals lying SSE. of it, and steer up the inlet in mid-channel, anchoring in 13 fathoms, about ⅓ mile from the head.

Tides.—It is high water at full and change in Nasparti inlet at 0 h. 0 m.; springs rise 12 feet.

Brooks peninsula.—Westward of Nasparti inlet is a peninsula, 9 miles long and about 5 miles wide, projecting SW.; its shores are for the most part very rocky and rise almost abruptly from the sea to upward of 2,000 feet. There are several offlying dangers around it, some of which extend upward of 1 mile from the shore.

Cape Cook, or Woody point, the SW. extreme of this peninsula and the most projecting point of the outer coast of Vancouver island, is 163 miles NW. ½ W. from the lighthouse on Tatoosh island. The cape rises abruptly from the sea 1,200 feet.

At 2 miles from cape Cook and off the southern side of the peninsula the depths are from 20 to 90 fathoms, and as a rule no vessel should approach nearer.

Banks reef, which covers at three-quarters flood, and on which the sea breaks heavily, lies 3 miles S. 44° E. (S. 69° E. mag.) from cape Cook and ¾ mile from the shore.

Solander island, nearly 1 mile westward of cape Cook, is bare, 580 feet high, and has two sharp peaks; between it and the cape the passage is choked up with rocks, and no vessel or even boat should go inside the island.

Brooks bay, on the northern side of Brooks peninsula, is a large open bay, about 12 miles wide and 6 miles deep; there are several dangers within it, and two inlets, Klaskish and Klaskino, which afford anchorage, but are very difficult of access, and no sailing vessel should attempt to enter either unless embayed and unable to get out of Brooks bay; the soundings are irregular, varying from 17 to 48 fathoms, shoaling generally to the northward.

Clerke reefs lie in the southern part of the bay, 5 miles north from cape Cook, their outer extreme being 2½ miles off the SE. shore of the bay. They cover an extent of upward of 2 miles; some are under water, others uncover, and no vessel should venture among them.

Cape Cook, bearing S. 4° E. (S. 29° E. mag.), leads 2 miles west of these reefs; and Small islet at the entrance of Klaskish inlet, in line with Leading cone at its head, bearing N. 85° E. (N. 60° E. mag.), leads 1¾ miles north of them.

Klaskish inlet, at the head of Brooks bay on the northern side of Brooks peninsula, and 10 miles NE. from cape Cook, is about 3 miles long in a northeasterly direction and 1 mile wide at the entrance; at its head is a long, narrow basin, the entrance of which is too contracted for a vessel to enter. There is an anchorage just within the entrance to the inlet on the south side, to the eastward of Shelter island, but it is difficult of access to a sailing vessel.

Caution.—The entrance to this anchorage is intricate and narrow, and, unless unavoidably necessary, no vessel larger than a coaster should attempt it, as there is generally a heavy sea at the mouth of the inlet.

Ship rock, lying 7½ miles N. 13° E. (N. 12° W. mag.) from cape Cook, 2 miles distant from the shore in the center of Brooks bay, and midway between Klaskish and Klaskino inlets, is of small extent, and has from 17 to 20 fathoms close on its southern and eastern sides; the sea generally breaks very heavily over it.

Surge islets, on the southern side of the entrance, 1,100 yards from the shore, are small, rocky, and about 40 feet high; foul ground exists among them, and when entering the inlet do not approach their NW. side nearer than ½ mile.

Shelter island, just within the entrance of the inlet on its southern side, is about ½ mile in extent, 300 feet high, with a hill at each end with a few stunted trees; some rocks extend a short distance from its eastern and western sides, but the northern shore is steep-to. The anchorage on its eastern side is about ⅓ mile in extent, with from 10 to 13 fathoms, well sheltered, but the bottom is irregular; the entrance to it, round the NE. side of the island, is less than 200 yards wide in the narrowest part. About 200 yards from the NE. point of Shelter island is Bare islet, 15 feet high, which on entering the anchorage should be passed close-to on its eastern side.

Between Shelter island and the northern entrance point of the inlet is a heavy confused sea, which is dangerous for sailing vessels, as the wind generally fails there.

Directions.—Entering Klaskish inlet, when coming from the eastward, and intending to anchor on the east side of Shelter island, do not bring cape Cook southward of S. 4° E. (S. 29° E. mag.), till Leading cone, a remarkable hill at the head of the inlet, about 500 feet high, comes in line with Small islet on the northern side of entrance bearing N. 85° E. (N. 60° E. mag.), which mark will lead into the inlet well north of the Clerke reefs and Surge islets; when abreast the latter, haul a little to the eastward, so as to enter midway between Small islet and Shelter island; pass within 200 yards eastward of Bare islet and anchor in 13 fathoms with the extremes of Shelter island bearing N. 38° W. (N. 63° W. mag.) and S. 74° W. (S. 49° W. mag.).

Tides.—It is high water, full and change, in Klaskish inlet at 0 h. 0 m.; springs rise 12 feet.

Klaskino inlet, the entrance to which is in the northern part of Brooks bay, 10 miles N. by E. ½ E. from cape Cook, is nearly 6 miles long in a winding direction to the eastward. Numerous rocks lie off the entrance, but there is an intricate passage through them, and there is a good anchorage on the southern side, 2 miles within the inlet. The depths vary from 10 to 20 fathoms in the lower part of the inlet, increasing gradually toward the head to 40 fathoms; the inlet here becomes narrow, with high and rocky shores, terminating in low land at the head.

Caution.—The entrance of Klaskino inlet is even more intricate than that of Klaskish, and should not be attempted by a stranger unless absolutely necessary for safety.

Nob point, the southern entrance point of the inlet, is rocky and covered with a few stunted trees, and close to its outer part is a rocky knob about 100 feet high. From Nob point a line of reefs above and below water with deep water between them extends fully 1½ miles in a NW. direction.

Twenty-foot rock, 800 yards NW. from Nob point, is bare and 20 feet above high water. It is conspicuous from the outside, and there are 19 fathoms close to its northern and western sides, but between it and Nob point the passage is choked up with rocks; the only channel into the inlet is westward of the rock, between it and Channel reefs.

Two rocks on which the sea breaks at low water lie southward of Channel reefs, and 1 mile distant from Nob point. The southernmost lies ¾ mile S. 71° W. (S. 46° W. mag.) from Twenty-foot rock.

Channel reefs, the SE. part of which is 700 yards W. by N. from Twenty-foot rock, are a cluster of rocks, mostly under water, extending in a NW. direction toward the northern shore of Brooks bay. There is deep water between them in many places, but the only safe passage into Klaskino inlet, upward of 600 yards wide with deep water, is between their SE. part and Twenty-foot rock.

Anchorage island, in the middle of the inlet, about 2 miles within the entrance, is of small extent and rocky; some small islets extend 200 yards from its NW. and south points. The anchorage between the eastern side of this island and the shore is from 600 to 800 yards in extent, and well sheltered, with from 9 to 10 fathoms of water; the entrance to it, round the southern point of Anchorage island, is about 200 yards wide in the narrowest part, with from 13 to 17 fathoms in the middle.

Between Twenty-foot rock and the entrance to the anchorage are several dangers; a rock 3 feet high lies 1,700 yards W. by S. from the southern point of Anchorage island, and another 2 feet high 600 yards SW. by W. ½ W. from the same point, and there is a reef which covers 200 yards W. ¾ N. from the latter rock. When entering the inlet pass northward of these.

Above Anchorage island some rocks extend nearly across the inlet, rendering it almost impossible for a vessel to go beyond them.

Red Stripe mountain, rising on the northern side of the entrance, abreast Anchorage island, is of a remarkable conical shape, 2,200 feet high, with a valley on either side of it; on its SW. part, facing seaward, is a conspicuous, red, cliffy stripe or landslip, easily distinguished from the outside.

Directions.—Bound for Klaskino inlet, when outside Ship rock bring Twenty-foot rock in line with the lower part of the red stripe on Red Stripe mountain bearing N. 54° E. (N. 29° E. mag.) and run boldly for the entrance with that mark on, which will lead 500 yards SE. of the patches southward of the Channel reefs; keep on this course till within 400 yards of Twenty-foot rock, when haul a little to the northward and round it on its northern side at a distance of 200 yards, after which steer about N. 85° E. (N. 60° E. mag.) for the southern part of Anchorage island, passing about 200 yards north of the rocks off the southern side of the inlet; when abreast the western point of the island haul quickly to the southward, round the rocks off its southern point within 100 yards, and anchor in from 9 to 10 fathoms midway between the eastern side of the island and the main, with the extremes of the former bearing N. 21° W. (N. 46° W. mag.) and S. 80° W. (S. 55° W. mag.); a large vessel should moor.

Three miles from Klaskino, in the extreme northern part of Brooks bay, is a large rivulet where boats may enter and find shelter in bad weather.

Tides.—It is high water, full and change, in Klaskino inlet at 0 h. 0 m.; springs rise 12 feet.

Lawn point, the NW. extreme of Brooks bay, lies 12 miles N. ¾ W. from cape Cook; it is low, and some rocks extend more than ½ mile in an easterly direction from it, inside of which a boat may find shelter; the sea breaks violently about this point and everywhere along the shores of Brooks bay. A vessel should keep a good offing.

The land in the vicinity of Lawn point appears very fertile, and is lightly timbered; it rises gradually from the sea to a height of 1,900 feet.

Boat shelter.—Between the entrance to Klaskino inlet and Lawn point is a deep bay, in which are several islets and reefs; it is unfit for anchorage, being open seaward, but at its head, north of Mayday island, there is good shelter for boats.

Quatsino sound, the northwesternmost of the deep inlets on the outer coast of Vancouver island, penetrates the island in a northeasterly direction for upward of 25 miles. At the entrance between Reef point (on the south) and Entrance island it is nearly 6 miles wide, narrowing to less than 1 mile at 5 miles within; the sound then takes a northeasterly direction, nearly straight for 13 miles, when it branches off in two arms, one (Southeast arm) extending to the SE. for 12 miles, and terminating in low land. The other (West arm) lies to the northward, and is connected with the sound by a straight, narrow pass about 2 miles long; it is 22 miles long in an east and west direction.

Just within the entrance of the sound on the northern side is Forward inlet, a much smaller arm, about 6 miles long in a northerly direction, in which are the best anchorages in the sound.

The shores of Quatsino sound are mostly high, and near the entrance very much broken; there are several small islands within and along its shores.

From outside the entrance Quatsino sound presents several remarkable features which render it easy to be made out; along its eastern side are several rocks and small islands; and on both sides of and within the sound the land is high, some of the mountains being very conspicuous. Among these are the Flattop and Entrance mountains northward of the entrance, and Nose peak and Gap mountains inside, Nose peak being easily distinguished by its sharp, rocky summit, 1,730 feet high.

There are several dangers along the northern side of the entrance; in the fairway are two very dangerous rocks, on which the sea only breaks in heavy weather, and it requires great caution on the part of the navigator to avoid them when entering or leaving the sound.

Reef point (Omannys), the southern entrance point of the sound, 14 miles N. ¾ W. from cape Cook and 1½ miles from Lawn point, the NW. extreme of Brooks bay, is low and rocky, but rises gradually to a well-defined mountain, 1,901 feet above the sea; the coast between it and Lawn point forms a slight bay filled with a number of rocks extending a considerable distance from the shore.

Boat cove, into which flows a small stream (Culleet river), and in which a boat can enter and find shelter in bad weather, is a small bight on the eastern shore of the sound, 5½ miles north from Reef point; the coast between the two places is indented by several bays and fringed by reefs, which extend in many places nearly 1 mile from the shore and over which the sea usually breaks very heavily.

Bold bluff, 7 miles northward from Reef point, on the southern side of the sound, is, as its name implies, a bold, rocky, salient bluff rising suddenly to upward of 200 feet, when it slopes gradually to a summit 1,609 feet high. At this spot the sound contracts to less than 1 mile in breadth.

Surf islands, 1½ miles SW. from Bold bluff and 3 miles within the entrance to Quatsino sound, are a chain of small islands nearly 1 mile long in a north and south direction, some of which have a few stunted trees and are about 40 feet above high water; a short distance from them are a number of rocks on which the sea breaks. Although there appears to be deep water between these islands and the eastern side of the sound, it is not advisable to use that passage, as it has not been sufficiently examined.

Entrance island, 5½ miles N. by W. ¼ W. from Reef point, at the NW. entrance point of the sound, is small and rocky, about 140 feet high, and covered with a few stunted trees. Westward of it is a narrow boat pass into the sound, about 200 yards wide, but filled with rocks, and passable only in fine weather. Breakers have been observed about 600 yards southward of the point westward of the island.

Danger rocks, on the northern side of the entrance, nearly in the fairway, are two very dangerous pinnacle rocks, of small extent, ½ mile distant from each other in a NNW. and SSE. direction, and steep-to on all sides. South Danger rock is awash at low water, and lies 1 mile S. 66° E. (N. 89° E. mag.) from the southern extreme of Entrance island; North Danger rock (Okookstaw) is 1,400 yards distant from the same island, and sometimes breaks at low water; there is deep water between the rocks. The sea very seldom breaks mag.), leads about ¾ mile east of them and midway between them when entering or leaving the sound.

Leading marks.—Pinnacle islet, in line with the eastern point of Low islets, in Forward inlet, bearing N. 8° W. (N. 33° W. mag.), leads nearly 800 yards westward of Danger rocks, and midway between the North rock and Entrance island.

Robson island, in Forward inlet, open north of Entrance Mount point bearing N. 37° W. (N. 62° W. mag.), leads 600 to 800 yards NE. of Danger rocks, and Village islet, on the eastern side of Forward inlet, just touching Brown point bearing N. 20° W. (N. 45° W. mag.), leads about ¾ mile east of them and midway between them and the Surf islands.

Bold bluff, in line with the gap in the center of Surf islands, bearing N. 41° E. (N. 16° E. mag.), leads nearly 1,600 yards SE. of South Danger. Between the Danger rocks and Surf islands, the passage is 1½ miles wide.

Forward inlet, on the northern side of the sound, is 1 mile wide at the entrance and about 6 miles long; it first takes a NNW. direction for 2 miles from its outer part, then, turning NE. for 4 miles, it contracts in breadth and becomes shoal at the head, terminating in large salt-water lagoons; in the upper part it contracts to less than ¼ mile in width in some places; there are two anchorages within it, North and Winter harbors; both are very secure and well sheltered.

Entrance and Flattop mountains, on the western side of Forward inlet near the entrance, are very conspicuous objects from seaward; the former is 1,275 and the latter 960 feet high.

Pinnacle islet, ¾ mile NNE. of Entrance island, is a small jagged rock about 40 feet high, with a few trees on its summit.

Robson island, in the bend of Forward inlet on the western side, 1½ miles from Pinnacle islet, is about ½ mile in extent and 385 feet high, and its shores are rocky. Between it and the SW. shore is a narrow passage of 2 to 5 fathoms of water.

Low islets, 800 yards SE. from Robson island, are small wooded islands which are steep-to on all sides.

Village islet.—A small village is situated on the eastern side of Forward inlet abreast Robson island, and close off it is Village islet, a small bare islet about 40 feet high, which is rather conspicuous.

Bare islet, lying 100 yards off the eastern entrance point to Forward inlet, is about 12 feet high and steep-to on the outside.

Burnt hill, 1,095 feet high, just over Brown point, ¾ mile NW. of Bare islet, is remarkable from the southward, being bare of trees and cliffy on its southern side.

North harbor, which lies NW. of Robson island, on the western side of Forward inlet, is a snug and secure anchorage, about 800 yards in extent, with from 4 to 6 fathoms; the entrance is 600 yards wide; it is perhaps the best anchorage within the sound, and from being only 4 miles within the entrance is very convenient. Browning creek, in its western part, extends 1¼ miles NW., and is very narrow, with from 2 to 5 fathoms in it, terminating in a shallow basin, dry at low water.

Observatory rock, which lies on the northern side of the entrance to North harbor, is a small bare rock, connected at low water to the mainland.

Winter harbor comprises that part of Forward inlet which runs in a NE. direction, and is a capacious anchorage with from 8 to 11 fathoms. Its shores are low and bordered by a sandy beach, and the harbor becomes shoal at a distance of 1 mile from the head; its breadth varies from 400 to 1,200 yards. There is a store here where provisions and clothes may be obtained.

Log point, just outside the entrance to this harbor on the eastern side, is low and bordered by a sandy beach; southward of it and extending 800 yards from the shore, is New bank, with 3½ fathoms on the shoalest part, and contracting the breadth of the entrance passage to the harbor to less than 200 yards between it and a shoal spit extending from the opposite shore; but, by keeping a little over to the western side when abreast North harbor, this bank may be avoided and a vessel may enter Winter harbor without danger.

At the narrowest part of the entrance to Winter harbor, above Log point, on the western side, is Grass point, bordered by a sandy beach, which is steep-to.

Pilley shoal, of 3 fathoms, on the northern side of Quatsino sound, is of small extent, steep-to on the outside, and marked by kelp. It lies 300 yards from the shore, and 1 mile west from Bold bluff.

Boat cove, on the northern side of the sound, is of small extent, with 5 fathoms inside; it would afford good shelter for a small craft. The northern shore of Quatsino sound between it and Bare islet is rocky and very much broken.

Bedwell islets, lying 5½ miles within the entrance, off a projecting point on the northern side of the sound, are of small extent, wooded, and separated from the shore by a very narrow boat pass, which is conspicuous from the entrance.

Monday shoal, 600 yards ENE. of them, has 4 fathoms (less water reported) on it, is marked by kelp, and steep-to on the outside; eastward of Bedwell islets no swell is ever experienced in the sound.

Rock.—About 400 yards WSW. of Monday shoal lies a pinnacle rock, showing 2 feet at low water springs; from the rock Rain point (Village island) bears S. 83° E. (N. 72° E. mag.) and the center of Plumper island N. 36° E. (N. 11° E. mag.).

Tides.—It is high water, full and change, in Quatsino sound at 11 h. 0 m.; springs rise about 11 feet.

Koprino harbor, 8 miles within the entrance, in the center of a bay on the northern shore of Quatsino sound, is a perfectly landlocked but small anchorage, affording room for one or two ships to lie moored within. It lies northward of Plumper island, which is about ½ mile in extent, low, wooded, and steep-to on all sides, there being a good passage on either side of it into the harbor. There is a store here where provisions and clothing may be obtained.

Dockyard island, in the western part of the harbor, midway between Plumper island and the northern shore, is small, and a ledge, the greatest depth on which is 4 fathoms, connects it with Plumper island.

Mud bank, about 300 yards east of Dockyard island, in the middle of the harbor, is a small patch of 15 feet; there is good anchorage 200 yards SW. of Dockyard island in 14 fathoms.

Wedge island lies at the eastern limit of the anchorage, about 200 yards NE. of Plumper island; it is very small and covered with a few bushes; a ledge extends a short distance westward from it; there is a deep passage on either side of it into the harbor.

Observatory islet, at the eastern extreme of the harbor, is bare and about 12 feet high; it is 400 yards NE. of Plumper island, and 600 yards from the northern shore, connected to the latter by a bank which dries at low water.

East cove, the head of the bight between Observatory islet and Prideaux point, appears to afford good anchorage in 6 to 10 fathoms; but the entrance to it has not been sufficiently examined to recommend its being used by a large vessel.

Prideaux point, the eastern entrance point of East passage, is low, bordered by a sandy beach. The northern shore of the sound from Prideaux point takes a general ENE. direction for 9 miles to Coffin islet, at the entrance of Hecate cove. It is bordered by a sandy beach, and Percy ledge, lying 6 miles from Prideaux point, is 400 yards from the shore and has 4 fathoms on its outer edge.

From Bold bluff the southern shore of the sound trends nearly parallel to the northern for 13 miles in an ENE. direction. It is high and indented by two bays of considerable size and some small creeks, none of which afford anchorage.

In Koskeemo bay, at 2 miles within Bold bluff, is a native village of considerable size (Mayhattee), and anchorage in 17 fathoms. Village islands, at the eastern extreme of Koskeemo bay, are of small extent and low; their outer part is steep-to. Shoal water extends 500 yards NNW. from the entrance of Maad river.

Brockton island (Quolaad), lying 400 yards from a projecting point on the southern side of the sound, 7 miles ENE. from Bold bluff, is nearly ½ mile long, but narrow; its west side is steep-to.

Limestone island (Maiclagh), 15 miles within the entrance and in the center of the sound, is nearly 3 miles long and about ¾ mile wide in the broadest part. Its shores are rocky, and the land is of moderate height. Quiet cove, on its northern side, is small and affords anchorage for small craft.

Foul islets, lying midway between Holloway point, the SW. extreme of Limestone island, and the southern shore of the sound, are small and about 600 yards in extent in an east and west direction. There is a deep passage, about 400 yards wide, on either side of them; the southern passage is to be preferred.

Single islet, ½ mile eastward from Holloway point and 600 yards NE. of the Foul islets, is low and bare.

Kultus cove, abreast Limestone island, on the southern side of the sound, is about ½ mile in extent, with irregular soundings of from 12 to 25 fathoms; it affords no anchorage, except for small craft.

Southeast arm, the entrance to which is 1 mile east of Limestone island and 18 miles within the entrance of the sound, is 10 miles long in a southeasterly direction and varies in breadth from 600 yards to 1 mile. Its shores are generally high and rugged, but terminate in low land at the head; the depths in it vary from 30 to 70 fathoms, and there is no anchorage, except for small craft; a bank dries off 400 yards from the head, and close to its edge is a depth of 15 fathoms.

Mist rock, 5 miles within the entrance and 800 yards from the eastern shore, is of small extent and covers at half flood; by keeping well over to the western shore a vessel will clear it.

Atkins cove, on the eastern side of the entrance to Southeast arm, is 800 yards long in a northerly direction and 200 yards wide, with from 5 to 7 fathoms; there is room for a small vessel to anchor in it, but the cove is open to the southward.

Whitestone point, at the separation of the two arms at the head of Quatsino sound, is a rocky point of moderate height, and lies ¾ mile eastward of Limestone island, and abreast Coffin islet. Bull rock, which covers and is marked by kelp, lies 600 yards SW. by W.

¼ W. from Whitestone point and 400 yards from the shore. Between Atkins cove and Whitestone point the coast is rocky and should not be approached nearer than 600 yards.

Hecate cove (Kagoagh), on the northern shore about 1 mile NE. of Coffin islet, indents the shore about ¾ mile in a northwesterly direction, is from 400 to 600 yards wide, and affords good anchorage near the center in 9 to 11 fathoms. In the inner part of the cove, near the NE. side, are some shoal patches, marked by kelp, with only 11 feet of water in some parts; the shores of the cove are moderately high and bordered by a sandy beach.

This cove is convenient for steam vessels or small craft; anchor in about 11 fathoms, with the entrance points bearing S. 25° W. (South mag.) and S. 21° E. (S. 46° E. mag.); a large vessel should moor. There is a depth of 18 feet at the end of the wharf.

There is a settlement of Norwegians on the west side of the cove; also a store and post-office.

Kitten island at the eastern side of entrance, is steep-to on the outside.

Round island (Quatishe), nearly in mid-channel, about 1 mile SE. of Hecate cove and just west of Quatsino narrows, is small and of moderate height; there is a clear passage between it and the northern shore, but the one south of it is filled with rocks.

At 600 yards SE. from it is Bight cove, of moderate extent, with from 8 to 10 fathoms inside, but as the tide runs strongly off the entrance and there are also some rocks, it is recommended for small craft only.

Quatsino narrows, 20 miles inside the sound and connecting it with Rupert and West arms, is 2 miles long in a northerly direction and 300 yards wide in the narrowest part; the depths in it vary from 12 to 20 fathoms; its shores are high and rocky. Turn point, at the SW. extreme of the narrows, is bold and cliffy, the coast turning sharply round it to the northward; a short distance off it are some strong tide rips.

Phillip and James points, at the northern end of the narrows, are bold and steep-to; off the latter, which lies on the eastern side, is a small island named Maquazneecht.

Tidal streams.—The tidal streams run through the narows at a rate of from 4 to 6 knots, and the streams turn shortly after high and low water.

Rupert arm, NE. of Quatsino narrows, is 5 miles long in a northeasterly direction and nearly 1 mile wide; its shores are high; its head terminates in low land, and a bank dries off it for 400 yards. The depths in this arm vary from 80 to 30 fathoms, shoaling gradually to the head, off which a vessel may anchor, in 14 to 17 fathoms, a short distance from the edge of the bank.

Marble creek, which lies ½ mile east of the narrows, at the entrance of Rupert arm, is of small extent and affords anchorage in from 5 to 6 fathoms; off its head a sand bank extends 800 yards and midway up the creek are some small islets on either side; if intending to anchor, pass between, and go just inside them.

From Rupert arm to Hardy bay, on the NE. side of Vancouver island, is a distance of only 6 miles, and a trail exists between the two places, frequented by the natives for trading purposes to the village and station in Beaver harbor, the old Fort Rupert of the Hudson Bay Company.

Hankin point (Ruanispah), abreast Quatsino narrows on the north side, is bold and rocky; it separates Rupert from West arm.

West arm trends in a westerly direction nearly 18 miles from the north part of Quatsino narrows and varies in breadth from 400 yards to 1 mile. Its shores are mostly high and rocky; the northern shore is indented by several small bays, and off it are some rocks and small islands. There are two anchorages, one at Coal harbor on the north side and the other at the edge of the bank extending from the head; the former is of moderate extent and the best anchorage northward of the narrows.

West arm gradually decreases in breadth to the westward of the Straggling islands; the head terminates in low land, and a bank extends upward of 400 yards from it; close to the outer edge of the latter are from 12 to 14 fathoms, where a vessel may anchor.

Coal harbor, 2 miles from the narrows, on the northern side of West arm, is of square shape, from 600 to 800 yards in extent, and affords good anchorage near the middle in from 12 to 14 fathoms. The shore is bordered by a sandy beach, and at the head are some fresh-water streams. This anchorage is easy of access; indications of coal have been met with in this vicinity. It was at one time worked to a small extent.

Pot rocks, which lie 2 miles west from Coal harbor and 600 yards from the north shore, are of small extent and cover at three-quarters flood.

Straggling islands, about 5 miles from the narrows, are a group of small islands and rocks extending upward of ½ mile from the northern shore; the depths among them and to the northward are irregular; when passing them do not approach their south side nearer than 400 yards. Just west of them on the north shore is a small patch of swampy ground, through which flow some fresh-water streams, and a bank extends 200 yards from it.

Directions.—Entering Quatsino sound from the southward, give Reef point, its southern entrance point, an offing of about 2 miles and steer N. 25° E. (North mag.) till Bold bluff comes in line with the gap in the center of the Surf islands, bearing N. 41° E. (N. 16°

E. mag.), which mark kept on will lead SE. of Danger rocks; when the west side of Robson island comes open north of Entrance Mount point in Forward inlet, bearing N. 37° W. (N. 62° W. mag.), or Village islet, on the eastern side of that inlet, is just touching Brown point, bearing N. 20° W. (N. 45° W. mag.), a vessel will be well east of these rocks. If bound up the sound, round the north end of Surf islands at a distance of ½ mile, or if going to Forward inlet, steer about NW. by N., taking care not to shut in the southern side of Robson island with Entrance Mount point, until Bedwell islets come open north of Bold bluff, bearing N. 69° E. (N. 44° E. mag.), when the vessel will be well north of Danger rocks. Pass from 200 to 400 yards eastward of Low islets and Robson island, and, rounding the north point of the latter at the same distance, enter North harbor and anchor in from 4 to 6 fathoms near its center.

If intending to anchor in Winter harbor, when abreast the northern part of Robson island, steer about North, keeping well over to the western shore to avoid New bank, and when past it enter the harbor in mid-channel, anchoring in 11 fathoms about ½ mile north of Grass point. Winter and North harbors are the best anchorages in the sound and available for sailing vessels, which could beat into the latter, and from being situated near the entrance their position is very advantageous.

Bound to Koprino harbor, which can only be entered by steam vessels or sailing vessels with a fair wind, round the NW. point of Surf islands at a distance of about ½ mile and steer up the sound in mid-channel until abreast the harbor. If in a large vessel, go through the East passage, keeping from 200 to 400 yards from Plumper island; enter the anchorage on either side of Wedge island, and moor immediately the vessel is NW. of it (with anchors north and south); a vessel may also enter by West passage and anchor in 14 fathoms SW. of Dockyard island.

When navigating the sound eastward of Koprino harbor the chart is indispensable, but a mid-channel course should be kept; large sailing vessels should not, however, go eastward of that harbor, as the anchorages beyond are rather difficult of access for them. If wishing to anchor in Hecate cove, enter it in mid-channel, passing north of Limestone island, and moor immediately inside the entrance points; the tidal streams run from 1 to 3 knots abreast the entrance and should be guarded against.

Going through the Quatsino narrows, keep well over to the northern shore, pass north of Round island, round Turn point close-to, and, guarding against the tidal stream, steer up the narrows in mid-channel; the narrows should only be attempted at slack water or with a favorable tide, unless in a full-powered steam vessel. The best anchorage north of the narrows is Coal harbor, and if wishing to go there, a northwesterly course for 2 miles from the narrows will lead to its entrance, and a vessel may anchor near the center in from 12 to 14 fathoms. In navigating the West arm keep well over to the southern shore when in the vicinity of Pot rock and Straggling islands.

From the westward.—Entering Quatsino sound from the westward, keep an offing of about 2 miles, till Entrance island bears N. 45° E. (N. 20° E. mag.), when steer to pass about 400 yards SE. of it, but not farther off. When abreast it haul to the northward, bringing Pinnacle islet in line with the eastern side of Low islets, bearing N. 8° W. (N. 33° W. mag.), and steer up with that mark on till Bedwell islets come well open north of Bold bluff, bearing N. 69° E. (N. 44° E. mag.), when enter Forward inlet, and proceed farther up the sound, as before directed.

If, when coming from the southward, Pinnacle and Low islets can be well made out, a vessel by keeping the former in line with the eastern part of the latter, bearing N. 8° W. (N. 33° W. mag.), will pass 600 yards west of Danger rocks; but as a rule it would be more prudent to pass eastward of them.

If the weather be so thick that the marks for clearing Danger rocks can not be distinguished, a seaman, if able to distinguish Entrance island, may enter the sound by steering for it on a NNE. bearing; give the island a berth of ¼ to ½ mile, hauling to the northward when abreast of it; by keeping ½ mile on a northerly course the vessel will be well clear northward of the Danger rocks, and may proceed anywhere up the sound. On a clear night in fine weather a vessel may also enter in the above manner.

There is room, with a steady breeze, for a smart working vessel to beat into the sound to the southward and eastward of Danger rocks, though without previous knowledge of the place it would be rather hazardous to attempt it. If obliged to do so, when standing to the northward toward Danger rocks, tack when Bold bluff comes in line with the center of the northernmost (wooded) Surf island, bearing N. 52° E. (N. 27° E. mag); and, in standing toward the eastern shore, tack when Bold bluff comes in line with the SE. extreme of the Surf islands, bearing N. 35° E. (N. 10° E. mag.). When the south side of Robson island comes open north of Entrance Mount point, N. 37° W. (N. 62° W. mag.), the vessel will be eastward of Danger rocks and may stand farther to the northward.

Beating between Surf islands and Danger rocks, tack at about 600 yards from the former; and, when standing toward the latter, keep Robson island open, as before directed, till Bedwell islets come open north of Bold bluff, N. 69° E. (N. 44° E. mag.); if going to North harbor, when inside Forward inlet, guard against New bank.

The coast of Vancouver island from Quatsino sound to cape Scott, the NW. extreme of the island, takes a general NW. direction; it is mostly rocky and iron-bound, indented by several bays, most of which are small, and from most of the projecting points rocks extend, in some places nearly 1 mile from the shore.

Caution.—When navigating between cape Scott and Quatsino sound do not approach the shore nearer than 2 miles.

Rugged point, 3 miles from Quatsino sound, is a rocky, rugged point, of moderate height, with 12 fathoms at ½ mile outside it. Open bay, which lies just inside it, affords landing for boats in fine weather on its eastern side.

The coast between Open bay and the entrance to Quatsino sound is high and cliffy; some rocks extend nearly 1 mile from it.

Topknot point, 5 miles NW. of Rugged point, is low, with a hill 300 feet high, shaped like a topknot, just within it; some rocks extend ½ mile southward from it.

Raft cove, 8 miles from Rugged point, is an open bight about 1 mile in extent, and affords no shelter whatever. Heavy breakers are reported, in moderate weather, with the northern extreme of the southern point of entrance to the cove bearing N. 49° E. (N. 24° E. mag.), distant ¾ mile.

Cape Palmerston, 11 miles NW. from Rugged point, is a bold rocky point rising to 1,422 feet; some rocks extend ½ mile from it.

San Josef bay, the entrance to which is 14 miles NW. from Rugged point and 8 miles SSE. from cape Scott, is an extensive open bay, 3 miles deep in a northeasterly direction; the breadth at the entrance is nearly 2 miles, narrowing gradually toward the head. Its shores are high, and off the south side are several offlying rocks; the depths vary from 11 to 4 fathoms, but the bay affords no shelter except with northerly winds, and should only be used as a stopping place in fine weather; generally a heavy sea sets into it, and a sailing vessel caught there with a southwesterly gale would inevitably go on shore. At the south side of the head of the bay is a fresh-water stream of considerable size, which boats can enter at high water and find shelter in.

Directions.—Intending to anchor in the bay, bring the entrance to bear N. 70° E. (N. 45° E. mag.) and steer for it, anchoring in 7 or 9 fathoms near the middle, with the entrance points bearing S. 25° W. (South mag.) and N. 65° W. (West mag.).

Sea Otter cove, just west of San Josef bay, is about 1 mile long in a northerly direction, and from 400 to 600 yards wide. There are 5 fathoms in the entrance, and from 1 to 3 fathoms inside it, also several rocks; the shelter within is very indifferent, and the place only fit for a coaster. Off its SE. entrance point, and separating the cove from San Josef bay, are some small islets extending nearly 1 mile from the shore; they are bare and yellow-topped, about 40 feet high, and conspicuous from the NW.

Cape Russell, 16 miles from Rugged point and immediately westward of Sea Otter cove, is a remarkable headland 870 feet high and the outer part of a peninsula formed by Sea Otter cove and a small bay NW. of it; some rocks, on which the sea breaks very heavily, extend nearly 1 mile south of the cape.

From cape Russell to cape Scott the coast, from 500 to 600 feet high, trends in a NNW. direction, and is indented by three open bays, which are nearly 1 mile deep, but afford no shelter whatever.

CHAPTER IX.

COAST OF BRITISH COLUMBIA (INNER CHANNELS)—QUEEN CHARLOTTE SOUND TO MILBANK SOUND.

VARIATION IN 1906.

Egg island..................26° 00′ E. Ivory island ....26° 45′ E.

The inner channels of the seaboard of British Columbia described in this chapter afford smooth water, together with suitable anchorages for vessels of moderate length, at moderate distances apart.

See Chapter I for routes usually followed.

These channels, therefore, offer facilities to steam vessels for avoiding the strong gales and thick weather so frequently met with in Hecate strait. They are also available for fore-and-aft schooners, when navigating between Vancouver island and Alaska.

Unless directed to the contrary, a mid-channel course is recommended when navigating these inner waters.

Cape Caution (Kakleesla), the northern entrance point of Queen Charlotte sound, is of moderate height and level, the tops of the trees being about 200 feet above the sea; the shore is white and of granite formation, with a few rocks off it; the land eastward of the cape rises gradually in a distance of 5 miles to Coast nipple, 1,350 feet high, 2 miles eastward of which rises mount Robinson, 2,100 feet high.

Sea Otter group, consisting of several dangerous rocks, islets, and shoals, which cover a space of about 12 miles in extent north and south and 10 miles in an east and west direction, lies at a distance of 6 or 7 miles from the seaboard of British Columbia, fronting the coast between capes Caution and Calvert.

Danger shoal, on which the sea is reported to break in heavy weather, is the southernmost outlying danger of Sea Otter group and lies 10½ miles N. 82° W. (S. 72° W. mag.) from cape Caution; near the center of this shoal a depth of 9 fathoms, rocks and stones, was obtained, with 22 fathoms close around. Shoaler water probably exists.

Clearing mark.—The southern extremes of Egg and Table islands in line, bearing N. 61° E. (N. 35° E. mag.), leads clear to the southeastward of Danger shoal and all other dangers on the SE. side of Sea Otter group.

Virgin rocks, near the western limit of the group, consist of three white rocks, the largest of which (50 feet high) lies 17 miles N. 64° W. (West mag.) from cape Caution. Southwestward of these rocks the 30-fathom curve is 4 miles, and in a northwesterly direction 6 miles, distant; rounding the rocks to the westward do not stand into less than 30 fathoms.

Watch rock, 74 feet high and black, lies near the northern limit of the group, 7¼ miles N. 33° E. (N. 7° E. mag.) from Virgin rocks. The rock is steep-to.

Pearl rocks, the northeasternmost of Sea Otter group, comprise several rocks above and below water, extending 1½ miles in a NW. and SE. direction; the largest rock (15 feet high) lies 3 miles S. 76° E. (N. 78° E. mag.) from Watch rock, and the SE. rock, on which the sea always breaks, lies 1 mile S. 31° E. (S. 57° E. mag.) from the largest rock.

Devil rock, the northeastern outlying danger, lies 1¼ miles N. 76° E. (N. 50° E. mag.) from the largest Pearl rock. The sea seldom breaks on Devil rock, and there is apparently deep water close around.

New patch, on which the sea generally breaks, is nearly 2 miles in extent and lies 4½ miles S. 14° W. (S. 12° E. mag.) from the largest Pearl rock.

Channel reef, the easternmost danger of Sea Otter group, has about 6 feet over it at low water; from the center of this reef Egg island bears S. 67° E. (N. 87° E. mag.), distant 4$\frac{3}{10}$ miles. The sea seldom breaks on Channel reef, and there are 60 fathoms close eastward of it.

Leading mark.—Addenbrooke island open of, and the eastern shore of Fitzhugh sound (beyond) shut in by, cape Calvert bearing North (N. 26° W. mag.), will lead midway between Channel reef and Egg island and up to the entrance of Fitzhugh sound. Allowance should be made for tidal streams; the flood sets to the eastward into Queen Charlotte and Smith sounds with a velocity at springs of nearly 2 knots.

Hannah rock, the southeasternmost outlying danger, on which the sea nearly always breaks, is situated about 2¾ miles S. 26° W. (South mag.) of Channel reef; Hannah rock is awash at high water, and from its center, cape Caution bears S. 59° E. (S. 85° E. mag.), distant 8 miles.

Caution.—Dangerous rocks have been reported as lying in a SW. by W. ¼ W. direction, 5 miles from Danger shoal and occupying a space of 2½ miles in diameter, but their existence is doubtful.

South passage, leading to Smith and Fitzhugh sounds from the southward, lies between cape Caution and the SE. limit of Sea Otter group, where it is about 7 miles broad, with irregular depths varying from 34 to 74 fathoms.

Blunden bay, a slight bend in the coast between cape Caution and Neck point, 2 miles northward from the former, is about 1 mile wide at its entrance and nearly 1 mile deep. Indian cove, which lies in the northern part of this bay, affords good shelter for boats; it is the rendezvous for Indians on their canoe voyages, when passing between Queen Charlotte and Fitzhugh sounds.

Hoop reef.—From Neck point the coast trends N. by E. for 2 mile to Good Shelter cove, midway between which lies Hoop reef, about ⅓ mile from the shore; this reef is ¾ mile in extent north and south and ¼ mile broad.

South Iron rock, on which the sea seldom breaks, lies ¾ mile westward of Hoop reef and nearly 1¾ miles N. 25° W. (N. 51° W. mag.) from Neck point.

North Iron rock, which dries 7 feet, lies nearly in the fairway of Alexandra passage, ¾ mile North (N. 26° W. mag.) from South Iron rock and 1 mile S. 30° E. (S. 56° E. mag.) from Egg island; there are 7 to 9 fathoms close-to.

Clearing mark.—False Egg island in line with West rock off Table island, bearing N. 10° E. (N. 16° W. mag.), leads 800 yards westward of South and North Iron rocks.

Egg island, immediately fronting Smith sound and standing boldly out from the coast, is the prominent landmark between Goletas channel and Fitzhugh sound. The island is 280 feet high, covered with trees, and is remarkable for its egg-like shape; it lies 5 miles NNW. from cape Caution. From the SW. side of the island rocks extend about 200 yards, and on the eastern side is a small island, which is separated from Egg island by a narrow gully, giving the appearance of a split in the island itself, when seen from north or south.

Light.—A revolving white light every 30 seconds, elevated 85 feet above high water, and visible in clear weather between the bearings of N. 19° W. (N. 45° W. mag.), through North and East to S. 31° W. (S. 5° W. mag.), from a distance of 15 miles, is shown from a square, white, wooden tower with red lantern, 50 feet high, and surmounting the keeper's dwelling, situated on the summit of the islet immediately westward of Egg island. The light is obscured from the northward and eastward by the high land of Egg island.

Fog signal.—A diaphone, operated by compressed air, sounds 1 blast of 5 seconds' duration every minute. The fog-signal building is a white building with red roof, which stands 100 feet northward of the lighthouse.

Egg rocks, on the NW. side of Alexandra passage, are a cluster of rocks, lying nearly ¾ mile NW. from North Iron rock and about 400 yards south from Egg island; these rocks extend about ¼ mile north and south, the northernmost being 30 feet high.

Denny rock is an isolated rock of small extent, seldom breaking and not marked by kelp, having a least depth of 7 feet at low water, with deep water on all sides of it; from the rock, Egg Island lighthouse bears N. 19° E. (N. 7° W. mag.), distant 1,300 yards, and North Iron rock S. 65° E. (N. 89° E. mag.).

False Egg island, bearing N. 18° E. (N. 8° W. mag.), its own breadth open of Egg Island lighthouse, clears Denny rock to the westward by about 600 yards.

Smith sound, 6 miles north from cape Caution, is about 10 miles long ENE. and WSW., with an average breadth of 3½ miles, the entrance between Jones and Long points being 4½ miles across in a northerly direction. At 6 miles within the entrance, on either side of a cluster of islands, is a channel leading into Smith inlet. In almost every part of the sound the depths are over 40 fathoms and there is generally a heavy swell.

The southern shore of Smith sound, for 4 or 5 miles from the entrance, is skirted by several small islands and rocks having deep water close-to; good shelter for boats will be obtained in a small cove about ¼ mile east of Jones point, the southern entrance point of the sound; also in a cove 1 mile SW. of Jones point, abreast Egg rocks.

The entrance to the sound is protected by a rocky plateau (Cluster reefs) and several islands, islets, and rocks, some above, and many under water, prominent amongst them being Egg and Table islands. Access to Smith sound may be had on either side of these islands.

Alexandra passage, the continuation of South passage into Smith sound, lies between Egg island and the southern point of entrance, the narrowest part between Egg rocks and North Iron rock being 1,200 yards wide; here, as elsewhere, however, the dangers are so steep-to that the quickest use of the lead is enjoined.

The northern edge of Surf islet in line with the southern edge of the islets south of Shower island, bearing N. 60° E. (N. 34° E. mag.), leads through Alexandra passage.

Beaver passage.—The northern channel into Smith sound lies between False Egg island and Brown island on the north, and John rock, White rocks, and Cluster reefs on the south. In Beaver passage the bottom is irregular, 20 fathoms being the least depth obtained.

The course through the passage is S. 60° E. (S. 86° E. mag.); the eastern extreme of Search islands, just open of the western end of Surf islet on that bearing, leads in between John rock and False Egg island, where the width is 1,200 yards.

White rocks, 35 feet high and very conspicuous, lie in the western end of Beaver passage at 3¼ miles N. 9° E. (N. 17° W. mag.) from Egg island and nearly 1 mile NW. of Cluster reefs.

John rock.—At 600 yards north from White rocks, and 1,400 yards SW. from False Egg island, lies John rock, which dries 3 feet at low water, with 9 to 20 fathoms close around, forming the northern danger on the southern side of Beaver passage.

False Egg island, resembling Egg island in shape, but smaller, is 150 feet high; it lies on the northern side of Beaver passage and is the outlying landmark for this northern entrance to Smith sound.

James rock.—At about 600 yards NW. by W. ½ W. from False Egg island lies James rock, the exact position of which is somewhat doubtful; the sea breaks on this rock at low water, and between it and False Egg island the bottom is foul.

Clearing mark.—The western part of the large Canoe rock bearing N. 25° E. (N. 1° W. mag.), or in line with Quoin hill (on Penrose island), leads ¾ mile westward of James and John rocks, and clear of all dangers at the entrance of Smith sound.

Table island, the largest of the group occupying the entrance to Smith sound, is about 1 mile long north and south and ½ mile broad, with the tops of the trees 120 feet above the sea, nearly flat, but when seen from abreast cape Caution it appears to have two hills.

A cluster of rocks, several of which are covered at low water, extend ½ mile from the western side of Table island, with 24 fathoms close to the outer rock.

Ann island, about ½ mile in extent, is separated from the northern end of Table island by a channel (200 yards wide in some parts) in which shelter will be found for boats.

Cluster reefs, consisting of several rocky heads and shoal patches, extend from Table island in a northerly and northeasterly direction into the entrance of Smith sound.

George rock, on which the sea breaks at low water, is the northwesternmost of the reefs, and lies 1 mile N. 5° E. (N. 21° W. mag.) from Ann island.

Edward rock dries 7 feet and lies east nearly ¾ mile from George rock.

Wood rocks, which are awash at low water, situated nearly ¼ mile S. 76° E. (N. 78° E. mag.) from Edward reef, consist of three rocky heads, and are the northeasternmost of Cluster reefs.

Bertie rock, with 3½ fathoms of water, on it, lies near the eastern edge of Cluster reefs; from the center of this rock the NW. extreme of Ann island bears S. 62° W. (S. 36° W. mag.), distant nearly ¾ mile.

Leading mark.—The western extreme of False Egg island in line with Kelp head, bearing N. 16° E. (N. 10° W. mag.), leads westward, and Limit point midway between Long and Shower islands, bearing S. 85° E. (N. 69° E. mag.), leads northward, of Cluster reefs.

Tidal streams.—Allowance should be made for tidal streams; the flood sets to the eastward into Queen Charlotte and Smith sounds with a velocity at springs of nearly 2 knots.

Long point, the NW. point of Smith sound, lies ¾ mile eastward from False Egg island; Tie island, which is nearly ¼ mile in extent, lies close westward of Long point and is separated from it by a boat passage, in which there is a depth of 4 fathoms. Ada rock, which is awash at low water, lies 400 yards south from Tie island.

Brown island, on the NE. side of Beaver passage, lies ½ mile S. 15° E. (S. 41° E. mag.) from Long point; the island is 250 feet high, nearly ½ mile long north and south, and ¼ mile broad, with 17 to 23 fathoms close to its southern point.

Surprise patch, on the northern side of Smith sound, lies 1¾ miles N. 85° E. (N. 59° E. mag.) from the southern extreme of Brown island; there is a depth of 5 fathoms on this patch, 7 to 17 fathoms close around.

Judd rock, with less than 6 feet of water on it, lies ¾ mile N. 88° E. (N. 62° E. mag.) from Surprise patch and ¾ mile NW. ¾ W. from Long island, the largest of the Barrier islands.

Barrier islands, in the middle of Smith sound, comprise several small islands covering a space of about 5 miles in extent ENE. and WSW. Blakeney passage on the northern, and Browning passage on the southern side of these islands, leading to Boswell and Smith inlets, are each about 1 mile wide, with no bottom at a depth of 40 fathoms.

Takush harbor, on the southern shore of Smith sound, 6 miles within the entrance, is 2 miles long NW. and SE. and 1 mile broad, and is the only anchorage to which a ship can resort for shelter when crossing Queen Charlotte sound. Vessels of large size can lie securely here.

The entrance is ¾ mile wide and has depths of 22 fathoms, rocky bottom, in the center of Ship passage, which is 500 yards wide, and is formed by Gnarled islands on the western, and Fish rocks (dry 3 feet at low water) on the eastern side. There is an Indian village here of the Quascilla tribe; the lodges are wretchedly constructed and the people miserably poor.

Petrel shoal, on which there is a depth of 15 feet, situated 200 yards S. 6° E. (S. 32° E. mag.) from the easternmost Gnarled island, is the principal danger in rounding into Anchor bight.

Fly basin, at the head of Takush harbor, perfectly landlocked, is about 1 mile long east and west and 200 to 400 yards broad, with 2¼ to 3 fathoms in the western and 6 to 8 fathoms in the eastern part of the basin. The entrance to Fly basin, which is about 200 yards wide, is contracted to 50 yards by a shoal extending from the eastern entrance point, with a rock (drying 2 feet at low water) and a patch of 9 feet on its western edge; between this shoal and the western entrance point there is a depth of 9 fathoms. If required, a small vessel could be taken into Fly basin.

Anchorage in Takush harbor will be found in 10 or 11 fathoms, mud, in Anchor bight, midway between Ship rock and Steep point, with the northern extreme of Bull point in line with Anchor islands, bearing N. 87° E. (N. 61° E. mag.), and the eastern extreme of Bloxam point N. 42° E. (N. 16° E. mag.).

Tides.—It is high water, full and change, in Takush harbor at 1 h. 0 m.; springs rise 14 feet, neaps 11 feet.

Directions.—When bound to Takush harbor, it is recommended to pass through Browning passage, and, after passing North point, keep the northern extreme of Bright island a little open north of that point bearing N. 79° W. (S. 75° W. mag.) until Berry point (south side of Fly basin) appears midway between the entrance points of Fly basin, S. 20° E. (S. 46° E. mag.), which will lead through Ship passage; and when Steep point is well open of the southernmost Gnarled island bearing N. 87° W. (S. 67° W. mag.), a course may be steered for the anchorage in Anchor bight, taking care to avoid the shoal ground south of Gnarled islands, passing midway between Anchor and Gnarled islands. Good steerage is required here; speed should be proportionately slow, the leads kept quickly going, and the water not shoaled to less than 7 fathoms.

Mamie rock.—Central island, the easternmost of the Barrier islands, lies 1½ miles NNE. from the entrance to Takush harbor, and 850 yards N. 82° E. (N. 56° E. mag.) from its eastern end is Mamie rock, which dries 1 foot at low water. There is deep water between the rock and Central island and also between it and Sound island to the northward.

Frank rock.—Oval islet, which is situated 200 yards NW. from Ripon point, is small, and 600 yards N. 75° W. (S. 79° W. mag.) from its western point is Frank rock, 5 feet above high water.

MacBride bay, on the southern shore of the inlet opposite Ripon point, is deep, but anchorage may be had in it, in 20 fathoms, with Central island shut in by the western point of the bay; Round islet lies 200 yards off the eastern point of the bay. There are two rocks in the entrance to the bay; the northern one has 6 feet over it at low water and lies 450 yards S. 60° W. (S. 34° W. mag.) from Round islet; the southern rock is 250 yards S. 15° W. (S. 11° E.

mag.) from the northern one and has 18 feet over it at low water. The entrance is between these rocks and Round islet, which latter should be kept aboard.

Smith inlet (Quascilla), the eastern continuation of Smith sound, is 1,200 yards wide between Ripon point and Round islet and extends nearly straight in an easterly direction for 6 miles to Quascilla bay. The shores are formed of rocky, precipitous mountains covered with trees, and the inlet has deep water.

Confined anchorage may be found in the cove in the southern bight of Quascilla bay. The water is deep in the cove, but there is a small rocky patch in the entrance with 9 fathoms of water over it.

At the eastern end of Quascilla bay there is a small tidal lagoon (Wyeclees) connected with the inlet by a short passage not navigable except by small craft. This lagoon connects by a stream with a series of lakes frequented by salmon in large numbers during the months of July and August. The inlet has not been surveyed beyond Quascilla; it extends in a northeasterly direction for a distance of 18 miles farther and has deep water to the head, where there is a large river (Laklekl) navigable by boats for 3 miles at high water.

Opposite Quascilla bay, on the northern side of the inlet, is a thickly wooded promontory, point Adelaide, which has the appearance of a cone from a vessel going up the inlet. This point is the southern entrance to Naysash inlet, about 200 yards wide. The inlet extends in a north and NE. direction for 13 miles. It is not navigable beyond 4 miles from the entrance. A cannery is situated about 1 mile up this inlet in Hickey cove; at the cannery there is a wharf with 12 feet alongside. The tide rises at the wharf in Hickey cove 16 feet at springs. The mountains around Naysash inlet are very high and steep, giving the place, the waterway being so narrow, a confined and gloomy appearance. Anchorage may be found in Naysash bay close northward of the cove in 30 fathoms, mud.

A rock, which dries at low water, lies 200 yards S. 81° E. (N. 73° E. mag.) from cape Anne, the eastern termination of Greaves island, with a depth of 9 fathoms close eastward of the rock, deepening rapidly to 45 fathoms.

Greaves island, forming the southern shore of Smith inlet from Takush harbor to Quascilla, is divided from the mainland by Ahclakerho channel, varying in breadth from 100 yards to about 1 mile, but as the western termination at Takush harbor dries at low water the channel is not navigable throughout.

Boswell inlet branches off from Smith inlet on the northern side, 4 miles east from Dsoolish bay; it has not been surveyed; Napier and Denison islands lie in its entrance.

The coast from Long point extends 2¼ miles N. ¾ W. to Kelp head, from which Cranstown point bears N. by E. ¼ E., distant 1 mile.

Fitzhugh sound, the entrance to which lies 3 miles northward of Smith sound, is 39 miles long in a general northerly direction, having an average breadth of 3 miles. The shores are mostly bold and rocky, the slopes are wooded and steep, and the elevation of the peaks from 1,000 to 3,400 feet. The southern entrance to Fitzhugh sound lies between Cranstown point (the southern entrance point of Rivers inlet) and cape Calvert, the southern extremity of Calvert island, which bears from Cranstown point NW. by W. ¼ W., distant 5 miles.

The sound at 4 miles north of Safety cove is contracted to 1½ miles in width by Addenbrooke and adjacent islands, which lie on the eastern side; the shores on both sides are, however, steep-to, and the depths in the channel from 80 to 140 fathoms.

Tidal stream.—The flood tide runs to the northward.

Canoe, Spur, and Paddle rocks lie about 1 mile off Kelp head and occupy a space of 1½ miles in a north and south direction, the space thus inclosed being foul and more or less covered with growing kelp. Canoe rock, the middle and most prominent one of these rocks, is bare, 25 feet high, and stands boldly out from the coast, making a good point for identification.

Open bay, on the NE. side of Cranstown point, affords anchorage in 7 fathoms, about 400 yards from the shore, during summer or with offshore winds, but there is generally a swell in the bay and it is only used by local craft as a temporary anchorage.

Cape Calvert, the southern extreme of Calvert island, is the southern termination of Cape range (2,000 feet high); it presents a broad face of rocky coast extending in a NE. and SW. direction, about 350 feet high, and covered with a thick growth of hemlock and pine trees. At 2 miles north of the cape is Entry cone (1,200 feet high), which is conspicuous and forms a good mark for recognizing Fitzhugh sound from the southward and westward.

Cape Calvert is fronted by the Sorrow islands, which are steep-to, of granite formation, and covered with gnarled and stunted trees; between these islands and the cape fair shelter may be found for boats in Grief bay (Telakwas), but during SE. or SW. gales more or less swell is experienced, rendering landing difficult and sometimes dangerous.

Those from the westward, bound for Fitzhugh sound, should use North passage, between Sea Otter group and Calvert island; this passage is about 3 miles wide.

Hedley patch, with 9 fathoms of water (possibly less), lies in the western end of North passage, 3½ miles N. 22° E. (N. 4° W. mag.) from Watch rock.

Schooner Retreat (Kapilish), on the eastern side of Fitzhugh sound, is the name given to the anchorages among a cluster of islands at the SW. part of Penrose island, which here separates Fitzhugh sound from Rivers inlet. The Retreat affords a secure stopping place, and with care may be safely entered by steam vessels. Karslake point (Joachim island), its southeastern entrance point, lies 7 miles NE. by E. ¾ E. from Sorrow islands. The entrance to Schooner Retreat trends in a NE. direction from Karslake point, where it is about ½ mile wide, contracting to 200 yards between Sea bluff and Grey islets; inside the narrows to the eastward it expands into Frigate bay.

Penrose island, which forms the northern protection to Schooner Retreat, lies in the mouth of Rivers inlet, a branch of the inlet passing on either side of it. Quoin hill, 880 feet high, is situated near the middle of the island.

Joachim island, the southeasternmost and largest of the cluster of islands at the SW. end of Penrose island, is 400 feet high, 1¼ miles long north and south, with an average breadth of ½ mile; the north extreme of this island is separated from Penrose island by a boat passage.

Ironside island, the eastern part of which is 200 feet high, is the next in size, and is separated from Sea bluff, the NW. point of Joachim island, by the channel into Schooner Retreat. Grey islets, on the western side of the channel into Schooner Retreat, lie close off the SE. extreme of Ironside island.

Safe entrance, between Joachim and Ironside islands, ¼ mile wide, has in the middle from 8 to 17 fathoms of water. On the western side of Safe entrance, about 50 yards from Grey islets, lies a rock awash; from it shoal ground extends 300 yards in a northerly direction, with 2 to 3 fathoms on it and 4 to 10 fathoms close-to.

Comber rock, on which the sea often breaks, is an outlying danger at the northern side of Safe entrance; the rock covers at three-quarters flood and lies 150 yards S. 36° W. (S. 10° W. mag.) from Surf point, the SW. extreme of Ironside island.

Frigate bay, the easternmost anchorage in Schooner Retreat, is about ½ mile long east and west and ¼ mile broad, with depths of 9 to 20 fathoms; it is formed by Joachim and Penrose islands on the south, east, and north, and it is protected on the west by Ironside and Maze islands.

Center islet, in the north part of the bay, of small extent, lies 450 yards from the northern end of Safe entrance; a shoal with from 2 to 3 fathoms on it extends for more than 200 yards from its eastern end in a northeasterly direction toward Penrose island. There are several other islets and rocks in the eastern part of the bay, from which a boat passage leads into Rivers inlet.

The best anchorage in Frigate bay will be found just within Safe entrance, off a clean sandy beach, in 13 fathoms, with the NE. extreme of Ironside island bearing N. 71° W. (S. 83° W. mag.) and the NW. extreme of Sea bluff S. 28° W. (S. 2° W. mag.). Vessels should moor.

Maze islands are a cluster of small islands on an extensive shoal projecting in a northerly direction from the NE. end of Ironside island; the NE. prong of this shoal extends nearly across to Penrose island, leaving a narrow channel with 5½ to 9 fathoms of water, which leads from Frigate bay to Secure anchorage.

Secure anchorage, NW. of Frigate bay, is about ¼ mile long east and west and 300 yards broad, with depths of 9 to 11 fathoms; it is protected from seaward by Ironside, Bird, and Highway islands. Verney passage, leading to Secure anchorage from the westward, between Ironside and Bird islands, is nearly 100 yards wide with 7 fathoms in mid-channel, but it is contracted to about 30 yards by the shoals on either side, and is only suitable for small coasting vessels. Chance rock, at the entrance between Folly and Stunted islands, renders this passage dangerous. This rock lies 150 yards NW. of Curlew point.

Directions.—When bound to Schooner Retreat use at all times Safe entrance; from the southward, Quoin hill (880 feet high), in the middle of Penrose island, should be brought in line with the hill 200 feet high, on the eastern end of Ironside island bearing N. 47° E. (N. 21° E. mag.); this will lead to abreast Karslake point, the western extreme of Joachim island, when Safe entrance will be open. After passing Karslake point steer very carefully and proceed at a moderate speed toward Sea bluff until Quoin hill is in line with Center island bearing N. 32° E. (N. 6° E. mag.), which will lead through Safe entrance in mid-channel and to the anchorage in Frigate bay.

Gales.—During SE. and SW. gales the gusts are furious, but with good ground tackle and care there is no danger in Schooner Retreat.

Tides.—It is high water, full and change, in Schooner Retreat at 0 h. 30 m.; springs rise 14 feet, neaps 11 feet.

Rivers inlet, the shores of which have not been surveyed, has an entrance on either side of Penrose island, but it is not known whether they are clear of danger. The inlet runs about 12 miles in a northerly direction, and then 10 miles northeastward to the mouth of Wannock river. Zero and Black rocks are dangers at the entrance of the inlet; the former is a small rocky islet, composed of white limestone, about 15 to 20 feet above high water, and about 400 yards in extent; the latter is a low, smooth, black rock, about 50 yards long and 3 or 4 feet high, with foul ground between it and the island to the northward.

A rock, with a depth of 4 fathoms on it, lies with Zero rock center bearing N. 71° E. (N. 45° E. mag.), distant 1,600 yards.

Pass northwestward of Zero rock and southeastward of Black rock, about 200 yards off each, in deep water.

Schooner passage, the entrance to which from Rivers inlet is on the western shore, about 10 miles up the inlet, and westward of Walbran island, has deep water, with low and densely wooded shores. This passage has a uniform breadth of about 400 yards, and is frequently used by local steam vessels, but it is not suitable for vessels more than 240 feet in length. There is a rock, which dries at extreme low water, at the western entrance of the passage, to avoid which a sharp turn is necessary, and the northern shore should be kept close aboard. A rock lies 50 yards offshore on the western side, about ¾ mile within the northern entrance.

Good anchorage is reported in the northwestern bight, in 10 to 20 fathoms, where the inlet turns to the eastward. Wannock cannery is on the northern shore about 2 miles eastward of this bight. At the mouth of Wannock river the village Oweekayno is situated on both sides; there is a cannery and wharf on the northern side, and a sawmill, cannery, and a wooden church are on the southern side. The water is too deep for anchorage off Oweekayno. The least water on the bar of the Wannock is 7 feet at low water, abreast the church, and the mark for entering is to keep a landslip, the middle of three situated about 1 mile southwestward of the church, bearing S. 57° W. (S. 31° W. mag.), astern. There is a wharf at the sawmill with a depth of 12 feet alongside. There are seven large salmon canneries in the inlet, each with a wharf. A mail steamer calls at the establishments in Rivers inlet once a month.

Swan rock is about ¼ mile in length NW. and SE., with depths of 1¼ fathoms on it, and lies with Lone island center bearing S. 64° E. (East mag.), distant 1$\frac{3}{10}$ miles, and Entry cone S. 48° E. (S. 22° E. mag.).

Addenbrooke island.—At about 8 miles NNW. from Karslake point lies a group of islands off the eastern shore of the sound abreast an unexplored opening. Addenbrooke, the westernmost of these islands, extends westward into the sound, narrowing the width of the passage between it and Calvert island to about 1¾ miles.

Safety cove (Oatsoalis), on the western shore of Fitzhugh sound, 7 miles northward of cape Calvert, is about 1 mile long east and west, and nearly ½ mile wide at its entrance, westward of which the shores of the cove extend parallel to each other 400 yards apart: there are depths of 9 to 17 fathoms within 100 yards of its shores, and 14 to 19 fathoms, soft mud, in the middle of the cove; a bank of sand and mud which dries extends 600 yards from the head with 7 fathoms close to its edge.

The shores, except near the head, are high, rocky, and steep-to, rising to an elevation of about 1,000 feet. There is a conical peak at the head of the cove which bears N. 71° W. (S. 83° W. mag.) from the middle of the entrance. North point, just north of Safety cove, has two small islets lying off it, which are useful in identifying the entrance, especially when coming from the northward. There is also a landslide on the south shore at the entrance, which is noticeable at night.

Anchorage.—Good anchorage will be obtained in 13 fathoms, mud bottom, in the middle of Safety cove. Entering at night, keep in the middle of the cove and, keeping the lead going, anchor as soon as 17 fathoms are struck. During SE. or SW. gales strong gusts blow across the valley at the head of this cove.

Water.—The stream which flows into the head of Safety cove affords excellent water, but it is difficult to obtain by boats. A waterfall on the northern shore will afford a good supply except in the summer, when it dries up.

Tides.—It is high water, full and change, in Safety cove, at 1 h. 0 m.; springs rise 14 feet, neaps 11 feet.

Kwakshua passage, between Calvert and Hecate islands, 7½ miles north of Safety cove, leads to the sea; this passage has been only partially examined; it has, however, been used by coasting vessels.

Hakai channel is 5½ miles north of Kwakshua, between Hecate island and the smaller islands lying off the southern side of Hunter island, leading to sea. Vancouver reached the sea by this passage in 1792.

Goldstream harbor, at the SE. entrance point of Hakai channel, affords good accommodation for small vessels; it is about 400 yards long north and south and 400 yards broad, with depths of 7 to 15 fathoms, sand and mud. The entrance to this harbor from Fitzhugh sound is through an intricate passage little over 100 yards wide, between the northern extreme of Hecate island, which forms the southern shore, and an island about 1 mile in extent which forms the northern side of Goldstream harbor.

Foul ground marked by kelp extends 200 yards from Kelp point, the north entrance point of the harbor. Evening rock, which dries 3 feet at low water springs, lies near the middle of the passage about 400 yards within the entrance on the north side of the channel; it would, therefore, be advisable, in the absence of good local knowledge, to place a boat near this rock (when covered) before entering or leaving the harbor, and, proceeding at slow speed, keep in mid-channel, where there is a general depth of 6 fathoms.

Tides.—It is high water, full and change, in Goldstream harbor at 1 h. 0 m.; springs rise 15 feet, neaps 12 feet.

Nalau island, separating Nalau and Hakai passages, is 4½ miles long north and south, 3 miles wide, and 650 feet high; it is situated between Hunter and Hecate islands.

Nalau passage, 4 miles northward of Hakai, is an unexplored channel leading to sea.

Namu harbor, south of the entrance of Burke channel, and 1 mile south of Edmund point, on the eastern side of Fitzhugh sound, lies 6 miles NE. by E. ¼ E. from Nalau passage, the intervening eastern shore of Fitzhugh sound being abrupt and bold. It is ¾ mile long east and west and ⅔ mile broad, with depths of 20 to 28 fathoms; at its entrance lies Kiwash, a round island, 200 feet high, ¼ mile in diameter, and covered with trees.

South passage, between Kiwash and Plover islands (150 feet high), the latter forming its eastern entrance point, is nearly ½ mile wide, with 23 to 28 fathoms; North passage, between Kiwash and Cliff islands, on the northern side of the harbor, is 600 yards wide, with 35 to 18 fathoms. Namu harbor may be entered either by North or South passage.

From the eastern side of Namu harbor two inlets indent the land about 1 mile; the northern is named Harlequin basin, the other, which is choked with rocks, is called Rock creek. At the mouth of the latter is Whirlwind bay, its entrance being marked by two small islands, Sunday island to the northward and Clam island to the southward, ¼ mile apart. Two or 3 miles eastward of the harbor a chain of mountains from 2,600 to 3,300 feet high extends in a NE. and SW. direction for 6 miles.

Anchorage.—Large vessels should anchor in 20 fathoms, in the center of Namu harbor, with the northern extreme of Kiwash island bearing N. 64° W. (West mag.), and the western extreme of Plover island S. 14° W. (S. 12° E. mag.). Small vessels may anchor in Whirlwind bay in 12 fathoms, clay, with the northern extreme of Kiwash island bearing N. 76° W. (S. 78° W. mag.) and the center of Clam island S. 26° W. (South mag.).

During the autumn and winter months the anchorage in Whirlwind bay is not recommended, as furious gusts blow over the mountains (3,000 feet high) in its vicinity. The anchorage is moreover confined by Loo rock, which dries at extreme low water, lying nearly in the middle of the bay, 400 yards S. 79° E. (N. 75° E. mag.) from the southern extreme of Sunday island. It is recommended not to bring Sunday island to bear westward of N. 45° W. (N. 71° W. mag.) when entering Whirlwind bay.

There is a large stream in Whirlwind bay.

There is a cannery and wharf in Namu harbor, where wood and water may be obtained.

Tides.—It is high water, full and change, in Namu harbor at 1 h. 0 m; springs rise 15 feet, neaps 12½ feet.

Burke channel, an inlet on the eastern side of Fitzhugh sound, 3 miles northward of Namu harbor, leads to Belakula anchorage at the head of North Bentinck arm, a distance of 55 miles in a general northeasterly direction from its junction with Fitzhugh sound. Burke channel lies between high, precipitous, rocky mountains, the sides of which are covered with stunted pine trees and mostly snow-capped, becoming more lofty as the head of the inlet is approached. Burke channel and North Bentinck arm, though not surveyed in detail, have been frequently traversed both by day and night.

Edmund point, the southern entrance point of Burke channel, is low and wooded and has several small islands south of it, lying off an indentation which has the appearance of affording sheltered anchorage. Some small islets also lie in the channel, eastward of Edmund point.

Walker point, the northern entrance point to the channel, is formed by an island situated 2 miles NNW. from Edmund point; this island is steep-to, but at 400 yards distance the water is not deeper than 26 fathoms, mud, bottom, deepening quickly at a short distance farther out, a position which might be used for anchoring in a fog.

Temporary anchorage, north of Walker point, might on emergency, with care, and sending a boat ahead, be taken up, but there are many covering reefs.

The first reach of Burke channel takes a NE. ¾ E. direction for 5 miles, and thence E. by N. for 3½ miles, the first part being a little over 1 mile wide, but the latter part only ¾ mile across. The tidal streams are strong in this reach, and several heavy tide rips are met with, but for the remainder of the distance to Belakula they are not much felt. Immediately facing the eastern end of this reach is a bay which might possibly afford anchorage. The water here is brackish.

Restoration bay (Tsekwai), at 4 miles from the NE. point of the first reach, is situated immediately under a high conical mountain, and has a sandy beach at its head, off which, at ½ mile, is a depth of 40 fathoms, shoaling gradually to 3 fathoms close to the shore. Several small streams enter the cove. Anchorage may be taken up in 18 fathoms at about 300 yards from low-water mark; the shore should be approached very slowly when coming to an anchor, as the bank is extremely steep-to and the water shoals very suddenly.

The second reach of Burke channel trends N. by E. ¼ E. for 10½ miles, ending abreast a low, wooded point at the foot of a high mountain; thence the channel takes a NE. by E. direction for 12 miles, another arm (Kwatna) branching off to the southward. At 200 yards from the SW. point (Mapalaklenk) of entrance to this arm is a rock, which uncovers at low water; it is the only known danger in Burke channel, and may be avoided by keeping the northern shore aboard.

Hence the channel takes an ENE direction for 4 miles along the base of a remarkably bare, stony mountain situated on the south shore, which is almost entirely devoid of vegetation. Thence the channel trends NE. for 6 miles, at which distance Labouchere channel branches off NNW., Burke channel continuing for 7 miles eastward to Menzies point (Taliuko), where it divides into the North and South Bentinck arms, the former taking an ENE., the latter a SE., direction.

North Bentinck arm is 8 miles long, and just within the entrance, on the northern shore, is a small bay affording anchorage for small craft. The head terminates in a sand and mud flat fronting low, swampy ground, covered with grass, which is submerged at high water. The inlet is here $1\frac{3}{10}$ miles wide.

Belakula, at the head of North Bentinck arm, affords indifferent anchorage close to the mud flat at the mouth of the river, on the south side east of Sutlej point. When taking up a berth, great care is required. A large vessel should moor in 45 to 50 fathoms, as the bank is very steep-to, deepening from 1 to 18 fathoms in a distance of 200 feet; a stern anchor may also be required, or a hawser laid out to the shore will be useful for keeping the hawse clear. Small vessels may find shelter during summer on the northern shore under Custom-House point. The country abounds in furbearing animals.

Belakula, or Nookhalk, river is a stream of considerable size and velocity, the deposit from which has formed the steep bank at the head of the inlet. The water is quite fresh alongside, and if pumped in at low water is fit for drinking. There are also several good places for watering on the north shore, opposite the anchorage, a boat being able to go underneath the waterfalls.

There is a Norwegian settlement here. A pier 610 feet long, with a depth of 16 feet at its outer end, extends from the shore near the settlement. A beacon, 8 feet above high water, situated to the westward of the pierhead, marks the northern extremity of the drying bank.

Tides.—It is high tide, full and change, at 0 h. 0 m.; springs rise 13 feet.

Winds.—The prevailing wind in Bentinck arm in summer is from the SW.; the westerly winds of the ocean blowing across Fitzhugh sound are led up the inlet as through a funnel, following the direction of the different bends. The breeze generally sets in about

10 o'clock in the forenoon and blows fresh until sunset, when it usually falls calm.

South Bentinck arm.—From Menzies point, South Bentinck arm branches SE., about 1 mile in breadth, with high land on both sides, for about 20 miles. At 9 miles from Menzies point an island lies on the eastern shore. The head of the arm is reported to be shallow, 5 and 12 fathoms, but it has not been surveyed and is seldom visited.

Kiltik creek.—From Nalau passage the coast of Hunter island extends 12 miles in a northerly direction, with only two openings; the northernmost of these, named Kiltik, on the western side of Fitzhugh sound, opposite Edmund point, is a narrow creek (less than 400 yards wide), extending nearly 1 mile in a westerly direction, with an average depth of 20 fathoms in the center, but shoal for ⅓ mile from its head. This creek, it is supposed, might be used by moderate-sized vessels, but has not been examined in detail.

The Trap.—At 13 miles northward from the southeastern point of Hunter island a small islet lies off an indentation of the coast, forming what has been termed the Trap. Strangers might be tempted to enter this opening; it is, however, extremely contracted, not affording room for a steam vessel to turn, and dangers are supposed to exist in the passage round the island; it should therefore be avoided.

Fisher channel, the continuation of Fitzhugh sound northward from the entrance to Burke channel, leads to Lama and Gunboat passages on the west and to Port John and Evans arm on the east. At 15 miles from Walker point Fisher channel divides into two, Johnson channel taking a NNW., and Cousins inlet a NNE., direction; the former, at a distance of 9 miles, splits into several arms (Roscoe and Sisters inlets on either side of Florence peninsula, and Bullock and Ellerslie channels on either side of Yeo island). Bullock and Ellerslie channels communicate with Seaforth channel, and from the northern point of Yeo island, at their northern junction, the main inlet continues northward for a farther distance of 10 miles to about lat. 52° 37′ N. These channels northward of Gunboat passage have not been surveyed in detail, and should, therefore, be navigated with caution.

Fog rocks, situated rather on the eastern side of Fisher channel and 3 miles north of Walker point, consist of 6 rocks above water, flat and of a whitish color, the highest of which is 25 feet high, with a few shrubs on it; close to the southernmost rock several small black rocks uncover at low water. These rocks (which appear nearly in mid-channel from the southward) may be passed on either side, but the main route lies westward of them, at a distance of about ½ mile.

Walbran rock, with 9 feet on it at low water springs and 4 to 10 fathoms close around, lies with the SE. extreme of Pointer island at the entrance of Lama passage, bearing N. 43° W. (N. 70° W. mag.), distant 550 yards, and Brend point N. 47° E. (N. 20° E. mag.). A red spar buoy is moored in 5 fathoms off the NE. side of the rock.

A triangular wooden beacon, 15 feet high and painted white, has been erected on White point near the eastern end of Lama passage. This beacon kept well open of the passage, bearing N. 41° W. (N. 68° W. mag.), leads outside Walbran rock.

Tidal streams.—About midway between Fog rocks and Lama passage the flood tide from the northward meets that from the southward.

Port John—Evans arm.—At 4 miles north of Lama passage, on the eastern shore of Fisher channel, is an indentation, in the northern part of which, immediately under Remarkable cone, 2,302 feet high, is Port John, southward of which is Evans arm, into which there are two passages, one on either side of Matthew island, 360 feet high, which lies at the entrance to the arm. The southern passage is ½ mile wide; the northern passage is only ⅓ mile wide, and this near the eastern end is contracted to 300 yards by a rock lying in the center.

Port John affords anchorage in 20 fathoms, but is much confined by Mark rock nearly in the middle, covering at half flood, and by a flat extending off the stream at its head. There is also anchorage at the head of Evans arm in 20 fathoms, which may be reached through South passage, but the immediate approach to it north of Boot island is foul, and a large vessel should be preceded by a boat. North passage should only be used after temporarily buoying Peril rock, which has 12 feet of water on it, and lies nearly in the middle of the eastern part of the passage.

Tides.—It is high water, full and change, in Port John at 1 h. 0 m.; springs rise 13 feet.

Dean channel leads out of Cousins inlet to the NE., in which direction it extends for about 12 miles, and there divides into three branches; one (Cascade inlet) taking a NW. direction; another (Labouchere channel) to the SE., and communicating with Burke channel; the third, the main inlet, extending in a north and NE. direction, with an average width of 1 mile for a distance of 18 miles, when it turns to the NNW. for 9 miles, terminating in low marshy land in about lat. 52° 52′ N. The river and village of Kimsquit are on the eastern side of the main inlet, 4 miles from its head.

Kimsquit.—Bound for Kimsquit, 4 miles from the head of the channel, round Raphoe point at the distance of ¼ mile and steer up mid-channel. As the head is approached the village of Kimsquit, and the river and sand bank off its entrance, will be seen on the eastern side; 2 miles above the river the inlet is contracted to about 1 mile in breadth by two low spits. Continue mid-channel between these spits and haul into the bay on the eastern shore, where anchorage will be found, off a pebbly beach, in 40 fathoms, with a large bowlder on the northern end of the beach bearing N. 19° E. (N. 8° W. mag.), and the NW. point of the bay N. 63° W. (West mag.).

Cascade inlet, so named by Vancouver, from the number of waterfalls, extends in a NW. direction for about 11 miles with an average width of ¾ mile. It, in common with the other branches of Dean channel, has not been surveyed in detail; its shores are composed of precipices, and several large cascades come down from the high mountains that overlook it.

Lama passage, between Hunter and Denny islands, is the main passage connecting Fisher channel (the northern continuation of Fitzhugh sound) with Seaforth channel and Milbank sound; its eastern entrance on the western side of Fisher channel, 6 miles north of Fog rocks, may be recognized by a conical mountain, 1,000 feet high, on the NE. point of Hunter island, and by Pointer island, on the southern side of the entrance, which is nearly 1 mile wide. Thence the passage trends WNW. 2 miles to abreast Serpent point on the southern shore, the breadth being about ½ mile, and the depths 130 fathoms in the middle, 25 and 26 fathoms near the shores; it then widens and trends 4 miles west to abreast Twilight point, the SW. point of Denny island.

Pointer Island light, at the junction of Fisher channel and Lama passage, is fixed white, elevated 42 feet above high water, and visible in clear weather from a distance of 12 miles from the bearing S. 31° E. (S. 58° E. mag.), through South and West, to N. 3° E. (N. 24° W. mag.).

It is shown from a square, white, wooden tower, 30 feet high, built up from the center of the red roof of a white wooden dwelling situated on the SE. end of Pointer island.

Fog signal.—A hand fog horn is sounded during thick or foggy weather when a vessel's fog signals are heard.

Long Point cove, to the southward of Pointer island, is an excellent anchorage for small vessels.

The entrance to Plumper channel, which is 1 mile wide, lies opposite Twilight point, round which Lama passage turns to the northward between Denny and Campbell islands, for 4 miles to Grave point, which has several Indian graves on it.

The northern shore of Lama passage is bold; a rock awash is reported to lie about 200 yards offshore. N. 55° W. (N. 82° W. mag.) from Serpent point. The southern shore, after the first 3 miles, is penetrated by a number of indentations, some of which afford shelter.

Cooper inlet, situated on the southern shore of Lama passage, 5 miles from the eastern entrance, is deep and contains several small creeks (the indentations already mentioned) off which lie a number of islets and rocks. In fine weather anchorage may be obtained in 14 fathoms under Westminster point.

Jane creek, in the SE. corner of Cooper inlet, may be used by small vessels. Charles point, its north point, has two reefs extending 200 yards from it in a northwesterly direction, the outer of which dries 9 feet.

Good anchorage may be had in this creek in 9 fathoms, with Charles point in line with the east point of Canal bight (on the opposite shore of the passage) bearing N. 23° W. (N. 50° W. mag.), and George point, the south entrance point of Jane creek, bearing S. 81° W. (S. 54° W. mag.). Large vessels may anchor in about 18 fathoms midway between Charles and George points. The bottom in this creek is mostly rocky.

Camp island, lying close to the SW. extremity of Denny island, and the turning point into the northern part of Lama passage, should not be rounded nearer than ½ mile, as the bottom is foul for 600 yards in a southerly direction from it, with patches that uncover 2 feet at low water springs.

McLaughlin bay, on the western shore of Lama passage, ½ mile south of Grave point, is a good stopping place; it is about 800 yards wide and 300 yards deep, with 8 to 14 fathoms of water. The southern point of the bay has a bare hill 150 feet high, which in thick weather is a useful guide to a stranger. The anchorage is in 11 fathoms off the center of the beach, about 200 yards from the shore, with Grave point open east of the SW. point of Narrows island bearing N. 22° E. (N. 5° W. mag.), and Archibald point open east of Napier point bearing S. 29° E. (S. 56° E. mag.) A spit extends from the western side of the bay with Bare hill bearing N. 65° W. (S. 88° W. mag.).

In this bay is the site of an old Hudson Bay trading post; there is a small quantity of cleared ground at the foot of a rocky hill, 200 feet high, ¼ mile from the beach, on the west side of which there is a lake. This is the only Indian winter residence between Queen Charlotte sound and Seaforth channel.

The Bella Bella natives migrated here from Bella Bella islands in 1868, and have now moved again to a site 1½ miles farther north on the same side of Lama passage, and opposite to Bella Bella islands. A number of modern houses have been erected, together with a wharf, hospital, and schoolhouse. The wharf has a depth of 15 feet at its outer end.

Tides.—It is high water at full and change in McLaughlin bay at 1 h. 0 m.; springs rise 14 feet, neaps 8 to 10 feet.

Bella Bella islands, lying ¾ mile north of Grave point, are bare and about 15 feet high. Temporary anchorage may be had to the eastward of Bella Bella islands off a green, bushy flat.

Kliktsoatli harbor, on the northern side of Denny island and 1½ miles eastward of Bella Bella islands, is about 1 mile in extent, with depths of 9 to 13 fathoms, and affords excellent shelter for vessels of any size. Harbor island, off the NW. point of Kliktsoatli, has a reef extending 200 yards from its eastern end.

Steamer passage.—The channel west of Harbor island is 200 yards wide, with a depth of 7 fathoms, and is suitable for small vessels; large vessels are recommended to pass north of Harbor island and through Wheelock pass, which lies between a 3-fathom patch near the center of the channel and Noble point, the NE. entrance point of the harbor, from which a 3-fathom shoal extends 150 yards in a southwesterly direction.

The west extreme of Cypress island in line with the east extreme of Meadow island bearing N. 6° W. (N. 33° W. mag.), leads through Wheelock pass in 11 to 19 fathoms, and when Harbor island bears N. 63° W. (West mag.) anchor in 12 fathoms. There is secure anchorage in 15 fathoms, with Harbor island bearing South (S. 27° E. mag.), distant 600 yards.

Kakooshdish creek, just east of Noble point and extending 1¾ miles in an easterly direction, is suitable for small craft, but is barred across by kelp, in 3½ fathoms.

There is an Indian fishing station at the head of this creek.

Main passage, leading from Lama passage to Seaforth channel, between the NE. extreme of Campbell island and Narrows island, is ¾ mile long NE. and SW. and from 400 to 600 yards wide, with depths of 20 to 30 fathoms in it. Care should be taken to maintain a mid-channel course, and in thick weather much caution must be observed, as the tidal streams are very strong.

Dryad Point light, on the extreme of Dryad point, the NE. point of Campbell island, is a fixed white light with red sector, elevated 36 feet above high water, showing white between the bearings S. 37° E. (S. 64° E. mag.) and S. 14° W. (S. 13° E. mag.); red between S. 14° W. (S. 13° E. mag.) and N. 18° W. (N. 45° W. mag.), through West; and white from N. 18° W. (N. 45° W. mag.) to N. 40° E. (N. 13° E. mag.), through North. In clear weather the white light is visible 11 miles and the red light 5 miles.

It is shown from a square, white, wooden tower with dwelling attached, 39 feet high, with red lantern.

Fog signal.—A hand fog horn is sounded during thick or foggy weather when a vessel's fog signals are heard.

Narrows island, situated about ¾ mile north of Bella Bella islands, is ¾ mile long east and west and nearly ½ mile broad; at 200 yards from the SW. side of Narrows island there is a ledge of rocks awash at high water, with 5 fathoms close-to.

Pole and Tree islets, situated about ¼ mile from the eastern extreme of Narrows island, are two small islets 400 yards apart in a north and south direction from each other; Tree islet, the northernmost, is 120 feet high, with a detached rock close to its eastern side. There are two rocky ledges between these islets and Narrows island.

Hodges reef, which dries 2 feet at low water springs, with 6 and 7 fathoms close-to, lies nearly in mid-channel between Tree islet and Deer island, the latter lying 800 yards SSE. from the former. From this reef the center of Tree islet bears N. 65° W. (S. 88° W. mag.).

Meadow island, ½ mile long east and west, lies 400 yards SE. of Pole islet. In the channel between them are depths of 5 to 15 fathoms, and a reef lies 100 yards from the northern point of Meadow island.

Deer and Cypress islands lie eastward of the above islands and are joined at low water; the former is ½ mile long in a NNW. and SSE. direction; the latter 1 mile long east and west.

Gunboat passage, between Denny and Cunningham islands, is narrow and intricate, containing many rocks and kelp patches; in some places the channel is not more than 100 yards wide. From its western entrance it trends easterly for 6 miles, thence NNE. for 2 miles to its eastern entrance, which is at the junction of Fisher and Dean channels.

Gunboat passage should not be attempted unless in small, handy, steam coasting vessels and with good local knowledge.

Seaforth channel, the main channel connecting Lama passage with Milbank sound, between Campbell island and the Bardswell group on the south, and Chatfield, Yeo, and Don islands on the north, is 14 miles long E. by S. and W. by N. with an average breadth of 1 mile; the land on both sides is much broken by islands with channels between leading north and south; the water is generally deep, and with the charts there should be no difficulty in navigating, in ordinary weather.

On the northern side three arms branch off northward; Deer passage, the eastern, between Cunningham and Chatfield islands, is about 7 miles long and communicates with Johnson channel; Return channel, the middle one, between Chatfield and Yeo islands, is about 3 miles in length and joins Bullock channel; and Spiller channel, the western, between Yeo and Don islands, extends 4 miles and connects with Ellerslie channel. These channels have only been examined in a casual manner, and their entrances are fronted by innumerable small islands, rocks, and reefs. On the southern side of Seaforth channel, at 9½ miles eastward of Sound point, is Hecate channel, about 10 miles long in a general southerly direction, with an average width of 1 mile, which leads into Queens sound.

Ormidale harbor, at the northern extreme of Campbell island, is about 1 mile deep in a southerly direction, and is protected from the NE. by Thorburne and Nevay islands, which lie across its entrance. The channel, nearly 1 mile SW. by W. ¾ W. from Grassy islet, lies westward of Nevay island; it is about 300 yards wide, with from 14 to 16 fathoms of water. Inside, the water is deep, the depth over the greater part being from 15 to 20 fathoms. Keep in mid-channel and anchor in 17 fathoms about 400 yards south from Nevay island.

The passage in is longer, but the berth is more convenient than in Kynumpt harbor directly west of it.

Kynumpt harbor, on the northern side of Campbell island, immediately west of Ormidale harbor (southern shore of Seaforth channel) and about 2 miles northwestward from its junction with Lama passage, may be recognized by Grassy islet, 20 feet high, and Regatta rock, both of which are conspicuous, lying in the middle of the channel 1¼ miles northeastward of the harbor, and also by White stone, a conspicuous bare rock, 12 feet high, lying 400 yards westward of the entrance.

The harbor, the entrance to which is between Shelf point and Low island, is 800 yards long north and south and averages 400 yards in breadth with 6 to 16 fathoms, mud bottom; the best anchorage is in 7 to 9 fathoms with the northern extreme of Berry point bearing East (N. 63° E. mag.) and the western extreme of Low island N. 41° E. (N. 14° E. mag.). A rocky patch with 6 feet on it lies on the western side of the harbor, with the SE. extreme of Low island bearing N. 86° E. (N. 59° E. mag.), distant 420 yards, and Shelf point N. 3° W. (N. 30° W. mag.).

It is high water, full and change, in Kynumpt harbor at 0 h. 30 m.; springs rise 14 feet, neaps 11 feet.

White stone—Beacon.—A square wooden beacon surmounted by a latticework drum, the whole painted white and showing 40 feet above high water, stands on White stone.

Grassy islet, small, 20 feet high, covered with long grass and bushes, and with two trees on it. lies nearly 1 mile N. 59° E. (N. 32° E. mag.) from the entrance to Ormidale harbor.

Regatta rock, awash at high water, 200 yards in extent ENE. and WSW., lies ½ mile N. 48° W. (N. 75° W. mag.) from Grassy islet.

Beacon.—A conical beacon surmounted by a latticework ball, the whole painted white and showing 25 feet above high water, stands on the SW. Regatta rock.

Wellington rock.—A rock with a depth of 18 feet over it at low water and deep water around, is situated with the SW. Regatta rock bearing N. 24° E. (N. 3° W. mag.), distant 1,200 yards, and White stone N. 71° W. (S. 82° W. mag.).

A tree, marked with white boards, on the western shore of Ormidale harbor, in line with the western extreme of Nevay island, bearing S. 5° W. (S. 22° E. mag.), leads over the rock.

Dall patch, a shoal with less than 6 feet of water on it, lies ⅓ mile NE. ¼ E. from the entrance to Kynumpt harbor; from the center of the patch Defeat point bears S. 30° W. (S. 3° W. mag.), distant 800 yards; it is marked by a platform buoy with pyramidal slatwork top, surmounted by a ball, colored black and red in horizontal stripes, in 2½ fathoms on the SE. side of the shoalest spot of 5 feet. A shoal of 3 fathoms extends 250 yards westward of Dall patch.

To avoid Dall patch it is recommended to keep White Stone beacon in line with the northern tangent of George point bearing N. 79° W. (S. 74° W. mag.); this leads between Wellington rock and Dall patch. If wishing to go northward of the patch, Grassy islet, in line with the southern extreme of Handyside island bearing S. 74° E. (N. 79° E. mag.), leads nearly midway between Dall patch and Regatta rock.

Dundivan inlet, on the northern coast of Dufferin island, about 3 miles westward of Kynumpt harbor, indents the coast about 1¾ miles in a southerly direction. It branches into several creeks, of which Lockhart and Rait are the largest, and there are several small islets just within the entrance. The water is inconveniently deep for anchorage.

Rait creek is said to be connected by a deep-water passage, called Jossa (Joassa) by the Indians, with Boddy creek, Hecate channel.

The southern shore of Seaforth channel, westward of Dundivan inlet, trends in nearly a straight line to Sound point, the SW. point of entrance. At 2½ miles eastward of Sound point Gale creek branches in a southerly direction and is supposed to connect with Boddy creek from the SE., thus separating Dufferin island from the remainder of the Bardswell group.

Edge reef, on which there is a depth of 4½ fathoms, lies nearly 800 yards distant from the southern shore, at 2 miles eastward of Sound point. Several patches lie between it and the shore.

Cod bank, on which the least depth found was 27 fathoms, sand, lies in the middle of the western entrance to Seaforth channel, 1⅓ miles N. by E. from Sound point; there are 58 fathoms on the southern side, and 163 fathoms, rock, close-to on the northern side, of Cod bank.

Hyndman reefs, the outer of several islets and reefs lying on the western shore of the entrance to Spiller channel, are nearly in the middle of that channel, and have a small rock only 3 feet above water at their southern end.

Midge reefs, on the northern side of Seaforth channel, dry 10 feet and extend 800 yards in a southerly direction from Bush point (Don island), and are 3¾ miles within the western entrance to the channel.

Mark rock lies 200 yards distant from the SE. point of Don island and 1 mile east from Midge reefs; between them is Sunk reef. Bare rock (black and low) kept just open southward of Surf point, bearing N. 67° W. (S. 86° W. mag.), leads ½ mile southward of Midge reefs, and the northern shore of Seaforth channel should not be approached within this distance.

Berry creek.—The southern shore of Don island is broken and rocky and has numerous islets and rocks skirting it. Berry creek is nearly 2 miles long in a NE. direction, but as the water in it is deep, and the entrance blocked by small islets, it is useless as an anchorage.

Blair inlet, 3 miles westward of Berry creek, is another indentation, useless as an anchorage on account of the numerous rocks with which the entrance to it is studded. Ivory and Watch islands form its southern side.

Ivory Island light is fixed white, elevated 66 feet above high water, and visible in clear weather from a distance of 13 miles between the bearings N. 79° W. (S. 74° W. mag.), through North and East to S. 26° E. (S. 53° E. mag.).

It is shown from a square, wooden lantern surmounting a small, white dwelling, 30 feet high, with red roof and lantern, situated on the southern part of Surf point.

Perrin anchorage.—If detained by fog at the entrance to the Seaforth channel, an anchorage may be obtained in 10 to 15 fathoms between Ivory and Watch islands. The passage east of Ivory island should be taken, a shoal patch of 1½ fathoms being avoided by keeping close to the eastern shore of the island. The passage from Blair inlet is foul.

Mouse rock, on which the sea sometimes breaks, has 5 feet over it at low water and is generally marked by kelp; it lies 1,500 yards N. 57° W. (N. 84° W. mag.) from Surf point, Ivory island. Idol point, kept open of Surf point, bearing S. 71° E. (N. 82° E. mag.), leads 400 yards south of Mouse rock.

CHAPTER X.

MILBANK SOUND TO CHATHAM SOUND—INNER AND OUTER CHANNELS.

VARIATION IN 1906.

Ivory island .... 26° 45′ E. | Yolk point .... 27° 40′ E.
Lawyer island .... 28° 15′ E.

Milbank sound has its entrance between the parallels of 52° 09′ and 52° 16′ N. and the meridians of 128° 33′ and 128° 42′ W. This spacious sheet of water is the main opening from seaward leading to Seaforth, Finlayson, and Mathieson channels.

At its entrance between cape Swain and Day point, the sound is nearly 9 miles wide, which breadth it maintains in a northeasterly direction for 5 miles; thence it trends to the northward for 10 miles, leading in that direction into Finlayson channel.

A channel of deep water 8 miles broad, with depths of over 100 fathoms, mud, extends southwestward of Milbank sound. Northwestward of this channel the depths decrease to 50 fathoms and less, off the entrance to Laredo sound, with a bottom of fine sand. Southeastward the depths are 76 and 80 fathoms, with a bottom consisting of sand, mud, and rock, at intervals.

In thick weather, therefore, or if overtaken by fog, when approaching Milbank sound from the southwestward, with due precaution, a vessel's position can be indicated by the deep-sea lead.

Landmarks.—Approaching Milbank sound from the southwestward, Helmet peak on Lake island, in the southern entrance to Mathieson channel, is conspicuous. This remarkable peak is 1,032 feet high and bears a striking resemblance to a helmet, with the sloping side toward the west.

Stripe mountain, on the northern side of Dowager island, at the entrance of Finlayson channel, is 2,020 feet high, pyramidal in shape, with a remarkable landslip destitute of timber and soil down its SW. side, but otherwise wooded to its summit; at its base is a comparatively level space scantily covered with vegetation, which is remarkable in such a thickly timbered country.

Nearing the sound the low wooded shores of cape Swain, the SE. entrance point to the sound, will be recognized. The shore northward of it is much broken, and the tops of the trees are about 120 feet high.

Day point (south point of Price island), the NW. entrance point of Milbank sound, has a group of wooded islets, rocks awash at high water, and sunken rocks, extending 2 miles SW. from it; the western island of the group (Outer island) is round, wooded, and conspicuous. The outer edge of these dangers lies $2\frac{1}{10}$ miles SW. from Day point and 1,600 yards S. 14° E. (S. 41° E. mag.) from Outer island.

White rock (Kamasik), lying about 5 miles within the sound, is 50 feet high, and ½ mile N. 37° E. (N. 10° E. mag.) from it is a smaller rock (Bare rock), 6 feet above high water. Both rocks are conspicuous, as lying well out in the sound, they show out against the dark background of pine and cedar, which line the shores of Milbank sound.

From White rock, a rocky ridge (on which the sea sometimes breaks) extends ½ mile to the southwestward; and a patch of 2 fathoms lies 500 yards eastward of the same rock.

A sunken rock, on which the sea breaks heavily, lies about 1½ miles to the southward of White rock.

Discovery rocks, situated off cape Swain, are two dangerous rocks lying NE. by N. and SW. by S. from each other. The southern danger, over which the sea seldom breaks, lies 1 mile N. 71° W. (S. 82° W. mag.) from cape Swain. The northern rock, which is usually indicated by breakers, lies N. 23° W. (N. 50° W. mag.), distant $1\frac{1}{10}$ miles from cape Swain.

West rock, situated on the eastern shore of the sound, is of small extent, 8 feet above high water, and lies ½ mile S. 68° W. (S. 41° W. mag.) from Sound point.

Several patches which uncover at low water lie between Sound point and West rock.

Mouse rock is a dangerous sunken rock on which the sea sometimes breaks, lying at the western entrance to Seaforth channel, 1,500 yards N. 57° W. (N. 84° W. mag.) from Surf point, Ivory island; it has 5 feet least water over it and is generally marked by kelp.

Bush point (north side of Seaforth channel) seen just open south of Surf point, bearing S. 81° E. (N. 72° E. mag.) leads southward, and Helmet peak seen just open of the western extreme of Mary island, bearing N. 35° E. (N. 8° E. mag.), leads westward of Mouse rock.

Vancouver rock, a dangerous rock which uncovers 12 feet at low water and is steep-to on all sides (there being depths of 13 and 14 fathoms within 200 yards of the rock), lies 4 miles N. 2° E. (N. 25° W. mag.) from White rock and 1½ miles N. 36° W. (N. 63° W. mag.) from Bowlder head. When visible this rock presents the appearance of a large whale and is conspicuous.

Cross point (south extreme of Lady island) in line with Bowlder head, bearing S. 56° E. (S. 83° E. mag.), leads 1,200 yards southward, and Low point seen just open westward of the North island group, bearing N. 27° E. (North mag.), leads westward of Vancouver rock.

Buoy.—Vancouver rock is marked by a whistling buoy, painted red, moored in 38 fathoms of water, northwestward of the rock.

Cross ledge extends 1,600 yards southwestward of Cross point and partially uncovers. There is a depth of 20 fathoms close southward of Cross ledge. Ivory Island lighthouse, bearing S. 53° E. (S. 80° E. mag.), leads southward of Cross ledge in mid-channel between Cross point and White rock.

Bowlder ledge, of sunken rocks, with depths of 1¼ and 5 fathoms, extends 1,800 yards in a southeasterly direction from Bowlder head; Bowlder bank, with 18 fathoms, rock, lies 1,400 yards S. 48° W. (S. 21° W. mag.) from Bowlder head. Ivory Island lighthouse, bearing S. 53° E. (S. 80° E. mag.), leads southward of the dangers off Bowlder head.

North ledges, which uncover at low water, lie northward of the North island group. The northern extreme of these ledges lies 1,200 yards N. 9° E. (N. 18° W. mag.) from North island, and the southern extreme 400 yards N. 71° E. (N. 44°.E. mag.) of that island.

Sandstone reef, situated close to the shore in the northern portion of Milbank sound, is a conspicuous narrow ridge, of sandstone formation, about 1 mile long in an east and west direction. The highest portion of this ridge is 4 feet above high water.

The western extreme of Sandstone reef lies ½ mile from the shore of Swindle islands and 1½ miles from the eastern side of Price island.

Price island, forming the western shore of Milbank sound, has a conspicuous ridge of hills (Jocelyn range) along its eastern shore, from 300 to 600 feet in height. From Day point the eastern coast of Price island trends in a NNE. direction for 4 miles to Aldrich point and is much broken into small exposed bays.

Boat cove, which affords shelter to boats, is situated ½ mile northward of Aldrich point. With this exception the coast of Price island, north of Aldrich point, is almost straight and unbroken for 8 miles, in a northerly direction, to the entrance of Schooner passage.

The eastern shores of Milbank sound are comparatively low and wooded, with pine and cedar trees predominating. In that portion of the sound lie two extensive channels (Mathieson channel and Moss passage), which branch from Milbank sound eastward and northward of Lady island, respectively. Lady island is low and wooded throughout. The western shores of Dowager island are also low and wooded, but are flanked by high mountains.

The SE. extreme of the island west of Lady island terminates in a high bold cliff (Bowlder head). Cliff island, which lies off the SW. side of Dowager island at the entrance to Moss passage, is small,

225 feet high, and its SE. extreme terminates in high, conspicuous, white cliffs.

North island is rocky, about 150 feet high, with some stunted trees growing on its summit.

Low point, the western extreme of Dowager island, and the SE. entrance point of Finlayson channel, is low and wooded.

Directions.—Approaching Milbank sound from the southwestward in clear weather, Helmet peak should be kept in line with White rock, bearing N. 57° E. (N. 30° E. mag.), which mark will lead nearly in mid-channel up the sound. When Ivory Island lighthouse bears East (N. 63° E. mag.), a vessel bound eastward may steer toward the lighthouse, or if bound northward a North (N. 27° W. mag.) course may be steered toward Finlayson channel.

In thick weather, with due precaution and attention to the deep-sea lead, the soundings will indicate the vessel's position.

Bound from Seaforth channel into Finlayson channel, keep Idol point well open southward of Ivory Island lighthouse, bearing S. 71° E. (N. 82° E. mag.), until Helmet peak comes open of the western extreme of Mary island, bearing N. 35° E. (N. 8° E. mag.), and then Ivory Island lighthouse should be kept astern bearing S. 53° E. (S. 80° E. mag.) for 3 miles, which will lead in mid-channel, 1¼ miles northward of White rock. From this position Cliff island should be seen open westward of Bowlder head, bearing N. 2° W. (N. 29° W. mag.), and a vessel may steer N. 36° W. (N. 63° W. mag.) for 3 miles, or until Low point is seen open westward of the North Island group bearing N. 26° E. (N. 1° W. mag.); thence steer N. 4° E. (N. 23° W. mag.) for 3 miles, or until Stripe mountain bears N. 60° E. (N. 33° E. mag.), when it may be steered for on that bearing, and the course gradually altered northward into Finlayson channel.

Tides and tidal streams.—The flood stream sets to the northward and divides near the middle of Milbank sound, one portion running toward Finlayson channel, another toward Mathieson channel, and another toward Seaforth channel. The reverse takes place on the ebb.

The strength of tide is variable, but it seldom exceeds 1 knot an hour in Milbank sound, but increases within the channels to 2 and 3 knots an hour.

Mathieson channel is an extensive arm of the sea running many miles northward from Milbank sound, eastward of Lady, Dowager, and Roderick islands, with depths of 103 and 105 fathoms in mid-channel. At 2½ miles within its southern entrance this channel is obstructed by islands, islets, and rocks, and a stranger should, therefore, not attempt to proceed farther. From the eastern entrance to Oscar passage, by which it communicates with Finlayson channel,

Mathieson channel extends in a northerly direction along the eastern side of Roderick island for over 25 miles to its junction with Mussel inlet; this portion of Mathieson channel is sometimes called Portlock channel; an arm, about 5 miles long, branches eastward at about 5 miles south of the junction; the channel northward of Oscar passage has not been surveyed.

St. John harbor (Cheekequintz) is on the SE. shore of Milbank sound, nearly midway between cape Swain and Sound point, and, though somewhat confined, affords good anchorage for small vessels.

The harbor is protected at its entrance by a reef awash and sunken rocks, which form a natural breakwater. Eastward of this reef, at the entrance, there is a clear channel, 400 yards wide, with depths of 10 to 30 fathoms.

At ½ mile within the entrance are two small islands, Wood island, the eastern and smaller one, being round, wooded, and conspicuous. The channel eastward of these islands is barely 200 yards wide abreast Wood island and leads into Anchor bay, which is the usual anchorage for small vessels. Westward of these islands the channel is wider and leads into Deep bay, which forms the SW. arm of St. John harbor.

There are depths of 9 to 20 fathoms in Deep bay and 11 to 14 fathoms in Anchor bay.

Rage reef extends 1,400 yards NNE. from the western point of St. John harbor and is about 400 yards wide. This dangerous reef consists of ledges which uncover, and rocks awash at high water, the northern extreme uncovering 4 feet at low water. Mark islet, 6 feet above high water, lies about the middle of the eastern side of Rage reef.

Ledges, which uncover, extend 200 yards from the eastern shore of the channel leading into the harbor.

Directions.—Approaching St. John harbor, cape Swain should be kept well open of the conspicuous quoin-shaped point situated 2 miles northward of the cape, bearing S. 32° W. (S. 5° W. mag.). On no account should Rage reef be approached inside that line, until Wood island (within the harbor) is distinctly seen, and North point bears S. 63° E. (East mag.). When Wood island is recognized, it should be brought to bear S. 4° E. (S. 31° E. mag.) and steered for on that bearing. Wood island on that bearing should be seen in line with a black high-water rock on the southern shore of Anchor bay, with a sandy bay immediately east of the rock.

Pass 100 yards eastward of Wood island and anchor in 10 to 11 fathoms, sandy bottom, in Anchor bay, with the eastern side of Wood island seen in line with the northern extreme of Rage reef, bearing N. 25° W. (N. 52° W. mag.), distant 600 yards.

Caution.—At high water, when Rage reef is nearly covered, it is difficult to distinguish the entrance into St. John harbor. At half tide, and at low water, the northern end of that reef and also the dangers on the eastern side of the channel, are visible, and a vessel can be guided clear of them by the eye.

Port Blakeney, formed between Mary and Don islands, on the eastern side of Mathieson channel, about 3 miles within the entrance, is easy of access and lies immediately at the head of Milbank sound. At its entrance, between Promise and Rain points, the port is 500 yards wide; thence it takes a southerly direction for about 1 mile, terminating in a small creek leading into Seaforth channel.

Cod reefs are a cluster of rocks awash, and sunken rocks, about 500 yards in extent in a NNE. and SSW. direction, at the entrance to Port Blakeney. The southern rock of this cluster is 4 feet above high water, and the northern rock, with 24 feet of water over it, lies 600 yards N. 48° E. (N. 21° E. mag.) from Promise point, with a clear channel northward of it 300 yards wide.

Oke reefs, situated about 400 yards northward of Cod reefs, extend 400 yards from the southern side of Oke island. The outer detached rock is 3 feet above high water, and between it and Oke island several patches of rock uncover at high water.

Clearing marks.—White rocks, off the southern end of Lake island, seen in line with the northern end of Passage island (between Lake and Lady islands), bearing N. 61° W. (N. 88° W. mag.), will lead between Oke and Cod reefs. Mark islet seen in line with Oke island, bearing N. 8° W. (N. 35° W. mag.) will lead eastward of those dangers.

Sand patch, with 24 feet of water upon it, is of small extent and lies nearly in mid-channel about ½ mile within Port Blakeney. Helmet peak seen in line with Promise point, bearing N. 9° E. (N. 18° W. mag.), will lead westward of Sand patch.

Anchorage in 10 to 12 fathoms, sandy bottom, will be found about ½ mile within Port Blakeney, with Helmet peak seen just open of Promise point, bearing N. 9° E. (N. 18° W. mag.), and Observation point on the northern shore of East bay bearing S. 81° E. (N. 72° E. mag.).

Tides.—It is high water at full and change in Port Blakeney at 0 h. 0 m.; springs rise 13 feet, neaps 8 feet.

Supplies.—Wood and water may be obtained in Port Blakeney. Rock cod and other fish may be caught in abundance on Cod reefs, and clams and cockles gathered in the sandy bays; they are readily obtained at low water by digging in the mud and sandy ground, especially in those places over which a fresh-water stream runs. Wild fowl are also plentiful in the season.

Directions.—Approaching Port Blakeney from the southward, Helmet peak should be kept just open of the eastern point of Lady island (Lang point) bearing N. 43° E. (N. 16° E. mag.), and when within ½ mile of the latter a N. 65° E. (N. 38° E. mag.) course should be steered toward Oke island, until White rocks are in line with the northern end of Passage island bearing N. 61° W. (N. 88° W. mag.); proceed with that mark on astern, and when Mark and Oke islands are seen in line bearing N. 8° W. (N. 35° W. mag.) a vessel will be eastward of Cod reefs, and may then haul into the harbor.

Moss passage (Toowitl) leads northward of Lady island from Milbank sound into Mathieson channel. At its western entrance this passage is over 1 mile wide; but at 3 miles within this entrance, and 1 mile from its junction with Mathieson channel, it is contracted by Squaw island to barely 200 yards; this passage is known as Sloop narrows. Beyond that position, therefore, it should not be attempted by a stranger.

Bird rock, at the western entrance of Moss passage, 600 yards S. 52° E. (S. 79° E. mag.) from the southern extreme of Cliff island, is 3 feet above high water with foul ground extending 400 yards eastward from it. The southern extreme of the North island group seen just open southward of the southern extreme of Cliff island, bearing N. 47° W. (N. 74° W. mag.), leads southward of Bird rock.

Morris bay, situated on the southern side of Moss passage, about 1 mile within its western entrance, is 500 yards wide, and extends in a southerly direction for 600 yards, terminating in a flat which dries at low water. Westerly winds send a swell into the anchorage, but the bay possesses the great advantage of permitting the state of the weather in Milbank sound being ascertained when at anchor, and if fog be prevalent (as is often the case) it can be seen from the bay.

Kitty patch lies at the eastern entrance to Morris bay, 200 yards from the eastern shore. This bank is 200 yards in extent north and south, with depths of 4 and 5 fathoms, sand.

Directions.—Approaching Morris bay, a mid-channel course should be kept between Bird rock and Salal point; and if Vancouver rock be uncovered, it should be kept bearing S. 82° W. (S. 55° W. mag.). When the south extreme of Cliff island is seen open northward of Bird rock, bearing N. 58° W. (N. 85° W. mag.), that mark kept on will lead to the entrance to Morris bay.

Anchorage will be found in 12 to 14 fathoms, sandy bottom, at 200 yards from the western shore, with the western entrance point of Morris bay bearing N. 81° W. (S. 72° W. mag.), and Detached island (north side of Moss passage) bearing N. 4° E. (N. 23° W. mag.).

Supplies.—Good water may be obtained in Morris bay. Clams and cockles can be gathered in abundance. Plover and other birds frequent Bird rock. Berries grow in abundance on Salal point.

Alexandra passage lies eastward of Vancouver rock and North island group. Small steam vessels, possessing local knowledge, make use of Alexandra passage, especially when coming from the northward to anchor in Morris bay; but this passage is barely 1,200 yards wide in its narrowest part, and in the event of an accident to the machinery a vessel using it would be in a dangerous position.

Cliff island is nearly steep-to, but the small islet close northward of it has foul ground extending from it 200 yards westward.

Directions.—If compelled by circumstances to make use of Alexandra passage, keep the western shore of Finlayson channel north of Jorkins point in line with Low point, bearing N. 6° E. (N. 21° W. mag.), which is the general leading mark through this passage. It is, however, recommended to alternately open and close these points, especially when nearing North island group, so as to keep in mid-channel.

Schooner passage, leading from Laredo sound into the NW. corner of Milbank sound, is obstructed by islands, islets, rocks, and sunken dangers, and no specific directions can be given for it. It is occasionally, however, made use of by small coasting craft, and the large canoes of the Queen Charlotte islanders also pass through it when making the passage to Vancouver island.

Finlayson channel, the entrance to which is between Jorkins and Low points, extends from Milbank sound in a NNE. direction for 3 miles, thence in a general northerly direction for 18 miles, and then NNE. for 6 miles to the head of Carter bay, with an average width of 1 to 2 miles. The land on both sides is from 1,000 to 3,000 feet high, the peaks closely approaching the shores and rising in a precipitous manner from the water's edge. Except where the vegetation has been removed from the mountain sides by landslips, both shores are thickly wooded, the pine and cedar predominating; occasionally their dark-green foliage is relieved by the bright light-green leaf of the maple.

Oscar passage, 4½ miles north of Low point, leads eastward out of Finlayson channel, between Dowager and Roderick islands, and is about 1 mile wide and 6 miles long to its junction with Mathieson channel.

Bulley bay, situated on the southern shore of Oscar passage, 3½ miles within its western entrance, though small, affords temporary anchorage in 15 fathoms at 200 yards from the shore, and is occasionally used by coasting vessels.

The Sisters, two small islets lying 400 yards from the eastern shore of Finlayson channel, 8½ miles northward of Oscar passage, are wooded and about 90 feet high. They lie NNW. and SSE. 800 yards from each other, and are joined by ledges which uncover at low water.

Otter cove (Nowish) lies ½ mile NE. of the Sisters islets, between Indian and Susan islands. The entrance, northward of Indian island, is 400 yards wide; the cove then extends SE. for ½ mile, narrowing near its head to 200 yards, and having on its northern shore, about 800 yards within the cove, a small bay, which affords anchorage for small vessels in 10 to 14 fathoms, sandy bottom, in the middle of the bay.

Tides.—It is high water, full and change, in Nowish cove at 0 h. 0 m.; springs rise 12 feet.

Jackson passage, an unexplored arm on the eastern shore of the channel, is 400 yards wide, and extends in an easterly direction from its entrance.

Mary cove, situated on the eastern shore, 5½ miles northward of the Sisters islets, is barely 200 yards wide at its entrance, and extends in a northerly direction for ½ mile, terminating in a sandy beach. There are depths of 24 and 7 fathoms in mid-channel within this cove.

Cone island, on the western shore of Finlayson channel, is 3¼ miles long in a north and south direction, and about ½ mile broad. The summit of this island, Bell peak, situated about 1 mile from its southern extreme, is conical in shape and 1,280 feet high; the eastern and western sides are precipitous, but the land slopes gently to the northward, terminating in Wedge point.

Klemtu passage, between Cone and Swindle islands, is about 3¼ miles long in a north and south direction and in some parts barely 200 yards wide. Its southern entrance, 200 yards wide, extends in a NNW. direction for about 1 mile; thence in a general northerly direction for 2½ miles, to abreast the northern extreme of Cone island. The depths in mid-channel are from 10 to 30 fathoms, sand and shells, with rock at intervals. Though narrow, this passage is safe (provided a mid-channel course be kept) and affords anchorage almost throughout.

Anchorage, suitable to vessels of moderate length, will be found north of Star islet, nearly in mid-channel, 200 yards from the shore of Cone island, at 1¼ miles within the southern entrance, in 12 fathoms, sand and shells.

Tides and tidal streams.—It is high water, full and change, in Klemtu passage, at 0 h. 0 m.; springs rise 13 feet, neaps 8 feet, and the neaps range 3 feet. The tidal streams are comparatively weak. The flood or north-going stream is but little felt, the great body of water passing into Finlayson channel. The ebb seldom exceeds the rate of 1 knot an hour.

South passage, between Cone and Jane islands, is ½ mile wide, with depths of 18 to 37 fathoms, rock.

Kelp patch, with 5 to 12 feet over it, lies 500 yards west of Reef point, the SE. extreme of Jane island, and is about 200 yards in extent in a north and south direction.

Berry point (eastern side of Swindle island) seen just open of Legge point (western side of Cone island), bearing S. 5° E. (S. 32° E. mag.), will lead westward of Kelp patch.

Wedge rock, uncovering at low water, lies 50 yards from the northern extreme of Cone island. Ripple bank, with 11 fathoms, rocky bottom, lies nearly in mid-channel of South passage.

North passage, between Jane and Sarah islands, is ½ mile wide, with depths from 22 fathoms to no bottom at 38 fathoms.

Danger patch, with 1 to 3 fathoms of water over it, lies 200 yards northward of Jane island.

Directions.—When proceeding through South passage, the southern shore should be kept aboard, passing 400 yards northward of Cone island. North passage is to be preferred to South passage when communicating between Finlayson and Tolmie channels. Keep nearer the northern shore, and pass 400 yards south of Sarah island.

Jane island, situated ½ mile north of Cone island, is about 1 mile long in a north and south direction, and ½ mile broad. It is low and wooded, the tops of the trees being 200 feet high.

Sarah island, the southern point of which is ½ mile northward of Jane island, is 15 miles long in a north and south direction, and 1 to 2½ miles broad. This island reaches its greatest elevation of 2,000 feet at 4 miles from its southern extreme. On the SE. side of the island, at 7 miles from the southern extreme, an unexplored bay faces southward, and at 3½ miles from the southern extreme of Sarah island, on its eastern shore, there are two high waterfalls.

Watson bay lies on the eastern side of Finlayson channel, 9 miles northward of Sisters islets. This unexplored bay is 1 mile wide at its entrance, and extends in an easterly direction.

Wallace bight lies 2½ miles northward of Watson bay. It is 1 mile wide at its entrance and takes a northerly direction for 1 mile. There is no bottom at 106 fathoms, between its entrance points.

Goat cove, situated 4 miles northward of Wallace bight, is ½ mile wide and extends in an easterly direction for ½ mile, terminating in a sandy beach. There are depths of 23 to 34 fathoms within this cove, the former being close to the head.

Sheep passage is nearly 1 mile wide, and leads eastward from Finlayson channel, just south of Carter bay. At 3 miles within its western entrance it trends northward until its junction with Mussel inlet.

Mussel inlet, which has not been explored since Vancouver's visit in 1793, takes a northerly direction for about 5 miles, when it suddenly turns to the eastward for about the same distance, terminating in Poison cove, so named by Vancouver, owing to several of the crew of the Discovery being poisoned by eating mussels found there. It is stated to have the same general characteristics as the other inlets.

Carter bay.—This excellent stopping place lies at the head of Finlayson channel, 26 miles within its entrance, and is easily recognized by the high cliffs on its western shore. The bay is 800 yards wide at its entrance, abreast the anchorage ground, and about 1,200 yards deep in a northerly direction, the head terminating in a large stream fronted by an extensive flat.

Anchorage will be found in 14 to 15 fathoms, mud bottom, at 300 yards from the eastern shore, and 300 yards from the sand flat at the head of the bay, with the entrance points of the bay bearing S. 11° E. (S. 38° E. mag.) and S. 54° W. (S. 27° W. mag.) respectively.

Supplies.—Water can be obtained from the large stream at the head of the bay, which is probably one of the best watering places along the coast. Trout abound in the fresh-water stream. Tracks of bear and deer were seen on the shore. Wild fowl frequent Carter bay.

Caution.—Shellfish, of whatever kind, should not be eaten.

Tides.—It is high water, full and change, in Carter bay at 0 h. 0 m.; springs rise 13 feet.

Hiekish narrows lies northward of Sarah island, and leads from Finlayson channel into Graham reach. This channel is about 5¼ miles long, in a general NNW. and SSE. direction, and from ½ to 1 mile wide. The depths are 31 to 73 fathoms in mid-channel, over a bottom of sand and shells.

Hewitt rock, a dangerous sunken rock with 10 feet over it and deep water close-to, lies at the western entrance of Hiekish narrows nearly in mid-channel.

The eastern shore of the channel should be kept aboard when navigating the northern portion of Hiekish narrows. The SW. point of Carter bay, seen just open of the northern extreme of Sarah island, bearing S. 27° E. (S. 54° E. mag.) leads eastward of Hewitt rock.

Tolmie channel, situated between Princess Royal and Sarah islands, is about 15 miles long in a general north and south direction, and from ½ to 1 mile wide.

On the western shore, 2½ miles northward of the southern point of Sarah island, an extensive arm takes a southerly direction, and is reported to communicate with Laredo sound. Abreast the northeastern point of this inlet a small islet lies close to the shore of Sarah island.

Caution.—The northern reach of Tolmie channel looks directly into this inlet; care is therefore necessary, when approaching from the northward, not to mistake this unexplored arm for the reach leading to Klemtu passage.

At 2 miles northward of the above-mentioned inlet, on the western shore of Tolmie channel, lies another unexplored passage, facing the SE.

Tolmie rock, on which is 4 feet of water, lies 100 yards from the shore of Sarah island, at ½ mile within the northern entrance of Tolmie channel.

Directions.—Tolmie channel, though not so wide as Finlayson channel, is preferable in some respects, especially if compelled to be under way at night. A mid-channel course should be steered throughout except when navigating the northern part of the channel, when the western shore should be closed to avoid Tolmie rock.

Tidal streams.—The flood stream sets to the northward, and is stronger in Finlayson than in Tolmie channel. The ebb, however, is stronger in Tolmie channel, and runs for 1½ hours after the ebb has ceased in Finlayson channel. In the narrow parts of these channels, both flood and ebb streams attain a velocity of 3 knots an hour at springs.

Graham reach, situated northward of the junction of Tolmie channel, with Hiekish narrows, is about 17 miles long, in a general N. by W. and S. by E. direction, and from ½ to 1 mile broad, with depths of from 38 fathoms, rock, to 150 fathoms, sand and shells. From the northern extreme of Sarah island this reach takes a northerly direction for 7 miles, to abreast Swanson bay, thence it takes a NNW. direction for 10½ miles to abreast Red Cliff point. In general features this reach resembles Finlayson channel.

Green islet lies on the eastern shore, 2 miles northward of Sarah island. This unexplored arm takes a southeasterly direction at its entrance.

Flat point lies on the western shore, 3 miles northward of Green inlet. This point is wooded, flat, and comparatively low. Abreast Flat point, on the western shore of the channel, is a remarkable, large, bowlder rock.

Swanson bay lies on the eastern shore, 7 miles from Sarah island. There is a conspicuous waterfall on the western shore of the channel abreast Swanson bay; in very dry summers this is reduced to a very small size, and occasionally ceases altogether.

Anchorage may be obtained in 19 fathoms, sandy bottom, in the northern part of Swanson bay, with the conspicuous waterfall on the western shore shut in with the northern entrance point, and Flat point shut in with the southern entrance point of the bay.

Khutze inlet is an unexplored arm extending in an easterly direction from the eastern side of Graham reach; its entrance is 6 miles northward of Swanson bay. One mile within the entrance a rocky spit, with 2 to 4 fathoms of water over it, extends from the southern side of the inlet to within 200 yards of the northern shore. Anchorage in 8 fathoms will be found 267 yards N. 47° W. (N. 74° W. mag.) from the low spit (Green spit) on the southern shore.

To reach this anchorage, stand up the inlet in mid-channel until Green spit, which is the first low land seen on the southern shore, bears East (N. 63° E. mag.); then proceed very slowly till a suitable depth is obtained.

The bar mentioned above has a depth of 10 fathoms on it near the northern shore. Above the bar the water seems to be deep; anchorage at the head is reported by the Indians.

Aaltanhash is another unexplored inlet on the eastern shore, 2 miles north of Khutze. In size and direction it is similar to Khutze, and is reported by Indians to afford anchorage.

Tidal streams.—The tidal streams meet abreast Aaltanhash inlet.

Red Cliff point, the turning point into Fraser reach, lies on the western shore, 17½ miles from Sarah island. This point terminates in a conspicuous cliff of a reddish-brown color, and is a good landmark.

Fraser reach, the channel northwestward of Graham reach, is 12½ miles long in a general NW. by W. and SE. by E. direction and ½ to 1½ miles wide. In features it resembles Finlayson channel.

Warke island is 1½ miles long in an east and west direction and ½ mile broad. The eastern extreme of this island lies 1 mile NW. from Red Cliff point. The channels on both sides of the island are deep, but that to the south is slightly the wider. There is a bay on the southern shore of the channel, abreast Warke island, at the head of which is a fine trout stream, communicating with a large lake. Fraser reach from abreast Warke island takes a NW. ½ W. direction for 5 miles, thence NW. for 6 miles to abreast Kingcombe point.

Klekane inlet, an unexamined arm on the eastern shore, abreast Warke island, is ½ mile wide and takes a NNW. direction from its entrance. Approaching from the southeastward this arm appears as the continuation of Graham reach. Anchorage may, from Indian report, be obtained at the head of Klekane inlet.

Kingcombe point, the turning point into McKay reach, is on the western shore 12 miles from Red Cliff point. The point is long, sharp, and conspicuous.

McKay reach, leading westward from Fraser reach into Wright sound, is about 8 miles long in a general east and west direction and from 1 to 2 miles wide; there is no bottom in mid-channel at

139 and 225 fathoms, the latter at 400 yards southward of Cumming point.

From mid-channel abreast Kingcombe point the reach takes a westerly direction for 4 miles to abreast Trivet point, thence W. by S. for 4 miles to abreast Cumming point. Westward of Kingcombe point a deep bay lies on the southern shore, between Kingcombe and Trivet points.

The land on the northern shore of the channel is high and bold, with mountains 3,000 feet high. The land on the southern shore is not so high; and near the summits of the mountains are some extensive bare patches of slate color.

Gribbell island, the shores of which have not been surveyed in detail, is of somewhat triangular form, about 11 miles long (north and south) and 7 miles wide. The Wimbledon mountains, along its southern shore, are from 2,000 to 3,000 feet high.

Ursula channel.—Between Pilot point, the SE. point of Gribbell island, and Fisherman cove, on the opposite shore, is the entrance to Ursula channel, which skirts the eastern side of Gribbell island for about 7 miles. Its shores are composed of steep lofty mountains rising abruptly from the sea and covered with pines and forest trees.

Fisherman cove, on the eastern shore at the entrance to Ursula channel, affords indifferent anchorage in 30 fathoms, with the southern point of the bay (a clump which is connected to the shore by a sandy neck covered at high water) bearing S. 29° W. (S. 2° W. mag.). When anchoring here feel the way with the deep-sea lead, as the water shoals very suddenly from 30 fathoms to 12 fathoms, the latter depth being at about 25 yards from the shore. A small stream flows into the head of the cove, off which a shoal extends some distance, its edge being very steep.

At 2½ miles northward from Fisherman cove is a small inlet where a hot spring was discovered, the color and taste of which resembled the waters at Cheltenham. At 8 miles northward from Fisherman cove is an inlet extending in a NE. direction.

Boxer reach, the continuation of Ursula channel NW. along the NE. side of Gribbell island, is about 6 miles long. On its NE. shore anchorage may be found in the NW. part of Bishop cove; this is a very good anchorage, and is formed by a narrow neck of sand extending from the land, terminated by a clump covered with trees, similar to that at Fisherman cove. The water shoals gradually up to the sandy neck, and a vessel might go into 15 fathoms.

There appears to be anchorage on the SE. side of the sandy neck, but the beach runs out shoal a long way on that side.

Verney passage leads from Wright sound to the southern end of Devastation channel and northern end of Boxer reach. From Money point, the southern point of Hawkesbury island, it takes a

NNE. direction between the SE. coast of Hawkesbury island and the western coast of Gribbell island for 10 miles to the northern end of the latter island, where it is entered by Boxer reach, and then continues about east for 6 miles to its junction with Devastation channel; its shores have not been surveyed.

Devastation channel, from its junction with Verney passage, continues northward along the eastern side of Hawkesbury island for 13 miles; its shores have not been surveyed.

Dorothy island, about 1 mile in extent in a north and south direction, lies in mid-channel about 6 miles from the southern end of Devastation channel.

An anchorage is reported in a cove on the western side of the channel, 4¼ miles northward from Eva point, the eastern point of Hawkesbury island.

Gardner canal, the entrance to which is on the eastern side of Devastation channel, turns off at Staniforth point to the eastward, in which direction it continues, with many sinuosities, for upward of 45 miles. The land is an entirely barren waste, nearly destitute of wood and verdure, appearing as a mass of almost naked rocks rising to rugged mountains, covered with perpetual ice and snow, whose towering summits, appearing to overhang their bases, give them a tremendous appearance.

Its shores have not been surveyed in detail, but there is reported to be anchorage on either side of Richardson point, on the south shore (SE. of Channel island), about 6 miles from the entrance, in from 18 to 5 fathoms; and also at Kemano bay, on the north shore, 20 miles farther up, but here the anchorage is said to be indifferent, as the water is deep and shoals very rapidly from no bottom at 25 fathoms to 3 fathoms; great caution is required in picking up a berth, and when entering keep over toward the eastern entrance point (Entrance bluff), as shoal water extends for some distance from the opposite point.

Kemano river flows through an extensive valley into the head of Kemano bay, and is a stream of some size, navigable in the summer by canoes for a distance of 8 miles from its mouth. Kemano bay is frequented by the Kitlup Indians during the houlican fishing season; their village, however, is at the head of the inlet. Bears are reported to be abundant in the Kemano valley, and mountain sheep in the mountains, but deer are scarce.

In the winter months ice forms at 25 miles from the head of Gardner canal.

Tides.—It is said to be high water, full and change, in Kemano bay at 1 h. 0 m. (June); springs rise about 9 feet.

Hawkesbury island, lying between Verney passage and Devastation channel on the east and Douglas channel on the west, is 23 miles long in a NNE. and SSW. direction, from Money point, its southern extreme, to Gaudin point, its northern, and about 11 miles wide. Maitland and Loretta islands lie close off the northern side of Hawkesbury island, being only separated from it and from each other by narrow creeks.

Kitimat arm.—From the northern end of Hawkesbury island the inlet continues in a northerly direction for a farther distance of about 17 miles to about lat. 54° 02′ N., where it is terminated by a border of low land with a shallow flat extending from side to side, through which a small rivulet, navigable only for canoes, discharges itself at the eastern corner. This termination differs in some respects from many of the others; its shores are not very abrupt but are bounded on each side by a range of lofty mountains, which, however, are not (as is usually the case) connected at the head of the arm, but continue apparently in a direction parallel to each other. The valley between them, 3 or 4 miles wide, is covered with trees, mostly of the pine species. An Indian village of the Kitimat tribe is located near the head of this arm; there are a mission and a store at the village.

Clio bay, on the eastern shore of the Kitimat arm, has been visited on several occasions by H. B. M. ships for the purpose of communicating with the Kitimat Indians; it affords good anchorage in 17 fathoms.

Kildala arm extends in an easterly direction for about 10 miles, branching off from the eastern side of Kitimat arm at about 11 miles from its head. Coste island, nearly 3 miles in extent north and south, fronts the entrance to Kildala arm.

Douglas channel, which extends along the western shore of Hawkesbury island for upward of 25 miles in a northerly direction, leading from Wright sound into the Kitimat arm at its junction with Devastation channel, has not been surveyed. It is about 3 miles broad, and the shores are very high. A rock, marked by kelp, is situated about ½ mile from the shore, in approximately lat. 53° 30′ N., long. 129° 13½′ W. There is another rock, which dries at extreme low water, situated about ¼ mile N. 23° W. (N. 51° W. mag.) from the above rock.

Kitkiata, an unexplored inlet, branches from the western side of Douglas channel in a southwesterly direction at 12 miles from Money point, the southern extreme of Hawkesbury island. Small vessels may anchor in 5 fathoms ½ mile within Kitkiata inlet. On the same side of the channel, 14½ miles northward from Kitkiata inlet, is another inlet which, 2½ miles from its entrance, divides into two arms, Miskatla and Gilttoyees, the latter extending for about 7 miles in a northerly direction.

Wright sound, a sheet of water 9 miles long in an east and west direction, and 2¼ miles wide at its narrowest part, lies between Gribbell and Farrant islands, with no bottom at 119 and 220 fathoms. It communicates eastward with McKay reach and westward with Grenville channel.

Verney passage and Douglas channel lead out of it to the northward, while Whale channel leads to the southward on the eastern side of Gil island, and Lewis pass, on the western side of that island, leads also to the southward into Squally channel.

Gil island, on the south side of the sound, culminates in a well-defined snow-clad peak 3,000 feet high.

The mountains northeastward of Holmes bay have bare patches down their sides.

Directions.—In thick weather, when the shores are almost obscured to the water's edge, Wright sound, with its different openings north and south, makes a very perplexing picture to a stranger. Under such circumstances it is well to remember that a N. 64° W. (S. 88° W. mag.) course leads across the sound from McKay reach to Grenville channel, the distance from point Cumming to Yolk point being just 7½ miles.

Promise island is on the northern side of the sound; its two dome-shaped mountains and cape Farewell, the southern extreme of the island, are conspicuous.

Holmes bay, situated on the eastern shore of Wright sound at the entrance of Whale channel, is 1,600 yards wide at its entrance and runs in a SE. direction for about 800 yards, terminating in a sand flat, which extends 200 yards from the head of the bay.

The northern entrance point is high and bold; a small islet lies off the southern entrance point of the bay.

Anchorage will be found in 14 fathoms, sand, with the southern extreme of Promise island in line with the northern point of the bay, bearing N. 46° W. (N. 74° W. mag.); and Gil mountain in line with the southern entrance point, S. 83° W. (S. 55° W. mag.).

Tides.—It is high water, full and change, in Holmes bay at 1 h. 0 m.; springs rise 13 feet, neaps 10 feet.

Fisherman cove was the name given by Vancouver to an anchorage on the southern side of Turtle point, the northern point of Gil island, nearly 1 mile southward from its extremity. The water is deep, and the anchorage reported indifferent.

Promise island, at the southern end of Douglas channel, is 8¼ miles long north and south, with an extreme breadth of 2 miles; it is covered with pine and cedar and culminates in two dome-shaped peaks 1,680 and 1,710 feet high, respectively. Cape Farewell, the southern extreme of the island, terminates in a high, bold cliff.

There is a conspicuous white cliff on the SW. shore, midway between cape Farewell and Thom point.

The eastern shore of the island is high. Dawson point, the northern extreme, is low and wooded.

Farewell ledge uncovers at low water and extends 400 yards SE. from cape Farewell. This ledge is steep-to, there being no bottom at 40 fathoms at 30 yards from it. Ledges extend 200 yards from the eastern shore of Promise island.

Dawson ledge extends 400 yards northward from Dawson point and uncovers at half ebb.

Coghlan anchorage, between the mainland and Promise island, situated about 1 mile westward of cape Farewell, is 600 yards wide at its entrance between Camp and Thom points and extends in a NNW. direction for 2 miles, widening within the entrance to 800 yards.

Thom ledge extends 100 yards SW. of Thom point.

Harbor rock is a dangerous rock of small extent, which uncovers 6 feet at low water, and lies nearly in mid-channel near the head of the harbor. This rock is steep-to, there being depths of 10 and 18 fathoms at 100 feet from the rock.

Gil mountain in line with Thom point, the eastern entrance point, bearing S. 21° E. (S. 49° E. mag.), will lead to the eastward, and Camp point just open of Observation point, bearing S. 16° E. (S. 44° E. mag.), will lead westward, of Harbor rock.

Otter shoal extends 300 yards from the western shore at the head of the anchorage, with depths of 3 fathoms and less upon it.

Anchorage in 6 to 7 fathoms sand, will be found near the head of Coghlan anchorage, with Gil mountain just shut in with Thom point, bearing S. 19° E. (S. 47° E. mag.), and Stephens point just open of Letitia point (Stewart narrows, southern side) bearing N. 60° E. (N. 32° E. mag.). When entering keep in mid-channel, to avoid the ledge which uncovers off Thom point.

Stewart narrows leads northward of Promise island into Douglas channel. The streams in this passage are strong and the channel confined; it is therefore not recommended.

Tides.—It is high water, full and change, in Coghlan anchorage at 0 h. 30 m.; springs rise 18 feet, neaps 14 feet.

Tidal streams.—The flood stream which enters Campania sound from the southward, divides off Passage island, and the main body of water passes up Squally channel. The lesser body, passing into Whale channel, skirts the northern shore of Gil island and unites, at 1 mile northward of Turtle point, with the main body of water which has entered Wright sound by Lewis passage. The flood stream from that position, sets directly across Wright sound, and impinging on Camp point causes very strong eddies off that point, and is then deflected toward Grenville channel.

A portion of the flood stream by Whale channel turns into McKay reach, and meets, abreast of Aaltanhash inlet, the flood stream from the Finlayson channel. Another portion proceeds into Douglas channel and Verney passage. On the ebb, the reverse takes place, the main body of water from Wright sound obtaining an exit by Whale channel.

The ebb streams from Wright sound, Douglas channel, and McKay reach, unite nearly midway between Maple point and Holmes bay, setting directly toward the latter, producing strong eddies at the mouth of Holmes bay. Thence the stream sets fairly through Whale channel, and passing north and south of Passage island, unites with the stream of Squally channel, and they pass out into Campania sound.

Both flood and ebb streams attain the velocity of 3 to 4 knots an hour, at springs, in the contracted portions of the channels.

Grenville channel leads northwestward out of Wright sound and is the usual channel taken by steam vessels when proceeding to the northern waters of British Columbia.

At its SE. end Grenville channel, abreast Yolk point, is 1,600 yards wide; thence it trends NW. for 4 miles to abreast Davenport point, with an average width of 1 mile. From this point the channel takes a NW. ½ N. direction for 11 miles, and narrows to 600 yards as Lowe inlet is approached, seldom exceeding 800 yards in width until northwestward of Evening point (Klewnuggit).

From a position in mid-channel westward of Lowe inlet, Grenville channel trends NW. ¾ N. for 7 miles, to abreast Evening point; thence it widens to 1 and 3 miles, and extends NW. ½ N. for 23 miles, to abreast Ogden channel. The depths in Grenville channel are 48 to 133 fathoms, rock.

The land on both sides is high, reaching an elevation of 3,500 feet on the eastern and from 1,000 to 2,000 feet on the western shore, and for the most part is densely wooded with pine and cedar.

The mountains rise almost perpendicularly from the water and cause the southern portion of this narrow channel to appear even narrower than it is (600 yards). But the general effect of so many mountains rising one behind the other renders the Grenville passage one of the most beautiful landscapes on this coast, equaled only by Klemtu passage.

The only directions necessary for navigating Grenville channel are to keep in mid-channel, except when passing Nabannah bay, and then the western, or Pitt island, shore should be kept aboard. The western shore for 4 miles NW. of Davenport point (Farrant island) is stated to be foul, but the dangers lie close in.

Tidal streams in Grenville channel are generally weak, in most places not exceeding 1 knot, though in the narrow part of the channel the ebb, or SE. stream, sometimes runs 4 knots at springs. The flood stream from the NW. meets that from the SE. abreast Nabannah bay.

Morning reefs extend NW. by N. nearly ¾ mile from Evening point and ½ mile from the northern point of Nabannah bay. The western shore of Grenville channel must be kept aboard when passing Morning reefs.

Bare islet (northern side of Klewnuggit inlet) kept open of Camp point (southern entrance point of that inlet) bearing N. 79° E. (N. 51° E. mag.) will lead northward of Morning reefs.

Lowe inlet (Kumowadah), situated on the eastern shore of Grenville channel, about 14 miles from Wright sound, is a little over 500 yards wide at its entrance between James and Hepburn points. From mid-channel, between the entrance points, the inlet extends in a N. by E. direction for ½ mile; thence NE. for 1,200 yards to the mouth of Nettle basin, and widens to 800 yards.

Nettle basin is nearly circular in shape, and ½ mile across; but between its entrance points the width is barely 200 yards. Within the basin the general depths are 15 to 17 fathoms, mud.

In the eastern corner of the basin is a large stream, with a waterfall close to its mouth, and several others within (Verney falls). This stream is reported to be connected by a chain of lakes with Kitkiata inlet (Douglas channel).

Landmarks.—On the west shore, at 2 miles southward of Lowe inlet, there is a remarkable bare hill 400 feet high.

Tom islet, a small and wooded islet, lies close to the eastern shore of the channel at 400 yards NW. of Lowe inlet.

On the SE. side of the inlet a remarkable mountain, with a conical summit (Anchor cone), rises to the height of 2,010 feet. From its summit the land slopes northward and southwestward. The latter spur terminates in the eastern entrance point of Lowe inlet, which when seen from the eastward appears as a long, low, wooded projection. Over the northwestern shore of the inlet mountains with bare summits rise to the height of 2,000 feet.

Highwater rocks, situated 200 yards from the western shore, at 800 yards within Lowe inlet, are awash at high water, and lie close to each other in a north and south direction. There is a depth of 23 fathoms at 100 feet eastward of the rocks.

Don flat, with depths of 3 fathoms and less upon it, extends 200 yards from the head of the bay south of Don point, on the eastern shore.

Whiting bank, at 400 yards within the mouth of Lowe inlet, having depths of 10 fathoms and less on it, extends across the entrance. Northeastward of that position the water deepens to 19 and 20 fathoms, mud.

Anchorage for vessels of moderate length will be found, in mid-channel, on Whiting bank, in 8 and 10 fathoms, sand and shells. In this position, Anchor cone should bear S. 75° E. (N. 77° E. mag.); and the southern entrance point of the harbor (Hepburn point) S. 8° E. (S. 36° E. mag.). For a long vessel, more convenient anchorage will be found higher up the harbor, in mid-channel, in 20 fathoms, mud bottom, with Anchor cone bearing S. 30° E. (S. 58° E. mag.).

Supplies.—Good water can be procured in Lowe inlet from the stream in Nettle basin. Trout may be caught in that stream, and clams are found on the flat at the eastern shore of Nettle basin. Whiting, in abundance, may be caught on Whiting bank.

A large salmon cannery, wharf, and store, are situated on the northern shore of Nettle basin.

Tides.—It is high water, full and change, in Lowe inlet at 0 h. 30 m.; springs rise 17 feet, neaps 15 feet.

Klewnuggit inlet lies 9 miles NW. of Lowe inlet, on the eastern shore of Grenville channel, and 1 mile north of Evening point. The entrance between Camp point (southern shore) and Leading island is 800 yards wide, and thence the inlet takes a southeasterly direction for 800 yards, and there divides; the longer arm (Exposed arm) extends in a southeasterly direction for 3 miles and terminates in a swamp fronted by a sand flat. The shorter arm takes a NNW. direction for 1¼ miles, passing eastward of Leading island, and is 500 yards wide.

Anchorage may be obtained in the NW. arm (Ship anchorage) in 15 to 20 fathoms, mud bottom, in mid-channel abreast Leading island.

Directions.—Entering Klewnuggit inlet, having cleared Morning reefs (Bare island open of Camp point, bearing N. 79° E. (N. 51° E. mag.), leads northward of Morning reefs), keep in mid-channel between Camp point and Leading island. Pass 400 yards south of the latter and anchor on its eastern side in Ship anchorage. In this position the SE. extreme of Leading island should be seen in line with a conspicuous cliff of purple color on the southern shore of Exposed arm, bearing S. 28° W. (South mag.).

Tides.—It is high water, full and change, in Klewnuggit anchorage at 0 h. 30 m.; springs rise 17 feet.

Stuart anchorage, situated on the western shore and just within the northern entrance of Grenville channel and 25¼ miles NW. of Lowe inlet, lies ½ mile NW. of a long, low, wooded projection, which serves to distinguish it.

Stag rock uncovers 13 feet at low water and lies 800 yards N. 46° W. (N. 74° W. mag.) from the above-mentioned point. This rock has foul ground extending from it 800 yards in a NW. direction, and a small patch, which uncovers at low water, lies 200 yards SSW. from the rock.

The whole of this foul ground is indicated by kelp during summer and autumn.

Anchorage will be found in 10 to 15 fathoms, rock, 400 yards N. 72° W. (S. 80° W. mag.) from Stag rock, with the southern extreme of Gibson island seen touching the NE. side of Pitt island (Calvert point), bearing N. 36° W. (N. 64° W. mag.).

Directions.—Proceeding for this anchorage, especially at high water, care is necessary. Pass 400 yards north of the foul ground extending from the Stag rock and anchor 200 yards SW. of the ridge.

Tides.—It is high water, full and change, at Stuart anchorage at 0 h. 30 m.; springs rise 17 feet.

The tidal streams meet abreast Evening point; SE. of that point the flood approaches from the SE. and NW. of the point from the NW.

At springs the flood stream in the narrow portions of Grenville channel attains the velocity of 2 knots and the ebb 4 knots an hour. The latter stream continues to run for 1½ hours after low water by the shore. Abreast Lowe inlet strong eddies will be felt on the ebb.

False Stuart anchorage lies on the western shore, 3 miles SE. of Stuart anchorage. On its NW. side there is a high, bold, projection. This point should serve to distinguish False Stuart anchorage from Stuart anchorage, as the latter has a long, low, projection on its SE. side. The water is deep close to the shore.

East inlet, an unexplored inlet on the eastern shore, 5 miles NW. of Evening point, is ½ mile wide at its entrance, and takes a northerly direction.

A rock which uncovers lies 400 yards SE. of the NW. entrance point of East inlet.

At 6 miles NW. from East inlet is Baker inlet, with a narrow entrance, but apparently opening out extensively within and trending in an easterly direction; a small islet or rock lies in the entrance. On the western side of Grenville channel, 3 miles westward from the entrance to Baker inlet, is a narrow but deep opening, which from Grenville channel appears to cut Pitt island in two, and may join the eastern arm of Petrel channel.

West inlet (Kumealon), an unexplored inlet on the eastern shore, abreast of False Stuart anchorage, has an entrance 400 yards wide and takes a northerly direction. Some small islets lie near the eastern shore of Grenville channel NW. of Kumealon inlet.

Gibson islands, situated in the NW. end of Grenville channel, at its confluence with Ogden channel, consist of an island, 160 feet high, about 1 mile in extent and wooded, and several smaller islets and rocks; the shores of the larger island are broken into several bays. On the SE. side of the large island is Bloxam island, of small extent, and Lamb islet lies 200 yards from the NE. shore.

Watson rock uncovers 18 feet at low water springs and lies 400 yards from the SW. shore of Gibson island.

Beacon.—A white, wooden pyramidal beacon, on a stone foundation, surmounted by a red slatwork top, the whole being 22 feet high, stands on Watson rock.

Bloxam shoal extends 1,200 yards eastward from Bloxam and Gibson islands, with depths of 1 to 3 fathoms over it.

Gunboat harbor, between Gibson and Bloxam islands, is a small harbor which faces the SE., affording temporary anchorage to small vessels, in 4 to 10 fathoms, 200 yards within the entrance, in mid-channel.

Bedford island, of small extent, lies ½ mile north from the larger Gibson island. Bedford spit extends 600 yards westward from Bedford island. The channel between Bedford and Gibson islands has depths of 4 fathoms and less in it; this passage is not recommended. Marrack island lies ¼ mile northward of Bedford island and is 1 mile in extent. Marrack rock, which uncovers, lies nearly in mid-channel between Bedford and Marrack islands.

Port Fleming, between Marrack, Bedford, and Gibson islands and the mainland eastward of them, is a good, well-sheltered harbor, of even soundings, from 3 to 7 fathoms, with muddy bottom, and very little current or tide.

The approach to Port Fleming from the north is by Arthur passage.

Kennedy island is 5½ miles long in a north and south direction, with an average breadth of 3 miles, is wooded, and, rising gradually, culminates near the middle in two conspicuous peaks, 2,765 and 2,470 feet high, respectively. The western and southern coasts of Kennedy island are bold and little broken; the northern and eastern coasts have not been examined in detail.

Cardena bay, an open bay on the SE. side of Kennedy island, is skirted by a mud bank, which extends over ½ mile from the shore, with depths of 5 to 10 fathoms upon it.

It is a good anchorage in case of fogs or darkness on reaching Chatham sound. Anchorage may be found on the bank in 7 to 8 fathoms, good holding ground, at 600 yards from the shore of Kennedy island; it is the best anchorage in the vicinity of Skeena river and is much used.

Good anchorage is reported on the western side of Smith island, opposite mount McGrath.

Arthur passage, between Kennedy island on the east and Lewis and Elliott islands on the west, is about 5 miles long, in a general NNW. and SSE. direction, and about 1 mile wide, with depths of 18 to 63 fathoms, mud.

Lewis island, situated 1 mile westward of Kennedy island, is low, wooded, narrow, and 2½ miles long in a NNW. and SSE. direction.

A shoal extends 600 yards S. 32° E. (S. 60° E. mag.) from Henderson point, the SE. extreme of Lewis island, with a depth of 9 feet at its extreme; a rock that dries 10 feet at low water lies 200 yards from the point in the same direction.

Herbert reefs lie on the western side of Arthur passage, about 800 yards from the northern end of Lewis island and 1,200 yards distant from Kennedy island. This dangerous reef consists of two rocks which uncover at low water, with depths of 7 and 9 fathoms between them, lying NNW. and SSE., distant ½ mile from each other. There are depths of 37 fathoms and over at 200 yards northward, and of 20 fathoms at 200 yards southward, of Herbert reefs.

The eastern and smaller Genn island, seen in line with the SW. extreme of White Cliff island, bearing N. 24° W. (N. 52° W. mag.), leads eastward of Herbert reefs.

Lawson harbor, on the northern side of Lewis island, is nearly ¾ mile long in a north and south direction and ½ mile wide. Anchorage for small vessels may be found in 4 fathoms, in mid-channel, about 200 yards within Lawson harbor.

Elliott island, NNW. of Lewis island, is low and wooded; it is about 1½ miles long in a north and south direction, with a greatest breadth of ¾ mile.

Bloxam passage, between Lewis and Elliott islands, and connecting Arthur and Chismore passages, is about 400 yards wide, with a depth of 21 fathoms in mid-channel.

Elizabeth island, NW. of Elliott island, is nearly 3 miles long in a NW. and SE. direction, with an average breadth of ¾ mile. With the exception of a hill, 334 feet high, near its southern end, this island is low and wooded.

Bamfield islands, a group of small islets, lie about ¼ mile from the NE. shore of Elizabeth island; 600 yards eastward from these islands are some reefs. A deep but narrow passage exists between Bamfield islands and the reefs.

Chismore passage, between Porcher island on the west and Lewis, Elliott, and Elizabeth islands on the east, is about 4 miles long in a NW. and SE. direction and from 400 to 1,000 yards wide, with depths of 4 to 21 fathoms, mud. It is obstructed by foul ground at its southeastern end, and is only accessible for ships by Bloxam passage.

Kelp passage, at the southeastern end of Chismore passage between Lewis and Porcher islands, is available only for boats.

Elizabeth rock, which uncovers at low water, lies 200 yards from the SW. shore of Elizabeth island, at 1 mile within the NW. entrance of Chismore passage.

Anchorage may be obtained, in mid-channel, in 7 to 10 fathoms, 400 yards from the western shore of Elliott island, with Genn islands seen midway between Elliott and Elizabeth islands, bearing N. 4° W. (N. 32° W. mag.), with good holding ground and excellent shelter.

Chalmers anchorage, on the northern side of Elliott island, is formed between that island and Elizabeth island.

Anchorage may be found in 13 to 14 fathoms, at 400 yards from the northern extreme of Elliott island, with that extreme seen in line with the southern extreme of White Cliff island, bearing N. 55° E. (N. 27° E. mag.).

White Cliff island, 260 feet high, situated in the northern entrance to Arthur passage, 1,200 yards NE. of Elliott island, is about ½ mile long in a north and south direction, its southern extreme terminating in high, bold, white cliffs. A ledge extends 400 yards southward from White Cliff island. Marble has been quarried at White Cliff island.

Cecil patch, seldom marked by kelp, has 4 fathoms over it, and lies 1 mile westward of the northern extreme of White Cliff island. There are depths of 7 and 18 fathoms at 100 yards from the patch.

The summit of Kennedy island (Elizabeth peak), seen in line with the southern extreme of White Cliff island, bearing S. 50° E. (S. 78° E. mag.), will lead NE. of Cecil patch.

Genn islands consist of two small wooded islands, about 120 feet high, lying close together in a NW. and SE. direction. The eastern and smaller island lies 2½ miles N. 24° W. (N. 52° W. mag.) from the SW. extreme of White Cliff island.

Bribery island consists of low rocks 6 feet above high water and lies 1,600 yards N. 74° W. (S. 78° W. mag.) from the western Genn island.

A rock with a depth of 2 fathoms over it is situated 250 yards N. 78° E. (N. 50° E. mag.) from the eastern apex of Bribery island.

Lawyer group consists of two principal islands, and several smaller ones, about 1 mile in extent, in a NNW. and SSE. direction. The southeastern and smallest island of the group lies ½ mile N. 73° W. (S. 79° W. mag.) from Bribery island. The ground between Lawyer group and Bribery island is foul.

Lawyer Island light is fixed white, elevated 55 feet above high water, and visible in clear weather from a distance of 13 miles from the bearing N. 46° W. (N. 74° W. mag.), through North and East, to S. 5° W. (S. 23° E. mag.); it is partially hidden by trees between N. 46° W. (N. 74° W. mag.) and N. 38° W. (N. 66° W. mag.).

It is shown from a square wooden tower, 48 feet high, surmounting a wooden dwelling painted white with a red roof, erected about 250 yards southeastward from the NW. point of the northern Lawyer island.

Cruice rock, with two heads showing 3 feet above high water, lies 250 yards N. 20° W. (N. 48° W. mag.) from the NW. extreme of the northern Lawyer island.

Client reef, with two rocks that dry 3 feet on its eastern edge, is situated on the northern side of Lawyer islands with the eastern apex of Bribery island bearing S. 15° E. (S. 43° E. mag.), distant 600 yards. From these rocks foul ground extends to the westward for nearly 600 yards.

Hunt point (Quilmass), the northern extreme of Porcher island, is about 3 miles NW. of Chismore passage. Temporary anchorage in offshore winds may be had east of the point in about 10 fathoms.

Rocky and foul ground extends northward of Island point (westward of Hunt point). A pinnacle rock with a depth of 6 feet lies 900 yards N. 31° W. (N. 59° W. mag) from Island point.

Malacca passage, situated between Porcher island and the Genn and Lawyer groups, is about 6 miles long, in a WNW. and ESE. direction, and about 1¾ miles wide, with depths of 21 to 31 fathoms, mud, the latter depth being found in the western portion of the channel.

Directions.—The summit of Kennedy island, Elizabeth peak (bare patches on NW. side), seen in line with the SW. extreme of White Cliff island, bearing S. 50° E. (S. 78° E. mag.), will lead through Malacca passage.

Skeena river, the largest river on the coast of British Columbia, northward of Fraser river, takes its rise in lake Babine, near the village of Naasglee, about 200 miles beyond Port Essington. At 120 miles from Port Essington the river divides into three branches, known as the Forks of the Skeena, the principal branch taking a northerly direction, the others a NW. and SE. direction, respectively.

The shores of the Skeena are said to be low, covered with small hard-wood and cotton trees; there are also good-sized white oaks, similar to those found on the banks of Fraser river. The shores at the entrance are densely wooded, chiefly with cedar and hemlock, and bear evidence of a remarkably wet climate.

17208——32

Caution.—Unless under the guidance of a pilot, as the channels of the Skeena are subject to periodical changes, it is recommended, before attempting them, to buoy the channel by boats or other means.

Navigable depths.—At 6 miles below Port Essington, the river divides into three channels, named North, Middle, and Telegraph passages.

North passage (The Slue) is suitable only for small craft. It is about 600 yards wide, with several sunken rocks and only 2½ fathoms of water, and the current is very swift. Middle passage is obstructed by shifting sand banks and is only fit for boats. Telegraph passage is the main passage with not less than 4 fathoms in the channel. The head of tidal water is about 18 miles above Port Essington. For about 20 miles above Port Essington the Skeena is available for vessels drawing 4 feet of water, though small sternwheel steamers of still shallower draft can ascend with difficulty about 15 miles farther; beyond that distance it is only navigable for canoes. The head of navigation, for vessels drawing over 6 feet, may be said to terminate 6 miles above Port Essington.

It is about 100 miles from tidal water, with a rise of 725 feet, to Skeena forks or Hazelton, a settlement not far from the abandoned Fort Stager.

Telegraph passage, the southernmost and principal channel into the Skeena river, leads, in a northerly direction, from Grenville channel between the mainland on the east and Gibson, Bedford, Marrack, and Kennedy islands on the west, with an average breadth of 1½ miles, and is about 11 miles in length from Gibson island to the SE. entrance point of the river, abreast De Horsey island.

Vessels from Ogden channel or Arthur passage should enter the passage between Kennedy and Marrack islands.

The western side of the channel is rendered dangerous by sand flats, some of which dry, extending from the eastern side of Kennedy island, but the eastern side has depths of 4 to 17 fathoms.

Anchorage may be had, in the southern part of the passage (Port Fleming), eastward of Gibson, Bedford, and Marrack islands.

Port Irving is situated on the eastern side of the passage, about 2 miles south of Hegan point.

Middle passage, situated between Smith and Kennedy islands, is obstructed at its western entrance by sand flats, some of which uncover.

A red spar buoy is moored in 5 fathoms 500 yards S. 72° W. (S. 44° W. mag.) from Hazel point, the SW. point of Smith island. to mark the northeastern limit of the Base sand.

In 1901 the least depth in the navigable channel was about 2¼ fathoms at average low water, 4 fathoms at half tide, and from 6¾ to 7 fathoms at high water.

North passage, between the Tsimpsean peninsula and Smith and De Horsey islands, has a depth of about $2\frac{1}{2}$ fathoms in some parts, and is not recommended. Mount McGrath, on Smith island, is conspicuous, 2,220 feet high. At the entrance to this passage several dangers lie nearly in mid-channel; the navigable channel lies on the south shore, and is barely 200 yards wide in some parts.

Near the entrance of North Skeena passage there is a considerable mining camp called Willaclagh.

From Inverness, on the northern shore of North Skeena passage, a narrow inlet extends westward of north, joining the sea near Coast islet; the inlet, continuing northwesterly, joins the large basin in which Oldfield island (containing mount Oldfield, 2,300 feet high) is situated. This basin enters Malacca passage between Lima point and Coast islet, and connects with Metlakatla bay through Venn creek. The land west of Oldfield basin, SE. from Metlakatla, has been named Digby island.

Caution.—The channels into the Skeena river, being subject to periodical changes, should not be attempted without a pilot.

Directions—Telegraph passage.—Enter the river by Telegraph passage, keeping about 600 yards off the eastern shore; pass 300 yards off Hegan point, and when Parry and Coffin points are in line, bearing about N. 68° W. (S. 84° W. mag.), cross the river steering about N. 40° W. (N. 68° W. mag.) for the highest part of De Horsey island, making allowance for tide. Keep along the De Horsey island shore at a distance of about 200 yards till the buildings of the North Pacific cannery can be seen open of Clara point; then steer N. 56° E. (N. 28° E. mag.) for Powell point; as Powell point is approached keep to the eastward, passing Veitch (Lambert) point at about 600 yards. Port Essington will now be in sight, and a N. 84° E. (N. 56° E. mag.) course may be steered to take up a berth abreast of the large wharf, distant $\frac{1}{2}$ mile, in 5 to 6 fathoms, mud.

Rocks.—Three dangerous sunken rocks lie in and near the fairway in Port Essington. The northern rock, which dries 2 feet at ordinary low water, lies with Veitch point S. 61° W. (S. 33° W. mag.), distant $2\frac{4}{10}$ miles, and the northern extreme of Village island, at the western side of the entrance to Ecstall river, S. 26° E. (S. 54° E. mag.). The center rock, which is the most dangerous, dries 1 foot at low water springs, and lies with Veitch point S. 68° W. (S. 40° W. mag.), distant $2\frac{6}{10}$ miles, and the northern extreme of Village island S. 10° W. (S. 18° E. mag.). The southern sunken rock is awash at ordinary low water and lies with Veitch point S. 72° W. (S. 44° W. mag.), distant $2\frac{4}{10}$ miles, and the northern extreme of Village island S. 26° E. (S. 54° E. mag.), distant 50 yards.

A black spar buoy is moored on the center rock lying on the edge of the shoal water northward of Village island. The buoy will lie flat at low water and is liable to be run under by the tidal stream.

Port Essington (Spŭksŭt) lies on the southern shore of Skeena river, about 11 miles from its mouth and 6 miles from De Horsey island, and affords extensive anchorage. The village is situated on the western side of a point forming the angle between the Skeena and Ecstall rivers. There are two wharves, a post-office, and two churches here.

The settlement Balmoral is on the eastern side of the mouth of Ecstall river. Steam vessels call regularly at the large cannery at Balmoral.

At 2 miles above Raspberry islands, on the southern shore, is a hot spring, 110° F., about 100 yards from the shore; the inhabitants use it for rheumatic affections.

Anchorage with good holding ground will be found abreast Port Essington, distant ½ mile, in 5 to 6 fathoms, mud.

A heavy cross sea is caused by strong winds from seaward between NW. and SE., and vessels are very liable to foul and trip their anchors at such times.

Raspberry islands, situated eastward of Port Essington, consist of two wooded islets lying close to the southern shore; they are joined at low water, and the passage between them and the southern shore is only fit for boats.

Supplies.—Potatoes of large size and good quality are plentiful; also berries, which are dried by the Indians for their winter food. The Skeena is a prolific salmon stream, and fish of the finest quality are procured here. Good timber is plentiful and of large size, especially spruce and yellow Alaska cedar.

Tides and tidal streams.—The tides are subject to considerable diurnal inequality. It is high water at full and change in Port Essington at 1 h. 0 m.; springs rise 24 feet, neaps 15 feet. The flood stream at the entrance attains the velocity of 4, and the ebb 5, knots an hour at springs, and the latter is at times much accelerated by freshets.

Winds.—During September easterly and southeasterly winds, accompanied by almost continuous rain, with frequent squalls, have been experienced.

Coal.—Kitsagatla, on Skeena river, is reported to be an extensive coal country, the seams being cut through by the river, and from 3 to 35 feet thick.

Ice.—The upper part of the Skeena is frozen over during the winter, and in severe winters the whole river as far as Port Essington. North passage is sometimes encumbered with ice during the winter, but it seldom reaches down as far as Kennedy island.

From Ecstall river comes the greater part of the loose ice which encumbers the Skeena in the cold season. Strong NE. gales in winter interrupt communication with the shore, and even if the river is not frozen over there is much loose ice, as also quantities of heavy driftwood.

Ships can not remain at Port Essington during the months of December, January, February, and March, and well into April. The snowfall has been as much as 6 feet on the level.

LAREDO SOUND TO OGDEN CHANNEL.

Laredo sound, between Price and Aristazable islands, is nearly 20 miles long north and south, and from 3 to 14 miles wide. Kititstu hill, on the eastern shore of the sound, is a well-defined summit 760 feet high. To the northeastward rise three remarkable mountains, North and South Needle peaks, 2,600 and 2,800 feet in height, and Cone mountain, 2,400 feet high.

The eastern shore is low, wooded, and fringed by numerous islets, rocks awash, and sunken rocks, 2 miles from the western coast of Price island. On the western side of the entrance of the sound a group of islands, islets, and rocks extends from Aristazable island for more than 5 miles in a southerly direction.

Entrance island, 250 feet high, and $\frac{3}{4}$ mile long NNW. and SSE., is the outer of the chain of islands lying off the southern extreme of Aristazable island.

Nab rock, a dangerous sunken rock, over which the sea breaks only at long intervals, lies $3\frac{8}{10}$ miles S. 30° E. (S. 57° E. mag.) from the summit of Entrance island. The ground is foul for 1 mile SE. from the rock, and several ledges uncover at low water between Nab rock and Entrance island.

The bank of comparatively shoal water stretching across the mouth of Laredo sound might serve to distinguish that sound, in thick or foggy weather, from Milbank sound, there being depths of over 120 fathoms at the entrance of the latter.

Don point, situated on the western shore of Laredo sound, 4 miles NE. from the summit of Entrance island, is a peninsula 150 feet high, but, when first seen, appears as an island. Close northward of Don point is a small cove, which affords shelter to boats.

Double island, on the eastern shore, is wooded, about 100 feet high, and divided near the center by a cleft which causes it to appear as two islands when seen from the southward and northward.

Low point, wooded and flat, lies $2\frac{1}{2}$ miles north from the summit of Double island. Low rock, which uncovers at low water, lies 800 yards north from Low point.

Schooner point is the turning point into Laredo channel, 7 miles N. by E. from Don point. Schooner ledge, which uncovers at low water, lies 600 yards northward of Schooner point.

South Bay islands, a group of small extent, lie at the head of Laredo sound. The larger islands are wooded and 250 feet high.

North Bay islands consist of three principal wooded islets, of small extent, 250 feet high. They lie 1½ miles NNW. of the South Bay islands.

Steep point, high and bold, forming the NE. entrance point of Laredo channel, lies 2 miles NE. from Schooner point.

Directions.—Small, sailing, coasting vessels, to avoid the light winds and calms which frequently prevail in the inner channels, make use of Laredo sound and the channels leading northward from it, as the wind seldom fails them there. Do not bring Outer island to bear southward of S. 64° E. (N. 89° E. mag.) until Schooner point bears N. 4° E. (N. 23° W. mag.); then stand up in mid-channel. Pass 1 mile off Schooner point and proceed through Laredo channel as hereinafter directed.

Laredo channel, between Princess Royal and Aristazable islands, is about 20 miles long in a general NW. by N. and SE. by S. direction, and from 2 to 5 miles wide. Fury point, on the southern shore, 4 miles NW. by N. from Schooner point, terminates in black, smooth rocks. A small bay, with a sandy beach at its head, and an islet at its entrance, lies close eastward of Fury point.

Bluff point lies 7½ miles NW. by N. from Fury point; it is high and bold, with a hill 400 feet high rising immediately over it. On the northern shore of Laredo channel, abreast Bluff point, is an islet at the mouth of a creek.

Beaver ledge uncovers at low water and lies ½ mile from the south shore, at 1$\frac{3}{10}$ miles northward of Schooner point. There is deep water close northward of this ledge.

Islet rock lies close southward of a small islet on the eastern shore at 1½ miles northwestward of Steep point.

South Channel islands are five wooded islands, 150 feet high and about 1 mile in extent, lying nearly in mid-channel, 6 miles from Schooner point. North Channel islands are two wooded islands of small extent. The eastern island of the group lies 1½ miles N. 30° W. (N. 57° W. mag.) from the western island of the South Channel group.

Channel rock is a dangerous sunken rock, lying nearly in mid-channel 1,200 yards S. 30° E. (S. 57° E. mag.) from the eastern islet of the South Channel group. A ledge of rocks, covered with kelp, which dries in patches, extends to the eastward of Channel rock for a distance of about 1 mile.

Seal rocks, which cover at high water and are of small extent, lie ½ mile from the western shore, 2 miles NW. from Bluff point. There is deep water at 400 yards northward of Seal rocks.

Sandspit point, 5½ miles NW. by N. from Bluff point, is white and conspicuous, with a ridge of bare hills, 700 to 950 feet high, immediately over it. Sandspit shoal extends ½ mile NE. from Sandspit point.

Devils point, the northwestern entrance point of Laredo channel, lies 4 miles NW. from Sandspit point. Over this point is a bare hill with a conspicuous bowlder or knob on its summit. Spray point, the NE. entrance point of Laredo channel, is bold, high, and lies 5 miles east from Devils point. A rock, covered by kelp, with a depth of 8 feet over it, is situated at a distance of 5¼ miles S. 7° E. (S. 34° E. mag.) from Spray point. A rock, covered with kelp, is situated in a position from which Spray point bears S. 8° E. (S. 35° E. mag.), distant 2 miles, and the westernmost of the Surf islands N. 42° W. (N. 69° W. mag.).

Directions.—Having rounded Schooner point at a distance of 1 mile, it is recommended to haul over to the NE. shore and keep it aboard until Spray point is passed, as the middle and SW. side of Laredo channel are reported to be very foul.

Tides and tidal streams.—In the wider portions of Laredo channel both streams attain a velocity of 3 knots an hour at springs.

Midway between Devils and Spray points, the flood or north-going stream from Laredo channel is met by the stream passing round the NW. end of Aristazable island, causing at springs dangerous tidal races in that locality.

The ebb stream having divided in mid-channel off Devils point, one portion sets round the NW. end of Aristazable island. The other sets fairly down Laredo channel and attains a velocity of 6 knots an hour, at springs, in Surge narrows. From Surge narrows the ebb stream sets directly toward Fury point, and thence sweeps along the southern shore of the channel, passing across Laredo sound to Low point, whence it is deflected and sets fairly to the southward.

Campania sound, between Princess Royal and Campania islands, is 5 miles long in a general north and south direction and 3 miles wide.

On the eastern side a conspicuous range of hills, with rounded summits, rises 900 feet, and ledges extend from the shore to a distance of ½ mile. On the western shore, 600 yards from the SE. extreme of Campania island, lies Eclipse island, a small wooded islet, 100 feet high; for 1 mile northward of Eclipse island ledges uncover to a distance of ½ mile.

South Surf islands, situated at the SE. entrance of Campania sound, consist of three wooded islands 250 feet high, with several small rocky islets close-to.

North Surf islands, 250 feet high, lying ¾ mile NW. from South Surf islands, consist of three wooded islands 1 mile in extent north and south.

Squally channel, between Gil and Campania islands, is 10 miles long NW. and SE., and from 2½ to 4½ miles wide. Gil island, which forms the eastern side of Squally channel, is 15 miles long north and south and 6 miles broad. Turtle point, the northern extreme of the island, is a peninsula, with small bays east and west of it. The southern extreme of Gil island is wooded, flat, and low.

Mount Gil, near the northern end of the island, attains the elevation of 3,000 feet, the summit being well defined and always clad with snow on the northern side.

Channel reef uncovers at low water, and extends ½ mile from the SW. extreme of Gil island (Ledge point), and fringes the shore of that island, at the same distance, for 1½ miles northwestward of Ledge point.

Windy islets form a group of three, the outer of which lies ½ mile from the western shore of Gil island, at 2 miles northwestward of Ledge point. Windy rock uncovers at low water and lies ½ mile S. 40° E. (S. 67° E. mag.) from the outer or southern Windy islet. There is a depth of 20 fathoms at 200 yards south of the rock.

Black rock, situated on the eastern shore of Squally channel at 400 yards from the western extreme of Gil island (Blackrock point), the turning point into Lewis passage, covering at high water, is small and nearly steep-to.

Violent squalls will often be experienced in Squally channel, descending from the high land of Campania island, when calms or light winds and smooth water will be found in Whale channel.

Lewis passage, between Gil and Fin islands, takes a northeasterly direction for 4 miles, and thence a NNW. direction for 4 miles into Wright sound, with an average width of 1¾ miles.

Fin island, 2 miles westward of Gil island, is 4 miles long in a north and south direction, with an average breadth of 1½ miles. Plover point, the NE. extreme, has a bay close southward of it, with several islets lying off the entrance; the bay dries throughout at low water. Four bare rocky islets fringe the northern shore of Fin island, at the distance of 200 yards. Fin rock, awash at high water, lies on the western shore of the channel, 400 yards from the southern extreme of Fin island.

Cridge passage, between Fin and Farrant islands, is 3 miles long in an east and west direction and 1 mile wide.

Farrant island, at the SE. entrance of Grenville channel, is 9 miles long NNW. and SSE. and from 4 to 6 miles broad. The land on the southern side of Farrant island reaches an elevation of 1,700 feet.

Blossom point, the southern extreme of the island, has a small islet lying close-to, with a ledge extending 200 yards westward from it. Block head, the SE. extreme, terminates in a high, bold, white cliff.

The coast between Block head and Yolk point is broken into several bays; the largest lies close under the latter point and has two patches of rock, which uncover, lying 400 yards from the shore at its entrance.

Yolk point, the NE. extreme of the island, lies 3½ miles NW. from the northern extreme of Gil island and 4 miles N. by W. ½ W. from Block head. Yolk point is smooth, bare, and rocky, and is nearly steep-to. Davenport point, the northern extreme of Farrant island, lies 3 miles NW. ½ N. from Yolk point.

Union passage (Matliksimtas), between Farrant and Pitt islands, enters Grenville channel about 4 miles westward of Yolk point. This passage has not been explored.

Whale channel, between Princess Royal and Gil islands, is 12 miles long north and south and from 2 to 3 miles wide. Leading point, on the eastern shore, 5 miles southward of Holmes bay, has immediately over it a conspicuous hill, 700 feet high. River bight, between Holmes bay and Leading point, is a deep indentation with a large river at its head. Maple point, on the western shore, abreast of Holmes bay, is comparatively low and wooded, with many maple trees growing.

Shrub point, on the western shore, 5 miles southward of Maple point, is comparatively low, flat, and wooded. Camp islet, a small, conspicuous, wooded islet, lying 400 yards from the western shore, at 9 miles southward of Maple point, is connected with the eastern shore of Gil island at low water. South of Camp islet there is a comparatively deep bay, 1 mile wide at its entrance, but which at low water is blocked by a ledge of rocks which uncover. Molly point, on the western shore, 1 mile SSE. of Camp islet, is the turning point of Whale channel into Campania sound.

Barnard cove, on the SE. shore of the channel, SE. of Trouble island, affords shelter to boats and small craft. Pass in mid-channel between Trouble island and the southern shore of Whale channel and anchor in 20 fathoms, mud, in the eastern part of the cove, at 400 yards from the eastern shore.

Passage island, situated at the junction of Whale channel and Campania sound, is 2 miles long in a north and south direction and 1 mile broad. It is wooded, the tops of the trees being about 250 feet above high water. Off the SE. side of Passage island a group of islets, rocks, and sunken dangers extends ½ mile in a southeasterly direction.

The passages east and west of Passage island are deep and 1,200 yards wide. On the eastern shore of the eastern channel several rocky islands extend from 200 to 400 yards from the shore, off the entrance to a bay.

Estevan sound, between Estevan and Campania islands, is about 15 miles long NW. and SE and from 2½ to 5 miles wide. At the SE. entrance are several islets and sunken rocks, nearly in mid-channel. To a stranger, therefore, Estevan sound can not be recommended.

If, however, circumstances should necessitate its being made use of, a course should be steered to pass ¾ mile northeastward of South Watcher islet. Thence a general course of NW. ½ N., cautiously followed, for 15 miles, should take a vessel into Nepean sound, keeping nearer the western shore of the channel, to avoid the dangerous ledges which extend 1 mile from the western side of Campania island.

Campania island is nearly 15 miles long NW. and SE., and from 1 to 4 miles broad. At 1 mile from its southern extreme the island has an elevation of 1,000 feet, increasing northward until it culminates in two bare mountains, with dome-shaped summits, 2,000 feet high. These mountains are of granite formation and furnish an excellent landmark when seen from seaward. From their summits, which are 4 and 6 miles, respectively, from the southern extreme of the island, the land slopes to the northward, the northern end of Campania island being comparatively low and wooded. The NE. extreme terminates in a high, bold, white cliff.

The western coast is low, wooded, and broken into bays and creeks, fringed by islets, rocks awash at high water, and at low water, to the distance of 1 mile.

The northern coast is bold and little broken. Marble rock, a small white rock, 6 feet above high water, lies ½ mile from it.

South Watcher is a small wooded islet, 100 feet high, lying nearly in mid-channel at the southern entrance of Estevan sound, 3$\frac{4}{10}$ miles W. by S. from Eclipse island; ledges, which uncover at low water, extend from it NW. and SE. for ½ mile.

North Watcher islet, 60 feet high, is small, wooded, and conspicuous; it lies 1$\frac{8}{10}$ miles NW. by W. from South Watcher islet; ledges which uncover, and sunken dangers, surround it to the distance of nearly 1 mile.

Blinder rock, over which the sea breaks occasionally, lies 1 mile S. 83° W. (S. 56° W. mag.) from the summit of South Watcher islet, and a little more than 1 mile S. 18° E. (S. 45° E. mag.) from North Watcher islet. Estevan ledge, which uncovers at low water, is 200 yards in extent, and lies 1,600 yards N. 63° W. (West mag.) from the summit of North Watcher islet.

Breaker point, the southeastern extreme of Estevan island, is low and wooded; Don ledge, which uncovers at low water, extends 1,200 yards eastward from the point. Breaker reef consists of three rocks awash, surrounded by sunken rocks over which the sea nearly always breaks; the outer rock lies 2½ miles S. 72° W. (S. 45° W. mag.) from Breaker point and nearly 1½ miles from the nearest part of Estevan island.

Trap rocks, some of which are awash at high water, extend 1,600 yards northeastward from the northern extreme of Estevan island and thence front the northern end of the island at the distance of 400 to 1,200 yards.

Guano rocks, on the eastern shore of Estevan sound, consist of a cluster of three white rocks, lying 1 mile distant from the western side of Campania island at 6 miles northwestward of Eclipse island. The highest rock is 30 feet above high water, and the group is surrounded by rocks awash and sunken rocks to the distance of from 1,000 to 1,400 yards.

Between Guano rocks and Eclipse island, ledges which uncover at low water extend from 1,000 to 1,200 yards from the shore.

Marble rock, ½ mile north of the NW. extreme of Campania island, is a bare rock 6 feet above high water, small, white, and conspicuous; it is nearly steep-to on all sides.

Nepean sound, between Estevan sound and Principe channel, is about 7 miles long and 4 miles wide.

Otter channel, between Pitt island and Campania island, connects Nepean sound with Squally channel, and is about 3½ miles long, and from 3½ miles at its western, to 1 mile wide at its eastern, end. Steep point, the northeastern entrance point of the channel, terminates in a high, bold, white cliff.

Otter passage leads southwestward from Nepean sound, between Estevan and Banks islands. This passage, though nearly 1½ miles wide, is obstructed on its northwestern shore by a group of islands (Block islets), islets, and rocks, which contract the navigable channel to barely 800 yards wide in places.

This narrow channel is rendered more dangerous by the strong tidal streams in it, the greater portion of the ebb stream finding its way out of Nepean sound by this passage at the rate of more than 6 knots an hour at springs, which, meeting the ocean swell at the western entrance of this passage, produces a most turbulent, breaking sea, dangerous to small vessels.

In no case should Otter passage be attempted except at slack water and with local knowledge.

Principe channel, between Pitt and Banks islands, is about 42 miles long NW. and SE. and from 2 to 7 miles wide. The western shore of the channel is bold, with mountains from 1,200 to 1,700 feet rising over it. The eastern shore is much broken into bays, especially about midway, in two of which, Ports Stephens and Canaveral, anchorage may be found.

Directions.—A mid-channel course should be kept when navigating Principe channel until nearing Anger island, when the western shore should be closed to avoid the dangers which extend off that island.

Deer point, at 4 miles northward of Block islets, is a small peninsula on the south shore, which when first seen appears to be an islet.

Gale point is prominent, bold, and high, and lies 5 miles northward of Deer point. A remarkable bare mountain, 1,250 feet high, is situated close to the shore at 4 miles northward from Gale point. Despair point, at 11 miles northwestward of Gale point, is bold, and nearly steep-to. Headwind point lies 5½ miles NW. of Despair point; thence the coast is bold and unbroken.

Deadman islet, a small wooded islet, lies close to the shore off the NW. end of Banks island, about 15 miles WNW. of Headwind point. End hill, an oval-shaped hill 450 feet high, lies close to the southern shore of Principe channel at 2 miles ESE. of Deadman islet.

Wolf point, the southeastern entrance point of Principe channel and the SW. point of Pitt island, is high, bold, and conspicuous, with several small islets close-to.

Brodie rock, a dangerous sunken rock, lies 1 mile west from Wolf point; it is about 200 yards in length and shows several heads at low water. Between Brodie rock and the shore the ground is foul to 2 miles northward of Wolf point. There is a depth of 66 fathoms at 400 yards south of Brodie rock.

Port Stephens, on the eastern shore, at about 8 miles within the southern end of Principe channel, is 800 yards wide at its entrance.

Guide islet, a small, bare islet, lies 1 mile southeastward of the port, with two small islets (the Sisters) lying midway between it and the entrance.

Bluff point, 8 miles NW. by N. from Wolf point, forms the western entrance point of Port Stephens and terminates in a high white cliff. Center point is the SW. point of an island lying toward the eastern side of the entrance of the harbor, ¼ mile northward from the Sisters islets; it is the largest and the southwestern one of a chain of islets extending from the eastern shore of the port in a SW. direction. From Bluff point the harbor extends in a general easterly direction for about 1½ miles, with several bays on its northern shore.

Directions.—Keep midway between the entrance points (Bluff and Center points) and steer N. 38° E. (N. 11° E. mag.) for ½ mile; thence N. 72° E. (N. 45° E. mag.) for ½ mile, keeping in mid-channel. Haul gradually to the eastward and southeastward as the harbor opens out and anchor in mid-channel in about 12 fathoms.

Tides.—It is high water, full and change, at Port Stephens at 0 h. 30 m.; springs rise 18 feet.

Oar point lies 6 miles NW. from Bluff point, the coast between these points being bold and unbroken.

Canoe islet, a small bare islet, not unlike a canoe in appearance when first seen, lies off the mouth of Mink Trap bay, at 1 mile NW. by N. from Oar point. Green Top islet, ¾ mile NW. by N. from Canoe islet, is small, with a patch of grass and shrub on its summit.

Mink Trap bay, about 8 miles NW. of Port Stephens, consists of two long, narrow creeks, separated by a peninsula; this bay has deep water in it, but it is useless as an anchorage for other than small vessels and boats.

At the head of the eastern arm is an Indian village, to which a tribe of the Kitkatlah Indians resort in summer for salmon fishing.

Anger island, on the eastern shore, 5 miles NW. of Oar point, is about 4 miles long and 2 miles broad; near its NW. end the island reaches an elevation of 730 feet. Trade and Storm islands are clusters of islets which extend from ½ to 1½ miles from the south and SW. shores of Anger island.

The narrow channel between Anger and Pitt islands is intricate and dangerous, with numerous rocks awash at low water which in July were free from kelp. The passage is used during the salmon season by small steam vessels collecting fish for the Skeena river canneries.

Wheeler islet is a small wooded islet, distant 5 miles NW. by W. from Foul point, the western extreme of Anger island. Cliff islets extend eastward of Wheeler islet to the entrance of Petrel channel. These islets are bare and rocky, with foul ground between them and the shore of McCauley island.

McCauley island is 17 miles long, 9 miles broad, wooded nearly throughout, and near its center 1,160 feet high. Almost midway on its southern side a bare hill with a flat top, 400 feet high, lies close to the shore.

Port Canaveral, near the SE. extreme of McCauley island, about 21 miles NW. of Port Stephens, is an inlet trending eastward for about ¾ mile with an average breadth of about 600 yards, and depths of 6 to 18 fathoms over it.

Dixon island lies on the western side of the port, with several islands and islets lying 400 yards off its southern and eastern sides.

Squall point, the SE. entrance point, is the termination of the spur from Hat hill, and is bold and conspicuous. Red point, on the northern shore, opposite Squall point, has a cliff of red-brown color over it.

Ethel rock, with a depth of 6 feet over it, lies in the approach to Port Canaveral, with Squall point bearing N. 59° E. (N. 31° E.

mag.), distant 1,100 yards, and Tonkin point, the SE. point of Dixon island, N. 23° W. (N. 51° W. mag.). This rock is surrounded by deep water, and at low-water slack is marked by kelp.

Alarm rock, with 8 and 10 fathoms close-to, is a dangerous sunken rock lying nearly in mid-channel at the entrance to Port Canaveral, at 300 yards N. 41° W. (N. 69° W. mag.) from Squall point and 500 yards from Red point.

Harbor bank, with 6 fathoms over it (probably less), lies 300 yards eastward from Alarm rock and midway between Squall and Red points.

Clown rock dries 3 feet and lies 550 yards S. 29° E. (S. 57° E. mag.) from Tonkin point, with foul ground between it and the shore.

Stephen rock, which just covers at high water, lies on the northern side at 300 yards from Dixon island. The outer portion of Stephen rock, which uncovers at low water, lies 400 yards S. 24° E. (S. 52° E. mag.) from Dimple point, the eastern extreme of Dixon island.

Directions.—The best way to enter or leave Port Canaveral is to pass close round Squall point, which is steep-to. Anchor about 300 yards SSE. from Red point in 14 to 15 fathoms, mud; the holding ground is good and the anchorage secure.

Tides.—It is high water, full and change, in Port Canaveral, at 0 h. 30 m.; springs rise 18 feet.

Bush and Dark islets are small, wooded islets, which lie close south of McCauley island, off the entrance to Port Canaveral, at 2 miles westward of Wheeler islet.

Petrel channel is an unexamined passage between Pitt and McCauley islands; its southern entrance is about 3 miles wide; thence the channel takes a NNW. direction for nearly 8 miles, when it divides, one passage going eastward, the other westward of Lofty island, and again joining at 2 miles eastward of Ogden channel. Noble mountain, on Lofty island, rises to a height of 2,874 feet.

Hankin ledges consist of rocks awash and sunken dangers, which extend nearly 1 mile from Hankin point (western extreme of McCauley island).

Tidal streams.—In Principe channel the flood stream, setting to the NW., comes principally by way of Estevan sound, being joined in Nepean sound by the stream which enters through Otter passage. At the northern end of Principe channel this stream is met by the flood which has passed up outside Banks island.

The ebb stream runs out principally through Otter passage. Both streams attain a velocity of 3 knots an hour at springs.

Browning entrance is the approach common to the south end of Ogden channel and the western end of Principe channel. It is included between the southern side of Goschen island and the NW.

extreme of Banks island, and between cape George and White rocks is 14 miles wide.

Ogden channel, situated between Pitt and Porcher islands, is about 16 miles long and from 800 yards to 1½ miles wide, and affords the shortest means of communication between Queen Charlotte islands (Skidegate) and the inner waters along this coast. At its southern end, Ogden channel is divided by Spicer island into Schooner and Beaver passages; at 1 mile northward of Spicer island the channel is obstructed by Channel islands, which reduce the width of the navigable channel to 800 yards.

On the eastern side of Dolphin island, close to the shore, Passage cone, 454 feet high, is a useful mark for indicating Schooner passage. On the NW. side of Spicer island a saddle-shaped hill rises 800 feet.

Spicer island, situated between McCauley and Dolphin islands, is 827 feet high. On its SE. side two small narrow bays indent the shore in a northerly direction; and off its western side, at ½ mile from the shore, are Christie islands, a cluster of islets and rocks, some wooded and others bare. Long island consists of two low wooded islets, lying close together at 1½ miles SW. of Spicer island. Channel island is a small wooded islet, lying nearly midway between Long and Spicer islands.

Channel group lies 1 mile northward of Spicer island. The large islands are wooded, and the southeastern islet of the group is small, bare, and conspicuous. Half a mile northward of the Channel group are some small islets, one bare (White rock) and another covered with vegetation (False Grassy islet).

South Twin islet is a small wooded islet on the eastern shore, ½ mile from the eastern islet of the Channel group and 1 mile northeastward of Spicer island. This islet, and the eastern bare islet of the Channel group, indicate the navigable channel, which lies between them. North Twin islet resembles South Twin islet, from which it lies north, distant ½ mile. The tops of the trees on North Twin islet are about 130 feet high.

Dolphin island.—There is an anchorage on the northern side of Dolphin island, in the bay off Kitkatlah village, in 11 fathoms, with Village point bearing S. 62° E. (East mag.) and the large white stone S. 28° W. (South mag.). There is a mission and store at Kitkatlah. The channel between Dolphin and Goschen islands is rocky and dangerous, with strong tides, and should not be attempted.

Kitkatlah inlet extends from Ogden channel in a northwesterly direction for 12 miles between Porcher and Goschen islands. A large island (Gurd or Guard island), which rises to a height of 550 feet, and several smaller islands lie near its western end. The land of Porcher peninsula at its western end is very low.

Beaver passage, between McCauley and Spicer islands, is the wider and better of the two passages leading into Ogden channel.

At its western entrance Beaver passage is about ½ mile wide, and takes a NE. direction for about 4½ miles, thence turning sharply to the NNW., toward the Channel group, for 2¼ miles.

North rock is always visible, and lies nearly in mid-channel at the southern entrance of Beaver passage, ½ mile SSE. from Long island.

Connis islet, small and wooded, is 600 yards SE. of the eastern point of Spicer island; close southwestward of it is a large flat rock which uncovers at low water.

On the eastern shore, abreast Connis islet, is a small, cone-shaped, wooded islet off a sandy bay.

Directions.—Having passed through in mid-channel between Long island and North rock, steer N. 58° E. (N. 80° E. mag.) for about 4 miles; pass midway between Connis islet and the cone-shaped islet on the eastern shore, and haul up to N. 29° W. (N. 57° W. mag.) for about 1½ miles; pass midway between South Twin islet and the eastern (bare) islet of the Channel group.

Schooner passage, between Spicer and Dolphin islands, is barely 400 yards wide in its narrowest part, and is about 3 miles long north and south. A rock, with a depth of 2 fathoms, is situated in Schooner passage, in a position from which the southern extremity of Dolphin island bears S. 61° W. (S. 33° W. mag.), distant 1$\frac{1}{10}$ miles, and the southwestern extremity of Spicer island in line with a small island S. 11° E. (S. 39° E. mag.).

Boys rock, a dangerous sunken rock, lies at the southern end of Schooner passage, 400 yards from the southern extreme of Dolphin island. There is a depth of 49 fathoms, rock, at 400 yards south of Boys rock.

Tidal streams.—The flood stream sets to the northward, and near the northern end of Ogden channel divides, one part turning eastward into Grenville channel, the other continuing northward toward Skeena river. The ebb streams from Grenville channel, Chatham sound, and Skeena river unite off the northern end of Ogden channel and pass out by it. The muddy water of Skeena river is usually distinguished against the blue water of Ogden channel.

Both flood and ebb streams, in the narrow portions of Ogden channel, attain a velocity of 4 knots an hour at springs.

Alpha bay, situated on the eastern shore, 4 miles within the northern entrance of Ogden channel, faces the west and is nearly 1 mile wide, but only 600 yards deep. Near its northern end a deep valley extends inland, and through it flows a fine trout stream.

From the southern entrance point of this stream a sand spit extends 400 yards toward the northern point of Alpha bay.

Anchorage may be obtained in 10 and 11 fathoms, at 300 yards from the nearest shore (Fish point), with the southern entrance point of the trout stream bearing N. 79° E. (N. 51° E. mag.), distant 500 yards, and the point on the western shore under Bareside mountain in line with the northern point of Alpha bay, bearing N. 8° E. (N. 20° W. mag.).

Tides.—It is high water, full and change, in Alpha bay at 0 h. 0 m.; springs rise 18 to 19 feet.

Peninsula point, the NW. entrance point of Ogden channel, is prominent, with a hill near its eastern extreme. Northward of the point, at the mouth of the river Oona, is Oona bay, about ½ mile wide and 1 mile deep in a westerly direction.

There is said to be anchorage in 8 or 10 fathoms of water on the northern side of Peninsula point, near the mouth of the river Oona.

CHAPTER XI.

OUTER COAST—CAPE CALVERT TO OGDEN CHANNEL.

VARIATION IN 1906.

Cape Calvert.................26° 10′ E. | Day point..................26° 45′ E.
Bonilla island...............27° 40′ E.

Calvert island, at the entrance to Fitzhugh sound, is 13 miles long north and south and 8 miles across at its broadest part. The southern and western coasts of Calvert island are but little broken, comparatively low, and thickly wooded.

Sorrow island, situated at the pitch of cape Calvert, the southern extreme of Calvert island, is conspicuous and an excellent thick-weather mark, from its cliffy formation, and by being covered with stunted, weather-beaten trees.

Mark nipple, an isolated hill, 350 feet high, at the SW. extreme of Calvert island, is a very useful landmark when approaching Fitzhugh sound.

Landing, with fine weather and offshore winds, may be effected in Grief bay (north of Sorrow island) and in other bights westward to Herbert point.

Bird rock, 20 feet high, lies about 4 miles NW. ¾ W. from the southern extreme of Sorrow island.

Wing rock, awash at low water, lies 500 yards N. 62° W. (N. 88° W. mag.) from Bird rock, and about 1,250 yards from the nearest part (Stafford point) of the shore of Calvert island.

Blakeney islet, 150 feet high, ½ mile from the SW. extreme of Calvert island, is small, wooded, and about ½ mile long.

Hedley patch, with 9 fathoms on it (probably shoaler), is of small extent, and lies 3¼ miles S. 26° E. (S. 52° E. mag.) from Blakeney islet.

Fitz Roy reef uncovers at low water and is about ½ mile in extent in a WNW. and ESE. direction. Its outer or western edge lies 1½ miles N. 54° W. (N. 80° W. mag.) from Blakeney islet and 1½ miles from the nearest shore of Calvert island.

Carrington reefs are a cluster of sunken rocks, the outer edge of which lies ½ mile from the western coast of Calvert island, at 1¾ miles N. 4° W. (N. 30° W. mag.) from Blakeney islet.

The coast of Calvert island, northward of the Carrington reefs, is foul to the distance of ½ mile.

Kwakshua is an unexamined channel between Calvert and Hecate islands. At its western entrance this passage is ½ mile wide and takes a northeasterly direction.

Kwakshua rock lies nearly in mid-channel, at the western entrance of Kwakshua channel. The sea only breaks at intervals over this dangerous sunken rock.

Hecate reefs fringe the western coast of Hecate island to the distance of 1,600 yards.

Hakai channel, between Hecate and Nalau islands, is about 7 miles long NE. and SW. and from 1 to 1½ miles wide. Sugarloaf hill, on the western side of Hecate island, is 500 feet high. Leading peak, about 1½ miles southward of Sugarloaf hill, has a sharp, well-defined summit.

South Pointers are a cluster of bare black rocks, of small extent, 2 feet above high water, surrounded by sunken dangers to the distance of 250 yards; they lie on the southern shore, at the western entrance of Hakai channel, 1½ miles westward of the Starfish group.

North Pointers are a cluster of bare rocks, of light color, lying on the northern shore at the western entrance of Hakai channel. The western or outer rock lies 2½ miles N. 9° E. (N. 17° W. mag.) from South Pointer rocks.

Breaker group, situated on the northern shore halfway through Hakai channel, is about 1 mile in extent, the larger islands being wooded, about 250 feet high, and the smaller ones bare. Breaker ledge uncovers at half ebb, and lies ½ mile SE. from the center island of the Breaker group.

Directions.—Hakai channel is not recommended to a stranger. If using it, steer midway between North and South Pointers rocks, and thence a mid-channel course toward a conspicuous mountain on the eastern shore of Fitzhugh sound, which will lead through into that sound.

Starfish group, wooded, from 70 to 150 feet high, lies on the southern shore and extends about 1½ miles NE. and SW. The group consists of three principal islands, much broken into long, rocky, narrow creeks with shores of white cliffs. Starfish ledge, over which the sea usually breaks, lies 400 yards from the NW. shore of Long island, the northernmost of the Starfish group.

East rock, off the entrance to Welcome harbor, is awash at low water and lies ½ mile N. 3° E. (N. 23° W. mag.) from the NW. point of Harbor island on the eastern side of the entrance to the harbor. There are depths of 23 and 25 fathoms close to East rock and 30 fathoms between that rock and Port reef, which latter is awash at high water, and lies 400 yards S. 60° E. (S. 86° E. mag.) from East rock.

Leading peak seen in line with Bluff point, bearing S. 6° W. (S. 20° E. mag.), will lead westward of these rocks. South Pointers bearing S. 49° W. (S. 23° W. mag.) leads northward of them.

Choked passage lies southward of the Starfish group; it is obstructed by rocks awash, reefs, and sand banks.

Welcome harbor, situated on the southern shore of Hakai channel near its western end, is 600 yards wide at its entrance and 1¼ miles long in a southerly direction. Though somewhat confined, it affords good shelter to small vessels, and within the harbor, on the eastern shore, there is a sandy beach where a vessel might be beached. Strong westerly winds send a swell into this harbor.

Exposed bay, situated just eastward of Welcome harbor, has a dangerous cluster of sunken rocks near the middle of the bay. White rocks lie from 400 to 600 yards NW. of the eastern entrance point of the bay.

Fairway rock, with 24 feet of water over it, lies nearly in midchannel at the entrance to Welcome harbor. There is a depth of 20 fathoms close westward, and of 9 fathoms close eastward, of the rock.

Leading peak seen in line with Bluff point, bearing S. 6° W. (S. 20° E. mag.), will lead eastward, and Sugarloaf hill in line with Leading island (a small, round, wooded island within the harbor) will lead close westward, of Fairway rock.

Harbor ledge, situated 200 yards from the western shore of Harbor island, is of small extent and dries 3 feet at low water. Codfish rock, with 12 feet of water over it, lies 100 yards off the south shore of Harbor island. Wolf rock, awash at high water, lies close to the eastern shore, at nearly 400 yards northward of Sandspit point.

Directions.—Having passed not less than ½ mile northward of Starfish group, the leading mark before given for clearing East rock should be brought on and steered for. Especial care will be necessary if the flood stream be making. Strong tide rips occur north of the Starfish group.

Having cleared East rock, pass east or west of Fairway rock as requisite and anchor in 7 to 9 fathoms in mid-channel between Leading island and Wolf rock, with the former bearing NW., distant 200 yards.

Tides.—It is high water, full and change, in Welcome harbor at 0 h. 0 m.; springs rise from 15 to 16 feet, neaps 12 to 13 feet.

The flood stream sets to the northeastward. Both streams attain a velocity of 4 knots an hour at springs.

Nalau passage, between the Nalau group and Hunter island, is obstructed by islands, islets, rocks awash, and sunken dangers, and is useless for navigation.

White Cliff island, situated 4 miles N. 46° W. (N. 72° W. mag.) from the western or outer North Pointer rock, is of small extent, bare, and 250 feet in height; its coast, consisting of high white cliffs, renders it conspicuous when seen from the south and west.

A reef, on which the sea breaks at low water, lies midway between White Cliff island and the North Pointers.

Queens sound, between Goose and Hunter islands, is about 12 miles long north and south and from 4 to 8 miles wide. At its northern end is a mass of islands and islets, which renders that portion of the sound intricate and dangerous.

Spider island, 250 feet high, on the eastern side of the entrance to Queens sound, is 3½ miles long north and south and 1½ miles broad; it is connected with Hunter island by a ledge of rocks awash, through which there are boat passages, and its NW. extreme terminates in high, bold, white cliffs.

Superstition point, on the eastern shore of Queens sound, 2 miles northward of Spider island, is the SW. extreme of a small island, which is connected with Hunter island by a narrow neck, awash at high water. Superstition ledge consists of high rocks, connected by rocks awash and sunken dangers, the outer extreme of which lies 1¼ miles WSW. from Superstition point. Strong tide races will be met with in the vicinity of this ledge, and the sea breaks upon it heavily at times.

Purple bluff, the SW. extreme of a group of islands on the eastern shore of Queens sound at the entrance to Plumper channel, terminates in high, bold, basaltic cliffs of a purple tint. The group consists of numerous islands, islets (wooded and bare), rocks awash, and sunken rocks, extending over a space of nearly 5 miles.

Purple bluff lies 5 miles NNW. of Spider island and 5 miles from the Goose island group.

Goose islands, forming the western shore of Queens sound, consist of four principal islands, connected at low water, the largest and northernmost being about 200 feet high and wooded; its NE. extreme terminates in conspicuous, high, white cliffs. Yellocki, an Indian fishing village, is situated on the eastern side of the westernmost Goose island.

Gosling rocks consist of numerous rocks, awash at high water, and sunken dangers, the outer extreme of which lies nearly 4 miles south from the Goose islands. West rock, awash at high water, lies 1 mile westward of the westernmost Goose island.

Plumper channel, between Hunter and Campbell islands, leads from Queens sound into Lama passage; its southern end is obstructed by numerous islets and rocks, and no specific directions can be given for entering it.

Hecate channel, between Campbell island and the Bardswell group, leads from Queens sound into Seaforth channel, and is also obstructed at its southern end by numerous islets and rocks. The two principal passages are Codfish passage and Brown narrows; no directions, however, can be given for entering them.

Broken group, situated 2 miles northward of the Goose island group, extends 2 miles north and south and consists of several islets and rocks, connected throughout by ledges which uncover at low water.

Fingal island is a small, wooded island, lying 1 mile N. 51° W. (N. 78° W. mag.) from the northernmost island of the Broken group. Fingal ledges extend 1 mile in a southerly direction from Fingal island, and consist of rocks awash, and ledges which uncover at low water.

Peveril rock lies 1½ miles N. 49° E. (N. 22° E. mag.) from the northernmost Goose island and is 8 feet high.

Middle rock, 6 feet high, lies 3 miles N. 35° W. (N. 62° W. mag.) from the NW. extreme of North Goose island. North breaker, a dangerous sunken rock, lies 1 mile north from Middle rock. There is a depth of 27 fathoms, rock, at 1 mile westward of the North breaker.

Limit island is a small wooded island, with foul ground extending ½ mile SW. from it. Rempstone rocks consist of two patches awash at high water, 1 mile apart, lying ESE. and WNW. from each other. The western or outer rock lies 1$\frac{3}{10}$ miles south from cape Swain.

Bardswell group, forming the eastern side of Milbank sound, consists of low, wooded islands, extending over a space of 7 miles square, the largest of which, Dufferin island, forms the western shore of Hecate channel. Among the islands are several boat channels, communicating between Milbank sound and Seaforth and Hecate channels. A deep-water passage, known to the Indians by the name of Joassa, exists between Rait creek, Dundivan inlet, and Boddy creek, Hecate channel. The passage is 7 miles in length, has many islands in it, and varies in breadth from 200 yards to ½ mile.

Price island, forming the eastern side of Laredo sound, has already been described. Outer island, about 2 miles WSW. from its southern end, when seen from the westward, appears round and well defined.

Entrance island, 1½ miles from the southern extreme of Aristazable island, has a small islet lying close south of it, and is the outer island of a group which extends from the southern end of Aristazable island. The larger islets of the group are wooded, the smaller bare.

Foul ground extends nearly 5 miles SSE. of Entrance island.

Aristazable island is about 26 miles long NNW. and SSE., from 1 to 10 miles broad, and wooded. South range, at about 8 miles from its southern extreme, is a conspicuous saddle-shaped hill 640 feet high. Near the northern end of the island, over the eastern shore, North range, a bare ridge of hills, with four conspicuous peaks, rises to the height of 950 feet.

Over the SW. extreme of the island there are some bare hills 350 feet high, and at the extreme northern end of the island there is a remarkable bowlder or knob on the summit of a bare hill.

White rock, 100 feet high, bare and conspicuous, situated 5 miles N. 39° W. (N. 66° W. mag.) from Entrance island, is the outer rock of a group extending 2 miles from the SW. shore of Aristazable island.

Sentinel island, 250 feet high, small, round, wooded, and conspicuous, lies off the SW. extreme of Aristazable island, 1½ miles from the shore, at 4 miles N. 55° W. (N. 82° W. mag.) from White rock. Several rocks awash and sunken rocks lie NNW. of Sentinel island, and there are also a number of them fringing the western shore of Aristazable island to the northward.

Gander islands (Chachekwas), islets, and rocks, extend 11 miles north and south, and 4 miles east and west, at about 6 miles from the western shore of Aristazable island. The larger islands of the group are wooded, the smaller ones bare; the tops of the trees are from 70 to 150 feet above high water.

Large Gander island, the northernmost and largest of the group, is about 2 miles long north and south, and ½ mile broad. Middle Gander islands are two small, wooded islands, lying close together, the northern island 5 miles south from the south extreme of Large Gander island. A bare rock, with sunken rocks surrounding it, lies 2 miles N. 7° W. (N. 34° W. mag.) from the Middle Gander islands. South Gander island lies 1 mile south from the Middle Gander islands; it is 900 yards long north and south, 100 yards broad, 70 feet high, and wooded. Southeast Gander islands are two small wooded islands 100 feet high, lying close together, 3 miles S. 30° E. (S. 57° E. mag.) from South Gander island; a reef lies midway between them and South Gander island.

Two small, bare, rocky islets lie 1½ miles NNW. of Southeast Gander islands.

Goose ledge, which uncovers at low water, lies 3 miles S. 43° W. (S. 16° W. mag.) from Southeast Gander islands and 3 miles S. 24° E. (S. 51° E. mag.) from South Gander island.

Sparrowhawk breakers lie, respectively, 4 and 6½ miles SSW. from Southeast Gander islands. There is a depth of 21 fathoms between these dangers.

Tide Rip islands, 2 miles northward of the Gander group, extend 12 miles north and south, are wooded and about 200 feet high; the northern and largest island terminates at its NW. extreme (Cliff point), in high, conspicuous, white cliffs, 2½ miles westward of Devils point, the NW. point of Aristazable island.

Gull rock lies 5 miles north of Large Gander island and westward of the Tide Rip islands. The rock is at the northwestern end of a rocky shoal which is nearly 1½ miles long.

Tidal streams.—The flood stream sets to the northward, both flood and ebb streams attaining at springs, among these islands, a rate of 4 knots an hour.

Caution.—An extended examination has not been made of the Gander and Tide Rip groups and their vicinity, and the tidal streams are strong; the channels between them, though deep, should not be attempted by a stranger. When approaching these groups of islands the lead and lookout should be especially attended to.

Breakers.—Extensive breakers are reported to exist at a point 16 miles N. 52° W. (N. 79° W. mag.) from the northern end of Large Gander island and 15½ miles S. 78° W. (S. 51° W. mag.) from Cliff point, the northern extreme of the Tide Rip islands.

Estevan island is about 14 miles long NW. and SE. and from 2 to 5 miles broad, the southern shores being comparatively low, wooded, and much broken into bays and creeks. Near the center it attains an elevation of 1,500 to 1,700 feet, forming a saddle-shaped mountain with the highest part to the westward.

Haycock island, small, bare, and 60 feet high, lies 7 miles W. ¾ N. from Breaker point, the southeastern extreme of Estevan island. Haycock rocks are three rocks awash, which lie, respectively, WNW. ½ W., S. by W. ½ W., and NE. ½ N., distant 1 mile, from Haycock island.

The passage between Haycock island and Estevan island should not be attempted.

Curtis point, on the SW. shore of Estevan island, 4½ miles NNW. from the summit of Haycock island, is low and wooded, with some rocky islets close to. Curtis rock, a dangerous sunken rock, over which the sea breaks occasionally, lies 1 mile SW. ½ W. from Curtis point.

Strong tide rips are encountered west of Estevan island, off Otter passage.

Cox point is the NW. extreme of Estevan island. Marchant rock, over which the sea breaks at low water, lies 2 miles S. 26° W. (S. 1° E. mag.) from Cox point and 1¾ miles from the nearest coast of Estevan island.

Cone islet, small, wooded, 250 feet high, and conical, is the southernmost of the Block islets and lies at the southern entrance of Otter passage, on the western side of that channel, at 2 miles from the coast of Banks island.

Breaker islets, which lie off the SE. shore of Banks island, at 1 mile westward of Cone islet, consist of a group of islets and rocks awash, the highest islet being about 70 feet high and wooded.

Banks island is about 41 miles long, NW. and SE., and from 5 to 10 miles broad. The SE. coast is wooded and comparatively low, seldom exceeding 150 feet in height, and is broken into bays and creeks, rendered useless as anchorages by numerous rocks awash and sunken dangers.

Calamity bay, at the southeastern extreme of Banks island, is 3 miles wide at its entrance and extends 3 miles in a northerly direction; it consists of ironbound shores, with rocky islets and sunken dangers occupying the bay nearly throughout.

Terror point, the southern extreme of Banks island, is high and bold, 200 feet above high water. From its outer extreme this point slopes inland, and when first seen appears as an island. Terror rocks consist of rocks awash and sunken rocks, over which the sea breaks heavily, extending 1 mile southward from Terror point.

Shrub islet, of small extent, 80 feet high, with a conspicuous patch of bush upon its summit, lies 3 miles S. 77° W. (S. 50° W. mag.) from Terror point, and has sunken rocks surrounding it to a distance of 600 yards.

Grief point, 8 miles NW. by N. from Terror point, is low and wooded. A ledge, consisting of rocks awash and sunken dangers, extends 1½ miles SW. from Grief point.

Foul bay, between Grief and Wreck points, is 5 miles wide and 2 miles deep; it is, however, useless as an anchorage, being obstructed by islets, rocks, and sunken dangers. Junk ledge, consisting of rocks awash and ledges which uncover at low water, extends nearly 2 miles southward from Wreck point.

North Danger rocks, 7 miles southwestward of Wreck point, consist of a dangerous cluster of five bare rocks of small extent, 10 feet above high water, and surrounded by rocks awash and sunken rocks for ½ mile. The center of the cluster lies 18 miles S. 36° E. (S. 63° E. mag.) from the summit of Bonilla island.

Vessels should keep southwestward of the line joining Shrub islet and North Danger rocks, and not pass between those dangers and Banks island.

Kelp point lies 8 miles NW. from Wreck point. Kelp ledge extends 1½ miles southeastward from Kelp point. Between Wreck and Kelp points the shore of Banks island is foul to the distance of 1 mile.

Halibut rocks consist of two dangerous clusters (covered at high water) about ½ mile each in extent, lying NW. and SE., distant 1½ miles, from each other. The center of the eastern cluster lies 8 miles S. 44° E. (S. 71° E. mag.) from the summit of Bonilla island and 4¾ miles S. 7° E. (S. 34° E. mag.) from Cliff point.

Cliff point, 6 miles NW. by W. from Kelp point, terminates in high, bold, white cliffs. Three small, rocky islets lie near the shore close southeastward of the point.

South rocks consist of two clusters of rocks awash at high water, of small extent, lying north and south, distant 1 mile, from each other. The southern or outer group, over which the sea usually breaks heavily, lies 3½ miles S. 4° W. (S. 23° E. mag.) from the summit of Bonilla island.

Highwater rocks, lying nearly midway between Bonilla island and Cliff point, consist of six rocks, awash at high water, about 400 yards in extent, at 2¼ miles S. 57° E. (S. 84° E. mag.) from the summit of Bonilla island.

Bonilla island, situated 9 miles S. ½ W. from the NW. point of Banks island and 4 miles from the western coast of the island, forms an excellent landmark. The island is about 2 miles long NW. and SE. and 1 mile broad, having on its SE. shore two small bays, with some rocky islets lying off them at 400 yards from the shore. Near the center the island reaches an elevation of 550 feet, the summit being dome-shaped, falling almost perpendicularly on its northern and southern sides, but sloping gradually to the westward. During the summer months, the sides of Bonilla peak are clothed with purple-tinted heather. Landing may be effected at the head of the southern of the two bays on the SE. side of Bonilla island.

Northwest rocks are a cluster, ½ mile in extent, lying 2 miles N. 30° W. (N. 57° W. mag.) from the summit of Bonilla island; the highest rock is 3 feet above high water.

North rocks, a cluster, about ½ mile in extent, and awash at high water, lie 1½ miles S. 85° E. (N. 68° E. mag.) from the center of the NW. rocks and 2 miles N. 5° E. (N. 22° W. mag.) from the summit of Bonilla island.

Middle rocks, two clusters, awash at low water, lie respectively 1¼ miles N. 40° W. (N. 67° W. mag.) and 2 miles N. 49° E. (N. 22° E. mag.) from the summit of Bonilla island.

A rock, drying 4 feet, lies 6 miles N. 6° W. (N. 33° W. mag.) from the summit of Bonilla island.

White rocks lie close to the shore at the northwestern extreme of Banks island; the two largest rocks are about 30 feet above high water, bare and conspicuous, with several smaller rocks surrounding them, and they form an excellent landmark when making Ogden channel from Hecate strait. Anchorage for small craft in fine weather is stated to be obtainable close northeastward of White rocks at the mouth of a creek. Anchorage is also reported to exist generally off the NW. coast of Banks island.

Supplies.—Game abounds on all the offlying islands. Notwithstanding the presence of wolves, deer exist in great numbers, especially on the southern shores, which appear to be their favorite resort. Water is plentiful at all seasons, the source apparently being springs. Trout may be procured in the streams.

Berries, especially the whortleberry, cranberry, and wild raspberry, have been found in abundance during July and August.

Cedar and pitch pine are the principal woods met with.

Browning entrance, between Banks and Goschen islands, leads into Principe and Ogden channels. It is 14 miles wide between White rocks and cape George.

The tidal currents in Hecate strait meet abreast the entrance to Browning entrance.

CHAPTER XII.

CHATHAM SOUND, EDYE AND BROWN PASSAGES, AND DIXON ENTRANCE.

VARIATION IN 1906.

Lawyer islands	28° 15′ E.	Pointers rocks	28° 40′ E.
North island	28° 00′ E.	Cape Muzon	28° 25′ E

Chatham sound is an extensive sheet of water, about 38 miles long and from 7 to 14 miles wide, lying between the Tsimpsean peninsula and Stephens and Dundas islands, the northern portion of the sound washing the southern shores of Alaska.

In the middle of the southern portion are the Rachael and Lucy islands, together with other detached islets and rocks.

At the northern end of Chatham sound, nearly abreast Port Simpson, there are some clusters of low rocky islets (Connis and Pointers rocks), which render that portion of the sound dangerous to navigation under certain conditions, and divide the sound into two navigable channels (Main and Oriflamme passages).

Chatham sound communicates with Hecate strait by three channels, Edye passage, in the southwestern corner of the sound, being the channel usually taken. Brown passage, south of Dundas islands, though comparatively wide, has strong and irregular tides near its western end; and a patch of rocks, awash at high water, lies nearly in mid-channel.

Dixon entrance, the principal channel north of Dundas islands, is about 5 miles wide, and is the channel usually taken by vessels proceeding northward along the coast of Alaska.

Landmarks.—On the eastern shore, in the SE. portion of Chatham sound, mount Oldfield and mount McGrath, 2,300 and 2,220 feet high, respectively, are conspicuous.

With the exception of a cluster of bare rocks (Gull rocks) off the mouth of Edye passage, the islets in that portion of the sound are wooded and of a conspicuous, dark color.

On South Dundas island there are four conspicuous peaks, the eastern and highest of which is 1,400 feet high. Northward of Metlakatla, Mission mountain, and Deer mound, of rounded form, will be seen rising from comparatively low land to 1,310 and 2,230 feet, respectively.

Coast mound, a conspicuous hill of oval shape, 750 feet high, will be seen on Middle Dundas island; a chain of wooded islets, of a peculiarly dark color, fringe the shore of this island.

Near the NE. extreme of North Dundas island, Table hill, with a flat summit, rises 700 feet, and is conspicuous. Southwestward of Table hill, Thumb peak rises 2,500 feet. With the exception of one small islet (Green islet), the islets and rocks in the northern portion of Chatham sound are bare and conspicuous.

At 2 miles southward of Port Simpson, mount Griffin (Waverly peak), a mountain with a sharp summit, rises to 1,410 feet. Southeast of mount Griffin the ridge has several conspicuous peaks rising to nearly 3,000 feet, among which are Leading peak and Basil lump 2,200 and 2,960 feet high, respectively.

Mount McNeil, on the eastern side of Work channel, has a snow-clad summit, of conical shape, 4,300 feet high.

Dangers.—The southern portion of Chatham sound is comparatively free from danger, the rocky clusters being of considerable elevation above high water and moderately steep-to. Northward of Metlakatla bay, however, ledges which uncover at low water extend in many places 2 miles from the eastern shore. On the western side of the sound also there are several offlying, detached, sunken rocks, with deep water close to them. Abreast Port Simpson, two clusters of rocks lie in the fairway of the sound, and being but little elevated above high water, render that portion of the sound dangerous by night or in thick weather.

Caution.—Northward of Metlakatla bay, during a fog, or if uncertain of the position, the eastern shores of Chatham sound should not be approached under 70 fathoms; nor the western shores under 40 fathoms.

Anchorages.—Anchorage will be found off the northern entrance of Skeena river, in Metlakatla bay, Duncan bay, Big bay, Pearl harbor, Port Simpson, Refuge bay, and in Qlawdzeet.

Gull rocks, consisting of three principal bare rocks, about ½ mile in extent, the highest rock being about 30 feet above high water, lie off the eastern entrance of Edye passage, 3 miles NW. ½ W. from Island point (Porcher island), and 3½ miles from the nearest part of Prescott island.

Ettrick rock, a dangerous patch of small extent, which uncovers 3 feet at low water, lies 1½ miles S. 29° E. (S. 57° E. mag.) of the center of the Gull rocks.

Havelock rock, of small extent and uncovering 6 feet at low water, lies 2½ miles S. 29° E. (S. 57° E. mag.) of the center of Gull rocks and S. 82° W. (S. 54° W. mag.) from Island point. Both Ettrick and Havelock rocks have deep water close-to.

A pinnacle rock, with 6 feet of water over it, lies 900 yards N. 32° W. (N. 60° W. mag.) from Island point. This rock is marked by kelp.

Green Top rock, 15 feet high, is small, with a patch of shrub on its summit, and lies 4¼ miles N. 32° W. (N. 60° W. mag.) of the western island of the Lawyer group.

A 3-fathom shoal lies northwestward of Green Top rock, with its shoalest point (9 feet) 500 yards N. 39° W. (N. 67° W. mag.) from the top of the rock.

Holland island, small, wooded, and 10 feet high, lies 1¾ miles S. 83° E. (N. 69° E. mag.) from Green Top rock.

Grace rock, between Holland island and Green Top rock, with 4 feet least water, lies 700 yards N. 72° W. (S. 80° W. mag.) from Holland island.

Dorothy rock, between Holland island and Green Top rock, with 4 feet least water, lies N. 72° W. (S. 80° W. mag.) from Holland island and 1 mile S. 86° E. (N. 66° E. mag.) from Green Top rock.

These are apparently identical with the two 9-foot rocks shown on the charts.

Kinnahan islands, two in number, each about ½ mile long, lie close together about 2½ miles from the shore of Tsimpsean peninsula; they are wooded and about 200 feet high. The southern extreme of the western Kinnahan island lies 1¼ miles north of Green Top rock.

Marion rock, awash at high water springs, lies 500 yards from the middle of the NW. side of the west Kinnahan island.

A rock, showing at low water, lies about 200 yards off the point on the western shore of the same island.

A rock, which dries at low water, lies 1,200 yards eastward of the SE. extreme of the eastern Kinnahan island.

Kitson island, situated off the mouth of North Skeena passage, is about 400 yards in extent and lies 1½ miles E. by N. from Holland island. Shoal ground, with depths of 6 to 8 feet at ordinary low water, extends about 1,200 yards in a SSE. direction from the island; near the outer end of this shoal ground the water deepens to 3 fathoms.

The passage between Kitson island and Leer point (southern extreme of Lelu island) is navigable only by boats.

Coast island, about 300 yards in extent, lies 2 miles east of the Kinnahan islands and the same distance NNW. of Kitson island. Foul ground extends between Kitson and Coast islands and nearly ¾ mile northward and westward of the latter island. The shore northward of Leer point should not be approached nearer than 1¼ miles.

Lima point, the southern extreme of Digby island, lies nearly 2 miles NW. of Coast island. A small island lies close to the point.

A rock, which is about 50 feet long east and west, with 10 feet of water over it, lies about 1½ miles S. 80° W. (S. 52° W. mag.) of the islet off Lima point. The position of this rock is doubtful; it may be an extension of the reef of which Chassepot rock is a part.

Chassepot rock, which dries at low water, lies ¾ mile S. 87° W. (S. 59° W. mag.) from the islet off Lima point.

Kestrel rock, awash at low water springs, lies ½ mile S. 8° W. (S. 20° E. mag.) from the islet off Lima point.

The rock is marked by a small spar buoy, painted red and black in horizontal bands.

Falcon rock, with a least depth of 29 feet at ordinary springs, lies 1,550 yards S. 36° E. (S. 64° E. mag.) from the islet off Lima point.

Jenner rock, with a least depth of 26 feet, lies 1 mile S. 40° E. (S. 68° E. mag.) from the islet off Lima point.

Beacons.—Two white beacons have been erected, one on the top of Coast island, the other on the mainland eastward of it. These two beacons in line, bearing S. 76° E. (N. 76° E. mag.), leads southward of the above-described dangers.

Tuck inlet has its entrance between Lima point and Coast island, and extends in a general northerly direction for 15 miles. Its entrance is nearly 2 miles wide, but abreast the southern end of Kaien island, where Fern passage branches to the northeastward, the inlet narrows to less than 1 mile. About 4 miles northward of Lima point, Venn creek leads northwestward into Metlakatla bay. Tuck inlet has not been surveyed.

Kaien island, 6 miles long north and south and 2½ miles broad, separates Tuck inlet into two channels, that on the eastern side being known as Fern passage. Two miles from the southern extreme of the island mount Oldfield rises to a height of 2,300 feet.

These waters have not been examined and should be used only with the greatest caution. Fern passage is reported closed to navigation by a succession of rapids.

Prince Rupert harbor.—This name has recently been applied to the southern part of Tuck inlet, this being the prospective terminus of the Grand Trunk Pacific railroad.

Rachael islands, two in number, about 1 mile in extent, wooded, and about 200 feet high, lie nearly midway between the Tsimpsean peninsula and Stephens island. The southeastern extreme of the southern Rachael island lies 5 miles S. 86° W. (S. 58° W. mag.) of the southern extreme of the western Kinnahan island, and about 3¾ miles from the northernmost Gull rock.

Alexandra patch is nearly circular, 1 mile in diameter, within the depth of 20 fathoms. This bank has depths of 10 to 17 fathoms, over a bottom of mud and sand.

The eastern edge of Alexandra patch lies 1 mile N. 27° E. (N. 1° W. mag.) of the northern Rachael island. There are depths of 46 and 50 fathoms, mud, at ½ mile eastward and northward of Alexandra patch.

Lucy islands, a group of islands and high-water rocks, the large islands being wooded and the small ones bare, lie nearly in the middle of the sound abreast Metlakatla bay, and are about 1 mile in extent in an east and west direction. The summit of the eastern and largest island is 200 feet high, and lies 5¼ miles N. by W. ½ W. from the northern Rachael island. This group is of great use when making Metlakatla during thick weather, as being comparatively free from danger it may be approached (except on the southern and western sides), and, when made, the easternmost island of the group kept astern bearing S. 80° W. (S. 52° W. mag.) will lead to the entrance of Metlakatla bay.

A ledge of rocks, 1¼ miles in length in a NW. and SE. direction, which partially uncover, extends from 800 to 1,800 yards southward and southwestward of the Lucy group, the outer rock lying 1,800 yards S. 28° W. (South mag.) from the summit of the eastern island of the group. The northwestern rock dries 3 feet and lies 500 yards S. 77° W. (S. 49° W. mag.) from the nearest island of the group, and is marked by kelp.

Tsimpsean peninsula is formed by Work channel, which penetrates the mainland in a southeasterly direction, the head of the channel approaching the Skeena river within 4 or 5 miles. This peninsula (which takes its name from a tribe of Indians residing upon it) is nearly 32 miles long, in a general NW. and SE. direction, with a greatest breadth of 9 miles.

The headquarters of the tribe of Indians inhabiting this peninsula are at Metlakatla and Port Simpson.

Metlakatla bay is formed between the shore of the Tsimpsean peninsula and the NW. coast of Digby island, and is protected from the northwestward by Tugwell island and the reefs which join that island to the shore of the peninsula. The bay from its entrance takes a general northeasterly direction for 1 mile, gradually narrowing as the settlement is approached; it then turns sharply to the east and SE., the latter being known as Venn creek.

Metlakatla village, an Indian settlement, founded as a missionary station, is situated upon Mission point. The houses forming the mission are built upon an elevated bank, about 100 feet above high-water mark, and are mostly whitewashed; the whole settlement from the offing presents the appearance of a picturesque English village, the most conspicuous buildings being the church, schoolhouse, and mission house. A wharf, 400 feet in length, with a depth of 15 feet at its outer end, has been built to the southward of the village, about 200 yards westward from Mission point.

Tugwell island lies about 2 miles westward of Metlakatla village, and those desirous of communicating with that place usually anchor off the eastern side of the island, or off its northeastern side in Duncan bay, according to circumstances. Tugwell island is about 1¼ miles long, in a north and south direction, with an average breadth of ½ mile, and is fringed by dangerous rocky ground, marked by kelp, especially on its southeastern side. It is wooded (the tops of the trees being about 200 feet high), and is connected at low water with Observation point, ⅜ mile westward of Mission point.

A black spar buoy, in 3½ fathoms, marks the SE. side of Tugwell Island reef, with Dawes point NW., distant 1,200 yards.

Dawes rock, awash at low water, lies 800 yards S. 55° W. (S. 27° W. mag.) from the southern extreme of Tugwell island (Dawes point). Between Dawes rock and Dawes point large bowlder rocks uncover at low water and extend along the western side of Tugwell island, generally marked by kelp.

Enfield rock has 5 fathoms on it and lies 1 mile S. 60° W. (S. 32° W. mag.) from the southern extreme of Tugwell island, with foul ground between.

Caution.—Vessels should pass westward of Enfield rock, in not less than 10 fathoms, at low water.

Alford reefs are a dangerous cluster of rocks, about 600 yards in extent east and west, lying at the entrance of Metlakatla bay. The eastern rock, which uncovers 2 feet at low water, lies 1,200 yards N. 29° W. (N. 57° W. mag.) from Quartermaster rock.

A red buoy, can, is moored in 6 fathoms 100 yards from the western end of these reefs.

The southern extreme of the large Cridge island, in line with Quartermaster rock, bearing S. 71° E. (N. 81° E. mag.), will lead southward of the reefs; the summit of Knight island kept midway between Pike and Shrub islands, bearing N. 52° E. (N. 24° E. mag.), will lead northwestward of them.

Cutch rock, with 1½ fathoms over it, lies ¾ mile S. 34° W. (S. 6° W. mag.) from the center of Knight island. It is not marked by kelp.

Quartermaster rock, a small black rock, 2 feet above high water, lies 800 yards N. 74° W. (S. 78° W. mag.) from the southern extreme of the large Cridge island. A rock, which uncovers 1 foot at low water, lies 300 yards S. 27° W. (S. 1° E. mag.) from Quartermaster rock. Midge rock, which uncovers at low water, lies ½ mile N. ½ E. from the small Cridge island.

Cridge islands, two in number, lie at the SE. entrance of Metlakatla bay; the eastern and larger island is 150 feet high, and lies

400 yards from the eastern shore of the bay (Digby island). The western island is small, 100 feet high, and lies 400 yards N. 73° W. (S. 79° W. mag.) from the southern extreme of the larger Cridge island. Both islands are wooded.

Devastation island lies almost in the center of the bay ½ mile eastward of Tugwell island, and is nearly ⅓ mile long, NE. and SW., and 200 yards broad. The island is wooded, 150 feet high, and two rocky islets lie close in to its SW. extreme; from the northern extreme of this island, a shoal, portions of which uncover at low water, extends ½ mile eastward.

Knight island, barely 10 feet high, small, with stunted scrub upon it, lies 800 yards S. 55° E. (S. 83° E. mag.) from the northern extreme of Devastation island. Armour rock, with 9 feet of water over it, lies S. 4° E. (S. 32° E. mag.), distant 200 yards, from Knight island.

Pike island, 100 feet high and wooded, is about ⅓ mile long NE. and SW., and its southern extreme lies 1,400 yards S. 84° E. (N. 68° E. mag.) from the northern end of Devastation island.

Carr islet, small, about 60 feet high, lies ½ mile N. 38° E. (N. 10° E. mag.) from the northern extreme of Devastation island, and is connected at low water with the spit which joins Tugwell island and Observation point.

Shattered reef.—Straith point, the southeastern point of Metlakatla bay, is fringed for nearly 300 yards offshore by a rocky ledge. Foul ground extends from its northern side for nearly 700 yards.

Shrub islet, 300 yards from the northern side of Pike island, is of small extent and low. A shoal, the outer portion of which uncovers at low water, extends nearly 400 yards from the northern side of Shrub islet, and is the outer portion of a bank of sand with patches of rock upon it, which connects Pike, Shrub, Gribbell, and Isabel islands at low water.

A small, square, stone beacon, surmounted by a staff and ball painted red, 8 feet above high water, stands on the end of the rocky ledge, 300 yards N. by W. ½ W. from Shrub islet. This beacon should not be approached nearer than 70 feet.

Kelp rock, a dangerous sunken rock, with another smaller rock 250 yards ENE. ½ E. from it, lies nearly midway between Shrub islet and Observation point, about 400 yards from each. The navigable channel between Shrub islet and Observation point is contracted by Kelp rock to barely 100 yards in width at low water; the channel is southward of the rock.

A black platform buoy, with pyramidal slatwork top surmounted by a drum, is moored close eastward of Kelp rock on the north side of the channel.

Gribbell island, situated on the south side of the channel leading into Venn creek, is about the same size as Shrub islet, from which it is distant ½ mile in a NE. direction. A small rocky islet lies about 100 yards off the northern side of Gribbell island.

Isabel island lies 300 yards NE. from the summit of Gribbell island, and 350 yards SSW. from Mission point.

A dangerous sunken rock, with 2¼ fathoms over it, lies in the center of the channel leading from Metlakatla bay to Venn creek, about 200 yards N. 68° W. (S. 84° W. mag.) from Isabel island.

A small isolated rock, with less than 6 feet over it, lies N. 47° W. (N. 75° W. mag.) 200 yards from Isabel island.

A black platform buoy, with pyramidal slatwork top surmounted by a drum, is moored close westward of the rock.

Venn creek takes a southeasterly direction from Mission point; it is only suitable for small vessels. There are several fishing stations upon the shores of this creek, in which the Indians obtain salmon. Venn creek at its head connects with the unexplored Oldfield basin (Tuck inlet), east of Digby island, which extends southward, connecting with Malacca and North Skeena passages.

Anchorage will be found in 11 to 12 fathoms, mud bottom, 600 yards off the northwestern side of Devastation island, with the southern extreme of Devastation island seen in line with the smaller Cridge island, bearing S. 6° E. (S. 34° E. mag.), and the southern extreme of Carr islet seen in line with the flagstaff on Mission point, bearing N. 70° E. (N. 42° E. mag.).

Small vessels occasionally proceed into Venn creek and anchor off Metlakatla village, in 10 to 12 fathoms, with the flagstaff on Mission point bearing N. 74° W. (S. 78° W. mag.), distant 600 to 800 yards. The channel into this anchorage is barely 60 yards wide at low water, when the dangers on either side indicate themselves, but the passage should only be attempted by short vessels of light draft, and at all times it would be well to place boats upon the rock which lies westward of Isabel island, and likewise on Kelp rock and the small rock 250 yards northeastward of it, should the buoys marking those dangers not be in position, and they can not be depended on.

Directions.—Approaching Metlakatla from the southward, if the Lawyer group of islands be kept in line with Green Top rock bearing S. 34° E. (S. 62° E. mag.), that mark astern will lead directly to the entrance of Metlakatla bay.

During a fog or in thick weather, when approaching Metlakatla from the southeastward, do not shoal the water to less than 40 fathoms, and on such occasions the Lucy islands should be cautiously steered for and sighted, taking care to avoid the reefs which extend from the south and SW. sides of the group. The large or eastern Lucy island should be brought to bear S. 80° W. (S. 52° W. mag.)

astern, and a N. 80° E. (N. 52° E. mag.) course should take a vessel to the entrance of **Metlakatla bay.** The bank of 10 fathoms (and less) extends 1 mile southward of Tugwell island, and the hand lead (if proceeding slowly) should indicate the position. During summer and autumn large quantities of kelp mark this bank.

To enter, Knight island kept midway between Shrub and Pike islands, bearing N. 52° E. (N. 24° E. mag.), leads into the bay, between Tugwell island and Alford reefs, in 25 fathoms.

Carr islet, just shut in with the western extreme of Devastation island, bearing N. 38° E. (N. 10° E. mag.), will lead southeastward of the foul ground off the southeastern part of Tugwell island. The southern extreme of the large Cridge island seen in line with Quartermaster rock, and touching the northern extreme of the small Cridge island bearing S. 71° E. (N. 81° E. mag.), will lead southward of Alford reefs and the dangers off Tugwell island.

Auriol point, just open north of Shrub islet, bearing N. 78° E. (N. 50° E. mag.), leads between the foul ground southward of Carr island and the ledge extending from the northern extreme of Devastation island, and when Ryan point comes open east of Carr island bearing N. 12° W. (N. 40° W. mag.) a course may be steered as requisite for Venn creek.

A vessel should at all times use the channel westward of Alford reefs, which is buoyed, and not navigate eastward of those reefs.

Tides.—It is high water, full and change, at Metlakatla at 0 h. 0 m.; springs rise 21 feet, neaps 17 feet.

Duncan bay, on the NE. side of Tugwell island, affords anchorage when desirous of communicating with Metlakatla during the prevalence of southeasterly winds.

The entrance to this bay between the northern extreme of Tugwell island and Ryan point is about 1¾ miles wide; the bay takes a southeasterly direction for about 1½ miles, terminating in the sand spit which connects Tugwell island and Tsimpsean peninsula (Observation point) at low water.

A shoal, with 3 fathoms (and probably less) water upon it, extends ½ mile northward of Tugwell island. Ledges, which uncover, and sunken rocks extend nearly ¾ mile from the northern shore of Duncan bay.

Hecate rock, with 10 feet of water on it, lies near the head of Duncan bay, 600 yards from the eastern shore and ½ mile N. 52° W. (N. 80° W. mag.) from Observation point.

Directions.—If desirous of anchoring in Duncan bay, pass 1 mile northwestward of Tugwell island, and when the southern extreme of Gribbell island is seen just open of Observation point, bearing S. 57° E. (S. 85° E. mag.), that mark should be steered for; a berth should be taken up on that bearing, in 8 to 10 fathoms, mud, with Chapman point, the northern extreme of Tugwell island, bearing S. 83° W. (S. 55° W. mag.).

Tree bluff, the southern entrance point of Big bay, lies 5 miles north from Ryan point, the northern entrance point of Duncan bay. The shore northward of Ryan point is low and wooded for 3 miles back from the coast, where it rises into high land. Two streams enter the sound on this part of the coast, and there are two islets lying close to the shore, respectively 1 and 2 miles northward of Ryan point. The former (Swamp islet) is covered with low grass and lies about ½ mile from the shore. The latter islet (Slippery rock) is bare and about 800 yards from the shore.

Immediately southward of Tree bluff there is a wooded hill close to the shore, 250 feet high.

Between Metlakatla and Big bays dangerous ledges extend offshore in many places to the distance of 2 miles. These ledges uncover at low water and are steep-to. Abreast Tree bluff the edge of the bank, which dries at low water, lies 1½ miles from the shore.

Hodgson reefs, a dangerous cluster, lie northward of Duncan bay; their southern part covers at half flood and lies 2 miles N. by W. ½ W. from the northern extreme of Tugwell island and 1½ miles WNW. from Ryan point. From that position dangerous sunken rocks extend in a northerly direction for 2 miles.

A black can buoy is moored in 9½ fathoms, about 700 yards westward of the southern part of the reef, with Ryan point bearing SE. by E. ½ E., distant 2$\frac{2}{10}$ miles.

The western side of Kinnahan islands, showing just clear of the southern end of Tugwell island bearing S. 26° E. (S. 54° E. mag.), leads westward of Hodgson reefs; and the eastern island of the Lucy group should not be brought to bear west of S. 17° W. (S. 11° E. mag.) (astern) until mount Griffin (over Port Simpson) is seen in line with the northern end of Burnt-cliff island N. 44° E. (N. 16° E. mag.); this mark leads westward of all dangers off the entrance to Big bay.

Big bay (Lakhou), the entrance to which, between Tree bluff and South island, is 2½ miles wide, takes an easterly direction for 3½ miles. At its head, which is skirted by a sand flat which dries about ½ mile from the shore at low water, several streams flow into the bay; this part is known as Salmon River bight.

There is confined anchorage southward of Swallow island at the head of Big bay in 4 fathoms, but the space is nowhere more than 600 yards across. The anchorage mark is the shipbuilding shed just showing along the bank of the river. The little rock, 1 foot high, on the southern edge of Swallow Island ledge, is a good guide when entering at high water.

Georgetown is a settlement on the banks of the river eastward of Swallow island. Two steam vessels, of 150 and 60 tons, have already been built. Mail steamers call and anchor in the 4-fathom bight.

South island, situated at the NW. entrance of Big bay, is small and wooded, with a sharp summit, 150 feet high, and connected with the mainland by foul ground, dry at low water, and 1 mile in width. A ledge of sunken rocks, with depths of 6 to 12 feet, extend ½ mile SW. by S. from the SW. side of South island.

Haycock island lies 600 yards SE. by E. ½ E. from the summit of South island. A sand bank, about 200 yards in extent, with 2 fathoms least water, lies about 500 yards S. 17° W. (S. 11° E. mag.) from Haycock island.

White Cliff island lies 1,800 yards SE. by E. from Haycock island; it is small and terminates in high, white, conspicuous cliffs. Shattock point, 600 yards eastward of White Cliff island, is the NW. entrance point of Salmon River bight.

A shoal, with a least depth of 30 feet, lies southeastward of South island; from the shoal Sharp peak, in line with the southern extreme of Shallow island, bears S. 73° E. (N. 79° E. mag.), and the summit of Haycock island N. 5° W. (N. 33° W. mag.), distant 1,100 yards.

A shoal, with a least depth of 18 feet on its northwestern extreme, lies 1,450 yards N. 30° W. (N. 58° W. mag.) from Reeks point, with Shattock point bearing N. 63° E. (N. 35° E. mag.).

A shoal, with a least depth of 28 feet, lies near the middle of Big bay, with Reeks point bearing S. 27° W. (S. 1° E. mag.), distant 1 mile, and Curlew rock S. 64° E. (N. 88° E. mag.).

Swallow island lies 1 mile SE. by E. from White Cliff island and 200 yards from the northern shore. Curlew rock is small, about 2 feet above high water, and lies ½ mile SSW. ½ W. from Swallow island, on the southern side of the anchorage.

Ripple bank, at the entrance to Big bay, is about 400 yards in extent in an ESE. and WNW. direction; the shoalest spot, near the eastern end, having 12 feet of water over it, sandy bottom, lies 1$\frac{1}{10}$ miles S. 47° W. (S. 19° W. mag.) from the summit of South island. This bank is usually indicated by tide rips.

Escape reefs are a dangerous cluster at the entrance to Big bay, southeastward of Ripple bank. The outer or western reef has 4 feet least water over it and lies 1$\frac{4}{10}$ miles S. 35° W. (S. 7° W. mag.) from the summit of South island. The eastern reef has 5 feet least water over it and lies ½ mile east from the western one. There are depths of 16 and 17 fathoms between these reefs. During the season kelp grows in great quantities upon Escape reefs and near the head of Big bay.

Anchorage will be found in Big bay, in 11 and 12 fathoms, mud, with Haycock island in line with the northern extreme of South island bearing N. 40° W. (N. 68° W. mag.), and White Cliff island in line with mount Griffin bearing N. 13° E. (N. 15° W. mag.).

Directions.—Approaching Big bay from the southward mount Griffin should be kept in line with the northern extreme of Burnt-cliff island N. 44° E. (N. 16° E. mag.) until Sharp peak on the ridge SE. of mount Griffin is in line with the southern end of Swallow island bearing S. 73° E. (N. 79° E. mag.); the latter mark will lead directly into Big bay; anchor with Sharp peak open south of Swallow island, in the position and depth above given. This range (Sharp peak and Swallow island) leads across the shoal, with 30 feet over it, that lies S. 5° E. (S. 33° E. mag.) from Haycock island.

To avoid this shoal take the passage south of Escape reefs, and bring Basil lump (2,690 feet high, NNE. of Shattock point) exactly in line with the 200-foot hill over Shattock point, bearing N. 68° E. (N. 40° E. mag.). This leads between Escape reefs and the 18-foot shoal northwestward of Reeks point.

Burnt-cliff island, situated northward of South island, is about ½ mile long north and south and wooded, its highest point near its northern end being 200 feet high. The northern extreme of this island terminates in high red-brown cliffs; the NE. extreme is cultivated, and from that point a long bank of shingle, awash at high water, extends 600 yards eastward. The whole space inshore of South and Burnt-cliff islands uncovers at low water.

A ledge, which uncovers at low water, extends 600 yards northward from the northern extreme of Burnt-cliff island. The channel between Burnt-cliff and One Tree islands is available only for boats.

One Tree island, 800 yards northward of Burnt-cliff island, is of small extent, with a sharp wooded summit 150 feet high. A low grassy point extends 100 yards in a northerly direction from the northern extreme of One Tree island, at the extremity of which a high, conspicuous, solitary tree was standing in 1868. One Tree island forms the southern point of entrance to Cunningham passage, and the western shelter of Pearl harbor.

A ledge, which uncovers at low water, surrounds One Tree island; its greatest distance from the shore being 500 yards in a northerly direction from the single tree.

Flat-top islands, a group lying NE. of One Tree island, consist of three wooded islands lying NE. and SW. of each other. The middle and largest island of the group is connected by a narrow grassy neck with the northern island and the latter has a flat summit, covered (in July) with long grass; also a single stunted tree growing upon it (1868). The southernmost and smallest Flat-top island lies 700 yards NE. ½ N. from the tree on One Tree island.

Ledges, which uncover at low water, and foul ground surround the Flat-top group for a distance of 300 yards.

Finlayson island, the largest in this locality, is 2½ miles long north and south and 1 mile broad, 200 feet high, and wooded. The southern extreme of the island terminates in cliffs; but the northern extreme (Gordon point) is long and comparatively low, with ledges which uncover extending 400 yards northward; on the NW. side of the island, and about ½ mile from the western extreme, is a large stream.

Red Cliff point, on the eastern side of Cunningham passage, ½ mile ENE. from Fortune point, the southern extreme of Finlayson island, is rendered conspicuous by the high red-brown cliffs over it and the small islet close-to. Immediately SE. of the point there is a bay, with a sandy beach, and a stream at its head.

Pearl harbor, situated eastward of One Tree island, is nearly circular in shape, and ½ mile across; on the eastern side is a bay which dries nearly throughout at low water. On its southern side, the high bank of shingle which extends from the NE. point of Burnt-cliff island effectually shelters the harbor from southerly winds.

Anchorage.—Good anchorage will be found in 9 to 10 fathoms, mud bottom, near the middle of Pearl harbor, with Fortune point seen just open eastward of the southernmost island of Flat-top group, bearing N. 14° W. (N. 43° W. mag.), and the tree on One Tree island, N. 83° W. (S. 68° W. mag.), distant 600 yards.

Otter anchorage, situated at the southern end of Cunningham passage, near the eastern shore, northward of Flat-top islands, is useful if communicating with the wood-cutting establishment abreast it.

Anchorage in 15 to 17 fathoms, sand, will be found with the center of the wood-cutting establishment in line with Leading peak, bearing S. 74° E. (N. 77° E. mag.), and the northernmost Flat-top island (Green mound) S. 18° W. (S. 11° E. mag.), distant 300 yards.

The wood-cutting establishment, from which the principal supplies for Port Simpson are obtained, is situated near the middle of a sandy bay, the northern point of the bay terminating in cliffs. The bay dries nearly throughout at low water.

From Otter anchorage there is a passage eastward of Flat-top islands into Pearl harbor, but this is not recommended to a stranger. A shoal, with 21 feet on it, lies South (S. 29° E. mag.) from Red Cliff point and 290 yards S. 87° E. (N. 64° E. mag.) from Green mound.

Sparrowhawk rock, a dangerous, sunken, pinnacle rock, on which is 5 feet of water, lies nearly ½ mile N. 12° W. (N. 41° W. mag.) from the tree on One Tree island, and nearly in mid-channel, between One Tree and Finlayson islands; it is steep-to, there being depths of 10 and 12 fathoms at 50 feet from it.

Sparrowhawk rock is marked by a steel can buoy, colored black and red in horizontal stripes.

Leading peak, a well-defined peak of triangular shape (the first to the SE. on the ridge from mount Griffin), in line with the northern extreme of Green mound, the northernmost islet of the Flat-top group, bearing S. 79° E. (N. 72° E. mag.), or that peak seen just open southward of the wood-cutting establishment abreast Otter anchorage, S. 77° E. (N. 74° E. mag.), will lead northward of Sparrowhawk rock.

Dodd rock lies a little over 400 yards SSW. ½ W. from Fortune point (Finlayson island); ledges which dry connect it with that point. Dodd rock only covers at the highest equinoctial tides, and is therefore a useful mark when entering Cunningham passage, as there is deep water a short distance southward of the rock.

Leading peak seen just open southward of the wood-cutting establishment abreast Otter anchorage, bearing S. 77° E. (N. 74° E. mag.), will lead southward of Dodd rock.

Directions.—Approaching Cunningham passage, Red Cliff point should be steered for in line with Fortune point, bearing N. 72° E. (N. 43° E. mag.), until Leading peak is seen in line with the northern Flat-top island (Green mound), bearing S. 79° E. (N. 72° E. mag.), when the latter mark should be steered for. When the western side of Burnt-cliff island is seen open eastward of the tree on One Tree islet, bearing South (S. 29° E. mag.), a vessel will be eastward of Sparrowhawk rock; and, if bound to Port Simpson, may haul to the northward into Cunningham passage.

If bound into Pearl harbor, a mid-channel course from the abovementioned position should be shaped between One Tree islet and the southernmost Flat-top island. Belletti and Shattock points, two conspicuous wooded points on the eastern shore, should be kept in line, bearing S. 29° E. (S. 58° E. mag.), when entering Pearl harbor.

Cunningham passage, eastward of Finlayson island, between it and the Tsimpsean peninsula, lies in a north and south direction. The southern portion of this channel is barely 700 yards wide; but northward of Sarah point (the eastern extreme of Finlayson island) the passage widens, attaining, between One Tree islet and Gordon point, a width of 1¼ miles. The depths in mid-channel are 16 to 36 fathoms.

A shoal, with a least depth of 24 feet over it, and 10 fathoms close-to all round, lies nearly in mid-channel in Cunningham passage, between Red Cliff and Fortune points. From the shoal the islet off Red Cliff point bears N. 78° E. (N. 49° E. mag.), distant 440 yards.

A shoal, with a least depth of 21 feet over it and 10 fathoms all round, lies 500 yards S. 30° W. (S. 1° W. mag.) from the islet off Red Cliff point and S. 83° E. (N. 68° E. mag.) from Fortune point.

Village island, at the SW. entrance of Port Simpson, at about 200 yards from the shore, with which it is connected at half tide, is about ½ mile long NW. and SE.; its southern side forms a bay, and following the trend of that bay and round the southern extreme of the island, the houses of one of the Tsimpsean Indian villages will be seen. Village island near its NW. extreme is about 50 feet high, having on it a high pole.

One Tree islet is about 100 yards long east and west, covered with stunted trees, lying close to the NW. extreme of Village island.

The shoal extending northward from Village island has a depth of 12 feet at a point situated 240 yards N. 31° E. (N. 2° E. mag.) from the western extreme of One Tree island, with the pierhead bearing S. 47½° E. (S. 76½° E. mag.).

Birnie island, at the north entrance of Port Simpson, is ¾ mile long NNE. and SSW. and a little over 400 yards broad, its greatest elevation, 330 feet, being near the middle of the island. The shores of this island are comparatively bold and unbroken. Knox point, the south extreme of Birnie island, lies 1¾ miles NNE. ½ E. from Finlayson island. Ledges which uncover at low water extend 200 yards from Knox point.

Light.—On Knox point is exhibited a fixed white light (unwatched), elevated 65 feet above high water, and visible in clear weather from a distance of 10 miles from the bearing of S. 38° E. (S. 67° E. mag.), through East and North, to N. 46° W. (N. 75° W. mag.).

Port Simpson, the most spacious harbor on this part of the coast, is nearly 1½ miles wide at its entrance between One Tree islet and Birnie island; thence it takes a southeasterly direction for about 3½ miles, contracting gradually as the head is approached, and terminating in a narrow bight, named Stumaun bay, which dries across at low water. At its head are several streams, where salmon are caught. The northeastern shore of the port is fringed with a rocky beach, compact and backed by rapidly rising high land. The southern shore is not so regular nor so steep-to, the rocks which dry at low water, near the eastern part of the bay, extending from high-water mark in some places for the distance of nearly ⅓ mile. Coal has been found here.

Port Simpson embraces over 4 square miles of water, from 4 to 20 fathoms deep, with muddy bottom, good holding ground, and free from rocks and shoals. It is easy of access from the sea, having no strong tidal streams, and well sheltered from all winds except the west, which here seldom blows. The prevailing winds are from SW. and NW., from which the harbor is perfectly protected.

Fort Simpson was formed by the Hudson Bay Company in 1831 as a trading post, on account of the good anchorage found in its vicinity and the facilities afforded to sailing vessels. The walls and bastions of the fort have been taken down, but the trading store and factor's house remain. The store stands near the SW. entrance point of the bay, close to the beach. A large entry gate faces the beach with a landing jetty of stones in front of it. A pier extends from the fort about north to the low-water edge of the beach.

There is a hospital here, post-office, two churches, and a station of the Provincial Constabulary.

The Canadian Pacific Navigation Company's steamers call fortnightly. Fresh meat and vegetables can be procured in moderate quantities.

Anchorage.—The usual anchorage is off the fort, in about 10 fathoms, mud bottom; a good berth being with Parkin island, seen just open eastward of Birnie island, bearing N. 17° W. (N. 46° W. mag.), and Gordon point, the NW. extreme of Finlayson island, in line with One Tree islet, N. 85° W. (S. 66°W. mag.).

Hankin reefs form a dangerous cluster, which partially uncovers, situated SW. of Village island. The SW. extreme of these reefs uncovers 6 feet at low water and lies a little over 600 yards S. 61° W. (S. 32° W. mag.) from the NW. extreme of Village island.

A shoal, 300 yards long north and south and 125 yards wide within the 5-fathom curve, lies southwestward of Hankin reefs. From the shoal the western extreme of One Tree islet bears N. 45½° E. (N. 16½° E. mag.), distant 800 yards. This shoal has a least depth of 12 feet. Depths of 15 and 18 feet lie to the southward and westward of this shoal, with the western extreme of One Tree islet bearing, respectively, N. 42° E. (N. 13° E. mag.), distant 900 yards, and N. 51° E. (N. 22° E. mag.), distant 900 yards.

The western extreme of the middle Flat-top island in line with the tangent to the land at Sarah point, bearing S. 4° W. (S. 25° E. mag.), leads westward of this shoal and Hankin reefs.

A platform buoy with pyramidal slatwork top, painted red, is moored in 8 fathoms of water, northward of Hankin reefs.

Harbor reefs, awash at high water, form a natural breakwater to Port Simpson, protecting the anchorage from NW. winds. This sunken plateau is about 1 square mile in extent within the depth of 5 fathoms. The SE. portion of these reefs only covers at the highest tides and lies 500 yards NW. ½ N. from One Tree islet.

A conical buoy, painted red, is moored in 6 fathoms off the northern extreme of the reefs.

A narrow rocky tongue extends in a southerly direction from the eastern ledge of Harbor reefs. On its southern extreme there is a depth of 12 feet, with the NW. extreme of One Tree islet bearing S. 81° E. (N. 70° E. mag.), distant 500 yards.

A black spar buoy is moored 100 yards northward of this shoal; it does not correctly mark this danger.

A shoal, with 18 feet on its southern end, lies with Birnie Island lighthouse bearing N. 5° W. (N. 34° W. mag.) and the northern end of One Tree islet S. 84° E. (N. 67° E. mag.), distant 1,300 yards. This shoal marks the southern limit of the western ledge of Harbor reefs.

A rocky head, with 24 feet least water, lies westward of Harbor reefs with Birnie Island lighthouse bearing N. 8° E. (N. 21° W. mag.) and the northern end of One Tree islet S. 57½° E. (S. 86½° E. mag.), distant 2,140 yards.

Lizzie hill seen well open southward of Birnie island, bearing N. 72° E. (N. 43° E. mag), leads northwestward, and Parkin island seen open of the eastern extreme of Birnie island, bearing N. 17° W. (N. 46° W. mag.), leads eastward of Harbor reefs.

Dodd passage lies between One Tree islet and Harbor reefs, and is 400 yards wide, with depths of 6 to 8 fathoms in it. This is available for small vessels, but local knowledge is necessary.

A shoal, with a least depth of 18 feet, 200 yards long east and west, lies in the middle of Dodd passage. Its eastern extremity is 380 yards S. 79½° W. (S. 50½° W. mag.), and its western extreme 480 yards S. 89° W. (S. 60° W. mag.), from the northern extreme of One Tree islet.

A small rocky head, with a least depth of 24 feet, lies in the middle of the eastern entrance of Dodd passage, with the northern extreme of One Tree islet bearing S. 19° W. (S. 10° E. mag.), distant 440 yards.

Anchorage patch, with 18 feet of water, sandy bottom, lies in the western portion of the anchorage ground off Fort Simpson, with the fort gate bearing S. 24° E. (S. 53° E. mag.) and the pole on the NW. extreme of Village island S. 72° W. (S. 43° W. mag.), distant 300 yards.

A rocky head, with a least depth of 12 feet, lies just northward of Anchorage patch, 460 yards N. 85° E. (N. 56° E. mag.) from the northern end of One Tree islet.

A rocky ledge, drying 2 feet, and 150 yards long east and west, lies in the approach to Stumaun bay. From its eastern end Lizzie hill bears North (N. 29° W. mag.) and Bath point S. 84° W. (S. 55° W. mag.), distant ½ mile.

Choked passage, situated northeastward of Birnie island, has several ledges which uncover and sunken dangers with deep water between them. This passage should not be attempted except in boats, and when using it keep near the northern shore.

Inskip passage, the northern and principal entrance into Port Simpson, is a little over ½ mile wide, and should invariably be used by a stranger. The depths in this channel are from 11 to 20 fathoms.

Directions.—Approaching Port Simpson from the southward by Cunningham passage, follow the directions already given for entering the southern end of the passage. When the western side of Burnt-cliff island is seen open eastward of One Tree islet, bearing South (S. 29° E. mag.), steer for the islet off Red Cliff point, course N. 48° E. (N. 19° E. mag.). When the NW. extreme of Burnt-cliff island comes open eastward of the SW. Flat-top island, bearing S. 16° W. (S. 13° E. mag.), haul to the northward and gradually bring the southwestern Flat-top in line with the NW. extreme of Burnt-cliff island, bearing S. 13° W. (S. 16° E. mag.). This mark on astern will lead through the passage until abreast Sarah point, when the mark for leading westward of Hankin reefs should be brought on astern. When the northern extreme of One Tree islet bears East (N. 61° E. mag.), alter course for Dodd passage.

If not wishing to enter by Dodd passage, when abreast Sarah point, bring that point in line with the southern point of a bay on the eastern shore of Cunningham passage, bearing S. 20° E. (S. 49° E. mag.) (astern), which mark will lead SW. of the Harbor reefs, midway between that danger and Finlayson island.

Entering Port Simpson by Inskip passage, Lizzie hill (on the northern shore) well open southward of Birnie island bearing N. 72° E. (N. 43° E. mag.) will lead 400 yards south of that island and 600 yards north of the Harbor reefs. When Parkin island is seen just open eastward of Birnie island, bearing N. 17° W. (N. 46° W. mag.), that mark kept on astern will lead up to the anchorage, in the depth and position before mentioned.

Indian villages.—Before the Hudson Bay post was built the villages of the Tsimpsean Indians were at Metlakatla, but the tribe being great traders, as well as hunters, traveling long distances inland, they naturally migrated nearer the trading post. They have therefore settled along the beach on either side of the fort and upon an island close opposite. Village island was formerly only connected with the main at half tide, but the Indians have constructed a trestle bridge, about 600 feet long and from 15 to 20 feet high, connecting the island and the main (Hay point).

Supplies.—Wood, water, potatoes, and stores of nearly every description can be obtained in Port Simpson.

Repairs.—The great rise and fall of tide at Port Simpson permits a vessel to be beached. A good site will be found for this purpose just westward of the fort. The bottom consists of hard sand with a covering of weeds.

Tides and tidal streams.—It is high water at Port Simpson at (approx.) 0 h. 14 m. after the moon's meridian passage; springs rise 22 feet, neaps 16 feet.

Chatham sound has very little tidal stream, not more than 1 knot. A strong stream sets out of Nass and Work channels in Chatham sound and then flows out through Dixon entrance between Dundas islands and Alaska, at the rate of about 2½ knots an hour.

Deviation.—For swinging to ascertain the deviation of the compass in Port Simpson, Table hill on Dundas island, 12 miles distant, is conspicuous. The bearing of the knob at the northern end of Table hill, from the anchorage in Port Simpson, is N. 76° 00′ W. (true).

Parkin islands lie close together, about 200 yards in extent NNW. and SSE.; though small, they are 250 feet high, wooded, and conspicuous. The southern extreme of Parkin islands lies about 1¼ miles N. 15° W. (N. 44° W. mag.) from the northern extreme of Birnie island and 1,200 yards from the nearest shore (Black point).

Maskelyne point, the SW. entrance point of Portland inlet and the NW. entrance point of Work channel, lies 3 miles S. by E. from Wales point.

Work channel, the entrance to which lies close northward of Maskelyne point, is a nearly straight arm stretching in a southeasterly direction for about 30 miles, the head reaching within 4 or 5 miles of the Skeena river; about 9 miles from the head a narrow arm, Quottun inlet, branches off, from the eastern side of the channel, in a northerly and easterly direction, and extends for about 9 miles. Its shores are bold and compact and surrounded by high, precipitous mountains.

Trail bay is situated on the westerly shore 6 miles from the entrance of the channel, and Trail Bay cove, on the western side of the bay, is small, and has a good anchorage in 9 fathoms.

Two miles southeastward of Grace point, a rock just visible at low water lies in the center of the channel. It is described as having a very small top with a depth of 130 fathoms close to it.

There is indifferent anchorage at the head of the main inlet in 35 fathoms, 400 yards from low-water mark.

The tidal streams at the entrance of Work channel run about 3 knots.

WEST SHORE OF CHATHAM SOUND.

Prescott and Stephens islands lie in the southwestern part of Chatham sound and are separated by a narrow passage which dries across at the southern end and is available only for boats. These islands together are about 12 miles long NW. and SE. Prescott island has an elevation of 820 feet.

Stephens island (Skiakl) attains an elevation of 1,340 feet near its eastern end; its southwestern shores are comparatively low, with some white cliffs near the center.

White Cliff point has several rocks off the SE. side of it; the outermost is 3 feet high, the inner ones awash. The extreme of White Cliff point is an islet which at high water looks from the eastward like two islets, each with some trees on the top.

Skiakl bay entrance is about 1 mile westward from White Cliff point; this bay has not been examined and appears to be foul.

Butler cove, 3 miles eastward from White Cliff point and lying between Joyce and Stephens islands, affords good, though limited, anchorage for small vessels in 12 fathoms, a little above the rock on the north side of the cove, which is always visible.

Rod islet, thickly wooded, lies off the southern point of Joyce island, and between it and the entrance to Butler cove are four rocks, the outer awash at low water, the others just showing at high water; the western of the rocks above water, well shut in of the western point of Joyce island, will clear the rock awash.

Tree-nob groups are a mass of islands, islets, and rocks awash at low water, which extend 6 miles in a northwesterly direction from the northern end of Stephens island. The larger islets are wooded and the smaller bare.

Arthur island, about 1¾ miles long east and west and about 200 feet high, lies on the southern side of Prescott island, from which it is separated by a narrow passage with several rocks in it; this passage should only be used by boats. Foul ground extends off the southeastern side of the island to the distance of 600 yards.

William and Henry islands lie close off the NW. side of Porcher island and south of Edye passage.

Edye passage, on the southern side of Prescott and Stephens islands, is the channel usually taken when communicating between Chatham sound and Hecate strait, as, by using it, vessels avoid the strong and irregular tides met with in Brown passage. It is over ½ mile wide in the narrowest part, between Porcher island and Prescott and Arthur islands, where it turns to the northward, with depths of from 12 to 40 fathoms in mid-channel. It is comparatively free from danger, and at its eastern end possesses an excellent anchorage (Refuge bay), in which a vessel may await a favorable opportunity for proceeding.

Caution.—The western approaches to Edye passage have not been surveyed; until they are examined vessels are recommended to avoid their use. If it be necessary to enter Edye passage proceed southward and eastward of Seal rocks.

Porcher island.—Approaching Edye passage from the southward, Oval hill, 630 feet high, near the western extreme of Porcher island, is conspicuous, and 2 miles northeastward of that hill lies Flat hill, 170 feet high. At 3 miles southward of the former the western shore of Porcher island terminates in high white cliffs.

The western side of Porcher peninsula has several rocks awash and sunken rocks extending 1 mile off it in a westerly direction.

Bass rock, 30 feet high, situated close to the shore of Porcher island under Oval hill, is small and bare.

A rocky ledge, with depths of 4 to 8 fathoms upon it, extends westward nearly 4 miles from the western side of Porcher peninsula, in the vicinity of Bass rock.

Goschen island, on the northern part of which is situated Nubble mountain, 1,400 feet high, is separated from Porcher peninsula by Freeman pass, leading from Kitkatlah inlet into Hecate strait, narrow and intricate, having many rocks, showing only at low water.

Seal rocks, a cluster of bare rocks of small extent, 10 feet above high water, the center of which lies 5 miles N. 38° W. (N. 66° W. mag.) from the summit of Oval hill and 4 miles S. 53° W. (S. 25° W. mag.) from cape Ibbetson (SW. entrance point of Edye passage), have depths of 12 to 31 fathoms at 400 yards from them.

Caution.—No vessel should pass between Seal and Warrior rocks; the passage is dangerous.

Warrior rocks, two bare rocks 30 feet above high water, lie NW. and SE., distant 1,600 yards, from each other. The eastern rock lies 3¾ miles N. 24° W. (N. 52° W. mag.) from the center of the Seal rock cluster.

Wallace rock, marked by kelp and with a depth of 8 feet on it at low water springs, lies with Seal rocks bearing S. 52° E. (S. 80° E. mag.), distant 1½ miles, and eastern Warrior rock N. 4° W. (N. 32° W. mag.).

Caution.—Depths of from 10 to 18 fathoms were obtained by H. B. M. S. Egeria when passing between Warrior rocks and White Cliff point, Stephens island. A depth of 11 fathoms was found with the center of White Cliff point bearing N. 47° E. (N. 19° E. mag.), distant 1¼ miles. Close southwestward of this spot a large patch of kelp, apparently attached to the bottom, was seen.

Depths of 10 fathoms were obtained with the North Warrior rock bearing S. 47° W. (S. 19° W. mag.), distant 1½ miles.

It appears, therefore, that dangers may exist in this region, and, until it has been examined, vessels are recommended not to pass between Warrior rocks and Stephens island.

Deep patch, situated in the western part of Edye passage, is stated to have 19 fathoms upon it; there is, however, probably less water on this patch, as kelp was observed growing upon it in August.

The patch is of small extent, and lies 1 mile N. 49° E. (N. 21° E. mag.) from cape Ibbetson. The southern extreme of Arthur island (View point) seen in line with the SE. extreme of that island bearing S. 83° E. (N. 69° E. mag.) will lead northward of Deep patch.

Truscott patch, with 16 feet of water on it, lies 1¾ miles S. 86° E. (N. 66° E. mag.) from cape Ibbetson and 1,200 yards from the nearest shore of Henry island.

Tidal streams.—The flood stream approaches from the westward, and both streams set fairly through Edye passage with an average rate of 2 knots an hour.

Refuge bay, situated on the NW. side of Porcher island, at the eastern entrance of Edye passage, is an excellent stopping place during southeasterly winds, or, if desirous of proceeding to sea from Chatham sound by the Edye passage, the state of the weather in Hecate strait can be ascertained. The bay is 1,400 yards wide between its entrance points and takes a southeasterly direction for about 1 mile, terminating in a sand flat which extends nearly ½ mile from its head. There is a cannery, wharf, and store on the western side of the bay; at low water the flat dries out to the end of the wharf.

The depths in the middle of the bay are from 14 to 23 fathoms, sand, shoaling gradually toward either shore.

Anchorage will be found in 12 to 14 fathoms, sand and mud, near the middle of the bay, about 400 yards from the northern and southern shores, with the northern entrance point (Table point) bearing N. 4° E. (N. 24° W. mag.) and Pearce point bearing N. 80° W. (S. 72° W. mag.).

Tides.—It is high water, full and change, in Refuge bay at 1 h. 30 m.; springs rise 17 to 22 feet, neaps 14 to 17 feet.

Brown passage, between Tree-nob groups and South Dundas island, is about 5 miles long NW. and SE. and 5 miles wide. Nearly in mid-channel, however, lies a cluster of rocks, awash at high water, which divides Brown passage into two channels.

Butterworth rocks are a dangerous cluster of rocks, the southernmost of which is 10 feet above high water, with several patches which uncover at low water extending ¾ mile northward from it. The southern rock lies 3½ miles S. 52° W. (S. 24° W. mag.) from Bare island, the western island of the Tree-nob groups, with that island in line with some wooded islands forming the northern cluster of Tree-nob groups (Osborne islands).

There is deep water between Butterworth rocks and Tree-nob groups.

Stenhouse shoal, a dangerous patch with 7 feet least water upon it, and reported to be 50 yards in extent, lies at the western entrance of Brown passage, 6½ miles S. 80° W. (S. 52° W. mag.) from Cape islet, at the southern extreme of South Dundas island.

North breaker, over which the sea usually breaks, is the outer known danger extending NW. from the Tree-nob groups, and lies 1 mile N. 40° W. (N. 68° W. mag.) from the northern Osborne island.

Hanmer rock, a dangerous shoal, nearly in mid-channel, 2¼ miles N. 38° E. (N. 10° E. mag.) from the northern Osborne island, and 2½ miles S. 35° W. (S. 7° W. mag.) from Cape islet, is awash at high water, with depths of 12 and 32 fathoms close-to; there are several patches, which uncover, extending from Hanmer rock ¾ mile NW.

Simpson rock lies on the northern side of Brown passage, ¾ mile S. 38° W. (S. 10° W. mag.) from Cape islet; this rock is 6 feet above high water, with rocks awash extending ½ mile westward and northward, and a depth of 17 fathoms at 800 yards southward of it; there is a patch, which uncovers 3 feet at low water, at 600 yards S. 18° E. (S. 46° E. mag.) of Simpson rock.

Beaver rock, with 12 feet of water on it, lies 1¼ miles S. 4° W. (S. 24° E. mag.) from the SE. extreme of South Dundas island (Deans point); several patches of rock lie between Beaver rock and the shore of South Dundas island.

Directions.—Brown passage is not recommended to a stranger, but should circumstances compel him to make use of it, the eastern peak of the Four-peaks range, on South Dundas island, should be steered for, bearing N. 61° E. (N. 33° E. mag.), until the eastern and highest Lucy island bears S. 85° E. (N. 67° E. mag.), which will lead through Brown passage south of Hanmer rock, or bearing S. 71° E. (N. 81° E. mag.), which will lead through, northward of this rock.

Tidal streams.—In Brown passage the tidal streams set fairly through at an average rate of 2 knots an hour. The flood stream sets to the eastward, and off the western entrance to this passage the streams are strong and complicated.

Qlawdzeet anchorage lies at the northern end of Stephens island. Qlawdzeet is exposed to the northward, is ¾ mile wide at its entrance, and 1 mile deep in a southerly direction.

Entrance reef, awash at high water, lies 400 yards northward of the eastern entrance point of Qlawdzeet bay.

Directions.—The entrance to Qlawdzeet bay will be made if the northern extreme of Tugwell island is kept in line (astern) with the eastern island of the Lucy group, bearing N. 55° E. (N. 27° E. mag.).

Keep in mid-channel when entering and anchor at 600 yards within the bay and 300 yards off the southern shore, in 12 to 14 fathoms, mud bottom, with the eastern entrance point of the bay bearing N. 66° E. (N. 38° E. mag.), distant 800 yards, and the western entrance point bearing N. 49° W. (N. 77° W. mag.), distant 1,200 yards.

Tides.—It is high water, full and change, at Qlawdzeet anchorage at 1 h. 30 m.; springs rise 17 to 22 feet, neaps 14 to 17 feet.

Bay islands, on the southern side of South Dundas island, are reported to afford anchorage off their NW. side.

The examination of this locality has shown the existence of many sunken rocks; the anchorage under Bay islands should therefore not be attempted.

Dundas islands, on the western side of Chatham sound, were so named by Vancouver; they consist of three islands, the northernmost being the largest and highest. A number of smaller islands (Moffat islands) lie close to the eastern coasts of South and Middle Dundas islands. The western coast of the group has not been thoroughly examined, but it is much broken into bays and inlets, with several small offlying islets.

South Dundas island is about 3 miles long, north and south, and 5 miles broad, its coast being comparatively low, wooded, and broken into bays on the southern and western sides. Near the middle of the island a mountain range rises 1,400 feet, with four conspicuous peaks which lie east and west of each other.

Middle Dundas island lies about 2 miles NNW. of South Dundas island, the passage between being obstructed by numerous low wooded islets, rocks, and sunken dangers. The island is nearly 5 miles long north and south, with a greatest breadth of 5 miles; it is mostly low and wooded, with numerous creeks and bays on its shores. Near the southern end of the island the land suddenly rises in an oval-shaped hill (Coast mound) 750 feet high, which is a useful landmark.

Connel islands, a group of small wooded islands, lie off the western side of Middle Dundas island. The outer or southwestern island of the group lies off the entrance to the passage between South and Middle Dundas islands, about 2 miles from the western coast of the latter and 8 miles NNW. from Osborne islands.

North Dundas island is about 12 miles long, NE. and SW., and about 7 miles broad near its northern end. This island, the highest and largest of the group, culminates in a mountain with a thumb-shaped summit, 2,500 feet high, about 4 miles from the SW. end of the island. Near the north extreme of North Dundas island there is a hill 700 feet high, with a flat top, and a knob near its north end (Table hill), a most conspicuous and useful mark.

The eastern coast of North Dundas island is but little broken and bold, with a range of hills about 300 feet high, rising immediately above it. On the northern side, nearly midway between Whitly point and White islands, there is a deep bay, useless as an anchorage, at the entrance to which lies a group of small wooded islets (Gnarled islands). Off the NW. extreme of the island, close-to, are two conspicuous rocks (White islands).

The western coast of North Dundas island has not been examined in detail. Several islands were, however, seen lying off that shore to the distance of 2 miles.

Captain Brundige put into a small harbor on the northern end of North Dundas island. He says: "I found a small river there which extended 5 miles or more into the island."

Zayas island is the largest of the islands which lie off the western coast of North Dundas island. The extent of this island has not been ascertained, but it appeared to be about 4 miles long, in a NNE. and SSW. direction, and about 2 miles broad, wooded, and about 250 feet high. A ledge of rocks, which uncover at low water, was observed to extend nearly 1 mile from the NW. extreme of Zayas island. From the west side of the island, rocks are said to extend 3 miles. One of these, known as McCullough rock, is about 3 miles westward of the northern end of the island.

Zayas island appeared flat and heavily timbered and probably 3 or 4 miles in extent.

It has been reported that an uncovering rock lies in mid-channel between Zayas and North Dundas islands, two more rocks rather close in on the northern side of Zayas, and three small islets less than 1 mile from its NW. extreme.

Channel islands are a group of wooded islands, about 100 feet high, extending across the channel between Middle and North Dundas islands. This group renders that channel useless for any but the smallest class of vessels. The passage, however, is frequently used by the Haida Indians, in their large canoes, when proceeding from Queen Charlotte islands to Port Simpson.

Moffat islands consist of six principal wooded islands and several lesser ones, the highest being about 250 feet in height. This group, which lies close to the eastern coast of the Dundas islands, extends 6 miles NNW. and SSE. When abreast, these islands show out well, being covered with pine trees of a peculiar deep-green foliage.

Ducie island is a small wooded islet, 350 feet high, lying 1 mile northward from the Moffat group. Two conspicuous white rocks, 30 feet high, lie 600 yards northward of Ducie island.

Whitesand islet is a small sandy islet, about 10 feet above high water, lying 1,200 yards eastward from Ducie island. A ledge of rocks, which uncover, extends 800 yards north and south from Whitesand islet.

Hammond rock, of small extent, with 9 feet of water over it, lies 1,800 yards S. 84° E. (N. 68° E. mag.) from the southeastern extreme of the southern Moffat island. This rock has 34 fathoms close northward of it.

Coghlan rock, with 3 feet of water and 6 and 7 fathoms close around, lies 2 miles N. 15° W. (N. 43° W. mag.) from Hammond rock. There are depths of 43 and 46 fathoms, mud bottom, at 1 mile northward of this rock.

Brodie rock lies 3¾ miles N. 18° W. (N. 46° W. mag.) from Coghlan rock. This dangerous pinnacle rock has only 3 feet over it at low water, with depths of 26 and 33 fathoms at a distance of 100 feet.

The Rachael group of islands, kept open eastward of the Lucy group, bearing S. 12° E. (S. 40° E. mag.), will lead eastward of the above-mentioned dangers; but during a fog, or in thick weather, the western shore of Chatham sound must not be approached under the depth of 40 fathoms.

Pointers rocks are a dangerous cluster of bare rocks, 3 feet above high water, about 400 yards in extent in a NNE. and SSW. direction. The southernmost and highest rock lies 3 miles N. 41° W. (N. 70° W. mag.) from the northern extreme of Finlayson island and 2¾ miles N. 83° W. (S. 68° W. mag.) from the northern extreme of Birnie island.

Connis rocks consist of several small rocks, nearly in the middle of Main passage into Chatham sound, abreast Port Simpson. The southernmost and highest rock, 15 feet above high water, is bare, and from it rocks extend 400 yards in a northerly direction. The summit of this rock lies 5 miles N. 86° W. (S. 65° W. mag.) from the northern extreme of Finlayson island and 3¾ miles S. 59° W. (S. 30° W. mag.) from Pointers rocks.

Green islet, situated on the western shore of Chatham sound, about 1½ miles from North Dundas island and 3 miles W. ½ S. from Connis rocks, is in two hummocks, lying close east and west of each other, joined by a low shingle beach, the eastern hummock being 46 feet in height and the western 20 feet; the islet is covered with long grass during the summer. The southern side of the islet is bold, but from the northern side a reef of rocks extends to some distance.

Light.—A flashing white light every 5.6 seconds, 81 feet above high water, visible 14 miles all round the horizon, except where intercepted by a chimney to the northward, is exhibited from a tower built on the southwestern point of Green islet.

The lighthouse is a square wooden tower, painted white, and surmounted by a circular iron lantern, painted red.

Grey islet is a small bare rock, of a grayish color, 34 feet above high water, 1,800 yards NNE. ½ E. from Green islet. A sunken rock, with 6 feet of water on it, lies 1 mile N. 41° W. (N. 70° W. mag.) from Grey islet. A rock, awash at high water, lies 400 yards N. 76° W. (S. 75° W. mag.) from Grey islet, and another rock, with 4 feet of water on it, lies 600 yards SSW. ½ W. from it. A large patch of kelp lies 400 yards westward from the islet.

Foul ground is reported to exist to the westward of these islets as far as Whitly point.

Main passage, between Pointers and Connis rocks, is 3½ miles wide, with depths of 92 fathoms at 1 mile NE. of Connis rocks. Both Connis and Pointers rocks may be approached to a distance of ½ mile.

Oriflamme passage lies westward of Connis rocks, between that cluster and Green and Grey islets. It is nearly 3 miles wide, with depths of 23 fathoms at 400 yards eastward of Green islet, and 65 and 70 fathoms, mud bottom, at 1,400 yards southwestward of Connis rocks.

Gnarled islands, a group of wooded islands, about 1 mile in extent east and west, lying off the northern side of North Dundas island, are from 150 to 250 feet in height; the eastern islet lies 2¼ miles NW. by W. from Whitly point.

The channel between Dundas and Gnarled islands is obstructed by ledges, which uncover, and sunken rocks.

White islands are two bare rocks, about 30 feet high, lying ½ mile from the NW. extreme of North Dundas island.

Dixon entrance is the channel between Prince of Wales and Queen Charlotte islands, passing northward of Dundas islands. Sunken rocks, of doubtful position, are reported to lie southward and southeastward, about 7 miles from cape Chacon, the SE. point of Prince of Wales island. Chacon breaker (existence doubtful) is reported 7 miles S. 27° E. (S. 56° E. mag.) of the cape.

A rock, upon which the sea breaks heavily at intervals, in a moderate swell, is reported off cape Muzon, southern end of Dall island. The rock lies about 1 mile southward of the cape with the tangents of the land forming the cape bearing approximately WNW. ⅜ W. and NE. ½ E. The coast-line of cape Muzon is incorrectly shown on the charts, and therefore the above bearings when plotted will not give the correct position of the rock relative to the shore.

In rounding the cape vessels should keep 2 miles offshore.

As a result of a triangulation carried out by H. B. M. S. **Egeria** it was found that the coast-line in the vicinity of North island should be placed 4 miles to the westward of its present position (1906) on the charts.

East Devil rock is situated about 4 miles northward of Zayas island, in (approximately) lat. 54° 41′ N., long. 131° 05′ W. East Devil rock is marked by a breaker and dries 2 feet at low water.

West Devil rock is a dangerous ledge, about ½ mile in extent, the shoalest part of which dries 10 feet, and is in (approximately) lat. 54° 40′ N., long. 131° 36′ W.

Broken ground extends northward from the shoalest part for 1⅛ miles, where there is a depth of 10 fathoms, over which the sea is said to break in heavy weather.

A shoal, on which H. B. M. S. Egeria anchored, in 9 fathoms, lies 2¼ miles S. 42° E. (S. 71° E. mag.) from West Devil rock. This shoal seems to be small in extent and steep-to, with 40 fathoms and more all round it.

A breaker, having the appearance of very shallow water, was observed on two occasions, in moderate weather, at a point ½ mile N. 5° W. (N. 34° W. mag.) from West Devil rock.

Foul ground, upon which the sea breaks, extends about ¼ mile southeastward of West Devil rock.

Vessels are recommended to give West Devil rock a wide berth.

McCullough rock, on which the sea breaks, lies about 3 miles westward from the western side of Zayas island, with the NW. point of that island bearing E. by N.

A rock, on which the sea breaks heavily, lies in the western end of Dixon entrance, about 8 miles N. by W. ½ W. from the NW. point of North island, of the Queen Charlotte islands, or in lat. 54° 22′ N., long. 133° 03′ W.; this position is doubtful.

Cape Fox, so named by Vancouver, lies about 7¼ miles north from North Dundas island and terminates in remarkable, high, white cliffs, with a conspicuous saddle-shaped mountain (Harry Saddle), 2,066 feet high, immediately over it.

Tree point.—From cape Fox the coast trends northwestward for 4 miles to Tree point, the eastern entrance point to Revillagigedo channel.

Light.—A fixed white light with a red sector, elevated 86 feet above high water and visible 15 miles, is exhibited from the western extremity of Tree point, on the eastern side of the entrance to Revillagigedo channel and about 4 miles northwestward of cape Fox. The light shows white between the bearings S. 24° E. (S. 53° E. mag.) and N. 33° W. (N. 62° W. mag.), through East and North; red between N. 33° W. (N. 62° W. mag.) and N. 43° W. (N. 72° W. mag.). The red sector covers Lord rock in the eastern end of Dixon entrance. The lighthouse is a white, wooden, octagonal tower 56 feet high, rising from a white building with black roof.

Two white oilhouses, with brown roofs, are situated eastward of the station.

Fog signal.—A Daboll trumpet sounds blasts of 3 seconds' duration every 30 seconds.

Lord islands, lying about 2½ miles SE. from cape Fox, are in two groups, separated about ¾ mile, the larger islands being wooded and from 100 to 250 feet high; the SW. island is distant 5¾ miles from the outer or northern island of the Gnarled island group.

Lord rock, bare, about 10 feet high, lies 1,600 yards S. 61° W. (S. 32° W. mag.) from the SW. island of the Lord group. Fleece rock, bare, about 12 feet high, lies ¾ mile southeastward, and Thistle rock, bare, about 10 feet high, 1 mile northward of the southwestern Lord island.

Nakat inlet has its entrance between cape Fox and Tongass island, and extends about 11 miles in a northerly direction. Craig rock, with 9 feet over it, lies in mid-channel at the entrance 1,400 yards N. 78° W. (S. 73° W. mag.) from the western extreme of Tongass island.

In Nakat inlet, in the SE. arm inside the group of islands, is a well-sheltered harbor with anchorage in less than 15 fathoms.

Tongass island, on the eastern side at the entrance to Nakat inlet, is about 3 miles eastward of cape Fox and about 16 miles NW. of Port Simpson. On the eastern side of the island are the remains of the old settlement and a deserted Indian village. The island is low and ledges extend from all sides of it except in Port Tongass.

Port Tongass is a small harbor formed by the passage between Tongass island and the mainland. It is sometimes used as an anchorage, but is not recommended; the bottom is hard, and with wind and changing tidal streams a vessel is liable to foul and drag her anchor.

Anchorage.—The approaches to Tongass settlement are intricate and require local knowledge; the anchorage abreast the fort is bad, with deep water, and limited accommodation even for a vessel of moderate length.

Directions.—The anchorage may be entered by three channels, but that between Tongass and Kannaghunut islands is not recommended. The main entrance is from the southeastward through Tongass passage, passing westward of Haystack island. In rounding Dark point to the anchorage keep the NE. shore aboard.

Approaching from the westward, keep the cape Fox shore aboard at a distance of from ½ to ¾ mile and pass north of Craig rock and in mid-channel west and north of Tongass reef (awash at high water), which lies at the NW. entrance.

Tongass passage is a deep, narrow passage, with very steep and wooded shores, between Sitklan and Wales islands, leading into the southern end of Pearse canal and forming the SE. approach to Port Tongass. The entrance from the southward is west of Haystack island.

Tidal streams.—The tides in Dixon entrance and Brown passage, especially in the western parts of those channels, are variable and complicated. The flood stream approaching from the southward up Hecate strait is met by the stream entering westward and northward of Queen Charlotte islands at about 15 miles eastward of Rose point or about midway between the NE. extreme of Queen Charlotte islands and the Tree-nob groups. Northward of that position this meeting of the streams produces tidal irregularities, and at spring tides or during bad weather the turmoil caused by the meeting of the streams is so great as to convey an appearance of broken water to that portion lying between Queen Charlotte islands, Brown passage, and Dixon entrance. In Chatham sound the tides set fairly through.

CHAPTER XIII.

PORTLAND AND OBSERVATORY INLETS AND PORTLAND CANAL.

VARIATION IN 1906.

Tracy island .... 28° 45′ E. Portland canal, head .... 30° 00′ E.

Portland inlet extends from Chatham sound in a northeasterly direction for upward of 20 miles, with a width of about 3 miles. It then divides; the western arm, Portland canal, continues in a general northerly direction for about 60 miles, with an average width of about 1 mile; the eastern arm, Observatory inlet, runs in a general NNE. direction for about 43 miles, with a varying breadth of from 1 to 4 miles. The water is generally very deep and the anchorages few and indifferent. Both shores are very bold and mountainous. Numerous large and small streams empty into the canal, and at its head the water is nearly fresh. In places the mountains rise almost perpendicularly from the water to a height of 6,000 feet and their summits are always snow-clad. With the exception of a few wooded valleys at the mouths of streams, the snow line is often very low, even at midsummer. The head of Portland canal terminates in the usual low, woody, swampy land, with Bear and Salmon rivers flowing through it. The shores of the inlet are comparatively free from danger beyond the distance of 400 yards.

Compton island, at the northern entrance of Work channel, is of triangular shape, with a base 2 miles long to the southwestward, the northern extreme of the island terminating in a long, low point. There is a boat passage into Work channel eastward of Compton island.

Emma passage, eastward of Compton island, is ½ mile wide and takes a SE. direction for 3 miles, thence NE. 3 miles, and terminates in a sandy bay. The depths throughout the latter arm are from 23 to 36 fathoms. Union bay, at the head of the SE. arm, affords anchorage for small vessels in 20 fathoms at 200 yards from either shore.

Somerville island, 2,000 feet high, on the eastern side of the inlet, is 8½ miles long NE. and SW. and 3 miles broad. The coast of this island is wooded and bold, the land on its western side rising almost perpendicularly from the sea. Elliott point is the southern extreme of Somerville island.

Truro island, off the SW. side of Somerville island, is about 1½ miles long NE. and SW. and nearly ½ mile broad. The island is wooded and culminates in two hills 800 feet high. Nob islet is a small, round, wooded islet, 30 feet high, lying close to the western shore of Somerville island, distant 1,600 yards from the northern extreme of Truro island. There is a remarkable white cliff just southward of Nob islet.

Start point, the northern extreme of Somerville island, lies abreast Lizard point, on the eastern side of Pearse island, and 2¾ miles from it; it is high and bold.

Somerville bay, close east of Start point, affords good anchorage in mid-channel in 12 fathoms, sandy bottom, Whitestone point on the west shore bearing WNW.

Steamer passage, eastward of Somerville island, has an average width of ½ mile, with depths of 28 and 40 or more fathoms of water throughout. Khutzeymateen inlet is an unexamined arm, 5 miles within Steamer passage. It is ½ mile wide at its entrance and takes an easterly direction. Quinamass bay, on the eastern side of Steamer passage, abreast the northern end of Somerville island, is ½ mile wide at its entrance and takes an easterly direction. At low water it is almost completely filled by a sand flat, rendering the bay useless as an anchorage.

Nasoga gulf, eastward of Mylor peninsula, extends in a northeasterly direction for 5 miles, is 1 mile wide, and terminates in comparatively high land. Anchorage will be found near the head of Nasoga gulf, in 10 to 12 fathoms, sand, in mid-channel, at 400 yards from the northern shore.

Mylor peninsula is a high and comparatively narrow strip of land on the eastern side of Portland inlet, between Nasoga gulf and Nass bay. A small islet (Ranger islet) lies off its SW. extreme, and there the land is comparatively low (450 feet); but it rises quickly to the height of 2,900 feet and forms high, bold, precipitous shores. Trefusis point, the SW. extreme of the peninsula, terminates in high white cliffs. Low point, the NW. extreme of the peninsula and southern entrance point to Nass bay, is wooded.

Wales island, situated on the NW. side of the entrance to Portland inlet, is about 7 miles in extent east and west and about the same north and south. Its eastern side is bold with some conspicuous red-brown cliffs nearly midway between its northern and southern extremes. On the southern side, about 1 mile westward of Wales point, the SE. extreme of the island, a deep bay faces southward, and within it are some patches, which uncover, and rocks awash. Tracy islet, a wooded islet about ½ mile long, in a NW. and

SE. direction, lies off the entrance to this bay, 1½ miles westward from Wales point.

Entry peak, situated about ½ mile northward of Wales point, is 1,400 feet high, of triangular shape, with a sharp, conspicuous summit. A mountain, with a flat summit, 1,100 feet high, is situated near the middle of the SW. side of the island.

Boston islands lie from ½ to ¾ mile off the SW. side of Wales island, 2¼ miles westward from Tracy island; the larger islands are wooded and about 150 feet in height. Proctor islands lie about the same distance offshore at 2 miles northwestward from the Boston islands, and are similar in character. Foul ground lies between the two groups. Haystack island, the western island of the Proctor group, is 450 feet high, round, wooded, and conspicuous; the entrance to Tongass passage is west of it.

Wales passage, which leads in a northwesterly direction from Portland inlet into Pearse canal between Wales and Pearse islands, has its entrance 3½ miles north from Wales point. It is about 4 miles long, and from ¾ mile broad at the southern end contracts to only about 200 yards at its northern end; it is free from mid-channel dangers, those that exist being very close to the shore. Center island, in mid-channel at its southern entrance, has a clear passage on either side; it is small, about 150 feet high, and thickly wooded.

Pearse island, which forms the northwestern side of Portland inlet northeastward of Wales island, is roughly oblong in shape, 16 miles in length NE. and SW., and between 4 and 5 miles broad. Over the eastern coast of the island the mountains attain an altitude of about 2,000 feet, rising to 2,600 feet at the northern end close over Portland point, the NE. point of the island and SW. entrance point to Portland canal.

Pirate point, 5 miles NE. from the entrance to Wales passage, terminates in high cliffs and has a small bay close southward of it. Lizard point is a prominent point 3 miles NE. from Cliff point. At 2½ miles northward of Lizard point there are some conspicuous red-brown earthy cliffs. From Lizard point the shore is comparatively low until near Portland point, which is high, bold, and nearly steep-to. Tree point, the northern extreme of Pearse island, is low, wooded, and conspicuous, with high land about 1 mile south of it. A reef extends ½ mile in a northerly direction from the point and is nearly steep-to.

Ramsden point, the southern extremity of the peninsula which divides Observatory inlet from Portland canal, lies 2¼ miles NE. from Portland point. A dangerous cluster of rocks, awash and sunken, extends a short distance southward from Ramsden point.

Nass bay, on the eastern shore, lies at the mouth of Nass river. It is 2 miles wide at its entrance, the points of which lie north and south of each other, and the bay preserves this width in a SE. direction for 3 miles, where it divides, one branch taking a northeasterly direction to the mouth of Nass river, and the other a southwesterly direction, forming Iceberg bay.

An extensive sand flat occupies nearly the whole of the eastern portion of the bay at low water. Low point is wooded. On the southern shore of the bay, ½ mile eastward of Low point, is Landslip mountain, 2,042 feet high, with a bare side facing the north.

North point terminates in a bold cliff, and 1 mile eastward is Mission valley; at 1 mile back from the coast is mount Tomlinson, a conspicuous mountain, 3,385 feet high. Through the valley a large stream runs, dividing near its mouth into two branches. Fort point, the NW. entrance point of Nass river, terminates in white cliffs, and on the eastern side of the bay some low, dark islands (Mud islands) will be seen.

Kincolith, a mission station situated east of the stream at the mouth of Mission valley, is fronted by a sand flat (Canoe flat), which renders communication by boat, except at high water, almost impossible. There are two sawmills here, one owned and worked by Indians. Gold is found here in small quantities and also coal. The temperature is very severe, the thermometer in some winters falling to from 40° to 50° below zero for weeks in succession.

Anchorage, in fine weather, may be had off Kincolith, nearly in the middle of Nass bay, on the line joining the mission station and Landslip mountain, in 10 fathoms, mud bottom, at about 1,600 yards from the northern shore, with the mission flagstaff seen in line with the center of Mission valley, bearing N. 39° E. (N. 10° E. mag.), and Leading point (southern side of Nass river) seen just open of Fort point (NW. entrance point of Nass river), bearing East (N. 61° E. mag.).

Caution.—A strong ebb tide will be felt in this position, and care must be exercised in taking up a berth, as Canoe flat is very steep-to, and it is recommended to use the deep-sea lead in approaching it.

Tides.—It is high water, full and change, at Nass bay at 1 h. 5 m.; springs rise 17 to 23 feet.

Iceberg bay, the SW. arm of Nass bay, is 3 miles long in a SW. direction and not less than 1,400 yards wide; the head of the bay, terminating in a low, swampy flat fronted by a sand flat, is only 3 miles from the head of Nasoga gulf.

At the entrance of Iceberg bay the depth of 10 fathoms, and less, will be found; but as the head of the bay is approached the water will deepen to over 40 fathoms. To enter the bay, when past the landslip on the southern shore, close that shore and give it a berth of 150 yards; round Double Islet point closely and steer for the anchorage.

Anchorage may be obtained at the entrance to Iceberg bay, in 7 to 8 fathoms, mud, with the northern entrance point of Nass bay (North point) seen in line with the NW. entrance point of Iceberg bay (Double Islet point) bearing N. 31° W. (N. 60° W. mag.), distant 1,200 yards from the latter.

Nass river flows into the NE. corner of Nass bay, the mouth of the river being obstructed by a sand flat, which dries at low water, and extends toward Iceberg bay. Ripple tongue, the western extreme of this extensive flat, lies 500 yards N. by E. from Double Islet point.

Within the river the navigation is difficult and dangerous, the channel at low water being barely available for large canoes; local steamers, however, drawing 6 feet of water, venture up, though they frequently run aground; it is recommended not to attempt the river until the strength of the flood tide has slackened. The channel is liable to change after freshets.

Nass river, at its entrance abreast Fort point, is 1½ miles wide, whence its direction is east for 7 miles, and then NE. for 7 miles, to abreast the Nass villages. The channel near the mouth of the river being tortuous, the distance by the channel from Fort point to the Nass villages is about 16 miles. The south, middle, and north villages are known, respectively, by the names of Kitminiook, Kitlahkumkadah, and Kitakauze. The river continues in a northeasterly direction for 25 miles beyond the lower Nass villages, and there divides, one branch taking a northerly direction. Kilawālāks, the head of canoe navigation, is situated on the northern branch 40 miles from the lower Nass villages.

Tides.—The time of high water at the lower Nass villages is uncertain, depending apparently upon the freshets down the river. There was no slack at high water, the water beginning to fall immediately it had ceased to rise (August, 1868). At low water there was slack for 1½ hours. In the month of August the flood stream was not felt above the Middle bank, and from Indian report this is the case at all seasons.

Ice.—The river is reported to freeze over down to its mouth during severe winters.

Fish.—The houlican, from which the nutritious oil is obtained, the principal sustenance of the Indians, are caught in great numbers during the spring, as also are salmon. There are two salmon canneries in the Nass river, one in Iceberg bay and the other ¾ mile eastward of Fort point.

Observatory inlet, northward of Nass bay, is called by the Indians Kitšahwatl; in some parts the shores are low and wooded, the land rising at a few miles back to 4,000 and 5,000 feet high. The low wooded shore has an undergrowth of thick moss, overlying rock, and saturated with moisture, which renders traveling difficult.

North point anchorage.—Anchorage may be had in the bight on the eastern shore, 2½ miles northward of North point, at a distance of 500 yards from the beach in 25 fathoms, sand. The northern point of the bight must be given a berth of 600 yards, as a narrow spit with 2 fathoms on it extends southward from this point.

Salmon cove lies on the western shore, 19 miles from Ramsden point and 39 miles from Wales point.

Richard point, the northern point of Salmon cove, is a long, wooded, conspicuous projection. From its NE. extreme the land trends in a southwesterly direction, for 1¾ miles, to the head of Salmon cove, which is barely 600 yards wide. A sand flat extends 400 yards from the southern shore at the entrance to Salmon cove.

Anchorage was obtained by Vancouver in Salmon cove "in 31 and 35 fathoms water, muddy and small stony bottom."

Brooke island, 2¾ miles long and ½ mile broad at its northern end, is low and wooded. The southern extreme of this island lies 4 miles northeastward of Richard point and ½ mile from the eastern shore. Several patches of rock, which uncover at low water, extend ½ mile northeastward from Brooke island.

Paddy passage is ½ mile wide, between Brooke island and the eastern shore, but near its northern end it is barely 400 yards wide between the eastern shore and the ledges extending northeastward from Brooke island; it is reported unsafe and should not be used.

Frank point, situated 5 miles northwestward of Richard point and 1¼ miles from the western shore of Brooke island, is low and wooded. Xschwan is the name of a salmon fishery which lies at the head of Goose bay on the western shore, 4 miles northward of Frank point.

Larcom island, situated nearly in mid-channel, at the mouth of Hastings arm, is about 5 miles long, north and south, with an average breadth of ½ mile; its southern extreme lies 1,200 yards NW. from Brooke island. The island is flat, wooded, and comparatively low. At its SW. end there is an extensive lagoon.

The channel westward of Larcom island is obstructed near the northern end of that island by several islets and rocks and is only available for boats.

A rock, with a depth of 5 feet over it, lies in mid-channel between the SW. point of Larcom island and an islet lying close offshore ¾ mile northward of Frank point. This rock is not marked by kelp.

Hastings arm passes eastward of Larcom island and takes a general northerly direction for 14 miles, until it terminates at the head of the inlet.

This branch of Observatory inlet is from ½ to 1 mile wide, terminating in a wooded swamp, fronted by a mud flat.

The water in Hastings arm is deep and it has no known anchorage ground. If proceeding into this channel, pass in mid-channel between Brooke and Larcom islands, taking care to avoid the foul ground which extends ½ mile northeastward from the former.

Alice arm, the eastern branch of Observatory inlet, from its junction with Hastings arm, runs in an easterly direction 12 miles. This arm is obstructed at its entrance by a small wooded island (Liddle island), which divides it into two channels 600 yards wide.

A rock, which dries about 5 feet at low water, lies 300 yards N. 61° W. (West mag.) from the southern end of Liddle island.

A rock, with 10 feet on it, lies with the northern end of Liddle island bearing S. 9° W. (S. 20° E. mag.), distant nearly 400 yards. The channel between this rock and Davies point has 6 fathoms in it and is recommended in preference to passing between the rock and Liddle island.

Alice rock, with 7 feet on it, lies southwestward of Hans point, with the northern end of Liddle island bearing S. 32° W. (S. 3° W. mag.), distant 1⅓ miles. There is deep water on either side of this rock, but vessels should pass eastward of it, the western extreme of Brooke island in line with the western extreme of Liddle island leading 100 yards eastward.

Perry bay, situated on the eastern shore at the entrance to Alice arm, is 500 yards wide and takes a southerly direction for nearly 1 mile, with depths of 14 and 18 fathoms, mud bottom, in mid-channel.

Off its western entrance point lies a small islet (Sophy islet). At the head of the bay there is a salmon fishery (Muckshwanne).

Anchorage may be obtained at the head of Alice arm, about 500 yards from the eastern shore and about the same distance from low-water mark at the head, in not less than 28 fathoms.

Tides.—It is high water, full and change, in Observatory inlet at 1 h. 05 m.; springs rise 23 feet, neaps 12 feet. Abreast Nass bay the ebb runs with great strength (estimated 3 to 5 knots), the blue water being clearly defined when meeting the muddy waters of the Nass river.

The strength of the stream in Observatory inlet depends upon the freshets caused by the melting snow.

Pearse canal, an entrance to Portland canal, extends from Tongass passage, northwestward of Wales and Pearse islands, in a general NE. direction for 23 miles to Portland canal. The general breadth is from ½ to 1 mile, but at the SW. end of Pearse island it narrows to under 400 yards; it is deep throughout. From Tongass passage to Wales passage it has several islets and rocks, sunken and awash, at varying distances from the shore on each side, and great care must be exercised in navigating this part of the canal. From Wales passage to Portland canal it is without dangers, except a rock, bare at half tide, that lies off a bight on the SE. side just SW. of the entrance to Winter harbor and a little southeastward of mid-channel; it is in line with the eastern shore southward of it.

Safa islands, mostly wooded, lie on the southern side of the channel at the western end of Pearse canal off the entrance to Wales harbor. A wooded island, about 150 feet high, lies in mid-channel ⅓ mile northward from the northern Safa island, and between them there is a rocky islet about 10 feet high having a few scrubby trees on it. One mile NE. from Safa islands, and nearly ½ mile from the southern shore of the canal, are two bare rocks about 10 feet high.

Entering Pearse inlet from Tongass passage, pass in mid-channel between point Phipp, the NW. point of Wales island, and the islands NW. of it; steer between the wooded island in mid-channel (150 feet high) and the rocky islet 10 feet high southward of it, and proceed in mid-channel, passing about 300 yards northward of the two bare rocks (10 feet high) above mentioned, being careful of the rock off the bight west of Winter harbor.

Wales harbor on the northwestern side of Wales island, southward of the Safa islands, affords good anchorage in from 15 to 18 fathoms, soft bottom, but its entrance is somewhat obstructed and caution is needed in entering. A reef extends westward from the NE. side of the harbor, the outer end of which is a rock with 12 feet over it lying 500 yards S. 39° E. (S. 68° E. mag.) from the southwesternmost Safa island; the channel is 350 yards wide between the end of the reef and the west shore. At the head of the harbor are three arms, the middle and largest one opening out into a basin about ½ mile in diameter. A good-sized island and a very small one close SE. of it nearly close the entrances to the western and middle arms; the channel for entering them is west of the islands. The usual anchorage is north of the larger island, in 15 to 18 fathoms.

Entering Wales harbor from Tongass passage, follow the Wales island shore giving it a berth of about 300 yards; pass in mid-channel SW. of the Safa islands, and when abreast the southwesternmost of the group a S. 42° E. (S. 71° E. mag.) course leads in to the anchorage. The basin at the head of the middle arm may be reached by passing westward of the island at its entrance and through the narrow arm, in which there is not less than 7 fathoms; it is suitable only for small craft.

Fillmore inlet joins Pearse inlet at the SW. end of Fillmore island and separates that island from the mainland; it extends about 2 miles northeastward beyond the island; a narrow entrance beyond the group of islands at the head of the inlet leads into two basins in succession, each of considerable size. The inlet has deep water throughout and all dangers are close inshore, but it has no value as an anchorage. A small group of islets and reefs lie on the western side of its entrance, which is north of point Phipp.

Willard inlet, having its entrance from the western side of Fillmore inlet just within its entrance, is a narrow inlet extending into the mainland for about 12 miles in a northerly direction. It is very narrow at the entrance, and the tidal streams run very strongly. This inlet can only be entered at slack water and has no value as an anchorage.

Edward passage separates Fillmore island from the mainland to the northeastward and connects Fillmore inlet with Pearse inlet: it is narrow, very foul, and not navigable except for small craft.

Winter harbor, at the southwestern end of Pearse island, having its entrance from Pearse inlet 1¼ miles NE. from Wales passage, is free from hidden dangers, landlocked, and affords perfectly secure though limited anchorage, with good holding ground and ample swinging room in the wider part. For 1¼ miles from the entrance the inlet is only from 200 to 400 yards wide; at this distance a broad bight makes into the western shore, filled by a small, wooded islet and several rocks, with flats connecting the islet with the shore; ¼ mile farther on the inlet widens out and affords an anchorage ½ mile long and ⅓ mile wide in 6 fathoms, muddy bottom. A rock, awash at high water, lies about 75 yards off the islet. The eastern shore is bold, carrying 4 to 10 fathoms close up to the shore, except for a short distance off the mouths of two streams, which may be known by the low grassy land. The head of the inlet contracts and ends in a flat dry at low water.

Approaching Winter harbor from the southwestward, be careful of the rock off the bight just west of the entrance, and in entering the harbor favor the western shore slightly until past the first stream; keep the eastern shore aboard when passing the islet, to avoid the rock off it, and anchor in the broad part of the harbor.

Hidden inlet, a narrow arm 5 miles in length, extends into the mainland in a northerly direction from Pearse inlet about 8 miles SW. of its junction with Portland canal. The entrance to this inlet is less than 150 yards in width, and through it the tidal streams rush with a velocity of from 8 to 10 knots, forming swirls that extend well into Pearse inlet. The main body of the inlet is about 3½ miles long, with from 30 to 70 fathoms, but there is only 2¾ fathoms at the entrance. It can only be entered at slack water and is of no value as an anchorage.

Portland canal.—At about 20 miles from Wales point Portland canal branches off to the northward and westward from Portland inlet. The first reach extends NNW. for 6 miles, with an average breadth of 1½ miles. Here Pearse inlet stretches SW. From this the canal trends in a general northerly direction for about 55 miles to its termination. It possesses few and indifferent anchorages.

In places the mountains rise almost perpendicularly above the high-water line to the height of 6,000 feet.

The two rivers, Bear and Salmon, at the head of Portland canal, are separated by a high ridge of bare mountains. On the eastern side of the valley of Bear river a mountain range extends in an ESE. and WNW. direction, mount Disraeli, the highest peak of the range, being a snow-clad pinnacle, 7,000 feet high. The delta of the Bear and Salmon rivers consists of a mud flat, which covers at high water and extends over 1 mile from the mouth of the former river. This deposit of mud is nearly steep-to, breaking down suddenly to no bottom at 40 fathoms.

During the month of August, a current of about 1½ knots an hour has been observed, setting down Portland canal, for 25 miles below the mouth of Bear river.

Timber, etc.—Pine and cedar are the principal trees met with, the former tall and almost bare to the top, and frequently above 100 feet high. Cedars are found in many places of great size, with branches close to the ground. Maple trees are occasionally seen, being distinguished by their light and variegated tints of green. Yellow cypress is also met with, being distinguished from the pine by its leaf, convex on both sides, and by its peculiar odor.

The wood of the yellow cypress is light, tough, and durable, and useful for repairing or building boats.

Dogfish bay, situated on the eastern shore, about 3½ miles northward of Ramsden point, is about 1½ miles wide, ¼ mile deep, and faces the SW.; it is, however, filled by a sand flat at low water, rendering it useless as an anchorage. Windy islet is small and lies close to the shore at the northern entrance point of Dogfish bay.

Tree point, on the western shore, the northern point of Pearse island, 4½ miles from Portland point, is low, wooded, and conspicuous, with high land at about 1 mile south of it. Tree Point reef extends ½ mile in a northerly direction from Tree point, and is nearly steep-to.

Spit point, on the eastern shore, 6 miles from Ramsden point, is the turning point into the northern reach. Between Spit point and Dogfish bay several small wooded islets lie close to the eastern shore and are connected with it at low water. A tongue of sand, which uncovers at low water, extends 600 yards SW. from Spit point.

Reef island, a small island lying on the western shore abreast Spit point, lies 2¾ miles north from Tree point, and 1¼ miles west from Spit point. Two small bays, with sandy beaches, lie under Reef island, in which a boat may find shelter. A reef, with rocks awash at high water, and sunken rocks, extends 400 yards SE. from Reef island.

Harrison point, a high, bold point, on the western shore, lies 2½ miles NNE. of Reef island. Dickens point is on the eastern shore, 4 miles from Spit point, the coast between them having a considerable curve to the eastward.

A small black rock, 8 feet above high water, lies close south of Dickens point, and a ledge of rocks which uncover extends 400 yards from the point.

Sandfly bay, situated on the western shore, nearly abreast Dickens point, is ½ mile wide and ¾ mile deep in a northerly direction, terminating in a swamp with streams in the NW. and NE. corners. Off the eastern point of the bay two small islets lie close to the shore. Sandfly bay is nearly filled up at low water by a sand flat, with deep water close-to, and is therefore useless as an anchorage.

Stopford point, bold and conspicuous, lies on the eastern shore, 3¼ miles from Dickens point.

Halibut bay, on the western shore, 15 miles from Ramsden point, is ½ mile wide at its entrance and extends back 1¼ miles in a northerly direction, having an extensive swamp at its head, through which three large streams flow. The bay is free from hidden dangers. Its shores are generally bold, but on each side near the entrance are sandy beaches about ¼ mile in length, with shoals extending 80 yards offshore and low grassy land running 100 yards back. Near the head of the bay extensive flats, bare at low water, make out from the western shore nearly all the way across, leaving a narrow channel close to the east side, through which 6 feet can be carried at low water, to a narrow basin with from 4 to 7 fathoms, suitable for small craft.

The anchorage in Halibut bay is in mid-channel, at 600 yards within the entrance, in 6 to 10 fathoms, mud bottom. The holding ground inside the 10-fathom curve is good.

Tides.—It is high water, full and change, at 0 h. 30 m.; springs rise 19½ feet, neaps 15 feet.

Cross islet, a small wooded islet, connected at low water with the shore, lies close northward of Halibut bay. A rude wooden cross was found on this islet, placed there at some remote period, apparently to mark a grave.

Logan point lies on the eastern shore, 3¾ miles from Stopford point. At 3 miles SE. of Logan point, is Dent mountain, 5,057 feet high.

Camp point, on the western shore, is the turning point of the northern arm, which abreast of that point changes in direction from NNE. to NNW.; it is wooded, bold, and precipitous.

Hattie island, situated nearly in mid-channel, abreast Camp point, is 400 yards long north and south with some stunted brush growing upon it. A ledge of rocks awash, and sunken rocks, extends 400 yards northward from Hattie island. The water is deep on either side of the island, beyond the distance of 400 yards from it, but the channel westward of the island is recommended.

Belle bay lies on the eastern shore, abreast Hattie island; a large stream flows into it, and the neck of land separating Portland canal and Salmon cove (Observatory inlet) is here about 4 miles across.

Car point lies on the eastern shore, 3 miles northward of Hattie island. Three conspicuous landslips are seen on the mountains south of Car point. Bluff point terminates in a high bold cliff and lies on the eastern shore, about 2 miles from Car point. The channel abreast Bluff point is 1 mile wide.

Breezy point, on the western shore, 4 miles from Camp point, is conspicuous, and the land recedes to the westward between Camp and Breezy points.

Tombstone bay lies on the western shore 7½ miles above Hattie island. At its entrance, the bay is about ¾ mile wide, and is divided into two bights, the larger, taking a southerly direction, narrows rapidly, until it terminates at ½ mile within the entrance, at the mouth of a river. Temporary anchorage for very small craft may be had in 8 fathoms near the head of the northern bight.

An extensive well-wooded valley lies at the head of the bay, and on the north side of the valley a remarkable mountain, with a snow-clad summit of dome shape, rises to the height of 6,500 feet. Trout are plentiful in the river flowing into this bay. Berries are found in abundance, especially the wild raspberry.

Maple point lies on the eastern shore, 3 miles from Bluff point. Maple trees grow upon this point, and when in leaf render it conspicuous. Half a mile south of Maple point is a small bay which affords fair anchorage for small craft. Anchor 300 yards from the southern side in 8 to 9 fathoms. Immediately northward of Maple point is a bay, with a large stream flowing into it, fronted by a sand flat. Swamp point, a low, marshy, wooded point, through which a river flows, lies 3 miles NNW. from Maple point. A sand spit extends ½ mile to the southwestward from Swamp point.

Pirie point, situated 2 miles NW. from Swamp point, is high, bold, and conspicuous. A sand spit extends 400 yards from the eastern shore midway between Swamp and Pirie points. White point lies on the eastern shore, 4 miles from Pirie point.

Turn point lies on the western shore, 1¼ miles from Tombstone bay, and is high, bold, and conspicuous. Steep point on the western shore, 6 miles from Turn point, is bold and steep-to. Two large streams flow into the sea, midway between Turn and Steep points.

White point, on the eastern shore, 2¼ miles above Steep point, has some white cliffs ½ mile northward of it. Bay islet, on the eastern shore, 2½ miles above White point, is small and wooded and lies 200 yards off a point which divides two sandy bays, being connected with the point at low water. Green islets are two small wooded islets, on the eastern shore, 1¼ miles from Bay islet. Close northward of these islets there is a considerable tract of comparatively low land, thickly wooded, through which a large stream flows.

Fords cove, on the eastern shore just north of Green islets, is a decided bight in the shore affording fair shelter from southerly, but none from northerly, winds. A rocky ledge extends northward from Green islets about 75 yards, partly showing at low water. The southern part of the cove is shoal for about 150 yards from the shore. A fair anchorage, with sufficient swinging room may be obtained in 16 fathoms, 400 yards from Green islets and from the eastern shore.

Slab point, terminating in a high, smooth, slate-colored cliff, lies on the western shore, a little above Fords cove.

Blue point, on the eastern shore, 5 miles from Green islet and 1¼ miles from Cliff point (on the western shore), terminates in high, bold cliffs, of purple-blue color and basaltic formation. Close south of the point, an extensive wooded valley extends to the northeastward, through which two large streams flow. A sand spit extends off their mouths to the distance of 400 yards. Cliff point terminates in high white cliffs and is steep-to.

Verdure point, on the western shore, lies 4 miles NNW. from Cliff point. The maple trees growing upon this point, when in leaf, render it conspicuous.

Midway between Cliff and Verdure points, there is an extensive wooded valley, through which a large stream flows in a southwesterly direction. Close northward of Verdure point is a bay, with a conspicuous sandy beach at its head. Landslip point, 1 mile northward from Verdure point, is conspicuous, having a high landslip over it.

Round point is the turning point, on the eastern shore, into the northern and last reach of Portland canal. With the exception of a small bay, which dries throughout at low water, the eastern shore northward of Blue point, for 6 miles, is high, bold, and almost inaccessible. The northern extreme of Round point lies 6 miles from Blue point.

Marmot river, on the eastern shore, immediately southward of Lion point, 2½ miles from the mouth of Bear river, flows through an extensive valley which lies in an easterly direction. A sand spit extends 600 yards off the mouth of Marmot river, and is steep-to. At the head of the valley, a mountain range with three conspicuous peaks, 4,000 to 5,000 feet high, extends in a north and south direction.

Seal rocks, on the western shore, at the entrance of the northern reach of the canal, are of small extent and lie 400 yards from the western shore. The highest rock is 6 feet above high water. Between Verdure point and the point off which Seal rocks lie, the coast curves considerably to the westward.

Salmon river, on the western shore, 1½ miles from Bear river, is separated from that river by the Reverdy mountains, a range of bare mountains 4,000 to 5,000 feet high. It is a stream of considerable size, and the valley through which it flows is ½ mile wide at its mouth; the river then takes a northwesterly direction and is flanked by high mountains.

Bear river flows through an extensive wooded flat at the head of the Portland canal and divides near its mouth into several streams, from which, during the summer months, when the snow is melting, a considerable body of water passes out into the inlet. The valley through which this river flows extends 10 miles in a northerly direction from the mouth of Bear river, and is thickly wooded, and flanked by the Gladstone mountains, 4,800 feet high; it terminates at the foot of the Disraeli mountains, a range which extends in an ESE. and WNW. direction.

The Bear and Salmon rivers have a mud-flat extending across their mouths, rendering communication, even by canoes, difficult at low water. Commencing at about 600 yards south of Salmon river valley, this deposit of mud extends across the canal in a northeasterly direction, passing over 1 mile from the mouth of Bear river. The edge of the bank is steep, breaking down suddenly to 24 fathoms.

Anchorage may be obtained in 25 to 30 fathoms, soft mud, about 600 yards below the Bear River flats, on the eastern side, with Eagle point, the northern point at the entrance to Salmon river, bearing S. 66° W. (S. 36° W. mag.). Vessels should not go above this bearing as the flat is uncovered only at low water and is very steep-to. The holding ground is good, but the anchorage is unprotected, being exposed to the southerly winds coming up the canal and the northerly winds that sweep down the Bear river valley.

Tides.—It is high water, full and change, at the head of Portland canal at 1 h. 30 m.; springs rise from 23 to 27 feet and occasionally 30 feet, neaps 15 to 20 feet. In August it was noticed that the night tides rose considerably higher than the day tides.

Tidal streams have an estimated maximum velocity of 2 knots on the flood and 3 knots on the ebb, diminishing toward the head of Portland canal and Observatory inlet. The streams turn shortly after high and low water by the shore.

CHAPTER XIV.

QUEEN CHARLOTTE ISLANDS.

VARIATION IN 1906.

Cape St. James	26° 20′ E	Lawn point	27° 25′ E.
Rose point	28° 10′ E.	Buck point	27° 00′ E.

North island..............28° 00′ E.

Queen Charlotte islands, consisting of three principal islands, may be regarded as a partly submerged mountain range—a line drawn from the southern extremity of the islands to their northwestern point representing its axis—which, together with several smaller islands, forms a compact archipelago, situated between the parallels of 51° 50′ and 54° 15′ N., and the meridians 130° 54′ and 133° 10′ W.

In general character these islands are mountainous and heavily timbered, and the mining resources are very extensive. The chief item of trade is in fur seals.

The channels between the principal islands are named Houston Stewart and Skidegate, the former, or southern, channel separating Kunghit and Moresby islands; and the latter, or northern, Moresby and Graham islands.

Climate.—The climate of these islands and of the offlying islands of the coast is influenced by the warm body of water which washes their shores. The climate is milder and the winters less severe than in the inlets. The vapor arising from this body of warm water is condensed upon the mountains forming the shores of the mainland and causes an almost constant drizzling rain.

Winds.—Southeast winds are prevalent and are generally accompanied with thick rain. Winds from the opposite quarter bring fine weather. No dependence can be placed on the weather for 24 hours at a time.

The heaviest rainfall takes place on the western mountains and often while it is raining heavily on the mountains it is clear over the strait to the eastward. Snow occasionally falls in winter.

Kunghit island (Prevost island), the southernmost island of the group, is about 12½ miles long north and south, with a breadth of 8½ miles. The land gradually rises northward from cape St. James (its southern point) till near Houston Stewart channel, where it has in places an elevation of about 2,000 feet, which heights, if the weather is clear, will be the first land seen on approaching Queen Charlotte islands from the southward.

The eastern coast of Kunghit island is bold, and in many places bordered by steep cliffs. This part of the coast, between cape St. James and East point, a distance of 12 miles, is indented by two bays or inlets, the southern apparently inconsiderable, while Luxana bay, the northern, is probably 3 or 4 miles in depth. From East point the shore trends northwestward 6 or 7 miles to Moore head, the SE. entrance point of Houston Stewart channel. The shore is much broken, being penetrated by inlets which extend back among the high hills. Several small islands lie off it, one of which (High island) is bold, densely covered with trees, and has a height of 150 feet.

The western side of Kunghit island, between cape St. James and the western entrance of Houston Stewart channel, for about 12 miles is apparently bold, but it is less known than the opposite side. The land near cape St. James is not so thickly wooded as that to the northward.

Cape St. James, so named by Captain Dixon who rounded the cape on St. James day, 1787, in the Queen Charlotte, is the southern extremity of Kunghit island. The southern point of cape St. James is a vertical cliff about the same height as the larger of the islets lying off it (180 feet).

The cape slopes gradually from a summit 1,000 feet high to the sea.

Kerouart islets received their name from La Perouse and consist of a chain of rocky islets and rocks which extend from cape St. James 3½ miles in a SSE. direction, corresponding with that of the mountain axis of the group. A sunken ledge is reported to extend 1½ miles farther in the same direction.

As seen from a distance of some miles to the NE., Kerouart islets appear to form three groups, the first lying close to cape St. James, consisting of two large rocks (Hummock islets) 180 feet high, the second of one large and several smaller rocks, and the third and farthest southward, of two or three rocks of 100 feet in height, and a number of lesser ones. These islets are remarkable, standing boldly up with rounded tops and vertical cliffs on all sides; the smaller rocks have the pillar-like form so frequently found where a rocky coast is exposed to the full sweep of a great ocean. They serve as secure breeding places for innumerable gulls, puffins, and other sea birds.

Danger rocks.—About 3 miles northward of the eastern entrance to Houston Stewart channel, and at about 2 miles off the low and densely wooded point between the eastern entrance of Houston Stewart channel and Carpenter bay, is a ledge of rocks, showing a little above water, on which the sea breaks violently and for a considerable distance around; other rocks encircle these, but they are under water.

Approaching Houston Stewart channel from the northward these rocks should be given a wide berth.

Houston Stewart channel trends westward from Moore head for 2½ miles to Hornby point, thence SW. for 3 miles to the entrance from the Pacific ocean. Opposite the bend formed by Hornby point is Rose harbor. Louscoone, at the western entrance of the channel and just within Anthony island, is said to be a good harbor, similar to Rose harbor. The country round this locality is mountainous, mostly rising steeply from the coast, and thickly wooded; the trees, however, are stunted and show much deadwood, the roots holding to the almost naked rock. There is no arable land, and the soil is poor.

Houston Stewart channel should only be used at slack water on account of the strong tidal streams and eddies in it.

Entering from the eastward.—This entrance may be known by its bold southern point, and the round thickly wooded islet. At about 4 miles from the entrance there is 90 fathoms of water, and the depth gradually shoals to 20 fathoms at 1 mile from it; from this distance off, the soundings are very irregular, varying from 30 to 7 fathoms over a series of ridges or bars of rock, sand, shells, and mud. In the entrance, which is about 1 mile wide, between Moore head and Langford point, there is 20 fathoms of water, rocky bottom.

Haydon rock lies on the southern side of the entrance about ¼ mile eastward of the NE. point of Kunghit island.

A rock which dries at low water lies on the line between Langford and Forsyth points and 650 yards from the latter.

Raspberry cove.—Within Forsyth point, at 1 mile westward of Langford point on the northern side, is a snug bay, bordered by a sandy beach, in which, at about ⅜ mile from Forsyth point, and at ⅓ mile from the beach, is a secure and convenient anchorage in 16 fathoms. In the NW. part of the bay is Raspberry cove, into which a stream of water flows.

Rock.—At ¼ mile westward of Forsyth point, and a little to the northward of the line of the direction of the channel, is a rocky patch with kelp on it, which dries at low water springs; do not, therefore, haul to the northward too soon after entering.

On the southern side of the channel are some small wooded islands (Charles, Annette, and Fairfax), here and there fringed with outlying patches of kelp, which latter should always be avoided.

Trevan rock.—Three-quarters of a mile eastward of Hornby point is Ellen island, the largest of the islands on the south side of the channel, and 600 yards north from its northern point and 1¼ miles nearly west from Forsyth point, nearly in mid-channel, and contracting the passage on its northern side to rather less than ½ mile, is Trevan rock, which covers at high water; close to the northern side of it the depth is 7 fathoms. Patches of kelp reduce the channel on the southern side of the rock, between it and Ellen island, to about 200 yards in width.

Anchorage.—There is a good anchorage, to the eastward of Ellen island, in a bay formed by that island and the rocky patch which covers at half tide, at nearly ½ mile eastward of the island. The anchorage is in 14 fathoms, mud, and the tidal stream is not felt.

Quadra rocks, in mid-channel, consist of a patch 120 yards long in a NE. and SW. direction and 60 yards wide, the two shoalest spots being at either extreme with 6 feet of water on them, 12 to 14 feet in other places, and 5 to 6 fathoms around. The patch can be seen at high water and is marked at times during slack water by kelp; with the tidal stream running it is distinguished by overfalls and tide rips. From the western extreme of the rocks, Hornby point bears S. 20° W. (S. 6° E. mag.), distant 1,100 yards, and the southern extreme of Ross island N. 81° W. (S. 73° W. mag.).

Tides.—The spring rise, in May, was observed to be 16 feet.

Rose harbor.—This secure and capacious harbor on the northern side of Houston Stewart channel, takes a northerly direction between Catherine point on the west and Ross island on the east, for 3 miles from its junction with the channel. For the first 2 miles the average breadth of the harbor is ¾ mile, the western shore rising boldly with deep water close-to; the eastern shore, although high, has kelp along it, with shoal water extending to a distance of 200 to 500 yards. The harbor then contracts to ½ mile in width between two low points forming its head, beyond which is a basin, about 2 miles in circumference, filled with rocks and wooded islets, having on its western side Sedmond river, a small stream abounding in the season with geese and ducks. The land on its northern and western sides is high and mountainous, while that on its eastern side is low. This basin is separated from South cove in Carpenter bay by a narrow neck of low wooded land.

Denny rocks lie about 400 yards NW. of Ross island; foul ground extends from them in all directions to a distance of from 200 to 300 yards; this ground is usually marked by kelp.

Pincher rocks lie nearly 400 yards S. by W. from the eastern entrance point of the basin.

Entering from westward.—The western portion of Houston Stewart channel is about 3 miles long and ¾ mile wide, with several small islands (Gordon isles) at its southern entrance. The shores on both sides are bold and densely wooded. Those from the southward bound in by this entrance, when abreast cape St. James, should close the land to 1½ miles, and after coasting it for about 12 miles the entrance will open. Two remarkable white stripes down the mountains, 6 or 7 miles to the northwestward, are excellent landmarks.

After passing at a convenient distance to the southward of Anthony island, the largest and outer island at the entrance, which is 200 feet high, with white cliffs (off the southern end of which an extensive ledge of rocks projects ½ mile in a SW. direction), the channel will show itself. Flat rock, 50 feet high and resembling a haystack, lies nearer the western than the eastern side of the channel, 1½ miles northeastward from Anthony island; it is a good guide and a vessel should pass between it and the Gordon islands to the southeastward. There is an Indian village known as Ninstints, of the Skangoi tribe, on the inner side of Anthony island; the natives are very wild, and persons visiting or trading with them should be on their guard.

Moresby island, the middle one of the three principal islands of the Queen Charlotte group, is 72 miles long, but explorations on its eastern coast have resulted (by tracing out the channels) in leaving it a mere skeleton, in places only 1½ to 2 miles in breadth. The highest and most rugged part of the island is probably in about lat. 52° 30′ N., where many peaks bear patches of perennial snow and attain altitudes of over 5,000 feet. Also on Louise island, and about the head of Cumshewa inlet, the land is very rugged, with many peaks of over 3,000 and 4,000 feet in height.

Carpenter bay, the southernmost bay on the eastern side of Moresby island, is between Iron point on its northern and Islet point on its southern side, a little over 2 miles wide, and extends westward about 5 miles. It is not quite landlocked, but is sheltered from the only direction otherwise exposed by a little rocky reef which extends out from its eastern side. On its southern side are two small bays, the western of which, South cove, approaches near to the head of Rose harbor. At its head is good anchorage for a small vessel in from 6 to 10 fathoms.

Carpenter bay ends westward in a narrow arm, which receives two streams. It resembles the head of Rose harbor in being filled with small rocky islands and rocks, making it unsafe for even a small craft. The general character of the country surrounding the bay is like that of Houston Stewart channel. In June there were many seals in the bay.

Off the entrance to Carpenter bay lie the Rankine islands, about 2 miles ENE. of Iron point and about the same distance from the southern entrance point of the bay. A small island lies 1½ miles north of the western Rankine island.

Collison bay, situated between Carpenter bay and Skincuttle inlet, is about 1¾ miles wide between Bluff point, its SE. point of entrance, and the NW. point, and has a probable depth of 2 miles.

It runs up into a narrow arm, which has not been examined. Several small islands and rocks lie off its entrance and it does not appear to be serviceable as a harbor.

Gull rock, 10 feet high, bears N. 82° E. (N. 56° E. mag.), distant 1¼ miles from Deluge point, and is ¾ mile off Moresby island, between Collison bay and Skincuttle inlet. Inner Low rock lies S. 4° W. (S. 22° E. mag.) from Gull rock and midway between it and the shore.

Skincuttle inlet is 5½ miles deep in a SW. direction, with a width of 4 miles between Deluge point on the southern and Granite point on the northern side of its entrance. The northern side of the inlet is formed by Burnaby island, and from the NW. angle Burnaby strait runs northward to Juan Perez sound and separates Burnaby island from the eastern shore of Moresby island. The shores of Skincuttle inlet resemble those of other parts of the islands already described. Near the NW. angle of the inlet the mountains rise steeply to a height of 3,000 feet or more.

The entrance to Skincuttle inlet is south of a chain of islands, called the Copper islands, lying ENE. and WSW. of each other, near the middle of the entrance. It is 1½ miles wide, but should be used with caution, as there is reason to believe that a rock, sometimes bare, lies in it. The passage to the north of the Copper islands is contracted and with one or more rocks in its narrowest part.

Granite point is a rather remarkable whitish crag, joined to the main shore by a narrow neck of low land.

Bolkus islands, five in number, with many small rocks and reefs, form a chain about 2 miles long, lying east and west of each other in the center of Skincuttle inlet. They are low, and on the western and largest of the islands the soil appears to be good, though now covered with dense forest.

A rock awash at high water lies midway between the Bolkus islands and the southern shore and at equal distances from the entrances to Harriet harbor and Huston inlet. Bush rock is situated 200 yards NW. from the eastern entrance point of Huston inlet, and 1,600 yards WNW. from Bush rock is Low Black rock.

Harriet harbor is 2 miles southwestward from the southern entrance point (Deluge point) and extends southeastward 1 mile. It should be entered by the channel on the western side of Harriet island, which lies in the middle of its entrance, and a vessel should be kept near the western side of the channel (as several small rocks covered at high water lie along Harriet island) and run some distance beyond the inner end of the island before anchoring, to avoid the shoal bank which lies off its southern point. The depth is about 8 fathoms, with good holding ground, and the harbor is well sheltered from most directions, though subject to heavy squalls from the valley at its head when a southerly gale is blowing.

Huston inlet, 1½ miles SW. of Harriet harbor, is a wide inlet which runs southeastward about 4 miles and then turns to the west, in which direction its extremity was not visited, but it approaches the western side of Moresby island to within about 1½ miles.

Tangle cove.—At the western end of Skincuttle inlet are three indentations of the coast, of which the southern is George bay. The northern, lying at the entrance of Burnaby strait, is Tangle cove, a well-sheltered anchorage for a small vessel, but a shoal, the extent of which is unknown, lies off its entrance. The entrance is between a small island at its southern side and two other little islets to the north, and in it is a rock which uncovers at low water. The mountains at the head of Tangle cove are steep and probably reach 3,000 feet in height; part of their upper slopes are bare of trees, but apparently covered with moss.

North side.—On the southern side of Burnaby island is a bay, with several small islands across the mouth of it, which may be a good harbor, but it has not been examined. Farther east, in the vicinity of an abandoned copper mine, are Blue Jay and Kingfisher coves.

Burnaby strait, between the western shore of Burnaby island and Moresby island, is 9 miles in length between Skincuttle inlet and Juan Perez sound, the southern portions of the distance of about 4 miles being narrow, but gaining at the northern end an average width of 1¼ miles. All parts of Burnaby strait must be navigated with great caution, as there are many rocks, and a large portion of them are covered at high water. Dolomite narrows, at 2½ miles north of the southern entrance, are not more than ¼ mile wide, and here the channel is crooked and obstructed by rocks and shoals having from 6 to 8 feet at low water. The tidal streams are not strong, but it can not be recommended as a passage for any craft larger than a boat or canoe.

Just south of Dolomite narrows, from the western side of the strait, opens Bag harbor, expanding within to a basin nearly 1 mile in diameter. The Twins, nearly abreast of Dolomite narrows, on Burnaby island, are two conspicuous mountains estimated to be 1,500 feet high.

Island bay, at 1½ miles north of the narrows, extends southwestward, and is 2 miles deep. It was so named from the number of small islands in it, about seventeen, and is probably too rocky for a safe harbor.

Skaat harbor, at the northern end of Burnaby strait, is a bay ¾ mile wide, with a depth of about 3 miles. Wanderer island and several smaller islets lie off the entrance. The harbor turns into a narrow inlet in its upper part and terminates among high mountains forming a portion of the axial chain of the islands. Skaat harbor has not been sounded or carefully examined, but from the character of its shores it would be likely to afford good anchorage, especially westward of Wanderer island, and if so, it is the best for large vessels in this vicinity. The harbor will probably be found deepest on the Wanderer island side, as there is an extensive field of kelp off the opposite shore.

All Alone stone and Monument rock form good marks to the northern entrance of Burnaby strait, near which lies the entrance to the harbor. The entrance to Skaat harbor on the southern side of Wanderer island is very narrow; at the angle formed between it and the shore of Burnaby strait are two small coves affording anchorage for a small vessel, but with wide tidal flats at their head, which a short distance beyond low-water mark fall away rapidly into deep water.

Limestone rock is a dangerous reef, dry only at low water, and lies 1 mile to the southeastward of Center island, with the eastern point of that island in line with the eastern point of Wanderer island; a second rock, also only dry at low water, lies a short distance SE. of it.

Huxley island, at the northern entrance of Burnaby strait, is nearly 2 miles long north and south and about 1¼ miles broad; it is bold and remarkable, rising rapidly from the beach to a height of 1,500 feet. Abreast the NW. point of the island, in mid-channel, a cast of 70 fathoms was obtained, with a fine sandy bottom.

Burnaby island.—The northern shore of Burnaby island, 5¾ miles in length ENE. and WSW., is nearly straight on the whole, though with a few shallow bays, one of which is called Section cove. Alder island lies off about the center of this stretch of coast; it is about ½ mile in diameter, nearly flat, with probably a good anchorage behind it, which should be approached from the NW., as Saw reef runs out from the shore of Burnaby island to the eastward, and this part of the coast is broken and rocky, with large fields of kelp extending from it. The hills on the northern side of Burnaby island are estimated at 300 to 500 feet in height.

From Scudder point, the northeastern point of Burnaby island, the eastern side of the island trends southwestward, allowing the outer of the Copper islands to be seen. A considerable width of low land stretches back from Scudder point, covered with an open growth of large but gnarled spruces. Small beaches of coarse gravel fill the spaces between the low, shattered, rock masses, apparently caused by the action of a heavy surf.

North of Granite point is a bay of considerable extent in a southwesterly direction; a high island lies in its mouth.

Juan Perez sound has at its entrance, between Burnaby and Ramsay islands, a width of 8 miles. The sound extends westward, a number of smaller inlets and bays branching off from it, and is continued in a more northerly direction by Darwin sound, by which it communicates with the upper ends of the long inlets which extend westward from Laskeek bay. From the center of a line joining its outer entrance points to the southern entrance of Darwin sound Juan Perez sound is 17 miles in length.

On its southwestern side are Werner bay, Hutton inlet, and De la Beche inlet, which terminate in narrow channels, or fiords, extending among the axial mountains of Moresby island, and which have not been examined to their heads. From Werner bay two small inlets branch. Hutton inlet appears to be about 3 miles long, and De la Beche nearly 6 miles, with a low valley, hemmed in by hills on either side, running northwestward from its extremity. The range of mountains southward of De la Beche inlet was given the name Sierra de San Christoval by Perez. None of these openings seem to be well adapted for harbors, as the shores are bold and rocky, seldom showing beaches, and the water to all appearances too deep for anchorage.

Bischoff islands, lying on the NW. part of Juan Perez sound, off the south side of Lyell island, are low, but densely wooded. There is sheltered anchorage for small craft between the two larger islands, but it must be entered from the westward and with much caution, owing to the number of rocks and sunken reefs which surround it.

Sedgwick bay, about 3 miles deep, on the southern shore of Lyell island, is too much exposed for a harbor, as southerly winds draw directly up Juan Perez sound.

Ramsay, Murchison, and Faraday islands are the largest of a group of islands forming the northern side of the entrance to Juan Perez sound.

Ramsay island is 2¾ miles in length east and west, has bold hills rising in the center, and is densely wooded. Its southern shore is high, with some rocky cliffs; two small islets lie off the NE. side, which is rugged and composed of solid rock. The NW. shore has several coves, but none suited for anchorage.

Murchison island is 2½ miles, and Faraday island nearly 2 miles, long; both are low.

Between Ramsay and Murchison islands is a small group composed of Hot Spring and House islets and a few smaller islets and rocks. On the southern side of Hot Spring islet is the spring from which it takes its name. Its situation is easily recognized by a patch of green mossy sward which can be seen from a considerable distance; steam also generally hovers over it. The temperature is so high that the hand can scarcely bear it with comfort. The water has a slight smell of sulphureted hydrogen and a barely perceptible saline taste. The Indians bathe in a natural pool in which the waters of one of the streams collect.

Between Hot Spring and House islets is a good anchorage for small craft, sheltered on all sides but the north.

Tar islands.—Extending northward from the NE. end of Murchison island is a chain of small islands about 4 miles long, named the Tar islands; the Indians report that on one of them bituminous matter is found oozing out among the stones on the beach. Agglomerate island, the southernmost, has apparently been burnt over, and is covered with standing dead trees. These islands are only approximately placed on the chart. Northeastward of them lies a single low island with a few trees on it, named Tuft island.

Rocks which dry at low water lie between Faraday and Murchison islands, and there are several small rocky islets and low-water rocks in the vicinity of Hot Spring and House islets.

Entering Juan Perez sound.—Those entering the sound had better do so to the southward of Ramsay island, till the narrower channels have been surveyed. No bottom was reached with 94 fathoms of line in the center of the sound south of Ramsay island, nor at about 1 mile SE. of the extremity of Bischoff island. The water is apparently deep throughout, but it has not been sounded.

Lyell island, about 15 miles long east and west and 9 miles north and south, is separated from Moresby island by Darwin sound. The island is composed of hilly land, rising generally at once from the shore to heights of 600 to 900 feet, and attaining toward the center of the island a height probably exceeding 1,000 feet. It is densely wooded, and on the low land there is some fine timber. The eastern coast has not been surveyed. Atli inlet, on the north side of Lyell island, has not been examined; it is about 3 miles deep, with two main arms, and does not appear to be a good harbor.

Halibut bank.—About 3 to 4 miles east of the NE. point of Lyell island is Halibut bank, with 23 fathoms of water on it.

A spot, on which the sea breaks at low water, is reported to exist about 1½ to 2 miles northward of Halibut bank.

Darwin sound lies between Lyell island and the eastern shore of Moresby island, and from its southern entrance to White point is 12 miles in length NNW. and SSE.; in width it is irregular, but is a fine navigable channel. In the southern entrance no bottom was found at 94 fathoms. When entering from the southward, Shuttle island appears to be nearly round. The channel on its eastern side should be followed, as this seems to be quite free from danger. Abreast the north end of Shuttle island in this channel a cast of 18 fathoms was obtained. One mile beyond this point, and in mid-channel, is a low rock which is not readily seen, with a second, uncovered only at low water, a short distance to the north of it.

Tidal streams.—The flood stream sets up Darwin sound from the southward into the various inlets, and then eastward to the open sea again by Richardson and Logan inlets. The ebb draws through from end to end in the opposite direction. The tidal streams run at the rate of 2 knots at the strongest.

Bigsby inlet.—The western side of Darwin sound for 5 miles from the southern entrance is rocky and broken, with several coves and inlets. At that distance is Bigsby inlet, extending 2½ miles in a westerly direction. It is a gloomy chasm, less than ½ mile in width, and surrounded by mountains probably as high as any in the islands. These rise steeply from the water, sometimes attaining in the first instance a height of 3,000 feet, and are in places nearly perpendicular, but are mostly well wooded. Farther back, especially to the southward and westward, massive summits of bare granite rise to a height of 4,000 to 5,000 feet with their gorges filled with drifted snow. The inlet is almost void of anything like a beach.

Shuttle island, though low, is rocky. The channel to the west of it is probably deep enough for vessels of any class, but should not be used until surveyed. There is a rock, covered at high water, on the west side of its northern entrance.

False bay, abreast Shuttle island, on the eastern side of Darwin sound, extends about 2 miles in a SE. direction. In the mouth of the bay are several small islands.

Echo harbor.—At 1½ miles northward of Shuttle island, and opposite the inner end of Richardson inlet, is Echo harbor. The harbor runs southward about 1 mile and then westward for a like distance and is surrounded by high hills which, toward its head, rise to rugged mountains. The outer part of the entrance has a depth of 10 fathoms in it; the sides then approach, leaving a channel scarcely 300 yards wide between abrupt rocky shores.

In the harbor proper the depth is everywhere about 15 fathoms, decreasing gradually toward the head for a short distance and then running steeply up to a flat which is partly dry at low water, and which above high-water mark forms a narrow grassy beach. The bottom is soft mud and excellent holding ground. A very narrow passage leads westward from the bottom of the harbor into a secluded basin, scarcely ¼ mile in diameter, which, with the exception of a channel in the middle, is nearly dry at low water. Into its head flows a large brook, coming from the mountains to the southwestward.

Klunkwoi bay.—At 2 miles west of the entrance to Echo harbor the shore-line falls back into Klunkwoi bay. The bay runs up in several arms, which have not been carefully examined, among the bases of rugged snow-clad mountains, which rise steeply from the shores, or at the sides of the valleys, by which the heads of the inlets are continued inland. The highest peaks are probably 5,000 feet or more in altitude. The mountains of Moresby island appear to culminate here and are not such a prominent feature farther southward.

Crescent inlet may be considered as forming the extension of Darwin sound northwestward. It turns gradually through nearly half a circle from a NW. direction to nearly SW. and is over 4 miles in length. It is a fiord, with steep mountains and wooded sides, but probably not so deep as most similar inlets, as there are stretches of beach of some length. It is not known if the Indians have any trail across to Tasoo harbor, to which, if correctly placed, the distance across can not be great. Red Top mountain, partly bare and about 3,000 feet high, is the most conspicuous peak in the vicinity, rising on the northern side of the inlet at the angle of the bend.

Laskeek bay is the name given to the wide indentation of the coast between the northeastern extreme of Lyell island and Vertical point, the southeastern point of Louise island, bearing NNW. and SSE. from each other, and 10 miles apart. From Laskeek bay four large inlets extend westward; of these the two southern, Richardson and Logan inlets, open into the head of Darwin sound.

The two northern inlets, Dana and Selwyn, communicate at their heads with the head of Cumshewa inlet to the northward.

Richardson inlet is about 11 miles in length in an east and west direction, with an average breadth of 1½ miles, and is straight, with moderately bold shores. The southern side is formed by Lyell island, Atli inlet being just within the entrance, and Dog island about 5 miles within it. Kunga, Tanoo, and Inner islands, from east to west, form the northern and western sides. Kunga island is about 1,500 feet high and forms a good mark for the entrance; there is a low rocky reef some distance eastward of the outer point of Kunga and a second off the southern coast of the same island. A small island lies 3½ miles ENE. of Kunga island. Near Dog island there are several small islets and rocks, and at about 3½ miles west of it on the southern side of the inlet is a cove, where a small vessel can find a convenient anchorage. probably the nearest stopping place to Laskeek village. The channels between Kunga and Tanoo and between the latter and Inner island are probably deep, though the first should be navigated with caution, and care taken to avoid the eastern end of Tanoo island, as several rocks and patches of kelp lie off it.

Laskeek or Klue Indian village is situated on the eastern extremity of Tanoo island. It is one of the most populous still remaining in the Queen Charlotte islands. There is anchorage off this village in 11 fathoms, about 400 yards east of the village. This anchorage is not a good one, being exposed to NW. and SE. winds. On anchoring, the houses should not be brought to bear west of WNW., as patches of rock stretch out two-thirds the distance across to the opposite shore from Laskeek point, so that going to or coming from the north, the eastern shore should be kept well aboard, it being steep-to. In the season, kelp marks the patches.

The western end of Richardson inlet is contracted to a width of about ¼ mile and obstructed by a small island and several rocks.

The tidal stream runs through Richardson passage with considerable strength and it is unsuited as an approach to Echo harbor, though the most direct way in from the sea.

Logan inlet is about 7 miles in length and nearly parallel to Richardson inlet, with Flower Pot island, a small bold rock, covered with trees, off its mouth. One other small island lies close to the shore on its southern side, but it is otherwise free from obstructions, and constitutes a fine navigable channel, the best approach to Echo harbor.

Enter to the north of Flower Pot island and keep in the center of the channel. Kunga island, as already mentioned, is high. Titul island, small and with low limestone cliffs, lies northward of it. Foul ground extends some distance northward of Titul island and it should be given a wide berth. Tanoo and Inner islands are also bold, rising to rounded hills of nearly uniform height of about 800 feet. They have some good gravelly beaches, though mostly rocky.

Timber.—In the inlets in the vicinity of Lyell island there is a considerable quantity of fine timber, trees growing in all moderately level and sheltered places.

Dana inlet runs about W. by S. nearly 8 miles, with bold shores; at its entrance is Helmet island, small, rocky, high, and of rounded form. A second small island is near it, and from most points of view the channel between the two is not seen, and care is necessary not to mistake this island for Flower Pot island, at the entrance to Logan inlet. At its western extremity Dana inlet turns northward, communicating by a narrow but apparently deep passage with Selwyn inlet, and thus cutting off Talunkwan island from Moresby island.

Talunkwan island is 8 miles long and 2 miles broad; the hills are rounded in form and from 800 to 900 feet high.

Selwyn inlet is nearly parallel to Dana inlet and about 10 miles in length, and near its head, turning northward, runs in that direction for a like distance, forming at high water a passage for canoes into the upper part of Cumshewa inlet, and separates Louise island from the main shore. The passage is narrow and walled in on both sides by mountains which rise very steeply from it. Entrance island is small and lies off the northern entrance point with a low rock about 1 mile southeastward of it.

After giving the islets off the northern entrance a wide berth, keep the northern shore aboard for a distance of 5 miles until the entrance of Rockfish harbor is reached.

Rockfish harbor is formed by a projection of low land, at the angle of Selwyn inlet, and extends in a westerly direction for about 1¼ miles, with a width of ½ mile, and an average depth of 15 fathoms. It is a secure and well-sheltered anchorage, more easily entered than Cumshewa. There is good anchorage in the head of the harbor in 14 fathoms. A spring of good water will be found on the northern shore at the head. Foul ground extends off the end of the spit which forms the southern side of the harbor.

The head of the northern branch of Selwyn inlet can not be more than 9 or 10 miles from Mitchell or Gold harbor (on the western coast), as a low valley runs some distance westward. At about 3 miles from the entrance of the passage leading to Cumshewa is the opening to an inlet about 3 miles deep in a SW. direction, approaching to within 4½ miles of Mitchell harbor. These upper arms of Selwyn inlet are environed by high and rugged mountains.

Reef and Low islands are situated in the outer part of Laskeek bay. The southern and first named is steep along the water's edge, and a reef runs off about ½ mile to the southward from it. Their exact position is not known.

Louise island is about 15 miles long east and west, and 8 miles broad, with high mountains, and doubtless the snow on them lasts throughout the summer. From Selwyn inlet the eastern coast of the island trends northeastward 8 miles, with several small bays, fully open to the sea, and mostly rocky.

Vertical point, the northern entrance point of Laskeek bay, projects at about halfway along this stretch of coast and is remarkable from the shape of the beds of gray limestone of which it is composed, aggregating at least 400 feet in thickness. North of the point are the two small Limestone islands, behind which the tide running southward along the coast forms a race on the ebb.

Skedans bay, about 2 miles from the entrance to Cumshewa, is strewn with sunken rocks and entirely open and should on no account be entered by vessels. A large stream enters its head, forming a high waterfall, which can be seen at some distance inland; this stream, according to the Indians, flows out of a lake of some size, high among the mountains. Skedans village forms a semicircle round the head of a small bay or cove, very rocky, which indents the southern side of a narrow isthmus, connecting two remarkable nipple-shaped hills with the main shore. This peninsula is situated at the southern entrance point to Cumshewa inlet, and between it and the Skedans islands the tide forms a race. Skedans islands, distant 3½ miles from the shore, are low and covered with trees.

Cumshewa inlet extends about 15 miles westward, with a prolongation southward connecting it with Selwyn inlet. It differs from the inlets to the south in the low character of the land on its northern shore. There is more beach along the shores than in the southern inlets, and wide tidal flats indicate shoaler water, which is found not only in the inlet itself but off the coast. Toward the head of the inlet the shores are quite bold in some places and the water probably deep.

In the entrance of Cumshewa inlet, to the north of Skedans islands, are depths of 20 fathoms, with a shell and gravel bottom. Off the northern point of entrance Cumshewa island, a small barren rock, and the Cumshewa rocks extend in a southeasterly direction nearly 1½ miles. When coming from the north, therefore, keep well off the shore till the rocks are passed and then stand in to the entrance in a northwesterly direction.

Kingui island, just within the northern entrance point of the inlet, is covered with dead trees and can be recognized easily. At about 1 mile within the entrance an extensive shoal, on which the sea breaks heavily, extends from the southern shore, leaving a channel about ½ mile wide between it and the northern shore of the inlet. The passage in is through this channel, in which it is reported there are depths of 7 and 8 fathoms. A few patches of the shoal dry at low water, but the greater part is indicated only by the kelp which grows thickly on it during the summer. The tidal streams run strongly in the mouth of the inlet.

McKay cove, just within the narrows, on the northern shore, is a cove where the shore dries out for some distance at low water, but off it a small vessel may find a pretty secure anchorage, though the tidal streams sweep round the cove.

Cumshewa village is situated on the northern side of the inlet about 1 mile westward of McKay cove, the houses being built along the shore of a bay facing southeastward, 3⅓ miles within the entrance. A small rocky islet, connected with the main at low water, lies off it.

Anchorage.—The best anchorage for a large vessel is probably to be found on the southern side, 5½ miles westward of Skedans point and abreast a stretch of low land, eastward of a stream.

The coast.—From the entrance to Cumshewa inlet the coast trends northwestward to Spit point, the southern point of Skidegate inlet, a distance of 17 miles. It is indented by two considerable bays. Copper bay, the northern, about 5 miles from Spit point, received its name from some copper works which were carried on there at one time. The land is low and very different in appearance from that of the coast southward.

The projecting points are mostly low and flat and formed of gravel deposits. With the change in the character of the land the beach becomes flat, and shoal water extends far offshore, the depths shoaling from 10 fathoms at 3 miles off Cumshewa island to 6 and 7 fathoms at 7 miles off Spit point. Near Cumshewa the beaches are almost entirely composed of bowlders, but show more gravel and sand toward Skidegate. The surface of the country is densely wooded with trees of large size.

Cape Chroustcheff, 2 miles to the southward of Spit point, should not be passed nearer than 5 miles; the cape is low and dark-looking. Coming from the southward, it shows very conspicuously; when abreast of it, Spit point, the low southern point of Skidegate, becomes visible.

Skidegate inlet, separating Moresby from Graham island, forms a spacious harbor communicating with the western coast between Hunter and Buck points, by way of Skidegate channel (Cartwright sound). Skidegate inlet from its entrance extends in a southwesterly direction for about 9 miles from the Bar rocks, where it contracts to a width of 1½ miles between Image point and Flowery islet on the northern side of Alliford bay.

Within these points it opens again, forming two expansions, separated by Maude island. That part of the northern expansion eastward of Lina island forms Bear Skin bay; the part westward of the island has several islands in it, with Anchor cove in the western end. Beyond Anchor cove it turns NW., forming Long arm, the total length of the inlet from Bar rocks to the head of Long arm being about 21 miles. The southern expansion forms South bay, in which is South island, its western side connecting, by East narrows, with Skidegate channel and the waters west of Queen Charlotte islands.

The shore of Skidegate inlet is not so bold as those of the fiords to the southward, and is mostly fringed with a beach. The surrounding country is densely wooded and, where the land is flat, timber of magnificent growth is found. This inlet would be convenient in many respects as a site for sawmills.

Spit point is low and wooded and composed of sand deposits which, extending northward, form the bar which stretches across the extrance to Skidegate inlet.

The bar or spit, with from 1 to 3 fathoms of water on it, extends in a northerly direction for about 9¼ miles to within nearly 1½ miles of Lawn point, the northern point of entrance. The spit slopes off very gradually seaward, while toward the inlet it rapidly deepens to 20 or 30 fathoms.

Bar rocks lie on the outer edge of the spit, 2½ miles from its extremity. The western one dries 5 feet and lies 6¾ miles N. 12° W. (N. 39° W. mag.) from Spit point and 2¾ miles N. 78° E. (N. 51° E. mag.) from Dead Tree point. The outer or eastern rock dries 1 foot and lies 600 yards eastward of the western rock. The sea does not always break on these rocks.

Lawn point is generally green, with a small sand cliff and a large bowlder 33 feet in height with a large white patch 24 feet square painted on its seaward face, in front of it; a hill 500 feet high rises immediately to the westward of the point. The coast southward of Lawn point is flat for 10 miles to Village bay and is covered with standing dead trees.

Dead Tree point, 3¾ miles to the southward of Lawn point, is a projecting part of the coast, but otherwise is not conspicuous.

Village islands, in front of Village bay, form good marks for Skidegate inlet; the northern one (Bare islet), 125 feet high, is almost bare, and the other (Tree islet), having trees upon it, is 153 feet high.

Village bay is a good stopping place; anchorage may be taken up between Bare islet and the beach in 14 fathoms. It is, however, exposed to SE. winds. Should one of these gales spring up, good shelter will be found in Alliford bay.

Skidegate village, nearly ½ mile in length, is situated on the shore of the bay and consists of many houses, with the usual carved posts, fronting the beach. The church near the northern end of the village is conspicuous. A wharf, with a depth of 10 feet alongside at low water, is situated to the southward of the village.

There is a wharf, 250 feet in length, with a depth of 7 feet at low water at its outer end, in the small bay westward of Image point. The post-office and store are situated near this wharf.

Two rocks, marked by kelp and with less than 6 feet of water over them, lie about 200 yards to the southward of the western point of this bay.

Alliford bay, on the southern side of the entrance, is an excellent anchorage, with good holding ground, in about 9 fathoms. The passage between Flowery islet and the northern point of the bay should not be used. Wood and water may be obtained.

Flowery islet, bare, 30 feet high, lies about 1,200 yards N. 60° W. (N. 87° W. mag.) from the northern entrance point of Alliford bay. Between Flowery islet and the point lie several small islands.

Bush islet lies ½ mile south of Flowery islet; Bare rocks extend ¼ mile southward from Bush islet.

Leading island, 3½ miles SSW. of Bare island, forms the western part of Alliford bay on the southern side of Skidegate inlet;

it is 400 feet high and appears round. The passage between Leading and Moresby islands is choked by small islands and rocks.

Maude island, at the junction of the north and south expansions of the inlet is nearly 4 miles long, WSW. and ENE., 1½ miles broad, and 1,260 feet high. On the island the Indians belonging to Gold harbor (on the western coast) have established a village on ground purchased from the Skidegate Indians. The Gold harbor Indians still preserve their rights over that region, and live there much of the summer, but find it more convenient to have their permanent houses near Skidegate.

Robber island lies 300 yards off the eastern extreme of Maude island and is connected with it by a reef.

Low Water rock lies about 1,100 yards NE. by E. from George point, the northern extreme of Maude island.

Bear Skin bay, on the northern side of the inlet, is formed by Graham and Lina islands. The head of the bay is shoal for a distance of 1½ miles. Roderick, Gooden, and Maple islands, about ½ mile apart in an east and west direction, lie ½ mile from the northern shore. Foul ground extends 500 yards SSW. from Gooden island and about 300 yards eastward from Maple island.

Channel islands.—This group extends ¾ miles SE. from the eastern end of Lina island, narrowing the channel between Lina and Maude islands to about 700 yards.

Burnt island.—A chain of islands, the principal being Tree, Angle, Wedge, and Burnt islands, extends northwestward from the western extreme of Maude island. The channel between Tree island (nearest to Maude island) and Angle island is about 700 yards wide, with 4 to 8 fathoms. Burnt island, 200 feet high, lies westward of Withered point, which extends to the southward from the western part of Lina island. Between Wedge island (320 feet high) and Withered point there is a reef, with two heads showing above water. Withered point is steep-to.

Noble rock lies 500 yards north of the NW. extreme of Burnt island; it dries 6 feet.

Triangle islet, 346 feet high. lies 2¾ miles WNW. from the western end of Maude island and a little more than 500 yards from the south shore at the entrance to Long arm. A 10-foot patch lies 300 yards eastward of the northern end of Triangle islet.

Treble islands, three in number, lie ½ mile WNW. from Triangle islet and the same distance SE. from the mouth of Slate Chuck brook.

Danube rock, in the fairway of the inner part of Skidegate inlet, with about 4 feet on it at low water springs, lies 600 yards NE. from the northern point of Triangle islet.

Anchor cove, situated 10½ miles from Village islands on the western shore of the inlet, affords anchorage in 5 fathoms; anthracite coal is found on both shores of the inlet, but principally on the sides of mount Seymour, 1 mile westward of the cove.

Ship islands lie ½ mile northward from the cove, about ¼ mile offshore.

Cowgitz coal mine is about 1 mile in a NW. direction from Anchor cove. The Queen Charlotte Coal Mining Company was formed in 1865 to open up the deposits of anthracite which had been discovered here. The project was abandoned in 1872.

Slate Chuck brook is the largest stream in Skidegate inlet, its mouth being about 1 mile north of Anchor cove. The brook receives its name from a quarry a few miles up its course, where the Indians obtain the dark shaly material from which they make carvings. In former years communication used to be kept up with the head of Masset inlet to the north by means of this stream, part of the distance being accomplished in canoe and part on foot.

Between South point, the SE. point of Anchor cove, and Steep point, to the westward, is Shoal bay, which is nearly filled by the flat extending from its head. To the southward of this bay, in the elbow formed by Long arm, is a group of islands. The northwestern, known as Gust island, is 300 yards distant from Steep point. Foul ground extends for upward of 500 yards from its western side. The Sandstone islands lie nearly in mid-channel with shoal ground extending 500 yards northward, and 800 yards westward, from them.

Directions.—A deep channel into Skidegate inlet may be found northward of Bar Rock spit by steering for Lawn point on a S. 71° W. (S. 44° W. mag.) bearing until within about 1 mile of the point, when the water will deepen to 15 or 20 fathoms; from this point a general southerly course may be steered, paying great attention to the soundings, until the western side of Leading island comes in line with the eastern side of Bare island, bearing S. 27° W. (South mag.), when steer as requisite up the inlet.

The deep portion of the channel from opposite Lawn point till past the northwestern end of Bar Rock spit (or until the bowlder at Lawn point bears NW. ½ W.) is only ⅓ mile wide; attention to the lead and steering, with a sharp lookout, is therefore very necessary.

The western side of Leading island, in line with the eastern side of Bare island bearing S. 27° W. (South mag.), leads over the Bar Rock spit, to the northward of the rocks, in 15 feet at low water, whence the depth is from 20 to 30 fathoms to Village islands; passing to the eastward of these islands anchorage may be found in the NE. side of Bear Skin bay in 12 fathoms, or, to gain shelter from a SE. gale, Alliford bay is recommended. To enter Alliford bay vessels are recommended to pass westward of Flowery and Bush islands and, to avoid the shoal southward of Bare rocks, close northward of Leading island.

Coasting vessels with local knowledge use a passage with 3½ fathoms over the spit, about 1 mile south of the Bar rocks, by keeping Dead Tree point bearing N. 86° W. (S. 67° W. mag.) until the leading mark comes on.

The channel southward of the Bar rocks appears to be shoaling, as several vessels using this channel, instead of the deep one near Lawn point, have struck heavily.

Approaching Skidegate inlet the water should not be shoaled under 6 fathoms at low water until Lawn point bears S. 71° W. (S. 44° W. mag.) or the leading marks are on.

Tides.—It is high water, at full and change, in Skidegate inlet at 1 h. 0 m.; springs rise 17 feet, neaps 14 feet.

The coast.—From Lawn hill, near Lawn point, at the entrance of Skidegate, to Rose point, the NE. extreme of Graham island, the distance is about 48 miles. The coast line is straight and open, with no harbor, and scarcely a creek or protected cove for canoes or boats for long distances. The beach is gravelly and sometimes stony to the Tlell river; beyond this it is mostly sandy to Rose point. For many miles northward cliffs of clay and sand are found alongshore, and for about 17 miles northward of Tlell river these frequently rise 50 to 100 feet in height. North of the range of cliffs the shore is almost everywhere bordered by sand hills, which are covered with coarse grass, beach pea, etc., and would afford fine grazing for cattle. Behind these are woods, in some places burnt, and the trees generally scrubby. This part of the coast is also characterized by lagoons, and is evidently extending seaward, by the banking up of the sand under the action of the sea. The largest lagoon, opening out at cape Fife, about 6 miles to the southward of Rose point, extends southward for some miles, and is reported by the Indians to communicate with a second lagoon, farther inland. The mouth of this lagoon forms a safe harbor for boats or canoes at high water, but is nearly dry at low water.

The coast between Skidegate and Rose point, having dangerous flats extending off it, which have not been examined, should be given a berth of 6 or 7 miles and the lead kept constantly going while running along it, the depths varying from 9 to 11 fathoms.

Tlell river enters the sea at 10½ miles north of Lawn point and is a stream of some size. For about 3 miles above its mouth it runs nearly parallel to the shore, separated from the sea by a low swampy strip of land only about ½ mile in breadth. This land is of comparatively modern formation, being composed of sand and gravel, and is partly covered with spruce trees of no great size. The water of the river is of a dark coffee, or amber, color.

Cape Ball (Kultowsis), nearly 20 miles from Skidegate bar, is very conspicuous, having a remarkable white cliff on it, with lower cliffs on both sides; it can not be mistaken. The Indians report that at very low tides patches of clay dry a long way off from the cape.

A rock with 2 fathoms on it lies about 6 miles ESE. from cape Ball.

Cape Fife.—Near this cape, on some parts of the shore, magnetic iron sand is abundant, with numerous colors of gold in it. There is anchorage off the cape with offshore winds; in this neighborhood the lead must be most carefully tended.

Rose point, the northeastern extreme of the Queen Charlotte islands, so named by Douglas in 1788, is known to the Haida Indians as Naikoon (long nose). It is a remarkable low promontory, apparently formed by the meeting of the currents and waves from the southward and westward round this corner of the island. The inner part of Rose point, near cape Fife, does not differ from the low wooded coast to the south; the Indians say there are many lakes and swamps inland. Farther out, where the point is narrower and more exposed, it is clothed with small stunted trees, which in turn give place to grass-covered sand hills. Beyond this the narrow gravelly point is covered above high-water mark with heaps of drifting sand and great quantities of bleached timber, logs, and stumps, piled promiscuously together. The apex of the point is a narrow steep-sided gravelly bank, which extends for a long distance at low water.

Rose spit.—A dangerous spit extends off Rose point in a northerly and then an easterly direction for, it is said, a distance of nearly 5 miles, but its exact extent has not been ascertained. H. B. M. S. Rocket struck soundings in 7 fathoms at least 3 miles from the end of the spit, over which the sea was breaking heavily, and which has four or five sandy hillocks on it. The point should, therefore, especially in darkness or thick weather, be given a wide berth. Several vessels have been lost on Rose point, which is a dangerous and treacherous point to round at any time, except in fine clear weather, and many Indians have been drowned there on different occasions.

Capt. R. Brundige remarks: "I examined Rose spit and found a strong current of about 2 knots. The spit or sand bank extends out about 4 or 5 miles, with bowlders and timbers or large trees buried in the sand. Soundings were found to be gradual, from 40 fathoms down to 5 fathoms close alongside; also good even sounding all the way to Masset, with sandy bottom. Ships could anchor under Invisible point in a southeasterly gale in 5 to 8 fathoms."

Hecate strait, between the Queen Charlotte group and the mainland of British Columbia, is 75 miles wide at its southern entrance, gradually narrowing to 25 miles between Rose spit (Graham island) and the Butterworth rocks on the eastern side of the strait. In the fairway of the southeastern part of Hecate strait the water is deep. From Skidegate across to within 10 miles of the mainland, in a NE. direction, the depths are from 8 to 25 fathoms; in some cases growing kelp was passed through by the surveying vessel Beaver (1866) in 8 and 13 fathoms.

With the center of Zayas island bearing N. 9° E. (N. 18° W. mag.) and the northern extreme of Stephens island N. 84° E. (N. 57° E. mag.), the depth is 15 fathoms. This bank of soundings was found very useful on one occasion, during a strong breeze from the SE., with thick weather, when H. B. M. S. Virago anchored on it and remained until it cleared up and the land became visible.

Northward of a line drawn from Skincuttle inlet, across the strait to Banks island, the depth does not exceed 100 fathoms, and is generally much less. A shallow area borders Graham island to the north, and it is also probably comparatively shallow for some distance off the western coast of the northern part of the same island. From the vicinity of Masset a bank of sand not exceeding 20 fathoms extends to the north and east, trending with Rose spit, and on the eastern side of the island extending southward toward Cumshewa, its eastern margin reaching the middle part of Hecate strait. The average depth of water is from 7 to 10 fathoms, but there are much shoaler parts. This bank was named Dogfish bank by Ingraham in 1791. Near its eastern edge he places, in lat. 53° 50′ N. and about 30 miles SE. from Rose (Invisible) point, a rock or shoal on which the ship Margaret struck in 1792, drawing 13 feet. Near the spot he notes 3 fathoms, deepening to 5, 7, and 12 fathoms eastward.

Shoal.—In lat. 53° 26′ N., long. 131° 06′ W., approximate, a shoal has been reported, but its position is doubtful.

Tidal streams.—In Hecate strait the flood stream sets to the northward. In Dixon entrance, the flood coming from the westward round North island, sets along the Masset shore, across Hecate strait for Brown passage, spreading for about 15 miles round Rose point, toward cape Ibbetson (Edye passage), where it meets the flood from the southward; consequently between Rose point, cape Ball, cape Ibbetson, and thence SE. 15 or 20 miles, the tides are irregular.

At spring tides, or during bad weather, the turmoil caused by the meeting of the streams is so great as to convey an appearance of broken water to that portion of the strait lying between Queen Charlotte islands, Brown passage, and Dixon entrance.

The direction and rate of the tidal streams are not regular, being greatly influenced by the winds. At full and change they run with great strength. Time of high water over the strait generally is about 0 h. 30 m.

Rose point to Masset harbor.—The shore between these two places forms a bay 22 miles in width. With the exception of a few small rocky points, the beach is smooth and regular and almost altogether composed of sand, with gravel in some places, sloping steeply above the ordinary high-water mark. Low sand hills generally form a border to the woods which densely cover the land. The water is shoal far offshore, and especially on approaching Masset harbor, where kelp forms wide fields at a great distance from the beach. In the northeastern part of the bay there is anchorage with offshore winds.

Hiellen river, at 9 miles southwestward from Rose point, is a stream of some size, which is frequented by great numbers of salmon in the autumn. Its mouth forms a good boat harbor. On its western bank is Tow hill, an eminence remarkable in this low country, facing the sea with a steep cliff 200 feet high, composed of columnar volcanic rocks on one side, while the other slopes more gradually.

Masset harbor is rather more than 22 miles WSW. from Rose point, and should be approached with caution; the entrance is between a low point, with a ledge of rocks covered with kelp extending ½ mile from it, on the western side, and the point of a long spit partly dry (the surf usually breaking the whole length of it) on the eastern side, the passage between having an extensive bar, upon which it is said there is a depth of 3 fathoms.

Just inside and round the eastern point of inner entrance is a bay, with a beach, containing the principal village (Uttewas), off the center of which there is anchorage in 10 fathoms. At this part the width of the harbor is nearly 1 mile, a large sand bank filling up its western side. The ebb stream runs very strongly, making this by no means a good anchorage.

There is a mission and store at Masset.

Masset sound, from its seaward entrance to the point at which it expands to Masset inlet, is 19 miles long in a general southerly direction and about 1 mile in average width. The depth, ascertained in a few places, varies from 10 to 12 fathoms. A number of small streams flow into it, most of which, according to Indian reports, have their sources in small lakes. At 3 miles up the sound a lagoon or arm runs off on the eastern side. Nearly opposite this place, on the west side is Maast island. It lies across a bay which seems at first sight to offer better anchorage than that already referred to. This island is low and sandy, and a great part of the bay or passage behind it is dry at low water. On the eastern side at 4½ miles from the southern or inner end of the sound, where its trend is nearly SW. and NE., a narrow passage runs off southward, joining Masset inlet and forming a large island, which is mostly lower than the surrounding country. This passage is partly dry at low water and is occasionally used by the Indians in canoes.

At its southern end the sound expands suddenly to a large sheet of inland water. The western half of the inlet is studded with islands and is rather irregular in outline, forming four large bays or inlets, with intervening mountainous points. The shores are steep, with narrow bowlder beaches sloping down at once into deep water. About the heads of the inlets, and near the mouths of the streams only, are small areas of flat ground found. Of these inlets, that which reaches farthest southward is called by the Indians Tininowe.

Tsooskatli.—On the southern side of the inlet is a narrow passage, the mouth of which is partly blocked by islands, but which leads into a second great inlet known by the Indians as Tsooskatli, or "the belly of the rapid." The largest of the islands in this passage is named Slipatia. Kelp grows abundantly in the channel on both sides of the islands, which, therefore, can not be very deep. The tide runs through them with great velocity, especially at ebb, when in the western channel it forms a true rapid, with much broken water.

Its eastern side is formed of low land, while its southwestern extremity is a long, fiord-like inlet. In this inlet are many islands; the largest, Haskeious, is nearly 1 mile in diameter and about 200 feet high. The eastern portion of the southern shore is rocky, with many small islets off it. On the eastern side of Tsooskatli, 2½ miles from its extremity, is Towustasin, a remarkable hill, with a steep cliff on one side. The northeastern part of Tsooskatli has a depth of from 10 to 16 fathoms. The depth of the northwestern part, about the center between the large island and the mainland, was 23 fathoms in one place.

Yakoun river.—Many streams flow into these inlets; the largest is probably that which is known as the Yakoun, and enters the southeastern corner of Masset inlet, in the bottom of a shoal bay. About the mouth of Yakoun are large sandy flats, dry at low water. It was formerly navigable for small canoes a long way up, and is reported to head in a large lake. On the western side of the bay at the mouth of this river are a few small houses, used during the salmon season.

The Mamin river joins the Tsooskatli inlet at its eastern end, and has a wide delta flat about its mouth. It is navigable by small canoes for several miles, but is much obstructed by logs.

The Awun river, west of the entrance to Tsooskatli, is said to rise in a lake.

Ain river, entering Masset inlet from the northwestward, is an important stream. There are several Indian houses, which are occupied in the summer, above its mouth. It is said to flow out of a very large fresh-water lake of the same name, the river itself being short. The lake is filled with islands, and in the winter is frozen completely over.

Tides.—The rise of a spring tide at the entrance of Masset sound was estimated at about 14 feet, but, owing to the length of the narrow sound, Masset inlet has a tide from 8 to 10 feet only; and Tsooskatli still less, about 6 feet. On one occasion, it was high water at the entrance of Masset sound at 1 h. 15 m. p. m., while in the narrow entrance to Tsooskatli, 23½ miles distant, the flood had just caused a reversal of the current at 0 h. 20 m. Owing to the great expansion of the upper part of Masset inlet the tide continues to run up opposite Masset for about 2½ hours after it is falling by the shore, while the ebb runs out for about 3 hours after the water has begun to rise on the beach.

Masset to Virago sound.—The coast between these two places is everywhere low and wooded, with occasional open grassy spaces, differing from the coast east of Masset in being rocky or covered with bowlders. No wide sandy bays occur, and the points are mostly of dark low rocks. The trees along the shore are not of great size, and are interspersed with occasional grassy spaces.

The water is shoal far offshore, with wide fields of kelp. The shore should be approached with caution, with the lead constantly going; there are some anchorages, in which a vessel might remain a night instead of keeping under way, or cruising about with a SE. wind, and thick weather.

Virago sound, the entrance to Naden harbor, is 4½ miles wide between its outer points, cape Edensaw to the east and cape Naden to the west, and 2½ miles deep to the narrow passage (which is 1¼ miles long and about ½ mile wide) leading into the harbor.

To the northward of the narrows the west shore between Mary point, the western entrance of the narrows, and Jorey point, a distance of 2 miles, is bordered by a flat extending to a distance of about ½ mile, and on the opposite shore, from cape Edensaw to Inskip point, a shoal also extends about the same distance; from the latter point a spit runs off to the westward for ¾ mile, with a depth of 2½ fathoms, contracting the channel, in which the least water is 3¼ fathoms, to a width of 800 yards.

Anchorage may be taken up, in 5½ fathoms, sand and shells, in the entrance to the sound on the line between cape Edensaw and Jorey point, with the opening to the inner harbor bearing S. 32° W. (S. 4° W. mag.).

The inner anchorage is inside the narrows, on the western side, just within Mary point, 400 to 600 yards distant from the shore, where a depth of 10 fathoms will be found.

Naden harbor.—This capacious and landlocked harbor is about 4 miles long NE. and SW. and 2 miles in width, with depths of 8 to 12 fathoms in it. Low land, densely wooded with spruce and hemlock of fine growth, borders the whole harbor. Rock appears on the shore only near the head of the harbor and in the narrows.

Naden river flows from a large lake, which, according to Indian account, must be 10 miles or more in diameter, and is much encumbered by fallen trees, and its banks, except in a few swampy flats, are densely wooded. At high water a boat can proceed about 2 miles up the stream. Stanley (Teka) river, in the western side of the harbor, is reported to be navigable for boats, and several other small streams enter the harbor. The spruce timber is excellent, and the harbor is well adapted for sawmills and the export of lumber. In August, the Indians say that halibut and salmon are abundant and geese and ducks come in large flocks.

Tides.—The rise and fall is about 13 feet.

Virago sound to cape Knox.—From cape Naden the shore and country behind is mostly low, though with some rocky cliffs of no great height, and the points are rocky, with wide gravelly or sandy bays intervening. Some rocks lie a little distance offshore, but there is no appearance of a wide shoal belt like that found east of Masset. Klaskwun point, 4½ miles northwestward from cape Naden, is a remarkable promontory, rising in the center to a hill about 200 feet in height, which, owing to the flat character of other parts of the shore, is visible for a long distance. In a rocky bay to the eastward of the point, and open to the northeastward, is Yatza village.

Halfway from Klaskwun point to the eastern entrance of Parry passage is Jalun river; its mouth forms an excellent canoe or boat harbor at high water. At 3 miles farther westward is a small promontory, on the eastern side of which is another excellent boat harbor.

The Pillar is a very remarkable columnar mass of sandstone and conglomerate rock which stands near the eastern side, about 25 feet in diameter and 95 feet high.

Parry passage separates North island (which forms the northwestern extremity of Queen Charlotte islands) from Graham island. The western entrance at the SE. angle of Cloak bay is ¾ mile wide, but is contracted to less than 600 yards by foul ground which extends in a northerly direction from a point on the southern side of the entrance. The passage proper is about 2 miles in length, with an average width of ¾ mile. This channel, between the ledges of rock which extend off the southern side for about 1 mile and North island, is clear, but the tide rushes through it, forming a race.

The flood stream runs eastward, leaving the eastern end of the passage with a northeasterly direction.

Parry passage toward its eastern end is separated into two arms by Lucy island, somewhat less than ⅔ mile long and ⅓ mile broad. The northern arm is not much over 200 yards wide; the southern or main channel is more than ½ mile wide. The soundings in the main passage are 30 fathoms, with a rocky bottom. The shores, except in the narrow western entrance, seem to be clear of dangers. The northern arm, while extremely narrow, is still farther obstructed by foul ground extending off to the northeastward from the eastern shore of Lucy island something less than ½ mile, and a similar bank from the opposite shore of North island. There is a narrow channel having from 8 to 11 fathoms, hard bottom, at the eastern end, and this increases to 15 fathoms in the western part of the arm.

A small islet lies about 1 mile eastward from the eastern entrance, and a rock awash is reported 2¼ miles N. 71° E. (N. 43° E. mag.) from the same locality and about 1¼ miles from the southern shore of North island.

Just without the eastern entrance of Parry passage, and on the southern side, abreast of Lucy island, is Bruin bay, affording anchorage in from 12 to 14 fathoms, sand. A line of kelp fringes the shore, which is studded with rocky patches and stones. This is not a good anchorage, as the flood sets into it from the passage, forming a number of eddies, and rendering it difficult to lie at single anchor without fouling it.

North island is above 5 miles in length, between North point and its southern extreme, and composed of low land, no point probably reaching a height of 300 feet. It is densely wooded. On the eastern side there is said to be a good anchorage in a bay which was formerly used by the vessels belonging to the old Northwest Company. A small rough high island situated close to North point, a prominent object in approaching, is named Thrumb. Remarkable wooden carvings are said to exist on the North island shore, or attached to the winter dwellings of the natives.

Caution.—A triangulation made by H. B. M. S. Egeria places the shore-line in the vicinity of North island 4 miles farther westward than shown on charts (1906).

Cloak bay forms the western entrance to Parry passage, lying between the SW. shore of North island and cape Knox. It is about 2¼ miles wide and the same deep; the depths in the middle of the bay vary from 30 to 17 fathoms, sand, gravel, and shells, and it is protected from all except westerly winds. Some rocks, on which the sea breaks only in heavy weather, lie some distance from the North island shore, and there are also a couple of remarkable pointed islands on this side.

On the southern side of North island, in Parry passage, is a snug cove named Henslung, in which whalers used occasionally to anchor. It is high water at full and change, at Henslung, at 0 h. 20 m., and the rise 16 feet.

Lucy island, on the northern shore of Parry passage, is separated from the southern side of North island by a narrow channel, on the northern shore of which is a small Indian village, called Tartanne, which was in former years a place of importance. A reef runs off the eastern end of Lucy island, and a wide shoal with kelp stretches eastward from the southern extremity of North island. Between these lies the channel with 8 to 11 fathoms of water. Abreast the Indian village the depth in the channel is 6 fathoms.

Cape Knox, the NW. extreme of Graham island, is a long, narrow tongue of land, on which are a few low hills. The cape may be considered as a gigantic dyke of igneous rock running in an east and west direction. Its southern side is bold, and off it lie several rocks in a westerly direction, the farthest out at a distance of about 3½ miles from the cape. On these the swell of the Pacific seldom ceases to break with great violence.

Directions.—On leaving Bruin bay or Henslung cove for the westward, a vessel may pass close to the cliffs forming the southern side of North island, and, keeping at about ½ mile outside the reefs that extend off the southern shore (Graham island), should get a good offing before hauling to the southward, to clear the rocks off cape Knox. When well out, the projecting point of Frederick island will be seen about 18 miles to the southeastward. At 2 or 3 miles to the southward of Parry passage is an indentation of the shore, which might be taken as its entrance by a vessel coming from the southward—a mistake that might lead to serious consequences, as the whole coast, as far as Frederick island, appears to contain several open bays with outlying rocks off each of them. The Indians, in their sketches of this part of the coast, do not draw any harbors, but merely exposed bays.

Frederick island lies about 14 miles south of cape Knox; the channel between the island and the main is about ⅓ mile wide and is reported to be foul, but has not been examined.

About 6 miles south of Frederick island is a prominent point, called by the Indians Tian Koon.

Thirteen miles southward of Frederick island is Port Louis, or Kiokathli inlet. The name Port Louis was given by Captain Chanal of the French ship Solide in 1791. The entrance is about 2½ miles wide, and is formed by two high bluffs with some small islets between them. This inlet is over 5 miles in length in an easterly direction and 3 miles wide; it contains five islands, and three streams flow into it. At the head is a beach and 9 to 10 fathoms of water.

Hippa island, lying 26 miles S. by E. from Frederick island, appears from a position 1½ miles seaward of Frederick island as high and bold; but from the south its outer end appears as a low point, and the inner end bold.

Directly eastward of Hippa island is an inlet about 4 miles in length, running about ENE., with regular shores and a breadth of about ¾ mile. This inlet is known as Skelu inlet or Port Ingraham. Three miles to the northward is another inlet, known as Athlow bay, of about the same size, with an island across the entrance. This island is about 1 mile in length and protects the bay from westerly winds. The entrance is north of the island and about 1 mile wide. The passage between Hippa island and the main is not recommended, as it has not been examined, and kelp has been seen in it.

A rock, on which the sea breaks heavily, lies between Skelu inlet and Rennell sound, about 3½ miles offshore, in approximately lat. 53° 26′ N., long. 132° 49′ W.

Rennell sound, the largest indentation on the western coast of Graham island, extends about 10 miles in a southeasterly direction and is 3 to 5 miles wide. There are five islands in the sound, the largest one, 1½ miles long, in the center, and a group of four islands near its head. Five streams flow into the sound, but none of them are navigable.

Tartoo inlet, about 2¾ miles in length and a mile wide, surrounded by steep and high mountains, runs in a northeasterly direction, from near the entrance, northern shore, of Rennell sound; there are two good salmon streams at its head.

Hunter point is the northwestern extreme of the entrance to Skidegate channel; it is a rather low and rugged point with high land at the back. A dangerous reef extends 1 mile off Hunter point.

Kano inlet, close northward of Hunter point, and between that point and Kindakun point, is about 2 miles in width and extends 4 to 6 miles in an easterly direction to near the base of some steep mountains, 2,000 feet high. The shores of the sound are rocky, with a river and fine sandy beach at its head.

Marble island (Guigatz), about 2 miles in circumference, is high and peaked and lies 4 miles NW. by W. from the southern entrance point of Skidegate channel. There are three small islets between Marble island and the main, and a rock, on which the sea breaks heavily, is ½ mile southeastward of it. A ledge of rocks extends ½ mile off its SW. extreme.

Keow inlet, 2 miles southeastward of Hunter point, runs in a northeasterly direction for about 2 miles and is nearly 1 mile wide. It is surrounded by high and steep mountains, down which plunge several cataracts.

Skidegate channel, the main entrance to which is about 3 miles northward of Buck point, is a little more than 1 mile in width and extends in an easterly direction for 6 or 7 miles to Log point, where it is 1 mile wide. Foul ground extends 1 mile westward from the southern entrance point of Skidegate channel.

Dawson harbor, on the northern shore of Skidegate channel, 4 miles eastward from Marble island, is reported to be a secure anchorage. The anchorage is at the head of the eastern arm in from 16 to 20 fathoms.

At Log point the West narrows commences, leading to Skidegate inlet. About 1 mile west of Log point a branch turns off to the southward for 1 mile and then westward to the Pacific, which it enters at about 3 miles to the southward of the main channel, forming an island 5½ miles long by 2 miles broad, which rises to an elevation of 1,000 to 2,000 feet.

This passage is only adapted for canoes or boats, as it is blocked by a bank at its eastern end, with not more than 4 feet on it at high water.

The tidal streams from the east and west meet about the East narrows, running through the channel with great strength, probably 5 knots in several places. The narrows must be passed at slack water of high tide, which lasts for a very short time, so that both narrows can not be passed in one tide.

Buck point, 8 miles SSE. ½ E. from Hunter point, is the southern entrance point of the arm which communicates with Skidegate channel 1 mile westward of Log point; it is high and bold.

Kitgoro.—Anchorage may be obtained at Kitgoro, 2 miles southeastward of Buck point, in 13 fathoms at the head of the inlet.

Kaisun harbor, 5 miles southward of Buck point, affords good anchorage in 17 fathoms, mud.

Inskip channel, leading round the north side of Kuper island, is about 8½ miles long and ½ mile wide. A short distance outside it there are some small islands on both sides, but there will be no difficulty in discovering the passage in. In the channel there was no bottom at 60 fathoms, but at the entrance a cast of 35 fathoms was obtained.

Moore channel, on the south side of Kuper island, is 5 miles long in an east and west direction and ½ mile wide, the shore on each side being steep-to, high, and covered with trees nearly down to the water's edge. In mid-channel there is no bottom at 70 fathoms. On the north side, just without the entrance, are some small rocky islets, named Moresby islands, and on the south side a few rocks close inshore off Denham point.

A heavy breaker, evidently on a rock, lies in the entrance to Moore channel in a position about 1,200 yards NW. by W. ½ W. from Denham point, the southern entrance point to the channel, or approximately in lat. 52° 57′ N., long. 132° 21′ W.

The eastern part of Moore channel is known as Port Kuper, and from its southern side three small inlets extend in a southeasterly direction—Douglas, Mitchell, and Mudge harbors.

Mitchell or Gold harbor, about 2½ miles deep and ½ mile wide, is surrounded by precipitous and densely wooded hills, from 700 to 800 feet in height, and at its head in Thetis cove is a sandy beach and a stream of water. The entrance to the harbor is about 6 miles from the entrance to Moore channel. At 1¾ miles up the harbor is Sansum island, a small islet covered with trees. The anchorage lies ½ mile farther on, in Thetis cove, leaving Sansum island on the port hand, the passage being 200 yards wide, with deep water. This cove is completely landlocked, but squalls, frequently accompanied by rain, come over the hills with considerable violence.

Thorn rock lies 1 mile inside the mouth of the harbor, on the southern shore, and has 3 feet on it at low water; it lies about 200 yards from the shore; and on the opposite shore, about 800 yards southeastward from Macneill point, the eastern entrance point to the harbor, but at not quite so great a distance from the land is another rock. These are dangerous to vessels working in or out; but there is nothing to fear in mid-channel.

At 1 mile to the westward of Mitchell harbor is the entrance to Douglas harbor, apparently very similar to the former, from which it is separated by Josling peninsula. Mudge harbor has not been examined, but presents an appearance similar to that of Gold harbor.

Directions.—The land, being very high on both sides of the channels leading into the above harbors, influences the direction of the wind, which blows either right in or out. Winds with any westing blow in, and those with easting in the contrary direction. A sailing vessel leaving Moore channel with a SE. wind should keep well over toward Hewlett bay, to enable her to fetch clear of the Moresby islands, as the wind will be very unsteady until well clear of the high land to windward.

Tides.—It is high water, full and change, in Moore channel at 1 h. 40 m.; springs rise 13 feet, neaps 10½ feet.

Tasoo harbor.—Cape Henry, which terminates in a very steep slope with a hummock at its extremity, is situated 6 miles southeastward of the entrance to Moore channel, and 4½ miles southeastward from it is the entrance to Tasoo harbor, the intermediate coast being high and rising abruptly from the sea. The entrance is short and narrow, with bold steep bluffs on each side, but the harbor itself is extensive, with deep water in many places, the anchorage being near some small islands on the port hand going in.

The coast between Tasoo harbor and cape San Christoval is an unbroken shore.

Between cape San Christoval and cape St. James are other openings, which, according to Indian report, lead into good harbors, the southernmost of which is that leading into Houston Stewart channel and Rose harbor. Inside Anthony island, and close to Houston Stewart channel, is an opening called by the natives Louscoone, and reported to be a good harbor, not unlike Rose harbor. This coast, excepting off Anthony island, is very bold. The land near cape St. James has fewer trees on it than that to the northward.

Supplies.—The banks in and near Hecate strait, swept by strong currents, with the shore line of inlets and fiords, constitute the feeding grounds of the halibut and other fish which abound in the vicinity of the islands. The halibut is the most important and is largely consumed by the natives; the dogfish is also very abundant and is taken for the manufacture of oil; salmon run up most of the streams in large numbers, especially in the autumn; herring are plentiful in some places, especially about Skidegate, at certain seasons; pollock or coal fish are caught on the northern and western coasts and supply an edible oil; flounders and plaice abound in some localities; cod and mackerel are also caught, and probably are abundant on certain banks at some seasons; while smaller fish and shellfish, oysters excepted, form an important item in the native dietary.

Immense flocks of wild geese and ducks visit the northern shores of the islands in the autumn. Potatoes grow in abundance in most parts, and thrive exceedingly well, forming an important article of food.

Bears are numerous, also martens and land otters, which are caught for their furs, and mostly taken to the Hudson Bay Company's establishment at Fort Simpson.

Caution.—From April to October the shellfish are said by the natives to be poisonous.

INDEX.

C.

D.

I.

J.

K.

L.

N.

Q.

R.

S.

X.

Y.

PRICE LIST OF BOOKS

ON SALE BY THE

HYDROGRAPHIC OFFICE.

THE FOLLOWING ARE THE ONLY BOOK PUBLICATIONS ON SALE.

Catalogue Number.	TITLE OF BOOK.	Price.
	SAILING DIRECTIONS.	
64	Navigation of the Gulf of Mexico and Caribbean Sea. Vol. II. Fifth edition. The Coast of the Mainland. 1907. Comdr. Holman Vail, U. S. N., retired.	$1.00
78	Newfoundland and Labrador, from Cape St. Lewis to Grand Point. Second edition. 1899. Ensign R. C. Ray, U. S. N.	1.00
-------	Do. Supplement. 1906	.10
84	West Coast of Mexico and Central America, from the United States to Panama, including the Gulfs of California and Panama. Third edition. 1902. Comdr. R. G. Peck, U. S. N., retired.	.50
-------	Do. Supplement. 1907	.10
86	Navigation of the Gulf of Mexico and Caribbean Sea. Vol. I. Sixth edition. West India Islands, Bahamas, and Bermudas. 1905. Lieut. Comdr. Harry Kimmell.	1.00
88	East Coast of South America. Third edition. 1904. Comdr. R. G. Peck, U. S. N., retired.	1.20
89	West Coast of South America, including Magellan Strait, Tierra del Fuego, and outlying islands. Third edition. 1905. G. A. Collie, Nautical Expert.	.80
96	Coast of British Columbia, including Juan de Fuca Strait, Puget Sound, Vancouver and Queen Charlotte Islands. Second edition. 1907. Lieut. Comdr. Glennie Tarbox, U. S. N.	1.35
99	Bay of Fundy, Southeast Coast of Nova Scotia, and South and East Coasts of Cape Breton Island. Third edition. 1906. G. A. Collie, Nautical Expert.	1.00
100	Gulf and River St. Lawrence. Second edition. 1897. Ensign R. C. Ray, U. S. N. (Under revision.)	.60
-------	Do. Supplement. 1906	.10
102	The Azores, Madeiras, Salvages, Canaries, and Cape Verde Islands. Third edition. 1898. Ensign R. C. Ray, U. S. N. (To be revised.)	.30
-------	Do. Supplement. 1906	.10

Catalogue Number.	Title of Book.	Price.
	SAILING DIRECTIONS—Continued.	
105	West Coast of Africa. Second edition. 1893. Ensign R. C. Ray, U. S. N. (To be revised.)	$1.00
......	Do. Supplement. 1902	.10
108A	Lake Superior and Saint Marys River. 1906. R. H. McLean, Nautical Expert.	.45
108B	Lake Michigan, Green Bay, and Strait of Mackinac. 1906. R. H. McLean, Nautical Expert.	.60
108C	Lake Huron and the St. Clair and Detroit Rivers. 1907. R. H. McLean, Nautical Expert.	.60
108D	Lakes Erie and Ontario, St. Clair and Detroit Rivers. 1902. Lieut. C. M. McCarteney, U. S. N. (Under revision.)	.50
115	The Hawaiian Islands, and Islands, Rocks, and Shoals to the Westward. Second edition. 1903. Lieut. Comdr. Hugh Rodman, U. S. N.	.40
	MANUALS AND TABLES.	
9	American Practical Navigator. Bowditch. Second edition. 1906. Revised by Lieut. Geo. W. Logan, U. S. N.	2.25
9:II	Useful Tables from the American Practical Navigator. 1905. (Being Part II of No. 9.)	1.25
30	List of Lights of the World. Vol. I. East and West Coasts of North and South America (except the United States) and the West India and the Pacific Islands. 1907. E. C. W. S. Lyders, Nautical Expert.	.30
31	List of Lights of the World. Vol. II. South and East Coasts of Asia and Africa and the East Indies, Australia, Tasmania, and New Zealand. 1907. E. C. W. S. Lyders, Nautical Expert.	.30
32	List of Lights of the World. Vol. III. West Coast of Africa and Europe, Mediterranean Sea, including the Adriatic, Black Sea, and Sea of Azov. 1907. E. C. W. S. Lyders, Nautical Expert.	.30
66	Arctic Azimuth Tables, for Parallels of Latitude between 70° and 80°. 1881. Lieutenants Seaton Schroeder and Rich'd Wainwright, U. S. N.	.30
71	Azimuth Tables, giving the True Bearings of the Sun at Intervals of Ten Minutes between Sunrise and Sunset, for Parallels of Latitude between 61° N. and 61° S. 1905. (Can also be applied to the moon, planets, and stars as long as their declination does not exceed 23° N. or S.) Lieut. S. Schroeder and Master W. H. H. Southerland, U. S. N.	1.00
87	International Code of Signals. 1905	3.00
106	Azimuth Tables, giving the True Bearings of the Sun at Intervals of Ten Minutes between Sunrise and Sunset for Parallels of Latitude between 40° N. and 50° N., inclusive. Fourth edition. 1906. Lieut. S. Schroeder and Master W. H. H. Southerland, U. S. N.	.50

Catalogue Number.	Title of Book.	Price.
	MANUALS AND TABLES—Continued.	
117	Table of Distances. (Temporarily out of print)	....
118	The Sun's Apparent Declination and the Equation of Time. From the Nautical Almanac.	$0.10
120	The Azimuths of Celestial Bodies Whose Declinations Range from 24° to 70°, for Parallels of Latitude Extending to 70° from the Equator. 1902. G. W. Littlehales, Hydrographic Engineer.	1.50
121	Manual of Symbols used on the Official Charts of the Principal Maritime Nations. 1903. The late Gustave Herrle, C. E.	.45
	MISCELLANEOUS.	
90	Development of Great Circle Sailing. 1899. G. W. Littlehales.	1.00
93	Ice and Ice Movements in the North Atlantic Ocean. 1890. Ensign Hugh Rodman, U. S. N.	.10
95	Average Form of Isolated Submarine Peaks, etc. 1890. G. W. Littlehales.	.30
103	Submarine Cables. 1892. G. W. Littlehales	.30
107	Wrecks and Derelicts in the North Atlantic Ocean, 1887–1893, inclusive. 1894. Hydrographic Office.	.10
109	Contributions to Terrestrial Magnetism, the Variation of the Compass. 1894. Lieut. Chauncey Thomas, U. S. N.	.30
109A	Contributions to Terrestrial Magnetism, the Variation of the Compass. 1895. G. W. Littlehales.	.30
110	The Gulf Stream. (A brief description.) 1894. Lieut. Comdr. John E. Pillsbury, U. S. N.	.10
112	Illustrative Cloud Forms. Sixteen color plates, with brief descriptive text. Litho. by Prang. 1897. Capt. C. D. Sigsbee, U. S. N.	1.00
....	The same in broadsheet (21 by 36 inches)	.60
114	Contributions to Terrestrial Magnetism. 1897. G. W. Littlehales.	.30
....	Catalogue of Charts, Plans, Sailing Directions, and other publications of the U. S. Hydrographic Office. Wm. M. Whiting.	.50

Remittance should be in advance by Money Order made payable to the HYDROGRAPHIC OFFICE, Washington, D. C.

AGENTS

FOR THE

SALE OF HYDROGRAPHIC OFFICE PUBLICATIONS.

IN THE UNITED STATES AND ISLANDS.

Aberdeen, Wash.—The Evans Drug Company.
Astoria, Oreg.—E. A. Higgins Company, 502–504 Commercial street.
Baltimore, Md.—M. V. O'Neal, 510 E. Pratt street.
Bath, Me.—Charles A. Harriman, 106 Front street.
Bellingham, Wash.—Chas. M. Sherman.
Boothbay Harbor, Me.—William O. McCobb.
Boston, Mass.—Charles C. Hutchinson, 152 State street.
Brunswick, Ga.—Frank A. Dunn.
Buffalo, N. Y.—Howard H. Baker & Co., 18–26 Terrace.
Charleston, S. C.—Isaac Hammond.
Chicago, Ill.—George B. Carpenter & Co., 202–208 South Water street.
Cleveland, Ohio.—The Penton Publishing Company, Browning Bldg.
Duluth, Minn.—Joseph Vanderyacht.
Eastport, Me.—C. H. Cummings, 101 Water street.
Galveston, Tex.—Charles F. Trube, 2415 Market street.
Gulfport, Miss.—Rolf Seeberg Ship Chandlery Co.
Honolulu.—Hawaiian News Company, Ltd.
Jacksonville, Fla.—H. & W. B. Drew Company, 45 West Bay street.
Key West, Fla.—Alfred Brost.
Los Angeles, Cal.—Cunningham, Curtiss & Welch Co., 252–254 South Spring street.
Manila, P. I.—Chas. F. Garry, 9 Calle Jaboneros.
Mobile, Ala.—E. O. Zadek Jewelry Company.
New Orleans, La.—L. Frigerio's Sons, 1015 Canal street.
Woodward, Wight & Co., Ltd., 406–418 Canal street.
Newport News, Va.—James E. Abbe, 126 Twenty-sixth street.
New York, N. Y.—T. S. & J. D. Negus, 140 Water street.
John Bliss & Co., 128 Front street.
Michael Rupp & Co., 39 South street.
R. Merrill's Sons, 66 South street.
Norfolk, Va.—Vickery & Co., 268 Main street.
Pensacola, Fla.—McKenzie Oerting & Co., 603 South Palafox street.
Philadelphia, Pa.—Riggs & Bro., 310 Market street.
John E. Hand & Sons, 222 Walnut street.
Portland, Me.—Wm. Senter & Co., 51 Exchange street.
Portland, Oreg.—The Chas. F. Beebe Company, 1–7 First street North.
Port Townsend, Wash.—W. J. Fritz, 320 Water street.
San Diego, Cal.—E. M. Burbeck, corner Fifth and D streets.
Loring & Co., 762 Fifth street.
San Francisco, Cal.—Geo. E. Butler, 310 California street.
Louis Weule, 106 Steuart street.
H. Lawrenson, 12 Market street.

Savannah, Ga.—J. P. Johnson.
Seattle, Wash.—L. W. Suter, 713 First avenue.
Lowman & Hanford Stationery and Printing Company.
Max Kuner, 94 Columbia street.
Sturgeon Bay, Wis.—D. S. Long.
Tampa, Fla.—Tampa Book and News Company, 513 Franklin street.
Washington, D. C.—W. H. Lowdermilk & Co., 1424 F street NW.
Wm. Ballantyne & Sons, 428 Seventh street NW.
Brentano's, SE. corner Thirteenth and F streets NW.

AGENTS ABROAD.

Belize, British Honduras.—A. E. Morlan, care of New Orleans News Company, 214 Decatur street.
Berlin, Germany.—Dietrich Reimer, Wilhelmstrasse 29, SW. 48.
Canso, N. S.—A. N. Whitman & Son.
Habana, Cuba.—José M. Zarrabeitia, 10 Mercaderes.
Halifax, N. S.—Robert H. Cogswell.
Hamburg, Germany.—Eckardt & Messtorff.
Montevideo, Uruguay.—Manuel Bottini, Calle Rampla 95-97.
Montreal, Canada.—Harrison & Co., 53 Metcalfe street.
Port Hawkesbury, C. B. I., N. S.—Alexander Bain.
Quebec, Canada.—T. J. Moore & Co., 118-120 Mountain Hill.
St. John, N. B.—J. & A. McMillan, 98 Prince William street.
A. B. Smalley & Son, 91 Prince William street.
Vancouver, B. C.—Albert Ufford, 140 Cordova street.

www.ingramcontent.com/pod-product-compliance
Lightning Source LLC
LaVergne TN
LVHW012209040326
832903LV00003B/200
9781344974561